Illustrated on the front endpaper

Peregrine; Pintail; Mallard; Jackson's three
horned Chamaeleon; Housefly; Ne-ne or
Hawaiian Goose; Bushbuck; Eyed Hawk
Moth; Thecadactylus Gecko.

THE EYE OF THE WIND

Also by PETER SCOTT

MORNING FLIGHT, 1935
WILD CHORUS, 1938
BATTLE OF THE NARROW SEAS, 1946
PORTRAIT DRAWINGS, 1949
WILD GEESE AND ESKIMOS, 1951
A THOUSAND GEESE (with James Fisher), 1953
WILDFOWL OF THE BRITISH ISLES (with Hugh Boyd), 1956
COLOURED KEY TO THE WILDFOWL OF THE WORLD, 1957
FARAWAY LOOK BOOK 1 (with Philippa Scott), 1960
FARAWAY LOOK BOOK 2 (with Philippa Scott), 1960

*A few short passages from some of these earlier
books have been quoted in this one*

Books Illustrated by PETER SCOTT

A BIRD IN THE BUSH—Lord Kennet
THROUGH THE AIR—Michael Bratby
GREY GOOSE—Michael Bratby
THE SNOW GOOSE—Paul Gallico
THE TURN OF THE TIDE—Richard Perry
COUNTRYSIDE CHARACTER (Blandford Press)
ADVENTURES AMONG BIRDS—by Three Schoolboys
HANDBOOK OF BRITISH BIRDS, VOLUME III—Witherby, Jourdain,
  Ticehurst and Tucker
LEMUEL—Ray Gregorson
AND CLOUDS FLYING—Ian Pitman
WATERFOWL OF THE WORLD, VOLUMES I, II AND III—Jean Delacour
THE MORLO—L. A. Knight
POPULAR HANDBOOK OF RARER BRITISH BIRDS—P. A. D. Hollom
TALES OF A WILDFOWLER—Arthur Cadman

1961

The author.

THE EYE
OF THE WIND

✳

PETER SCOTT

HOUGHTON MIFFLIN COMPANY BOSTON
THE RIVERSIDE PRESS CAMBRIDGE
1961

TO
PHILIPPA

Eye of the wind, whose bearing in
A changeful sky the sage
Birds are never wrong about
And mariners must gauge—

The drift of flight, the fluttered jib
Are what we knew it by:
Seafarers cannot hold or sight
The wind's elusive eye.

That eye, whose shifting moods inspire
The sail and trim the sheet,
Commands me, though I can but steer
Obliquely towards it.

C. Day Lewis.

FOREWORD

I AM without question the luckiest, and I believe the happiest man I know. As this is to be a story about me, I must make this plain at the outset: I am basically a happy person. I have gone through life supposing myself also to be quite simple. This may in itself be an over-simplification or perhaps I am just too lazy to enter into any lengthy introspection. My story tells what has happened to me rather than what I am or have been. It looks outwards rather than in, with an eye for events and adventure.

An autobiographer would be unnaturally lacking in vanity if he did not hope that his reader would entertain some sympathy for him by the time his story was told. Inevitably I hope that my story may lead to the ultimate conclusion that I am not a bad fellow really. Those parts of my life which might not lead to this conclusion are likely to be omitted, and though I suppose few autobiographical books set out to tell the truth, the whole truth and nothing but the truth, a certain ingenuousness (coupled with the danger of being found out) forces me to give this warning at the beginning. Stories which I have been telling for years with great conviction, believing them to be true to the smallest detail, have proved after careful research among my papers to be greatly garbled. Such stories can be corrected, but what of the host of other reminiscences of which no contemporary record remains? Must I water them all down in the sacred name of truth, or can the reader be trusted to apply the 'Scott reduction index'—an arbitrary figure of between twenty and fifty per cent by which all lengths, breadths, weights, distances and vehement statements should automatically be reduced? As an old Cambridge don once said to me: "My poor boy! Let this be a lesson to you only to believe half of what you hear."

Peter Scott

ACKNOWLEDGMENTS

MY PUBLISHERS have allowed me this page on which to say 'Thank you' to all those who have made this book possible. As it is the story of my life this ought to include all those who have made my life possible—beginning with my parents. I hope however that my indebtedness over this wide field will emerge from the book itself. To acknowledge my gratitude to those who have actually helped to create the book, as a book, is a more manageable task. Especial thanks first to my wife Philippa for endless encouragement through the "I-can't-think-who's-going-to-want-to-read-this-stuff" stages of the writing; then to Elizabeth Jane Howard for bringing the monstrous original typescript to reasonable and publishable proportions ("You know, half a million words is really too long for *any* book"); to Douglas Eccleston for turning the spatch-cocked and much-pinned together manuscript into a comprehensible typescript; to Michael Garside for much assistance directly and indirectly connected with the book; and to my long-suffering publishers for their forbearance during the considerable period between the 'absolutely final dead-line' and the ultimate delivery of the typescript—a delay caused, at least in part, by the purchase of a new glider with the advance royalty on the book. I was particularly touched by their acceptance of the excuse that I was gathering material for the penultimate chapter.

Having sought in vain for a quotation which incorporated the book's title, a possible alternative seemed to be a poem especially written for the purpose. For writing such a poem (and such a lovely one, too), my grateful thanks are due to Cecil Day Lewis.

I should also like to thank Messrs. *Country Life* for permission to quote from my earlier books, and to the following for permission to quote from letters and other documents or to reproduce photographs:

H.M. The Queen.	Dr. Finnur Gudmundsson.
The First Lord of the Admiralty.	Dr. W. J. L. Sladen.
Karl Müller.	Mrs. Michael Warr.
Dr. Gerald Gibbens.	

CONTENTS

PART 2

PART 3

LIST OF ILLUSTRATIONS

*   *   *

Key to Acknowledgments

1 Madame Yevonde
2 C. Hulse
3 John Bratby
4 C. Hills
5 Beken & Son
6 Oil Paintings by Peter Scott
7 Central Art Library
8 *Eastern Daily Press*
9 Water colour by Peter Scott
10 Ismail Khodjeste
11 Eric Bruce
12 *Life* Magazine
13 Dr. Gerald Gibbens.
14 Pen and ink drawing by Peter Scott
15 Associated Press
16 J. V. Beer
17 *Country Life*
18 Philippa Scott
19 Bill Sladen
20 Finnur Gudmundsson
21 *Homes & Gardens*
22 Fayer
23 Shaw Wildman
24 *Sunday Times*

THE COLOUR PICTURES

PART 1

CHAPTER I   *The Window*

ALL animals have interested me, and birds more than others, but wild geese have an almost mystical importance. Long ago I decided that my home must always be within sight and sound of the winter wild geese, which, in itself, drastically limits the choice of locality. There is only a small number of places in Britain where, from one spot, one can be sure of seeing and hearing wild geese daily through the winter months. On such a spot, close to the estuary of the River Severn, stands the house in which I live with my family. We built it on that precise spot for that precise reason, and in winter time the White-fronted Geese feed in the fields all around us. At dawn they stream over us on their morning flight and under the full moon the night echoes with their wild cry. It is just as I planned it long ago.

As I start to write this book on 29th March, 1957, I am sitting in the window of my studio. It is no ordinary window, for it is ten feet across and eight feet high, and it looks out upon water and birds and the green fields of Gloucestershire. From my armchair the window frames a picture of endless beauty, activity and diversity—a picture which gives me a peculiary intense pleasure, because its composition is my own creation. A pool with islands reflects the flash of the setting sun in the ripples made by the ducks and geese that are swimming on it. There is a great crowd of birds, 300 or more, of many different kinds from all over the world. They have not long been fed and the nearest are dibbling at the water's edge less than six feet away from where I sit. Many of the birds are tame ones, brought from distant countries to live together here in the Vale of Berkeley—Ringed Teal from Brazil, Barrow's Goldeneyes from Iceland, Ruddy Ducks from North America, Ne-ne Geese from Hawaii, White-winged Wood Ducks

3

from Siam . . . But many too are wild ones from far away breeding grounds which have elected to spend their winter at the Wildfowl Trust on the Severn Estuary, and to come in to feed in front of my window—Pintails, Wigeon, Shovelers, Pochard, Tufted Ducks, Coots . . .

There is a grey ruffle on the far water from the light wind, which is coming from just a touch north of west. The precise wind direction, the very eye of the wind, has always been important in my life for the things which have depended on it: the flight courses of birds, and the drift of their migrations; the angle that a sailing boat will point, and the advantages to be gained over an opponent by tacking if the wind changes by the smallest amount; the wind that will enable me to hold altitude in a glider on the ridge of the Cotswold, or the wind that will drift the glider as it gains height in a thermal up-current on a cross-country flight. The study of birds, sailing, soaring, all depend at one point or another upon the eye of the wind and an appreciation of its precise bearing.

Against the sunset there is a continuous coming and going of birds; a courting party of Shovelers takes off with drumming wings; a family of Barheaded Geese sweeps round low across the window, their great wings gloriously spread across the evening sky as they bank steeply to land on the grass. It is a much steeper bank than I should dare to make at low altitude in my glider, but I know something of what it must feel like to them. In great profusion Mallards cross and recross the sky in pairs and little teams, splashing down from time to time in a glitter of ripples in front of me, where the long-maned Goosanders and the exquisite white Smews, almost invisible in the dusk, have been diving incessantly for food.

This window is a dream come true, a dream born of other windows and of many ideas evolved and crystallised over the years. Neither it, nor the slightly curved room it enriches, nor the pool in front of it, existed at all four years ago. All were created from a bunch of rough drawings which I had handed to a dragline operator and an architect with the instruction to "get on with it". The window is also a magic window, for as well as the picture I see through it, there is a picture of the room itself which I can see reflected in it, and the reflection grows stronger as the sunset fades and the warm red-shaded lamps become the dominant part of this curious double image. I see myself, my wife, my children, my books lining the walls at one end, my easel and painting cabinet at the other, and the shelves of half-finished pictures, and below them the gramophone and the shelf of records.

The light has gone, but still very dimly I can see the black birds moving about on the dark blue water and the black shapes of them as they fly against the dark blue sky; the whole background of the picture beyond the window is ultramarine in contrast to the red light of the room, which lies across it in reflection.

A pair of ducks circles round over the pond, out over the pollard willows until the two black specks are lost against the loom of the elm trees beyond and in the red reflection of the lamp shade behind me. I project their line of flight, following the course they will take if they come round again, and up they sweep out of the red glow and above the elms, round as they head the wind and . . . splash . . . down on to the pond. The elms line one of the fields where the wild geese feed in winter. The wild Whitefronts of the Severn Estuary have gone east on the first stage of the long migration which will take them to their breeding grounds in Arctic Russia; they left a fortnight ago, and only a week or two before that I was out under those elms in the rain-soaked dusk. We were setting a net to catch the geese in order to mark them with rings on their legs; and before daylight on the following morning we were back again putting the finishing touches to our work before the geese should come. For me it was a memorable morning; its dawn was cold and grey and cheerless with a south-easterly wind which promised rain.

A single goose called out of the darkness and then passed low over the field, only just visible against the sky. He was the mysterious and still unexplained scout, the forerunner of the great skeins, who flies yelping over the feeding-ground in the early gloom a few minutes before the main flocks arrive. Then above the song of the wind in the old elms we heard the first clamour of the main flight. We ran to the hedge, and stood there half hidden by it, as wave after wave of geese passed low over our heads. It was too dark for them to see us through the thin hawthorn branches and to us the birds were no more than black silhouettes against the low grey clouds.

To each of the five of us watching they meant something different. To one they were a wholly new experience, to another his habitual quarry as a wildfowler (here flying much lower than usual); to the third a newly acquired object of scientific study, and to the fourth familiar birds whose behaviour had occupied his time as a professional biologist for the last eight years. To me they were something different again. They were the single continuing passionate interest of my life, as a painter, and as a naturalist—

just as exciting and moving as they had been thirty years before when I first fell under their spell. Familiarity had done nothing to lessen the thrill; the tingle still ran down my spine at the sheer beauty of the sight and sound. But then there was additional enjoyment that stemmed from this very familiarity itself. The first geese had landed just where I expected. From long experience I was able to forecast and explain their movements. In this context I had specialised 'know-how' in which I took particular delight. Small though the context might be I was an established expert and proud of it. In the process of 'knowing more and more about less and less' I had done my best to learn how to become a wild goose. In my efforts to understand the animal completely, I had achieved only a moderate reincarnation, for I could fly with them only in spirit; but with this approach I had found that more and more of the unsolved problems had fallen into place. I had by now a very fair idea of what it felt like to *be* a goose.

In the twilight of the dawn the geese had landed in the next-field-but-one to our nets because it was still too dark for them to see the stuffed decoy birds which we had set out. Wild geese have surprisingly poor vision when they are flying in the half light. Once the first geese were down, the great flock began to build up in a thick mass in the centre of the grass field they had chosen. As some of the later skeins came swinging over the elms and set their wings to glide down, testing their drift and heading directly into the eye of the wind, I knew that they were too high to make a landing. I knew that they would have to flap up and go round again, and I knew it long before the geese themselves realised it. My judgment of their flying accuracy from the ground was better than theirs from the air.

When the whole flock was assembled—3,000 strong—and the daylight had come, I knew that my appearance at a precise point in the field beyond them would lift the whole mass and send the bulk of it in a great clamouring wave over the field in which our nets were set: and this in fact they did exactly as I hoped, so that we had a great crowd of geese in our field. The geese, in combination with the weather, finally beat us and we never released our nets, but my thoughts for most of that day were those of a White-fronted Goose, and so, too, were the thoughts of the biologist who was with me and shared this understanding. Yet there were also things we did not fully understand, the things that nobody knew, the challenge of discoveries still to be made. What was the true explanation of the single scout before dawn?

1910

With my father and mother.

1920

With my Zonure and punting a canoe.

Punt-gunning in an oilskin skirt on Wigtown bay and a three-jump on the Kulm rink at St. Moritz.

Why, when I flushed the geese from their first field, did two small lots go off into the distance instead of yielding to the powerful mechanisms which hold the flock together? Small mysteries these, leading up to the much larger mysteries of migration and navigation and the evolution of the traditions which order the life of a wild goose. To a naturalist these were signposts on a road whose end was far over the horizon; and I had been a naturalist ever since I could remember, for I had become a naturalist by the design of my parents.

A few days before he died in his tent in the Antarctic on 29th March, 1912, forty-five years ago to the day when I began this book, my father wrote to my mother:

"Make the boy interested in Natural History. It is better than games. They encourage it at some schools . . ."

I was two-and-a-half-years old then and I cannot remember a time when I have not been interested in Natural History. But my first memory is of fire and panic at a Christmas party.

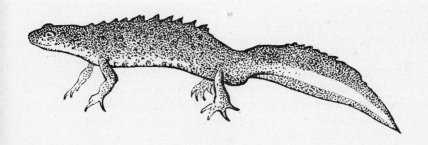

CHAPTER 2   *Morning Mist*

FIRST memories of early childhood must always be of things that
made a deep impression. How otherwise would they stay with us
down the years?

The candle fell from the Christmas tree; the tinsel and the paper
decorations caught fire at once, the parcels and the crackers fed
the blaze and even the cotton wool 'snow' burned fiercely. There
were thirty children at the party and pandemonium broke out
among them and their parents and nannies—screams and
hysterics and near-panic. I can remember being hauled from the
room by my mother, and looking back as the flaming tree fell
over to the left with a burst of sparks. We dashed away, out of
the front door and straight home in a four-wheeler. The incident
is recorded in my mother's diary for 11th December, 1911, when
I was just two years and three months old.

A more clouded memory is even earlier. It is an impression of
the arrangement of the furniture in the drawing-room of our little
house in London, the house which no longer exists, where, on
14th September, 1909, I was born. The Green Line Coach station
now stands where 174 Buckingham Palace Road used to be. It was
a typical small early-Victorian terrace house with a tiny garden
in front and a studio built out behind. I can dimly remember a
man sitting on the sofa in the drawing-room at a time when I
cannot have been more than one-and-a-half years old. My father
left for the Antarctic when I was that age and although his
departure cannot have meant much to an eighteen-month-old
baby, it is just conceivable that the emotions of my parents reached
me strongly enough to create a lasting memory. Soon after my
father left, the furniture was moved and the sofa was put into a
different part of the room, where it remained for the next twelve
years. It is hard to know whether that is a true memory or whether

8

my mother reconstructed the scene in my mind. "Don't you remember," she might have said, "sitting on your father's knee when the sofa was over there?"; and to bolster this memory there is an excellent photograph of me doing so.

A brighter scene comes out of these early mists of memory. It concerns a captive balloon and a primitive motor-car. The captive balloon was a bulbous sausage-shaped spot with a tinier speck, its basket, hanging beneath it. It moved slowly, almost imperceptibly down across a backdrop of the brilliant orange sunset with the high shapes of cumulus clouds cut-out in grey silhouette. I stood entranced on the back seat of the open car facing backwards and leaning on the folded hood, while my mother gripped the seat of my trousers with a firm anchoring hand. The balloon was being hauled down into the trees at Roehampton.

I must have been quite young when my mother found herself sitting one night at a dinner next to Lord Baden-Powell, the Chief Scout. He was ambidextrous and showed her the advantages of being able to write and draw with both hands. It would be nice, she thought, if her son too was ambidextrous; so from then onwards she started taking the pencil out of my right hand when I was drawing and putting it into my left. This might have achieved what she intended had she not slightly overdone it, so that I have been left-handed ever since. That is the story she used to tell, although privately I think I might have been left-handed anyway.

Another story she would tell whenever the subject of telepathy was raised is also recorded in her diary. Early in 1912 news came that Amundsen, who had set off for the Antarctic after my father's expedition and without telling him, had reached the South Pole before him. On March 11th, when my father was returning from the Pole and the bad weather had set in, he wrote, "Oates is near the end. What we will do, God knows." On that same day my mother's diary, which she was keeping especially for him, begins: "Peter said this morning, 'Mummy, is Amundsen a good man?' I said 'Yes, I think he is.' Then he said, 'Amundsen and Daddy both got to the Pole. Daddy has stopped working now.'" My father probably died about 29th March, 1912, but this was not known until February 1913. I do not think my mother really believed that there was anything paranormal in this, for she was basically sceptical of all such things. Certainly in later years she regarded it as a combination of coincidence and her own anxiety at that time.

I remember (back again in my very early youth) a garden party held by Queen Alexandra at which there were Chinese acrobats and jugglers. But the memory is overlaid by my mother's account of how I formed up behind the Queen saying, "Now let's be a train," and taking her firmly by the bustle proceeded to shunt her up the path. "*Chuff*, chuff, chuff, chuff, chuff. . . ."

The front windows of our London house looked out over a large area of railway lines immediately outside Victoria station. It was a lively and fascinating scene at a time when the expressed ambition of most small boys was to become an engine-driver (although it was never mine). In the afternoons the sun shone from behind our house full on to the railway yard and its colourful activity. I can still see the green engines shunting down to the turn-table in front of the engine shed in the right-hand corner of the panorama, or stopping to fill their side tanks from the hanging hose. Painted on their sides were the letters LB & SCR (standing for 'London Brighton and South Coast Railway') and occasionally engines carrying the letters LC & D (for 'London Chatham and Dover', a company which had been described as the 'run-down smash-up and turn-over'. I remember I thought that was hugely comical).

Across the sky above this railway-scape, on one exciting day, drifted a bevy of free balloons at the start of their race. They were none of them close enough to see any detail, but the very fact that there were men up there in those hanging baskets made the imagination boggle. "What," said my nurse, "will they be up to next?"

A hundred yards down the road from our house was a hansom-cab rank across against the high red-brick wall of the railway. Every morning up the slope from Pimlico came the Guards in red tunics and bearskins with band playing on their way from Chelsea Barracks to the Palace. On ceremonial occasions the column was led by a white billy-goat. There were still horse-buses in those days and I can remember catching one at the corner of Grosvenor Gardens and Buckingham Palace Road and getting off again at Hyde Park Corner. I think it was the only time I ever rode in a horse-bus, for the internal combustion engine had arrived—the first motor-buses were on the streets and so too were the early taxi-cabs. One of them caught fire one afternoon just opposite the Grosvenor Hotel. I can remember telling the taxi-on-fire story unendingly to my youthful cronies. I dined (or more accurately tea-ed) out on it for months. I would tell them vividly how this taxi came to the kerb and its sloping bonnet—it was a Renault, I think—was thrown open by the taxi-man and flames ten feet high burst out of it. I used to describe, because after all I was standing only a few yards away, how the fire-engine arrived and how another taxi ran over the hose which stopped the water, and how finally the driver of yet another taxi was so busy looking at the flames that he ran into a Carter Paterson's horse van in front. Such things were very novel in those days. I was always sure of an attentive audience for this story, and it lost nothing in the telling.

We had a small coast-guard's cottage near Sandwich called 'Shingle End'; it stood in a small group of cottages among the dunes at the far end of Princes Golf Course. There was no road to the coast-guard station and we had to walk more than a mile along a sandy path among the golf bunkers, carrying all stores and provisions.

Sandwich was my first 'seaside', a paddling and bathing beach, with shells and sandhoppers and wading birds and glass balls washed up from the fisherman's nets. The striped curtains in the cottage smelled of damp and the rush mats were full of sand and there was an earth closet at the bottom of the garden. It is all part of the pattern of my childhood, though I cannot remember when I first went there.

We were at Shingle End at the outbreak of the 1914 war and I can quite clearly remember the newspaper next day. There was a picture of a battleship on the front page but I cannot be quite certain that the headlines I see above it are not the headlines from every epic movie covering that period.

The war brings a jumble of memories from Sandwich, for example the air-raid when a party of German Gothas came across the Channel and divided almost over our heads at Sandwich, half of them going towards London and the other half turning south to bomb Deal and Dover. There was an aerial battle—a primitive prelude to the historic fighting in those same summer skies twenty-four years later. One of the Gothas came down in flames in a cornfield near Ramsgate, but I did not see this, for I was made to take cover in the cupboard under the cottage stairs as soon as the aeroplanes came close enough to be really interesting. Mme. Rambert, the dancer, who came regularly to stay, was with us at the time of this raid and she also, I remember, occupied the tiny cupboard under the stairs, kneeling in prayer for our

B

deliverance. I was too young to be frightened by bombers; I was merely curious. Needless to say no bombs were dropped within ten miles of us. Mimi Rambert taught me to do cartwheels—a minor accomplishment which I still retain, and for which I shall always be grateful to her.

My mother and I used frequently to sleep out on the beach at Sandwich so that I became quite used to it. One night as we lay there in the foothills of the dunes, a great black shape of a Zeppelin came quite low across the coast, blotting out the stars as it passed on its way to drop bombs on London.

It was at Sandwich that I first discovered my own weakness at the sight of blood. A fisherman had badly cut his leg on the beach about a mile away from our home. The coast-guards were called upon to go out with a stretcher and I went with them. It was my first sight of blood in quantity and I disliked it very much indeed. My father also shared this weakness and, as my children seem to do the same, I suppose it to be hereditary. In nature red is often a warning colour, and no doubt it is more than mere chance that danger signals are the colour of blood—but so are roses and strawberries. For long periods, as for example during the Second War, I have been able to control this phobia. Many a surgeon, I reflect, has mastered the same instinctive horror and eventually become indifferent to the sight; there are few things to which man cannot become accustomed. But there are still times when I must keep a tight rein on my imagination not to be possessed by an extreme revulsion at the very thought. I remember a rather shaming incident in my University days when I had been invited by Sir Almroth Wright to see his work at St. Mary's Hospital. Soon after my arrival I had been introduced to a quiet Scotsman sitting at a microscope at one end of the laboratory—a Dr. Fleming, the then unknown discoverer of penicillin. He showed me some blood slides, on which, as I recall, he was making some bacteriological counts, and I was immediately fascinated by the bacteria which he pointed out under the high-powered lens. It was at this stage that an assistant came in with a large glass jar of blood which was to be put through the centrifuge on the next bench. I remember strolling nonchalantly towards the window, and hoping that my white face would not be noticed. Perhaps fortunately it had been and, probably only just in time, I was led out on to the fire escape by Sir Almroth—a sad ending to an interesting afternoon.

But the shrimp fishermen on the beach at Sandwich also had

pleasanter associations in my early youth, for as they waded
waist-deep, pushing their wide-framed nets through the beds of
sea grass far out at low tide, they collected many species of small
fish and other less edible creatures than shrimps—crabs and dabs
and gobies and pipe-fish. These were named for me by Denis
Lillie, biologist on my father's last expedition, and also by Julian
Huxley who often came to stay.

Around the group of coast-guard cottages at Shingle End ran
a grey brick wall covered with yellow lichen. The turf lay against
the bottom of the wall, and if in summer you worked your way
along it searching in the crack between grass and bricks, you could
find if you were lucky the Common or Viviparous Lizard. These
were the first lizards with which I ever became acquainted—the
first of a long line of lizards which I have counted among my
friends (the last in the line are the Marine Iguanas of the Galapagos Islands).

The turf around our cottage was rich in pink Rest Harrow
flowers, and yellow Birdsfoot Trefoil on which the caterpillars of
the Six-spot Burnet used to feed, and at times the sand dunes were
alive with the glossy black and red moths as they hatched from
their strange papery cocoons on the grass stems.

Here I first became conscious of the song of the Skylark. At
Shingle End there was always a lark overhead. And if my mother
quoted Shelley I could lie on my back and watch the bird doing
just what the poet said it should: "And singing still dost soar, and
soaring ever singest."

There were sea birds too, especially waders, and ducks—and
once Brent Geese. That was at a time when the beach was lined
with barbed wire entanglements and trenches zig-zagged through
the dunes, for invasion was threatened. There were perhaps
forty Brents formed into a V with unequal arms and they flew
low over the sea. As they passed the afternoon sun shone full upon
their bright white sterns. I did not know what they were at the
time, but I carried the picture in my mind until long afterwards
when I realised without doubt what I had seen—my very first
wild geese.

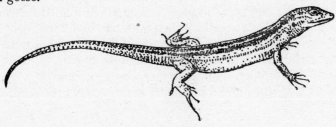

THOSE earliest memories are mostly of action, of events rather than people, of fire and aeronautics and blood and animals. Others who have had a happy childhood may have similar memories, for in those circumstances *people* are largely taken for granted. Alternatively this may be an indication of my own particular character—my greater preoccupation with action and things than with thoughts and people.

Long years later my wife told me that when she was a child she had imagined me as a dark-eyed tragic little boy living under the perpetual shadow of my father's death in the Antarctic, and I record it merely because as a conception it is so very far from the truth. Never having known my father I was brought up without any sense of loss. My mother could never have tolerated any kind of continuing tragedy. She was one of the gayest people I have ever known. Financially our future had been secured to a modest extent by funds contributed soon after the news of the disaster became known. Thus we could continue to live in the house in London in which my parents had lived ever since their wedding, and also to have the little cottage at Sandwich for holidays. Furthermore my mother was a professional sculptor (she hated the word sculptress for its concession to feminism) who had studied her art in Paris and been a pupil of Rodin. She was immensely energetic and in my early childhood she was already well known, especially for her vigorous portraits. Her larger-than-life-size statues of my father were in place in London and in Christchurch, New Zealand; her small statuettes, often including delightful babies, were exhibited regularly at the Academy and at the Salon in Paris; but in particular the distinguished men of the times came to her studio, and many of them became her lifelong friends. Of all this, and much more besides, she wrote brilliantly in her diaries which were published after her death as a book, *Self Portrait of an Artist*.

But what influence, if any, did these great men have on *me* as a child? Not, perhaps, very much. If the Prime Minister came for tea and was tired, as frequently happened in the early days of the First World War, I was not allowed to play the pianola. But, though I was allowed to call him 'Squiff', I doubt if Lord Oxford and Asquith had any wider influence on my life. If the Chancellor of the Exchequer came to lunch, my interest went no further than the hope that he would take a message about a goldfish back to his sons, Michael and David McKenna, who were my friends. As for the men of letters and of the arts such as Galsworthy, Yeats and Granville Barker, these were shadowy figures when they came to my mother's studio, and remain familiar only from the portraits she made of them.

I suppose I was a slow developer as a child and certainly I was late in learning to read and write. Even now I read so slowly as to find it a handicap, for my speed is not much greater than it would be if I were reading aloud. I am sometimes told that this is an advantage in that what I read I am more likely to remember. But I am far from sure that this is so. In fact this slowness means that I read very little—perhaps on the average no more than two books a year, and this I greatly regret.

But if I learned to read late I began to draw early. Racing free-balloons and taxi-cabs figure on the earliest pages, and not much later came the aeroplanes, all mixed up with zoo animals. (My mother flew with Graham-White in 1912 or '13 and knew Gustav Hamel and Charles Rolls, both of whom she sculpted.) I can remember enjoying drawing in a positive sort of way at a very early age, but the results in those days were sadly lacking in artistic merit. Like so many children I was obsessed with minute detail and accuracy—a fascination from which I have never been able to escape completely.

The front and back rooms on the first floor of 174 Buckingham Palace Road had been knocked into one drawing-room but were still divided by heavy black velvet curtains. I can remember a time when it required an effort after dark to push through those curtains into the blackness of the back drawing-room which was the only way out. In this back drawing-room was an elaborate column-like piece of ornate mahogany furniture which was the forerunner of the cinematograph projector. If one peered through a rectangular lens in the box at the top of an adjustable stalk (I

had to climb on to a chair to do this), a series of positive photographs mounted on a wheel flicked past like the pages of a book,
and produced a perfectly realistic action lasting for perhaps ten
seconds. The only 'reel' we had was one of myself at the age of
three in the front garden of the house throwing a ball more or less
straight towards the camera. My first appearance, therefore, in a
motion picture was in 1913 in a 'star' role, though my impression
was that the scene had been under-rehearsed.

In the front drawing-room was a much more important instrument—a grand piano which was also a pianola. It used paper rolls
longitudinally perforated. I was allowed to operate this machine
from the time my feet would reach the pedals. It was an instrument ideally suited for the creation of an interest in music, for to
any child it was an irresistible toy. The mechanism was pneumatic
in principle and the pedalling required exactly the right amount
of energy; the little levers which controlled the speed and volume
allowed enough variation to call for 'a performance' on the part
of the operator; the works could be played louder or softer, faster
or slower and with more or less feeling at the whim of the pedaller.
We had a limited number of rolls which lived inside the piano
stool. All were of famous music, which soon became well known
to me. Many were special piano renderings of orchestral, even
operatic, works. I can remember every one of them today; the
G minor Ballade and the Polonaise Militaire of Chopin, a Liszt
Hungarian Rhapsody, plenty of Beethoven—the Moonlight and
Kreutzer Sonatas, the 1st Piano Concerto and the 4th; the Eroica
and 5th Symphonies; Schubert's Rosamunda and the Unfinished;
the Overtures and principal melodies from *The Magic Flute* and
Cosi Fan Tutte; Rossini's music used in *Boutique Fantasque* and one
or two more.

I shall never forget the thrill of hearing these works for the first
time in the concert hall. The first, it so happened, was Beethoven's
1st Piano Concerto. To know the tunes intimately and then suddenly to discover what it was really supposed to sound like made a
tremendous impact. Although later on—perhaps through lack of
aptitude, or perhaps through unimaginative teaching—I never
learned to play any musical instrument, this introduction to music,
followed by singing at school and the possession of various
gramophones, has led me to some of the most intense enjoyments
of my life. I am quite ignorant of all its technical aspects, but I
am easily and deeply moved by music—perhaps the more so
because I do not understand its mechanisms. There are parts of

the Brahms Violin Concerto, and of Sibelius's First Symphony, and of Beethoven's Ninth, and of the very end of *Rosenkavalier*, which, quite apart from their spiritual uplift, give me a purely physical sensation which can be compared on level terms with any other extreme of sensuality. I am writing of a time, however, when for me no such comparison was yet possible and when music itself meant little more than a convenient way of burning up surplus energy after tea.

Our house was about half-way between St. James's Park and Chelsea Gardens. Hyde Park and Battersea Park were only a little further, and yet St. James's was always the favourite, which must surely have been because of the pelicans and the ducks. This early association with ducks may or may not have had a deep psychological influence and may even have been the true fore-runner of my life-long passion for the *Anatidae*.

It seems that I also had a great many human friends in the Parks, to judge from the number of times, even now, that it is used as an opening gambit: "I believe we played together in the park" they say, and I expect they are right.

No account of my early youth would be complete without men-tion of my beloved 'Winkie', who with one short break looked after me for five years before I went to boarding school. Winifred Parker—Winkle or Winkie—was the daughter of the rector of Hook in Dorset. She had grown up in the country and she had an infectious enthusiasm for all country things, and especially for animals and plants. She was twenty-one when she first came to Buckingham Palace Road, small and freckled and bright-eyed and gay. I adored her for all of those five years. When she had finally seen me off to my Preparatory School she married Captain Woodgett, the last Captain of the *Cutty Sark*, who was a great many years her senior, and made for him a happy home in Norfolk for his declining years.

In 1917 my mother accepted a job in the Embassy in Paris and took me with her. For a short time I went to school there and must have learned a little French. We lived in the Hotel Alexandre III at the Rond Point des Champs Élysées. Its name had been changed from the Hotel Meyerbeer because of the anti-German feeling. I can quite clearly recall trying to imagine how people could hate other people so absurdly much.

In those days there were roundabouts at various places along the Champs Élysées. These were my special delight, for as you took your seat on the wooden horse you were given a spike with a wooden handle and each time as you whizzed round you tried to collect on your spike one of a row of little rings which hung from a board. If you succeeded, another ring dropped down into the place of the one you had spiked. There were normally ten revolutions per ride and if at the end you had ten rings on your spike you were given a free ride again. I must have been the despair of the roundabout proprietors, for in the end I became proficient enough to ride all afternoon for the original fee. The roundabouts were not crowded, which was perhaps why they did not seem to mind; and they got to know me quite well, so that there were friendly smiles when I arrived and sympathetic exclamations whenever I missed a ring. No doubt this was something to do with the *Entente Cordiale*.

While we were in Paris the war was going badly; at one time the front line was less than 40 miles from the city and the taxicabs were requisitioned for troop movements. There was also Big Bertha, the huge German long-range gun which fired into Paris. I can well remember the day it opened up. There was an absolutely clear blue sky and it was very hot. Quite early in the morning the shells began to fall on the city and continued with an extraordinary regularity about every half hour. A good deal of panic arose, and together with the rest of my school I spent the whole day in the cellar. For a long time it was believed that an 'invisible aeroplane' was operating and a young pilot, who had been dining with my mother the night before, was sent off in his aeroplane to look for it. His mission was unsuccessful, of course, for there was no ghost bomber to find, but I remember a few nights later sitting in my pyjamas in our hotel sitting-room with my eyes popping out of my head while he told us about it. Twice during the day he had climbed high into the cloudless sky, creeping laboriously up to the maximum ceiling of his aircraft. He made it sound so exciting and so beautiful that aeroplanes immediately became wonderful romantic things whose only object was to climb as high as possible into a clear blue sky. (Now that I can do this without an engine, in a glider on a day of dry thermals, it is no whit less romantic and wonderful than he said—even when there is no ghost bomber to seek.)

In due course the situation became so bad that it was thought inadvisable for my mother and me to stay on in Paris. We arrived back in London late one night and took a taxi from the station. As we were driving along The Mall an air-raid developed, and the taxi-man stopped his cab. Leaning back, he opened the taxi door to tell us that he could take us no further. We must get out at once, he said, here and now, beside the Victoria Memorial and proceed to take cover in the nearest shelter. My mother was quite firm with him and said in imperious tones, "Don't be so silly! You must take us home at once," whereupon he shut the door and drove us home. I remember this incident particularly because, leaning against the door in the corner of the taxi, was an ash stick which had been cut for me during a holiday in Scotland and when he opened the door it must have fallen out, for I never saw it again.

CHAPTER 4

"Well, My Little Man"

BECAUSE of the Antarctic story I was, even as a small child, regarded as 'fair game' by the press photographers and reporters. At an early age I was frequently recognised in the street—a state of affairs which, as I have discovered more recently in a different context, has its advantages and its disadvantages. During my childhood, my mother made great and, on the whole, successful efforts to protect me from the effects of this notoriety, but it was inescapably one manifestation of being my father's son. There were others; the arch people who said, "Well, my little man! And are you going to follow in your father's footsteps when you grow up?" Or the ones who genuinely admired my father and expected me to be like him. All these things have had specific effects on my life. First of all, being the son of a national hero set me a standard. Whether or not I could live up to it, it was at least there. Secondly, it provided an incentive to succeed in some quite different direction entirely on my own unaided effort; and thirdly, it inoculated me, to some extent, against the Antarctic story with which I grew up. This meant, and still means, that I know rather less about the intimate details of my father's explorations than many of my contemporaries. Of course, my mother read the story to me as a child, but I did not set out regularly to re-read it and so the details were gradually forgotten. Thus when I am asked about those more technical parts of the expeditions which I am naturally expected by others who are interested to have at my finger tips, I frequently find myself at a loss.

In polar exploration my father had achieved a position to which I could not possibly aspire. In that field (even if I was not prepared to accept the theory that ability skips a generation) I could obviously never be more than a pale shadow desperately trying to emulate him, to be dogged all my life by direct and unfavourable comparison. If I was not to live in reflected glory only, I must strike out on a line of my own. I could not follow in my father's footsteps; but to follow his wish that I should be interested in Natural History was something quite different. About this my mother was very ingenious, for she did not thrust the subject down my throat, but instead put me most subtly into the way of naturalists and biologists of all kinds, many of them famous men who were prepared to give time to me because of the passage in my father's letter.

I used for example to stay occasionally with Sir Arthur Shipley, the Master of Christ's College, Cambridge, and I have to this day a copy of his masterpiece *The Minor Horrors of War* (surely the wittiest biological text book ever written) inscribed to 'Peter M. Scott, F.Z.S.', for I had been made a Life Fellow of the Zoological Society of London as a christening present. A proprietary interest in a zoo and its animals is a wonderful thing for a child, or at least it was so for me.

The most vivid memory I still have of my visits to Christ's is of swimming in the lily pond in the Master's garden. In doing the breast stroke my finger tips almost touched both sides at once, but not quite.

It must have been when I was between seven and ten years old that I used to go quite regularly with my mother to tea with the great zoologist Sir Ray Lankester at his home in Oakley Street. He always had some kind of specimen to show me and often for me to take home—an insect, a fossil, a feather, a vertebra—and the specimen led to pictures in books (often his own) and to a dissertation. Once it was the earbone of a sperm whale, another time a series of snail shells and on another a fly in amber. On his mantelpiece there were photographs (or at least a photograph) of a native woman with huge warts on her face hanging down almost like the wattles on a turkey. I remember that this made a deep impression on me—indeed I can still see the dreadful picture quite clearly in my mind's eye.

These tea parties must have been predominantly in winter time, for I see the room as rather dark, with a pool of light over the desk which was covered with books and papers and specimens. I think it was in this room that I first looked through a microscope. Sir Ray must have retired from the Natural History Museum some time before, and I believe that most of his time was then occupied with writing books and articles. Looking back I cannot help thinking that he must have taken a good deal of trouble to plan an exciting evening for me. To establish a sympathetic audience in the first place, his proposition was that only he and I appreciated all these strange animals; we could not expect my mother to do so, because, by and large, women did not like that sort of thing. It worked very well and followed by the fascinating exposition of the evening's specimen, it led me to look forward immensely to my tea-time visits, which went on until his death.

A more romantic approach to animals came from the books of Ernest Thompson Seton. My copies of *Lives of the Hunted* and *Wild Animals I have Known* had previously belonged to my father. They are inscribed (I have them still) with his signature and "Discovery, Winter Quarters, February 1903". They and the others—*The Trail of the Sandhill Stag, Rolf in the Woods*, and *Wild Animal Ways*—must have influenced me considerably and even lastingly. My favourite story was 'Tito, the Coyote that learned how'. At six years old I knew it more or less by heart.

In those days I took Thompson Seton for granted. The books were a part of my life: they were without question classics: every aspiring naturalist had obviously read them. Only now, looking again at the worn and dilapidated volumes and re-reading the stories, do I fully realise his genius. In the days before animal behaviour became an exact science, he was a good enough naturalist to avoid making his animals think like humans, he was tender and sad, and simple enough for children, without ever being sentimental. His illustrations were brilliantly drawn and he was a pioneer in the field of decoration by line drawings in the margins —a device I copied in my first (joint) publication as a schoolboy, *Adventures Among Birds*. It seems possible that Thompson Seton's achievement in introducing thousands of children to the wild woods will be increasingly valued by future generations of mankind.

One of my two godfathers was Admiral Sir Clements Markham, President of the Royal Geographical Society at the time of my father's first expedition. It was he who had selected my father to lead it, and it was for him that I was christened with the middle name of Markham. My second godfather was the Scottish playwright Sir James Barrie, who had met my father in 1905, soon after he returned from his first Antarctic expedition in the *Discovery*. In describing the meeting Barrie says that having found him he was unable to leave him: "In vain he escorted me through the streets of London to my home, for when he had said goodnight I then escorted him to his, and so it went on I know not for how long through the small hours."

For all the time that I knew him, Barrie lived on the top floor of Adelphi Terrace House, overlooking the river. The room in which he wrote was dominated by a huge open hearth piled high with wood ash, and with a high-backed settle in the inglenook on one side of it. The room, so far as I recall, was scarcely altered at all in the twenty-five years that I knew it. It was full of pipe smoke and books. As a very small boy I used to go there for tea, sometimes with my mother, sometimes alone and feeling very independent. There is no doubt that Barrie knew all about how to get on with children. Although there were often long silences I cannot ever remember feeling shy in his company.

He wrote delightful comic letters, often in rhyme, and always full of invention.

```
                                    3, Adelphi Terrace House,
        january            18              Strand.
                    1 9 1 4
          M y      dear      Peter
                 H A L L O    i
        a m       so      glad       too
        g e t        y o u r      R i p p
        i N g   L E T T E R          I T
        i s      A      LOVLY       LET
        TER      T H E       R E A S o
        N      I      HAVE       NOT
        W̶R̶O̶T̶E̶              W̶R̶I̶T̶
        R O T            B E F O R E
        i s      B E C A U S       i
        H A V E       B E E N      I N
          S W I T S E R L A
        N D      W I T H       N I
        K O L A S      AND       M i
        K A L      A N D      THEM
        U T H E R          B O Y S.
        i      H O P      U      WILL
        COME       WITH          M E
          S O M      DAY      TOO
        A N D      H A V E      F U N
          i     A M     gL A D     N O
        O N E      HAS       STOLE
          YOURE          BEAR
        Y E T.      T H E R E      is
```

```
A  L O T        OF       Sc o u N.
D R E L S           A B O U T.
IT    I S    TIME        U
S A W E D           P E T E
R      PAN       I       A M
T O O        RING       Y O U R E
M O TH E R           U P
A B O U T    IT    T O M O
R ROW.    HE    is       B R
A V E    H E    C A N    F L Y
      I  A M
          Y U R E       L O V I N
      g
                GODFATHER
  U R E           FOTOgRAFS        is
  g RAND          THEY    is    ON    MY
      BOOKSHELF
```

Nicholas and Michael were of the Davies family whom Barrie looked after when their father died in 1905. A short while later he duly took me to *Peter Pan* and we sat in a box. Having seen the play several times since, I cannot now remember what impression it made upon me this first time. I was, after all, only four-and-a-half years old. But Barrie always described how he asked me in the taxi on the way home which part I had enjoyed the most. "I think," I am supposed to have said, after some deliberation, "that I enjoyed it most when I dropped the programme on the fat lady's head in the interval."

Peter was played that year by Madge Titheradge who had followed eight years of Pauline Chase. Much later I twice saw Jean Forbes-Robertson in the part.

The next letter from Barrie, also addressed from Adelphi Terrace House in May 1914, came after we (ostensibly I) had sent him as a present a small bronze statuette of a boy by my mother which she had had cast as a table bell. The letter is headed:

P O E T R Y

Hurray, Hurray
I got today
A Bell shaped like a Boy
Hurroo hurroo
It came from you
And fills my heart with joy

Hurrump Hurrump
It's such a trump
A gem without a blot
Dido Didum
I like it some
I'm glad it came from Scott

Hullo hullo
I love it so
For nothing could be sweeter
Ding dong, ding dong,
Oh that's the song
I sing in thanks to Peter

Ta rum ta rye
I proudly cry
You, postman, do not tarry
To whoo, to weet
Please take to Pete
The thanks of poet Barrie

Adelphi Terrace House,
Strand, W.C.

Dec. 30, 1914.

Dear Peter,

When I look upon my Box,
With pride and joy I rocks,
From my head to my socks,
And everybody knocks
At my door, and flocks
To see my Box.

Signed by The Author.

The writes of translation are reserved.

Your Loving,
Godfather,

J.M.B.

23 Campden Hill Square,
Kensington.
22nd December, 1917.

My dear Scott,

I am sitting here smoking the tobacco out of your pouch. It is a lovely pouch and I watch people in case they try to steal it. Who steals my purse steals trash, but if anyone tries to steal my pouch he had better look out.

I am hoping to see you soon. I am with my boys and they are as rowdy as ever.

My love to your mother and you.

I am
My dear Scott
Your humble servant
Barrie.

Adelphi Terrace House,
Strand, W.C.2.
April 9, 1918.

My dear Peter,

Your mother thinks I do not write clearly, but I expect this is jealousy. It is funny to think of your being at a French school, parleyvousing with big guns firing and bells ringing and hooters hooting. What a lot you will have to tell me when we meet again. Michael and Nicholas are here just now, and tomorrow we are going to Wales for 10 days. Michael won the competition at Eton for flinging the cricket ball farthest. Peter [Davies] is where the fighting is heaviest, near Amiens. I think Brown [his man-servant] will have to go and be a fighter now, as he is under 50. It will be queer if I am the only person left in London and have to cook the food and kill the cow and drive the bus. It will be rather difficult for me to be engine-driver and guard at the same time and also take the tickets and sweep the streets and sell balloons at the corner and hold up my hand like a policeman to stop the traffic every time a taxi comes along. Then I shall also have to be the person inside the taxi at the same time as I am sitting outside driving it and if I run over anybody it will have to be myself, and I will have to take my own number and carry myself on a stretcher to the hospital, and I will need to be at both ends of the stretcher at once. Also I will have to hurry on in front of the stretcher so as to be door keeper when the stretcher arrives, and how can I be the door keeper when I have to be the Doctor, and how can I be the Doctor when I have to be the nurse?

You see I am going to have a very busy time, and I expect that a letter from you would cheer me up. I will have to be the postman who delivers it.

Your loving
Barrie.

Edgerston,
Jedburgh,
Scotland.
14 August, 1918.

My dear Scott,
Oh what rot,
I'm far away from you,
I'm up in Scot.
But you are not
What is a bloke to do?

There aint a trout
To be hooked out
In all this northern land
No rain at all,
And streams so small
They've lost themselves in sand.

Till August ends
(Or I offends
My host, and have to hop)
I here remain
Awaiting rain
Then scoot to the metrop.

If in Septem.
You say the same,
That you're expecting me,
Why then, I'll try
(And bring a fly)
To hurtle down on thee.

I am
Yours
Barrie. P.N.N.F.
(Poeta nascitur, non fit.)

One of the best is, alas, incomplete and undated, for the letter has been lost and it is recorded here from memory.

Dear Peter, though I'm far away
I envy you your négligé
Here in the Highlands it's so hot
I wish I was attired like Scott.
With him I'd leap o'er moor and fell
Although I shouldn't look so well
I'd dance for you, you'd sing for me
We'd have the Highland Fling for tea
The pools and streams are full of trout
All shouting "Peter fish us out"
Oh life would be a better joke
If Scott the scientific bloke
Were with us here—the poppinjay
All shining in his négligé.

> Eilean Shona,
> Acharacle,
> Argyllshire.
> September 3, 1920.

My dear Peter,

How are you all on your island? We are very well on ours. Can you say "Acharacle"? It is rather bad for the teeth; by the time you have succeeded, it is advisable to see the dentist. I expect you are having a good time and feathering your oars in grand style, and I hope you are asserting yourself as Head Man. See to it that the domestics come to you for *Orders*. Say to your *mother* in a *firm* voice, "You had better lie down now for a little." Insist on being *obeyed*, without giving *reasons*, which are always ticklish things.

This is a regular Robinson Crusoe sort of island. It is about 8 miles round and very mountainous, and you should see me facing the mountains with my staff, and then deciding to stroll along the shore instead. I wish you could land quietly some morning, and let us find your footprints on the sand like Man Friday. We are alone on the island, and people on the mainland have to blow a horn, and then we go across for them. I am afraid we are too comfortable tho' to be real Robinsons, as we can get provisions. We are more like the Swiss Family Robinsons, who when they wanted butter, looked up and saw the butter tree. I wish I could look up and see the Peter tree. My love to your mother and yourself.

> Yours,
> Barrie.

CHAPTER 5 *No Clothes*

MY mother believed that hardiness could be induced by habit and training—cold baths and not too many clothes. I had always been a thickset little boy, inclined to be podgy, and before going to school (except for a period of Greek influence when I wore hand-printed tunics which my mother bought in Paris from Isadora Duncan's brother Raymond) I had worn clothes which are more or less standard dress for children nowadays—a shirt and shorts, a jersey in winter and in a hot summer perhaps just the shorts. This led, however, to the exaggerated comment of often (though not always) well-meaning people which has dogged me for most of my life: "Of course I used to know you when you were a little boy; you wore no clothes." The impression was relative rather than literal, for in the days of my youth the normal children's outdoor wear was thick overcoats, scarves, gloves and buttoned gaiters. A contemporary press cutting records with shocked amazement that I was usually *bare-headed*.

This rugged upbringing had been supported by my Guardian and his family. When my mother set off on the abortive journey to meet my father in New Zealand on his expected return from the South Pole, I was left in the charge of Sydney Holland, Viscount Knutsford, and was looked after by the younger of his two daughters, Rachael, now Lady Malise Graham. Lord Knutsford was known as the Prince of Beggars; he was a pioneer in the art of raising large sums of money for charity. Hospitals were his special interest and the London Hospital in particular. He was known to me as Uncle Sydney and I went frequently to stay with him for holidays or whenever my mother was travelling abroad. He lived at Kneesworth Hall just outside Royston where he had installed an organ and kept ornamental pheasants and ducks and fished for trout, with which he had stocked the small lake. He also played the clarinet and kept very tame bullfinches and Labradors (which he trained to land the trout), and I adored him. For the whole period of my boyhood, he and his serene wife, known to me as Lady Mary, and his two daughters, made a happy place for many of my holidays. In his later years Uncle Sydney became very deaf, but he had an unending string of jokes about it which he told with magnificent gusto, so that I have always had an especial sympathy for this particular disability. In my schooldays he introduced me to Scotland and deer stalking and trout fishing, and this led to a whole new range of outdoor activities.

I was ten years old when I was sent to West Downs, a Preparatory School near Winchester. The headmaster was Lionel Helbert —a man of original ideas and tremendous vigour, but by the time that I arrived there he was already gravely ill and he died during my first term. The headmastership was taken over by Kenneth Tindall, who was very popular with his boys and whom I have greatly admired ever since.

At breakfast one morning when I had been a week or so at West Downs one of my neighbours had a letter from home. Delightedly I leaned over to see what it said. To my surprise it was hastily pulled away with a cry of "Don't crib!" But it did not end there. "Sir!" said quite another boy, "Sir! Scott's been cribbing Lakin's letter."

"I don't suppose he meant to."

"Oh but he did, sir, he said 'Let's see what it says.' I heard him."

"Did you say that?"

"Well, yes, sir. I wanted to know."

"It was none of your business what was in Lakin's letter, and you had no right to try and read it."

"Sorry, sir."

I had never heard the word crib before and not until then had I ever been told that letters were private and should not be cribbed. I felt horribly flushed and my eyes were brimming with tears, but I was determined not to 'blub'. Worse things still happened to people who blubbed. I held on. I discovered that the worst of all happened to those who lost their tempers and blubbed with fury. They were deliberately baited for sport. It wasn't exactly bullying because that wasn't allowed, it was just . . . well, baiting. But I was fortunately found not to be baitable and suffered not at all.

When I first went to West Downs my mother made a special arrangement with 'L.H.' that I need not wear a coat. I was to be as much as possible in shirt sleeves, though, of course, all the other boys wore coats. I still vividly remember being thus conspicuous. Nowadays, however much the health aspect might dictate such a plan, it would probably be ruled out on psychological grounds. Possibly my two terms of coatlessness had some slight influence on my character, but who is to say what that influence was? If I was 'a slow developer', was it because of this that I developed slowly? Or was it because of this that I ever developed at all?

My mother's efforts at physical toughening do not seem to have had any great or lasting effect on my capacity to face cold weather. I 'feel the cold' no more, but on the whole I believe no less than anyone else.

My Natural History interests were well served at West Downs. Butterflies and moths and especially their caterpillars swam for the first time into my ken. One of the masters—C. A. Ranger (who subsequently became headmaster of another 'prep. school') knew about 'bug-hunting', and under his encouragement I found my first Poplar Hawk Moth caterpillars on the leaves of the young poplar trees in the neighbouring nursery of Messrs. Hilliers. My first Lime Hawk caterpillar was found in the row of limes above the cricket field; my first Puss Moths slept like black and green kittens on the leaves of the willows at the back of the miniature shooting range.

By this time I was deeply committed to Natural History, and one day when I was going down by train to Sandwich for the holidays I made an astonishing and wholly useful discovery about the powers of suggestion. I was standing in the corridor looking at a map on the swing door which divided the second class from the third class carriages (corridor trains had not long been invented in those days), and leaning against the door which was suddenly opened from the far side. To save myself from falling I put out my left hand and gripped the door-post for support. A man came past me and behind him the door swung back on to my thumb. I felt very little, but when I looked down at my hand I was rather horrified at what I saw. The flesh of the whole top of my left thumb was removed from the bone and hung like half a plum separated from its stone. I ran back into the carriage saying apparently in rather matter-of-fact tones, "Look Mummy, my thumb's come off." Later when the numbness wore off it hurt terribly. We got off the train at Tunbridge Wells where I was treated by a doctor. As it was being dressed my mother said, "Think of the nicest thing you can think of." At that moment the nicest thing I could think of was a fully grown Privet Hawk Moth caterpillar and I thought hard of its glorious velvety greenness, the purple and white diagonal stripes and the curved shiny black and yellow horn on its tail; above all, I thought of the satisfying bigness and fatness of it. I concentrated fiercely on this image and suddenly no pain remained in my thumb.

The doctor in Tunbridge Wells was not prepared to undertake the tricky job of stretching the fragment of skin by which the tip of my thumb was still attached and popping it over the bone like a thimble; for this I had to return to London and be treated under general anaesthetic at St. George's Hospital. "He will have no feeling in that thumb," said the surgeon cheerfully, "and will probably never be able to bend it again"; but in due course the only after-effects were an inconspicuous scar, and a slight malformation of the thumb nail. Much more important was the discovery that a concentration of thought could so strikingly affect physical pain. I seemed to have a sort of safety curtain which I could lower between my imagination and reality. It has been a useful standby many times since then.

At West Downs I made two other discoveries which were unexpected: I could swim faster than most, and I had what was considered to be a reasonably good soprano voice. No doubt the swimming originated from visits to the swimming baths in Buckingham Palace Road at a very early age. My mother was determined that I should swim before I could walk. In this she always claimed that she succeeded, and as it seems to be true that very small children have no innate fear of water, I may well have swum at a year old. Certainly I can remember swimming 'dog-paddle' quite happily and successfully at a very early age. I also remember a curious period of a year or two—at about the age of five—when I lost confidence and could no longer swim. But then suddenly the confidence returned.

In bathing there was one particular game which had always especially appealed to me. On a sandy shore I delighted in pretending to be a seal, and cruising along in the shallows, propelled by my hands on the bottom. I record this because forty years later, when I first discovered the delights of watching fishes on a coral reef through a face mask my earlier life as a seal came back to me most vividly. It was for this, I thought, that I was training myself in those far-off days.

The fact that I was unbeaten over the 'six lengths' distance in the school swimming baths went some way to offset my undistinguished performances on the cricket and football fields. My left-handedness led me to bowl (mostly wides) with my left hand, though I batted with the ordinary right-handed stance. But I was also left-footed, so at soccer I was placed at outside left. But neither here nor at public school was my heart ever in organised games, though I doubt if my father's expressed preference for Natural History was responsible for this, unless it was at a subconscious level.

With an acceptable treble voice, and a capacity to sing in tune, I soon found myself singing the solos in chapel and taking part regularly in all the concerts. These were the days before gramophones and no recording was ever made, so I can safely assert that my voice was altogether outstanding. At all the school concerts, term after term, year after year, I used to sing 'Polly Wolly Doodle all the Day', and I wonder whether the audience got more bored with the song than I did.

For the Christmas holiday immediately after the end of the First World War, my mother decided to take me to Sicily. She had planned to go to Syracuse. Sitting opposite to us in the train compartment as we left Rome was an old gentleman, his knees covered with a great travelling-rug. He was wearing steel-rimmed dark glasses, which were rare in those days, and to me he looked impressive, mysterious, almost sinister. He turned out to be Axel Munthe. When he asked us where we were going and my mother answered Syracuse, he suggested that at least we should break our journey at Capri. After that we could decide whether we should go on to Sicily, although he personally did not advise it. So to Capri we went; such was the magnetic influence of the famous Dr. Munthe, who was at that time a complete stranger of whom my mother had never before heard. We stayed at the Piccolo Marina and went often to the Villa San Michele. Of all the beautiful things in this remarkable house I remember most vividly a large square biscuit tin containing two or three shrunken heads, which came, so he told us, from somewhere near the source of the Amazon, the first of these macabre objects that I had ever seen. That I should remember them so well at this distance of time suggests that they must have made a sharp impression, but much more perfectly I can picture in my mind the beautiful adult male Wall Lizard of the green form which I caught in Dr. Munthe's garden. On a rocky islet, only to be reached by boat, there was (and may, for all I know, still be) a strain of green Wall Lizards which were lacking in yellow pigment so that they were a beautiful clear blue, striped with brown in the usual way. I was shown one of these beauties, but to my sorrow, I was not allowed to try the precipitous climb onto the towering rock. A rowing-boat took us to the famous Blue Grotto where we waited for the right wave and then hauled ouselves in by the chain under the low arch into the magical place, lit by its ethereal submarine reflections.

We did not go on to Syracuse, but stayed in Capri until what should have been the end of the holiday. But in Rome on our way home we met a party of Americans who were travelling by car round Italy on a Reparations Mission. They invited us to go with them, and on impulse my mother accepted. It was the sort of snap adventurous decision she loved to make, and it was a splendid idea to me, for it meant missing a term of school—not that I disliked school, but a tour of Italy was obviously a good exchange for a winter in England. The only sad part, in looking back on it, was that at nine I was just too young to get the best from the great pictures, the sculpture, the architecture. To be sure, I can still feel satisfied by the memory of the fat black-and-white horizontally-striped pillars of the cathedral in Siena, but the Uffizi Gallery in Florence is chiefly memorable because I did cartwheels when the attendant was not looking. On the other hand I can clearly remember the golden richness and shining blue of the mosaics at Ravenna. We went to Rimini and up to the little Republic of San Marino; to Bologna and Padua, Verona and Venice. A Venetian gondolier, who had been engaged by the Americans for the whole of the week we were there, taught me to handle the sweep in his gondola, and allowed me finally to take charge on the stern, which I remember as an immensely proud moment. As near as no matter I was a gondolier.

Boats had come my way in England in earlier holidays and I had learned to propel a Thames punt with a pole. I had even carried the system a stage further and learned to use the pole when standing in a Canadian canoe. These were my earliest essays in boats. The Norfolk Broads and my first sailing boats were still to come.

Above Venice in the foothills of the Alps we visited the battlefield of the Piave, motoring up into cloud and snow. Along the road which zig-zagged up the mountain towards the pass were hastily dug trenches, where, beside other abandoned equipment, we found a short-handled entrenching spade which returned with me to England as a souvenir. It was my first visit to a battlefield, and it did not seem to be difficult to imagine the noise and smoke of battle, and the disorder of the retreating troops. As we stood looking across the valley where the battle had been fought so recently the mist came down on us again. It was part of a snow cloud, and in a few seconds the whole scene was silently overcome by a falling curtain of white.

Before we got to Milan I was told that the cathedral looked 'like bride-cake'. As I did not know what bride-cake was, I had no idea what the cathedral would look like when I saw it. Indeed I still imagine bride-cake as Milan cathedral rather than Milan cathedral as bride-cake. I was taken up to the roof and I can remember climbing the steps among the forest of white statues.

On this long tour of Italy we had punctures which happened very regularly in those days of motoring: we used to walk on ahead while the tyre was being mended and I caught wall lizards and geckos and kept them in a small meat-safe. How often I used to long for another puncture . . . and another. Terrace walls in Italy are usually built with frequent holes, vertically rectangular and often a foot or so high, which are left open for drainage. These are the homes of many lizards, and especially the sand-coloured Moorish Geckos which come out to bask in the hot sun just outside the hole. With the first approach of danger the Gecko runs back into the hole, but often stays just inside without re-tiring into the crevices at the back. It is then that a stealthy approach out of sight of the animal followed by a lightning (but perfectly controlled and gentle) grab can result in a successful capture, perhaps once in a dozen attempts. Certainly my meat-safe did not get overcrowded. I can still see those Geckos, and the terrace walls, and the grey olive leaves against the blue sky, and the almond blossom.

One day an Italian child of about six ran across the road in front of the car. The American driver tried hard to avoid him but it was too late; he was overtaken and fell, and the car apparently ran over his legs. Amazingly he was scarcely hurt at all, but there was an agonising period from the time it became clear that we must hit him until the welcome discovery that he was not dead. It was the first motor accident in which I was involved and still the only one in which anyone has been even slightly injured.

We stayed in many hotels during this tour—hotels which I chiefly remember for my rather destructive habit of bouncing vigorously up and down on the beds. To me the quality of the hotels was in direct proportion to the bounciness of its beds.

By the time we were back in England, the Easter holidays had arrived. I had missed a whole term at West Downs, but I doubt if I suffered any serious ill-effects from it.

One day in holiday time the Captain of an airship came to lunch at our little house in London. He said that when he flew over St. James's Park on the following afternoon he would drop a message addressed to me. Next day I was out with a cousin in the Park when the dirigible came over and suddenly we saw the message fall. It was an object which trailed streamers and which fell over towards Victoria Street. We began to walk in that direction, and by a strange chance met a policeman carrying the rubber tube with its strips of silver fabric. We told him who we were and said we knew that the message was for me, but he said, "Oh no; I'm afraid I can't give it to you, it's evidently a very important message and I must take it back to the station for instructions." In due course it was delivered at our house and the container, complete with its streamers, went at once into my own small private museum.

Apsley Cherry Garrard, author of *The Worst Journey in the World*, and a member of my father's expedition, lived in Hertfordshire at Wheathampstead, and from time to time we used to go there to see him. Lamer Park was a large house, and once when we arrived the hall was dominated by a new statue—a bronze figure of Christ by Epstein. My mother did not like it, and had a long argument with Cherry about it. Secretly, although I could not have said why, I was on his side. The work was impressive to me even at this early age. And yet surely my mother could not be wrong; after all, she *was* a sculptor and she must know.

Cherry had written rather critically about my father but in spite of that my mother liked him. I was mainly concerned with the Crested Newts in the pond in his kitchen garden.

Bernard Shaw also lived near-by at Ayot St. Lawrence. He was a very old friend of my mother, and was also involved in the argument about Cherry Garrard's criticism of my father. Shaw did not have a particularly sympathetic manner with children, so that at this stage I have no special recollection of him, though for most of my life he was a regular luncheon guest at our house and sometimes came to stay. During a summer when we had taken the Rectory at Streatley he spent about a fortnight with us, while my mother worked on a small statuette of him. We bathed in the Thames before breakfast every morning (Shaw swam a curious side-stroke) and after lunch each day he used to read to us. Because of his general preposterousness in conversation he became to me an unreal figure; and this was accentuated by the very precise manner of his slightly Irish accent. Surely he could not mean half the extravagant things he said, diverting though they were. Surely he was just a little bogus. It was not until much later, when I heard him read the whole of his new play *The Applecart* just before it was first produced, that I suddenly recognised this familiar and vaguely comical white-bearded figure as a great man. The reading was at Cliveden at one of Lady Astor's week-end parties, and although much of the political significance was lost on me at that age, I was immensely impressed not only with the play but also with the way Shaw read it. At that time there were great discussions and indecisions about who should play the lead and whether or not it should be Cedric Hardwicke (who finally played it).

Shaw told us once that he got most of his household stores and food free. As he never signed autographs, his signature was apparently more valuable than the amount of the cheque, so that his cheques were seldom cashed. Much later I remember watching Shaw, as an octogenarian, catching a bus outside our London house, after he had walked across the park to have tea with us. "If I can do that at eighty," I thought, "I shan't be doing too badly."

CHAPTER 6   *'Bill'*

ABOUT half-way through my time at West Downs a new character appeared on my horizon, Edward Hilton Young, who was later to become 'Bill', my stepfather, a Cabinet Minister, and Lord Kennet of the Dene. He had a profound and wholly beneficent influence on my life. He was a naval hero of the war; he had lost his right arm in the Zeebrugge Raid; he had commanded an armoured train in Russia; he had won a D.S.O. and a D.S.C.; he had written a book about the war, and he was a Member of Parliament. He was quiet and brave and he knew about birds. What more could there be? It was some time before I realised that my mother was going to marry him, but when I did I was completely delighted. So far as I was concerned it was all a splendid idea, and this it has remained ever since. They were married in the crypt of the House of Commons in March 1922.

The three of us went to Tunisia for a holiday, which was the farthest afield that I had yet been. Travel had already become an important activity in its own right. My mother had travelled widely, and I had been abroad more than most children of my age.

Tunis is chiefly memorable because it led to my first ride on a camel (outside London Zoo). We went south from Sfax to Gabes and rode in a caravan of camels westwards into the desert. The camel is not perhaps a particularly difficult animal to ride, but I still remember the glow of pleasure when I was first allowed to take my camel away from camp on my own, to go looking for animals. In a shallow pool at a small oasis one evening I found a terrapin. I slid down to catch it and had a difficult time thereafter trying to persuade the camel to kneel down again for me to remount. I had visions of having to return ignominiously to camp leading the beast behind me; and then suddenly and most unexpectedly it knelt, and in a moment I was up on its back. There was nothing now to mar my triumphant return—complete with terrapin.

At West Downs I became first a Wolf Cub and later a Scout. My patrol was the Buffaloes. In the course of my scouting career I set out optimistically, along with all my brother Scouts, to pass as many badges as possible. A letter to my stepfather indicates a certain over-confidence:

"My Dear Hilton,

In our scouting their is such a nice badge called the stalkers badge in which you have to take 20 photos of wild beasts so that they are recognised in the photo, quite easy here because there are so many birds. We are acting a Shakespeare play 'The Taming of the Shrew'. I'm Hortensio for I am sure you know the play by heart!!

How is unemployment getting on? Are you in Scotland and if so is it nice and fine? I hope so as I think it is unpleasant where there is a Scotch mist hovering round the house all day. There is a Robin here who has a family, who have not yet dispersed and feeds them. She's very tame and we give her biscuits and bread which she will take out of our hands . . ."

But tame though the Robin was, I do not think I ever achieved the stalker's badge.

The naturalist's badge, on the other hand, involved being able to identify a certain number of birds from pictures in a book. The names under the pictures had, of course, to be covered up in order that the identification should be fairly made. I had a copy of T. A. Coward's *British Birds* in the Wayside and Woodland series, a famous book which I often carried about with me, jammed into the slightly split pocket of my blazer. If the names must be covered I would stick stamp paper over the printing under each of Thorburn's beautiful plates. Of course I knew all the pictures by heart, so it was not very fair, and when I came to take the test, the Scoutmaster very sensibly disallowed my copy of Coward's *British Birds*. I had to do it from some other book, but to my surprise I found that I knew most of the birds anyway. I still have that copy of Coward's book, still with the stamp paper stuck over the names.

I went in for my entertainer's badge by giving a lantern lecture on prehistoric reptiles. It was my first attempt at public speaking and I was dry in the mouth with fright, but hoped I was managing to conceal it. Those who heard it said they would not have known that I was nervous, but they had to admit that it was rather a boring lecture, though the slides, they said, were good; I had acquired them from an outside source, but I cannot remember from where. Earlier on the same evening Edward Ford, son of the Headmaster of Harrow, had given a lecture which was excessively witty and flitted airily from subject to subject for no apparent reason. Everybody laughed a great deal and afterwards we were told we had both just scraped through our badge. Edward had won it for the manner of delivery and the lightness of touch, though his subject matter was described as 'thin'. My lecture, they said, had meat in it, but not enough humour. I can well believe it.

My interest in butterflies and moths at school led to a delightful friendship with Miss Evelyn Cheeseman, the distinguished entomologist. She was Curator of Insects at the London Zoo at the time, and was invited to come to Streatley. The Rectory had a lawn which ran down to the Thames, and the idea was that Miss Cheeseman should come over for the day and we should hunt for water insects. Alas, the day did not go according to plan, for poor Miss Cheeseman had been train-sick on the way and arrived feeling very unwell. In spite of that and the pouring rain she gamely set forth with me in the punt to look for dragonfly larvae in a backwater below the weir. But I remember looking down into the water on one side of the punt, and suddenly seeing poor Miss Cheeseman's lunch coming down from the other to feed the Bleak and the small Roach below. The expedition was abandoned, though a second plan was more successful, and not long afterwards she invited me to make a drawing of a Privet Hawk Moth caterpillar for an insect book on which she was then working. This was the first of my drawings ever to be reproduced in a book.

My Zoo visits had long been regular, for my christening present of Life Fellowship had enabled me to sign in my nannie with a cross even before I could write my name. At one of the Zoo's stormy General Meetings in 1958 I was able to put forward my point of view as the senior Fellow in the room, with 49 years of Fellowship behind me.

It seems from my letters home from West Downs that birds were already becoming especially important in my life. As ever, I was optimistic, particularly in listing the extreme rarities which I believed I had seen.

"My dear Hilton,
     We have seen such nice things. A Spotted Flycatcher's nest with four eggs, two Willow-wrens' nests and a Chiff-chaff's, and

a Cole Tit's. We saw a Wall Creeper, a grey-backed shrike, and a Pied Flycatcher, as well as a Spotted Flycatcher and a Long-tailed Tit, a pair of Redpolls, a pair of Goldfinches and a Nut-hatch going into its hole. My only reason for bileiving that the Wall Creeper was genuine is that it was rather like a Tree Creeper only it was climbing up a wall. It had a slightly longer beak than a Tree Creeper and was more curved. Yesterday we saw a family of Gold Crests in a fir tree and a pair of Bullfinches."

It was in the year before my mother married again, when I was eleven, that she decided our summer holiday should be spent in France. She went there to see a villa which she planned to take on the island of Noirmoutier off the mouth of the Loire, and she wrote to me describing it glowingly. This was my reply from West Downs:

"Mummy,

Noirmoutier sounds *lovely*. Where did you see the Redshank? How exciting. Can't wait; take me there now. Oh! If you only could. Yesterday we saw a pair of Bullfinches and a family of Gold Crests and saw the nest high up in a fir; we could only see it through glasses."

When later we arrived at Noirmoutier it was as wonderful a place as she had said, and it became our summer holiday home for the next two years.

La Solitude was a small villa set in the pinewoods perhaps fifty yards from an uncrowded beach. The sand was smooth and white—a perfect beach with a rocky outcrop at one end. There were boats drawn up on the sand at the other end of the beach in front of a holiday hotel called the Beau Rivage. The sand dunes and the pinewoods were full of lizards and my cup was full.

"My dear Hilton," I wrote to my stepfather-to-be, who was then Financial Secretary to the Treasury,

"You absolutely must come here, it's too divine—fishes, birds, lizards, butterflies, sea, woods and everything.
We have caught 4 kinds of lizards

        Sand lizards
        Green lizards
        Common lizards
        Wall lizards.

It's hot all the time and gorgeous.

                Pete."

The letter was adorned with drawings of the lizards.

The invitation was accepted, though no doubt my letter had only minor influence.

For the young, one of the objects of a holiday abroad is to learn the language. For an hour each morning Mlle. Herbulin, an elderly spinster, used to come to La Solitude to teach me French. She did not care for frogs or toads or lizards or caterpillars, but she told me she knew of a little animal called a Cochon d'Indes. I had no idea what this could be. I listened most carefully to the description, but somehow it never occurred to me that she was simply describing a guinea pig. I was fascinated; I thought this must be the most rare and wonderful animal—something between a Bushbaby and a Kinkajou. "And you can keep them as pets too," she said. "I will bring you one tomorrow morning." Excitement ran high, as may be imagined, until the guinea pig arrived. Deep disappointment followed. Here was a piece of zoological snobbery. The animal was charming to look at, tame, cuddly, easy to feed, an ideal pet. . .and yet it was 'only a guinea pig', the type specimen of an experimental animal, zoologically wholly unromantic. It was, curiously enough, my first guinea pig and inevitably it was not long before it laid strong claim to my affections. Without doubt it was a delightful pet; and yet it was some time before my faith in Mlle. Herbulin was entirely restored. True to the traditions of French teaching, Mlle. Herbulin invented phrases which I must say after her and learn by heart. In this case they had nothing to do with my aunt's pen. "Jeudi prochain," she used to say, "il y aura une fête de charité a l'Hotel Beau Rivage . . ." There followed a list of the diversions and entertainments which were to be included in these festivities, though I cannot now remember them all. On one of the stands, however, some novelties were to be offered for sale by members of Mlle. Herbulin's family. "J'ai des cousins qui a fait des jolies coussins avec des coquillage." I remember thinking at the time how extraordinarily uncomfortable these would be.

But more important than Mlle. Herbulin and the fête at the Hotel Beau Rivage were the caterpillars. Two species are indelibly imprinted on my mind. One was an adult Pine Hawk Moth larva which I found walking across the sand just outside the door of our villa, looking for somewhere to pupate. It was the first of these that I had ever seen, it was beautiful and rare (at least in England) and it was an incomparable prize. It finally buried itself in a box of sandy earth which I provided for it, and in due course failed, so far as I can recall, to hatch out. The other was a whole colony—some dozens—of the caterpillars of the Humming Bird Hawk Moth which I found feeding on bedstraw in the sand dunes just behind the beach. These adult caterpillars were of two colours some green and some purplish brown. They had longitudinal stripes and carried on their tails the characteristic Hawk Moth spike. Again they were the first of their kind I had ever seen and each new one that I found was a new excitement; for the whole day on which I discovered this colony I was in a seventh heaven of delight.

Noirmoutier was reached from the mainland across a causeway at low tide. In both directions from the causeway the road led through salt pans, and salt marshes and low-lying meadows in which there were always Yellow Wagtails. Driving with the chauffeur I went frequently to Nantes, which was the nearest railway station, in order to meet visitors who were coming to stay with us. These drives were especially popular with me because I was allowed to steer the car while leaning across from the other seat. At times, too, I was allowed to use the accelerator pedal. It was wonderful.

Boats figured too in the delights of Noirmoutier. There was a small class of double-ended dories, with coloured lug sails, and steered with an oar—fishing dories converted for racing. I was never allowed to sail in these boats during a race, but I can remember going out fishing in one and watching dolphins leaping ten feet out of the water and falling back with a splash to be heard half a mile away.

At the rocky end of the beach there was a fish trap which consisted of a rough wall of weed-covered rocks with a couple of grids. At low spring tides the area enclosed by the wall was almost dry and the small pool was full of large Wrasse and quantities of flat fish. As the tide went down there was tremendous excitement trying to determine what fish had been caught inside.

The summers at Noirmoutier are still a kaleidoscope of bright pictures; even by the next term at West Downs I was full of nostalgia in a letter to my mother:

"My dear,
    How nice it is to think of La Solitude, picking blackberries and catching lizards on the last day, and how good the cackes were from the paticerie, and that evening in the woods, our bathe by moonlight, the thunder storms; all to be repeated next summer. Those lovely starfish; the fisherwoman's horn; walking round the walls of St. Malo."

All these delightful reminiscences, however, did not prevent me from enjoying the school term that followed. Of all school activities

C

in winter I remember enjoying most a game which was known as Table Touch. It was played in a long room which had once been the school chapel but was now used for carpentry and indoor scouting activities. Before the game began the tables and benches, all of which were fortunately very solidly constructed, were arranged round the room at jumping distances apart, to give a series of different routes. At one side two long forms were secured in the bench vices, so that they made a ramp down and up. The game was then played like ordinary touch, but no player might tread on the floor. It was, of course, slightly dangerous, though the casualties were not heavy. It required immense nimbleness and jumping precision. In due course, when someone sprained an ankle, it was suppressed. Still, after forty years, I think that decision was probably a mistake, for I doubt if any irreparable harm would have come to us. As a game to watch it must have been lively; there was often quite a crowd in the doorway of 'N' room shouting exhortations. But to play it was utterly satisfying. We flew through the air in magnificent leaps, we twisted and turned, bluffed and double-bluffed on which direction we would jump, hurtled down the sloping ramp and up the other side. As a game it had a primitive quality, for it had no winners or losers. You just went on playing until you got tired and then someone else took your place. Without doubt the most skilful player— though I might not have admitted it at the time—was 'Boy' Somerton, now the Earl of Normanton.

Out of the dim past of those days comes a moment of shame. It was in the holidays and concerns a very large eel. My mother and I were staying at Beaulieu Abbey with the then Lord Montagu and were to spend the day operating a seine net in the Beaulieu river. During the morning the catch had been small. By far the most notable fish had been an eel which was almost as thick as a man's arm and must have weighed about 10 lb. For a silver eel it was truly a monster, and Lord Montagu could talk of nothing else at the picnic lunch. After lunch I went to have another look at the monster. It lay on the bank, apparently dead, among the other and lesser fishes of the catch. It had wriggled in the dust and was caked with dried slime and earth. It would, I thought, look much better if the dirt were washed off. I lugged it to the water's edge and dipped it a couple of times. A dry eel is not so difficult to hold, but as soon as it was wet again it became slippery and I nearly dropped it. I must be careful, I thought, because it really would be too awful if I lost it. Eels can live for a long time out of water; this one had been on land for two or three hours already, and seemed quite moribund until I came to give it that last dip before returning it to its place among the rest of the catch. Then it gave one violent wriggle and was gone for ever. I fear that Lord Montagu did not suffer this kind of foolishness very gladly. Having to tell him what I had done and his irate reaction still form part of a terrible nightmare.

Small boys can, of course, be excessively tiresome; they can also at times be fairly poisonous, particularly in bulk. Individually they are, I suppose, poisonous in varying degree. Schoolmasters no doubt have a scale by which to measure it, and from their wide experience can forecast just how poisonous a boy must be to succeed in later life. West Downs had its fair share of the little horrors, many of whom became Cabinet Ministers and the like. No less than fourteen of my contemporaries are members of one or other of the Houses of Parliament, yet without doubt the most unusual of my fellows was poor Jack Amery, for whom the twists of fortune were finally to take such a disastrous and terrible turn.

However successfully or unsuccessfully a school may provide 'the happiest days of one's life', holiday memories are likely to stand out most plainly. Many of our holidays were spent with the Austen Chamberlain family. Joe was a little older than me, Diane a year younger (and I was going to marry her for sure), and Lawrence younger still. I remember a simple and sad little story of deflation which happened when both our families were staying in the seaside village of Trebeurden in Brittany. We children had been ranging over the gorse-covered hill looking for Dartford Warblers and we thought it must be nearly lunch time. Approaching us was a French-man who looked as though he would have a watch; but who was to ask him the time? Was it not I who spoke French like a native—and why not? Had I not been to school in Paris (for three months) and spent summer holidays in Noirmoutier? Was there not the redoubt-able figure of Mlle. Herbulin in the background? Diane had more faith in me than the others. She looked at me as if to say, "You're brave and clever, you must do it," and then she looked at the others as if to say, "Now just you watch this."

I stepped into the road "Pardon m'sieur" in the faultless accent of the parrot, "Est ce que vous pouvez me dire le temps?" There was a giggle from behind me. "Please can you tell me the weather?" How could I possibly have made such an elementary error? I can still remember the hot shame of it; and Diane is happily married to someone else.

When our house in Buckingham Palace Road was scheduled for demolition to make way for the Green Line Coach Station, we moved to Bayswater Road—to a house which the family still occupies to this day. On the corner of Leinster Terrace, overlooking Kensington Gardens, stands a two-storey semi-detached house with an oval window in its side wall, a small garden in front and a larger one behind. It has variously been called Leinster Corner House, Leinster Corner, or 100 Bayswater Road. At the far end of the back garden, which has a small formal pond and fountain, was a building which, at the time when we first moved in, my mother had just converted into a studio for her sculpture. Leinster Corner had, by a strange coincidence, once been Sir James Barrie's home (I have a letter written from it to my father in 1906) and in what was now to be my mother's studio he had written *Peter Pan*.

This new house was in many ways much nicer than the old. Like any house which has served a family for thirty-five years, its memories cover almost the full scale of emotions, but for me it is overwhelmingly a happy place. My half-brother Wayland now lives there with his large family. He had been born at Buckingham Palace Road in 1923 and was three years old when we first moved into Leinster Corner.

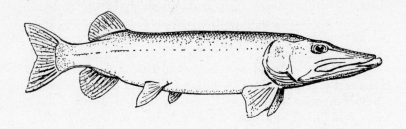

CHAPTER 7   *"Come on, Oundle"*

H. G. WELLS was a family friend. He was interested in Oundle
School and greatly admired Sanderson who was then Headmaster.
He strongly advised that I should go there. My mother had also
heard good report of it from Lady Fisher Dilke, an old friend, whose
second son, Michael, had already been there for a couple of terms.
It was agreed that I should go there in the autumn of 1923.

The school was then principally renowned for its enlightened
attitude to science and technology. Engineering was its special line,
but the natural sciences were well served. For zoology, it seemed, I
could hardly do better. To send me there was a snap decision made
only a few months before. In the preceding Easter holidays, it was
arranged that I should join a special course which went annually
from Oundle School to the Marine Biological Association at Plymouth. It was here that I first met William Orton, a marine biologist of distinction. At Sandwich I had learnt a little about the
animals of a sandy shore, and now Dr. Orton showed me for the first
time the animals of a rocky coast, and those which were brought up
on to the deck of the Association's trawler *Salpa*, in the trawls and
dredges from deeper water. But to me the greatest enjoyment of that
first course was shore collecting at Wembury Bay. At low spring
tides our party went far out on the rocky shore, each armed with a
'collecting basket' which contained one large jam jar, and a number
of smaller ones. As we turned over the big stones, the profusion and
diversity of the animals we found underneath was to me sheer
delight. Rocklings, Blennies, Cornish Suckers and Butterfish; the
beautiful carpet patterns of compound Ascidians, the delicate
branching hydroids, the brittle stars and the quick-moving Poly-
chete worms. Here were real riches in my currency. With enthusiasm Dr. Orton would talk of the ingenuity of evolution, the
nicety of the balance in the struggle for existence, the range of

variation within a single species, and suddenly I realised that there was more in zoology than putting a name to every animal you saw. All the time the beauty of shape and colour and the newness kept me enthralled. The course at Plymouth was a tremendous success.

Sanderson died suddenly just before I went to Oundle and his place was taken by Kenneth Fisher, who was Headmaster for the whole of my time there. In my day he was known to the boys as 'Bud' (after Bud Fisher, the artist of a strip cartoon in the *Daily Mirror*). I was to join School House, Bud's house, but for my first term I was to be 'living out' with four or five other boys at The Firs. This was the house of an assistant master known as 'Pa' Bray, who taught French. At a previous interview when told that I had a little French he had answered with an explosive and never-to-be-forgotten "Ah! Bon!"

I arrived at the School in company with Michael Dilke. He was a keen ornithologist and of friendly disposition but he had already been two terms at Oundle; I was considerably junior to him, and therefore very much pleased at any encouragement that he might give me. I remember that during that first term I and a contemporary caught a pike in a pool of the River Nene. We caught it by the unconventional method of stretching a line, with spoon bait attached, from the far end of the pool to the bridge; the bait was then thrown in, while the operator on the bridge hauled in rapidly. The method was crude but it succeeded, though the pike we caught was a small one; I should think it weighed a pound or at the most a pound and a half. I remember telling Michael Dilke the same evening that we had caught this fish; I told him with tremendous pride and excitement and his comment was "Ye Gods!" I had never heard the phrase before and I thought, "This is it. This is a grown-up phrase and this chap who is older than me and after all really knows a thing or two, has said 'Ye Gods' about something which I have done. This is the greatest thing that ever happened."

We fished a great deal at Oundle, for the River Nene is famous for its coarse fish; and besides the river, there were near-by lakes and ponds well stocked with fish. According to local legend the ponds in Biggin Park were originally laid out by the monks. In one pond there were roach and in another rudd, while in a third there seemed to be a population of roach-rudd hybrids. There were also bream, and in one of the ponds rudd-bream hybrids. All these peculiar fish interested me so much that I made detailed drawings of them which I took in due course to Dr. Tate Regan at the Natural History Museum in London. The specimens from which I made these careful drawings were all caught on hook and line. It was exciting fishing, by the standards of those days—paste or gentles, or perhaps a red worm, on the smallest possible hook, a quill float, touch and timing.

Late one winter Sunday afternoon when ice was forming at the pond I hooked a much larger fish than usual. As I hauled it in, it suddenly clattered out on to the thin ice and I realised that my hook was no longer attached. There the great fish lay on the ice like an upturned carving dish, within easy slithering distance of the patch of open water through which I had been fishing. The ice was much too thin to bear my weight, so thin indeed that I expected the fish itself to break through at any moment. There seemed to be only one thing to do. I must jump into the two feet of water and grab the fish in my hands before it could make its escape. I can still see that fish slipping about on the ice in the cold frosty winter's dusk. I got it to the shore and it proved to be a rudd-bream hybrid. It weighed, if I remember right, about two and a half pounds, and I kept it alive, as I often kept the larger and more interesting fish in those days. There was trouble about the sodden and creaseless pinstripe trousers of my Sunday suit.

The ponds in Biggin Park produced an even more dramatic encounter with a shoal of very large Perch. On one wonderful afternoon when I was fishing with a lob worm there was a great rush as I pulled in to recast. I tried again and a splendid Perch came after it, taking the bait as I paused to give it the chance. The fish weighed 2 lb. 10 oz. A few minutes later I hooked another in exactly the same way. By the end of the afternoon I had four Perch of over two pounds, and a fifth which weighed 3 lb. 2 oz. Two of the largest of these were sent some time later to the Aquarium at the London Zoo. For Perch they were exceptionally large.

I remember, too, from these days a four-pound Tench caught with a noose as it cruised in the clear shallows of the lake at Blatherwyke, a fish which also went to the London Zoo.

But, apart from Pike, the largest fish we caught at Oundle were Bream. They were in larger schools and of larger size, so it seemed, in the river itself and they were most easily caught at night. The problem was to get out of school at night. It involved a certain amount of subterfuge, and a certain amount of climbing, but it was fairly frequently achieved. On one particular night near Barnwell, on a bend of the Nene which was famous for its bream, two of us had three ledger lines down, when the bream shoal came past. In half an hour we had caught a dozen bream, the largest five-and-a-half pounds. Under each rod hung a loop of line with a small piece of paper folded over it. When the fish took the bait the paper jumped up, and this could easily be seen in the dark. As each of us played a great plate-sized bream, I can still see the third piece of paper jumping up and remember the moment of panic; what do we do now? I forget how that particular panic was resolved. But I know that in half an hour we had caught a dozen splendid bream. We had to leave them out there that night in order to bring them back legitimately on the following afternoon.

Fishing was not always smiled upon at Oundle, particularly if it prevented attendance at football matches. I had a strong aversion to being made to watch other people playing football. I have never enjoyed watching other people doing anything so much as doing it myself. In this context I became a violent rebel. I could not bear standing frigidly on the touch line shouting wanly "Come on, Ounderl" in unison with a lot of equally bored contemporaries. In vain did they try to appeal to my community spirit. If it was a House Match, where was my pride in my house, if a School Match where my loyalty to the school? Did I not mind how each of them fared on the football field? The sad thing was that I did not. Of course, there was a tariff for this kind of delinquency. In the last analysis it came down to corporal punishment. The first two times it was four strokes with the cane from the duty House Prefect, then six from the Head of the House, then six from the House Master and finally six from the Headmaster. This scale usually lasted me through the winter, for of course it was not every time that I got caught. On match-watching days I could be seen hobbling down the steps from School House with a stiff leg caused by the fishing rod hidden in my trouser leg.

To show the extraordinary futility of these attempts to achieve conformity, I can remember quite late in my public school days having tea with a contemporary in his study. He had been made a House Prefect and I had not. As we began our tea a message was brought in to say that it was known I had not watched the match that day. As Duty Prefect it was his job to deal with the matter. "Of course," he said, "I've got to give you four—that's the standard thing. Shall we get it over with or wait till we've finished tea?" The reason that the punishment was so useless was that no stigma attached to it. On this score and others I was probably beaten more than any other boy in my house. Perhaps I was not proud of the fact, but it certainly brought me no shame.

There were, of course, also effective punishments. After a winter sports' holiday at Font Romeu in the Pyrenees I had become keen on skating and in the following term at Oundle the ponds froze. Until it was certain that the ice would bear, the school was expressly forbidden to walk or skate on it. But I went to a small horse pond, hidden away in the far corner of a field. I found that the ice was thick enough and had a delightful afternoon's skating. As I was taking off my boots to return to school, by the merest ill-luck an assistant master passed by. "And who," he asked, "made that figure of eight out there on the ice? Not you by any chance?" Next day the Headmaster announced that skating on the big flood would be general for the whole school "except for Scott". On the day after, Bud relented, which was unexpectedly lenient, for after all I had quite deliberately disobeyed a very reasonable order. His gesture was skilful, for I could not feel aggrieved and was therefore left feeling slightly ashamed, and with a greater respect and admiration for my Headmaster.

Bud was a slight figure, rather bald, with a small moustache and high colouring in his cheeks. To look at he was not impressive, yet his authority with the boys was immense. This stemmed almost entirely from two things, his sense of justice and his sense of humour. If you were in trouble you knew that you would be treated fairly, but you could not hope to pull the wool over his eyes.

There were times when fishing was quite legitimate. I remember standing on the bridge which spans the River Nene near Oundle station, fishing for chubb, when I saw Bud approaching down the road. There was nothing illegal in fishing from there or at that particular time, but somehow I felt it would be best if the rod were concealed. Unfortunately at that precise moment the bait was taken by a goodly chubb. As the Headmaster approached deep in conversation with an assistant master I turned my back on the bridge parapet and held the rod just below the edge. I could only use one hand for this, for the other would be occupied with taking off my straw hat to the Headmaster as he passed. He stopped suddenly when he was abreast of me. "Well, Scott—not fishing today?" "Well, sir, 'Yes' and 'No', sir." "Oh well. Good luck!" and he was walking on again, while I returned to the problems of landing my chubb.

Kenneth Fisher was no discourager of enterprise and individuality, provided that it did not get out of hand. We were not supposed to go into the houses in the town for the very good reason that we might pick up epidemic diseases and spread them in the school. Nevertheless I had for some time kept a ferret which for the most part was boarded out at the home of one of the school

C*

employees. We caught many rabbits with this ferret and did not always have the necessary permission to do so. One afternoon I was returning from a sortie with the ferret, and was carrying over my arm, and concealed by my raincoat, two rabbits which had been caught in a dried-up culvert alongside the main road, rabbits which soon afterwards I should be presenting at the poulterer's shop in exchange for some welcome additional pocket money. I was about to turn into the little yard leading up to the ferret's home, when I chanced to look round and see the Headmaster walking in company with the assistant housemaster. They were twenty yards behind me and deep in conversation, but I thought that it would be unsafe to turn into the narrow yard, and the only alternative was to walk the full length of the High Street ahead of them. It was not until after I had left the school and Kenneth Fisher was a guest at my Lighthouse home, that I learned that three inches of the rabbits' ears had extended below the folded mackintosh and that he and the assistant housemaster had been laughing about it all the way along the High Street.

Not all the masters at Oundle were so understanding. There was, for example, Mr. John King, the housemaster at New House, a magnificent and forthright character who did not believe in nonconforming boys. At some periods and especially immediately before a rabbiting excursion my ferret used to accompany me to the classrooms, living quietly in a makeshift 'poacher's pocket' which I had created by cutting a hole at the top of the lining of my coat. She was a small ferret and very tame, and normally she made very little trouble in class. But inevitably sooner or later the giggling or the unexpected movements in my coat gave away her presence. Eventually I was hauled up for a stern rebuke. "Supposing . . .", said Mr. King. "Supposing 550 boys all kept ferrets in their pockets . . ." The absurdity of this classic argument against individuality made a deep impression on me, and my belief in the 'lone wolf' attitude was perhaps too greatly strengthened thereafter.

The chapel had only lately been completed when I went to Oundle. Some years before, my mother had made a nude bronze figure of a boy with upraised arm as a War Memorial for West Downs. Another cast of this statue was bought for Oundle and placed on a rather lonely and exposed site in front of the chapel. As legend under it, it carried the answer of the boy Samuel, "Here am I, send me!" The model for this statue had been an Italian boy, the son of Fiorini, the caster who for many years cast all her bronzes. I had never posed for it, and it was not at all like me, but it was useless to say so. It was (and I believe still is) widely held to be me. The assumption was only once useful to me, when I went back to lecture to the school after the Second World War. The notion that I had gone to the Admiralty at the beginning of the war with my right hand raised saying "Here am I, send me" had somehow tickled my audience, and from then on the lecture was made.

But if I have given anywhere the impression that I was not happy at school, this must immediately be remedied. On the whole the school gave great freedom to its boys and I managed to pursue my interests, which were almost entirely concerned with animals, with extraordinarily little interruption. By most present-day public school standards we were more limited in our range of operations because bicycles were not then allowed. In spite of this we managed to wander far and wide by devious means (often by the then little practised device of hitch-hiking).

Michael Dilke and I made a collection of the skins of British mammals. It was started when two dead badgers were brought to us, which had been run over on the railway line. Clearly they had been caught out on the far side of the line, had tried to get back to their setts when they heard the train coming and had been run down before they could do so. To these skins we added a fox skin and later an otter, and then we began in earnest to collect the skins of the smaller mammals, stoat, weasel, water rat, brown rat, black rat, the field voles, the wood mice, and the shrews.

Collecting, of course, can become a mania with children and perhaps I was fortunate in not being much bitten by this particular bug. Michael Dilke, to be sure, had a modest collection of single eggs of British birds and I was content to help him in the building of it. But apart from this and our mammal skins I was never a collector at school. No butterflies, nor moths, nor stamps, nor autographs. Nevertheless a large number of pet animals figured prominently throughout my school years. Among these I particularly remember the bats which we found living in a colony behind two loose stones in the wall of the house. These stones were fitted into special holes intended to accommodate scaffolding in any future maintenance or repairs. The spaces behind the stones were each the home of half a dozen Pipistrelles—the smallest and commonest of the British bats.

For the first twenty-four hours of captivity these bats always refused food but after that they became so hungry that if offered a suitable fly they would take it from the hand. We had extensive fly-catching forays round all the school windows in order to keep them supplied. After a while they became extraordinarily tame. We

designed a special box for them and made it in the school's wood
workshop. The next stage was to give them their liberty again and
yet keep them tame by hand feeding. We hung the box out on the
wall near their original home and for a week or two the bats continued to use the box in preference to the hole behind the stone. The
advantage of the box was that it could be opened, and food offered
without actually dislodging and therefore disturbing the bats. But
after a while they seemed to decide in favour of a little more privacy,
and by the time the term ended only two bats were still living in the
box.

Owls became a special line during my last two summers at
Oundle. We had established a fairly extensive trap-line in connection with our mammal skin collection and this provided a ready
supply of food for owlets. We reared owls of the three common
species, Tawny, Barn and Little. The Barn Owls were the most
difficult, the Tawnies the nicest and the Little Owls the fiercest.
Their diet was augmented with rabbits caught with my ferret and
sparrows brought from a sparrow-trap on the school farm.

Then of course there were caterpillars. In summer time the
window-sill of my study was always lined with small Petrie dishes,
muslin-topped jars and boxes, and larger breeding cages full to
bursting with the caterpillars of British moths, especially the Hawk
Moths, which I always thought of as the *crème de la crème*.

I worked quite hard in school, and in due course found myself in
the Biology VIth. I enjoyed the work as it had to do with animals,
though too often dead ones, when the live ones were so much more
exciting. I had a certain facility in drawing which enabled me to
record neatly and tidily what I saw down my microscope, what I
saw when I was dissecting my cockroach, my frog, my dog-fish or
my rabbit (or my badger, for we dissected the badgers whose skins
went into our collection. They were extremely high for it was warm
weather; one of them was a female full of quite large embryos). I
was also able to make drawings of the birds I saw, and although they
were the animals I enjoyed most, and enjoyed drawing most, I was
left in no doubt that this was to be regarded as 'play'—it was certainly not biology.

Drawing itself was taught, of course, as a subject in its own right.
My mother did not believe that art could or should be taught. There
were perhaps some complicated techniques in art where time could
be saved if you did not have to learn everything by trial and error.
But the idea that anyone should be taught that there was a right and
a wrong way to compose a picture, right and wrong combinations

of colour, right and wrong ways of applying paint—this was to her a heresy, and liable to stifle the original artist, and perhaps disastrously influence the whole future of his art. She believed the object of art classes or art school was to present an unlimited opportunity for practice and a little cheerful encouragement. These views were evidently to some extent shared by our delightful and very tall drawing master, E. M. O. R. Dickie, an Irishman who, it must be admitted, spent more time reading (inimitably) the works of Mr. Llyn Doyle to us than he did in teaching us drawing. But he once said something important to me after I had drawn a picture of a stuffed Kestrel. He said, "That's all right, I know you can draw a stuffed bird. What I really want to know is whether you can draw a pudding. If you can draw a pudding really well you can draw anything. Go and draw a pudding." These were sage words, for it is certainly much easier to draw an object which has a complex outline, or a detailed pattern; but if you can draw a pudding really well you can draw anything.

Oundle School was noted for its music. The music master, Clement Spurling, had the brilliant and original idea of using the whole School, whether they could sing or not, as a sort of diapason in the great choral works which were performed each year. Those who had an ear for music joined the School Choir which represented perhaps a third of the boys, and the rest, who could not sing in tune, formed the 'Non-choir'. They came in at specific places to swell the fortissimo passages.

During my four years at Oundle I took part in four great choral performances. In my first year I sang treble in Bach's B *minor Mass*; in the following year in Bach's *Christmas Oratorio* I sang alto. The year after that I sang tenor in Handel's *Messiah*, and in my last year I was a bass in the B *minor Mass* again. Unfortunately these performances were never recorded, for recording in those days was a professional affair; but I have the feeling that they were rather important musical events. The four soloists were professional singers who came for their love of the music. Miss Carrie Tubb (who had a son at Oundle) was one of them and perhaps it was through her that the others came. Margaret Balfour was the contralto soloist and Topliss Green was the bass. I shall never forget the almost unbearable beauty, as it seemed to me, of the soprano and contralto duet in the *Christe eleison*. But apart from the beauty of the final performance, consider for a moment the effects of the rehearsals on the boys. For a school of 550 boys to be going around for a whole term humming and whistling the tunes of Bach must surely have played a significant part in the formation of their musical taste.

Kenneth Fisher was a keen ornithologist and from my earliest days at the School he used, from time to time, to take one or two of us to the flood waters further up the River Nene at Lilford and Aldwincle—floods which in late winter stretched almost all the way to Thrapston.

On the flood waters, which spread across the great meadows on either side of the old disused Lilford Decoy in its triangular wood, there were thousands of Wigeon, Mallards, Teal, and a few Shovelers, and a small number of Pintails which according to the books were 'rare inland'. To me the Pintails had a special appeal. They were so graceful, their plumage so perfect and the scientific name of their genus—*Dafila*—which was then still in standard use, so pleasantly euphonious; though I did not then think that I might one day use it to name one of my daughters.

But the most exciting things on the floods were the Grey Geese. These were the first Grey Geese I had ever seen and we used to find their identification difficult. There were sometimes as many as 200, and nearly all of them, we finally decided, were White-fronted Geese, although there were small family parties of Pink-footed and Bean Geese. This then was my first aquaintance with the White-fronts and the Pinkfeet which were to play so important a part in my later life. Casting my mind back to those school days I can quite easily recapture the excitement with which we crept along the railway cutting to get a closer view of these wonderful birds. Already geese were to me more than just big birds. They had some aura of romance and mystery around them.

Michael Dilke was also a regular member of the Headmaster's bird-watching parties to the winter floods, and to the lake at Blatherwyke eight miles from the school. We used to go in Bud's open Sunbeam car to catch diving ducks (among them an occasional Smew) and bramblings (on a great heap of chaff) and to see the feral flock of Canada Geese and the single wild Greylag which lived and hybridised with them. At this time Michael and I were working on a book; it was to be a book about birds in which I was to make the illustrations while Michael provided the text. He came of a family with a tradition in writing and his own literary talent was already emerging. Our book was almost complete and rather secret when John Brereton, a contemporary in the same house, somehow discovered about it and asserted that he could arrange for its publication: and so in due course a limited edition of 525 copies of the book appeared, privately printed by Messrs. Knapp, Drewett and Sons

Ltd., under the title *Adventures Among Birds*, a title which had already been used, although we did not know it, by W. H. Hudson. The anonymous authors were described as 'Three Schoolboys'. (This to make sure that the sponsors could not be charged with trying to exploit my Antarctic connections.) My drawings were placed in the margins of the text. They were very primitive little drawings made with pen and ink and I encountered for the first time one of the great problems which to this day bedevils the artist who would make small black and white book illustrations for inclusion in the text. My drawings were printed either crooked or, in the worst cases, upside down. A Little Grebe swam steeply down hill, a pigeon leaned perilously forward, a squirrel which should have been looking round a tree trunk was printed looking over a horizontal log, and a pair of Hooded Crows were shown in inverted flight. It seems that there is still no accepted method in the printing trade whereby an artist who draws something which is unfamiliar to the operator who sets the type can be assured that it will appear at the right angle. Perhaps one day a foolproof method of alignment will be devised. Until then my drawings will surely continue to be set crooked in the text, or even upside down.

All our adventures were not among birds. In those days most things seemed to be quite adventurous. It became, even then, almost a 'way of life'. I wrote home after the adventures of a summer weekend in which bicycles were allowed by special dispensation and hired for the day:

"Mother dear,

"So sorry not to have written on Sunday, but it was half-term. Lord! What a busy life! I don't know where to begin.

"On Friday Michael and I went to Blatherwyke. He had met the keeper before so we went to him. He was awfully nice. About a mile from Blatherwyke M. had a puncture. I took the bicycle to a place where the man was to return at 5 oc. We went off and walked round the lake, and had fun, seeing lots of birds. On the way back we found a rabbit's nest pulled out, and five young rabbits meandering around. They were about four inches long. We took them. I expect and suspect a badger or fox. They opened their eyes on Saturday, and one was crushed by the others sitting on him. Sad, but we still have four. They gallop around the floor. They are now about eight inches long; very short ears.

"Anyway, to continue, we went to get the bicycle at 7.30. We were to be back by 9 oc. to show our experiment to the Master and

Wardens of the Grocers Company. We found the bike not done, and we took it to someone else. He was going to be some time, so I gave my bike to M. who cannot ride fast, and he started off. At exactly 8 oc. I started. I rode a mile and a half and then realised that my back tyre was flat. I rode for two-and-a-half miles on a flat tyre. The cover came right off twice! Then I thought of a ruse, so at the next farm I arranged to swop bicycles temporarily, and caught up M. We arrived at ten to nine, which is twelve minutes shorter than the previous record. Then, of course, the Grocers did not come until ten past ten, so the hurry was useless. Our experiment, or rather demonstration, was a chart of useful and harmful birds to Agriculture, Horticulture, and Game-Preservation. (I hope you can read all this. I am writing at lunch, it being the only spare moment in the day.)

"Well, the next day, chapel in the morning, speeches, dull and boring. Did some sleep in order to make up for early school— lunched with Mrs. Margesson [her son was a contemporary] at the little place where she is staying. There were some other parents who had a racing BENTLEY and took all of us for a 'spin'. After lunch, afternoon demonstrations. Most people were interested, chiefly in the Game Preservation. Lots of shooting tenants all wanting to know if a Kestrel was good or bad. It is good on the whole.

"Sat. night, dinner with Lady Greig [mother of another contemporary]. Concert after. Performance of Choral. I am tenor. During the concerts when you are not performing, and have no parents, you can stroll anywhere you like in the market place.

"Gale and I found a Scarlet meeting with a Bolshi on a box. We listened, joined in (fortunately he knew less about what he was talking about than we did). We muddled up his argument, and got the crowd, twenty-five strong, on our side. He was preaching Strike, so we thoroughly routed his arguments. He told a lie or two which made us stronger. People refused to listen to him, and at last a bad egg from the back of the crowd shut him up. Gale and I then got up in turn, and being careful of what we said, roused a cheer at every word, and when it was time for us to be homing, we were carried through the crowd and cheered. It will always be a boast of mine that I was the instigation by which a Socialist meeting was wrecked! It really was a triumph, and quite thrilling.

"Sunday, lunch Mrs. Margesson, tea Sir John Russell [father of another of my friends in School House] who is the greatest agricultural scientist of the day. He experiments on corn parasites, and on the system of lesser fleas, destroys earwigs, etc. by the million. He shipped one hundred million earwig parasites to Australia last week. He has invited me to go and work at Wrothamstead, his experimental farm, in the last week of the holidays. What a chance! I must not on any account miss it. Dinner again with Mrs. Margesson. Altogether rather a hectic half-term. Added to which I race in School House second boat tomorrow as ever is, and also I have to sweat for a School Cert. besides having the bugs to tend (I have an Eyed Hawk caterpillar), and four young rabbits and Moctaques [a big Eyed Lizard from the South of France]. You can perhaps imagine what a life it all is.

"By the way, Bill's big Cecropia [a Silk moth which my stepfather had given to me as a pupa] has layed many infertile eggs, which we are experimenting on with

  a) Oxidising agents which stimulate
  b) Strong metals—Uranium, etc.
  c) Sudden shocks, rupture of cell walls, etc. which is what
     a sperm does to the egg.

"The solutions are injected with a glass capillary tube. Very hard. Tell Bill, it might interest him."

The eggs did not hatch, but rather surprisingly the rabbits were reared to maturity.

In my day Oundle had no swimming bath; we swam only in the river. I found, when I had the competition of 550 boys, instead of only eighty, that I was not so good as I had thought I was, though I swam every year for my house. In the summer I used to row on the river, rather than play cricket which was the alternative. I rowed for the principal reason that it was possible to take a single-handed skiff and go down the river for the afternoon. This meant that I could troll a spoon bait on a pike line from the outrigger, and many were the small pike that I caught, though curiously enough I never caught a big one in this way. At rowing I finally stroked my House four, but I did not like it enough to go on with it at Cambridge.

Being a member of the O.T.C. was a dreary business, I thought, except for Camp at the end of the summer term which was always rather enjoyable. It was during one of these camps at Tidworth that I had my first opportunity to fly. A party was to be taken over in a lorry to the aerodrome at Old Sarum. All members of the party had to have a signed paper from their parents to say that they were permitted to fly, but unfortunately no such paper had arrived for me, for, as I sadly knew, my mother was away; yet I was determined not to miss this chance and I was sure that she would have signed the paper had she been at home. (I am supported in this by the following passage in her diary written for my father when he was in the Antarctic, though of course I did not then know of it.)

"Nov. 18th, 1911. What nonsense that virtue is its own reward! What reward have I for refraining from getting my pilot's certificate? There is nothing I want so ardently to do as to learn to fly. Almost every day I have actively to restrain myself. Everybody is shocked at my flying even as a passenger. 'My duties to my husband and son!' I see their point, but I want to fly, and what reward have I? Worse—I believe you'd like it if I did fly. Damn!"

Somehow or other I managed to smuggle myself into the lorry without disclosing that I had no paper. But it was evidently going to be very difficult when we arrived at Old Sarum. On the way over I could not make up my mind whether to claim that the paper was lost or whether to own up that I had not got one. When the time came honesty prevailed, and was unexpectedly rewarded. Someone must have taken a risk in order not to disappoint me, with the result that a couple of hours later my turn came up and I found myself sitting in the observer's seat of a Bristol Fighter.

The first flight of one's life must surely have been a memorable thrill for everyone of my generation. In future it may well be no more momentous than one's first trip in a car or a boat. But for me it was miraculously exciting. I can remember every windswept detail of the take-off, the breathtaking 'moment-of-truth' when the bumping of the wheels ended and I realised that I was airborne for the first time ever; the shadow of the plane getting visibly smaller as we climbed; the vertical bank over the earthworks of the Roman Camp; the long glide down with the engine throttled back; and the delightful relief of tension as the landing was successfully completed. I discovered, that day, and have confirmed it many hundreds of times since, that flying is unlike any other sensation in the world and well above most.

CHAPTER 8

Sailing and
Stalking

HOLIDAYS from Oundle are now in my mind merged together. But there are special memories which may have some bearing on the story, and particular events on the Norfolk Broads which had their influence. We took a converted wherry, the *Golden Hind*, from Messrs. Loynes of Wroxham and made our way through the broads along the usual route by the wooded broads of Salhouse and Ranworth, up the River Ant to Barton, and in due course up the Thurne and the Kendal Dyke, through Heigham Sounds to Hickling, where I met for the first time Jim Vincent, the Warden of Lord Desborough's then quite new bird sanctuary at Hickling Broad. Jim showed me his young bitterns, his young Montagu's Harriers, and his Bearded Tits, for the first of many times. He remained a delightful friend until his death twenty years later.

After Hickling came the Meadow Dyke leading to Horsey Mere, which was later to become our regular summering place. On this first passage through the Meadow Dyke, I found for the first time the beautiful striped caterpillars of the rare Swallowtail Butterfly. The wide landscape of the Broads has a character and beauty of special and perhaps specialised appeal. From this earliest visit it has been the setting of two of my life-long enthusiasms—water birds and sailing.

At Potter Heigham I remember that my stepfather had hired a half-decker. This was a comparatively safe eighteen-foot half-decked sailing boat, carrying a balanced lug, and it was in this that he gave me my first lessons in sailing. By the time we went on our next holiday to the Norfolk Broads I was already quite handy in a boat and could sail on my own.

Many of my holidays from Oundle were spent at my stepfather's cottage in Wiltshire. It was called The Lacket and was on the outskirts of the village of Lockeridge near Marlborough. It was, and

still is, one of the most perfect thatched cottages I have ever seen. It
nestles amid ancient yews, its garden enclosed by a great bulging
box hedge like the fat green forearm of a giant. It lies at the farthest
end of the village in a shallow valley called a dene. If you look up
the dene from the village, the foreground of the landscape is a grass
meadow scattered with great grey boulders or sarcen stones. Behind
the cottage the hill rises steeply to the Downs; and across from the
cottage there is a gentle slope of fields to the West Woods. These
woods were our particular delight, and we had our own names for
all the places in them, which we marked on our own special six-
inch-to-the-mile map—Archer's Dene, Brock Dene, Pleached
Alley, Mole Joke. It was to Archer's Dene in April 1926 that I took
Lord Grey of Fallodon to hear his first Wood Lark. He was then
almost blind, but the bird sang beautifully for more than half an
hour: and because Lord Grey was so moved I too shall never forget
that clear flute-like song. Often we used to walk far over the
Downs to Temple Wood, and Hackpen and Barbary Camp;
and up and down the Kennet Valley; and into Savernake
Forest.

Always on these walks I used to collect wild flowers and bring
them home; and while my stepfather read aloud to us each
evening I would draw the flowers meticulously and paint in the
colours in water-colour. I made quite a complete collection of small
water-colour drawings of the common wild flowers that grew around
The Lacket. These we identified from Sowerby's beautiful Flora.
Often when I found interesting caterpillars on the plants I added
them to the plates in the book. Alas, my additions were not so
skilfully made as the exquisite hand-coloured drawings which
formed the illustrations of the book itself.

Being read to aloud was always an excellent stimulus to my drawing. Among my papers I found, the other day, a list in my stepfather's handwriting of the books which he had read aloud to us, in
whole or in part, during my school holidays. I wonder how it would
compare with a boy's book list of today:

Kidnapped	*Rip Van Winkle*
St. Ives	*Great Expectations*
Quentin Durward	*The Shaving of Shagpat*
Feats on the Fjord	*The Rose and the Ring*
Peter Simple	*The Scouring of the White*
Huckleberry Finn	*Horse*
Vicar of Wakefield	*Bevis*

King of the Golden River	*Old Mortality*
The Casting Away of Mrs. Lecks	*The Ebb Tide*
and Mrs. Ayleshine	*Martin Chuzzlewit*
Travels with a Donkey	*Pickwick Papers*
Prescott's Mexico	*Island Nights Entertainments*
King Solomon's Mines	*Odtaa*
Tom Sawyer	*Path of the King*

Menabilly, which is now the home of Daphne du Maurier and was the original Manderly of her novel *Rebecca*, stands back in the Cornish woods from the Gribbin Head to the west of Fowey. It was our summer holiday home for three widely scattered summers. The house was large, rambling and agreeably sinister; much of it was unused in our day and in near ruinous condition. The woods were full of hydrangeas and cyclamen, and a hidden smugglers' path ran down to a tiny bay with a bathing beach. The grounds were extensive and secret. We bathed and went fishing for mackerel, collected shells and wildfowlers and had a tame cuckoo. In my earliest memories of Menabilly my companions were Michael and David McKenna, the sons of the Chancellor of the Exchequer in the Asquith Government. They, and their mother Pamela, and their mother's sister Barbara, who later became Lady Freyberg, used to come to share the big house with us. I remember how the whole McKenna family was fascinated by hunting for Cowries to be found only on certain parts of certain beaches. The enthusiasm which I caught from them has persisted, and I can still spend a happy hour at that needle-in-haystack operation of looking for the tiny pink Cowries on an English beach.

In another summer at Menabilly while exploring the roof we discovered a colony of a hundred or more Greater Horseshoe Bats all hanging like pears from the rafters. When I went there thirty years later and explored the same roof with Daphne du Maurier's children we found this same colony of Greater Horseshoes still hanging from the same rafters, though no doubt there had been very many generations of the bats in between.

Menabilly was the scene of a sad little romance in the last summer that we spent there, when I was sixteen and learning to drive the family Austin Seven. Help in the kitchen was provided at times by a pretty dark girl of my own age. She was Cinderella and as I saw it there was only one part I could play. I remember standing in the rather dank shrubbery at the back of the great house watching her washing the dishes in the even danker scullery. I do not believe we ever spoke to each other. Our whole romance was conducted with meaning looks and occasional half-concealed smiles. Once I brushed past her in the kitchen but that was all. And then suddenly and without explanation she came no more.

Overlooking near-by Fowey harbour in those old days lived the writer 'Q'—Sir Arthur Quiller-Couch. We were invited to use the terrace of his house on regatta days in order to watch the racing. 'Q' was always among his guests, a frail old man, impeccably dressed in white flannel trousers, with a rather high stiff collar and a small yachting cap. To me he was gentle and charming and eminently venerable.

The most striking small boats racing in Fowey harbour at that time were called Jolly-boats and I shall not easily forget the impression that these boats made on me at that age as they returned from their race on a rough day. They had been nearly planing as they came in through the harbour entrance (although Uffa Fox had not yet designed the real planing dinghy hull) and when I looked at them I thought that they must without doubt be the most marvellous small racing yachts in the world. The extent of my sailing ambition at that stage was to own a Jolly-boat.

Later in the same summer I found myself in a small hired dinghy having entered for the all-comers race. It was to be my first sailing race, and the course was twice round Fowey harbour. For crew I was to be accompanied by a young man whom I had scarcely met before called George Tozer. He afterwards became Captain of the Cambridge University Sailing team and included me as its most junior member; but on this occasion George and I were strangers and as he was to be my crew he was suitably deferential. He had brought with him a stop-watch, an essential part of the equipment of a racing yachtsman, as the start is timed from guns fired ten and five minutes before. But in those days I had not the least idea what a stop-watch was used for in yacht racing and I sadly betrayed my ignorance to my crew. We started and finished last by a very long way.

I was about seventeen when, at the end of the summer holidays my guardian, Lord Knutsford, invited me to stay with him at the shooting lodge which he had taken in Scotland, Tournaig, in the deer forest of Inverewe on the west coast of Ross and Cromarty. This was my first introduction to stalking, a sport which had delighted 'Uncle' Sydney for very many years. And perhaps because my family had been basically opposed to blood sports, my introduction induced something of a reaction. The shooting of my first stag was steeped in the romantic traditions of the sport, and overnight I was an enthusiastic stalker.

I had two great days stalking on Inverewe, one on each side of my seventeenth birthday, and I wrote about them both at the time.

"13 Sept. 1926. Started out at 9 a.m., Alec Urquhart, the stalker's son, having reported deer on the western slopes of Ben Aridchar. We went by car to Kernsary, the stalker's house, and found Donald Urquhart a hundred yards up the road at the spying place. He was a large man with wonderful physique and a long grey beard, aged, apparently, 71.

"From the point where we spied we made out a large herd of beasts near the march with Ardlair, and about halfway up the hill. There were also four beasts higher up. Donald decided to make for the fifteen lower beasts and risk their crossing the march before we got there. So we started off, Donald leading, me next, Lucy Holland [Lord Knutsford's elder daughter] third and Alec bringing up the rear. We stopped once again to spy. Some of the deer had crossed the march but most were still on this side. We began to climb almost straight towards them. When we had been climbing for about two and a half hours Donald went forward. He returned after a few minutes and directed that I should go on with him, while the other two waited there. Apparently the deer were in a corrie, the burn of which was the march. In order to get the shot we had to cross a ridge in full view of the deer at about 250 yards after which there would be fairly good cover. Donald tried to cross the ridge at the lowest end but found this very difficult. We therefore ran hard round behind and up the hill to try to cross higher. This we could not do, so we returned and tried again lower down still. We crawled over the ridge in view of some of the deer which were on the far side of a little hollow. They had all been walking towards the march, some having crossed; but now they were returning. We got to a gap between two rocks. It had been raining all the time and my hands were frozen. From here we could see about four stags. The best beast—a large eight-pointer, rather pale coloured—was sitting facing us. We waited a quarter of an hour and he had not turned. We were just deciding to try another beast when he got up and turned round so that he was facing away from us. Then he turned broadside and I fired. I went right over his back and they all galloped off. They stopped just before crossing the march and one turned broadside. I fired another shot to no avail. The other two thought I had hit a beast, for a very small stag went away lame, but this was not the one I had fired at. We had lunch and walked home. Saw a lot of Golden Plover. There was a wild cat in Donald's trap."

The last three sentences of the contemporary account give no clue to the desolation which possessed me during that long walk home, and which I can remember to this day. Two days later I was on the hill again:

"15 Sept. 1926. Having heard the day before that the deer had begun to come down from the high tops, we set out in the morning, picking up Donald Urquhart and going by car almost to Loch Fionne. Here we got out and walked west across low ground. Donald spied two medium-sized stags and we set out to stalk them. However we put two hinds and a calf over the crest of a hill and they moved our beasts. We moved on after them, and then stopped for lunch. Afterwards we proceeded, spying as we went for our two beasts which had run up-wind. On walking round the side of a small loch we saw our two beasts, which had been behind a knoll, running away down-wind. Donald and Alec went on to spy for new beasts, while Lucy and I watched two Golden Eagles soaring. Donald came back and reported a party of two small stags, one of which was shootable, and two hinds. He said that beyond and rapidly going round the hill was another stag, but that it could not be stalked because of the four which were nearer. We had, however, to stalk down the slope of a hill in full view until we reached the buttress which divided two corries. This we did crawling, all of us keeping as much behind Donald as possible. We finally gained the cover of the buttress; but the deer had walked down the opposite slope to meet us. Standing off the buttress was a small round mound. Leaving Alec and Lucy behind it, Donald and I stalked round the right-hand side of it. Donald said 'Keep your body down, damn ye!' We looked round the edge of the mound and saw our beasts about 150 yards away. Donald wanted me to shoot, but as he was on the outside I could not, as I could not get far enough out. We were going to retire and get to the other side of the mound when one of the hinds saw us. We had to freeze and yet all the time our stag was walking across so that at any moment he might get our wind. Finally we managed to get back behind the mound and, passing Lucy and Alec, we ran to the other side. Donald said 'Tak' 'im noo!' before I even saw the beast, for again he was on the outside. When I did see him, he was only about seventy yards away and on the alert.

I fired and he dropped like a stone. Donald said, 'Ye're no out of the wood yet', and we lay still, letting the other beasts go right away and waiting to see if this one would try to get up, for he seemed to be hit in the shoulder. Finally Donald went in and killed him. I went to help and Donald, with great guile, sloshed my face with blood saying 'I s'pose ye ken the custom!' I watched the gralloch: and so home to tea.''

After that I acquired all the famous books on stalking and read them as fast as I could (which, as I have already explained was not very fast). Later this led me to begin to draw deer and for this I went frequently from the Lacket to watch them in Savernake Forest where at that time there was still quite a large Red Deer herd.

That there could ever be any serious conflict between the outlook of the naturalist and the sportsman did not occur to me then, or for many years thereafter. I was an uninhibited hunter answering quite simply the instinctive urge to kill. If any concessions were to be made, the conventions of traditional hunting and shooting and fishing were more than adequate. The statutory close seasons, or the code of what was done and what was not done in sport—these were the guiding principles. If they were followed it was quite unnecessary to have other doubts. The issues were of delicious simplicity in one's school days.

My stepfather was at this time a delegate to the League of Nations at Geneva and some of my school holidays were spent there. I remember making a drawing of the Assembly during a speech by Briand, the French statesman, and hearing for the first time the astonishing art of the interpreter who followed Briand by rendering the same speech in English with almost greater emotion than the original. Later in the debate the same man translated my stepfather's speech into French and again it lost nothing in the telling. The interpreter was a French Canadian and must surely have been an orator in his own right. This particular art of translation must now be dead, for it has been replaced by the almost schizophrenic performance of the modern conference interpreter in a soundproof booth who is busy saying the last sentence in one language while listening to the next as it is spoken in the other.

While in Geneva I had hired a sailing boat and this had encouraged Briand to disclose that he had always longed to go sailing. Thus it came about one afternoon that I found myself embarking him in his black suit and black patent leather boots. Fortunately it was an afternoon of extremely light breezes. In the hour that we were afloat together we sailed no more than a mile from the quay. I was required to give instruction and explanation, and for a part of the time M. Briand was at the helm. Curiously enough, the Press never found out about it, so that the event was not marred by publicity.

I had read in a book that the black Alpine Salamander was to be found in Switzerland only above the 1,000-metre line, and I was determined to find one. From Geneva the simplest way to reach this altitude was to take the train eastwards along the north side of the lake, past Lausanne and Montreux, and up the valley to the south as far as Bex. I decided to do this by myself as a day excursion. Arrived in Bex I simply started up the nearest hillside. There was some kind of path, but the hillside was thickly wooded and I climbed on until I calculated from my map that I had achieved the necessary height. I stopped to get my bearings and my breath, and then moved off the little path into the thick woods and turned over the first loose stone I could see. Underneath it was an Alpine Salamander. It was slimmer in build than the yellow and black species—smooth and shiny and all black. I could hardly believe that my mission had succeeded so easily. It took twenty minutes and at least twenty more stones to find the next one and most of the day to catch a dozen which I put into the small brown cardboard suit-case in which I had brought my sandwich lunch.

Up on the hillside I met a chamois hunter returning from an unsuccessful stalk who told me of his adventures as we made our way down into the valley, he to his home and I to my train. Just before we parted he insisted on looking at my Salamanders, and assured me that he had never seen one before.

"You are the successful hunter," he said. "I, the unsuccessful."

"But tomorrow it will be the other way round; you will surely get your chamois."

"Ça se peut." He shrugged his shoulders. "Eh bien, c'est la chasse!"

CHAPTER 9

The Red Herring

IN the letter to my mother which my father wrote from the tent in the Antarctic in which he died he included a passage about me which read . . . "Above all he must guard, and you must guard him, against indolence. Make him a strenuous man; I had to force myself into being strenuous as you know, had always an inclination to be idle." But my father made himself strenuous and my mother was always strenuous too, so 'idleness' in the accepted sense was not, for me, the most serious danger. The direction of strenuousness and enthusiasm into the right channels was much more difficult.

At Oundle I had had a fair capacity for work and had finished up not top of the Biology Sixth Form, to be sure, but quite well placed. I won no scholastic prizes and at the very end of my time there had only just scraped into being made a prefect. How would it be at Cambridge?

In the autumn of 1927 I went up to Trinity College to read Natural Sciences, Zoology, Botany, Physiology, and later Geology. The Master of the college at that time was J. J. Thompson, the famous physicist. I remember having tea with him at the Lodge early in my first term and being miserable because my shoes were dirty. I had managed to get not only into College but into Great Court, by dint of sharing rooms with Humphrey Trevelyan (son of the historian who was to be the next Master of the college and who was a close friend of my stepfather's). I have often wondered how Humphrey stuck it out for the whole academic year, for without question I must have been a tiresome room-mate. For a start there was the aviary which occupied half my bedroom, extended onto the roof and incorporated the sitting-room window. Then there was the Flying Phalanger . . . But Humphrey remained good-natured all the time. My second year was spent in

Neville's Court and my third year back again in Great Court with another attic room. If environment can have any effect on the development of character, I must surely be a better man for having lived for three years surrounded by the architecture of Trinity.

My career at Cambridge began quite respectably. I went to all my lectures and demonstrations, and worked away at my books. For exercise I went out beagling three times a week with the Trinity Foot Beagles, whose Master, at that time, was Bill Hicks Beach, now Member of Parliament for Cheltenham. One day after trotting across the upland fields we ran down through a little marsh, and as we ran snipe jumped up on all sides of us. Running beside me was one Francis Wayne, a Wykehamist who was up at Magdalene, and between puffs he told me that he knew . . . of a place . . . where we could go . . . snipe shooting. This was a new and exciting idea to me and I sent home for my father's old Cogswell and Harrison gun. A week later (it was in November 1927) we found ourselves on the Washes at Earith. The Washes are not to be confused with the Wash into which they eventually run. They consist of a wide strip of grass-land, lying between two high banks, which can be flooded as a sort of safety valve for the drainage systems of the fens. There are Washes on three of the Fenland rivers—the Welland, the Nene and the Ouse, and those of the Ouse are also known as the Bedford Levels. Because the level of the flood waters was affected by the tide, these Washes were long held to offer free shooting to the wildfowler.

On that first day as we walked over a rough field of brown grass with water at its roots that squelched underfoot, there was suddenly a 'frrp' and a snipe jumped up at my feet. With a 'scarp-scarp' he twisted and turned, close to the ground, but just as he started that great upward curve I found the gun at my shoulder, and with the feeling that the rest was in the hands of Providence, I fired. And Providence had done me proud, for the snipe had fallen into the grass. It was my first shot with a 12-bore, and my first shot at a flying bird (and for quite a long time the only successful one). It seemed to be an occasion for comment if not for celebration, but the rest of the party walked on as if nothing unusual had happened, and I walked with them. At the end of the field Francis shouted across to me:

"You picked up that snipe all right, didn't you?"

"What?" I said, casually. "Oh—the snipe—oh yes, I 'picked' that all right."

But for all the nonchalance, that snipe constituted the entire day's bag. If this monumental fluke had not come off perhaps I should never have become a wildfowler and should now be quite a different sort of person. Or perhaps I should be just the same, because of some other fluke.

Of the party that day was my old friend from Oundle, Michael Dilke, now also up at Trinity. Before long beagling had for me been entirely replaced by regular visits to the Washes. The flood-waters were teeming with birds. Great flocks of wigeon grazed on the puddly fields, mallards and teal sheltered among the flooded thistles and when the water became deeper as the winter advanced there were rafts of tufted ducks and pochards and coots.

In the heat of the enthusiasm we founded the Trinity Duck Hunt —and not long afterwards disbanded it, when we discovered that wildfowling was an individual activity for which a large 'field' was inappropriate. But two new friends soon joined our excursions— Dick Hull (later to become Deputy Chief of the Imperial General Staff and C.-in-C. Far East), and Christopher Dalgety. Both had been longer at Cambridge and both had wider experience of shooting than Michael and I.

I began to keep a wildfowling diary from the first day of my new-found delight. Its title-page carries the following inscription in ornate Gothic lettering:

A book containing sundry
short accounts which
purport to record
The WILDFOWLINGS
and other sportings
of
P. SCOTT Esquire.
Starting in the year of
Our Lord MDCCCCXXVII
and finishing, God willing,
not until the end of
his days on earth.

The diary is by and large—and I have faced it—a rather tedious document; it is concerned too much with the very precise details of our movements which would no doubt have served to remind me of the occasion for a year or two, but which in most cases no longer conjure up a living picture of any kind, and too little with the thoughts and sayings of the principal characters in the story.

"Thurs. 17 Nov. 1927" is a good example:

"Went with C. T. Dalgety and R. A. Hull to a morning flight at Sutton Gault. I waited on the southern of the two westerly corners of the first withy bed in the black canoe. I had lots of shots and brought one bird down, but couldn't find it afterwards. The other two collected four ducks and a coot."

Or another:

"Tues. 29 Nov. 1927. Went with F. S. Chapman [author of *The Jungle is Neutral*] by motorbike to Oxlode. Arrived 2 p.m. Others went by train. I shot at a Goosander. Stalked coots and shot at them out of range. Met Thomson [professional wild-fowler] with three duck. Told Wayne we had shot them. Swallowed it! Had to keep it up. Ha! Ha! They had got two wigeon (MD.) and found FTW's teal of three days before. F.S.C. shot Peewit in flight. We used black boat."

Sutton Gault is on the upper stretch of the Bedford Levels where the flood-water of the drainage rivers is only about a third of a mile wide. Oxlode is a few miles further down, where there was often, in those days, three-quarters of a mile of open water between bank and bank.

The diaries record much irrelevant detail. They say very precisely how I went here and someone else went there. Occasionally they are unconsciously funny, very occasionally they are useful for reference, but they give no real impression of the places or the people and it is sad to think of the number of hours so largely wasted in writing them. They fill six thick volumes covering the next six years —a fascinating monument to the misapplication of time. Yet perhaps they have some bearing on the kind of chap I was at the age of eighteen.

Boats are mentioned in both the entries I have quoted above— black boats, because they were very old and tar or pitch were in those days the only practical materials for making an old boat watertight. But black boats are conspicuous on the water and any self-respecting duck-punt must be painted in a much paler colour. On the upper stretch of the Washes at Sutton, Christopher Dalgety had installed such a punt which he had bought second-hand at Keyhaven on the Solent. She was a single-handed sea-going punt, about twenty feet long with a two-and-a-half foot beam and her name was *Penelope*, because that is the Latin name for a Wigeon. On her bows he mounted a punt gun borrowed from Cornelius Smith, landlord of The Fish Inn at Sutton Gault: it was a small muzzle-loading gun that fired only about eight ounces of shot and one-and-a-half ounces of powder, and it was one of those guns which might or might not go off and probably would not.

One bright November afternoon Christopher and I stalked hopefully down upon a company of diving ducks sitting in the open water. Our progress consisted of a series of violent zig-zags, for the art of pushing a gunning punt with a short pole requires practice which at that time neither of us had, and when two people are trying to conceal themselves in a cockpit that was only made for one, the ensemble is liable to be more conspicuous than it should be. Owing to some reeds and thistles, however, our quarry were still unsuspicious, and already we were drawing into range. We nearly spoiled it all when we ran aground on a submerged bank, but by an almost superhuman effort we got off, and in a moment we were all ready for the shot. 'Popwooomph', it was almost a 'hang-fire', and a cloud of blue smoke filled the air—well, at any rate she had gone off, and we jumped up to see what we had shot. There on the water lay one single drake pochard. He was stone-dead and we pushed up and collected him.

Two days later we were out again in *Penelope*. Christopher and I had borrowed a motor-bike, and we stopped to spy from a point of vantage near a tiny pub called The Jolly Bankers. In front of us were the floods and on a spit of grass sat three grey geese. What matter that it involved rowing a mile and a half against the stream; we intended to go after them. It was a long stalk across open water. By the time we reached the spit it was beginning to get dark. There were a lot of ducks there, most of them seemed to be shovelers, but nowhere could we see the geese. We navigated a difficult gap in the spit through which the stream was running fast, and emerged on the other side—but still no geese. So we sat up in the punt—and then towards the west, where the stormy sky was brighter, I saw reflected in the water three large black silhouettes. In an instant we had flattened ourselves, and I was making all speed in their direction. At about ninety yards the geese decided that we looked dangerous, and spread their great wings; there was a movement in front of me, and a click which was followed by a loud curse—the gun had misfired.

We shot a mallard from the punt with a twelve-bore just before dark, and then we went back to the river and rowed down with the current, which was running like a mill-race. We had a bridge to go through, and there were a few breathless moments as we sped down peering into the darkness in front for the great black shadow which we knew to be there. Suddenly it came, and we were under it in a flash, narrowly missing one of the pillars. We pulled quickly to the shore, made fast the punt and went up to the bank to The Fish just as it began to rain.

To me these adventures were irresistible: the beauty of dawn and dusk, the planning of the campaign, the slight risks to be taken, and above all the animals—not only the quarry but the others who had business on the floods, the Otters, the Peregrines, the Harriers and the Shorteared Owls.

Mallards returning to the Broad at dawn.

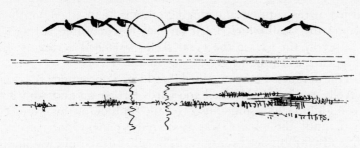

CHAPTER 10

The Lure of the Geese

THE flood-waters of the Bedford Levels were exciting enough in those early days, but if we were to be wildfowlers, then wild geese must be the real quarry. According to the books, the place to go for wild geese was Wells-next-the-Sea on the north coast of Norfolk. This it seemed was the true Mecca, and there Michael Dilke and I decided to go for a week of the Christmas vacation.

Upon some personal recommendation we had selected as our guide the well-known professional wildfowler, Sam Bone, and went round to see him on the evening of our arrival.

Unfortunately we had chosen the time of the full moon, which, because of the tides, he told us, was not the best time to shoot geese at Wells. But we had seen few geese in those days, and we were content to see them even if we never fired a shot, though we did not say this to Sam. That night as I got into bed and lay awake for a while wondering what luck the morning would bring, I suddenly heard the magic sound of geese and ran to the window. Outside the moon shone brightly from a clear sky, and from over towards the marsh came the call of the Pinkfeet. There must have been a big lot on the move, for the sound seemed like a single singing roar made dim by the two miles of marsh that lay between. I thought of the only time when I had heard geese before, the Whitefronts on the flood-waters away inland in the middle of Northamptonshire. Now the sounds came mingled with the murmur of the sea. I jumped back into bed with a feeling of strange exuberance.

Next morning we stood at the end of the bathing huts on the shore. There was an orange glow in the east, and out of it came skein after skein of geese, delicately traced patterns on the deep blue of the sky above. Since then I have seen pink-footed geese in flight many thousands of times, in all their winter haunts in Britain; I have followed them to their breeding grounds in Iceland, I have

D

assisted at the capture and ringing of more than 20,000 of them; and yet the thrill which I felt on that first morning is repeated again every time I see the great skeins stretched across the sky. The spell is as strong as ever.

In the darkness I had imagined that I was alone among the dunes at Wells, except for Michael 200 yards farther on and Sam Bone beyond him. I had soliloquised on the solitude of this wonderful dawn, until the silence was shattered by stentorian sneezing. Evidently the gunner twenty yards behind on my right was finding the morning chilly, and when one of the great skeins of geese came over, there was a thunderous roar as the gunner forty yards on my left tried out one of his new four-bore cartridges. Now, as it got light, I could see movements and shadows hidden in almost every hollow along the dunes; but, for all that, 3,000 geese had gone in to feed in the green 'fresh marsh' so high that they were far out of reach of any of them.

During the day Sam took us to Stiffkey salt-marsh and there we tramped about, crossing the creeks by the old tumbledown bridges built by the men who had business on the marshes. Here redshanks abounded and curlews were sometimes to be found. Sam persuaded us that redshanks were suitable game, and we returned to lunch after many miles of tramping, with, I believe, three of them.

I think it was Christopher Dalgety who first heard about the saltings at Terrington, to the west of King's Lynn. They were comparatively unknown to wildfowlers in those days. Michael and I went with him on the first exploration there. Christopher was the leader of the party. He was fair-haired and slight with a small fair moustache and a quick temper. No one could pour scorn more quickly or effectively on inefficiency. He did not suffer fools gladly and when you were foolish you were not suffered. For many years afterwards he was one of my most regular wildfowling companions and I believe his strictures upon me had some considerable influence. I did not think he was always right, indeed I often *knew* him to be wrong, but if ever I was feeling too pleased with myself, Christopher was the master of deflation. For most of our time at Cambridge he kept at least two dogs. My favourite was a small liver-and-white spaniel called Pansy and I used to think Pansy worked better for me than for Christopher, perhaps because I did not shout at her so much. She had her limitations, for she would only retrieve from water. If she found a wounded bird on land she was fairly likely to administer her own *coup de grâce*. But in those days the finding of it was what mattered, and except from water, retrieving was for the most part an unnecessary refinement.

Pansy was certainly with us on that first expedition to the shores of the Wash at Terrington. We kept the place darkly secret, inventing our own code name for it, 'Sandbanks', for it was only forty-four miles from Cambridge—an hour and a half's drive in Christopher's square-nosed Morris. Nowadays the marsh has been found to be privately owned and is controlled by a Wildfowlers' Club, so the secret need no longer be kept.

'Sandbanks' consisted then of a rough salting half a mile wide, bounded on the seaward side by mudflats, and on the landward side by a sea-wall protecting mile upon mile of flat neatly ditched fields. The salting was finely divided by a network of deep muddy creeks which branched and wriggled their way in from the sea. The flatness of the scene was broken and at the same time emphasised by a single stunted willow tree which grew just behind the sea-wall. But the sky and the birds made it for me a place of incomparable beauty and romance.

It was out on the salting here that I shot my first goose when the moon was just turning from gold to silver on February 6th, 1928. There had been a great flight of mallards that night. For half an hour they had whispered overhead, high above the salting, and now the geese were beginning to move, out at the edge of the tide. In little parties they were starting in across the marsh to find good grazing or to pass on over the sea-wall into the black potato fields.

I could follow them by their calling as they circled and passed wide of me. Then, from almost behind, I heard the low intimate talking of another bunch, heading, it seemed, straight for where I sat. Almost at once the black line of them appeared, a dozen geese full low and passing close behind me. I swung round and fired one shot over my left shoulder, and throwing myself on my back I fired the second. As I watched, one of the geese seemed to be separating from the others. At first, being upside-down, I did not realise that it was falling, but as I jumped up I heard a thud on the soft muddy turf. I ran to the spot, and there he was stone-dead on the salting— my very first goose.

He turned out to be a Bean Goose—a considerable rarity. But at the time he was to me a plain wild goose, and that was all that mattered.

Success was rare in those early days and when it came my enjoyment was very great—the primitive enjoyment of the hunter. If anyone asked me, and they frequently did, how I could equate the killing with my evident love of the living birds, my answer was given without hesitation. They were man's traditional quarry and it was part of man's instinct to hunt; it was part of the birds' instinct to be hunted. My delight and admiration for wild geese was based as much upon their supreme capacity to remain watchful and to look after themselves as it was upon their beauty and grace. There was nothing sentimental about my regard for them. Our relations were simple and straightforward, to be carried to the logical conclusion— to the death; and there, when I was eighteen, the argument ended. Today I find that it goes a good deal further and its conclusions are rather different, but we are dealing with the year 1928.

CHAPTER II   Grey Goose

EXPEDITIONS to the coast from Cambridge were only occasionally possible, but the flood-waters were more easily accessible, although as the winter advanced boats became more and more essential. At Sutton there were *Penelope* and the 'black canoe', but at Oxlode there was only the 'black boat', a leaky vessel with pointed ends and vertical sides which was clearly of great antiquity. We borrowed it locally and sometimes graced it with the name of 'punt', but if it was far from perfect in this capacity it provided us with some agreeable adventures, although it was clear that for our purposes she was too old and too primitive. She could with advantage, we felt, be returned to the service from which we had borrowed her, of occasionally ferrying a farm hand across the New River. For wildfowling we must have a proper punt, and a boat-builder in Cambridge was commissioned to start work on one forthwith, to be made from our own designs.

He was very quick and had it completed within ten days, for a price that was only a little over £10. On February 2nd she was launched in the Cam, in the pool just above Silverstreet Bridge.

We poled her up the little backwater there to the mill pool and practised stalking with hand paddles and pole. The diary records that "she is very stable and yet light to punt. Colour which is almost white on top and *quite* white on sides, is an attempt at 'protective colouring'. Dimensions: Length overall 19 ft. Breadth 3 ft. 8 inches. Height above water 8 inches. Draught, light 1½ inches, loaded 3 inches." We christened her *Grey Goose*, and arranged for her conveyance to the fens on the very next day. Meanwhile we had bought an old muzzle-loading punt-gun, which fired half a pound of shot—small for a punt-gun, but it seemed large enough for our purpose. Of its age and history we knew little, but in those days we were prepared to risk much.

So next morning *Grey Goose* was hoisted on to a one-ton Ford lorry and, perilously balanced on the top, the journey to the fens began. It was nerve-racking, for every bump in the road I felt sure would break the boat's back; and the road to the fens in those days was particularly bumpy. But at last, after an hour of agony, we arrived at Earith Bridge at the head of the flood-waters.

Here *Grey Goose* was lifted from the lorry, found to be intact, and launched in the river. We had then about nine miles to go on the flood-water to Oxlode. On the way we should pass the reaches we already knew from our adventures in *Penelope* and as we expected to find ducks there, we decided to be cleared for action.

The first thing to do was to test the big gun. Laboriously we loaded it, ramming down only a light charge of powder, a tow wad, a charge of shot and some hay to keep it in: then, standing well to one side in the shallows, I pulled the trigger. The roar, the spatter of shot on the water, and the cloud of smoke were all perfect. So with high hopes we reloaded again and set off down the river.

After about a mile we saw some birds in front. At first we thought they were coots, but soon we discovered that they were a pack of tufted ducks, and lay down to stalk. Our way lay through the bare stems of an old thorn hedge that had been used by the cattle as shelter when the fields were dry. Once through this we should, we thought, be in range. But the ducks had begun to swim away, and it was not until we were half-way across the next field that a chance presented itself as the ducks bunched together. The gun went off with a terrific roar and a burst of flame. Was this usual with punt-guns? We supposed so, and jumped up anxiously to see our luck. Not a bird had been struck, and disappointedly we pushed to a bank opposite the Jolly Bankers to reload. Only then did we find that the gun had blown up; half the nipple-holder in the breach had blown out sideways—a piece of metal about the size of a wine cork, and it had fortunately gone out without making a hole either in us or the punt.

The rest of our journey was carried out under sail, and late in the evening we arrived among the more familiar washes of Oxlode. We were met by the rest of our usual team, who had not shot anything either, and my diary records that on the way home the car radiator boiled twice and we had a geyser in Ely.

It was a long time before our new punt brought us any luck. A week later I find a sad little cry at the end of a diary entry:

"One failure after another. We must succeed with the punt soon. I suppose my one and only goose has really made up for all the hellish discomfort of this bloody game."

Curiously enough the first success, which was three weeks and many expeditions after the launching of *Grey Goose*, came on a day when I was accompanied by a newcomer to wildfowling. This was George Tozer who had crewed me in my first sailing race in Fowey Harbour. The morning that he came punting was calm and bright. At our first shot we killed one mallard duck, and at our second four mallard drakes, and I record that we went back for breakfast 'justly elated'. But later in the day our troubles began again. The hammer of the big gun went wrong, caused a misfire and, at the next potential shot half an hour later, flew off and hit me in the face, fortunately with no worse damage than a cut and subsequently swollen lip. "We poled home in darkness and the customary dejection; the success of the morning seemed to belong to another age."

It was not until the following winter that I scored my first right and left of geese. The tide was just flooding those same saltings at 'Sandbanks', filtering up through the grass, and shimmering golden under the moon as she rose like a great orange in the east. The place where I knelt was still dry, but behind, between me and the security of the sea-wall, the creeks had filled and the marsh was covered.

The geese were farther out also on a dry part of the marsh, but I knew that the tide must reach them at any minute. Before long, however, I should be plainly visible standing alone surrounded by glassy, white water; but if they came soon, not only should I be hidden on the black island of salting, but the island itself would be a landing-place for them. Then all at once there were geese every-where. They came with hardly a sound. Many went on inland, but suddenly I saw a little bunch of six quite close and very low. They were going to settle beside me. I crouched down as low as I could, and they came on with set wings. Geese have comparatively poor eyesight at night, and they did not see me at all until it was too late. Indeed, one of them never did see me, and another only for a second. So fell my first right and left of geese.

The feeling of achievement was complete, long looked forward to, cleanly executed, utterly satisfying to contemplate. I do not think at the time I experienced any trace of regret at the destruction of these beautiful creatures, such as I should feel were I to do the same thing today. I was simply the successful hunter, and as I walked home with my two geese I might have been returning to my cave.

Moonlight flighting was without doubt the most exciting kind of wildfowling we did in those days, even though no boats were involved, for geese were the most worthy quarry, to be placed far above any other fowl. Soon after the rising of the full moon they would move in, some perhaps on to the salting but others over the sea-wall into the potato fields. When the tide had filled the creeks on the out-marsh we usually waited behind the high bank, or in the fields themselves. While the moon was still low and red, the first geese, often a family party of six or seven, would cross the bank and sweep silently round the chosen fields. Sometimes they murmured to each other as they flew, but more often they came in with no sound at all but the 'frp-frp-frp' of vibrating pinions as they settled. Later the bigger flocks would stream in on the same flight-line. Often we ran feverishly to try to get under the line, or to intercept a bunch we could hear approaching; and almost as often they went straight over the place where we had been. Although the main flight was usually over by nine o'clock, there were always a few geese going out to the shore to drink throughout the night. By eleven, though, these movements were so sparse that we gathered for hot curry from a Thermos flask. If we had been out on the salting and had wet knees and bottoms we would start the car and dry our clothes by sitting on the radiator.

By about two in the morning we often thought it was time for some sleep, either in the car or in a straw stack, but it was usually too cold, and after a while we would have to turn out and run about to get warm. At four-thirty it was time to start out for the edge of the mud and wait for the geese coming out again, and the ducks, and the sunrise—and perhaps fall asleep in a creek. Then after the high tide, at about eight or nine, we would start back for breakfast. Sometimes the geese would defeat us completely and we would return empty-handed. Always there were *some* regrets. But however it went the nights were permeated by one sound—the wild call of the geese.

Sometimes after such a night on the Wash, I would return to Cambridge the next evening, very tired, and walk across the Great Court of Trinity, bright in the moonlight; drawing level with the fountain, I would hear the water splash out into the calling of Pinkfeet. Then I could imagine them gliding in over the chapel on set wings, and with a great vibrating of quills, dropping on to the green lawns, which are as good grazing as any goose could desire.

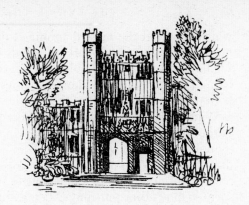

CHAPTER 12

Applied Climbing

ENTHUSIASM and moderation do not go easily together. My enthusiasm for the wild marshes and the birds and the chase was immoderate, and occupied an altogether excessive amount of my time. We were of course entitled to be away from college on a limited number of nights during the term, but the restriction meant little, for it was not difficult to climb out of college in the corner of 'I' Court, a small courtyard opening out of the Great Court. This corner had what is known to climbers as a 'chimney'; by operating with back and knee against the two sides of this 'chimney' it was possible to reach the top of the fifteen-foot wall even when carrying guns and coats and rubber boots, and to drop over on the outside into a little yard which connected with Trinity Street. This, combined with a scheme by which the bedclothes on our beds were ruffled as necessary to indicate that we had slept in college when we had not, enabled us to spend as many moonlight nights down on the shores of the Wash as our consciences would allow, which, of course, was a great many more than our tutors or directors-of-studies could have approved.

Climbing out of college was only one aspect of climbing. Roof climbing, although it had a less practical application, was a well-supported activity in the University in my day; indeed I was required to provide a number of drawings for a new edition of the *Roof-climber's Guide to Trinity* which was published during my second year. I was one of the party which made the first complete circuit of Trinity Great Court, not perhaps a very difficult climb but an achievement of minor distinction because of the problems presented by the Great Gate. Also in the party that night were Gino Watkins, Laurence Wager and Jack Longland. The climb that frightened me most was the ascent of St. John's College Chapel. There was an overhanging cornice about sixty feet from the ground

D*

which required the most determined disregard of my indifferent head for heights. Gino Watkins was also on this climb, and Bunny Fuchs, and I think also Bobby Chew, now headmaster of Gordonstoun. I never extended these activities to rocks and mountains, perhaps because the call of the marshes was too insistent.

Wildfowling was a new subject for my drawing and painting. Hitherto of course I had drawn birds in not much greater numbers than I had drawn other kinds of animals. There had been line drawings of ducks and geese in the book that we had published at school. But now I found a new delight in painting the birds that I spent so much time pursuing. My pleasure was to recreate the tense excitement that I felt when I was out on a marsh, recapture some of it each time that I looked at the picture, and convey some of it to those who had shared the experience. If those who had never seen the birds flighting at dawn and dusk and under the moon also happened to like the pictures, that was purely incidental and of no significance to me. Basically I was painting on the roof of my cave just as the Cro-magnon hunters had painted their quarry on theirs. Perhaps, like them, I was seeking some kind of magic which could be exploited to bring wildfowling success if the paintings were good enough.

My paintings of geese and ducks and snipe led to a small exhibition of my works at Messrs. Bowes and Bowes, the Cambridge booksellers. I do not now remember the number of water-colours in this my first one-man show, but there must have been a dozen or twenty and I remember that at prices up to five guineas they were nearly all sold, which made a welcome addition to the funds available for future wildfowling expeditions.

One such expedition in the Christmas vacation took Christopher and Michael and me to the Solway Firth, upon the recommendation of Rachel and Malise Graham. This was an unspoiled area for the wildfowler in December 1928. On the salt-marshes between the Lochar and the Nith there was still a great flock of more than 2,000 Barnacle Geese, a flock which, many years later, disastrously declined in numbers to a few hundred and is now spectacularly increasing again under protection, and the establishment of a new Wildfowl Refuge.

There were in those days great flocks of Greylag Geese but no Pinkfeet at all in that part of the Solway. I remember on the first night of our arrival at Glencaple leaning out of the window of the Nith Hotel in the darkness and hearing the Greylags drifting up the river past the quay with the flood tide.

In the ten days that followed we had exceptionally good luck, so that by the end all three of us declared the expedition an unqualified success. In the middle of it came an opportunity to go punt-gunning with an acknowledged expert, Major C. W. W. Hulse, from whom we learned a great deal.

CHAPTER 13   *A Likely Night*

CRIME has a fascination for most of us. Some are content to read
about it, while some go the whole hog and get hanged for it.

It was in connection with Canada Geese that temptation reared
its ugly head in our young and irresponsible days. During the wildfowling season Christopher and Michael and I had shot each of the
six wild species of geese that come regularly to this country, and we
felt the need to bag a Canada. There are several parts of the country
where Canada Geese have been established for so long that they are
now practically wild. Their introduction is so widespread that
the species has at last been given a place on the British List, although
it was not so at the time of which I write. Probably, like the Snow
Geese, occasional wild Canadas have taken a wrong turning and
found themselves on this side of the Atlantic. It has usually been
assumed that any odd bird like this which may have turned up must
surely have escaped from a park or be descended from an 'introduced' flock, but I should be surprised if a truly wild Canada had
never set foot in Britain.

However that may be, the feral park-bred flocks seem to become
surprisingly spry in some areas, especially late in the shooting
season. Certainly the Canadas in the marsh we had chosen for our
project were exceedingly wild. Our plan required, in accordance
with the song, 'a likely night, in the season of the year'.

The likeliest night was one of bright moon with snow on the
ground and a hard frost which had frozen the ditches so that they
would bear our weight. With white pyjamas over our clothes, we
should be invisible alike to man and goose.

By midnight on 19th February, 1929, Christopher and I had
walked three miles and were at the edge of the marsh, listening for
our quarry. There were grey geese feeding in the marsh under the
moon but on that night they meant nothing to us. We could hear

the Canadas further on. Half an hour was spent dangling a pyjama cord down the barrels of one of the guns which had become blocked with snow. After it had been cleared we came to a track which led through the marsh at right angles. By the sound of them the Canadas were on the left of the track, a big pack spread, it seemed, over a fairly large area. The nearest were on a line at an angle of about forty-five degrees to the track. By pacing along the track until they were at right angles and then (in spite of feeling like Lewis Carroll's Beaver who "recollected with tears how in earlier years it had taken no pains with its sums"), making a brilliant calculation, we determined roughly how far away from us they were. After a short discussion we took a ditch apiece and started to stalk in, one of us on each side of the nearest bunch. As the ditches were all frozen and rubber boots were not compatible with a quick getaway, we were wearing ordinary shoes, but very soon, running along the ice, I came to a thin place and one foot went through. My way led me along the side of a railway. There was a ditch of open running water which I came suddenly upon. It was full of ducks and teal which rose with a terrible clatter and clamour. It seemed that if anyone were abroad that night they must surely hear it and wonder at the cause.

I turned off down another ditch of thin ice, which crackled ominously, and I still had one dry foot. So I crawled along the edge of it. The moon was now hidden by cloud, but the snow made the world surprisingly light. There was a little bank in front and when I looked over this I thought at first that the moles had been very busy since the last snowfall. But a moment later I realised that the dark spots were not mole hills, but Canada Geese.

I crawled over the bank to get closer but they saw me and in a flash they were up. It was a long way to the nearest bird, too far for a shot in normal circumstances, but it seemed to me that we had been long enough in the marsh, so I fired. It was a lucky shot; the goose fell dead, and with that the whole marsh seemed to rise. With a tremendous clamour the great flock curled away, and I heard a surprisingly distant 'pop-pop' as they went over Christopher. I picked up my bird and without any delay, set off towards the shore. A Canada Goose is a bulky bird, and while I knew that in our white clothes we ourselves were nearly invisible, I felt that to an observer a goose careering across the marsh hung up by its neck might arouse suspicions. Once, when I looked behind, I saw a man running past a bush. So the keepers were out and this one was close on my heels; what should I do? Double back past him, or head on for the shore? I stopped to make sure which way he was moving and then realised that the bush was a moving sheep, and the supposed man only a gate post. But I was worried now. I came to a fast running main drain that was quite unfrozen and dared not wait to find a bridge. So I plunged across in water nearly to my waist, but I had no time to be cold.

The worst part was to come. As I approached a dark strip of pine wood through which I had to go, I realised that if anyone was in it and watching my approach, he could move along silently in the wood and pounce as I entered it. When I was about ten yards from it, I turned suddenly and ran hard for 100 yards parallel to it. No one, I thought, could run fast inside the wood without cracking a stick, and since there was no sound, I dived through and reached the shore with a great sight of relief. It was a mile to the rendezvous which we had fixed and Christopher had arrived less than a minute before me. In our white pyjamas we had walked along no more than 100 yards apart and neither had been aware of the other. My goose was our entire bag but we had achieved our object. The ducks began to flight to sea over our heads on the re-maining mile-and-a-half walk and dawn was breaking as we set off for Cambridge in the car.

In February 1929 the whole coast had been gripped by a hard frost since some time before our 'likely night'. The foreshore all round the Wash was covered with great cakes of ice, like miniature icebergs, scattered along the tide-line in a jumbled mass, some of them a foot thick, and three or four feet high, as they lay canted over on their sides or upended, leaning on their neighbours.

Nowhere, I remember thinking on one particular morning, could have been more romantic and beautiful than our secret marsh at 'Sandbanks'. It was an icy orange dawn with that smokiness along the horizon which only comes with hard frost. The Pinkfeet had been rather irregular in their flighting, as they often are in a frost, because the potatoes are too hard for them to nibble and the land too hard and jagged for their feet. We did not expect to see many at flight time. About 300 of them flew in when it was still fairly dark. They came in half a dozen skeins, flying low, for they had come from the edge of the mud, only a few hundred yards in front, and they passed to the eastward silhouetted against the sky. By now it was much lighter, and from our creeks we could see that no more remained where they had been sitting. The flight seemed to be over, when suddenly a very distant murmur could be heard, gradually increasing in volume. At first I thought it was the tide moving the ice cakes in my creek, but no—it was geese.

When at last they came in sight they were very high in the air, a single thin line of them stretching for half a mile, it seemed in each direction. A hundred yards behind came another line, not quite so long, and behind that a third. They flew in very high over us, 2,000, perhaps 3,000, calling in chorus, and disappeared inland over the top of the mist that was rising from the marsh behind us.

After that the tide really did flow into our creek and start tumbling the ice cakes one over another; it surged and swished past them, eventually carrying them with it as the water rose higher and higher. There was a bunch of about thirty Brent Geese drifting in on the tide—which were rare on our marsh except in a frost; and there were hundreds of mallard and wigeon, sitting out among the floating ice cakes, and hundreds of knots and dunlins sitting on them. The marsh was alive with birds, their plumage brilliant by comparison with their white surroundings, although their bodies were probably thin enough underneath.

I suppose our marsh was really no more beautiful than many others. Probably it was only knowing it well that made it seem so much better to us, in spite of its soft and sticky mud.

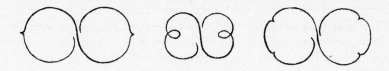

CHAPTER 14   *Mainly Summer Pursuits*

THERE is not much doubt that wildfowling occupied too much of my winters. But what of my summers at Cambridge? That might have been the time to work doubly, trebly hard to make up for it. But alas for my academic career, there were still plenty of birds to watch.

Many ducks nested in the near-by fens, and in the 'breck country' of Norfolk around Barton Mills and Brandon and Thetford, there were Crossbills and Wood Larks, Stone Curlews and Ringed Plovers. Set in the dry expanses of the brecks there were a handful of small meres surrounded by bracken-covered slopes and a few pine trees. Tufted Ducks nested there frequently, and there was a small breeding colony of Gadwalls, rare in other parts of England, the duck in which the male has no bright colours in his plumage, but looks at first glance sombre and leaden in his greyness. Only at a range of a few feet is the glorious intricacy and subtlety of the pattern of the drake Gadwall revealed to the human eye, though the avian eye can probably see it clearly at much greater distances. Once, and it was a great event, we found the nest of a Pintail—the first time that it had ever been officially recorded breeding in East Anglia. Great secrecy attached to the whereabouts of this nest, for among undergraduates in those days there was a strong body of egg-collectors. This secrecy, I remember, caused some friction at the time within the Cambridge Bird Club, for we were unwilling to disclose the details of the Pintail's nest until after it had successfully brought off its young. Freddy Spencer Chapman was the Secretary of the Club at that time; after he had been sworn to secrecy I took him to see the nest and when we got there we found that the eggs had been stolen.

Much nearer to Cambridge lay Quy and Fulbourn Fens. These and the Cambridge Sewage Farm were easily accessible haunts of birds.

Skating was another red herring, though (except occasionally in winter) it could not become an additional diversion from work in term time, for there was no skating rink nearer than London. My enthusiasm for skating had arisen from the school holiday in the Pyrenees when there had been too little snow for skiing, and had been followed up with regular visits to the Ice Club in Westminster and later to Grosvenor House and Queen's Road—which was very close to Leinster Corner. It was at the Ice Club that I collided violently with (among many others) an ebullient character called James Robertson Justice. But beyond the collision there is not much to record of that first meeting.

Some indications of moderate proficiency in skating had led to Christmas holidays at the Kulm Hotel, St. Moritz, for the purpose of intensive training, so that gradually my skill had increased. But while I was happy to leap about on the ice, to dance and spin, to master the Axel Paulsen jump, the double Salchow jump and the double loop-jump, I was not so diligent with the school figures that were necessary for competitions. My counters were passable, my rockers were usually rockers, I could even get round a bracket-change-bracket in a sort of a way, and my one-foot eights were impeccable; but there arose a curious 'block' in my progress. I simply could not do loops. Nor did I ever master these comparatively easy figures. Loops were my Waterloo, and skating is not the only field of endeavour in which I have encountered my 'loops'. But in spring time in Cambridge my thoughts were rather of Elizabeth, a small, dark and adorable Canadian girl whom I loved very much indeed, than of loops, and rather of Garganey Teal than of either.

We were convinced that at least one and perhaps two pairs of Garganeys were breeding at Fulbourn Fen. Two drakes had been there all spring, rattling away to each other like a couple of fishing reels, and their wives had now disappeared, but finding the nest was another matter. Even when we had pinpointed one duck to one particular field it involved working backwards and forwards methodically so that every inch of it was searched. The grass was not particularly long and at first it seemed quite a simple task; therein lay our principal set-back, for when we finally found the nest we had already walked past within a yard at least three times. We could not believe that she would sit so tight. The tiny nest was in a horse's hoof-print and superbly concealed. It was the first Garganey's nest ever to be recorded in Cambridgeshire. On that same evening I remember returning full of triumph after the long hot afternoon (the third or fourth running that we had spent searching) and sipping orange squash in the rooms of a friend in Trinity College who had a gramophone, on which he played me Mozart's Symphony No. 40 in G minor. It was the first time I had heard it, and thereafter we played it over and over and over again. It became and still remains one of my favourite works. Because of the excitements of the day on which I first heard it, we called it for many years the Garganic Symphony.

But the summer was not only for birds; at week-ends there was also sailing, for I had joined the Cambridge University Cruising Club. At that time the great boom in small boat sailing had not yet begun. Dinghies were the kind of boat you used to take you from the shore to a larger and more respectable yacht and were not in their own right regarded as yachts at all. The Cambridge University Cruising Club had, as its name suggested, been primarily concerned with cruising rather than racing, but it had a long and respectable history; and H. Yule Oldham, a splendid character who was a don at King's, and one of whose comments is quoted in the Foreword of this book, decided that if small boat sailing was to be undertaken at Cambridge it must be developed under the aegis of the C.U.Cr.C. of which he was then Commodore. Thus I found myself one Saturday afternoon in a fairly primitive and heavy cat-rigged dinghy, with a balanced-lug, racing on a stretch of the river at Ely which was scarcely more than fifteen yards wide. I was decisively beaten in my race by a Carthusian who was a contemporary at Trinity and spent his holidays sailing on the Norfolk Broads. His name was Stewart Morris. After the racing we repaired to the inn for tea at which Yule Oldham, huge and bald and rubicund, presided beneficently, and then we all took the train back to Cambridge. This became the pattern of many a week-end in the summer term. I did not, of course, recognise that this first meeting with Stewart Morris, Olympic Gold Medallist and now probably one of the half dozen best helmsmen in the world, was of any importance. I could scarcely have guessed at the influence it was to have on the future course of my life. Without doubt his enthusiasm and subsequent skill was responsible for my interest in dinghy sailing and thereafter in the wider world of yachting. In those early days at Ely, George Tozer, my erstwhile crew at Fowey and punting companion of the Washes, was selecting a team to represent Cambridge against Oxford, and although Stewart was an obvious choice, it was far from certain until the last minute who would occupy the sixth and last place. After winning a single-handed race at Ely in a strong breeze, I just scraped into the selection and sailed annually against Oxford for the rest of my time at the University.

The Varsity Regatta was always held at sea in boats which were borrowed for the occasion, and quite unfamiliar to all the competitors. The authorities had not yet been persuaded to award a Half-Blue for sailing as is done now. Another member of that early team—and a subsequent Captain—was Francis Usborne, now Secretary of the Royal Yachting Association.

Stewart was always the principal spur. I was invited by his parents to stay on the Broads in their beautiful converted wherry *Sundog*; she moved from regatta to regatta with a string of racing dinghies and one-designs towing astern, all superbly kept in trim by Cubitt Nudd, one of the best 'paid hands' in all Norfolk. For these holidays I was usually Stewart's crew, but when his new fourteen-foot dinghy *Clover* was built for him by Morgan Giles in beautifully selected teak, I wondered if I would be considered good enough to crew him in important races. Much later, when I had crewed in less expertly handled dinghies and finally graduated to my very own fourteen-footer, I wondered if I would be good enough to beat Stewart? Without this friendly rivalry over the years I should never have been selected to represent Great Britain at the Olympic Games (with Stewart as my spare man) in 1936; I should never have won a Bronze Medal there—and likely enough I should never have become (quite accidentally as it transpired) the President of the International Yacht Racing Union.

Most of the races at Ely were sailed in deadly earnest, and it was a good training ground, for in so narrow a river inches counted and fine judgment could be cultivated. A well-rounded buoy passed less than a foot away down the boat's side as a matter of standard practice. A boat's length was to be gained when 'going about' by shooting up along the bank before filling away on a new tack.

On occasion the sailing was more light-hearted. There was an afternoon when an unofficial prize had been offered for the helmsman who, sailing single-handed, contrived to capsize his boat first after the starting gun had been fired. The Commodore had not been informed of this plan; he walked up the bank with his megaphone, shouting "Let the sheet go, you stupid boy, you'll have the boat over in a moment if you're not careful." But his warning was of no avail and a few seconds later I won the prize.

CHAPTER 15   *Of Pinkfeet and Punts and Blue Geese*

DURING our Christmas holiday on the Solway we had heard rumours that very large numbers of geese assembled at the head of the great estuary upon their first arrival from the Arctic in late September. Between the River Esk and the River Eden is a vast merse covered only by high spring tides and for a few years this was used as an assembly point for what must have been at times something like thirty per cent of the world's Pinkfooted Geese. Nowadays no such concentrations of geese are to be found on Rockliffe Marsh as we saw there in the autumns of 1929 and 1930. Great numbers of Pinkfeet still come to the Solway, but not in any concentration until well into October, and their headquarters is now ten miles further to the westward around the Lochar mouth and the sanctuary provided for them on the Kinmount Estate near Annan.

On 20th September, 1929, I set out from London alone in the family's Austin Seven and arrived at Sark Bridge Farm, Gretna, eleven hours later. Next morning I found that many thousands of geese had already arrived at Rockliffe. All that day more were coming in. This was the first time I had ever seen geese arriving on migration. There were little bunches coming in high over the Metal Bridge, heading the westerly wind and planing down on to the marsh —some in threes and fours, some in groups of a dozen or twenty. The little parties were scattered about the sky almost wherever you looked. It is a pattern I have seen many times since, but never more impressively than on that first day. I know now that the geese were coming from Greenland and Iceland, but in those days Spitzbergen was thought to be the breeding ground of most of the British Pinkfeet. But wherever they came from, it was far away in Arctic or Sub-Arctic lands, and it added immeasurably to the mysterious appeal of these wonderful birds.

Rockliffe Marsh was private shooting, but by crossing the Esk in a boat it was possible to intercept the geese at the marsh edge, or from 'lying-pits' out on the sand. In the week that I was there I shot twelve geese and was vastly pleased with my success. More recently I believe Manorial Rights extending to the river channels of the Eden and Esk have been substantiated, but in 1929 this had not been clarified and the sand was widely, if erroneously, held to be free shooting.

Digging in on the sand is not now regarded as a wise procedure, for if it is extensively practised on a goose roost it seems eventually to drive the geese away. This may have been one of the contributary causes of the abandonment by the grey geese of Wells and Holkham, though I do not think it influenced their change of habits on the Solway. But in that first autumn on the Solway digging lying pits on the sand seemed only to be a practical if difficult method of goose shooting, and a number of my geese were bagged while shooting from their scanty cover.

For my last two days in Scotland I moved westward to Wigtown Bay in order to go punting with Major Hulse—the Expert as we called him. I joined him at Creetown and we spent the two days afloat in pursuit of wigeon, which confirmed my earlier conclusion that punting was the best that wildfowling had to offer. Our bag was meagre and the occasion was chiefly memorable for my meeting with Adam Birrell and for a stirring return journey in the punt in a gale of wind. I had met Adam very briefly at the end of my previous day's punting with Major Hulse, but now for the first time I recognised this was no ordinary fisherman-wildfowler. He was a first-class naturalist, with an astonishingly wide (self-administered) education. He was delightful company whether on a fowling expedition or bird-watching or fishing, and we remained in fairly regular communication thereafter for a quarter of a century.

After the two days' punting I set off from Creetown in the Austin Seven at a quarter to eight in the morning and arrived in London at a quarter to eight in the evening, having stopped for half an hour in Carlisle and three-quarters of an hour at Boroughbridge where I had lunch. It is an interesting commentary on the Great North Road and motoring conditions in 1929 that I was able to make the 380-mile journey in a seven-horsepower car at an average speed of just over 35 miles per hour. It is also perhaps worth recording that my ten days in Scotland had cost me almost exactly £10.

On the flood-waters of the Bedford Levels we had *Penelope* and *Grey Goose*, but we still had no sea-going double punt for the Wash, and this must clearly be remedied. Mr. Mathie, a boat-builder in

Cambridge, was commissioned to build one, based mainly on the design and specifications of the Expert's punt. She was to be twenty-four foot long, four-foot beam, with a twelve-foot cockpit, and she was to be called *Kazarka*—the Russian name for the Red-breasted Goose.

Kazarka was launched just below Magdalene Bridge in Cambridge on 11th December, 1929. On the following day I set out with a companion, David Lewis, to sail her to the coast. There was a south-westerly wind which was very strong at times and we made good progress until just before Ely, when there was a stretch which came closer to the eye of the wind and the lee boards could not really cope with it. But a passing sugar beet tug took us in tow as far as the Ely beet factory. Thereafter we sailed without difficulty to Brandon Creek which was to be our staging point for the day. There is a fascination in the bareness of the Fenland river banks. Trees are few and far between, and the river runs artificially straight or nearly so for many a mile, broken only by an occasional bridge. From the punt we had no view into the distance, for the high green banks rose steeply on either side to the skyline at most fifty yards away. The flat fenland fields, mostly below the level of the river, were hidden from us; and yet I remember that the passage, the testing of our boat on her maiden voyage, the anticipation of her arrival on the fowling grounds of the Wash, the pleasure of spinning along under the small sail, all added up to a sheer delight which I can clearly recall today —just thirty years later. Christopher Dalgety came to meet us at Brandon Creek, and we took David Lewis to Ely to catch a train (which he missed) and then went on to the Globe Hotel at King's Lynn which was our coastal headquarters.

Re-reading my shooting diaries in 1959 in the course of writing this book I came upon the entry for the following morning, Friday, 13th December, 1929, which is of more interest than I realised at the time. There was a moderate west-south-westerly breeze blowing as we walked out along the old drove at Terrington (past a pole evidently set up on the salting long ago as a landmark and known inevitably as the North Pole) and out to the edge of the salting. "I was in position at 6.40," says my diary, " 'streak of dawn' having been at 6.10. As it got light geese began honking all round. A lot of mallards had been sitting at the edge of the mud as I came up and now a lot more came over. I could have had several shots but the geese were all round. At last I saw about eight geese coming straight towards me. They sagged away on the wind and passed rather wide. I had a shot but without success. The sound of the shot put up a big lot of about 200 which had been sitting farther to the east. These pitched again about 200–300 yards away. I looked at them and thought that one on the left of the flock looked different. With the glass I could see at once that it was a white goose. His head, neck and breast were pure white and his back was dark brown, darker than the surrounding Pinkfeet. From the fact that he was a head taller than the rest (and longer in the leg) and also that his bill was very large and thick, I felt no doubt that he was an albino Greylag. In general size he was much larger than the Pinkfeet and was much more on the alert. He had his head up the whole time—once when only three other geese in the whole 200 had their heads up. After the flock had walked towards me a little, they sat for a while, and then I think they must have scented me, for away they went, crossing my creek further down and joining some more geese on the mud to the west."

Well, there it is! There is the first record of the Blue Goose for Europe. The description is perfect. We even know that he was the rather less common form in which the white of the head extends on to the breast and belly. I may have exaggerated the size a little, and I gave him (and his fellow Pinkfeet) a sense of smell which I do not now believe could have accounted for their departure. But the thick bill, the upright stance, the extra-dark back, all seem to me conclusive evidence. That the bird was a Blue Goose I do not have the smallest doubt. His wariness, however, does not entirely preclude the possibility that he had escaped from some collection or zoo—though at that time I should think it at least as probable that the bird was a genuinely wild one.

When the morning flight was over at 'Skeldyke' (our new code name of Terrington Marsh since the old one—'Sandbanks'—was already too widely known), we returned to breakfast at King's Lynn quite unaware that we had seen a new European bird, and an hour later we were off to Brandon Creek to see that all was well with our new punt. It was, and that day we took her to Lynn. On the next she reached her anchorage in a big creek on Terrington Marsh. *Kazarka* was a better sea boat than we imagined, and we tested her several times. Here is one of them.

Monday, 23rd December, 1929 began badly. According to my diary "Christopher forgot the sandwiches which I left in his care." According to Christopher, as far as I can remember, I forgot the sandwiches which he had left in my care. It was a misty morning on 'Skeldyke' saltings and the geese were flying all over it, so that in spite of our bungling, and particularly of my bad marksmanship we bagged a Pinkfoot each and three Mallards and two Curlews as well. These we took back to the car and then set out for the punt. The mist had now cleared and our plan was to take *Kazarka* round into the River Nene four miles direct but three times as far by water at low tide, so as to leave her there while we all went home for Christmas. On the way round of course we hoped for some opportunities for a stalk. It must have been noon by the time we reached the punt, to find her bridging the creek, supported only by the extreme stem and stern. However her back was not broken and we got her into the water only just in time, before the last of the tide went out of the bottom of the creek, leaving a narrow, winding and unnavigable trickle of water. In the course of the afternoon we made two rather small shots with the punt-gun, one at Knots, and one at Wigeon, with the result that we had not done more than about a fifth of our journey by dusk. After picking up the six Wigeon and reloading the gun, we started on down Scotsman's Sled.

The light was already beginning to fade and the S.S.E. wind which had been freshening all day was now blowing really hard—also it had begun to drizzle, and we had had nothing to eat since 5.30 a.m. In the face of all this it was madness to attempt to go round into the Nene channel, which we did not know, on such a night. However, with neap tides we hoped to be able to cuff a good many corners: to turn back now would have meant a very long wait in the dark and cold before the tide would flood us to the marsh-heads again. So we set off, rowing round 'the hairpin'. We came to a shallow 'eye' with a bar at the top which we could just cross. There were a lot of mallard in the water ahead, but we had no time for them. We set sail as quickly as possible and tore off down the 'eye', periodically touching the ground and nearly getting pooped by our own wake.

I think it was when we reached the end of this lead and had to jump out and pull the boat over a sand bar that we really began to realise our folly. Outside there was a big sea running, and it was nearly dark. Just as we ran into the sea I managed, with considerable effort, to get the big gun off the breeching ropes and bring it in board: then turning up the hinged coamings I just managed to get aft again before she burrowed. At each big wave she only just lifted clear with water pouring off the decks.

We could make out on our port beam a wreck on the sand, which was marked on the chart, but we couldn't find any channel leading to the left, in fact we were sailing straight down wind and away from our destination. By the last of daylight we made out the corner and turned into a very shallow lead. We soon came on to a lee shore, for we had not got the lee boards out and she wouldn't make to windward at all. As soon as she was aground we got the sail down at once and tried to row. There was a shallow bar in front which we had to cross and we thought we had better hurry, as the tide was still falling. Rowing was no good, so we poled on to the bar—then jumped out and pulled the boat across. As soon as we were over Christopher got out the lee boards. He had some difficulty in putting them together, but eventually, after much swearing and hammering with the short pole, they were ready and he hoisted the sail. During this delay we had drifted some way down wind and we were also in deep water—over ten feet. However, we knew that if we sailed on a beam wind, after a mile of open water we must eventually reach the far bank of the Nene channel. If the wind veered there would be the lights of the fairway buoys outside in the Lynn channel behind us to give us direction. We could see them fairly well in spite of the rain. We were in deep water, however, and there were, of course, big waves. This was perhaps the nastiest moment. I found myself with a very dry mouth and I doubt if Christopher was any happier. I gave him the chart, and he got out the torch and tried to read it, but said all he could see were the words 'Inner Westmark Knock'. This was in fact the very sand we were going round, but the chart seemed to bear very little relationship to what we could see, and indeed the sandbanks and leads were constantly changing. Anyway it was not the best kind of night for dead reckoning; and our hands were fairly full with baling, too.

After what seemed an age, during which the boat went well on a beam wind, and, all things considered, shipped comparatively little water, we decided that it was, nevertheless, about time to take off our rubber boots, and prepare to swim; but at that moment we thought we could see land ahead, and a minute or two later, with infinite relief, I touched bottom with the ten-foot pole. We ran ashore, and as it was obvious that we shouldn't want to sail any more (as our way lay into the wind), we stowed the mast and sail. Now, at any rate, we were safe, for we could leave the boat if necessary, and walk across the mud. However, we decided to stick on as long as possible. Rowing was obviously useless on this lee shore with almost a head wind. We tried poling and found that equally useless. The only way we decided was to walk and push the punt. At first we leant on to the punt and walked slowly along. However, so many waves were breaking in that it soon became obvious that the boat would sink unless something was done about it. So we arranged then that Christopher should tow in front with one of the breeching ropes walking in the water, whilst I sat on the stern and baled out the water as fast as it came in. At first I could only just keep it down and was kept pretty busy.

Then after about three-quarters of an hour of this the water got fairly suddenly calmer and we could see a bank opposite. I suggested crossing to it, but Christopher said it would be best to stick to the west side. Then we came to a dead end with shallow water all across. Over the sand on the east side we could hear the seas breaking, and we knew there was a channel there. At first we waited about to see if the tide was flowing, but it wasn't. Then Christopher said he would walk out to the west and see if he could find salting. He took the short 'sprit' and walked out, leaving me to shine the torch intermittently to direct him back again. All this time there were strange glows in the sky, some of which suddenly brightened and must have been cars on certain corners of the main road. They seemed incredibly close and comforting, but they must have been four miles away at the least. Other glows were from the towns—Lynn, Sutton Bridge, Long Sutton.

After about twenty minutes Christopher returned. He had seen nothing but mud and one creek running south, which was entirely wrong. We then had a stale ham sandwich, of which we found about half a dozen in the cartridge magazine. We lay down in the punt to get out of the wind and I think I went to sleep. When I next sat up the tide really had begun to flow, but very sluggishly, and it looked like a long wait. I walked over to the channel, which was only 100 yards away, whilst Christopher got some water out of the punt. Then he walked over, and when he returned we decided that the sea wasn't too bad and it would be best to go back a bit and get into the channel. After all, the longer we waited, the worse would be the sea. We went back, Christopher towing and me sounding. Finally we got into the channel again, but the sea was not terribly bad, and although an occasional wave came into the punt I had no trouble in keeping her fairly dry inside. We passed a beacon, a post with a place for a lamp on top—but no lamp. 'Buoys' were marked on the Admiralty chart, and I supposed that these were they.

Then an unexpected difficulty came. The bank along which we were towing became a little cliff and, being on a lee shore, we could tow no more. At first I pushed the punt out and kept her going with the ten-foot pole, but the bank became too high—the waves were breaking nastily, also there was a little side creek. We decided to try to row and got out the oars. The boat had a lot of water in her and we had some difficulty in getting off the lee shore. When at length we did get about three yards out, one wave came the whole length of the punt and took Christopher green, in the back. We then really had got some water aboard. The floor of the boat was floating with Knots and anchor rope. I said, "We must go ashore and get the water out," and Christopher said, "We'll be swamped if we do," so whilst he pulled off the shore I feverishly rowed and baled alternately. In this way I managed to get the water down before any more came in. However, it was some time before I had her empty and by that time the water had become calmer. It became so gradually calmer that one hardly noticed it, and soon we were rowing with great relief in comparative comfort. We had passed lots of beacons, all poles with something—either a gorse bush or an unlighted lamp on too; so we knew we must be in the right channel. Then at last we came into the straight, which we knew from the chart: the 'finishing straight' we called it because that made it sound as if we were nearly there. We had a mile or more of this and we crossed to the sheltered side of the river. When we had come in sight of the old lighthouses we crossed back again: we heard geese not far off on the salting to the eastward, though why they were so far in on a black-dark night we could not think. We pulled into the little 'gull' by the sea-wall then, after collecting and tying up the birds—some of the Knots had been baled overboard—we climbed up the mud slope and walked along the bank to the lighthouse, immeasurably relieved to be on dry land that we knew would not be covered by the tide.

One of the cottagers further along the bank gave us cold milk to drink, and jolly good it was, but so cold as to give us an 'ice-headache' if we drank too fast. Then we set off to walk three miles to Sutton Bridge. We got a lift in a car for the last bit. There we hired a car for the remaining ten miles to Lynn.

"We arrived at 11.30," my diary concludes, "having had two stale sandwiches each and a glass of milk since 5.30 a.m. The whole thing turned out very well, but we never deserved to get off so lightly. We undertook a very dangerous thing almost without knowing it until it was too late to turn back, and had any mishap occurred we should have been done—there was no margin of safety. Anyway it gave us both a nasty scare. I never remember to have been so frightened for so prolonged a period. The whole thing was madness, but very good experience and the boat stood up to the seas surprisingly well."

Kazarka was indeed an unqualified success. She was built to the

designs of Major Hulse, the Expert, incorporating all the modifications and refinements which he had thought of since his own
punt was built. She was probably then the best double punt in the
country. In spite of learning fast by bitter experience, it was some
time before our skill was a match for our boat. But luckier times
came later in the season, when we took her back again to her creek at
Skeldyke. The basic pattern of our punting days was always much
the same, for we could only navigate in and out of our creek at 'full
sea', or within an hour of it, which meant that our trips were, either
a brief sortie for an hour at high water, or else, at a minimum, ten
hours long; often we made use of the high tide at both ends and
were out for fourteen hours.

Coming home at the end of the day, our marsh was at its most
mysterious. In those early days we were not very sure of the way,
and as the light failed on a dull evening there were no landmarks
at all, just an expanse of grey, a little darker on the landward side
because it was mud instead of muddy water. As we drifted up from
Scotsman's Sled, there was no line to distinguish the sea from the
sky; they merged into one another, so that we had to glance back
to the boat to make sure that it really *was* like that and not our
eyes that were failing.

There was a curious silence about the mudflats: an occasional
rustle of wings as a pair of belated mallards went inland to feed, and
a few lost dunlins in ones and twos, flying low over the water; a
very lonely world, until suddenly the geese would call and chatter
out on the water, the sound rising in a crescendo as two families
quarrelled and then dying away again. If a shelduck flew past and
'laughed' harshly, it seemed to echo in the emptiness and made one
shiver a little. The mudflats were rather frightening in the days
before we knew them well. But even then they were our new world,
strange and different from any environment we knew, yet infinitely
romantic and irresistible.

By now punting had perhaps for this very reason become, for me,
the most enjoyable of all forms of wildfowling (and therefore by
definition the most enjoyable of all activities). The marshes were
wild, but the mudflats were wilder still—the wildest remaining part
of this over-populated country. At sunset on a clear day, drifting
homeward on the tide, we would look to the westward across the
waste flatness into a brilliance of scarlet and gold. The flat land
beyond was a thin black line. Above it, only the serrated edge of a
distant spinney, or the outline of the old lighthouses at the Nene's
mouth encroached upon the sky. Below it, a little dimmer and more

broken than the sky itself, the wet mudflats stretched to our feet. In our ears was the bubbling of the flowing tide and the call of curlews.

Although my ideas about killing have changed since then, I can still relive the incomparable thrill of stalking a great pack of wigeon or geese lying flat and hidden in a craft which only showed a few grey inches above water, and drew even fewer below. As the punt swept silently closer the excitement grew, until one felt as if one had just run 100 yards 'all out'. If one was pushing the punt there was good reason for this feeling, for punting with one hand from a prone position was as gruelling an exercise as could be devised. The stalk had always to be done as fast as possible, and the 'pusher' usually felt as if he had run a mile rather than 100 yards by the end. But the 'gunner' had no excuse for being out of breath except just plain excitement.

The beauty of the setting and the immediate thrills of the chase were not the only things. A punting expedition was a campaign. It required organisation, generalship, and seamanship. It was difficult and arduous—usually disappointing, and sometimes dangerous. I felt that it was one of the few remaining sports which offered adventure. Inescapably I was a devotee.

Punting was also, even in those days, controversial. There were a good many people who believed that it was too easy, or that many birds were wounded, or who did not believe that many birds should be shot with one shot. The great cannon mounted on the bows of the punt suggested to them wholesale slaughter. These were the arguments of the conventional game shooter; they did not touch on the basic question of whether birds should be shot at all; they were concerned only with how the job was done once it was agreed that it should be, and as arguments I believed (and still believe) that they were false. The punstman's bag of wildfowl was always smaller than the game shooter's bag of pheasants or grouse or partridges. If many birds were to be bagged at all, why many with many shots more than many with one shot? And what about the wounding of the birds? Here, too, punt-gunning when properly conducted stood up quite well to the comparison.

When punting the number of wounded birds that were lost was very small. People might say, "How can one know how many are struck?" We have used portable X-ray equipment since then to demonstrate that in all kinds of shooting many birds carry away shot (although it does not seem to do them very much harm). But in this respect punting is no worse than game shooting. A man who kills fifty partridges with 100 cartridges would be considered a reasonably good shot. Of the other fifty cartridges not all represent clean misses. After a punt-gun shot the wildfowler has a great deal of time, during which there is nothing to do but collect the wounded—more time than is usually left for that purpose after a partridge drive.

For those who thought that punting was too easy my advice used to be "Just you try!"

I felt secure in these arguments and at that time I had no inclination whatever to embark on the much wider issues of whether or not any killing for sport can be justified. Nowadays when I do not really think that it can, I still look back and wonder just how different my life would have been had I never been a fanatical wildfowler. The pursuit of ducks and geese with immoderate enthusiasm was an essential ingredient in my painting and in my specialised study of the *Anatidae*. How would it all have been if instead I had continued to run three days a week with the Trinity Foot Beagles and gone more regularly to my university lectures?

CHAPTER 16   *Brents with the Expert*

YOU may feel that you have already been overburdened with the pursuit of quarry, the excitement of the chase. But it would not, so it seems to me, be possible to present a balanced picture of the metamorphosis of my philosophy as a naturalist without taking you with me through the earlier wilderness. To understand the sequence I must attempt to turn you—at least for the time being—into a fanatical wildfowler.

The expeditions to the Wash continued and some success began to attend them, but although we were rapidly gaining experience and improving as marksmen, successes were still very elusive. For example I find a diary note for 23rd February, 1930: "I cannot think of a less successful morning. We walked disconsolately home." And yet were not the failures part of the appeal? The sight of the great conclaves of birds, the mastery of punt-handling, the beauty of marsh and mudflat, sea and sky—were not these the main point of it all? The diary records a morning at 'Skeldyke' when I had shot one Mallard and "ought to have finished the flight with half a dozen at least . . . By now it was getting light and it was a most wonderful morning. Thick black rain clouds to the north-west with tremendous rain storms trailing underneath them and great masses of cotton-wool clouds showing pale against the blackness behind. To the south-east it was clearer and the sky was pale cream-coloured with flat blue-grey clouds. But the most remarkable thing was the absolute clearness. Hunstanton looked only a mile or so away, and the trees of Lincolnshire were incredibly close. The old windmill along towards the coast-guard station stood out sharply against the sunrise . . . We had some breakfast sitting on the old bank, and a superb rain storm came past over Horseshoe Hole Farm and Balaclava. Great curtains of rain reached down to the ground from the very low clouds, and seemed to be dragging on it in murky streaks. It was a wonderful thing to watch, especially as we were perfectly dry only half a mile away."

As the wildfowling season of 1929–30 drew to a close, we planned a three-day excursion to the Wash as a finale. The party was Christopher Dalgety, Dick Hull, Mervyn Ingram and the Expert himself. Major Hulse was held in considerable awe by us all, and we thought it a great compliment that he had elected to join us. It is interesting that in spite of this awe, he was known to us not by his Christian name, nor as Major, not even as the Expert (a title which we coined for him some years later); he was known quite simply as Hulse.

The last day of the season (which was the most interesting of these three) was Saturday, 1st March, 1930. Hulse and I had arranged not to get up early, but to go out to the punt after full sea. When we got up at six o'clock we were surprised to find that the rest of the party, in spite of their intentions of the night before, were still in bed.

After breakfast Hulse and I went down to the marsh, and walked out along the now well footprinted path across the saltings to the punt. Nearest to the sea-wall the out marsh was covered with short green grass on which the Wigeon often fed at night, but outside this strip the vegetation was thicker and coarser. There were small patches of coarse Spartina, the alien grass which has colonised so many English estuaries, but most of the salting was covered with 'crab grass' or Sea Purslane (*Halimione portulacoides*) with grey-green, almost succulent leaves. Between the patches of Purslane the short, bright green grass interspersed with small tidal pools made good grazing for the geese and the Wigeon. Nearer to the mud most of the cover of the salting consisted of the dead heads of a flower which looked very much like a Michaelmas Daisy. This was *Aster tripolium*, the Sea Aster. Here too grew patches of Sea-blite (*Suaeda maritima*), its tiny fleshy leaves tinged with red. Further out still, the very outermost colonists of the silting mud, were beds of Glasswort or Samphire (*Salicornia stricta*) luscious and fingerlike and salt-tasting.

As we reached the punt a pair of Mallards rose from the creek and flew once all round us before going off to seaward. A moment later I saw seven dark birds landing at the edge of the salting; but almost at once they were up again and making off to the eastward— seven Brent Geese. Brents were by no means common at 'Skeldyke' and I was excited to see them, for they are the traditional quarry of the punt-gunner, and in theory the most difficult of all to approach.

As there were no more than a few duck about the mouth of our

creek, we decided to wait hidden in the marsh edge for the tide to
fall; then we drifted slowly down on the last of the tide. The banks
of shiny wet ooze sloped with a soft bulging curve to the water.
Our heads were almost level with the flat mud on top. We were
gliding silently, secretly through this stark landscape which
belonged to the birds. From a punt was the only way it could thus
be seen and enjoyed, for if we struggled out into this no-man's land
on foot and managed to avoid the bottomless soft places along the
creek sides, not only were we grotesquely conspicuous as a man
might be who was walking on smooth water, but each of us left a
great black herringbone track behind him like a scar, which
needed a month of subsequent tides to heal it. Only by sitting low
in the punt and slipping down without a sound on the receding
tide could we feel part of the scene which delighted us so much.

Where the mud gives way to sand the Mallards sat to the west of
us with every indication that they would move down to the Wisbech
Eye rather than the Sled. There must have been nearly 3,000 of
them three-quarters of a mile away lining the lop of the high sand
through an arc of sixty degrees. To the east were a few scattered
bunches of Wigeon, nothing more.

It was a lovely sunny morning now, but the north-east wind was
already strong and seemed to be freshening. It was blowing up white
horses on the open water at the edge of the ebb tide. The chances of
getting the punt round the Westmark Knock, scene of my frightening adventure with Christopher two months before, seemed rather
unlikely.

Round the hairpin bend we came upon a party of a dozen Mallards, and Hulse pushed me up to them. I misjudged the range
and thought they were too far away until they rose, when it was too
late. But it was no very good chance, though we might perhaps have
had five or six. Lower down were some more, but these were more
spread out and wilder, so as soon as they were gone we sat up to row.
On the left bank of the corner leading round into the Sled lay a seal,
away up on the high sand thirty yards from the water. He was a
rather small Common Seal, grey with a tinge of yellowish or olive
brown. We lay down and stalked him, just to see how close we could
get, but he had seen us and when we were about 100 yards away he
started for the water's edge. After a feverish shuffle he finally made it
when we were still thirty yards from him, wriggled in and swam out
watching us. Then with a long sigh (I could not be sure if he was
breathing in or out) he sank down tail first and disappeared. A
minute later there was a splash on our beam: evidently he had come

E

up rather closer to us than he expected. Next time he came up a little further away and took a long look at us. He had a delightfully appealing expression in his eyes.

Afterwards, we found this was a favourite low-tide basking place, and we always called it Seal Corner. "Stupidly" (says my diary) "I had forgotten my camera and so lost a nice chance of a photograph. As we came round the corner about thirty Wigeon sat in the mouth of the East Lead, which is no more than a minute creek at low water. I pushed down to them, and then had to turn round and push up the creek. I misjudged it, and did not allow enough for leeway in rounding the point, which had a soft muddy end. We ran aground and I had the greatest difficulty in getting the gun to bear on a bunch of eight or nine birds which sat thirty yards closer than the rest, and still a long shot away from us. Just as we swung on to them they put their heads up and Hulse, aiming by the bottom of the V of the back-sight, fired. The result was that he shot under them, and the bag was one Wigeon, which I collected after tramping through the very soft mud. Then and only then . . ." (this is the nearest to a reproachful comment about the Expert to be found anywhere in my diaries), "Then and only then could I impress upon Hulse that one had to aim with the *top* of the back-sight. After reloading the big gun we did the obvious thing—we blocked the back-sight with mud flush with the shoulders."

After this we spied down the Sled and saw that there were white horses all along the western shore. In this weight of wind it was clearly no place for us, so the Wisbech Eye project had finally to be abandoned. There were no more ducks in the Sled, so there was nothing to be done until the tide turned. We ate some sandwiches and then pulled down the sheltered eastern shore towards Hull Beacon and walked over the hard brown sand until we had a view of the Lynn Roads in which quite a sea was running.

When the flood began we rowed up into the Hairpin Reach, and spied a bunch of eight ducks on the north shore. To these I pushed Hulse at great speed and it looked quite a good chance, for they had not seen us at all at 150 yards. But when they did, at ten yards less, they were up and away on the instant, and we were sadly crestfallen. The whole distance covered by the punt on such a day as this was perhaps no more than ten miles in twelve hours, and with the tide behind her when rowing or pushing the punt probably made three or four knots. Thus there were, of necessity, long periods of sitting and waiting for the tide to ebb or to flow. There was now a long wait while the tide filled in ahead of us. Up the Hairpin Reach on the tide came a little grey and white bird with a slender neck and a long pointed bill. At first I took it for a Great Crested Grebe, but as it came closer I realised that it was too small. And then by the shape of its bill and the very white cheeks which contrasted with the slightly darker neck and breast I realised that it was a Red-necked Grebe. The light was so good that I could see every detail of the bird—the first Red-necked Grebe I had ever seen. Having come to within about fifty yards, he then swam off down the Sled against the incoming tide, diving perpetually for food. When I last saw him his white cheeks shining in the sun were his most conspicuous character.

Hulse and I sat talking after he had gone. He was not usually much of a talker; his delight was in doing things in a skilful and expert manner, and most of his speech was in clipped mono-syllables. He had a small repertoire of unprintable stories. In one the pay-off line was "It might have been worse" but it was ren-dered in broad Scots as "It micht ha' bin whaur", and was obviously of very wide application to our activities. But Hulse was at his best talking of his wildfowling adventures in Scotland and in Ireland, and it was of these that I most wanted to hear. When the Red-necked Grebe had gone he began to tell me of a visit to Tralee Bay in the west of Ireland. The local wildfowler had estimated the numbers of Brent Geese there at two and a quarter millions, but with a twinkle Hulse said he thought this "might be an exaggera-tion" because his own estimate at the same time had been 4,000.

Great numbers of ducks had meanwhile been sweeping in from the sea and from the Wisbech Eye, and settling on the mud high above us to the east. It was a wonderful thing to watch them swirling in and rounding up to settle. But there was nothing we could do to get near them; so we rowed on up the creek where we caught up the first of the tide and found a small bore going up ahead of us, with a wave six or eight inches high breaking on either bank.

During another long wait an aeroplane passed to seaward, and we suddenly heard a great clamour of geese. We quickly lay down in the punt and a pack of Bean Geese came over. As they came up we both remarked how much more like Greylags than Pinkfeet they sounded. When they were exactly overhead and about fifty yards up, I got the glasses on to them, and by the light of the setting sun I could see their almost dazzlingly orange legs. As they passed over us the clamour, which had been tremendous—a deep buzzy note—suddenly ceased and they departed eastward with only an occasional honk. There were sixty-nine birds in the flock. They flew a mile or so to the east and then pitched.

As the light began to fade we were determined to profit by our mistakes of two days before. This time we would wait in the creek for the ducks to come drifting up to us with the flood tide, and only push out towards them at the last minute. I lay down to the gun and Hulse lay down to push, holding the punt against the bank of the creek. Slowly the black line of ducks in the water came closer, but again we were impatient and again we went out a little too soon. Again the birds lifted at 150 yards. We retired at once into our creek but we had cleared its immediate neighbourhood of ducks and that seemed to be the end of our day—and of our season (for it was the 1st March). Hulse suggested we should unload the big gun while there was still enough daylight to see what we were doing, but I was for waiting a little yet. I was about to stand up and spy with the binoculars when Hulse said, "Quick, lie down." Seven geese had pitched at the edge of the salting 200 yards away to the east ; but unfortunately they had seen me, and they rose again at once and flew a few hundred yards further. With the glass I could see that they were Brents.

There was nothing to do but wait and we spent a quarter of an hour in an agony of suspense, wondering if the light would still be good enough when the tide enabled us to get across towards them. To add to the difficulty the geese were walking away from us, feeding all the time as they went.

The light was going fast and there came a moment when I had to accept the conclusion that the project was hopeless. It was a bitter moment too, for Brents were to me the most exciting quarry of all, and I had never stalked them in a punt. "Of course," said Hulse, "if they'd been over to the west of us, against the sunset, it would have been all right. We could see to stalk that way for another twenty minutes." I looked round towards the bright sky and the bright water below it, and there silhouetted were seven geese. I could hardly believe my eyes. They were less than 150 yards away and I could see at once that they were Brents. I peered back into the gloom and could just make out the original seven, still feeding away from us along the shore. This then was a new lot.

As quickly as we could we began to turn the punt round by swinging the stern out into the current. I remember I was tremendously excited as I lay behind the gun, for I felt that our chances were good. Perhaps our luck would change and our day would be redeemed at the eleventh hour. The stalk was going to be difficult because the strong wind kept blowing us sideways on to the shore of the creek, and the punt was continually running aground. We had lost the shortest pole two days before and now we really missed it. Had I been able to push off from my position just behind the gun, I could have kept the bows out, while Hulse drove her forward. I got out the little hammer from the tool kit for the big gun and managed to fend her off with that. We were still broadside on to our geese going down the creek, and they were only a little over 100 yards away. At last we thought there would be enough water to turn left and head towards the quarry. Hulse was pushing with his right hand, which was now exposed to the waves breaking over the point. Suddenly the stern of the punt ran aground and we began to ship water in earnest through the open shutter. I looked round and had a glimpse of Hulse trying to keep dry as the water poured in and across the floor boards. From his language I concluded he was not succeeding.

Meanwhile the bows were swinging round and something drastic had to be done. I plunged my left arm overboard and held her up with the hammer. Hulse got the shutter in, and in another ten seconds we were afloat again. But the geese had seen us, and were swimming rapidly away, all bunched together. We gave chase at high speed. Now thoroughly suspicious they stopped, spread out, and prepared to jump. But they seemed to think better of it and turned to swim away again, bunching as they did so. We were gaining on them now, and Hulse was fairly driving the punt along.

When the Brents headed the wind for the second time I decided that this would be the last opportunity. Four of them were fairly well bunched together on the left, the other three being spread out to the right. Hulse in an urgent and breathless voice said, "Now's your chance!" I steadied the gun on them and pulled the string.

The smoke cloud blew away from us straight towards the birds and from the side of it three of them flew off. I remember that my arithmetic was not at its best and I said to Hulse, "We must have got three"; but when the smoke had cleared four geese lay on the water. I got out and cautiously waded in eight inches of water to pick them up. They were all adults of the Dark-bellied form.

We pulled back into the creek. Hulse was soaked and very uncomfortable. I was also pretty wet and my left arm was soaked almost to the shoulder, but I was vastly pleased at the result of my first stalk at Brents.

At the usual mooring place we put the punt covers athwart the coamings and collected the sail which we had left out to dry. *Kazarka* looked rather more like an aeroplane than a boat as we took her on up the creek to the nearest point to the sea-wall, anchored her and set off for home.

So ended our three days in the magic world of the wildfowl— to me, at that time, the only world of reality. The University of Cambridge might have been upon another planet.

CHAPTER 17   *Dogfish v. Sunrise*

THE mechanism by which my absence on the Wash should have
remained unknown to those in authority had broken down and
serious trouble was only averted by assigning the three days to
those normally permitted, and staying up for three extra days at
the end of the term. News of my absenteeism, however, reached
my stepfather, who wrote more in sorrow than in anger.

This was my reply:

University Pitt Club

"Dear Bill,

"It was true—and I was away for three nights—the last of the
shooting season and no doubt the last I shall do for a long time.
I suppose it was very bad and I merited all you said and more.
I suppose it was a case of not sticking to it; but I am not entirely
convinced. Somehow or other being out in the wilds seems so
much more necessary to me than learning the fossils of the
Devonian period that I cannot quite manage to 'put it from
me'.

"It's such a rare thing to be able to enjoy and understand a
wild place; that sounds stupid I know but it's what I feel.
Anyone can learn the names of fossils and the classifications of
animals but I don't want to do things that anyone can do.
Anyone can't paint—and I suppose that's why I like it, and
anyone can't 'understand' (I use the word for lack of a better
one) and get the best out of the elements and the wastes—the
places where 'anyone' wouldn't even want to go.

"I suppose it's scope for imagination that I want and there
isn't any that I can find in the inside of a dogfish. I think I have
a rather particularly vivid imagination (I don't know whether
everyone thinks that they have); but not only do I think that I

should use it, but I know that I must use it or I shall just fade away and lose it.

"This isn't really an excuse and I don't really expect you to understand it. I can't express it properly either which makes me sure that I could never write.

"Do please come next week and I will get my very bestest friends.

"I know it was naughty to go away but of course I have to put in the three days at the end of the term just the same.

Yours,
PETE."

The assessment of my literary potentialities may well have been sound but there are a good many other things in this letter which now seem foolish and unimaginative. Particularly, perhaps, it is strange that I was then unmoved by the romantic aspects of geology and comparative anatomy. In my mind they did not touch that part of zoology which interested me most, the behaviour of the living animal. But this was only part of a wider reappraisal. I was approaching a major decision.

It is established that in my enthusiasms I lacked (and perhaps still lack) a sense of proportion, that I did not (and perhaps still do not) readily distinguish work from play, and that so far as my academic work was concerned I had become totally irresponsible. There were three factors in this, the nature of the work, the appeal of the diversions and my own character. I was in a mood to consider only the first. If the University could not keep me interested in Part 1, Zoology, there was either something wrong with the University, or something wrong with Zoology, or both. There was too much dissection, there were too many specimens in bottles. In those days the science of animal behaviour had scarcely begun and the word 'ethology' was unknown in this context. To know about live animals was something less than science, nor was it apparently significant to know about animals in relation to their habitat. The modern science of ecology was scarcely born. The suggestion that an intimate knowledge of saltings and mudflats and their plants and animals could in themselves add an important element to my University studies would not have impressed those in charge of my education.

And what of my painting and drawing? It was, of course, satisfactory that I could turn out a reasonably neat and realistic drawing of the central nervous system of my dissected dogfish, or frog, or rabbit, or cockroach; but there was no excuse for spending working time on a reconstruction of the Brent Geese against the sunset, as seen from the punt. Art simply did not seem to be getting a look in, and yet I wanted to be painting for most of the time that I had to be indoors. I had begun to make a few portrait drawings of my friends, and was commissioned by the Editor, Lionel Gamlin, to do a series of University personalities for the *Granta*. What with these and my exhibition of water-colours at Bowes and Bowes, and the illustrations to the new edition of the *Roof-climbers Guide to Trinity*, was I not perhaps becoming more of an artist than a zoologist?

Both at school and at Cambridge I had been specialising in science and I came to realise that I had no education whatever in the humanities. I could draw a little, but I knew practically nothing about art, nor literature nor history.

As my academic career in Natural Science held no great promise I decided to change horses in midstream, and to complete my time at Cambridge by studying 'History of Art and Architecture'. At the same time my primary objective in life changed. Instead of a scientist I would be an artist.

I have never regretted this great and momentous decision, for at one sweep my whole outlook on life was changed and enlarged. I saw it as the missing half which had suddenly come up into balance. Perhaps I was going to be complete after all. In order to take a degree in the new subject I stayed a fourth year at Cambridge, and worked a good deal harder than I had done in my first three.

I had to move out of College and had rooms off Jesus Lane just behind the University Pitt Club. It was fashionable in those days for members of the Club to wear a hat, though few other undergraduates did so. When I joined I bought a hat for the express purpose, but either I lost it or else I felt rebellious about it. I remember that this pained my friend Lord Hinchingbrooke. We had been at West Downs together and our families were close friends, but he was a couple of years older than me, and was also a good deal taller. One day I met him in the hall of the Pitt. "My dear Peter," he said, "you simply can't go in and out of the Club without a hat." "No, I suppose not," I said meekly, and went straight out after lunch and bought another. But a week later it too was lost or left behind. Except for my wartime service in the Navy, I have never worn a hat since.

The summer of 1930 was the summer of *Clover*, the International

E*

fourteen-foot dinghy built by Morgan Giles for Stewart Morris. When I agreed to be Stewart's crew for the season, I was entering a new world of sailing.

Clover was built of teak and was dark nut-brown instead of the usual chestnut-colour of the mahogany hulls. She was No. 216 in the class, which had only become 'International' three years before: it was a class of open boats—entirely undecked. At the outset H.R.H. the Prince of Wales had given a Challenge Cup which has remained the blue riband of small boat sailing in this country ever since. In 1927 at Cowes the Prince of Wales's Cup was won for the first time; the winner was Cecil Atkey in *Irex 2*. In the following year the entries for the race at Lowestoft included a new boat called *Avenger*, which was to be sailed by its designer, a young boat-builder and Sea-Scoutmaster named Uffa Fox, who had been second in the original race. *Avenger*'s fame had preceded her, for in earlier races she had swept the board in the Solent, and her designer had sailed her with three on board from Cowes to Le Havre in a strong wind, so strong, in fact, that when four miles out from the island they had met a fifty-ton cutter also bound for Le Havre, with three reefs in her mainsail, running back for shelter. Having won her two French races *Avenger* sailed back to Cowes in the teeth of a fresh nor'-wester.

Avenger won that second Prince of Wales's Cup by more than five minutes, and in all that season she took fifty-two first prizes in fifty-seven starts. In the following year Uffa Fox won again in *Daring* when the race was in Plymouth Sound.

The secret of these successes seemed to be that the bows of these new boats were V-shaped in section rather than U-shaped as most of their predecessors had been. This, combined with a rather flat run aft, made them lift out of the water and 'plane' along the top whenever the wind was fresh. Sailing boats which 'planed' had existed already for many years, but this was the first time that so small a boat as a dinghy had been made to 'lift and go'. *Clover* was Morgan Giles's reply to the challenge of Uffa Fox.

By 1930 Uffa had decided not to compete again himself for the Prince of Wales's Cup, but of course he continued to build ever faster and faster boats each year. For Tom Thornycroft, who had been second in the two previous years, he built *Goldeneye*; for Phyllis Richardson who was crewed by her husband, Colonel Henry Richardson, he built *Filibuster*; and for 'Bee' Mackinnon, an Oxford undergraduate against whom Stewart and I had raced in the previous 'Varsity Match', he built *Flame*.

Stewart and I sailed *Clover* in the regattas on the Broads for practice and were moderately successful, but the real opposition would come when the racing began at sea off Lowestoft.

The Prince of Wales's Cup is usually held on the Thursday of a week's racing, so that if the race has to be cancelled because of too much or too little wind, there are two spare days in hand. On this particular Thursday the day dawned with no wind at all. The ten o'clock start was postponed for half an hour and then a second half hour in the hope that a breeze might spring up. Just before eleven the forty dinghies lay kedged in the strong south-going tide and when the gun went we all pulled up our anchors and drifted away to the first mark off Pakefield where we quickly dropped them again. The atmosphere was rather tense among all the boats lying almost alongside each other, for although there was nothing we could do until the tide turned or a breeze set in, we were, after all, competing in the premier small boat race of the year. Stewart made it plain that I was not to forget this.

In due course the tidal stream eased off, and at the same time the very lightest of zephyrs began to fill in from the sea. Slowly the boats ghosted out to the outer turning mark and on round the triangle. It should have been a six-round race, and I forget now whether the course had been shortened, but late in the afternoon the wind began to die away again and by this time the tide was running strongly to the northward.

We were lying somewhere about tenth when it became necessary to kedge in order not to lose ground. Our kedge-anchor held beautifully but many of the boats ahead of us began to drag. Slowly, inexorably, they dragged past us so that only three boats remained ahead of us. If the wind were to freshen now, a place in the first six in the great race would assuredly be ours. But of course the wind was not going to freshen. At that time of day in that sort of weather there was only one thing it could do, and that was to stop blowing altogether, which very soon afterwards it did. Tom Thornycroft had been in the lead since the beginning and was still there when the motor-boats came round to tell us that the race had been abandoned and to tow us in.

Next day the performance was repeated; there were the two half-hour postponements, the kedging before the start, the drift with the tide to the Pakefield buoy, and the prospect of the same long wait in the noonday sunshine for the tide to ease and the sea breeze to set in. The mood was rather different from the day before. There was a good deal more bonhomous chatter among the crews.

Windjammer had got her kedge foul of the moorings of the turning buoy, and although rules disqualify a boat which touches a mark of the course above water, the underwater part does not count. Eric Morris, Stewart's cousin, was dispatched by Quiller Gold, his helmsman, to dive down and extricate the submerged anchor, taking care to avoid touching any part of the buoy which was above water.

These activities led to a good deal of light-hearted banter, and it was not long before I had my Captain's permission to go swimming for the fun of it, and to get cool. I swam from boat to boat thinking what fun it was until suddenly I saw that the seaward ones were hauling up their kedges against the arrival of the sea breeze. Immediately I swam back to *Clover*, but by the time I got there several boats had recovered their anchors and were already sailing away. Tom Thornycroft had worked out a lead of fifty yards already towards the seaward mark. I climbed aboard shamefacedly and hauled in on the kedge line; by the time it was up twenty boats were away ahead of us.

But the wind that came in that day was even more fickle than it had been the day before, and almost at once it died again. Half an hour later, in order to save a repetition of the day before the race was officially abandoned, and once more we were all towed back to harbour. Once more Tom Thornycroft was in the lead when we all stopped.

As in the previous year, my family had taken Horsey Hall from Tony Buxton for the summer holidays, and I was returning there each night. On the Saturday morning conditions at Horsey seemed to be exactly the same as they had been on the two previous days. It was dead calm and nothing seemed more certain than that the race would be postponed for half an hour at least, probably for an hour. I set off to motor the twenty miles in the family Austin Seven; as I saw it, there was no kind of hurry. As I came down past the lighthouse on the hilltop at the north end of Lowestoft there was a ripple in the leaves of a big poplar tree. Could I be wrong? If there was no postponement I was cutting it pretty fine—in fact I'd be late. But after all for the last two days there *had* been a postponement, and it was just the same kind of day.

But as I came down the hill and in sight of the harbour I could see that the flags were blowing out in a light breeze. I also noticed that there were no fourteen-footer sails or masts in the harbour. I hurtled to the club steps, and down them into a motor-boat which cast off at once and took me out to the harbour mouth. The ten-minute gun had gone, the dinghies were manoeuvring at the starting line in a light but steady easterly breeze; with Stewart in *Clover* was the professional skipper Cubitt Nudd. The dinghy rounded up alongside. As Cubitt climbed out I climbed in, murmuring something about a mythical puncture, and as we pushed off the five-minute gun went.

I do not remember much about the race. Stewart made a poor start from which we never extricated ourselves and we finally finished eleventh. Tom Thornycroft won by eleven minutes from Mrs. Richardson with 'Bee' Mackinnon third and *Windjammer* fourth.

Perhaps *Clover* was no match for the new Fox boats even in light airs, perhaps at that stage Stewart's skill and experience was no match for Tom Thornycroft, but at the back of my mind was the inescapable thought that I had been a thoroughly unsatisfactory crew. What with swimming and late arrival I was simply not to be depended upon.

In the following year, when *Clover* was superseded by *R.I.P.*, designed and built by Uffa Fox, Stewart wisely invited his brother Jack to crew him in the Prince of Wales's Cup, instead of me, but although they led for the first part of the race in a heavy wind, they filled up with water at one stage, and later lost their rudder pintle and had to retire.

In its final stages the race was very exciting. *Nil Desperandum*, sailed by Chris Ratsey of the famous sailmaking firm, who had been in the lead, was passed by Harold Edwards in *Swift*, and now from astern came a challenge from Morgan Giles the veteran designer himself, sailing *Catherine*. He had been gaining off the wind and losing to windward, but now there was nothing left but the final run. It was blowing very hard but in spite of that he told his son to set the spinnaker. He was rolling wildly but closing the gap. Could he get to the finishing line without capsizing? Harold Edwards, who because of the wind strength had left his spinnaker ashore, hoped fervently that he could not, but *Catherine* planed down that reach as fast as any Fox boat, overtook *Swift* and won the race by six seconds. As the winning gun fired Morgan Giles relaxed and at that moment his boat capsized. It was a dramatic and splendid victory in the best race for the Prince of Wales's Cup that had been sailed since its inception. Not for another seven years was there to be so close a finish and then I was myself to be intimately involved.

CHAPTER 18   *'The* Bolero *Term'*

MY first pictures of wildfowl to be published, apart from the little
drawings in the schoolboy book, had appeared in *Country Life* in
August 1929. They were rather simple water-colours of wild geese,
reproduced in monochrome and accompanied by a bloodthirsty
little article, of which I am not now very proud, describing my
wildfowling adventures. The birds were poorly drawn and I had
as yet no idea of how to make the air support them; they were
simply stuck on to the sky. But the compositions were quite pleasant
and already I had begun to understand that the movement of birds
through the air could more easily be suggested by the pattern of the
flock than by the shapes of the individuals. After that my paintings
appeared regularly in *Country Life*, about twice a year, for many
years to come.

This outlet for my work may have played a very small part in
my decision to become a professional painter, although I never
seriously believed that there was likely to be any commercial
demand for my work. If I had ever hoped that the painting of birds
could provide me with a modest livelihood, I had long since dismissed the thought. "Portraits," they had told me, "ah, now there's
money in them—but birds . . ."

My last term at Cambridge was the autumn term of 1930, and as
I have already recorded I was no longer able to live in College. It
was for me 'the *Bolero* term', for the occupant of the rooms immediately below mine had a gramophone and a new recording of Ravel's
Bolero. He played this record incessantly for many weeks on end.
As with so many things in life there were two courses open to me.
One was to protest violently to my landlady that my work was being
interfered with; the other was to learn to like the music. The latter
seemed to be the line of least resistance and quite soon I found
myself humming and beating time to it, and even calling on my

neighbour so that I could hear it better than through the floor. The *Bolero* term' was otherwise important for two reasons.

First came Fulbourn Fen, the marsh in which we had first found the Garganey breeding, and had watched the Ruffs dancing in the spring of the two previous years. But now it became a syndicate shoot which four of us had rented for £20; the other three were Aylmer Tryon, Michael Adeane and Peter Maclean.

What seemed most remarkable about Fulbourn was perhaps that it was full of wildfowl although only three miles from the middle of Cambridge. It had, too, a certain magic about it because of the dawns and dusks that we spent there.

The Fen consisted of about thirty acres of flooded fields in which a reed bed had grown up, and to which some hundreds of wild ducks came to drink when they were feeding in near-by stubble fields, to feed when we provided barley and the potato peelings from the kitchens of Trinity College, and to rest by day when they were not too greatly disturbed. Along one side of it was a path bordered by a hawthorn hedge which gave way in places to patches of thorn bush scrub. Across the far end of the marsh ran the Lode, a raised water-way into which the surrounding marshes were drained by pumping. The bank of the Lode was old and leaky, and where the water rats had been at work the water trickled through into the fen and spread out across the two wet fields. When repairs had been made to the bank the fen tended to dry up and grow smaller until hardly any open water remained. But fortunately the water rats only needed limited help and encouragement for the fen to remain in being.

The Fulbourn syndicate were gentle people, perhaps less ruthless and determined than some of my usual companions on the Wash. They laughed at me for being so serious-minded about it all and so tediously 'efficient'. "After all," said they, "ultimate efficiency is a rather pointless objective in something which you are doing for fun." All kinds of philosophical paradoxes are implicit in this simple assertion; surely games should be played for fun and yet a game is scarcely worth playing if you are not trying your hardest to win. It raises the whole question of competition between human beings; there is a strong argument which says "if you want competition then go and play golf, or sail races, or go into politics, or industry, or the City; but if you want to enjoy wildlife and the beauty of the natural world you must leave human competition behind and below, and rise to a more rarefied plane." I do not think the Fulbourn syndicate cared particularly for any such rarefication. They were simply concerned that the member who seemed to think the most of himself should not so consistently hurl insults at his fellows whenever they did anything which in his view fell short of 'ultimate efficiency'. Poor things! They had an uphill row to hoe. But I learned a good deal from them.

The rules of our shoot permitted the invitation of guests from time to time. During the long vacation term and soon after the contract had been signed with the farmer, I was staying just outside Cambridge at Elsworth with Geoffrey Webb, a distinguished and bearded teacher of architecture, who was attempting to put into my head the final details about 'History of Art and Architecture' in which I hoped to take my degree. My diary records that on 17th September, which was a pouring wet day, Geoffrey Webb and I enlisted the support of Bunny Garnett, the novelist, who lived near-by at Hilton. I do not record that this was the same Garnett who was author of the best-selling novels *Lady into Fox* and *The Grasshoppers Came*. All that the diary notes is that he went up the south side of Fulbourn Fen to butt No. 5 while I went up the north side, that there were a good many snipe, that I missed one of them and that I also missed an easy Teal. It is rather a sad commentary that of my short acquaintance with this distinguished author I recorded only these few irrelevant facts. "One could have gone on shooting for another twenty minutes but I thought Garnett and Webb would be bored so I returned and met them. Garnett had not shot anything but seemed to have enjoyed himself. We tied the ducks up and went home drenched to the skin and dined at Garnett's house at Hilton."

The '*Bolero* term' was also significant because of my first meeting with a Marlburian who was up at Sidney Sussex College and who was then known to his friends as Malpas Bratby. I record that on "Wednesday, 29th October, I went to Childerley Hall with Malpas Bratby. It is a shoot taken by him for £40." The principal bag on that day, I remember, was pigeons.

William Michael Malpas Bratby was a remarkable character. There was nothing unusual about his appearance: of average height, slight build, wearing glasses, you had only to listen to him for a few minutes to realise the originality of his mind. It was closely linked with his sense of humour and he might easily have become a comedian or a funny writer but for his flair for finance, which later led him to such delight in his work as a very successful stockbroker. In Cambridge days he was already a glorious deflater of pomposity, and he also had a line in sheer fantasy, so that he could give a long and detailed account of supposed adventures which bore little relation to the truth—nor were they meant to—and kept all of us who listened in fits of laughter. This particular capacity at times amounted to inventive genius. Here I realised was a splendid new companion for our various adventures. He remained one of my closest friends from then until the day he died in 1959.

Although when I first met him at the University he was introduced as Malpas Bratby, Michael was the name he used for most of his life. He had a large collection of gramophone records of American railroad songs and western ballads. He could not himself carry a tune but in a curious monotone he hummed these songs perpetually on car journeys and the like. I found myself singing them too, interspersed with Ravel's *Bolero*. I was well aware by this time of the extraordinary power of popular tunes to associate themselves with occasions and adventures. During our wonderful Christmas expedition to the Solway Firth a year before I had been humming two tunes from a gramophone record sung by Mr. Frank Crummit. On one side was 'The Year of Jubilo' and on the other 'Down in the Cane Break'. I have only to hum these tunes to see again the tightly packed flocks of Barnacles sweeping in over Caerlaverock Merse from the 'Blayshie Bonk' or the Greylags coming out from inland and tumbling down to the shore. And I have only to hear Ravel's *Bolero* to take myself back to Fulbourn Fen and Childerley Hall and my last term at Cambridge. 'Casey Jones', 'The Wreck of the Number Nine' and 'The Wreck of the Ninety-Seven' and the 'Wreck of the *1256*', 'Ben Dewbury', 'The Wreck of the Royal Palm', 'The Jealous Lover of Lone Green Valley', 'Frankie and Johnny': I have carried the words of these songs in my head for thirty years. Occasionally they are trotted out as a party piece, sung unaccompanied. How much I wish that I had learned to play a guitar or perhaps even one of the easier stringed instruments!

This repertoire of songs was strengthened by some songs from *Riverside Nights*, an intimate revue—words by A. P. Herbert—which had had a short season in Cambridge. I had been enormously impressed with the performance of Miss Elsa Lanchester, especially her moving rendering of such works as 'I was a Beautiful Baby' and 'Please sell no more drink to my father'.

The memorising of lyrics and verse is quite a common way in which we fill the pigeon holes of our minds. I can remember hearing Sir John Simon, the great Liberal lawyer-statesman, when sitting for the marble bust which my mother cut of him (and a very striking likeness it was), reciting page after page of *King Lear* from memory;

after half an hour or more of Shakespeare he would change to Milton.

Of serious poetry I have never memorised much—a little Keats, rather inaccurately, some Browning, *The Revenge*—no more. But at a fairly early age I took the trouble to commit the whole of Lewis Carroll's *Hunting of the Snark* to memory, and have retained it down the years. I have found it very useful, not only for whiling away any dull half hour, but more particularly perhaps for its quotability. There is a verse which is appropriate for nearly all occasions, especially nautical ones.

In the winter of 1930 we had established the punt again at 'Skeldyke', though for this last term I only went seldom because of my exams. It was important to get a degree in my new subject and this I duly achieved. Mervyn Ingram and I took our degrees together on the 17th December and went snipe shooting on the same afternoon. A couple of days later, with Christopher Dalgety and Michael Bratby, we were off to the Wash. This was a swan song, and the end of my season, at least, for I was to go abroad almost immediately to study my new trade: I was to attend the State Academy at Munich to learn to be a painter.

CHAPTER 19

Pair-Formation and Pan

AS 1930 draws to a close—a momentous year in my life—I must pause to take stock of the major influences. Painting was now to be my profession. Natural History was deeply embedded in my system. A zoological training was part of my background. Wildfowling was my obsession. Sailing was my summer's delight; fourteen-foot dinghies had entered my world and seemed likely to stay there. Skating was primarily a winter interest, and although it did not compete on even terms with wildfowling, it was my principal contact with the juvenile females of my species, which gave it a significant place.

By this time I was moderately proficient on the ice, especially in free skating. This involved fitting together a sequence of movements in what was called a 'programme', but which was in fact a dance lasting a specified number of minutes, and performed to almost any kind of music, usually a *passo doble*, or the March of the Gladiators. There were complicated steps, and simple ones (which often looked more effective); there were jumps and spins, spirals and spread-eagles, and if the ice was empty they could all be performed in sequence without interruption. But, competitions and demonstrations apart, the ice was seldom empty. Skating at the crowded ice-rinks in London was divided into 'sessions', and just before each session began, the keener spirits would form up at the entrances ready to rush out at the bang of the gong and stake their claim to a 'centre'. This was enough space in which to perform the school figures, based more or less upon a figure of eight. Less advanced skaters had to have enough room to perambulate round in a clockwise direction so that the 'centres' had to be in the centre of the rink; and oh! the daggers which flashed from the eyes of those who met trespassers upon their 'centre'. After about half an hour most people were bored with school figures and ready for something more dashing. Sometimes newcomers took over their centres, but sometimes the area became available for free skating—for dashing about. I was always glad when the dashing about began, for I was still weak on my figures, principally because of my failure to master loops. But free skating was the best fun: it was exhilarating and there was a wonderful feeling of achievement when a difficult jump came off. There was something else too: it was rather nice to bring it off if anyone happened to be watching.

Once Michael Bratby and two other friends had said they would like to go skating and we had motored from Cambridge to the newly opened and immensely crowded Golders Green ice rink. There were so many people on the ice that the prospects of finding space in which to jump or spin seemed negligible. But in Golders Green at that time they had not seen much skating and in a few minutes quite a large patch of the rink was opened out and lined with skaters who had stopped to watch. I had all the space I needed, and my afternoon was made.

What a strange thing is modesty! Perhaps less strange is the lack of it. Skating was for me a mixture of many urges. If I was skilful, and that after all was what I practised for, then people looked at me; if I did not want to be looked at, why then did I practise to become more skilful? On the more sophisticated ice-rinks there was seldom room in those days for a free skating sequence, but there was usually enough space to try a difficult jump. If there was an audience finesse was called for in the presentation. The jump could be tried several times running. Failure was followed by much shaking of the head and perhaps a run back over the spot to look at the mark on the ice, and an implication that the ice itself had something to do with the failure. If an unfortunate skater got in the way at the crucial moment, it all helped to build up sympathy and tension in the audience. "Let's see if he does it this time—oh, bad luck, but it was a good try! That beginner got in his way. Now here he comes again. Oops! Oh, well done, a jolly good double loop jump . . . you didn't see; you weren't watching; you can't bear the way the fellow shows off? Oh well, I expect you're right, really."

But the best part of skating was the thing itself—the magic of the swift smooth movement over the ice. There was pure physical enjoyment in the speed and the power, the steepness of the curve in a spiral, the neatness of a grapevine, the freedom of a high three-jump: it was fast and glossy as silk. There was also pair-formation.

In birds pair-formation usually involves a ritualised display of some complexity. In the human species it is no less complex, and the display on ice was no less ritualised. My comparative skill in waltzing and the Ten-Step ensured for me an array of charming partners of varying degrees of skill and beauty. I have written already of Elizabeth, whose skating abilities were the least part of her appeal. Tiny, dark-eyed Elizabeth was much adored; but in due course she returned to her native Canada and short of following her, what could I do? I was not cut out for the waiting game. One wonderful afternoon my eye lit upon a new princess working quietly at rockers on her centre in mid-ice-rink. I watched spellbound. She was good, too—very good. It did not take me long to discover that she was the champion skater of her own Scandinavian country. But there was more to it than this, for she was quite different from the majority of the girl champions. She did not have the thick muscular legs of the Axel Paulsen-jumping girls, nor did she fill her free skating with ever faster and faster scratch spins. She was not so much an athlete as a dancer, not a sportswoman but an artist. My little champion knew how to move, how to dance—she also, I discovered, knew how to draw, and she was delightfully pretty.

So long afterwards I find it difficult to assess this romance of thirty years ago, but it was something gentle and tender and altogether happy. In skating and in all else I felt a clumsy clodhopper in her company. I discovered real humility for perhaps the first time in my life. There were no ifs and buts; I was not (as in most previous humiliating circumstances) hardly done by. I simply was not good enough for her.

It had been decided that during my year's study at the State Academy School in Munich, I should stay in the family of one of the Professors of the School who was himself a distinguished painter of animals, particularly of horses. The Herr Geheimrat Professor Angelo Jank's family consisted of his charming and rather stout wife and five children—two boys and three girls. The eldest boy and the eldest girl were already grown up and living elsewhere but still at home were the three younger ones—Ruli, a very tall, fair-haired, sardonic lad of about my own age, Anna-Louise (who was also called Mouse) and Jula (who was thirteen and irrepressible). They lived in the Karl Theodor Strasse in Schwabing, an eastern suburb of Munich. It was a large house and typically German in its architecture; its floors were mostly carpetless, its doors fitted on to rather than into its walls, and were characteristically handled; for most of the day it smelled strongly of the popular table relish Maggi, so that as we came in we murmured "Ah, Maggi!" instead of "Ah, Bisto!"

For some reason I was not able to go at once to the Academy and spent a term at a private art school. This was perhaps as well because when I arrived in Munich I had no single word of German. It was obviously necessary to learn at least the rudiments of the language before I could expect to get anything from the professional training.

My mother believed any school was good enough provided it gave you a model to draw and unlimited time to draw in. Although this may have been an overstatement, there is some truth in the notion that artists are born and not made, and that individuality can easily be suppressed and overlaid by excessive teaching.

During my first weeks in Munich, however, no one stood much chance of influencing my artistic individuality in any direction for lack of a common language. But in a very few weeks Frau Bermann (the twice-weekly successor to Mlle. Herbulin) had established the first bridge across the chasm. It was purely by chance that I was living in the house of the Professor of the Animal Painting School, but when the time came to enter the Academy it seemed sensible to go into his class, although the animals involved were horses and cows and pigs, and did not ever seem likely to include such extraneous and irrelevant animals as wild geese and ducks. The Herr Professor himself was a kindly man, and I can remember showing him the first oil painting which I had ever made—a picture of geese against the background of a sunrise. The sky was very dark, the birds almost black, silhouetted against a streak of fiery orange. It was an undistinguished picture, but it had a snatch of the atmosphere about it and I was inordinately proud of it. The Professor's criticism was in friendly vein but it was plain to see that he did not think much of it and that he did not understand at all why I had painted it.

Soon after my arrival in Munich it was Faschingsfest, a festival of dancing and merrymaking, and with 'the family' I was invited to some dances. It was here I discovered that dances are for pair-formation. Dancing requires a certain skill, and when that has been acquired, it can be very enjoyable if there is room to exercise your skill. But at most dances there is no such room, and often no partners prepared to do more than shuffle round in the crowd. Dances, I decided, were not for dancing.

One day I was taken to a tea-party out in the country. Frau Jank told me before we left that I should particularly like it because the daughter of the house was 'altogether charming'. I must by this time have acquired some slight knowledge of the language (it is astonishing how fast a language can be learned if needs must). Already I could understand most of what passed in conversation, and could even occasionally make myself understood. Here I was, then, for an afternoon and evening at a house in the country some twenty miles from Munich.

We had arrived by car soon after lunch and I had been introduced to the daughter of the house. Charming she might well be, but pretty she most certainly was not. Her face was rather podgy and held that curiously heavy emotionless expression which is not uncommon in Bavaria. To be sure, her figure was agreeable enough, and she was, I thought, very becomingly dressed in a high-necked jersey with a well-fitting skirt. But the most striking thing about her appearance was her honey-coloured hair. It looked enchanting, and made her plain face sadder still.

It was suggested that she and I should go for a walk while Frau Jank and her mother remained indoors for a good gossip. She showed no great enthusiasm for the idea—I wondered if she ever showed enthusiasm for anything—and for her the prospect was obviously dreary, for conversation between us would be strictly limited by language.

We had not long been walking along the road through a countryside of hedgeless and fenceless fields, sparsely snow-covered, and broken here and there with belts of evergreen woodland, when I saw a group of half a dozen Roe Deer. They were some hundreds of yards away, looking small and black by the edge of the trees, and I pointed them out to the girl. "Oh, Ja," she said without enthusiasm. Later there was a crackle in the undergrowth quite near, and across the road in front galloped a beautiful Roe-buck. He ran up a steep bank and stood for a few seconds on the top, looking back at us, Pan-like. His coat was very dark against the shade-blue snow, his horns were sharply outlined like thorns. It was the best view I had ever had of a Roe Deer, but when I looked at the girl, I could see that she was quite unmoved. To me it was a piece of magic, but she was evidently no Pantheist. I felt sad for her as we returned towards the house. The light was beginning to fade by the time we were back and we went into the warm drawing-room for tea. There was an open wood fire which was unusual in Bavaria, for ornate stoves provided the heat in most houses there, even in the country. It was also a surprisingly English kind of tea—laid on a lace cloth with a silver kettle singing over a little spirit lamp. They asked us about our walk and the girl began to describe the Roe Deer we had seen. She told them about the little buck running across the road and how he had stood and looked back at us, "'swar fabelhaft . . ." and her eyes brightened and then she went on to describe him in detail and finished, after a pause, with "I wonder where he is now." I was surprised that she had noticed so much about him.

We ate little sweet biscuits with our tea. Outside the light was fading. In contrast to the red embers of the fire the window was a deep-blue picture on the wall. The room was now so dark that the figures round the table were dim shapes, their faces pale blurs. I looked across to where the girl sat in a big armchair. The conversation flowed on unceasingly between the older women; neither I nor the girl were required to take part in it, and as the darkness fell we ourselves seemed to be fading away from reality. Above the dark transverse line of her high-necked jersey the girl's face was a plain smudge, but there was nothing in the image my eyes transmitted to my brain which told me that it was a plain face. This I knew only from the daylight of the afternoon. Supposing that the afternoon had not been real at all. Who could tell, with the great god Pan and his magic spells about the place?

The fire flickered a dim flame, glinting in the honey hair, and suddenly I was imagining. It was a simple beauty which I saw, the perfection of simplicity and the simplicity of perfection. Everything about the face, the shape of the features, the colouring, the expression—all were completely perfect. In savouring the image I had created, I knew nothing of the sense of limitation in technical skill or in the selected medium which must have plagued Pygmalion. Mine was for me the infinity of beauty, and it was dreadfully sad, I reflected, that the Creator had got so far as to make this possible in twilight, and then made such a hash of the finishing touches. "Dear me," said our hostess, "I had scarcely noticed how dark it was." She reached out and twisted the bell pull on the wall. "I will get Karl-Heinrich to bring the lamps and clear away the tea."

For a few seconds more my dream could live on, and then it would be shattered, unless the great god Pan could really work his magic. Perhaps when Karl-Heinrich arrived with the lamp, the girl would be as I imagined, perhaps even more beautiful, for in her face would also be the subtleties which had been beyond my imagination. "Come on, little Roe-buck, now's your chance . . ."

But although the great god Pan must have been busy elsewhere that evening, the idea appealed to me enough to write a fairy story about it. In it Karl-Heinrich was rather a long time bringing the light, which gave plenty of time for the consideration of the alternative possibilities. During the wait I began to be certain that my imagination would fail, that the girl could not possibly have changed. But when Karl-Heinrich finally appeared in the doorway with the lamp flooding the whole room with light, there was my girl blinking in the new brightness and still as beautiful as anything I had ever thought of. I was speechless, and had eyes only for this glorious creature so that I did not see the reactions of her mother or Frau Jank, and not until some time later did I think it curious that neither of them made any reference to the transformation. There remained only one more small and perhaps irrelevant thing to record: as we drove away in the hired car half an hour later the little Roe-buck ran across the road in front of us, brightly lit by the beam of the headlights.

CHAPTER 20   *Poker with Strauss*

ANOTHER guest in the Professor's family was a rather earnest young American. As we laced up our skating boots on the edge of the lake in the Englischer Garten, I remember he asked whether I liked opera. "Not much," was my reply. "You see, I really don't care for the human voice unless it sings in chorus." "Well, of course," said he, "there are choruses in some operas. Take *Meistersinger* for example . . ."

I had never been to an opera in my life and my taste for choral music came from the works we had performed at Oundle. All the same I must have realised that I was on thin ice, for I have remembered the exchange to this day. The ice of the Englischer Garten lake was thick enough to bear, and face was regained rather spectacularly when the skaters cleared a space for me as they had done at Golders Green.

Die Meistersinger von Nurnberg was the first opera that I ever saw —in the theatre in which it had first been produced sixty-three years before—and in spite of its great length I was at once a fanatical devotee of opera and of Wagner.

As a student I was entitled to a 'Student Card', which among other things reduced all opera tickets to half price. It was not long before I had seen all the Wagner operas in the company's repertory, and most of the Mozart operas, which were usually produced in the glorious little Baroque Residenz Theater. The Verdi and Puccini operas were not supposed to be so well rendered in Munich as those of the German composers, but in truth I enjoyed them almost as much. There were three special favourites in the repertory which I never missed: Smetana's *The Bartered Bride*, Rossini's *Cenerentola* and Weinberger's *Schwanda*. There was a song of homesickness in Schwanda; Babinsky (a part normally taken by the brilliant young Viennese tenor Julius Patzak) sang:

Auf unserem Hof daheim
Hört mann die Gänse schrien
Kräht auch der Hahn.
Dass du meinen Sehnen bist
Liebster zu jede Frist
Denk ich daran.

"At our house at home one can hear the geese calling." If I was ever homesick in Munich I could think of my marshes and hear again the wild geese cry. If according to the song one also heard the cock crow too—what of it!

Julius Patzak was my hero. In 1931 his greatness had not yet been recognised. He was, I felt, my own discovery, and I was prepared to eat all my words, raw and unseasoned, about not liking the solo human voice. When Patzak sang Florestan opposite Lotte Lehmann's Fidelio I did not believe that music was capable of any greater perfection.

On my student card I used to go to the opera two or three times a week. When I knew the opera well I sat at the back of the gallery where for a two-shilling ticket (reduced to a shilling by my student card) I could listen and walk forward whenever I particularly wanted to look down on to the stage. The music students sat all round me reading their scores, but I usually took some drawing paper. Of all the operas I saw in this way I suppose I was most impressed by those of Wagner. Apart from the beauty of the music, I was prepared to boggle at the immensity of the undertaking, the gigantic achievement of one man in creating a whole opera— story, words and music; and so many of them, and all so long! It is doubtful whether, even at Bayreuth, the productions of Wagner could outshine those of the State Opera House in Munich in the early 1930s when Bruno Walter and Hans Knappertsbusch were the conductors.

I heard the whole cycle of the *Ring* three times, and was in the audience when the veteran tenor Heinrich Knote sang *Siegfried* on his sixtieth birthday. There were various moments of hilarity in the performance; one in particular was when Siegfried strikes the anvil with the newly forged sword and cleaves it in twain. A special catch is fitted to the stage anvil so that when struck by the sword it falls apart, but poor Knote did not have the knack, or else the catch was faulty. He struck and struck to no avail and finally bent down to release the catch by hand. But at the end of the performance, no mean feat for a man of sixty, Knote was cheered to the echo at I do not know how many curtain calls. His voice may have been past its prime, and Siegfried is no old man's part, but the occasion was inescapably memorable, and the audience acknowledged it. Knote lived to the ripe old age of eighty-three, and finally died in Garmisch-Partenkirchen in the Bavarian Alps in 1953.

Richard Strauss's opera *Rosenkavalier* was written in Garmisch-Partenkirchen, and completed during the week after I was born in 1909. By 1931 it was the most frequently performed opera in Germany, and the composer was to conduct a performance in Munich. I had to be there. I believe it was my first hearing of the opera, and I cannot be sure whether Lotte Lehmann sang the Marschallin that night, for it was only later that she became so famously associated with the part. There are parts of *Rosenkavalier* which I did not like then, and have never liked since, but the last minutes of the last act contain music of such ineffable beauty that I have often wondered whether the opera's popularity does not largely depend on it. So perfect an ending must send contented audiences away, declaring that they have heard the most beautiful opera, and cannot wait to hear it again. After the performance that night I went with a music student friend to the flat of Hans Knappertsbusch where Strauss was staying. My friend (who was also a namesake, Michael Scott, although no relation) had previously enquired whether I could play poker, "because," he said, "you will almost certainly be involved in a game". Fortunately I knew the rules and had already played it since arriving in Germany; and this was as well, for I had no sooner been introduced to the great man— then in his sixties, tall and thin and quite unlike the popular conception of a composer—than we were sitting down round the card table. The game went on until the small hours and after various ups and downs I left, as I recall, some five marks richer than when I arrived. This game of poker with Richard Strauss is likely to remain my greatest claim to fame in the sphere of music.

I had not been very long in Munich before I decided to attend the World Skating Championships in Berlin. In order to do this without interfering with my work at the Academy I decided to travel by air. Air line travel at that time was still a comparatively adventurous business. I embarked in an archetypal Junkers three-engined airliner of the Lufthansa with seats for about a dozen people. It was constructed of corrugated aluminium and looked very much like the Ju. 52, which became well known as a troop-carrier in the war, and which I met with again on the freight run

in New Guinea in 1957. But back in 1931 this was to be my second
flight ever.

Last to climb into the cabin was a middle-aged man who was
obviously a pilot himself. It later transpired that he was a Lufthansa pilot on passage back to Berlin. He had no sooner strapped
himself into his seat than he settled down to sleep. This to me
seemed incredible. How could anyone think of sleeping during
anything so exciting as flying—least of all before the supremely
thrilling moment of take-off. Could he really genuinely want to
sleep or was this some elaborate affectation? Evidently he was just
tired, for he slept soundly all the way.

I had never been to Berlin before, but I found my way by tram to
the Sportpalast where the Skating Championships were being held,
and there among the competitors was my Scandinavian love. For
three days I watched the skating. Winner of the men's title was Karl
Schäffer from Vienna with a marvellously unhurried free skating
programme, with great slow three-jumps and single loop-jumps
(Rittbergers they were sometimes called in those days) in which he
seemed to linger in the air. Women's Champion was the young
Norwegian girl Sonja Henie, with a programme full of fireworks.
My girl was third or fourth, as I recall, but that did not matter, for
I was still sure that her free skating had more artistry in it than all
the others put together. Perhaps her jumps were not so high, perhaps her spins were not so fast. But her performance was a dance
and that, I thought, was more than could be said for most of the
others. It is of course possible that my judgment was not wholly
based on skating technique.

Watching the competition was the British teacher and stylist
Bernard Adams, a gentle little man with white hair and moustache
and black eyebrows. He had never himself been a great performer,
but he was acknowledged as one of the greatest of all teachers of the
art. In London I had known him well and had some lessons from
him. Here in Berlin he made me an interesting offer. "Loops or no
loops," he said, "if you will give me your time uninterrupted for
the next two years I will make you World Champion." It was an
interesting thought. Did I really want to give up everything else to
become a champion figure skater? Sitting beside the rink in Berlin
as the World Championships took place before us, this seemed to be
an uncommonly attractive proposition. But when I had returned to
Munich and was back at my painting, I thought to myself "Perhaps
not." At the back of my mind was the thought that skating was
an art, not a sport. Who ever heard of a World Champion Ballet

Dancer? The objectives seemed somehow to be muddled. Sport or art, amateur or professional, all these seemed to confuse the issue, seemed to be far removed from the delights of the skating itself. Perhaps, too, Bernard Adams would never be able to get me over those loops, and even if he could, did I really want to give up two years of my life to this particular and rather limited objective? On balance I felt that I did not.

Twenty-five Karl Theodor Strasse, although it was a large house, was always very crowded, for apart from the Professor's family there were young people from many foreign lands who were staying there in order to learn the German language. So crowded was it that for most of the time I shared a room with Ruli, and this was useful for the progress of my German, in spite of his quite good English. We were both studying at the Academy although he was in a different class and at school we only met for 'life-drawing' in the afternoons. He was a clever draughtsman and a devastating caricaturist. No one escaped. It was he who first suggested that we might go one night and listen to Hitler. In 1931 this indifferent imitator of Mussolini was not taken very seriously; indeed, he had not long been out of gaol, and as Ruli said, "How could a man with a moustache like Charlie Chaplin expect to be taken seriously anyway?" So we went to a public meeting in the Bierkeller in the middle of the city, where he spoke for an hour. One could not fail to be impressed by the oratory, even if I did not understand more than about half of the speech at all, and had little or no conception of the implications. But as a piece of rabble-rousing I, as part of the rabble, was duly roused. Ruli came out murmuring something about the Fascist shirts at least being black, and why had Hitler chosen dung-colour for his. Next day there were some new and magnificently comical drawings in Ruli's caricature book.

Although the eldest daughter of the Jank family was living and working elsewhere in Munich, we met often enough, for we had danced together at Faschings dances and had agreed that there must be more enjoyable kinds of dancing than the crowded social functions. We decided to go dancing where there was space to dance —at the Thés-dansants at the big hotels. It was not long before we decided, on the principle that if a thing is worth doing at all it is worth doing well, to take dancing lessons together. Was it once, was it twice a week, that we went to our dancing school? In due course we emerged reasonably skilled in the German style ballroom dancing of the day. We even went in for a competition and were, surprisingly, third. Our dancing and my acquaintance with my musical friend suggested the composition of some dance tunes; so many of them seemed to be ruined for dancing by what seemed the irrelevant requirement for singable words. I began to make up dance tunes in my head but I had no idea of how to write them down. Here I was helped by Michael Scott, who faithfully committed to paper the tunes which I hummed to him. I took the best of them to Herr Kohl-Bossé, the leader of the dance band in the famous Four Seasons Hotel. To my surprise he was interested. "Yes," he said, "I like it. Give me a couple of days to teach it to the band, and I'll let you hear it." He played it on the piano a few times more, and eventually changed the final phrase, which had been the most original part in my view. Looking back on it now, it is more than ever clear that I was right about this. The pay-off line of my wordless tune had been thrown away and replaced with a ghastly nineteenth-century-Punch explanation which ruined it all. But adulterated as it was I was still thrilled when the band first struck up my tune. For want of a better name we had called it 'The Elephant's Cake-walk'.

Herr Kohl-Bossé played it at least four times at that first Thé-dansant. It was on the last time, as they struck up, that I overheard a tall, very smart young man, who was something of a rival in dancing skill, say to his partner, "Good God! Don't they know any other tunes, this band?" Dear Herr Kohl-Bossé! He did not over-hear it, and every time we came to dance in his hotel I could be sure that my tune would be played at least twice. There were other tunes and other bands later, but this first time was the great event.

In 1956, on my way to visit my friend Konrad Lorenz at his new field station and laboratory in Bavaria, I stood again in that central room of the Vierjahreszeiten Hotel, which amazingly escaped destruction in the wartime bombing. If I listened hard I could still hear the echo of Herr Kohl-Bossé's band as it knocked out 'The Elephant's Cake-walk'.

The second daughter of the family with whom I lived, the one called 'Mouse', was seventeen when I first went there and the youngest daughter was still at the Bavarian equivalent of St. Trinian's. To me the important one was Mouse. She had deep brown eyes, a high forehead and a turned-up nose. Her eyes were the darkest thing about her. She was very shy and during the whole of a meal she would scarcely look up from her plate, but when she did you could not avoid her gaze, and the gentle half smile that hovered at the upturned corners of her mouth. Mouse, I was sure, had hidden depths.

There was also staying in the house an attractive and dashing young English girl, who later became an intrepid parachutist. There was my flying visit to Berlin to see my skating champion. But at every meal there was Mouse. Once she rolled up the sleeves of her jersey which looked, as I thought, especially attractive. I told her so, very foolishly, in the hearing of her merciless younger sister. First she threatened and finally told her brother. His ragging had to be explained to her mother, who said she did not think it very becoming. But in spite of the persecution Mouse's sleeves were always rolled up after that. She was the Cinderella of the family. Only once was she allowed to go with me to the opera, just occasionally might she come skating with me in the Englischer Garten, and ballroom dancing was for her elder sister but not for her. After lunch and dinner we played Mühle—a game which has something in common with draughts and something with solitaire. Mouse was particularly good at Mühle. She was gentle and calm, and her deep brown eyes looked steadfastly at me and seemed to ask nothing in return.

Dear Mouse—she was a constant nymph and I found that I loved her very much. If I was not to have a Swedish wife, perhaps I would have a German wife. Mouse came on a brief visit to England in the following year, and stayed with my family in Norfolk and I was as enchanted with her as ever. I cannot remember when I was not enchanted with Mouse, right up to the time when I received an invitation to her wedding, to which, alas, I could not go. I hope she was happy and still is.

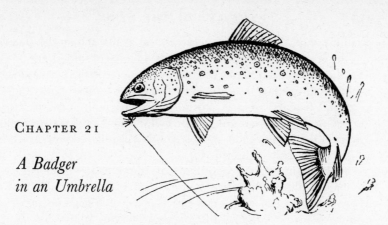

Chapter 21

A Badger
in an Umbrella

AN hour and a half from Munich in the electric train is the village of Oberau, nestling in the foothills of the Alps beside the River Loisach whose milky melt water thunders down from the high snows. It was early spring when I first went there with Stevie Johnson, a young Englishman who was also learning German in Munich. Stevie was a fly-fisherman and the Loisach and its tributaries were full of trout. The valley was so beautiful on that first week-end that we had to go again for the next, and the next and the one after that. It was spring—lovely and full of living things, of Roe Deer, and water birds, and butterflies, and all the spring flowers of the Alps. Only then did I realise how much I had missed the wild countryside during my city winter in Munich.

The Loisach valley floor at Oberau is about a mile wide. At the sides the wooded mountains rise precipitously. The road and the electric railway occupy the comparatively narrow strip between the river and the western hillside; across the Loisach the water-meadows are wilder and more remote. I knew them well for all that summer and for part of another. To me now they are a collective picture of all the seasons, full of gentians and orchids and columbines and great beds of lily-of-the-valley. I remember the excitement of the week-end when Swallow-tail butterflies were everywhere, I remember the dippers which lived on the rapids, the Firebellied Toads which came out after rain, the trout and the grayling and the chubb.

Flowing into the Loisach a mile or two below Oberau was a tributary stream which drained the opposite side of the valley. In contrast to the milky waters of the main river this tributary was as clear as a chalk stream in Hampshire, and here we fished with a dry fly. The trout we caught there did not ever weigh more than a pound and a half and you were almost as likely to catch a chubb or a grayling, but there was always the chance of something bigger. In the clouded melt water of the main river the fish certainly ran bigger—we caught them up to three pounds, missed one of about four, and listened wistfully to tales of seven pounders—but there they could only be caught by spinning, and I preferred the clear waters of the Lauterbach, even if my line usually arrived in a heap on the water long before the fly.

One late summer's day, walking up the river along the edge of a hay field, I almost stumbled over a small reddish animal curled up in the tall grass. It was a day-old Roe Deer fawn, and of all the animals I have ever seen I think it was the most appealing. He was tiny, with long coltish legs, unafraid eyes, a bulging forehead and huge expressive ears. He was deep russet and handsomely marked with sharp white spots in a row down either side of his back and spreading down his sides and flanks. He was almost too beautiful to be true. He seemed to be entirely without fear and lay confidently in my arms; he sucked my little finger, he stood quietly while we photographed him and was finally happy to be left in his original nest. His was a perfection that suited the perfection of our valley on that sunny morning.

Fierce thunderstorms were common there; they built up, black and brooding, over the mountains to the south, flickering among the high peaks and then burst with an exciting fury in the evening; lightning almost without pause shone golden pink through the curtains of rain, and the crack and boom of the thunder echoed from the steep walls of the valley in a continuous bombardment of sound. For me it held no sinister associations in those days. From Paris in 1918 the rumble of the guns had been too distant; the Blitz was still to come. I found these Alpine thunderstorms stimulating, awe-inspiring, beautiful, but annoying because the rain brought the river down like pale coffee and ruined the fishing. It was on a day when thunder threatened that we encountered the badger, and caught it in an umbrella. I do not suppose that many people either before or since have caught a badger in an umbrella; indeed I would hazard a guess that I am the only person who ever has caught a badger in an umbrella.

I was walking home from the Lauterbach as the great cumulus clouds gathered at the head of the valley. The fish had not been rising and I had given up fishing and bathed instead. Over one shoulder was a damp towel, my trout rod over the other, and hanging on my arm was an umbrella against the threatening storm.

It was tea-time and I was thinking of the mountainous plate of wild strawberries topped with whipped cream which would be waiting for me at the Gasthof. Crossing a recently cut hayfield I came towards one of the little wooden huts in which the hay is stored in most of these Alpine meadows. As I came round the corner of the hut there, sitting right out in the open, was a baby badger. The moment he saw me he started to run for his sett which was actually underneath the hut, and thinking it would be interesting to have a look at him, I jumped to head him off. We both had about ten yards to go, but as I went I had a brainwave: I pushed my umbrella about half-way open and blocked the hole with it. The badger finished a close second and went full tilt into the umbrella. It was a well-grown baby and it looked quite savage down at the bottom of the umbrella, so I wrapped my bathing towel round my hand and gave it to him to bite. He seized hold of it and while he was busy biting it, I picked him up with the other hand and had a good look at him. Then I thought I would take him back to show the others, so I carried him back to the inn. As we went he spent the time alternately biting my towel-padded hand and rolling himself up into a sort of ball, almost like a hedgehog.

After tea we decided that he was altogether too old to be tamed, but the thunderstorm was upon us and we decided to keep him overnight in a box in the garage. Next morning we found he had eaten a large plate of bread and milk, and escaped from his box, but he was still in the garage and still as ferocious as ever. I carried him back to the little hut by the hayfield and popped him down his hole. Then I listened. I heard the rumble as he ran down and then a great babel of grunts and squeaks. Greetings, scoldings, recriminations? Who knows what treatment a young badger can expect from his family after a night out?

Perhaps Oberau really *was* an enchanted place or perhaps it came at a romantic period in my life. In my memory it echoes with Wagnerian leitmotivs, with arias from *Don Giovanni*, with the fast accordion waltzes to which we danced the Schuhplatl in the Gasthof on Saturday nights. I see pretty Kathi whose portrait I painted in water-colour against the deep blue of the summer sky; I smell the new mown hay; I taste again the exquisite flavour of the wild strawberries; I dream again of the five-pound trout which may take my fly if only I can lay it immaculately at the downstream side of that overhanging willow.

In 1956 I went back to Oberau, ready to wallow in the nostalgia of my lost youth. We had been making a film of Konrad Lorenz's wonderful new research station at Seewiesen, near Starnberg—then only just begun; my companions were Winwood Reade and Tony Soper, both of the B.B.C. It was soon after I had taken up gliding with my usual obsessive immoderation, and no sooner had we climbed out of the car outside the familiar little Gasthof, which had scarcely changed in a quarter of a century, than we saw a glider sailing silently overhead. The launching ground was over on the far wild side of the valley. It was perhaps the only single cause for which I could condone the invasion of my beautiful place. We spent the afternoon discussing glider types, launching winches, wave lift and training methods. "By the way," I said to Winwood as we walked back through the water-meadows, "you see that hut over there? That's where I once caught a badger in an umbrella."

In the Tiermahlschule at the State Academy in Munich the old bay mare that we were painting spread her heavy hind legs and deluged the cobblestone floor. One or two of the students put down their palettes and brushes and waited for the animal to resume its original pose. The sickly sweet stench came up at us. The place would be hosed down at the lunch break, but not before. The Herr Professor came round to me and stood for a long time in front of my picture. I stood back with him and the longer the silence lasted the greater was my despair. The proportions of course were right; the thing was inescapably a horse . . . inescapably *that* horse. As a portrait it was really quite a good likeness, but as a painting it was dull and pedestrian to a sad degree. There was nothing rich or interesting about tone or colour or composition. I had been an effective colour camera but no more; I had made no contribution of my own. Nor did I need the Professor to tell me this: I knew it quite well. After you have looked at a picture for a long time—as you do when you are painting it—it is easy to become blind to the most glaring faults. It is worth cultivating the capacity to turn away from the canvas and clear your mind of its image, and then to turn back and see it with a fresh eye. I had tried to do this as the Professor moved from the last painting to mine, and what I saw appalled me. Perhaps I should go back to biology or become a skating champion after all. At last my teacher spoke. "I do not think you are moved by this horse," he began. "It does not seem to interest you in the same way as the Roe Deer you painted last week out of your head, or the jumping trout. Technically the picture's not too bad," and he passed on to the next pupil. He was, as I have said, a kindly man.

Next week in the Tiermahlschule there was a cow, and in the afternoons from four to six in the main building there was life drawing from the nude human figure. There was opera, the zoo at Hellabrunn, the pictures in the Alte Pinakothek, German Lessons from Frau Bermann, Mühle on the big top-floor landing at 25 Karl Theodor Strasse . . . and the dark brown eyes of Mouse.

One day at dinner the family had received some shocking and disastrous news. The son of some close friends had married, but the wife he had chosen was a Jewess. Frau Jank was a kind and tolerant soul, friendly and charitable, it had seemed, about everyone; but her voice was pitched high in incredulous emphasis "Eine *Judin*. Ja, *wie* ist dass *möglich*?" How was it *possible* that this nice young man could have been so *foolish* and so *unkind* to his parents as to marry a *Jewess*? There was no other topic of conversation for the whole of that meal and it came up again at many more. None could offer any explanation of how such an extraordinary and terrible thing could have happened to so respectable a family. The year was 1931 and Hitler's moustache was still compared with Chaplin's. It was the first time I had met racial prejudice, and it was as frightening to me as the social instinct of a swarm of wasps. It was something I did not understand, how this strange, unreasoning hatred could exist in the hearts of people I thought I knew so well and had hitherto liked so unreservedly. I was quite certain that anti-Semitism was wrong. Impressionable though I still was in many ways I would not budge on that: it ran counter to all my beliefs. Once I said of the young man's fall from grace, "Does it matter so very much? Perhaps she is very nice and very pretty and very talented. Perhaps she's an artist."

"Maybe," said the eldest son, "but she is a Jewess."

When we talked of international politics it was easier; there was no particular tension then. The Treaty of Versailles was in those days the root of all evil. "If you drive it to the edge of a cliff," said Frau Jank, "even a rabbit will turn and face you." I was doubtful about this as natural history, and even more doubtful of it as politics. Even in 1931 the German nation seemed to have little enough in common with a rabbit.

But they were my friends, these people, and I knew and loved them well. Whatever their views might be, violence was not in their thoughts. This may have been the soil in which to grow pogroms and

Auschwitz and a second world war, but in 1931 the seeds had not yet been sown at No. 25 Karl Theodor Strasse. Even in 1938 when I passed through Munich and called on Ruli, now a conscripted soldier in barracks, I found him a most unwilling Nazi, and surprisingly free with his critical speech.

CHAPTER 22   *The Far Cuillin*

AT the end of the academic year in Munich I returned to England.
In the following year I was to go to the Royal Academy Schools
in London. But meanwhile there were invitations to Scotland for
the summer holidays. Stevie Johnson, my friend and fishing
colleague in Bavaria, had invited me to stay at Strathaird, a large
estate in the southern part of the Isle of Skye. It included three
beautiful lochs famed for their sea trout fishing and the fine
mountainous country around them—the Red Cuillin and the
eastern face of the Black Cuillin (the 'far Cuillin', which according
to the song was 'putting love on me').

Skye was much more wonderful in the reality than I had been
able to imagine it from the descriptions I had been given in
Germany. At once it became for me an apotheosis of Scotland.
When I arrived at Kilmarie Lodge on the south-east side of the
estate I met Stevie's father and mother, his younger brother
Mark, and a small house party. Kilmarie was an attractive and
comfortable white house standing up the hill from the sea and
fitting pleasantly into the landscape of bracken-covered slopes and
birch woods. It was beautiful, and eminently Scottish; our days
were peopled with delightful Scotsmen—stalkers and gillies; there
were sea trout to be caught and stags to be stalked, and grouse to
be chased. I was very happy.

On the second day of my visit I was sent out with the stalker
John McIver for a day on the hill. There were no great quantities
of deer on Strathaird in those days, and the Skye stags did not
grow so large as they did in some of the deer forests on the mainland, but the country was steep and difficult and the stalking was
rugged and exactly as I thought it should be, although the first
day we never saw a stag.

On the following day we went round to Coruisk. There were

two ways of doing this, either by boat or by walking, first of all over the hill to Camasunary and then round the foot of the Black Cuillin to the loch itself. This time we went round by motor-boat. Stevie and I fished all day in Coruisk, the long sliver of water lying between the two razor steep ridges of mountain. We sat one at each end of the boat drifting and casting on the principle which has been described by scornful river fishermen as 'chuck and chance it'. It may require less skill than dry-fly fishing in a chalk stream but I found it very exciting all the same. We caught some good trout too; my largest was three and a half pounds, and I got another of three; and then on the way home we stopped for some sea fishing and caught about fifty Cuddies—small pollock.

The next day was to be given over to a haddock fishing expedition in Loch Scavaig, the sea loch below Coruisk. We spent a calm sunny day in the sturdy motor-boat, which rejoiced in the name of *Whiffin Goffin*, but the haddock were not to be found and we only caught a few rock cod. But we saw a ten foot tunny.

The main object of our expedition was the night fishing on Coruisk. Stevie's younger brother Mark (then usually called 'Ski') was to fish with me, and Johnny Mohr, the fishing gillie, rowed us up the loch in the dusk. The Black Cuillin towered above us blacker than ever against the sunset sky. In our little row-boat out in the loch we seemed so tiny, walled in by the steep darkness all round us. Yet there was nothing sinister about it. The evening was still and friendly, the anticipation of the monster sea trout we might catch glowed enthusiastically within us. This, I thought, was tremendous.

We fished until it was almost dark, casting blindly out as far from the boat as possible. Occasionally the water would be dimpled by the rise of a trout to our dry fly, a speck of reflected sky against the black reflection of the Cuillin. By half past nine in the evening Ski had caught nine fish, all small, and I had only caught two, both so small that they had to be thrown back. Soon it was getting too dark to see and we had to start for home, without the five- and six-pounders we had been dreaming of. We stumbled over the rocky path from Coruisk to the sea, rowed out to the *Whiffin Goffin* and chugged round the headland in the gentle darkness.

Then came another day out stalking. We rode the ponies uneventfully to Camasunary, then past Loch na Cray and Loch an Arn. A shepherd with two dogs walked with us. It was the last day of August—a grilling day without a cloud in the sky, and in all the morning we saw not a beast. It looked as though we had drawn blank again and after lunch we joined Arthur with the ponies and began the long ride back. From the mouth of Harta Corrie we had a last spy and saw several hinds and two small stags —too small to stalk. Arthur went back his way and we rode down towards Loch an Arn where we spied again, I with my binoculars, McIver with his telescope. There is something tremendously exciting about spying. You lie as comfortably as you may and in front of you is the whole face of a hill. There are perhaps many places where a red deer may be hidden from your view. Even should there be a stag there, it is a gamble whether he will happen to be in sight when your glass passes across the hill face. After ten minutes of searching there is always the temptation to try once more—one last desperate throw of the dice and perhaps a great stag will have walked into view since the last time your line of sight swept by.

McIver lay back in the heather, one knee raised, his long crook'd stick leaning vertically against it to form a rest for his telescope. "There's four beasts here," he said quietly. "Three of them's hinds but the fourth looks a heavier animal." I picked them up at once; the 'heavier animal' was feeding but suddenly it raised its head and it was a stag. He was a very small stag, we thought, and from that distance we could not see if he was clean— if all the velvet had dried and been rubbed from his horns. We moved closer and then I had to go back for my glasses which I had foolishly left where we spied. When I rejoined McIver he said that the deer had fed into a hollow and were now out of sight. But we decided to go up and have a look at them; so we waited for the shepherd to come up and hold the ponies. Then we started to climb, doubting much that the stag would be shootable. After three-quarters of an hour we reached the place, loaded the rifle and advanced with caution. We found that the deer were deep in the hollow, a hollow which looked as though it did not exist. After a while we saw the back of a hind and we knew at least that we were in the right place: so McIver gave me the rifle and I lay in the heather behind a rock while he went higher up to see if he could see the stag. I sighted the rifle on a rock and having completely got my breath I felt quite confident. I put my head down and when I looked up a moment later I saw a very red beast standing there. As I put the glass on it I realised it was the stag. At a glance I could see that there was no trace of velvet, but I could not so quickly decide upon his size. I pictured myself shooting a small and promising stag and being thoroughly unpopular with

F*

my host. I saw at once that he had a very round and handsome head, though small. Then I counted the points, seven of them, he was an eight-pointer minus one bay antler, and he had longish points except for the brow on the same side. The left horn was a nice shaped eight-pointer, the right horn a bad six-pointer.

I had just decided he was shootable, as he stood there broadside, and was picking up the rifle when he suddenly cantered to the left and disappeared. Then I heard an avalanche of stones crashing down the hill behind me and a moment later McIver was pulling me down with him and we were rolling and sliding down to the next knoll. "There he is," said McIver when we got there. "A fine broadside." And I peered over and saw the stag stern on looking over his shoulder. "Be quick now, take your time," said McIver in classical contradiction, and I levelled the piece. "Man, cock your rifle." And I pressed over the forgotten safety catch and sitting bolt upright, craning through the heather without any rest at all, I fired and the stag cantered off. I fired again. "I think ye've hit him," said McIver and we rolled and crashed down to the next knoll in time to see the stag at the bottom of the corrie. I was taking aim when McIver said "No, that's the hinds." And by the time he too had decided that it was the stag, the animal had moved on and was across the burn. As he trotted up the far slope McIver said, "Och, he's no' hit at all!" and the stag galloped round the hillside.

I had left my stick where I had first lain 100 yards up the hill. I could not be bothered to fetch it . . . I felt too miserable. We climbed down the hill with scarcely a word and my diary records that "the three hours' ride home seemed like three days".

One morning Johnny Beg, the fishing gillie (the small Johnny, not to be confused with Johnny Mohr, the large Johnny) came to Kilmarie as he did each morning to join us for the boat trip to Camasunary and the day's sea trout fishing. "We hear you've a baby," we said on this particular morning. "So I believe!" was his answer in measured tones. We fished for most of the morning in Loch na Cray and I caught a two-pounder which jumped splendidly three times. But after a while the wind had freshened so much that we went to the small hut at the head of the loch where we made a fire and brewed some tea. We stayed there for most of the afternoon but fished again for a while unsuccessfully and then back to Camasunary for tea. It seemed that Johnny Beg was anxious to get home and see his baby. "Boy or girl?" we asked. "I really couldn't say, sir." So he had come away for his day's work knowing his child was born, but without knowing its sex; and all through the day until now he had said no word about it. The homeward passage in the *Whiffin Goffin* was rough and very wet.

Blaven, which is a shortening of Blath Bheinn, is usually counted as one of the Red Cuillin. It is 3,042 feet high according to the map, and we set off one morning to climb it in search of ptarmigan. It was a long haul up the mountain. We found some ptarmigan droppings on the way, but all we saw at the top was one very large hill fox. From the summit we had a noble view. Loch na Cray was at our feet and it looked as if you could toss a biscuit on to the Isle of Soay. To the east across the head of Loch Slapin lay the Red Hills of Beinn Dearg Mhor and Beinn Dearg Bheag and in the distance the sound of Sleat and Loch Alsh, and Ben Screel on the mainland beyond. A rain storm blew across from the west and blotted out the Black Cuillin; and then they reappeared magically and majestically one by one. In the distance behind us we saw a golden eagle soaring high over Garven.

From Skye I went on, in the second week of September, to Struy Lodge near Beauly for some more stalking at the invitation of Lady Lucas from whom, years before, we had taken Horsey Hall in Norfolk for the summer. The pattern at Struy was to send the guests out with the stalkers in pairs, two to each 'beat' of the deer forest. On the first day my companion was a young soldier, John Boyle, and after a very strenuous all-day walk on the home beat we drew blank; neither of us got a shot at a stag. But on the next day, accompanied by one Andrew Maxwell, I was off on a two days' journey to the Corrie Harabie beat of the forest. According to the map the correct spelling is Coire Chairbhe, but perhaps it is easier to spell it as it is pronounced.

"The first part of the journey up Glen Farrar was by car till we met the gillies and the ponies. The plan was to stalk out on the first day, spend the night in a small bothie at the far side of the beat and then stalk back again the next day.

"In the morning we drew blank. Hinds we had disturbed took seventeen stags over the march into the next forest. After lunch the only stag in sight was a single beast we had seen first of all lying down. On closer inspection we found him to be a good deal better than we had supposed; there were now a number of hinds who had appeared from around the corner and were lying just beyond him. We started our stalk, trying first a burn, but that did not go close enough so we climbed up again and

began a much more difficult approach along the top, straight towards the stag. Finally we had to crawl about fifty yards, stopping
at one point and then finding that we could get closer. When at
last we got into position we could not at first see the stag, but then
we made out his horns with eight points and the ridge of his back.
He was lying down with his head flat. The plan was to wait until
he should get up to feed. It was already 3.30 in the afternoon,
and deer always feed in the evening. We hoped it would not be
too long a wait. I took sighting aims at various hinds beyond and
at two young stags with them—two knobbers. After about
twenty minutes the stag lifted his head. The range was no more
than 100 yards, so in high excitement we waited. Rory McCray,
the stalker, kept saying, 'You're not excited now, are you, sir?'
and when I took aim at the stag's head for practice, 'You're
shaking with excitement a little, sir.' And then at last, after
more than half an hour, the stag stretched his neck. Two of the
hinds which had been getting up periodically and sitting down
again, had now got up and begun feeding. 'He's thinking about
it,' said Rory, then, 'He's getting up.' And so he was; first his
hind legs, then his front and he was up, facing us, scratching.
Then he took a few paces downhill and began feeding broadside
on. 'Wait till he stands,' said Rory, and a moment later he stood
stock still.

"The aperture sight was up and I took careful aim and began
to squeeze, but the rifle would not go off and at last in despair
I pulled right through, forgetting the first pressure, and when it
went off it was nowhere near the stag. 'Over his back,' said Rory,
and I reloaded.

"At the shot the stag had looked up and stood with hind legs
slightly bent ready to jump away at any moment, but he did not
know which way to jump. Said I to myself, 'Now then, pull
yourself together or you'll make a hash of it again.' So I took
careful aim and squeezed. There was a thud and the stag fell.
My first sensation was one of intense relief that I had saved the
situation, if only by a hair's breadth: I flopped backwards and
sat down with a bump in a pool of water. The stag was a good
eight-pointer with a very wide head and he was a fairly heavy
beast."

Looking back on it I can remember a dim awareness of remorse
at having killed that beautiful creature, but it was overwhelmed by
the sense of success after the days of failure in Skye and the blank

day we had already had at Struy. For those days I had walked and walked over the hills with one express object in view—to shoot a stag. I had taken good exercise, I had steeped myself in the atmosphere of the Highlands, I had seen all kinds of animals from Red Deer to Fox Moth caterpillars; I had learned something of the art of stalking, and the use of dead ground, how to flatten my body as I crawled, when to move fast and when to move slowly, the importance of the precise direction of the wind and the eddies which might carry my scent. All these might have been objectives in their own right, but they were subsidiary to the single much simpler and more easily recognised objective of shooting a stag. Success in this main object was not yet to be soured by feelings of remorse. The physical exertion and the excitement easily banished all misgivings, which were not even mentioned in my diary.

Late in the evening a new stalk developed but this time it was Andrew's turn to shoot and he successfully bagged a rather smaller stag. Then we walked to the wee bothie—a wooden hut standing close by Rory McCray's house. It had two cubicles with beds and a kitchen. After an excellent supper of soup warmed up on the stove and a very good cold pie, we slept the sleep of the hunter home from the hill.

Three days later (which was my twenty-second birthday) I started for Corrie Harabie again with John Boyle. My diary records that he won the toss, took the first stalk and had a successful shot:

"We left John's stag and climbed on to the spur between Glas toul Mhor (Grey hole big) and Glas toul Beg (Grey hole small) to look at the stag we had seen in the morning. The hinds got our wind and the stag was very small but we saw some beasts on the far side of a little chimney-like corrie on Sgurr Chairbh. So after watching a pair of Ring Ouzels for a few minutes we set off to stalk this new bunch, a long slanting pull up from the burn. When we were very near the corrie we suddenly felt the wind on our right cheeks and knew that we were in an eddy and sure enough the beasts had winded us and were away. About thirty hinds went over the ridge in front of us and finally a great stag, a nine-pointer with a splendid broad head and so they trotted over the top while I cursed and Alec said, 'What a peety, he wass a good stag whatever!'

"When they were gone we started down the corrie to cross it and follow the deer. Suddenly Rory stopped dead. Just up the corrie we could see a stag feeding away from us, and a little above him was another. Alec said they would do. I took the rifle and climbed up to a ledge on the side of the corrie. I saw four stags and asked Rory which was the best. 'The top one,' he said, and so indeed I could see that it was. Alec said that it was 'as good as the one that went over'. There were five stags altogether and the big one was the furthest. He was a dark beast and near the bright horizon to the west I sighted with the aperture but could see nothing and so put it down. Then I drew a bead with the open sight and fired. Probably I went high but the stags ran together, paused, and then ran down the corrie a little, before starting up the slope opposite. Then they stopped and I fired again and was again high. In a second I was ready once more and 'This time,' said I to myself, 'we won't be high.' At the shot the stag turned and galloped fifty yards at breakneck speed down the steep bank, almost overrunning his pace and when the bank flattened out he went straight into the ground and lay stone dead. He was a seven-pointer and he weighed fifteen stone four pounds."

He could not have known much about it, but it had been a clumsy piece of work. He and my earlier eight-pointer were the two heaviest beasts of the season, and the twenty-eight-inch span of the first one made it the best head too. These were causes for congratulation, but the seeds of doubt were there.

I only ever shot one more stag after that—a year later on the steep slope above Loch na Cray in Skye. The doubt became a certainty. Stalking was wonderful, but killing stags was not for me. So now I do not walk for days over the wild hills; I see the high tops only in memory. There is no doubt that I am the poorer in mind and body for this, and it is questionable whether the Red Deer are the better for it. What I learned of stalking probably saved my life one day in Normandy, but unless I were starving I could not now be persuaded to shoot a stag.

CHAPTER 23   *The Lure of Serendipity*

BACK in London in the autumn of 1931 I became a pupil at the
Royal Academy Schools in the dark bowels of Burlington House.
My teachers were Russell, Monnington and Jackson. I was two
years at the school, two happy years of drawing and painting.

I motored daily from Leinster Corner in the Austin Seven, and
parked it in a tiny space in the narrow lane leading down from
Burlington Gardens to the back door of the Academy. Recently
John Bourne, a fellow student, has formed the Reynolds Club for
old boys and girls of the Academy Schools, but I find that only a
handful of my contemporaries are members. What, I wonder,
has happened to those brilliant ones who drew so much better than
I did, whose artistry was quite clearly of greatly superior calibre?
One or two of them are famous, not necessarily the expected ones,
but there were young artists of staggering promise whose names I
have not heard of since. At the time it was vastly discouraging to
find so many who were so much better at it than I. This may be
true in any school, but in an art school it seems more significant
because inborn talent seems more than ever important. But the
two years were, on the whole more stimulating than discouraging.
Endless discussions on purity of line, cubism, abstraction; romance
in the dark passages; copying old Masters in the National Gallery;
painting up canvas-covered decoys for netting wild geese; and
painting and drawing and drawing and painting. I won no prizes
at the competitions, I had no very advanced ideas about the future
of art, the girl I liked best married a sculptor, and my copy of
Bellini's 'Agony in the Garden' was by no means meticulous, though
it taught me something of composition. Only the canvas goose
decoys, stretched over frames of sculptured wire netting were
wholly successful. Yet I believe my training at the Royal Academy
Schools was of the greatest value to me.

But in this period of my life, as it had been in Cambridge days, my most serious limitation was an unbridled propensity for adventure. I wanted things to *happen*; I was not so much interested in the causes of their happening, nor in the human conflicts and relationships which made them happen, but rather in the effects of the happening on my day-to-day life. For me to be happy things had to be happening, and in a curious way they seemed to happen all the time. It seems that I was serendipitous.

Adventure was indispensable and wildfowling provided it. Thus the winter week-ends found me back on the old familiar beautiful marsh on the Wash, sometimes with my original companions, sometimes with new. Punting still held its special appeal, now more perhaps for the boat handling, the silent and secret comings and goings in the creeks, the intimate views of the wild creatures, than for the shooting; though it would not yet have been worth the long days if the guns had been left behind.

A new character must now be introduced into my story: David Haig Thomas. I had met him as an undergraduate at St. John's College before going to Munich, a boyish, round-faced enthusiast with dark brown curly hair and no great scholarship. His father was the distinguished rowing coach who trained the Cambridge crew for the best part of a generation. David himself rowed bow in the Cambridge boat for four years. He was uncomplicated, unpredictable, unafraid and completely friendly. He had ideas, many of which were less good than others, but he had them in profusion about every conceivable subject. Soon after I first met him he propounded a scheme for capturing the popular song market by re-writing all the current hits upside down with the high notes low and vice versa.

I had first met him one frosty November morning shooting on the Wash, where he was wading in bare feet because he had over-spent his allowance and was unable to afford rubber boots. His shoes tied by their laces were hanging round his neck. David was tough, ruthless, irresistibly charming and cheerfully good-looking. I never knew him to be more than momentarily downcast, and he was basically absolutely kind. In our adventures he was an enchanting companion and a staunch friend. In due course I was best man at his wedding.

David and I spent Christmas Day, 1931, out in *Kazarka*, in the familiar haunts off Sandbanks. We floated down the creek, round 'the Hairpin' and 'Seal Corner' into Scotsman's Sled. It was, according to my diary, a red-letter day although the bag was quite small. Our enjoyment had ceased to be in direct proportion to the success of our operations. Indeed by then there was a vague misgiving that perhaps we were getting rather too good at it.

Christopher Dalgety had acquired a motor-boat as a tender to *Kazarka*. She was a small ship's lifeboat with a cabin built over the foremost two-thirds of her length and she had a rather unreliable engine. Her name was *Havelle*, the Norwegian name for the Long-tailed Duck which is based on the musical call of the bird. Long-tailed Ducks (rather sadly called Old Squaws in North America) are dumpy little birds and the name was curiously appropriate to our dumpy little motor-boat.

Another new character in my story was a Lincolnshire farmer who was not in the usual mould. Whereas, in our earlier wildfowling days, it had seemed that the Pinkfeet fed mostly in the fields close to the sea-wall at Sandbanks, we now found them flighting up to twenty-five miles inland across the Fen country, especially after the New Year. When we followed by car we found them feeding in fields where they had been unknown only a few years before. Our pursuit led us to meet many farmers, some of whom became lifelong friends. When I first met him at the very end of 1931 William G. Tinsley had lately reached his fiftieth birthday. He was unmarried and lived at the Poplars in Holbeach Marsh. It was a flat 'marsh' farm, which in that area indicates that the incredibly fertile silt soil will produce up to twenty tons of Majestic potatoes per acre.

Will's father had died about a year before I first went to the Poplars and most of the farm business was undertaken by 'Gran', his magnificent and matriarchal stepmother, who had in fact brought up Will, his three brothers and his sister. Will's preoccupation was birds. He had little inclination for farming although in fact he spent his days doing it. His great interest was wildfowl and particularly the geese which came to feed on his potato fields. He had shot them and had kept the wounded ones alive; he had brought in and hatched the eggs of Shelducks which nested locally under the stacks. Around a small pond at the back of his garden were most of the common species of British ducks, pinioned in an enclosure, and in the orchard were a number of geese. His enthusiasm was immediately impressive.

At once I recognised in Will Tinsley a kindred fanaticism: "A very quiet person," I wrote that evening, "with a strange shy manner and remarkable feeling for wild things. A most unexpected find on a Lincolnshire farm."

After a second visit a week or two later:

"Then we called on Mr. William Tinsley who was in great form. We looked at his ducks and geese for some time. He said some nice things: that of all animals the Pinkfoot was the finest; that if it were not for his duck pond in these hard times he would give up farming; and finally when we went away: 'Come again soon, most of the people who call talk about nothing but potatoes.' "

In those early days his collection of waterfowl was small, though later it was greatly enlarged. How his observations during the Second World War influenced the establishment of the Wildfowl Trust on the Severn Estuary will be described later in this book.

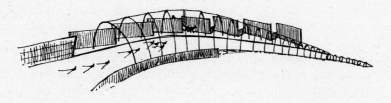

CHAPTER 24   *Eende Kooi*

"TOMORROW," said Will Tinsley, "we'll go over and see Billy."
I had been staying at the Poplars for the week-end and on the
following morning he piloted me twenty-five miles inland to
Borough Fen Decoy, near Peakirk.

It lies within sight of Crowland Abbey in the flat land close
to the River Welland, which, like the Nene and the Ouse, is
artificially canalised between great banks as it runs through the
low country. The river is bordered on one side by Cowbit Wash,
the wide expanse of grassland which acts as a safety valve in
time of flood, and half a mile from the upper reaches of 'the
Wash' lies the decoy. We approached it along a straight lane
lined with pollard willows leaning outwards from the road over
the flanking ditches. This impressive avenue was called 'The
Chase' and it led to a gravel yard surrounded by agreeable farm
buildings, the coach house topped with a weathercock on which
sat the sheet metal silhouette of a duck.

At the door of the farmhouse itself we met Billy Williams,
the decoyman—a small man of about fifty, with twinkling bright
blue eyes, and a responsive robin-like welcome. His family, famous
in the annals of early duck decoys, had worked Borough Fen since
it was built. Billy had followed old Herbert Williams as decoyman,
and had married old Herbert's daughter Annie, who was his
first cousin.

Borough Fen Decoy was certainly in existence in 1670 and may
have been built some years before that, which makes it one of
the earliest, though probably not the first, of the two or three
hundred duck decoys built in Britain. The idea came from Holland,
and the name Decoy comes from the two Dutch words Eende,
meaning ducks, and kooy or kooi, meaning cage or trap. Probably
it is a simple contraction or perhaps just enough Dutch was

known to recognise the first three letters as the same as the indefinite article and thus to imagine 'een dekooi'.

Two great family names were connected with British duck decoys: Williams and Skelton. Billy's and Annie's ancestors had built and operated many famous decoys besides Borough Fen. Old Tom Williams, who worked one of the decoys at Wrangle in Lincolnshire in the eighteenth century, moved to Lakenheath in Suffolk where he may have built, and certainly worked, the eight-pipe decoy there. He is said to have died at the age of 109. *Young* Tom worked the decoy at Methwold in Norfolk until he fell into a drain and was drowned in 1870, at the age of 100.

Then there was the Shropshire branch of the family and the delightful epitaph to 'Andrew Williams, born A.D. 1692, died April 18, 1776, aged 84 years, of which time he lived under the Aston family as Decoyman 60 years.

> 'Here lies the Decoyman who lived like an otter
> Dividing his time 'twixt the land and the water;
> His hide he oft soaked in the waters of Perry
> While Aston old beer his spirits kept cheery.
> Amphibious his life, Death was puzzled to say
> How to dust to reduce such well-moistened clay;
> So Death turned Decoyman and 'coyed him to land,
> Where he fixed his abode till quite dried to the hand;
> He then found him fitting for crumbling to dust,
> And here he lies mouldering as you and I must.'

I had, of course, read something about duck decoys but I had no very clear idea of how they worked until my first visit to Borough Fen on Sunday, 5th March, 1932. The decoy wood lay 200 yards from the farmhouse—eighteen acres of trees, among them tall poplars, elms and oaks standing out in the vast bare expanse of fenland fields. Inside the wood was a small secret pond of two and a half acres, of a regular but complex shape. It had eight very small bays, from which led eight curved tapering ditches each about sixty yards long and five yards wide at the mouth. The plan was like an eight-armed starfish. The ditches were spanned by hoops made of ash or willow saplings, over which tarred string netting was stretched to make a tapering tunnel, curving to the right as it went farther from the open water of the pond. Along the outside of the curve were ranged a row of screens made of reeds, three or four yards long and six feet high, set up in an overlapping pattern like a Venetian blind, which could be seen through from one direction but not from the other. These eight devices, radiating from the central pool were called the 'pipes' and Borough Fen was therefore an eight-pipe decoy.

To operate a decoy it is necessary to entice some of the ducks which have collected on the pond (often in thousands) to come into a pipe, and this may be achieved in three ways. First, the banks of the pond can be made vertical except in the pipes, so that ducks which want to go ashore and preen and sleep can do so only on the 'landings' in the pipe or at its mouth: this is called 'banking'. Alternatively, the birds may be encouraged to come to the pipes with food spread on the 'landings'. But the most surprising and interesting method is the use of a trained dog. In this the decoyman exploits the curious behaviour pattern of ducks in the presence of a predator. If, for example, a fox appears before them when they are sitting on the water, they appear to feel safe enough to swim up within a few feet and mob it. The behaviour of small birds round a hawk or owl, and the behaviour of young cattle round a dog is clearly analogous. The attraction seems to be all the greater if the predatory animal is retreating. The application of this principle in Holland in the sixteenth century is still today the operating basis of most of the duck decoys which remain in existence. The dog is trained to run round the overlapping screens, appearing, retreating along the screen and disappearing again progressively further and further up the pipe as the ducks follow it. At Borough Fen, as in many other decoys, the dog jumps over a two-foot-high screen called a 'dog leap' and appears with a startling suddenness which seems to be even more stimulating. The 'dog leaps' occupy the space between the ends of the high screens making, in plan view, a zig-zag pattern.

When as many ducks as possible have been lured under the archway of netting, the decoyman appears suddenly at the mouth of the pipe. Because of the overlap of the screens he is still invisible to the ducks out on the pool but is in the full view of those which are in the pipe. They dare not fly back towards him, for he appears to have cut off their retreat to the open pond. Instead they fly away from him up the pipe, thinking perhaps to escape round the bend, but there they find the pipe growing ever narrower. The decoyman is following close behind them as they run up the final slope from the narrow channel, into the detachable tubular net at the pipe's end. From this 'tunnel net' they are removed, and in the days when I first went to Borough Fen Decoy they were

speedily killed and sent to market in London. Nowadays Borough
Fen Decoy, and some others (including our four-pipe decoy at
Slimbridge, built in 1845) are used exclusively for ringing and
measuring ducks, which are thereafter released.

Back in 1932 I was tremendously excited with my first introduction to this fascinating technique. To be operating silently
within a few feet of the ducks, and within 100 yards of perhaps
thousands of them, was a new thrill, and in addition there were
the historical and antiquarian associations, the traditions, the
lore and the superstitions.

On that first day Billy Williams was confined to the house with
a bad cold and we were taken down to 'the ʼcoy' by old Hill, who
had been assistant decoyman under Annie's father. It was a day of
cold winter sunshine and the wood was thickly sprinkled with
snowdrops. We crept noiselessly from pipe to pipe, peeping through
a tiny vertical crack in the screen which gave a sadly limited view
of the birds. Each of us carried a small piece of smouldering peat
which was supposed to drown our own human smell. This I took
at the time to be a superstition. I knew that the existence of an
acute sense of smell in ducks was not accepted by scientific ornithologists, but since then I have caught ducks hundreds of times in
many different duck decoys, and I am satisfied that ducks downwind can smell human beings quite well at short ranges. It may be
that their sense of smell is only a little better than our own, and
in no way comparable with the capacities of deer and other
mammals. But if they can smell at all, the idea of carrying lighted
turf in a decoy may well have been practical in the days when every
marshland cottage burned a turf fire. Nowadays the smell of burning turf might be more unusual to the ducks than the smell of
man, and they might even become conditioned to the idea that it
foretold danger. For these reasons no burning turf is now carried
either in Borough Fen Decoy or in Berkely New Decoy at Slimbridge, both of which are worked by the Wildfowl Trust for
ringing.

If the lighted turf could not entirely be considered a superstition, the old hats surely were. When the ducks were to be
driven up the pipe from the 'show-place' it was useful to have
something in your hand to wave. It could effectively be a handker-
chief, but when I first went to Borough Fen it had to be an old
hat. There were three grey felt hats, folded like forage caps, moth-
eaten and almost worn away by the waving. Tradition had it
that although they were never worn it was only by waving one or

other of these old hats that really successful catches could be made, and an old hat had solemnly to be collected from the black hut near the decoy gate on each and every occasion, together with 'the strings'—some special loops of stout, rather hairy twine for carrying up the dead birds.

The ducks were killed, neatly, instantaneously and without mess, by breaking their necks. I took some pains to learn how this was done, so that I could use the method for destroying wounded birds. If killing must be done it is important that it should be done quickly and certainly: it must not be bungled. But even as Billy showed me how to do it, I knew that this was the part of the business he hated. The ducks which went to market were his livelihood, but he hated killing them as they came out of the net, and welcomed the chance of saving the few which were to be kept alive in captivity.

Many times Billy and I talked of the days when it would be possible to kill no more in the decoy, but to ring and release the catch instead. This was not finally achieved until 1955, only two years before Billy's death. For several years before that, only Mallards had been killed, all other species being sent away with rings on their legs.

Using the family 16mm. ciné camera I set out to make a film of the decoy in action. It was the first time that I had used a film camera and the results were not particularly impressive. But the attempt clearly showed that the decoy lacked an observation point from which the ducks on the pool could be surveyed, photographed, counted and studied; and such a place seemed eminently desirable. I hoped that Billy would allow one to be built.

In the early summer of 1932 my appendix was removed by Lord Moynihan at a nursing home just opposite the B.B.C. in Portland Place. After my springtime visits to Borough Fen I had bought the only two available books on duck decoys and during my time in the nursing home I read them both from cover to cover: *The Book of Duck Decoys* by Sir Ralph Payne Gallwey and *British Duck Decoys of Today, 1918* by J. Whitaker.

Soon after the operation I talked to Billy on the telephone at Borough Fen and made arrangements to go there as soon as I was convalescent. At the same time I proposed the new Observation Hut, of which he seemed to be in favour.

It was June when I arrived at the decoy and we selected a site for my observation hut on one of the 'pointings' jutting out between the north and the north-east pipes, from which with the prevailing south-westerly wind we should get a good view of the ducks without risk of disturbing them. It involved cutting a path with axe and slasher through a thick blackthorn thicket and then building a small reed thatched hut at the far end—not perhaps the best light activity for the first weeks after an abdominal operation, but I was desperately keen to get the job finished before the decoying season began in August.

The hut was successful: it could be reached in secrecy and gave an excellent view of the ducks on the pool, with a chance to count them, to assess the relative abundance of the different species, and check sex ratios. Although it remained there for a good many years I was never quite sure that Billy Williams entirely approved of it. But in the first winter after it was built it was a novelty and was much frequented by visitors to the Decoy.

One morning in the following February when the ice on the pool was half an inch thick, my diary records that we went down before dawn to break it and to feed the house pipe: "The birds came in very early so that we had to leave it before we had finished and go back to the house; after breakfast there were a few ducks and Wigeon in the house pipe. Then we went into the hut where the sight was simply staggering. Filling the pond from edge to edge was a huge mass of birds. There must have been 3,000 ducks sitting on the ice, possibly 4,000. There were quantities of Wigeon and Pintails and about forty pairs of Shovelers. The sight was so amazing, even after seeing the usual 1,500 to 2,000 which one habitually sees from the hut, that I went straight up and telephoned to Kenneth Fisher, my old Headmaster at Oundle, for him to come over and see it. Unfortunately he had lately had 'flu and could not come out. In the afternoon I took a camera down and photographed the great concourse."

My initial idea of an observation hut which could be entered and left without the knowledge of the birds seemed to be a success. It was the prototype of many huts built since, and perhaps it was fortunate that the first attempt should have proved so satisfactory.

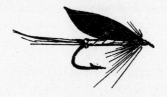

CHAPTER 25   *Of Trouts, Skates and Paints*

MY introduction to sea trout fishing in Skye, after our adventure in the clear rivers of Bavaria, led me to spend a week in the following year at Loch Boisdale in the Island of South Uist. By this time I was competent enough as a fisherman; this Hebridean sea trout fishing was mostly done from a boat on a loch, which so far as casting accuracy is concerned required much less skill than river fishing. The 14th September, 1932, my twenty-third birthday, was spent fishing in the Mill Loch for sea trout:

"I put on a 'butcher' and late in the afternoon I got into a fish off the Yellow Rock. I thought it was about two pounds as it was very sluggish to start with. Eventually after about ten minutes I landed it and it turned out to be four and a half pounds—an admirable birthday fish. The other two were fishing on Lower Kildonan and got four fish, the best two and a half pounds. A couple of eyes nicely wiped, I thought . . . or just duffer's luck."

Inescapably I am and have always been a competitive sort of person. I cannot seem to undertake anything without sooner or later wanting to be able to do it better than others. It is a defect which I clearly recognise, but cannot eliminate. In skating I had always wanted to compete but had always been excluded from top-flight figure-skating competition by my failure in loops. Pair-skating, however, was a type of competition in which no school figures were required, and as there was to be a Pair-Skating Competition at the Ice Rink in Westminster, I decided to enter for it with a young skater from Manchester named Joyce Macbeth. It required a good deal of concentrated practice, designing the programme which we could do together, memorising the sequences of steps, spins, and jumps, and then trying it out until we could perform it in unison. When the great day came, a remarkable thing happened: suddenly we found that we were *better* than we had ever been in rehearsal. Perhaps after all we could scrape a third prize. Luck was with us too; neither of us fell, the timing appeared almost perfect, and our programme apparently had greater variety than any of the others. To our astonishment we were declared the winners.

Based possibly on this pair-skating success, I found myself in demand for a more acrobatic manoeuvre—a spin called 'the aeroplane' in which you seized your partner by one hand and one skate, and having achieved 'flying speed', swung her off the other skate so that she swooped alternately high in the air and low over the ice. It looked a good deal more hazardous than it really was, and all the budding girl champions of the day demanded to be so swung. "Aeroplane, please," they used to pipe —for there were eight- and ten-year-olds—as soon as I appeared on the ice. The boldest of them, and I think at the time the smallest, was young Megan Taylor who subsequently became British Champion. She was the daughter of a skilful professional skater, Phil Taylor, whose speciality was jumping barrels and skating on stilts. Cecilia Colledge was another candidate for 'the aeroplane' and so too was Belita Jepson Turner, both of whom grew up to be famous skaters.

I was still living at Leinster Corner, the family home overlooking Kensington Gardens. Here I would stay so long as I studied at the Academy Schools, but after that I had decided to make a home of my own in the country among the birds, perhaps at or near the Decoy. I also had my eye on one of the two old lighthouses which we could see in distant silhouette against the evening sky from our beloved marsh at Sandbanks.

A significant reference to it appears in my diary:

"Sunday, 30th October, 1932. I went down to the East Lighthouse at Sutton Bridge which I am anxious to get hold of. It is a very nice place, grand situation, and the house apparently in good repair. No road to it and no fresh water for birds but otherwise splendid. The only trouble is a right-of-way along the bank used largely by Kenzie Thorpe and other poachers.

"Then I went back to Holbeach where I met Mr. Maples, who is the head of the Spalding Gentlemen's Society founded in 1710. The Society had a large collection of stuffed birds and I am to show the Decoy film to them in three weeks' time."

There is a pattern of disaster which even nowadays attends amateur film shows. In those days such vicissitudes were even more frequent, and perhaps to that extent less disastrous. My first address to the Spalding Gentlemen's Society was the first 'lecture with film' that I had ever given and the first of a long series of entertainments to be marred by technical hitches of one kind or another:

"Saturday, 26th November. After tea we went to Spalding where I was showing the Decoy film.

"When the people arrived I lectured for ten minutes with diagrams on the Decoy before starting the film. When I *did* start it, the lamp blew. A man in the audience went to fetch another—his own private one. Meanwhile I drew geese and ducks on the blackboard for the amusement of the audience. When the lamp arrived it also blew; then we found the resistance was set wrong. Another man went to fetch another bulb and eventually we got started. It was very dim for those at the back of the hall. There were about 130 people there. All however went reasonably well, and I showed them a sailing film and Skye afterwards. They seemed to like it . . ."

For that summer holiday we had taken Catfield Hall in Norfolk, which lies on the east side of Barton Broad. It was the home of Lord William Percy, one of the world's greatest experts on ducks. As a summer guest my stepfather had invited an old friend—the painter Duncan Grant. This, my parents thought, was a chance for me to learn something about painting from a distinguished artist.

Duncan Grant went out to paint on the marshes and I walked out with him, but not to paint; I was too busy cutting reeds in anticipation of a great duck flight which I had planned. Grant gave my family one of the little paintings he made at Catfield, and it still hangs at Leinster Corner. I was looking at it the other day, an enchanting landscape, painted with great assurance and a superb economy. I was there when it was being painted but I had not time to watch how it was done.

A year later, with the Academy Schools behind me, I had got to start making my way as an artist. I went to live at Borough Fen Decoy. I was likely, I thought, to paint best those things which moved me most. That meant my wildfowl. They had never been painted in the way I saw them. The great Swedish painter Bruno Liljefors, also a hunter, had come nearest to it; but even he did not *know* them quite as I knew them. Frank Southgate, a Norfolk water-colourist of some distinction who had died in the

First War, had come some of the way from the conventional painters of birds in the direction I wanted to go. For the rest, they had been trying to do something different. Old Archibald Thorburn, who painted the feathers of birds with exquisite truth (and may, in that field, never be surpassed), had come to Leinster Corner at the age of eighty to criticise my drawings of birds and deer. His advice had been wise and useful at the time, but it was not his road that I now wanted to extend into the jungle. What I wanted to do was extraordinarily simple and easy. I had only to put on to canvas to the best of my oil painting capacity the birds as I had seen them at dawn or dusk or moonlight, or in storm or frost or snow, and I could not fail to be doing something original. It remained to be seen whether those who looked at the pictures would be moved in the same way as I was when I watched the flight of the wild geese, and heard their music.

I painted hard during the winter, picked out what I thought were the three best pictures and sent them in for the summer exhibition at the Royal Academy. To my surprise and delight two of them were accepted.

During the winter at the Decoy I had painted about forty pictures and these, with a few earlier works, were accepted as a one-man show by Messrs. Arthur Ackermann & Son of 157 New Bond Street. The exhibition was opened by Sir Samuel Hoare in the summer of 1933. Nearly all the pictures were in oils, and the highest price was £25. During the month all but two or three were sold.

The show led to a number of commissions. One was for a large painting to hang above the stairs in the hall of Sir John Beale's country house at Oulton Broad in Norfolk. The dimensions of the canvas were to be eight feet by five feet, and I was considerably alarmed by the prospect. It was more than four times larger in area than any picture I had ever painted before. For a long time I was frightened of starting it, but Sir John Beale was not a man to be fobbed off with excuses or postponements. A deadline was agreed, and Sir John said that he was coming to see the picture on a certain day the following week. "As it is already half finished," he said, "I'd like to see how it looks. Perhaps it won't be too late to make small alterations . . ." The pristine canvas was hastily taken from the wall against which it had been standing for so long. It was plain and white and vaguely terrifying. But I had in my mind the sort of thing that I meant to do; so, with my biggest brushes I started to slosh on the sky.

By the end of that day there was also a reed bed, some water and the outlines of the birds. I still had two days in hand and if I worked very hard I might paint up the birds and still get in the tall reeds which were to sweep up the foreground of the picture. Towards the end of the third day, after the initial background had been given time to dry, it was evident that I was not going to get the reeds done. There were a lot of tall *Phragmites* stems to go in, reaching almost from top to bottom of the picture. It was a matter of a few minutes to indicate where they would be, but the actual job of painting them in, the long fine line of the reed, the dark line of its shaded side, the thinner paler line of the highlight along each—these took time and there were a minimum of twenty reeds to be painted. The only answer was to enlist the active assistance of my mother. She went to work on the reeds on the left-hand side of the picture while I plodded on with those on the right. When Sir John came the picture was virtually finished and he seemed delighted with it. For the rest of his lifetime it hung in his house at Oulton Broad and was sent later to a Royal Air Force mess. Meanwhile it was to be reproduced as one of the illustrations in a new book, *Morning Flight*, to be published by *Country Life*. The title of the picture in the book was 'Norfolk Spring—Shovelers and a pair of Garganey Teal', but there was a misprint in which the dash had been replaced by a hyphen. They appeared as Norfolk Spring-Shovelers and all Shovelers have been Norfolk Spring-Shovelers ever since.

This title was too long when the picture was acquired for reproduction by the Medici Society, and they called it 'Taking to Wing', under which corny name it has since sold more than 350,000 copies.

Morning Flight was first published in a signed and numbered de luxe edition in 1935. I had written about 50,000 words of my wildfowling experiences to go with the lavish illustrations and in spite of its then high cost of three guineas the book was unexpectedly successful. The first edition quickly sold out and a cheaper one appeared in the following year, which was kept in print by new impressions for the next ten years.

Some adventures which are essential to my story were recorded in *Morning Flight* and have been retold here. The rather frightening intensity of my feeling for birds in wild places was illustrated by a passage in the last chapter of the book under the heading 'Wild Music':

"Sound has a powerful effect on man's emotions, perhaps more powerful than sight, and whether the sound is of man's designing or of nature's, it may bring us near to tears by its beauty. Heard above the rushing of the wind, the cry of wild geese can be overwhelmingly sad.

"The nightingale and the blackcap and the curlew are nature's soloists but the geese are her chorus, as rousing, over the high sand, as the 'Sanctus' of Bach's B minor Mass. As they flight at dawn one can imagine that each successive skein brings in the fugue, *Pleni sunt coeli* . . ."

CHAPTER 26   *The Ultimate Sanction*

NOT far from my old school at Oundle was the Lilford estate where
on the floods we had watched the White-fronted geese in my
school days. Near the Hall was a fine collection of captive birds
presided over by Mr. A. F. Moody, who was Lord Lilford's
curator and had previously looked after the famous collection of
W. H. St. Quentin at Scampston Hall. Mr. Moody was the author
of a standard work on the care of birds in captivity. On visits to
the Wash we had saved many birds caught in flight-nets (now
happily illegal) and had taken them to the aviaries at Lilford—
Curlews, Redshanks, Knots, Dunlins, Grey Plovers and others;
we had also brought wing-tipped geese both for him and for Will
Tinsley's collection in the orchard beside his farmhouse in Holbeach Marsh. The idea of keeping birds alive had suddenly become an important new objective.

To be sure, we still liked to go wildfowling as often as possible
on our beautiful marsh at Terrington. It had now reverted to its
original code name of 'Sandbanks' because Skeldyke had in turn
lost its secrecy. We still went far out into the Wash in *Kazarka*,
and we still went excitedly each year to the Solway Firth. But
gradually the idea of a wider interest in the birds was catching hold.

I am writing, still, of a time which was long ago, when my
views on many things were different from the views I hold today,
and in order to put those youthful thoughts into perspective I
must now digress on the subject of killing.

As I have said earlier in this book, it is man's instinct to hunt
and kill the animals which he required in his primitive state to
keep himself alive. Among those animals were ducks and geese.
He caught them in late summer when they were moulting and
flightless; he killed them with thrown stones, with stones from
slings, with spears and arrows and snares and blow-pipe darts and

nets, and finally with guns. Not until the modern punt-gun and the modern double-barrelled ejecting shoulder-gun had been invented did anyone seriously think that the scales were weighted in favour of the man rather than of the bird. It was widely held that wildfowl were wild; they asked for no quarter, they needed none, and there was no reason why any should be given.

With the exception of certain wisdom buried in folk lore, the moral obligations of conservation are a comparatively new conception to civilised man. To me they were still new a long time after I became a keen wildfowler. I have already explained that my parents were not interested in shooting—indeed, they were opposed to it. In the days when we lived near Marlborough the lads with whom I used to walk through the fields and woods had carried 4·10 shotguns and I had envied them. At fifteen I had wanted a shotgun for my birthday, and when told that I could not have one I had sulked. I had dragged twenty yards behind for most of a walk through the West Woods and when asked why I had mumbled sub-tearfully, "I want a shotgun." This my mother repeated in misquotation ". . . want a popgun" she mocked, by which I was incensed. At fifteen one might reasonably want a shotgun but not a popgun. It was a palpable injustice to be thus misrepresented. I got no 4·10 for my birthday, and perhaps this was why, when I finally came to use my father's old Cogswell and Harrison twelve-bore (which I believe he bought only for the special occasion when he went grouse shooting with King Edward VII at Balmoral), I was at once such an enthusiastic shooting man. Soon, as we have seen, I was painting and drawing the animals that I liked to hunt, just as the cave-dwellers of old drew the bison and the deer on the roofs of their caves.

I have already explained the way in which I resolved the main problem in those early days. When people said: "I don't understand how you can draw those beautiful creatures and at the same time want to kill them," I used to answer that this was admittedly a strange paradox, but that my particular regard for them was not a sentimental one; it was not a 'dear-little-dicky-bird' attitude, but rather a respect for a wild creature which was supremely able to look after itself, and which did so, by and large, very effectively in spite of all my wiles. It was in fact, I would say to them, this capacity to look after themselves which primarily attracted me to wild geese. This simple argument no doubt left many in disagreement.

932

Michael Bratby.

934

With two punts on Morecambe Bay:
Michael Bratby, John Winter and Brian D'Arcy Irvine.

c. 1935

The East Lighthouse at Sutton Bridge, where the Nene runs into the Wash.

1933   1933

A Roe Deer fawn and a Badger cub that was caught in an umbrella—both at
Oberau in Bavaria.

Man's relationship with other animals is complex, and contains intellectual factors which have become a part of civilisation. It is, after all, no longer the shooting man's excuse for going out that he is hungry and wants some birds to eat. He is concerned with the battle of wits between man and beast, and with exercising the ultimate sanction—the power of life and death. If the beast is difficult to outwit, his enjoyment is the greater; but for many the ultimate sanction is more important than the skill and chance of the chase.

If it is the wildness of a bird which makes it attractive to outwit, it is in turn man's shooting habits which make the bird wild and difficult to outwit. So here is a complex between man and bird each part of which depends upon the other. A large part of the fascination of getting close to a wild goose, of photographing it, and studying it, is that it is excessively wary and difficult to get near; if geese were no longer shot they would no longer be wary and much of the fascination would be lost. To watch from a hide geese which are unaware of your presence although they are within easy shot—that magic and so rarely achieved distance —would be vastly less significant if guns had never been invented. In those parts of the world where wildfowl are unmolested, they are tame, and the shooting of them palls. In other places they become so wild that the pursuit of them enters into the main structure of civilisation, as it has done in the United States of America, where there is a strange and ubiquitous phenomenon known as 'duck-hunting', and where practically every able-bodied male is anxious to be classed as a 'duck-hunter'.

But there comes a time for some men when their first reaction even to the traditional quarry is no longer to kill. (Thoreau writes of leaving the gun and the fishing pole behind the door.) They reach a certain stage, or age, some sooner, some later, when the old phrase which is supposed to epitomise the English country gentleman, "It's a lovely morning; let's go out and kill something," is no longer funny but obscene. Whether this has to do with the agony of the two great wars, or whether it arises from new ideas about humanity and suffering, I do not know. Nor do I know if this outlook is more common than it was, though I suspect it may be.

After many years of wildfowling the first inklings of this changing attitude came to me on a marsh where, one early spring day in 1932, David Haig Thomas and I had shot twenty-three Greylag geese. Among them were two wounded ones, and as soon as we

G

had picked them up we hoped that they might not die. The birds which a few moments before we had been trying to kill, we were now trying to keep alive. Here was something of the awful paradox which faces a man in war who is called upon to kill his fellow men. ("Do you mean," the Eskimos had said to David in Greenland, when he described the First World War to them, "Do you mean people were trying to kill people they'd never even *met*?")

The two geese survived and we kept them for many years. Having got this far it began to seem strange that we should ever have taken delight in killing geese at all. And yet we had, and to a certain extent still did. When a bird was cleanly killed in the air there was a satisfaction of good marksmanship, but was it any greater than the satisfaction at breaking a 'clay pigeon' fired unexpectedly from a spring? And if so how much greater, and why? When a bird crashed with a thud on to the ground, how could I ever have thought the sound satisfying, even though I had not then heard the noise which follows an unopened parachute?

Then came the problem of wounding. I was a moderately good shot in the days when I kept myself in practice, which meant, if I was shooting geese and employing the essential self control only to fire when the birds were in proper range, that I was likely to bring home one bird for every three cartridges I fired. On inspired occasions over a short period I could bring home one for every two cartridges, but hardly ever better; even the best shots cannot improve much on fifty per cent in practical wildfowling. Yet, when you are firing a pattern of pellets, is it likely that the other fifty per cent of cartridges are all clean misses?

I once heard a keen wildfowler say that he had "the satisfaction of hearing his shots slap into the birds" although none of them came down. I have taken a wildfowler round the pens of the Wildfowl Trust and heard him say when a flock of Snow Geese came low over his head—"My word, I could knock a couple of those down." When those same Snow Geese landed at our feet and walked up to feed from my hand I could sense that he was very much ashamed of the remark. The expression suggests a blunt stick to beat the beautiful birds out of the sky. Are these phrases the healthy symptoms of 'man the hunter' or something less healthy; or are they perhaps quite superficial—a relic of the tradition which has persisted from the time when the only reaction to a bird (more particularly if it was rare) was to fetch a gun and kill it?

Back in the 1930s that tradition was not yet dead, though it was dying. But already my own desires to exercise the ultimate sanction were beginning to be superseded by the desire to catch the birds alive. This involved achieving the power of death over the quarry without exercising it. It seemed at once to be a step forward. There was the initial objective of keeping the captured birds until they became tame, and thereby learning more about them; and when enough had been caught for these purposes there was still the technique of bird ringing—then fairly recently developed—which would require a virtually unlimited number to be captured.

This advance, if advance it was, was no sudden change in my outlook. I was still much too captivated by the 'ritual' aspects of wildfowling to give it up altogether. So many things went with the actual shooting—the beauty, the natural history, the exercise, the memories, and particularly the technical skills which in the course of years I had acquired. Especially was this so of punting; the seamanship, the boat handling, the knowledge of weather and tide—all these appealed to me as much as ever.

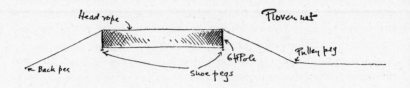

CHAPTER 27   *First Pulls with the Net*

IT was one thing to decide to try to catch geese alive and quite another to find a way of doing it. We scoured the literature and considered all the methods which we had ever heard of. Not for twenty years did we perfect a means of catching wild geese by the hundreds, but our final success adds some interest to these early beginnings.

The best system seemed to be that developed by the Plovernetters of the Fens—a modification of the double Clap Net in which a single net, attached to two poles, swung over like the page of a book at the release of a springy stretched rope.

At the end of August 1932 Will Tinsley and I went over to see an old Plover netter, Barney Shawl, who gave us a demonstration of how his net worked. I took careful notes of the way in which the rope was pegged down, from the back peg through the pulley peg to the operator, of the way the twenty-two-yard-long net was attached to the rope, and how the heels of the two six-foot poles were set into 'shoe pegs'. My diary records the special devices for release, so that both poles go over simultaneously. It goes on:

> "In this way I am perfectly convinced we can catch numbers of geese with the use of judiciously placed decoys [dummies of cardboard or canvas stretched on wire netting].
> "Netting geese will, I believe, prove much more exciting than shooting them, and with the tremendous advantage that never a wounded bird will be lost, and that the prize will be a bag of fine live geese instead of bloody corpses."

Two months later two nets, one seven-inch mesh and one four-inch, had been delivered and we set both of them in the same field. But the day was not promising; most of the geese went on inland,

and we started to pack up and leave it for another day. I dissuaded my colleagues from springing the nets until the last. It seemed to me that we should pack everything else up first—just in case some more geese came. While we were all standing out on top we suddenly saw about a dozen geese just over the field. Of course they had seen us and they cruised on over the next field. They did not go down, however, but went away across towards Wolferton on the other side of the Wash.

A minute or two later we saw a great skein of geese coming from far inland. Quickly we jumped into the ditch and pulled the bushes we had cut for cover down over ourselves. The geese had already curled in towards us and obviously intended to settle. Then they saw the decoys; they circled the first time high up and a few split off from the main lot which circled a second time. This was the thrilling moment; the critical high circle was over and they had not seen us. This time they would be likely to land. There were 200 in the party and they made a great clamour as they finished the second circle, still without having detected us, and rounded up to settle. They passed over the four-inch net and the first one settled in a direct line with the seven-inch head rope.

"I judged that about thirty were behind the head rope; the rest settled further upwind. Immediately I pulled and up came the net ten yards this side of them. They did not seem greatly scared, and I believe they would have settled back had they not seen us as they swung out over the ditch. So they went out to sea instead.

"We packed up quickly, for by this time I was very late and had to drive like hell to Ely in order to take part in a sailing race with Stewart Morris."

By mid-November I was not so sanguine about the goose nets:

"I have come to the conclusion that it is not going to be so easy to net these geese as we fondly imagined. We have had an easy time so far in concealing the net. Stubble fields and clover make good cover. Setting them on bare plough, where footprints count, is going to be a very different matter. Our net is twenty yards long and three yards wide and covers twice that area in the course of swinging over, but this is still only about one-fortieth of an acre. It looks a pretty small patch in a field of eighty acres.

"I don't think that catching them as they fly over will ever be a success as it is extremely difficult to judge the lead to give them. The only chance of a flying shot would be if they were to pitch downwind of the net; it *might* then be possible to put them up and pull on to them before they got too high. One does not realise how big a goose is. When he looks as though he is only a few feet up he is probably twenty feet in reality. After all, the net's height is just under twice the wing span of a goose. I think if we go at it we might catch some, but it will be very difficult and we shall never catch as many as we can shoot in the long run. But still a live goose in the net is worth ten dead ones."

The most serious limitation of the Plover net device was the length of tautly stretched rope leading to the point where the operator was to hide. If we could get away from this there seemed a much better chance of catching geese. Some other way than a stretched rope must be found for the motive power. We turned our thoughts to break-back mousetraps and wondered whether the poles could not be pushed over in the same way.

By the beginning of December I had brought these plans to a practical stage and my diary records:

"During the week I had springs made to throw the poles over. They were not finished but I brought them down to test them—two torsion springs, the coil four inches in diameter with legs about eighteen inches long and the whole made of seven-sixteenth-inch spring steel. They were made to be set through three-quarters of a revolution but this could not be done until they were completed without a risk of distorting the spring. My idea is that with a spring we can do away with the all-too-visible 100 yards of springy rope, which will leave nothing but the poles to conceal, a much easier proposition."

Then came a day of special significance:

"Monday, the 5th of December. David Haig Thomas and I took the net with the new springs down to Holbeach. Jack Caudwell, the farmer, met us to help set it out, and Christopher Dalgety arrived a little later. It was still dark when we got there but I was afraid we had not left enough time to set the net properly. The geese started to come when we were still experimenting with the release; the main causes of the trouble were that we had not perfected the release mechanism and that the poles were too weak (being made of deal and full of knots); we had to pin them down in the middle instead of at the opposite end, which meant that we had much less leverage. The pressure on the release peg was so great, in fact, that the fishing line which Christopher had brought was not nearly strong enough and broke at once. Binder twine was substituted, also broke twice, but eventually seemed to work from close quarters. Then the pieces of stick under the release pegs began to bend and others had to be cut from the hedge. When the mechanism was working from close quarters I found that I had pegged down the guy rope in the wrong place. Finally in a trial shot the frozen knobbles of earth (which caught at the net and held it back) prevented the poles from going much past the vertical.

"Meanwhile the geese had been pouring in in fifties and hundreds, and Christopher had been keeping them away from the decoys by flapping his coat. It was amazing how close to him they came. Eventually about 1,000 geese arrived in one huge mass and landed in the next field downwind. We set the net for one last try, and . . . snap, one of the poles broke in half.

"So ended ignominiously the first attempt with the springs and richly I deserved all the scathing comments of Jack Caudwell and Christopher, who said they had never expected it to work anyway. The whole idea, they said, was wrong and we must start again at the beginning without a thought of Plover nets. That was Christopher's view, but I do not think he had thought about it very much. Only David remained faithful, although *he* said his confidence had been badly shaken. We drove disconsolately to London, David and I, discussing nets *all* the way."

Not long after this, though, I was still sufficiently confident to place bets with David Haig Thomas, Mervyn Ingram and Christopher Dalgety, "five pounds to a shilling that I will not get twenty geese at one pull of the net this season".

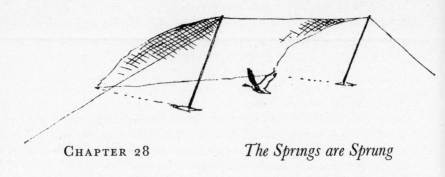

CHAPTER 28   *The Springs are Sprung*

WHEN the new springs and their modified release mechanism were complete, hopes were very high and I went for the Christmas holiday to stay at the Poplars with Will Tinsley. We set the net in various fields in Holbeach Marsh. The whole of Christmas Day, for example, was spent unavailingly sitting over the net. Boxing Day was a thick fog and then came Tuesday, 27th December.

"I went all by myself to Trevathoe Farm. I was none too early and while I was setting the net some geese came on to the next field. Very soon a little lot of three geese came. Fortunately they did not see the thirty or forty geese on the field next door, nor four others on the far side of my own field, so in they came to perfection and pitched. I looked up and saw at once that they nicely covered the area of the net. One of them must be under, so I pulled. There was a clang as the new tubular steel 'poles' swung over. In the first instant I saw two geese getting up and sweeping back to the left. The wind was blowing almost along the net and they had got it under their great wings and had shot back on it. But the third . . . what of him? Then suddenly I saw him jumping and straining in the meshes of the net. I should think I covered the intervening sixty yards in something under six seconds and was on the spot to extricate the very first goose ever caught in my net.

"The extrication was a great deal more difficult than I had anticipated; he was completely 'taffled up'. I had to reset the net in order to get him the right way up and then I set to work; I should say it took five minutes to get him out. When I eventually did so he was a somewhat bedraggled object but he was nevertheless my first netted goose. I returned to the dyke and popped him into the bag I had brought for the purpose. I had got one anyway."

Two days later on the same farm I caught another single goose. Our first attempts had been made in fields to which only small numbers of geese were coming, but on 1st January, 1933, I found a field where:

". . . we were confronted with a very remarkable sight. At first glance I took it to be a field of deep plough, the sods of which were shiny in the sun, as they so often are. But the 'sods' were geese; the whole field was covered with them. There were 2,000 at least and probably 3,000. Something put them up and the whole great phalanx flew out to sea.

"When we got back to the Poplars for lunch I rang up the farmer who owned the field and asked if I could set my net there for the morning, but he said that he was planning to shoot the geese there himself.

"After lunch I went down again to see if the geese were back. It was raining a little and they were there in full force. I watched them with the glasses, looking for the white goose, the albinistic Pinkfoot, which had been among them in the previous year, and suddenly I saw him. He did not seem to be quite as pale as last year's 'pink' goose but on the other hand he was quite easy to pick out. So back I went to Will Tinsley's house and telephoned the farmer again and said: 'Look here, if you let me net on your field tomorrow, I'll lend you my decoys the next day and promise you some shooting.' And to this he agreed.

"So we tore off down to the field where the net was still set, hauled up the springs and gear and then tore back to the new field. By this time it was nearly dark and we had a job to hit on a suitable place to set the net, but eventually everything was fixed. The field was a 'tatey bottom' which had not been ploughed or drilled, but just 'scuffled'; it was fairly rough with quite a lot of rubbish on it and only twenty-two acres.

"When we left the net was set only sixty yards from the ditch. It occurred to me during the night that this was not far enough out, and so we got up early next morning and made a very stupid mistake. We moved the net in the dark and as a result got very belated and hectic. The geese were beginning to come, although it was very dark, while I was still messing about with the net. One side suddenly sprung and since I had no one with me who knew how to reset it I was in great trouble.

G*

However eventually all seemed ready and we took cover in the ditch. I had the cut side of a turnip to mark the far end of the net but only a small metal peg marked the near end. By this time the geese were coming in 'good and proper'; in the half light they pitched down beside the decoys which were eighty yards downwind. But very soon they had spread upwind as they came in a solid stream from the shore. I decided not to pull until I could definitely see both the markers of the net. The geese I knew must be all over it, but I would wait until the light showed me just how many were in the area. Then a most unfortunate thing happened: some of the geese pitched on the wheat field behind me. Geese coming from the sea saw them first and pitched there too, flighting on to our field low over me in twos and threes, which made it exceedingly difficult to watch the net. By the time I could get up and bring my periscopic binoculars to bear, there were geese everywhere except for a little bare patch round the net. There is no doubt that earlier they had been all over the net, but had walked off it. Even now five geese sat at the very edge of the catching area. They walked in and appeared to be leading more in but then turned and walked off again. One mistake was that I was not in close enough touch with my release. I think that it probably needs two people, one to watch with the glasses, the other to wait for the word and then pull.

"Anyway there were still at least two geese within the catching area and several more perhaps within the catchable range after they got up, though I could not count on this as the wind was pretty strong. Then the geese dealt with my net in another way. They would walk up to within fifteen feet of it —only a few feet outside the catching area—and then get up and fly ten yards over it, pitching a few feet upwind.

"But in spite of all these difficulties there still seemed to be a chance of a good pull: only five or six feet outside the catching area were a dozen or more geese. About fifty yards downwind of the net was a beautiful adult Whitefront who was being rudely chased about by the surrounding Pinkfeet. He had a large white blaze on his forehead and very prominent black bars which first drew my attention to him.

"All this time there were so many geese between me and the net that it was only with difficulty that I could see my marks. All seemed to be well; it seemed to be just a question of waiting; and then suddenly all the geese got up. The wind was such that in an instant they were twenty feet up and there was no possibility of a flying pull. The cause of this was later apparent. Two schoolboy friends coming to join me had stalked down the far ditch and had put them up from the upwind end. As it turned out, however, it was fortunate that they did so. When I went out to the net to see that all was well I found that in my haste in the dark I had left in one of the safety pegs which held down the springs during the time of setting. Removal of the two safety pegs had to be done last when setting was complete, and I had forgotten one of them. Only one of the 'poles' would have gone over had I pulled. This of course was largely the result of having moved the net in the dark, a completely unnecessary performance.

"On the following morning, the farmer having extended netting permission for another day, I got up by myself and went down to the net. It was blowing hard and streaming with rain, altogether one of the nastiest mornings I ever ventured forth upon. I put on my new oilskin cape over my old oily and armed with three torches for marking the net so as to know where to put the guy pegs I started work on setting up in a new position on the opposite side of the field. While kneeling down the wind blew under my cape and blew it over my head, my hands were full with a spring half compressed and by the time I could get the peg in the cape had gone. Hastily leaving a torch to mark the net I went off after it and found it nearly 100 yards away, which gives some idea of the strength of the wind—not a very hopeful day for netting for that reason. I had no decoys with me, trusting to the field being full again as before.

"Everything was ready and I had dug myself a reasonably good hole in the dyke side when it got light, but no geese came and as it gradually grew lighter and lighter I began to fear that they would not come at all. I saw a very distant bunch making in to the west, which looked even worse. Perhaps they had all gone that way. Then four geese came in low and would definitely have pitched had there been decoys but without them they would have none of the field and came on over me, only a few yards above my head. This made me think that the decoys would be needed after all and I set off at once to get them. I was half-way across the field when I saw some geese making very slow progress against the wind but straight to my field. It was a double lot and they drew in well, but only the back lot pitched and they went down in the field beyond the end of mine. I started to stalk back along the ditch and saw as I did so a wave of 1,000 geese coming, followed by many more. Some dropped into the head end of my field, others in the next, some even opposite the head of my dyke, looking down it; but they soon moved away and at last I managed to get back to my hole.

"There was no sun today and as shadow is one of the best forms of cover and this dyke was far shallower than yesterday's, I was not surprised that some of the geese saw me as they swung round to settle in my field. On the ground the geese were incredibly thick. The whole of the 2,000 must have been sitting on five or six acres. But so far they were all upwind of the net except for a tongue of geese feeding rather on the far side of the middle. These were walking very rapidly downwind, their feathers ruffled on their backs. Next to my ditch was a ridge of slightly higher ground. I had a big clod stuck up in front of me but this afforded no protection from the side so I had to cut away a fresh sod and push it gently up into view. In this way I could look at the net without being seen by the geese to one side of me.

"There were very soon geese within ten yards, and once I saw a goose's head in the field behind me, about fifteen yards away. He looked at me and I at him, but then he walked away without giving the alarm. I was still hoping for a big pull, hoping that perhaps the sun had been responsible for yesterday's failure in showing up the net and that today, without sun, they would notice it less and come closer to it. So I decided to bide my time. I wanted a nice bunch close up to the net. If on the other hand any geese were to sit for long in the catching area itself I should probably pull. I saw several sitting just downwind of the net with their heads up ready to jump, and before I could pull they had flapped up and pitched down on the other side. Again the release was too far from my hole. Then I saw a pair of geese settle, one of them actually on the net; he sat for ten seconds and then moved on. I should perhaps have pulled but I felt in no experimental mood, so I let him hop off.

"I knew after that that I would sooner or later get one that had made a mistake but I hoped still to get a couple or three. I looked back to the very close geese and they were very uneasy. A single goose paused for a long time at the extreme edge of the catching area and then finally flipped up and over the net.

This made me decide to pull for the very next goose which gave a chance. By this time it must have been eleven a.m. and as the geese had come in soon after seven-thirty I was beginning to get chilled, and there was quite a risk that something would disturb them.

"The next time I looked at the net there was a goose beetling across the catching area straight towards the far spring. I rushed for the wire and pulled, there was a roar of wings and half the geese got up. Some pitched again and some went away to the next farm. I looked up and there was what looked like one tiny goose caught in the net. I got up and walked out to it. In fact it was a very nice female in beautiful condition. I suppose it was after looking at the geese for so long through glasses that I had the illusion of its smallness. It had been a very poor throw and the goose was only caught in the very top of the net. Nor was it so firmly tangled up as its predecessors, although it took several minutes to extricate. I took her back to the dyke and cut her primary feathers; and there she was, the third Pinkfoot ever to be caught in my nets."

My diary entry concludes:

"These two days have been two of the most enjoyable I ever spent in pursuit of geese; and the total bag has been one goose . . . but alive."

Bagnes

CHAPTER 29

The Breaking Wave

MANY of our Norfolk summers
were spent at Horsey Hall where
we sailed on Horsey Mere—the easternmost of the Norfolk Broads
—which belonged to the estate. The coarse fishing was good too:
I once caught a Rudd there of one pound five ounces. I can
remember still the golden flash deep in the brown bog water
as I hooked it.

The Bitterns boomed and the Marsh Harriers hawked over
Horsey Breydon, the caterpillars of Swallowtails were still to be
found on the clumps of Milk Parsley along the banks of the
Meadow Dyke, and the rare Giant Sowthistle grew along the
Waxham Cut.

At Horsey the Norfolk coast is one long sandy beach backed by
high sand dunes. We used to play an exciting version of 'prisoner's
base' which required careful stalking among the dunes. The
sixteen-millimetre ciné camera which had been given to my
mother (with which I had filmed the decoy) was used in the summer holidays not so much for 'holiday snaps' of the family growing
up, as for short dramatic charades in which the family and guests
took part. As a small boy my brother Wayland was delightfully
innocent in a drama of piracy on Horsey Mere. Geoffrey Eley, the
banker, was nothing less than brilliant in the same film as the
principal villain, hiding behind the hollyhocks in the herbaceous
border.

When, as a schoolgirl with theatrical ambitions, Judy Campbell
came to stay, she was an obvious choice for the leading part in a
powerful drama which I had written. I was to direct the picture
and to play opposite her: its title, proposed by my stepfather,
was *The Breaking Wave*.

Shooting the film took a great deal of time that summer, but
at last it was completed. Then came the editing, which alas was

neglected. The film still exists, but only in the form of 'rushes'.
This was the story:

A young artist is standing among the tall marram grass of the
sand-dunes, painting the sea shore. He scarcely notices the figure
of a young girl walking down across the deserted beach. She goes
directly towards the sea's edge, but instead of stopping she walks
on fully dressed into the waves. Suddenly the painter's suspicion
is aroused. Does she really mean to drown herself? He lays down
his brushes, still uncertain. Then he starts down the beach
after her, as she wades deeper and deeper and finally disappears
from view in the sea. He is now running all out, but inevitably it is
some seconds before he reaches the water, and wades in after her.
For a moment he cannot see where she is, but a wave trough discloses her; he reaches her and carries her out over his shoulder.
He lays her on the sand and then begins artificial respiration.
He has laid her face downwards, her head turned sideways and
resting on one raised arm. He kneels beside her, pressing rhythmi-
cally with both hands in the small of her back, and watching her
profile and beneath it her hand. In time with the rhythm of the
artificial respiration he sees in his mind's eye (in the film by a
series of 'mixes') all the rhythmical things which the girl herself
might have been doing—combing her hair, playing a piano,
swaying to dance music, and gradually he falls in love with the
character he has given her and with the beauty of her face. He
works alone on the sand there for an hour, for two hours, for three
hours, until he is almost exhausted. He listens from time to time
to hear whether there is any return of the heartbeats, and finally
when there is none he realises that his love had died of drowning
before ever he found her.

I told the story one day to my godfather, Sir James Barrie.
He only said three words after I had finished: "That's rather
good." I fear it was more good manners than literary praise, but
I was very pleased.

There had been a break in my early tea-time visits to Adelphi
Terrace until a letter in April 1930:

". . . having heard a glorious rumour that you are growing
rather like your father I want very much to see you again, could
you come in and lunch with me on Wednesday or Thursday at
one-thirty. I should be very glad if you could. Yours sincerely,
J. M. Barrie."

I went often after that and, after my training as a painter in

Munich and London, I asked Barrie if I might paint his portrait. I knew that he had not previously allowed this to be done, and he told me that he did not think he should break his rule, "but I would very much like you to paint a picture of this room, and, who knows, when you have finished it you might find me sitting in a corner of it".

In January 1934 I found myself taking a canvas thirty inches by twenty, a box of oil paints, and a small portable easel into the famous room in the top flat of Adelphi Terrace House. The centre of my picture was to be the open hearth piled high with wood ash, surrounded with various characterful fire irons, a pair of bellows with long handles, and a brass kettle. On the left was to be the leather-covered pouf, on the right the inglenook containing the high-backed settle on which I hoped Barrie might sit as the picture advanced; and so in due course he did. I learned more of Barrie during the next few weeks than I had discovered in all the years of casual visits. He was no longer a godfatherly institution which rated a visit at about the same intervals as the zoo and the Natural History Museum; instead of a literary legend he was at last a real person. If he was older than he had been, so too was I, and our talk was easier than it had ever been. Often there were long silences which embarrassed neither of us. I painted and he sat gazing into the fire, enveloped in clouds of smoke from his pipe, and sometimes coughing alarmingly, so that I would suggest he smoked too much. Once I asked him whether he had ever planned a conclusion to his one-act play *Shall We Join the Ladies*. I told him that I had tried to work out plausible second and third acts for it, but had not been successful. He said, "I never could make out which of them did it, and I don't suppose the mystery will ever be solved"; then, "Most of them must be dead now anyway."

I asked him whether he would write any more plays, but he said he was seventy-four and he doubted if he would. I said something empty like "Oh, what a pity", and there it might quite easily have ended, but evidently he wanted to go on thinking about writing. Suddenly he began to talk—excited talk of the days when he first came to London, of the Davis boys whom he had brought up after their father died, of how *Peter Pan* grew out of them; he talked about village cricket and about the Outer Hebrides and the origins of *Mary Rose*, he talked about the theatre in a friendly, loving way. I asked him how long it was since he had been to a play and he said three years. I said I thought

this should be remedied; I had just seen a play which I thought
he should see.

I have already recorded my greatest claim to musical fame—
that I once played poker with Richard Strauss. I come now to
record my greatest claim to literary fame which is perhaps more
firmly based. It happened thus.

Soon after I began painting Barrie I was taken to Margaret
Kennedy's play *Escape Me Never* in which the Viennese actress
Elisabeth Bergner was appearing at the Apollo Theatre. Ever
since reading *The Constant Nymph* I had greatly admired Margaret
Kennedy and it seemed that she had produced, if not a perfect
play, at least a perfect vehicle for the art of Elisabeth Bergner.
Her performance as the young waif Gemma Jones moved me so
much that I went to see the play again. It chanced too that my
mother was instrumental in finding a house in Hampstead for
Bergner and her husband, Paul Czinner. I went to the play a
third time and a fourth.

When I first proposed to take him to the Apollo Theatre, Barrie
was full of excuses. He said that he did not go to the theatre these
days and did not think that he would enjoy it very much anyway.
But I was not prepared to take no for an answer. I made a careful
plan with Frank Thurston, his manservant. "I'm coming to dinner
with you on Wednesday, and if you feel like it, we'll go to the
theatre afterwards," I said, and left it at that. I had already
bought the tickets and when the day came we dined together in
his flat, delightfully as ever. After it Frank appeared with his coat.
"Time to go now, Sir James," he said, and the pressure from both
of us was too great. A few minutes later we were off to the theatre
in my car. At the interval Barrie said nothing about the play or
the performance. It would have been quite wrong to ask. We sat
in silence. I scribbled a message on a programme and sent it
round to Bergner saying that I had Barrie with me and might I
perhaps bring him round to see her afterwards. Curiously enough
there was no reply at the next interval; I must have given inadequate details of where we were sitting. But in spite of this I felt
so sure that she would like to see him that we went.

In the last scene of *Escape Me Never* Gemma Jones breaks down
into hysterical laughter from which I had always noticed that she
was in tears at the final curtain call. When we found Bergner in
the passage just outside her dressing-room she was still in tears.
Without saying anything at all she took Barrie's hand and held it
for rather a long time while fresh tears coursed down her cheeks.

We hardly stayed with her at all. Barrie said, "Will you come and have tea with me on Friday?" She said, "Yes, where do I come?" I stepped in quickly and said, "Never mind about that, I will fetch you." And their first meeting was over.

I took Barrie back still in complete silence; it was not for me to break in on his thoughts. I was still not quite sure whether it had been a success.

Next day I was round at his flat and at work on the painting again. Barrie was pacing up and down as he so often did, smoking his pipe, coughing a little, his voice occasionally crackling, one eyebrow raised:

"You've unsettled me . . ."

"Oh dear," I began to apologise.

"I told you that I had given up writing. Since last night I've decided to take it up again." Then after a pause: "I haven't felt like this about an actress since the first time I saw Pauline Chase."

"What will the play be about?" I asked foolishly, but he did not answer. Thank goodness he hardly seemed to have heard the stupid question. In pigeon-holes in his mind he must have had many ideas, but the theme of his last play, *The Boy David*, seems to have come from Bergner. For the rest of the afternoon, as I painted, we reminded each other excitedly of the play we had seen. "Do you remember where she says . . . ?" "Did you notice her hands when he came in in Act Two?"

I did not know until long afterwards when I read it in Cynthia Asquith's *Portrait of Barrie* that he had taken her to *Escape Me Never* on the very next night after I had taken him.

The picture was not completed for a week or two after that, but it was clear that the new play was not only secret but also taboo as a topic of conversation and I never returned to it. Nor was I ever allowed to be present when Bergner had tea with Barrie, although for some weeks I maintained the illusion that his flat was too difficult to find without an experienced guide. Twice a week, and sometimes more often, I would go to collect her in my car at Frognal and deposit her at Adelphi Terrace, returning for her after tea and driving her home again.

It was not for another two years that the new play finally went into rehearsal and thereafter every conceivable kind of bad luck attended the production—illness, unfounded rumours, a string of postponements, and the Abdication, which burst upon London at the same time as *The Boy David*. When the play began its run I was abroad and by the time I returned it had been taken off. Four months later my godfather died.

My picture, with Barrie sitting in the corner of it, had been bought soon after it was completed by Elisabeth herself, who was just as enchanting off the stage as on it. My heart had been lost to her from her very first entry as Gemma Jones on the first time that I saw *Escape Me Never*. She liked to drive in my rather dilapidated Morris touring car with the hood down, and she liked to be taken to the cinema, wearing dark glasses so as not to be mobbed. She had never, she told me, seen any of her own films, and could not bear to do so, but I remember taking her especially to see a film in which Marlene Dietrich's daughter, who was I think her god-daughter, was appearing; and on another day to see Katherine Hepburn in Barrie's *The Little Minister*. A few days before I had taken Barrie to see it and it had been a disastrous flop. The idea had been his and I had been very reluctant. I felt fairly sure that they would have taken terrible liberties with Barrie's story and I doubted whether Hepburn's art would appeal to him anyway. The combination seemed doomed to failure, but Barrie said he had steeled himself to it, so in mid-afternoon we went. But the picture had been on for less than ten minutes when he leant over and murmured "Shall we go now?" Perhaps it was her curiosity to know what Barrie did *not* like which made Elisabeth want to see it.

Once she came to tea at Leinster Corner and arrived half an hour early. She had been shown into the drawing-room, and I found her curled up in a chair like a kitten, fast asleep. Once I got into terrible trouble for sitting in the front row of the stalls at her play (it was the only seat I could get and the seventeenth time I had seen it). "How could you!" she said indignantly. "How *could* you do it!" I must have looked very crestfallen and bewildered, for she ran laughing across the room and kissed me as a signal of forgiveness; time stood still just long enough for me to recognise that this was something I should never forget in all my life.

CHAPTER 30

The Lighthouse

THE stretch of saltings lying between King's Lynn and the River Nene, which had been variously known by us as 'Sandbanks', then 'Skeldyke' and then 'Sandbanks' again, is marked on the map as Terrington Marsh. At the western end it is sharply bounded by the artificial cut which brings the River Nene out into the Wash. The completion of this cut, built at the end of the eighteenth century as a final stage in the draining of the Great Fens, was commemorated by the construction of two small ornamental lighthouses, one on each side of the river at its mouth. They had been a landmark to us ever since we first began to visit these marshes, and no doubt they were a landmark to ships coming up the river, but they were never lit. According to the legend they had once carried a light shining from the round windows of their top floors, but as they were sited for ornament rather than for navigation, they had only confused the mariners, so the story went, and brought shipwreck and disaster until their lights were dowsed.

Although I had been thinking of trying to acquire the disused East Lighthouse for some time, it was not until 1933 that I made an approach to the Nene Catchment Board for a lease, which was immediately granted at a rent of £5 a year. My new home was then still in use as a 'hailing post' of H.M. Customs and Excise. Two officers were stationed at Sutton Bridge, three miles up the river, and one or other of them arrived half an hour before high water; with a megaphone he hailed any ship that might be entering or leaving the river, and half an hour after high water he left again.

Earlier the lighthouse had been in more continuous use as a dwelling-house for a man who worked on the river bank and his family, but it had been condemned as too damp and had stood vacant (but for the Customs officers' short visits) for several years until I took it over, re-pointed the brickwork, and lined the walls inside to make it reasonably dry.

As you turned down towards the lighthouse, following the river from the swing bridge for road and railway across the Nene, you could see your destination three miles away. The road was good for the first part, past farms and cottages, but for the last half mile you had to drive along the grassy top of the sea-wall on which the car slipped and slithered. I was perpetually surprised that no one ever skidded into the river; nor was any car ever seriously stuck, though I once had to go to the rescue of my old headmaster, Kenneth Fisher, who, in the dark, thought he must have missed the way, for no one surely could regularly take a car along so perilous a bank.

The Nene had a rise and fall of about thirty feet and at low water there was a steep slope of soft mud held together by often renewed faggots. At the point where the sea-wall, running east and west to protect the reclaimed fields, met the bank of the river running north and south, you arrived at a gate, and seventy yards beyond it stood the East Lighthouse on a short projection of the river bank which jutted out into the saltings. A hundred yards away across the river stood its twin—the West Lighthouse. Nowadays the reclamations of the Wash have pushed far out over those saltings, but in the 1930s the spring tides surrounded my lighthouse on three sides, covering the great expanse of saltmarsh to the foot of the bank.

It was a conical brick building looking rather more like a windmill without sails than a conventional lighthouse. It had four storeys, the bottom one sixteen feet in diameter and above it three rooms in which the diameter became progressively smaller until, in the top one it was little more than six feet. There was only just room for a divan bed up there, but it was a room with a wonderful view from each of its two opposing round windows, one looking up the straight river on a scene of parallel lines converging at the vanishing point, the other down over the Wash and its sandbanks and mudflats and saltings.

The floor below this was my bedroom; on its pale green walls flew ghostly geese, outlined in white, for ever circling the room. Below the green room was the pink room on the first floor—a double-bedded sitting-room. Its two beds hung on stout ropes from each corner to the ceiling. A system of blocks and tackles was used to haul the beds up to within a few inches of the ceiling when they were not in use, so that the room could be a sitting-room.

Whereas the upper rooms were reached by ladders through trapdoors, the first floor was connected with the ground floor by a curved stairway which followed a sector of the wall. It debouched into the ground-floor room with a simple but attractive Georgian banister. In the early days this room, which was living-room and studio, was also shared at high water with the Customs Officer.

As a lean-to on the ground floor was a small room which had evidently been built on at a later date than the original house. This was used as a kitchen and I built a small bathroom beyond it. There was also a basement room reached by outside steps in which a rather splendid nomadic character called Charlie had his home when he was not sleeping under a hedge. Charlie was a great big friendly red-headed man who collected cockles and samphire in the summer and did handyman jobs in the winter.

At first I had visualised the lighthouse as a temporary head-quarters for wildfowling week-ends, in which some of the gear might be stored in the dry until the following week-end. It was not for several months that I began to see it as a potentially permanent dwelling-place. It was necessary, for example, to pipe fresh water to it and this could only be done across the river from a main near the West Lighthouse. It was easier than I had expected: we simply started out from the far shore with a boatful of pipes and joined one on to the next, allowing them to sag down on to the bed of the river and continuing the process until the boat reached the other side. The supply was secure only so long as no ship came up the river, as they were reported sometimes still to do, steaming stern first and dragging an anchor up the river bed. But the pipeline lasted without breakage for the next five years.

The East Lighthouse was my home until the beginning of the Second World War. During those five years there were, of course, many developments. I added, for example, a flat-roofed studio overlooking the marsh, a larger bathroom and a bunk room con-nected with the garage and boathouse which I had put up initially. The additions included a new front door leading from the gravel driveway into a small hall. This was altogether more respectable than the original entrance through the kitchen. With a front door it became a proper house.

But the arrangements for keeping live waterfowl on the marsh all round the house were even more important.

Although I like to remember the lighthouse in its final form—as it was for the last two or three years I was there—the original primitive and ignorant ideas we put into practice for housing the birds we had caught with our nets are worth recording if only to show how it should not be done.

Already the collection at Lilford, visited in school and university days, had encouraged us to think in terms of keeping live birds ourselves. Michael Bratby was keeping some Canada Geese and a few ducks at his home in Cheshire; Mervyn Ingram had some ducks at his home in Kent; Christopher Dalgety, who now had a house near Denver, also had an enclosure for geese and ducks; my new friend Will Tinsley had his collection on the little pond and in the orchard at the Poplars. Clearly I must have some kind of enclosure for birds near the lighthouse.

For some time we had been sending birds caught in the flight-nets on the saltings at Sandbanks to Mr. Moody at Lilford. One dark night more geese than usual flew into these nets and next day about a dozen were offered to us by the flight-netters. I decided that these must form the nucleus of my own collection, to which would be added the three I had caught with my spring net, now in temporary residence at the Poplars.

First an enclosure must be made and this had to be done quickly; at the ironmongers in the village of Sutton Bridge I bought a fifty-yard roll of six-foot wire netting and some metal stakes. This roll was set up round a little pool on the salting within a stone's throw of the lighthouse. It could only be twenty yards long and five yards wide and into this tiny area the fifteen geese were introduced. Soon I realised that something very much larger was necessary, and this required a certain amount of planning and could not immediately be provided.

The fifteen geese had only been there a week when, during a fog, some wild geese settled on the marsh close by. One of these flew into the pen, but was very soon chased out again by the ganders in possession. The newcomer was a young bird and he refused to be driven right away but walked up and down just outside the pen where he was safe from the attacks of the pinioned birds inside. He stayed there for a week or so and became quite tame; for security when anyone appeared he would flap up over the fence and into the enclosure. We called him (for no reason that I can remember) Egbert, and I tried to get a close up film of him rising and settling. The trouble was to make him fly and we used to do this by throwing small lumps of mud or potatoes at him;

even then only a direct hit was effective. He became quite expert at dodging even the best aimed missiles, and when he was hit he would jump up about ten feet into the air and then settle again. All this time it was possible to stand within three or four yards of him and watch him behaving as unconcernedly as if he had been far out on the mudflats, or sitting in the middle of a fifty-acre potato field.

One day in the middle of February when there was a strong north-east wind and a big spring tide the waves raced in over the saltings and right up to the sea-wall. They beat on the wire netting of my little goose pen and the weight of the debris, the dead leaves of the marsh plants and other flotsam, lay against the wire until it collapsed. Out swam the fifteen geese and half an hour later I saw the little flotilla far out among the breakers nearly a mile from the shore. When the tide began to fall the geese had long since disappeared from view. It was very cold with sleet and searching with glasses out of doors was almost impossible. That night we went to bed feeling very miserable, and wondering how our pinioned geese would fare.

Early the next morning I went up to the round window at the top of the lighthouse to spy the marsh with glasses. To my astonishment sitting in the middle of the mangled remains of the pen was a goose. I thought at once that it must be Egbert who had flown back, but it was not: it was one of the pinioned birds who had walked back into the middle of the pen and was sitting there apparently feeling quite at home, and waiting for his breakfast. That day a local wildfowler brought another back. We made up the pen again and on the following morning I was awakened by a familiar honk; running to the window I was just in time to see Egbert circle round and settle again in his usual place just outside the pen. Of the rest of the geese, as far as I know only one met with tragedy: he was shot. All the rest were caught and all but three were returned to me, the three being sold to someone else before I heard of their capture; but I was assured they had gone to a good home.

Egbert developed a rather dangerous habit of flying down to the river to wash, and as the new pen which I was then in process of building contained perfectly good washing accommodation, I thought that this habit should be discouraged. I was not at all sure that some unscrupulous character with a gun might not shoot Egbert from the river bank, even if he knew full well that it was Egbert. So I stretched a net over half the pen and then walked the geese under it. Twice Egbert flew up, refusing to go under the net, but each time trying to settle on top of it. When he found that awkward he flew down to the river. But each time after a few minutes he came back, swinging in over the wire and settling in the open half of the pen. At the third attempt he walked under with the pinioned birds. His escape was quickly blocked and soon afterwards Egbert could no longer endanger his life in that fool-hardy way.

In due course the new enclosure of about three acres of salting was completed and the twelve Pinkfeet (including Egbert, now in permanent residence) were released into their new home, there later to be joined by ducks and geese of many other species as my small collection grew.

In the earliest days the 'tame' geese at the lighthouse were far from tame. In the larger pen I found that they spent most of their time keeping as far away from the observer as possible. In order to see them closer we had to hide in the garage and peep out of the window at them. I had still to learn that the two secrets are use and example. There is hardly anything which a goose (and it applies to many other animals too) will not get accustomed to if it happens often enough without any disastrous result. To make my birds tamer they must see more people, not less. But it also helps if there is a nucleus of hand-reared birds thoroughly accus-tomed to seeing people near-by and unwilling to be disturbed by it. When once these principles were understood the birds round the lighthouse quickly grew tame and soon many of them came to feed from my hand.

The lighthouse itself was in the middle of my new enclosure. The geese would finally hardly move out of the way of cars or people as they came along the top of the bank.

Birds need regular feeding and it was necessary to employ someone to look after them. Charlie, who lived in the basement, had shown himself not to be sufficiently reliable, and he had finally neglected the birds and remained absent for several days. Probably I had been over-optimistic in believing that he was employable. His independence had to be admired, but I could not afford to pay him good money unless I could be sure that my birds were fed.

His place was taken by a no less unusual character who was well known as a local poacher. Kenzie Thorpe had Romany origins; he was a middle-weight boxer, a skilled wildfowler and an invet-erate poacher. But he knew something about the local wildfowl and I could not help liking him, in spite of the circumstances of our first meeting.

One morning at Sandbanks several years before, David Haig Thomas had shot a goose which slanted away across the ditch on the other side of the field. From far to one side a long shot had been fired at the bird which was already half-way to the ground, and Kenzie and a companion had jumped out of the ditch and gone to collect it. When David went over to fetch his goose Kenzie refused to part with it, disclosed that he was poaching, and threatened to sock David on the jaw if he came any nearer. I had joined in the argument when we met him on the outmarsh later in the day. From then onwards I had met him only occasionally, but on the principle that poachers make good gamekeepers I decided to engage him to look after my collection. By and large the arrangement worked well, and Kenzie was soon quite expert in the care of live waterfowl.

There came a time when it seemed that if the Customs Officers had a small hut for their hailing station and sited it on the other side of the river, it would be altogether more convenient for everyone. When this had been done and my new studio had been built, the lighthouse was as near perfect for all my purposes as I could make it. I began to paint hard.

CHAPTER 31   *Bond Street*

OIL PAINTS rather than water-colours, and large canvases rather
than small . . . I selected both because I wanted to escape from
the preoccupation with tiny detail which had so greatly affected
my early work. I painted from memory, which is to say that I
did not find it necessary to have what I was painting in front of
me as I worked. In the case of flying birds this would in any case
scarcely have been practicable. I had in mind a conception of what
had stirred me when I had seen it out on the marshes. The picture
became a mixture between this image which I could still dimly
see and the chosen subject expressed in words. By this I mean
that the completed work was in part a direct visual translation
of what I had seen and in part an indirect, almost, literary translation of what I imagined it ought to look like. The preponderance
of one influence over the other varied from picture to picture.
There is nothing unusual in this combination. It is a formula
probably used for the majority of paintings now executed. Both
kinds of translation give scope for artistic individuality—in one
case it is what the artist sees, in the other what he thinks. What
he feels may shine through either or both.

My earlier works painted at the decoy had shown a certain
hasty and ignorant crudeness. Now at the lighthouse I seemed
to have advanced beyond that stage, but there was always the
danger of losing the original freshness and vigour.

I quickly discovered that if I worked for too long on a painting
I was quite capable of ruining it. Working fast was the secret of
quality as well as quantity. But I was also brimming over with
new ideas. I could not wait until one picture was finished before
starting the next, and I soon found that this was in fact a practical
method; the first stage of one picture could be drying while the
next was started. It also gave me the chance to adjust my work to

my mood. If I was feeling creative I could start on a blank canvas, if not, I could go quietly on with the chores—putting on a large area of blue sky, or laboriously painting up flocks of birds whose shapes and pattern I had already determined. I painted in bouts of intense energy, working all day and long into the night with two Aladdin mantle lamps, one at either side of the canvas; often I had no idea how the colour would look when I saw it again in the daylight. I can remember the tremendous excitement of coming down in a dressing-gown in the morning to see how it looked; and the bitter disappointment when my corrections for the artificial light had been faulty and half the picture had to be painted all over again. I can remember often, too, going to bed when a half-finished work was on the easel and just before I went to sleep seeing the picture finished in my mind's eye—in that moment of truth between waking and sleeping—and then being furious that it had gone from me by the morning. But in those wonderful days there were few frustrations. I was not trying to do anything very complicated. I set out to put my birds and my wild places on my canvas and, by and large, my training allowed me to put them there more or less as I meant to. Sometimes the conception rather than the image took charge—the idea 'on paper' dictated a sequence of developments in the picture which swamped the original memory so that it finished up quite unlike what I had initially imagined, but sometimes rather better.

I was painting hard for another exhibition after the unexpected success of my first in 1933, which had been opened by Sir Samuel Hoare. I had to produce about forty more pictures. At the speed I worked this was not difficult, and I still had plenty of exciting ideas—far more than I could ever undertake.

My exhibitions at Ackermann's Galleries followed annually. Forty new oil-paintings and a few drawings a year, mostly of my beloved wildfowl with occasional portraits or pictures of sailing boats. If one of the requirements of a portrait was to paint a likeness, the same requirement must surely, I thought, apply to a picture of a bird. Gradually as the years went by, the likenesses of the birds in my pictures improved, and my earlier works, when I saw them again, left me dissatisfied. Why did I not see when I was painting it that the shape of that wing was all wrong? It sticks out a mile now; but I suppose I just did not know enough then. How could I have let such careless ignorance of the anatomy of that leg go by without correction? And so the anatomy got better, the lighting became more true, the creatures came to life. But these improvements in my work went unnoticed by all except the few who really knew the birds. The study and the loving care which made my pictures have greater truth did not necessarily make them have any greater artistic impact on the inexpert eye of the majority who came to see them. To many the whole business was repetitious . . . without detectable progress.

In the social and financial fields however the exhibitions were increasingly successful. In 1934 the opening was performed by John Buchan; in 1935 by Hugh Walpole; in 1936 by Sir James Jeans, the astronomer; in 1937 by G. M. Trevelyan, the historian; in 1938 by James Stephen, the poet; in 1939 by Vincent Massey, the High Commissioner for Canada. Each of them came to New Bond Street on a summer's afternoon, said a few well chosen, often witty words, and launched me into another London season. It had all become alarmingly, dangerously, but delightfully fashionable. I used to go daily to the gallery, which was a pleasant opportunity of meeting my friends. A continuous stream of them turned up, unexpectedly, and in the most improbable juxtaposition; I very often found myself forgetting all about meals because so many entertaining people came in at lunch time.

One very hot June afternoon an old friend from Cambridge days walked into the gallery rather smartly dressed and carrying a straw hat. He was looking as handsome and charming as ever. I had not seen him for a year or two since he had spent part of a summer holiday with us in Norfolk. He told me that he was trying to get a job in films and had that morning been calling on Mr. Sam Goldwyn. It appeared that Mr. Goldwyn had paid little attention to him, being much too preoccupied with a new young actor called Franchot Tone. "But," said my friend, whose name was James Mason, "I think I'll go and see him again later. I don't like taking 'no' for an answer."

The first royal visit to one of my exhibitions began disastrously. I was sitting on one of the print cupboards in the outer room of the gallery, dangling my legs over the edge and talking to Betty Gilbert, who helped to sell the pictures, when two ladies came in. One of the faces was vaguely familiar, so I smiled, nodded benefi-cently and went on talking to Betty. The two ladies passed on into the inner room. Betty said, "Wasn't that the Princess Royal?" "Great heavens! Of course it was—how awful!" In confusion I dashed through to apologise, but Her Royal Highness would allow it no further thought and in a moment we were discussing the Whooper Swans which came to the lake at Harewood.

The Queen [H.M. Queen Elizabeth the Queen Mother] came to a later exhibition and bought a fiery picture of Pinkfeet coming out from inland to the mudflats of the Wash at dusk. She told me she had once seen them against such a sunset on the Wolferton marshes below Sandringham. Queen Mary also came to Acker- mann's Galleries during the series of pre-war exhibitions, but gave no real indication of what she thought of the pictures. Perhaps she liked them, for she came again some time after the war, in a wheel chair.

It seemed that success in Bond Street was a handicap in artistic circles. My pictures were less readily accepted by the Royal Academy, though I knew they were better than the earlier ones. From time to time they would take a very large oil-painting of flying birds, chiefly, I think, because they thought it would be comparatively easy to hang. A great sky full of birds could with justification be 'skied'—would indeed look the better for being hung at the very top of a wall of pictures. Recognising this partic- ular niche which it seemed possible I might continue to fill, I sent in each year an elongated, freeze-like picture of wild geese in flight against the sky, with no ground in the picture at all.

Reproductions of my works in print form were now beginning to sell well. *Norfolk Spring-Shovelers* or *Taking to Wing*, published by the Medici Society, had already had some success; proofs in colour collotype printed by the Chiswick Press for Ackermann's in a limited edition, in accordance with the provisions of the Fine Arts Trade Guild, were appearing twice a year and being sold out. Each 'Artist's Proof' in these editions of 550 copies had to be signed in pencil. Signing one's name 550 times in quick succession is a curious task. To begin with I found it impossible to think of anything else except signing my name. If my mind wandered I began to write other words than my name. Signing the 550 proofs in those early days seemed an endless business. Perhaps under the influence of the autograph-hunting craze or perhaps only because of longer practice, the ceremony has largely lost its terrors. I find now that I can carry on a lively conversation about entirely extraneous subjects while signing my name con- tinuously and that, by sloping the pile and with someone to turn back the signed ones and the interleaved tissue paper, 550 prints can be signed in slightly under three-quarters of an hour.

I had not long been living at the lighthouse when I had my first introduction to the film industry.

The Private Life of the Gannet was a documentary film which had a great success. At the instigation of Julian Huxley, it had been made for Alexander Korda on the island of Grassholm off the Welsh coast. Korda was anxious to follow it up with a new natural history documentary and someone had suggested to him that it might be about wild geese. Accordingly I was engaged, in an advisory capacity, to make what would, in effect, be *The Private Life of the Pinkfoot*. Two cameramen, Bernard Brown and Donald Gallai-Hatchard, were assigned to the project and arrived in due course at the lighthouse. For some weeks we collected film material on the Wash and in the neighbouring Fens.

But whereas the gannet is a large white bird which assembles in huge numbers in midsummer on an island where it goes about its business supremely unaffected by the proximity of human beings, a Pink-footed Goose is a dark grey bird which, in Britain, assembles only in winter when the days are short, the weather bad, and the light poor, and which minds very much when human beings attempt to come closer than 300 yards. This was a distinction which I had tried to make plain when the project was first put to me by Korda, but which was only finally recognised after many weeks of almost abortive filming.

Once when watching 'rushes' in the projection theatre of London Film Productions a film test had to be sandwiched in between two of our reels. A very nervous young foreign actress sat down beside me. It was her first film test and she was in despair about the piece of Juliet she had done for it, though I could not see why; I thought she played it beautifully. The executive who sat the other side of her was inscrutable, but she got the part. Her name was Lilli Palmer.

This was the heyday of Korda's film making. *Sanders of the River* with Paul Robeson and Leslie Banks was in production and I was allowed to watch the shooting of some of the studio sequences. The film industry had its glamour and watching Zoltan Korda directing *Sanders* was immensely fascinating, but now, too, I had experienced the preposterous extravagance and inefficiency. My cameramen had arrived on the Wash in a Daimler, with a uniformed chauffeur. Car and driver had remained with us for three weeks at £5 a day. The cameras could have ridden in my car for the cost of the petrol.

Try though they might—and both 'Brownie' and 'Hatch' were hard workers, full of early-rising keenness and enthusiasm for the magic of the geese—they could not get the shots they wanted. The Pinkfeet and the English winter combined to beat us, and the film was never completed. We had some lovely shots, but not enough, and we had spent our budget. In the long winter evenings 'Hatch' had written a delightful dance tune called 'The Turn of the Tide', and I had offered him a neater last line to his melody which to my surprise he had accepted. I had learned a little about filming wild life and a lot more about the geese. My small excursion into the film industry had revealed the dangers and difficulties and frustrations, and left me with the determination to explore it no further. But it had all been very interesting while it lasted.

5

Whisper leading in the Prince of Wales's Cup race in Osborne Bay, Nicky Cooke sitting out well. A few minutes later the mast fell over the side.

1937   An early portrait: John Winter.

CHAPTER 32   *My First Fourteen-Footer*

THE family had now spent its summer holidays in Norfolk for a
good many years and for me the sailing had been growing more
and more important. There were regattas which could not be
missed, and particularly the week of racing on Oulton Broad
followed by 'Sea Week' at Lowestoft with the Royal Norfolk and
Suffolk Yacht Club as headquarters. There were one-designs and
dinghies to crew in, and occasionally to sail, and there was a
growing circle of Norfolk friends. My Cambridge contemporary
Stewart Morris was still the most promising young helmsman.
In 1932 at Torquay he had won the Prince of Wales's Cup—the
Championship of the International fourteen-foot dinghies—for the
first time. Stewart aroused all my competitive instincts. If he
could be a 'champ' why should not I be one? But it would mean
having to have my own dinghy . . . Could I afford it? Perhaps
with the success of my first exhibition I could; but more important, did I really know enough about boats to look after it
properly? And was I going to come across the sailing equivalent
of those tedious skating loops? The first thing seemed to be to sail
in as many races as possible. Here my benefactors were the Colman
family of mustard fame. Old Russell Colman, father of the family,
had been a great helmsman in his day, and I can see him now at
the helm of his Broads One Design during Sea Week. More
clearly I remember him sitting at the club-house on Regatta days
telling inimitable stories in Norfolk dialect, making net bags and
giving them away as soon as they were finished. His sons Geoffrey
and Alan, his grandson George Lockett, his splendid old skipper
Ernie Drake, the Colman boat-house and lawn . . . all were part
of the pattern of those late summer regattas at Oulton Broad in the
1930s.
    Alan Colman had invited me to 'crew' him in his International

fourteen-foot dinghy *Telemark*, and I had accepted with alacrity; this seemed to be the very chance I needed to get more experience. *Telemark* was a new boat built by Uffa Fox by the new stressed skin method which required no conventional ribs. For a year or two he built a number of these boats—known as 'the boneless wonders'—until it was found that they did not hold their shape well enough, and the system was abandoned.

The Prince of Wales's Cup of 1933 was raced in light airs at Lowestoft, and *Telemark* was not in the prize list. As far as I can remember we were somewhere about twelfth. Stewart Morris won for the second year running, Chris Ratsey of the famous sail-making firm at Cowes was second, and Sir John Beale's eldest son, James, was third.

Alan, nothing daunted by my shortcomings as a crew, invited me to crew him in America: a team of three boats was to be taken over to demonstrate the capabilities of the International fourteen-foot class. The other two boats were to be sailed by James Beale and Phyllis Richardson.

Mrs. Richardson was very tall with white curly hair and an air of slight puzzlement. She had sailed all her life and was always crewed in her dinghy by her husband, Colonel Henry Richardson. They had two teenage children who did not much care for sailing, and they lived in a fine Georgian house overlooking Lough Erne in Co. Fermanagh. 'Aunt Phyllis' as she was afterwards called by most of the dinghy sailors when her nephew Brian became one of them, had been in the prize list of nearly every Prince of Wales's Cup since it began, but she had never quite managed to win it. Each year she brought her dinghy to Oulton Broad and Lowestoft; the regattas would not have been the same without her.

Uffa Fox was also to accompany us on the trip to America. Uffa, named after an early Saxon king, must have been about thirty then and already he had built up an impressive reputation as a designer, as a helmsman and as an *enfant terrible*. He had black curly hair, a laugh which stopped all conversation in a crowded room, and an irresistible urge to shock the strait-laced. He liked to be unconventional; the only shoes he brought with him to America were white gym shoes, and he resolutely wore them at all the evening parties. In public speaking his choice of unexpected words kept his audience (especially those who were fellow guests) on the edges of their chairs. He had a rugged common-sense philosophy, he sang sea shanties, liked beer, and was basically kind. I thought him a great man at the time and having known him well ever since, in good times and in bad, I have no reason to change my view.

We took the dinghies over in the liner *Olympic* and raced them not very successfully at the Seawanhaka Yacht Club in Oyster Bay, Long Island. We stayed in various different houses near-by, all belonging to millionaire yachtsmen who talked of the America's Cup and considered that nothing smaller than a Six Metre could really be regarded as a yacht. But the interest that we aroused in the fourteen-footers was to have large-scale results in the more distant future. Meanwhile the trip had immediately widened my own sailing experience. Alan Colman having financed my passage to America, it was only fair that I should look after his boat. I was determined that everything should be in absolute readiness when he arrived before a race, and that I alone should be responsible for putting the boat to bed when we got back. There was a paid hand who went over too and he and I in fact looked after all three boats. By the end of that trip to America I reckoned I knew as much about the care and maintenance of a dinghy as I needed to know in order to justify becoming the owner of one myself. Before we started back I had commissioned Uffa to build me my first International fourteen-foot dinghy. At that time Uffa built his boats in a converted 'floating bridge'—one of the old chain ferryboats which had been used between East and West Cowes. He had moored her near high water-mark on the flats of the Medina a mile or so above East Cowes. In the early spring I went down for the launching of my new boat, and soon afterwards for her first races.

In the car with me were two acquaintances who were to become lifelong friends—John Winter and Beecher Moore. John was the eldest of three brothers. His father, who taught engineering in the University, had been Rear Commodore of the Cambridge University Cruising Club in the old days when I had sailed at Ely. The Winters lived in the beautiful mill house at Grantchester, overlooking the pool below the bridge. John had been brought up in small boats. At an early meeting at Ely he had shown interest in *Kazarka* and later he had come out punting with me on the Wash for a couple of days. He was tall and dark and good-natured, with a wide friendly smile, and as a dinghy sailor he was already obviously destined to be a champion. He owned a fourteen-footer called *Lightning*, although he was to sail a borrowed boat at this first meeting of the season.

In the Prince of Wales's Cup of the previous summer John had been crewed by a young American, Beecher Moore, who worked in his father's firm—Moore's Modern Methods—in London. I had first been introduced to Beecher at the Ice Club by the American skating champion Maribel Vinson, and it was pleasantly unexpected to meet him again in dinghy sailing circles. Beecher was large and heavy and strong, yet John reported that he was surprisingly nippy about the boat. He usually looked mildly surprised—an impression which may have been conveyed by his eyebrows, or by his brown hair which stood up on his head almost like a shaving-brush. He was above everything an enthusiast, and he turned out to be an excellent crew. My beautiful new boat acquitted herself well, and I was once more absorbed and absolutely happy in the technicalities of my new endeavour.

Eastlight's initial success so greatly encouraged me that I decided to keep a detailed record of her every race. As ever I began to indulge my capacity for recording useless details. Just as I had recorded every bird and beast that was shot during our wildfowling expeditions, I now recorded the exact position of *Eastlight* in every round of every race that I sailed in her.

More than twenty years later when I was bitten by a new sport, gliding, I found myself recording in exactly the same way every detail of every flight that I made. I think I am an incurable recorder.

CHAPTER 33

Eastlight *in Canada*

SAILING a fourteen-foot dinghy—my very own fourteen-foot dinghy —was utterly satisfying. I enjoyed it most in a breeze of wind. Beating to windward I sat on the gunwale, shoulder to shoulder with my crew. With our toes tucked under a special strap we both leant as far out as we could to bring the boat upright, trying to counteract the heeling moment of the wind. If our combined weight was not enough, then by easing the mainsail a little the heel was reduced. In one hand I held the mainsheet leading from a block on the transom, and I played the wind as one might play a fish. In the other hand I held the tiller extension or 'joystick' hinged out at right angles to the tiller so that, leaning as far out as the strength of my tummy muscles would allow, I still had perfect control.

The boat was deliciously sensitive. A tiny movement of the hand holding the tiller was instantly reflected in a movement of the jib luff along the horizon. The heel of the boat could be controlled also with the helm. If I luffed up a little she came upright. To keep her as upright as possible was my aim, and at the same time to work her as close to the wind as she would go. In my two hands were the controls which could be operated in various sequences and permutations. My raw materials were the wind, varying slightly in force and direction, and the waves, varying perpetually in their obstruction to the hull that I was driving through them.

What I was trying to do with my hands seemed as much of an art as modelling in clay. It came more easily with practice, but the feel which got you to the weather mark before the others was something with which you either were or were not born.

Once round the weather mark, and planing away on a reach there were new problems and new skills to be acquired; but still there was the inescapable factor of touch. 'Planing' is without doubt the most exciting sensation to be had from a sailing boat. There is a sudden acceleration, a sudden smooth rush as the boat lifts and flies *over* the water instead of through it. If the wind is strong enough and the water smooth enough, the boat may stay on top, planing away at full speed. Fourteen-footers may perhaps reach eleven or even twelve knots during such bursts of planing. Down hill it may be faster still; in a seaway it is sometimes possible to ride the slope on the front of a wave like a surf rider, perhaps for short periods moving over the sea at fifteen knots. Again the interplay of the main sheet and the tiller requires an extreme exility of touch. Whereas I could make my *Eastlight* go to windward in a blow better than any other boat in the fleet, when it came to planing I still had much to learn. John Winter and Stewart Morris were far ahead of me in the art. I remember one of the great exponents of planing—'Shorty' Trimmingham of Bermuda, who won the Prince of Wales's Cup in 1954—describing how he sailed his boat down wind as if he were trying to balance the mast on his nose. He was, he said, always trying to steer the boat underneath the masthead. At the same time he played his mainsheet in a series of violent jerks.

But although some could make their boats plane faster than others, *Eastlight* could dash along in a cloud of spray quite fast enough to be gloriously exhilarating. (What matter if we had also to be soaked to the skin!) Yet this was not all that yacht racing had to offer. There was also the chess-like quality of the tactics. In sailing the race is not merely to the swift. It is not only legitimate, but an integral part of the game that a boat which is in front may do all in her power, within the framework of the rules, to hold back a faster boat which is behind. The simplest way to do this is by interfering with the power supply—the wind; and this in turn requires an intimate knowledge of the rules.

In 1934 a new transatlantic team racing fixture was organised—largely by Sir John Beale. This time it was to be a three-cornered contest between Canada, the United States and Britain, and the races were to be sponsored by the Royal Canadian Yacht Club at Toronto. As reigning Champion, Stewart Morris was to be Captain of the British team. Four boats with their helmsmen and crews sailed in the *Empress of Britain* for Canada on 7th July, and *Eastlight* was one of them. Stewart was to be crewed by Roger D'Quincey, John Winter by a namesake of mine though no relation, Tom Scott; David Beale, Sir John Beale's younger son, was to be crewed by Oscar Browning and I by Nicholas Cooke. Nick was the son of a distinguished Cambridge surgeon, a very tall strong lad who had been in the University sailing team. I think of him still as a lad, because a continuing youthfulness was one of his most engaging qualities, but he was twenty-one years old, dark-haired with a pointed chin and an infectious grin. We called him 'the Grasshopper', partly because of his long legs, and partly because of his habit of suddenly jumping up and rushing off to do something different. But for the next two years he was my cheerful, hardworking, boundlessly optimistic crew, though we had not sailed more than a dozen times together when we set off for Canada as part of the British team.

Once more Uffa Fox came with us as team manager.

When we took the boats out of their covers at Toronto we found that in each had been screwed a small, carefully painted black cat, wishing us luck from the ship's staff of the *Empress of Britain*. These black cats became mascots of great value to us. To have raced without them would have been to court disaster. They were painted on a small piece of cardboard and then varnished, and they are still to be found in some of our boats even today.

The Canadian dinghies which opposed us were quite different from our own. To begin with they were not open boats like ours but had fairly extensive decks; they were also a good deal lighter in construction, but they were not made for planing and in the event they were no match for ours. The American boats were less good than the Canadian. As a result we beat Canada in the team race by three races to one, and the United States was beaten in all its races by both the other two teams.

Eastlight scored one private triumph by winning the Wilton Morse Trophy for a separate individual race, which at that time was regarded as the most important of the year for Canadian dinghies. With a so much faster boat no great glory attached to helmsman or crew, though the race was in light airs which did not favour our boats so much. A Canadian boat was second and Stewart Morris third.

But although Nick and I might style ourselves Canadian champions, the most memorable race of the whole trip was one of the team races. So unusual and exciting was it that I wrote an account of it soon afterwards: it was the second race of the series, four boats a side, and the course was twice round a triangle, six miles in all, out in the open lake.

Lake Ontario is thirty miles wide at Toronto, and being fresh water it can provide a shorter, steeper, nastier sea than you will find anywhere on salt water. This particular day, however, 19th July, 1934, dawned calm and hot and in the morning the race between Canada and the United States had been abandoned owing to lack of wind. When we started out from the harbour after lunch it was still almost dead calm and as Nicky Cooke and I were a heavy combination, it seemed doubtful whether *Eastlight* would have a chance to show her paces. We all had on our newest and most beautiful light weather sails, but with little hope of finishing within the time limit of two hours.

We were towed out in a long string by the Committee boat, and as we came into the open lake whose surface was like glass, we could see, away to the west, a cloud. Our Canadian opponents with long faces began hurriedly reefing their sails. Having heard something of these squalls, we immediately followed suit, although reluctantly because it was likely to ruin our beautiful light weather canvas. But the cloud was getting bigger and blacker and a black line was gradually approaching across the water. Suddenly the squall hit us. It was a stiff breeze and, from being becalmed, we were all at once scudding along at ten knots. From our point of view in *Eastlight* this was a most agreeable turn of events because in 'planing' weather our chances against the Canadians were greater than ever.

At this time we were still waiting for the preparatory signal which was due at any moment but before the gun was fired, and almost as suddenly as it started, the weight went out of the wind and we were left with a pleasant light breeze. The squall, we thought, was over and we hastily hoisted full sail, a fairly simple procedure with our roller reefing gear, and congratulated ourselves that we had not had enough wind to spoil the set of our light weather mainsail. There had been no rain to wet it and its shape was still perfect.

Soon after this the ten-minute gun was fired and, in manoeuvring for the start and checking all the gear we did not watch the weather so carefully as we might have done. Without warning the wind suddenly hit us again, and it was only the great quickness of Nicky that saved us from being overpowered. Almost before I could tell him he had started to reef and in a few seconds we had seven rolls of mainsail round the boom and were planing along the top of the water like a speedboat. This time the wind showed no signs of abating but rather blew harder and harder every moment.

The five-minute gun had now gone and I remember looking back at a most memorable sight. The blue-black cloud had descended until it seemed quite dark. The water was inky black, dotted and streaked with white horses, and the other boats, with new sails looking creamy yellow against the dark sky, were dashing hither and thither each enveloped in a cloud of spray. By this time we too were wet through from spray. One of the Canadian team seemed to be in trouble and had lowered his sails, we saw a motor-boat trying to take him in tow. This was bad luck, but all in the game, and we thought it a most encouraging sight. We now had only three boats to beat with our four.

When the starting gun went, I think that most of the British team were more occupied with keeping their boats afloat than with the finer points of racing tactics. To add to the confusion thunder began to crash all round and the lightning flashes left our eyes full of purple streaks. The waves were short and very steep, and every other one came in solid and inky black over the bows. My crew was holding the jib sheet which he did not dare to belay because of the cannon-ball puffs. He held it in one hand and was baling hard with the other, and at the same time trying to 'sit out' in between scoops so as to keep the boat upright.

When we escaped from the *mêlée* at the start and took stock of our situation we found that two of our decked opponents were ahead. One of them, Atwell Fleming in a boat named *Judy*, was some way ahead—perhaps 200 yards, and Charlie Bourke, their Captain, in *Riptide* was thirty yards away under our lee bow. The first leg of the triangle had been a beat to windward but as the wind was following the storm round, it became a reach and the waves were now so big that it was hard to see the buoy; the rain which had started to fall in torrents made it harder still. Owing to our weight, however, *Eastlight* was now lying third and well in front of all the rest. We rounded the mark and found that the wind had so changed that the next leg too was a beat, but we were sailing across the seas instead of into them and so not shipping as much water. This enabled us to sit out a good deal more and that made us go faster so that we were rapidly catching the two leaders. When *Riptide* tacked we were ahead of her and at the next buoy only twenty yards behind *Judy*. Now was our chance to break through, because off the wind our boats were likely to plane along on top of the water at great speed, which the Canadian boats could not do.

But as we rounded the buoy, all ready for the killing, to our

H*

dismay the wind died light as suddenly as it had arisen; there was not nearly enough to make us plane. At the same time a thick mist arose off the water. We hoisted full sail and a spinnaker both of which my crew did so smartly that, even without the planing, we blew past *Judy* and out of the mist. We were leading by twenty yards as we passed the Committee boat at the beginning of the second round.

But the wind had become light and flukey and although we kept *Judy* behind us, as team tactics demanded, some of the others who had taken a different course were ahead when next we met. We found ourselves fourth with *Riptide* second and two of our side first and third.

All four of us were close together when suddenly the mist came across again. First it enveloped the buoy for which we were heading and then, one by one, we sailed into it ourselves and were swallowed up. It was like an ice-cold blanket around us and still the rain was falling in great cold drops. We could see about twenty-five yards, and beyond that only the tops of the sails. The mist was a layer over the water about six feet thick. Standing up on the mast thwart Nicky could see over it, and I told him to stay there in the hope that the top of the buoy, which could not now be much more than 100 yards away, might just be visible to him. We were scarcely moving, so light was the wind.

Nicky stood up there for a good while and when I told him to come down he was reluctant because it was "lovely and warm up there". Certainly the mist itself was unbelievably cold, and as we had only thin shirts on, which clung clammily to us, I could not blame him for climbing up again. And it was as well that he did, for suddenly he saw the buoy fifty yards away and well to leeward of our course. We called softly to one of our team mates, without letting our opponents hear, and it was some seconds before they noticed, from the top of our sail over the mist, that we had altered course. By that time they were almost past the buoy although still much closer to it than we were, but they had to turn at right-angles and run, while we were still reaching. So much faster do sailing boats go when reaching with a light wind abeam than when running, that although we had twice the distance to go, we got there first, with *Riptide* close on our tail. Then we stood up and laid a course over the fog on the Committee boat and the finishing line—a broad reach home. Soon after this we ran out of the mist and, still leading *Riptide*, we crossed the line first by twelve seconds in the most unusual race I have ever sailed.

During the series we lived at the delightful Royal Canadian Yacht Club, on the island which spans Toronto Bay. The hospitality was magnificent and our success in the series seemed generally to be welcomed. The Press in Toronto reported the races fully, fairly and accurately; but the technique of their headline-writers was a constant source of delight and amusement to us.

"ARRIVE IN TORONTO FOR INTERNATIONAL SAILING" (—but who?)

"BRITISH DINGHIES RATE AS MAGNIFICENT BOATS" (We agreed.)

(Over a picture) "RIP, THE CHAMPION ENGLISH DINGHY BOAT".

(Over another) "PICTURESQUE SCENE AS ENGLISH DINGHIES BEST COMPETITORS".

And when the Canadian team beat us in one race the column was headed:

"CANADIAN DINGHIES FIRST ACROSS LINE

———

Give English Nice Trouncing in Some Wild, Hard Racing

———

GET SECOND AS WELL

———

Canadians Receive 20¼ Points—Had To Do Dipper Work".

On the same day another headline read:

"CANADIAN TARS BEAT BRITISH

———

States Were Losers All Along Line—British Boats Superior".

Back in England *Eastlight*, like the rest of the team, was entered for the Prince of Wales's Cup which was to be held at Falmouth. My family had taken a house called 'Greatwood' near Restronguet and overlooking Carrick Roads: it was full of dinghy sailors, their crews and their girl friends. Nicky and I should have been in good racing trim for the big race. We had both been sailing all summer and had finished with an excellent working-up cruise in Canada. Surely we should be well up in the prize list. There were thirty-nine starters and as usual six replicas of the

Cup would be given; it seemed that at least we had a good chance of gaining a replica. But we reckoned without three things: first, the snorting cold which descended on me the day before; next, the glassy windlessness of the day itself; and finally, my own lack of 'big race' experience. The Big Race is indefinably different from all other races, and requires an extra 'something' if it is to be won, over and above the ordinary skills of sailing—a new power of concentration, a determination to think only of winning especially when ill fortune befalls.

It was a long and gruelling race, in which at one point we were becalmed in the lee of a large anchored merchant ship, and dropped from fifth to twentieth. In the end *Eastlight* finished sixteenth. John Winter in *Lightning* won by seven minutes from Mrs. Richardson, with Stewart Morris sixth. It was a bitter, but doubtless salutary disappointment.

In seventy races in 1934, *Eastlight* scored fifty-one guns, twenty-three first prizes, twelve seconds, fourteen thirds; she finished fourth ten times, and fifth six times. Except for four races in which she retired she was only once below fifth and that was sixteenth in the Prince of Wales's Cup, the one time when I really wanted her to be in the first six. On reflection it seems that the fault may have been as much mine as hers.

But if I had failed in my first attempt to become the Dinghy Champion, and must wait for another year to come round, there were some compensations at 'Greatwood' when the Big Race was over. There was a sudden release of tension and the house party could begin to enjoy itself. Besides, Deirdre was due to arrive next day.

There had really been no need for Mrs. Richardson to call my attention to her at Oulton Regatta a year before. I was not unobservant. The Broads One Designs, the old 'Brown Boats' as they were called because of their graceful varnished hulls (not to be confused with the Yare and Bure One Designs, the old 'White Boats'), had lately finished their race, and far behind lagged the last of the fleet, a retired Colonel at the helm. One of his crew was a girl of striking appearance.

"Who's the Greta Garbo?" said Aunt Phyllis as the boat went by. "I don't know," I replied, "but I think I must find out." And then, nonchalantly, in case that should sound too eager: "She's quite pretty, isn't she?" But she was much more than 'quite pretty'; there was no doubt that in a serene and simple way she was very beautiful.

So it was not only sympathy with the Colonel in the slowness of his boat which led me to suggest that if I joined his crew one day I might perhaps discover why he always finished last.

That was how I first met Deirdre, and now she was staying with us at 'Greatwood', for the dinghy races at Falmouth. She loved sailing, she loved dancing—and danced superbly, she loved me and I loved her. If this were another kind of story Deirdre (who was called by some other name) would play a leading part in it. She could not be taken for granted then, but you must take her for granted now, (though I still cannot, and never will).

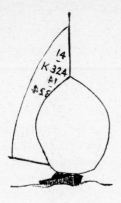

Chapter 34

Whisper *and* Daybreak

IN the race for the Prince of Wales's Cup at Falmouth third place was taken by *Whisper* belonging to David Drew. She was probably no faster than *Eastlight* but she was the prettiest of all the boats in the fleet; her timber had been very carefully selected and the most glorious grain continued across her sides from plank to plank, so that she appeared to have been carved from the whole trunk of a tree. Her colour was that beautiful purplish-chestnut of some kinds of mahogany whereas *Eastlight*'s colour was yellower, and seemed less mellow. *Whisper* was so lovely, and incidentally had done so well in the light airs, that I decided to sell *Eastlight* and buy her. The price, as I recall, was £130. *Eastlight*'s number had been 318, *Whisper* was 324; although she was six boats later, the vintage was the same, and her performance was almost identical.

In 1935 the Prince of Wales's Cup was to be raced for in Osborne Bay in the Solent and again Nicky Cooke was to be my crew. We had tuned up *Whisper* to a high degree, and had done well in the earlier part of the season. Once more we were full of confidence.

On the day before the big race we were out in front, doing very well in a fresh breeze, when one of the rigging wires of the mast broke and the mast itself bent alarmingly. I let the sheet go just in time and the mast was saved. The wire which had parted was the bottom diamond wire on one side, part of a stressed structure of single-strand wires on spreaders of aluminium tube which kept the mast straight. Congratulating ourselves that it had broken the day *before* the big race and not during the race itself, we got the boat back to Cowes, whipped out the mast and took it up to Uffa Fox's yard where the boat and its spars had originally been built. A new diamond wire was fitted in the place of the broken one, and all seemed to be ready for the race the next day.

It was another day of strong winds, which suited us perfectly. Nicky and I went off on the first beat without a care in the world, and before long it was clear that we were in the lead again, just as we had been on the day before. As we approached the weather mark I suddenly saw that the mast was bending as badly as yesterday. The wire had not broken, but it seemed to have stretched, or else the wire knot had slipped at its attachment. We went about quickly on to the other tack, and found that the mast stood up quite straight. It only needed one more short starboard tack to get ourselves round the weather mark, still first by nine seconds from Stewart Morris. On the broad reach Nicky did his best to tighten up the slackened diamond wire, but it had stretched too much and the rigging screw would not take up enough to get it taut again. Round the leeward mark we came on to a port tack where the mast stood up quite well. We plugged on, but in due course we had to tack and as soon as the sails filled away on the starboard the mast began to bend again. We gilled along gently not daring to fill the sails, and then, as we sailed only at half power, we found ourselves overtaken by Willie Hicks from North Norfolk, who had been going very well on the wind. He crossed us once and we were faced with a major decision. There were three and a half more rounds to the race. If we sailed on at half power we should drop down and down. There was just a chance that if we drove her hard, the mast would bend until the slack diamond wire was tight, without actually breaking. We decided to haul in the sheet, drive her as fast as we could, and hope for the best. As we hauled in, the boat surged forward again, but the mast bent like a bow; it was clear that it would not last long. A moment later we came over the crest of a big wave and with a splintering crack it broke. The rest of the fleet sailed past, and that was that.

I was bitterly angry. I felt we had been let down by bad workmanship, though no doubt the chap who had fitted the diamond wire had done his best. I found it especially hard to be a 'good loser', even though I knew I would lose more by being a bad one. Our misfortune in the Prince of Wales's Cup of 1935 was doubtless very good for the character.

Stewart was the winner, John Winter was second and Willie Hicks third. It was small consolation that *Whisper*, with a new mast, won the race on the following day in identical conditions over the same course. It was *not* for the Prince of Wales's Cup.

The venue of the championship changed annually, but for weekend racing the keenest competition in the fourteen-footers was in

Chichester Harbour where a strong fleet, including most of the best helmsmen in the class, was assembled at Itchenor.

One day after a race as we were hauling our boats out of the water at the end of the club jetty, I noticed a small sailing dinghy lying a few yards offshore. At her tiller was a boy wearing a pair of blue bathing pants. He was mahogany brown from sunburn, his hair bleached to the colour of straw; and his blue eyes were almost popping out of his head with excitement at seeing, at close quarters, the beautiful International fourteen-foot dinghies which he had watched only at a distance during their races. I did not know that he had sailed round from Emsworth especially for the purpose, but I could see how much he wanted to look at them more closely, so I called across to him:

"You can come up the slipway if you like and look at mine."
Stewart looked reproachfully at me.

"He can't possibly come up unless he puts a shirt on," he said.
"The older members wouldn't like it." So I called across.

"Have you got a shirt?" And the boy said "Yes" and put it on. After he had examined the dinghies for some time I could see that he longed for a sail in one.

"All right," said I. "Next week-end, if you come over, I'll take you out in *Whisper*; by the way, what's your name?"

"Charles Curry."

"Right, see you next Saturday."

With a fresh breeze Charles and I took *Whisper* down the harbour a week later and planed backwards and forwards at speed in the most exhilarating clouds of spray. After about an hour when we were thinking of coming back an upper diamond wire suddenly parted and the mast fell over the side again. We drifted in to the shore, waded through the mud to the saltmarsh and walked disconsolately back to the club to get a motor boat to go down and tow the dinghy home. That was Charles Curry's first introduction to the fourteen-footers.

Early in the summer of 1936 I decided to enter for the trials for the single-handed sailing in the Olympic Games. The event was to be sailed in the German Olympic monotype, or Olympia-jolle. Three of these boats had been obtained by F. G. ('Tiny') Mitchell, Commodore of the Royal Corinthian Yacht Club and brief eliminating trials were held at Burnham-on-Crouch. By some extraordinary chance I won these trials. I still do not quite know how it happened, but I suppose you cannot have bad luck all the time. Stewart was second and became my spare man for the

Olympic Regatta at Kiel. At the time the importance not only of the trials, but of the yachting events in the Games themselves was surprisingly low. It may seem extraordinary now that neither Stewart nor I (nor indeed any of the fourteen-foot dinghy sailors), rated the Olympic Yachting as in any way comparable in importance with the Prince of Wales's Cup. In this judgment we were probably right. The general standard of skill shown by competitors in the Prince of Wales's Cup was almost certainly higher than in the single-handed Olympic contest.

Chronologically the Prince of Wales's Cup came first. It was to be held at Hunter's Quay on the Clyde and we had been told that light weather might be expected—indeed the Clyde was famed for it. So I agreed to sell *Whisper* to Michael Bratby and from Uffa Fox I ordered a new boat, to be called *Daybreak*; she was to have the minimum beam in order to reduce the wetted surface, and would therefore be less good for planing. This was the gamble I had to take.

Immediately before the Prince of Wales's Cup races we were to sail a series of team races against the United States. My crew, both for the team races and for the Prince of Wales's Cup itself, was once more Beecher Moore.

As well as being narrower than most of the other boats of her class *Daybreak* had a secret weapon: we had decided to try a wooden centreboard. We had no idea whether this would be effective, but until we knew, we were determined that it should remain a secret.

At this time the centreboards of most of the dinghies were made of a single plate of phosphor-bronze—a dull, brass-like metal—weighing something like 100 pounds; the wooden centreboard weighed ten pounds. The boat would be enormously lighter. But should we miss the stability of the lower centre of gravity? In order to preserve our secret we painted the light board with brass paint, and whenever we carried it, we put on a great pantomime of weight lifting.

Beecher believed in preserving the right state of mind in his helmsman. More recently he has compared the relationship of crew to helmsman with that of a farmer to his prize pig. I was treated to every kind of luxury in order to put me at my ease, and on the Wednesday—the day before the Cup—I was not allowed to race, but spent a most delightful day in the hills to the north of the Clyde with Beecher and his wife, trying to think about something other than sailing.

But on the Thursday, it blew a gale, so hard that the Committee decided to postpone the race. Although a gale of wind was not likely to suit our *Daybreak*, Beecher and I were fairly heavy and competent when it was blowing hard, so we felt annoyed and frustrated when the race was postponed. On the following day— the Friday—the wind was as strong as ever and there was another postponement. Again we made our protest to the Committee. The only other person who minded was Robert Hichens, a Falmouth solicitor who had a home-made boat called *Venture*.

By the Saturday morning, the last day of the week, the gale had abated a little though not very much. At about nine a.m. Robert and I, having protested, were asked by the Committee at Uffa's suggestion, to sail out as guinea-pigs. We were to test the course and see if the weather was fit for the race to be held. Out we planed, from the shelter of the town and the hillside into a strong wind and a very big sea. We could almost feel the eyes watching us from the shore. With our mainsails reefed we were never overpowered. When we got back Robert and I agreed on our report.

"Yes, it is just fit to sail today, but it would certainly not have been on Thursday or Friday and we both unreservedly withdraw our protests."

The start was postponed till one o'clock in the hope that the wind would moderate, but there was little change. It blew and blew and rained and rained.

We made a good start and got to the weather mark thirty-one seconds ahead of the rest of the fleet. This was a dramatic and impressive lead. To windward it seemed that *Daybreak* was un-beatable, but there were two more legs of the triangle and three more rounds after that. How would she compare at planing for which she had not really been designed? I remembered the saying, which was still true, that in no previous race for the Prince of Wales's Cup had the boat which led at the first mark in the first round ever been the winner.

The old gang was out in front again. John Winter rounded second, with Stewart only seven seconds behind him in a field of thirty-one. Then the planing began. *Daybreak* planed very fast, but *Lightning* planed much faster. She did the second leg of the course in one minute six seconds less than *Daybreak*, planing through our lee in a great sheet of spray. It was depressing, yet no more than we expected; not only was *Lightning* designed as a planing hull, but John was far better than me at starting his boat off, and keeping her planing, even if I could usually beat him to windward.

We stayed second for another round, then Stewart who had been biding his time, came up on the reach and planed past us just as John had done. John led for the third round but I had the feeling that Stewart was awaiting his chance to pounce. Not only was he planing as fast as John but he was going very fast to windward too. Then John struck a bad patch; he had shipped a lot of water in his boat and his crew was forced to bail on the beat. While that was happening Stewart took the lead and won the race for the fourth time. John finished second for the second time and *Daybreak* came third to win my first replica for me. Phyllis Richardson was fourth and Robert Hichens sixth. Charles Curry had been sailing *Whisper* at the invitation of Michael Bratby who crewed him, and they were doing quite well until they capsized at the gybe in the second round.

So it had not been 'third time lucky'. Perhaps in *Eastlight* or *Whisper* it would have been a closer thing, but the truth was that two helmsmen in fourteen-footers were still substantially better than me; although I could often beat them in lesser races, and had managed twice now to get myself out in front at the beginning of the Big Race, they were in front of me at the time it mattered most—when crossing the finishing line.

The excursion of the fourteen-footers to the Clyde was memorable for a delightful story to which Michael Bratby bore witness. The two postponements of the big race had greatly disorganised the plans of those who wanted to return south at the end of the week. After finishing fourth in what must have been the most strenuous race of her life Aunt Phyllis was eager to catch the night train. Leaving her husband to pack up the dinghy, she was driven to Glasgow by Michael. They arrived at the barrier just as the guard was waving his green flag. The wheels had already begun to move when Aunt Phyllis, drawn up to her full six feet, shouted in an imperious voice,

"Stop the train—I'm Mrs. Henry Richardson."

The name could have meant nothing to the guard but the tone of voice was not to be denied; he blew a shrill blast on his whistle and waved his *red* flag. The signal was repeated farther up the platform and the train stopped.

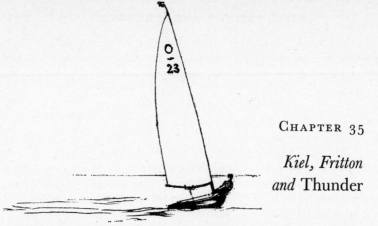

ALTHOUGH we had placed the Olympic Games far below the Prince of Wales's Cup in importance in the season's racing, my failure to win the Big Race became an additional spur in the regatta at Kiel.

Apart from the initial trials my only experience of the boat I was to sail had been a week on the Buiten Y, a part of the Zuider Zee near Amsterdam, in early June. Dutch, German and Norwegian helmsmen were racing and Stewart Morris and I were both lent boats for the regatta. In spite of the distraction of low-flying Spoonbills flighting out from the Naarder Meer, I had managed to win the points cup for the week, with two firsts and two seconds, and Stewart came fourth with one first and three thirds. Neither of us had liked the Olympic Monotype as a boat, but of the two Stewart seemed to like it the less. In spite of the Clyde, I was determined not to allow any inferiority complex to prevail. After all, I had won at Amsterdam.

In Germany, Stewart was much more than my spare man; he was my team manager and my coach, and looked after me and my boat with meticulous care.

The series began on 5th August, 1936, and in the first race it blew hard. In that weather I had the measure of all the other competitors, many of whom had very little experience either of strong winds or of the Monotype. The more it blew, the more I felt at home, though the boat, of course, was fairly new to me too. She was sixteen feet long, rather beamy, and was 'cat-rigged' which means that she had only a mainsail—no jib. The rather heavy mast was stepped very near to the bows, and the boat became extremely difficult to control off the wind in a blow. The tiller was a huge wishbone affair, which was the standard continental method of getting over the difficulty of a helmsman who has to steer while leaning far out of the boat. Its weight and inertia alone greatly reduced the delicacy of the control. By comparison with a fourteen-footer the Olympia-jolle seemed a very blunt instrument.

The German word *Jolle* is etymologically related to the English 'jollyboat' and the English 'Yawl', but in yachting circles a *jolle* and a yawl are very different vessels: a *jolle* is a small dinghy; a yawl is a yacht with mainmast and mizzen, and is usually of several tons register. The soft j of *jolle*, however, led to an ignorant translation of Olympia-jolle into Olympic Yawl, by which name the class became known throughout most of the British Press.

On that first windy day I went away to win quite comfortably from the German Willi Krogmann, and that night we dried the sail in the cruiser *Neptune* which was lying in the harbour at Kiel. But in the next few days the wind fell away and my performance was gradually outshone by the Dutch helmsman Dan Kaghelland.

By 11th August—the day of the last race in the series—Dan was so far ahead on points that he had won the Gold Medal. He had no need even to start, though in fact he did so. Willi Krogmann and I had an exactly equal number of points, but again we were so far ahead of the Brazilian who was lying fourth that he could not possibly overtake us. So far as the gold, silver and bronze medals were concerned, the last race had only to decide whether Willi or I should have the silver one.

At the start we manoeuvred with eyes only for each other and Willi got the better of it and went away ahead of me. Then followed a spirited race in which we ignored the other twenty-five competitors entirely. By the second round when we lay respectively thirteenth and fourteenth, I was coming up on Willi fast. The wind had freshened and it was quite clear that in a short while I should overtake him. He tacked to cover me and we sailed along side by side going to windward on a starboard tack. At the outset of this tack his boat lay about fifty yards to weather of mine, and he was therefore in effect still about fifty yards ahead. In the fresher breeze we both lay out to the very limit of our strength. This was it. If he could hold me back now, the silver medal was his, if I could get past him it was mine. I was gaining on him by sailing an infinitesimal amount closer to the wind. The two boats remained level, almost stem to stem, but their courses were gradually converging; I was shortening that fifty-yard lead. As I sat out on the starboard gunwale Willi was directly behind me. I did not need to look round at him; I could hear his bow wave, and by its direction I could tell that we were both sailing at the same speed, but by sailing closer to the wind I was still closing the gap.

Of a sudden the wind changed its direction very slightly and both of us were able to point a little higher than we had been pointing. This minor change in our positions relative to the wind's eye, meant that the wind shadow from Willi's sail now fell across my sail. There was nothing for it but to tack immediately. I scarcely looked behind and flung the boat around. To my consternation I felt a little tap as she went round and realised that I had nicked the stern of Willi's boat. This of course I had no right to do; it was a collision and the fault was most certainly mine. Although I knew I had been gaining on the German boat, I could not believe I had reduced that fifty-yard lead to a boat's length in so short a time. But there was a second reason. In the quick glance behind me I seemed to have room to tack astern of him, but I was thinking in terms of a fourteen-foot rather than a sixteen-foot boat. My familiar fourteen-footer would have cleared him easily but the Olympic Monotype did not.

The damage was done; there was, as I saw it, no alternative but to retire immediately. I dropped the mainsheet, bore off down the wind and sailed out of the race. It was a very bitter moment and small solace that it was regarded as the correct thing to do.

One way and another 1936 had been a full year: apart from winning a replica of the Prince of Wales's Cup and an Olympic Bronze Medal—in spite of disappointments, I was very proud of both—my book *Morning Flight* had been published in its first 'Ordinary Edition', I had had an exhibition of pictures at Ackermann's and had illustrated my stepfather's book *A Bird in the Bush* which was published that autumn. It was very well received and reviewed, but I was not at all satisfied with my drawings. I knew that they were not in the same class of excellence as the text. A few of the designs were fine and bold but with too many of the small birds I was groping for a likeness. For so exquisite a book the illustrations should have been perfect and I was sad that they were not. It was a poetical book and by chance Bill was President of the Poetry Society, as well as Minister of Health, when he wrote it.

Birds and sailing had met on the common ground of East Anglia for so many summers now that my family decided we should have a permanent country home in that part of the world.

So we came to live in holiday times at Fritton Hithe, an unob-trusively Victorian house thatched with Norfolk reed, which overlooked Fritton Lake, near Great Yarmouth. In front of the house, which rambled about, mostly at ground floor level, was a wide lawn leading down to the reed-fringed lake side and a small jetty from which we could bathe and fish and sail, though the lake was so sheltered by the surrounding woods that there was seldom a steady breeze. This did not prevent us from sailing a small fleet of eight-foot Corinthian Otter 'prams', with tiny balanced lugs. We had two of them and our neighbour across the lake, General Sir Thomas Jackson, had two more for his family of two sons and a daughter. It was in these that my brother Wayland learned to sail.

The care of the 'prams' was my stepfather's special province, and I think it was this that led him to study knots and splices. It was astonishing that he could make the most complicated turk's heads, and could sail those tiny, tipply boats with only one arm.

He had lately retired from politics and had become Lord Kennet of the Dene, his title taken from the river and the little valley at Lockeridge. At one time it had seemed that he might go from the Ministry of Health to the Exchequer, but Baldwin withdrew his offer, and there was then no alternative but the House of Lords. In face of what was a palpable breach of faith my stepfather showed no signs of disappointment or bitterness, though my mother was not so charitable about the Prime Minister's change of mind, and particularly about the way it was done.

I never admired Bill more than during the critical time when his political career was in the balance. Had he become Chancellor of the Exchequer then, he could conceivably have been the next Prime Minister, but at home it was impossible to tell that any such things were in his mind. Basically, perhaps, he was not ruthless enough for the political pinnacle.

At the east end of Fritton Lake were three decoy pipes still operated by our landlord, Lord Somerleyton, on a minor com-mercial scale, and in winter there were frequently large flocks of ducks in the hidden corner of the lake. In summer Great Crested Grebes displayed at the foot of the lawn.

My mother took great delight in the garden at Fritton. There was a brilliant herbaceous border, on which, in season, great numbers of Comma Butterflies were to be seen, and once a Large Tortoiseshell. At the back of the house were two small green-houses—in one of them a splendid vine which kept us in grapes for half the summer it seemed; in the other exotic plants like *Pamianthe peruviana*, *Gloriosa rothschildii* and a few orchids. It was the first time we had ever had greenhouses and my mother was very proud of the beautiful things she grew in them.

Fritton was a part of my life for about twelve years—a home for a family in peace and war. Distinguished musicians played on its two grand pianos, artists, writers and politicians came for the week-end or the holidays and played parlour games (J. B. Priestley as a St. Bernard dog was never to be forgotten), but in particular the house was full of young people, contemporaries of my brother and me. This was especially so during the regattas in the summer.

Sea Week at Lowestoft in 1937 was more than usually important because the Prince of Wales's Cup was to be held there again. For this, my fourth attempt, I had commissioned Uffa to build me a new dinghy, called *Thunder*. (As owner of *Lightning* John Winter claimed that his must always come before the thunder, but I was not to be deterred.) I had persuaded Charles Curry to be my crew.

In the previous year *Daybreak* had been designed for the light airs on the Clyde and we had raced in a gale. The weather at Lowestoft was anyone's guess, but as my best chances seemed to be in a strong wind I had decided to gamble again—to have a dinghy with a planing hull. Already I knew that sailing to windward in a blow there were few who could beat me. If I could plane fast off the wind I should have a good all-round chance in fresh breezes; but by the same token if we had the light weather we should have had in Scotland I would be at a similar disadvantage in reverse.

Thunder was the most beautifully finished sailing boat I had ever seen. This perfection of functional efficiency was reflected in the boat's appearance and was part of its particular appeal. Not only were the fourteen-footers thoroughbreds, but they looked like thoroughbreds. They were built with the precision and artistry of a violin; Uffa had set new standards of workmanship in boat building, and to own one of his fourteen-footers in the 1930s was to own the most perfect little boat in the world.

Although Stephen Potter had not yet invented the phrases, there was plenty of gamesmanship and even lifemanship to be practised in dinghy sailing. For several years a secret preparation had been applied to the bottoms of certain boats on the morning of the Big Race. It was called 'Elgo', was supposed to make the boat 'go like 'ell', and consisted of the whites of half a dozen eggs applied with a rag and allowed to dry. Almost certainly all traces of it were washed off by the time the boat had been in the water five minutes, but for many years it persisted as a supposed secret weapon available only to a privileged few. Before the 1937 race we decided that a new gambit was required. I let slip that I had been secretly examining the cost of an ultra-light aluminium mast for *Thunder*. On the day before the race we rubbed down the existing wooden mast and painted it with aluminium paint. Until that time all dinghies had had varnished masts, but the silver colour looked in many ways more attractive and racey than the yellow varnished silver spruce. On the morning of the race we stepped the old mast in its new colours and all round the dinghy park tongues began to wag. In the course of the morning one or two people came up, tapped the mast gently and immediately realised that it was only wood. But among the fleet of forty-six dinghies, few had time to do this and there were many who believed that we were sailing with the expensive advantage of a lighter mast. This went only a little way to offset our misgivings about the weather. The day had dawned absolutely calm and there was little hope of more than a zephyr all day. I still owned *Daybreak* but had chartered her to David Pollock, and now it was *Daybreak*'s weather. There was nothing I could do about it but watch David take the lead almost from the start. In the very light airs the windward leg of the race had to be sailed close in to the beach because of the strong south-going tide. The whole fleet stood in towards the shore and for a mile short-tacked among the groynes and holiday bathers, and past the Claremont Pier with its hazard of fishing lines.

We were away close behind David and stayed close upon his tail. I felt confident that we should find an opportunity to pounce on him at a later stage in the race but to begin with he was offering us no chances. We were a good deal more concerned that John Winter and Stewart Morris were not very far behind us. Early in the third round *Thunder* went into the lead and as we tacked up the shore we had a difficult decision to make. Each tack was very short—perhaps forty or fifty yards out into the tide, then 'about', and forty or fifty yards back again towards the beach, the crew with his hand on the centreboard rope ready to pull it up the instant it touched. The wooden breakwaters jutted out at frequent intervals, making helpful tidal eddies, but complicating the defensive tactics required of a leading boat. I must try all the time to 'cover' the next astern—to be on the same tack as her, and whenever possible to get between her and the eye of the wind, so as to reduce her motive power. Every time John tacked I too must tack so as to be similarly affected by any small change in the direction of the wind. Being in front my tactics were to maintain the *status quo* and take no chances. The boat behind on the other hand was always trying to get on to the opposite tack.

In this case, however, John was covering Stewart so that in looking after one I was looking after them both. But my problem was suddenly complicated when John allowed Stewart to break tacks and go off on his own. My two most important rivals were now on opposite tacks. Which of them should I cover and make sure of keeping behind me? Stewart was four times winner of the Cup and was sailing *Alarm*, in which he had won the race in the two previous years. John had won the race once at Falmouth and was still sailing *Lightning*, the boat in which he had then triumphed. Since then he had twice been second in the same boat. *Lightning* was older than *Alarm* and if either was to get through it might be easier to catch *Lightning* again. If I could not catch her it was John's turn to win rather than Stewart's and victory for so old a boat as *Lightning* would be good for the class and maintain the value of second-hand boats. I decided to let John go, and tacked to cover Stewart. The wind was altering all the time very slightly; now that John was on the opposite tack to us any small alteration of wind which headed us on our tack freed him up on his and doubled the effect of the alteration on the relative positions of the two boats. This could work the other way, too, and might have favoured us, but as it turned out the next time we came together with John, he crossed ahead of us and was in the lead at the weather mark. There was little change on the next two reaches except that John opened out from us and rounded the leeward mark almost exactly one minute ahead. By now the tide had fallen slack and it was no longer necessary to go close inshore. We were going to have the whole sea for manoeuvre on the last beat to the finishing line. As we came to the buoy with one more mile of windward work ahead of us, I said to my crew, "It is a pity we couldn't win, but it's rather nice that old John in his four-year-old boat should be winning it, don't you agree?" This released a tirade from Charles, the gist of which was that he had never expected to hear such defeatist talk from me, that it was absurd to say that the race was already won and why didn't we get on with it?

"But," said I, "you know as well as I do that with competent operators in boats as nearly even as these are it is not possible to pick up a minute in a mile."

"Well, you'll never know whether it is or not if you don't try!"

And so we set to and tried as never before; and at that critical moment there came a freshening of the breeze. After a couple of tacks we were sitting full out to keep the boat upright and driving her as hard as we could go. At the same time John and Tom Paxton (who were a good deal lighter than the combined weight of Charles Curry and me) were beginning to look back over their shoulders—beginning to realise that the freshening wind could beat them yet. Perhaps they were getting a little tired too, and earlier in the year John's appendix had been removed, which may have been a factor. Whatever the reasons, there came a time when the impossible seemed almost within our grasp. Up till now we had been carefully covering Stewart as well, and John of course had been covering us—tack for tack. Now we decided to wriggle and try to escape from John's control. We took a couple of short tacks, got him slightly out of step and unbelievably we were through. On the next port tack, we crossed his bows by about five yards, tacked to cover him, killed him with our wind shadow and crossed the finishing line sixteen seconds ahead of him after a race of three and a half hours. Twenty-two seconds after *Lightning* came *Alarm*, closely followed by James Beale and Mrs. Richardson.

It was a moment of immense elation. During the last minutes of the race there had been no time to savour the golden instant when we took the lead again. Now the gun had gone; the unbelievable had happened; at the fourth attempt we had won the Big Race. The years of failure had perhaps built it up to a disproportionate significance. But even now I look back on those few minutes after the finishing gun as among the most triumphant and utterly satisfying moments of my life.

Apart from his skill as a crew and his knowledge of sail trimming, Charles Curry had undoubtedly given me a touch of the whip at exactly the right moment. His part in our victory had been much greater than is usual for a crew.

Although, sailing in his own dinghy, he competed in most of the Prince of Wales's Cup races during the next twenty years, and won the Olympic Silver Medal in the single-handed class at Helsinki in 1952, it was not until twenty-two years later when the Big Race was again at Lowestoft that he finally won it, by the even narrower margin of four seconds.

After our triumph in 1937 one of the newspapers carried the
headline:

"Elemental, My Dear Yachtsmen.
Thunder, *Lightning* and *Alarm*
take first three places in
Championship."

In small-boat sailing circles we always winced in those days
when the word Championship was used in connection with the
Prince of Wales's Cup. There was, and still is, a curious snobbery
in yachting circles which suggests that it is slightly vulgar to call
the winner of the principal event in each class the Champion.
These races are held by respectable Yacht Clubs for particular
cups, often from distinguished donors, and to call them Championships is thought to subject them to some kind of indignity. I have
never really understood the force of the argument, and at the time
I certainly had no objection to being regarded as 'the Champ'.

Later that summer came the regatta at Torquay, to commem-
orate the Coronation of King George VI. Stewart Morris had
been invited to sail the six-metre yacht *Coima*, and the owner,
Bill Horbury, suggested that he might select his own crew. Stewart
asked me to join him as mainsheet hand; the rest of the crew consisted of the owner and Sandy Wardrop-Moore, with Charles
Curry as foredeck hand.

The regatta was chiefly memorable for some spirited races
between *Coima* and *Norna IV* sailed by His Royal Highness The
Crown Prince Olav of Norway. In the long run he was too good
for us and carried off the six-metre cup, but we were second by
three-quarters of a point in seventy at the end of the fortnight's
racing. We believed that a beautiful little red spinnaker carried
in the Norwegian boat, and known as Monsieur Stalin, was chiefly
responsible for our downfall.

A minor crisis arose during this regatta. We had devised a new
gadget which we believed would improve the six-metre's performance on a close reach: it was a light spar which was fitted on to
the forestay and into the clew of the jib, following the mitre
seam and holding it out in a flatter curve when the sheet was eased.
This device we had christened 'the Google' but before using it we
thought it essential to discover whether our distinguished foreign
competitor was prepared to allow its legality; although we
believed it to be legal we must obviously be careful to avoid an
international incident.

With this in view I remember going over in a motor-boat one morning, before the racing started, to call upon His Royal Highness who was staying on Tom Sopwith's yacht *Philante* (which was long later to become his own Royal Yacht, *Norge*). I outlined the principle of our device and told the Crown Prince why we thought there was no rule to prevent it. There was a very slight pause and then, very firmly: "I do not think it is legal and if you use it I shall immediately protest."

The Google was dead. We were sad about it at the time, but in retrospect I am satisfied that the Crown Prince was right. It was an awkward gadget anyway.

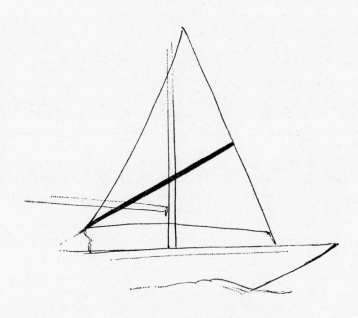

CHAPTER 36   *Wild Goose Chase*

IN the early spring of 1936 I had been invited by *The Field* to go as their special correspondent to the great plains of Hungary during the northward migration of the wild geese. My companion was my cousin Eric Bruce (known always as Brucie) with whom I had fished for sea trout in the Outer Isles. He was on leave from his job as District Commissioner in Sarawak.

We went to the Hortobagy (pronounced Hortobarge to rhyme with canal barge) by train from Budapest and at once began looking for geese in the sky as we trundled through the Hungarian countryside, but although we saw one flock of 200 not very far from the capital, it was not until shortly before our arrival at Nagyhortobagy that we saw any more. At first there were small groups in the distance, but all of a sudden we were amongst them on both sides of the railway, at first scattered and then gradually thickening till the climax by a little copse where there were not less than 10,000. Nearly all were White-fronted Geese.

Nagyhortobagy is a tiny village in the middle of the *puszta*—a vast grassy plain thirty miles by twenty, or bigger. The surface in the spring was of beautiful short green turf with small pools all over it—some large, some small, all shallow. There were no ditches or drains of any kind and no enclosed fields. Here and there were wells with thirty-foot lever arms for drawing water for the cattle in summer.

The inn or *Csarda* was the principal building in Nagyhortobagy, with a steep-pitched red-tiled roof and white walls. The rooms opened on to a long arcaded loggia, like one side of a cloister, and the chimney was specially constructed to carry its stork's nest. From this we went out each morning in a cart to lie in wait for the geese in specially dug holes, or pits, in the clay soil. The principal guide was Farkhas Istvan, who knew exactly where the holes should be dug and could dig them with expert speed, rectangular and five feet deep with a seat on one side.

It was the first time that I had seen geese in really big numbers. On the second morning when I climbed down from the cart which had taken us out in the darkness and took cover in my pit, there were geese murmuring upwind in a semi-circle. It was a cloudless dawn and cold—thin ice on the splashes. Suddenly there was a noise like a train; and a grey mist appeared just above the horizon in front of me: it seemed that all the geese in creation were in the air. They flew round and settled, and a few minutes later as many again were up over on the right. Then a grey mist lifted above the horizon on the left, and another behind me. There were not less than 5,000 geese in each of these flocks and not less than five flocks within a couple of miles of my pit. All this was at least eight miles from where we had seen great numbers on the previous morning. If there were not more than 100,000 geese, there were certainly not less.

The shooting was too easy: a bag of 100 geese to one gun is altogether excessive and nothing to be proud of. But those morning flights were memorable for the wide variety of birds we saw—the Great Bustards, the Cranes, the Eagles, and particularly for the Lesser White-fronted and Red-breasted Geese. Those geese which were only slightly wounded I kept alive for bringing back to the collection at the lighthouse. Already in the first days I had assembled a group of Common Whitefronts which I planned to take back; I hoped that I might perhaps manage to add Lesser Whitefronts and Red-breasts before the end of our week.

One morning the cart arrived to pick me up at my pit with Brucie already on board. He called me to look under the front seat where we always kept live birds. Sticking out from under the rug which hung down from the seat were the primaries and tail of a live goose. I was not unduly impressed as I had five live ones in my pit; but Brucie said "Wait" and then dramatically lifted the rug like a theatre curtain, and there, peering at me, was a beady eye surrounded by an eyelid ring of brilliant yellow. It was our first live Lesser Whitefront. When we got back to the Csarda we cut two splints from some firewood, bandaged them on and then put the bandages right round his body. Next day the bandages were invisible as the bird had preened his feathers over them, and in the afternoon he was eating corn. Lesser Whitefronts were called 'Kis Lilliks'. Lillik comes obviously from the call and Kis (pronounced Kish) means small. Common Whitefronts were called 'Nagy Lilliks' (pronounced narge to rhyme with large which is what it means): Red-breasts were 'Vörös nyaku liba' (Vörös, red —nyaku, neck—liba, goose).

I had not expected to find Red-breasted Geese in Hungary, but there were two skins in the small museum at the Csarda which had been set up by Nemeth Ur, the enterprising proprietor, who also owned the Queen of England Hotel in Debrecen. I had been told that Red-breasts were *very* rare, but I decided particularly to keep my eyes open for them.

After my very first day I wrote to Michael Bratby:

"The *pièce de résistance*, the high spot of the morning—three geese coming low on my right. One of them has a very short neck, it is very dark and small. As it passes there is a flash of chestnut. Eighty yards out and shining in the sun passes the first Red-breasted Goose I have ever seen alive. There are two Lesser Whitefronts with him. When he is past I can see that his tummy has much more white than the others—and so he goes off to be swallowed up in 10,000 geese which are sitting three-quarters of a mile away. I'm sorry about the present tense, but it *was* an event, wasn't it?"

On the following morning I saw a flock of them.

". . . Almost immediately afterwards a big wave of geese came over. High above and behind them I heard a new noise, short but very squeaky, not unlike a Whitefront but fairly easily distinguishable. By now it was quite light and I grabbed the glasses. Were they? Weren't they? *They were*—thirteen of them, *Rufibrenta ruficollis*. I did not see much of the colour, but the shape was more compact and perfect than in any other goose.

"A little later I heard the noise again in the distance. It was another little bunch—sixteen Red-breasts and one Lesser White-front planing down with set wings from a great height. Their flight is almost reminiscent of a golden plover, so short are their necks."

At the end of the week the Lesser Whitefront came safely back with me to the lighthouse in company of a number of Common Whitefronts and a Bean Goose. But among 100,000 wild geese on the Hortobagy 'puszta' there seemed to have been no more than thirty or forty Red-breasts; the chances of getting any of them alive seemed negligible. Nevertheless a few weeks later, a letter came from the proprietor of the Csarda.

1936

Painting in the studio at the Lighthouse.

937

The Prince of Wales's Cup at last, won at the fourth attempt, at Lowestoft.
Helmsmen and crews of the first three boats, *left to right:* Tom Paxton, John
Winter, P.S., Charles Curry, Stewart Morris, Brian Whinney.

1937

Duck catching with flare, gong and hand-net in a Persian *Murd ab*.

1937

In the Lesser Whitefront marsh near Kara Tappeh in the south-east corner of the Caspian.

"My Dear Sir," it began, "I am very glad to inform you that I procured a red-breasting goose, however a living one. Alas it is yet very ill. Our veterinary surgeon dressed the wounded wing of the bird saying that it has also got an inner wound, because it has fallen from a great altitude, but has perhaps also got a stomach-shot. I put before it cornwheat and plenty of water. I keep it in my own room for being treated well. In the daytime I put her box on the sun. We try everything that it might be kept in life . . ."

But soon after came another letter to say that the poor little red-breasting goose had not survived.

In the following autumn I went again to the plains of Hungary. This time there were only four Red-breasts among the migrating hordes. Further east, I thought, there would surely be more, and I pushed on through Roumania to the Black Sea and the Danube Delta.

I arrived at the same time as a blizzard, and in three days the continental winter had descended on the land, driving all before it.

On the second day at a place called Gropeni I drove in a sleigh past a flock of 500 or 600 geese on some meadows by the side of the Danube. They were mostly the familiar White-fronted Geese and they were feeding sitting down so as to keep out of the wind and to keep their toes warm.

"I looked at them with the glass but it was hard to make them out, as they all looked black in the snow and there was a mist of powdered snow blowing past in front of them, but suddenly I saw some white streaks and there they were, seven little Red-breasts, their white flanks showing plainly. Part of the flock moved and when they settled again they were further away and there were twelve Red-breasts and still two stayed with the near lot. We walked fairly close, but it was too cold to hold the glasses up for long. As we left I took a last look at them over on the far grass where they had settled—a place where the wind had blown most of the snow away. They all turned and walked down wind picking their way among the Whitefronts—fourteen little Red-breasts all in a row."

From Roumania I went back again to the Csarda at Nagyhor-tobagy to collect a group of live geese which had been assembled for me. From the bags of the autumn wildfowlers sixteen birds had been saved and put into a temporary pen; among them were a Bean

I

Goose and four Lesser Whitefronts. The Csarda was officially closed to visitors, but Nemeth Ur came out from Debrecen to see that I was comfortable.

"I have to wait here until Wednesday," I wrote to John Winter, "because I cannot get permits for the live geese before then. Nemeth Ur has just sent away to the next village, ten miles away, for my favourite gypsy violinist, and he has just arrived by the train and is now playing 'Nem tudom ehn mivon vellem . . .' This really is rather a sweet place. Everyone treats one as if one had come home . . . tremendous welcomes. When we left for Roumania a fortnight ago the gypsies brought their instruments out and played us into the car and away. And now they are playing my favourite tunes in honour of my return, including one they have composed about Scott Peter and his hunt for the Vörös nyaku liba."

When the permits arrived I set off for England with the live geese in three large crates. At Budapest they were loaded into an aeroplane and we flew to Vienna. At Vienna there were reports of bad weather and fog ahead. I and the geese were the only passengers and the pilot told me that if the fog were bad we would not stop at Prague but go straight on to Leipzig.

But the fog was bad at Leipzig too, and we had not enough petrol to go on. We came down gingerly, dropping into the grey blanket of fog, saw a chimney-top flash by, and zoomed up again into the sunshine. Three times we tried unsuccessfully to get down, and then flew a few miles to a military airport at Erfurt where we found, as the wireless had reported, a thin patch in the mist and we landed safely. We refuelled there with 400 gallons poured from tins, and then we took off again and flew to Cologne.

At Cologne the service was suspended. England was enshrouded in fog. There had been a bad accident at Croydon, with the loss of fourteen lives, that morning, and the geese and I could go no further by air. There was a chance, they said, that I might catch the boat train to the Hook and be in London the next morning; and I was anxious to do this because the crates were small and the geese unfed, for I had been counting on a short journey. But I had so arranged my affairs that I had only just enough money for my taxi in London, so that I might obviate the currency restrictions on the journey across Europe. By the time that the airline had refunded the exact railway fare necessary there was hardly time to catch the train. The bus hurtled from the airport to the station to the great discomfort of the other travellers, and accompanied by two airline porters I dashed in to buy my ticket. One of them, carrying my baggage, came with me, while the other took charge of the geese.

"You have luggage to register?" asked the booking clerk. "Then you will have to pay extra for it." "Yes," said I, "but my train is due to leave, I will have to pay on the train."

"You must pay now."

"I have no more money," I replied, and threw down a few pfennigs which was all that I had. The porter pulled me by the arm. "Never mind him," he said, and we dashed up the steps on to the platform.

There was a train moving past the platform at a good speed. The other porter ran up. "Your geese are in there—in the front van," he shouted, and I could see that there was not a chance of loading my baggage on to that fast-moving train. But the geese were going to the Hook: baggage or no baggage I must go with them. So I leapt on to the running board, shouted back to the porter, who said, "All right, I'll send them after you," and pulled myself up into the train.

Once inside I took stock of my position. All that I had with me was a Hungarian fur-collared overcoat, a volume of short stories by Somerset Maugham, and a cheque book. I had no money and I had had no food since a roll at Vienna at ten in the morning. As I walked along the train and through the dining-car I was tortured by the smell of the dinner which my fellow travellers were already enjoying.

I appealed to the head waiter of the dining-car, but he had no suggestions to offer.

When you are hungry it is bad to think about food. I went and sat in a carriage further up the train and thought about food for half an hour. I had just started to think of something else when the little bell sounded in the corridor and the attendant announced the second service. A few moments later an official came to inspect my passport.

"Are there any English people on the train?" I asked him.

"Yes, there are one or two."

"Which of them would be most likely to lend me a pound?" and I tried hard to look as though I were not a 'confidence man'. But he looked so suspicious that I had to tell him my story and when he admitted that he had heard the geese honk as he passed through the luggage van I knew that I could count on his support.

He led me to a benevolent-looking Englishman who, when I had told my story over again, willingly cashed a cheque for me, and ten minutes later I was eating a hearty dinner.

From then onwards the journey went smoothly enough and by the following evening we had all arrived safely at the lighthouse —eleven Whitefronts, four Lesser Whitefronts, one Bean Goose and I.

The following year I decided to extend my search for Red-breasted Geese to the Caspian Sea. This, according to Alpheraky's great monograph, *The Geese of Europe and Asia*, was their true wintering ground, and I took careful notes of their reported whereabouts, especially an account by one Zhitnikov—a traveller who saw thousands of them in the trans-Caspian Steppes.

I set off alone on my wild goose chase in November 1937. It was a more ambitious journey than any I had made before. My destination was the Persian shore of the Caspian because the more northerly Russian shores were even then almost impossible of access to a foreigner. I travelled out by way of Beirut, and took the Nairn transport, a glorified motor-coach, from Damascus straight across the desert to Baghdad, a journey of sixteen hours, steering mostly by compass course. From Baghdad after a week staying with the Ambassador—Archie Clark-Kerr—I travelled up by car to Teheran.

I knew from Alpheraky that the Red-breasted Geese wintered in large quantities on the Mughan steppe in Russia, and I hoped that when, in the middle of winter, this steppe had become snow-covered, the geese would migrate southward to a lagoon near Pahlevi, in the bottom left-hand corner of the Caspian. I also knew that thirty years before Zhitnikov had seen them on the River Atrek, which flows into the Caspian in its bottom right-hand corner.

My first port of call, therefore, was the lagoon at Pahlevi. I was driven by hired car from Teheran, over the Elburz Mountains by the mountain road through the Chalus Pass—an impressive piece of engineering. From the top of the pass we dropped down into the Caspian forest. Instead of the dry brown plateau, there was rich vegetation. I had expected this to be a tropical forest, but it was just like an English woodland with beech trees, oaks, boxwood, brambles, and bracken as well as acacia and tamarisk. But although these looked like English woods I was told that they contained in their inner fastnesses tigers, leopards, wolves, deer, wild pigs, porcupines, and wild pheasants.

The big lagoon at Pahlevi was a great gathering place for wild-fowl, including in aggregate literally millions of ducks which fed at night in the rice fields. I had never dreamed that my favourite group of birds could exist together in such concentrations. They rose almost like smoke from the edges of the reedbeds. At the time I thought there might be 20,000,000 ducks on this one lagoon, which is thirty miles long and about ten miles wide, bordered by mudflats, reeds and marshy broads, but I expect this was an over-estimate. Most of the ducks were Mallards, Teal and Pintails, but there were, in varying quantities, most of the ducks of Europe and many of the Asiatic ones too. Here I first saw the White-headed Duck—a Stifftail and the Eurasian counterpart of North America's Ruddy Duck; and unexpectedly I saw large flocks of Smews.

Of geese there were also large numbers, but only Eastern Greylags and Whitefronts—alas, no Red-breasted.

On several days I watched flocks of Pelicans, perhaps nine feet across the wings, rising into the sky and circling upwards in a great spiral. They gained height without moving their wings at all—merely by soaring in an upward current. As they turned the pinkish-white of their plumage looked whiter than white and the sun shone on the tops of their steeply banked wings. As a back-ground to all these magnificent birds was the frieze of snow mountains—the noble peaks of the Elburz range.

I learned that in the great lagoon or *murdab* near Pahlevi the wildfowlers or *murdabchis* had an extraordinary way of catch-ing wild ducks at night. To discover how it was done and how to do it myself I went to stay for ten days in the charming village of Siah Derveshan.

At night great numbers of ducks come to feed in specially preserved broads surrounded by trees and well grown with low vegetation through which waterways have been cut. The *murdab-chis* go afloat in two boats. In the bows of the first, burning on a tiny earth-covered foredeck, is a flare consisting of bullrush fluff soaked in kerosene. Immediately behind this is a hood of rush matting and behind this again stands the duck-catcher with a great elongated hand-net. He and the rest of the boat are in darkness, shaded from the light of the flare by the intervening hood. The boat is propelled with a punt pole from the stern. The second boat is propelled also with a punt pole but surprisingly from the bows. In the stern sits a man incessantly beating a gong. It seems that the object of the gong ringing is to drown all other noises of the approaching boat and to bewilder the ducks so that they do not fly until it is too late. The gong makes a noise which is difficult to locate. The sound rises and falls and it is hard to tell how far away it is. Often when I was in the front boat I thought that the gongster's boat had been left far behind, but when I turned to look there it was in the shadows just astern. There are many places in that neighbourhood where the flickering flare and the ringing gong go nightly through the marshes—the nearest thing in reality to the Dong with the Luminous Nose. The ducks must get used to them, and think of them as some strange predatory animal from which they must hide in the thickest cover. Often it is difficult to persuade them to fly at all. They swim along with their heads low on the water hoping not to be seen. The *murdabchi* makes a high-pitched squeak such as you might make to attract a dog and which seems to be heard above the ringing of the gong. Immediately the bird jumps into the air, the *murdabchi* makes a swipe with the net and the duck is caught. It is even sometimes possible to pick the ducks up by hand as they swim against the boat. I caught one like this myself. Many species of ducks are caught with flare and gong and hand-net in these marshes and sent to market. My *murdabchi* who owned the particular marsh—a man of tremendous skill with the duck net— told me that one year, rather earlier in the season, he had caught over 600 in a night.

After a little practice I became fairly proficient with the net, and one evening I caught a dozen myself under the watchful eye and with the helpful tuition of my host.

The south-western corner of the Caspian had failed to produce Red-breasted Geese. I travelled eastward along the coast, past Ramsar with its huge new hotel, where by chance I met Prince Peter of Greece who was travelling in the opposite direction. (We dined together enjoyably and did not meet again for twenty-five years.)

At Babol I collected an interpreter—a Persian lad named Ismail Khodjeste who spoke a few words of German, and for a short period I was joined by Christopher Summerhayes, the British Consul at Teheran. I had stayed with him there, and a few weeks before he had taken me exhaustingly to the top of a mountain before dawn to hunt ibex.

We hired a large sailing boat to explore the lagoon at Bandar-i-Gaz and were accompanied by a guide who had looked carefully at my reasonably realisitic water-colour of a Red-breasted Goose.

Yes, he said, he knew them well. They were locally called 'Ghazal Goz' and he could show us thousands. Two days later when we had sailed far up the lagoon he pointed proudly to his flock of Ghazal Goz. They were flamingoes. My drawing, though perhaps not perfect as a likeness, deserved better than that. We decided that our guide had not been entirely honest with us, but the flamingoes —15,000 strong—were very beautiful; their pink, made doubly pink by the rising sun, outshone the pinkness of the mountain snows beyond.

From Bandar-i-Gaz we drove across the steppe to Gumbad-i-Kabus, a magnificent tenth-century tower built by one of Genghis Khan's lieutenants and still in astonishingly good repair. It is a round brick tower of great height with a conical roof and beautiful angular flutings in its walls.

The south-east corner of the Caspian makes a sharp corner and we headed northward in our tumbledown car across a corner of the great plain which stretches away and away north and east to Bokhara, Samarkand and Tashkent. The unending expanse of the steppe was vastly impressive. We were travelling along scarcely defined tracks, over ground where the car was often bogged, and once horses from the nearest village took half a day to haul us out. But at last we reached the Russian frontier, only to find the great marshes of the River Atrek virtually devoid of geese of any kind. We saw Red-crested Pochards, and I mastered the handling of the smallest and most tipply dug-out canoe that I had ever seen, but a small party of Greylags were all the geese that we saw. If there were Red-breasts there thirty years ago on that very date (as Alpheraky's book stated most categorically that there were) then they must have changed their habits. Neither the officer in charge of the frontier post nor any of the local Turkoman tribesmen seemed to know of the bird.

During the night we heard Lesser Whitefronts passing southward on migration and next day on a romantic and unmapped lake called Atagel we saw a small bunch of them resting. But of Zhitnikov's hordes of Red-breasts there was not a sign.

We followed the Lesser Whitefronts back towards the mountains and our quest led us back to the lagoon where we had seen the flamingoes. It transpired that on the voyage in the sailing boat we had gone to within two or three miles of a magnificent marsh where huge flocks of these little geese were wintering, but we had turned back just before discovering it. Now we decided to explore it fully—it was our last chance of finding the elusive Red-breasts.

The marsh is dominated by a small hillock on top of which stands the romantic looking village of Kara Tappeh. The words mean 'black hillock' and it looked strangely black across the green marsh on a clear day. I spent about a week living in the headman's house—for as usual in that country I was received with almost embarrassingly generous hospitality. Although the people of the village knew the Red-breast as a straggler in small numbers, I satisfied myself that there were none there now among an estimated 30,000 Lesser Whitefronts which might have been twice as many.

So finally and reluctantly I abandoned the search and headed for home.

The birds I had come so far to see had completely eluded me. I had not seen a single one; and yet I had seen a thousand other new and exciting sights. The thread on which I had hung my journey mattered scarcely at all by comparison with the journey. I had become a traveller.

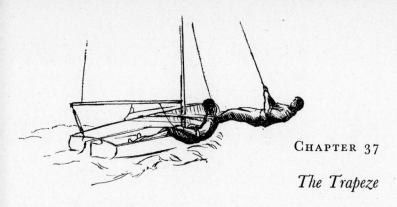

CHAPTER 37

The Trapeze

As the summer of 1938 approached I began to think of our new sailing plans. John Winter and I had long had a theory which we had now decided to put to the test.

We believed that the crew rather than the helmsmen should be responsible for the tactics of a dinghy race. The helmsmen's attention should be exclusively occupied with watching the luff of the jib and sailing the boat, especially to windward. The crew was in a very much better position to look all round at the other competitors, assess the tactical situation and decide when to tack. Neither of us had ever had a crew we could entirely trust to do this, so we had sailed our boats by feel while we ourselves looked around to see how the tactical situation was developing.

There was the additional advantage in the new idea that, in sitting out, the helmsman uses rather different muscles from the crew; if we sailed one round each of a long and gruelling race, by changing over we should be much fresher, and therefore much less likely to make mistakes or to be clumsy in our exhaustion. Some years before we had planned to join forces—become joint owners of a boat in which we could put our theory to the test. Until this year there had been one difficulty about the plan. I was unwilling to join forces with John until I had won a Prince of Wales's Cup on my own account. My pride demanded first a success without John, the winner of 1934, to show me how. But having finally won the Big Race in *Thunder* at Lowestoft the way was now clear, and we had commissioned Uffa Fox to build us a new boat. In order to make it quite plain what the new boat was and how the system would work she was called *Thunder & Lightning*. John planned to retain *Lightning* and I retained *Thunder*. If the idea did not work we had our escape routes ready.

We had also had another idea—the device which is now

universally known as the trapeze. Some years before I had crewed Beecher Moore in his Thames Rater at Surbiton to which he had fitted a 'Bell rope' attached to the mast at the 'hounds' and one member of the crew hung on to this and was thereby enabled to lean much further out than without it. Uffa, Charles Curry, John and I had discussed taking the invention a stage further by the use of a harness to be worn by the crew which could be hooked on to a wire hanging from the 'hounds', that is to say from the point of attachment of the main shrouds to the mast. In this way the crew would lean or even sit in the harness with his feet on the gunwale and his body horizontally stretched outboard. If it really worked this device would give enormously greater driving power to the boat than had ever been possible with toe-straps in the middle of the boat and the crew leaning out just as far and as long as his belly muscles would sustain him. The Canadian dinghies had also used a method of belaying the jib sheet to a cleat on a sort of breast plate strapped to the crew. Our harness would combine the two.

As well as this trapeze, we felt that the very light wooden centre-board, which I had tried out in *Daybreak* but which I had not dared to use in heavy weather, might be operated in combination with the new trapeze method of keeping the boat upright. We hoped to keep her up with the trapeze and at the same time have the advantage of the greatly reduced all-up weight off the wind. *Thunder & Lightning* was completed only very shortly before the Prince of Wales's Cup Week, which that year was at Falmouth. As a result there was no chance to try out the trapeze in realistic conditions. First, it had to be kept secret, or moderately so, and secondly, during the early races of the week the winds were quite light.

On the evening before the big race John and I sailed out from Falmouth Harbour, round the corner into Carrick Roads and there, safely out of sight of all our competitors we tried out our new device in a very light wind. If I sat out to leeward and pulled the sheet in tight, it was just possible for John to go out to wind-ward on the wire. The device seemed practical. How would it affect our performance? Of this we still had no clue.

There was in our minds no doubt that the trapeze was legal. Outriggers were not allowed, but nothing solid protruded from the boat in this system, and a wire hanging from the mast could not possibly be described as an outrigger. However, so that there should be no doubt of the legality if we used it, on the night before the race, when it was too late for anyone else to apply the system to their own masts, we leaked the information in the bar. There were cries of derision. We even showed them the harness and breast plate, which had been made for us. It brought loud and ironical laughter, and the cry, "No big race has ever yet been won by a gadget."

The day of the race again dawned utterly calm. We had to consider whether or not we should put in our light centreboard. The trapeze, its concomitant, could be used at will, but the selected centreboard had to be fitted before launching the boat. Was it to be the one made entirely of wood, or the one ballasted with fifty pounds of metal? We dashed by car up to the headland and looked out over Falmouth Bay. The race was to be held in the open sea and there was the merest cat's paw of a breeze lying across the face of the water. Sitting on a seat overlooking the bay was an old man in a navy blue jersey and peaked cap. "What do you make of the weather?" we asked. "How much wind will there be by midday?"

"Well," said he, "I think that'll blow. You wait till the sea breeze sets in and you'll find you've got all you want out there." This was a most encouraging prophecy, but how good was the prophet? We were disposed to be convinced that none was better.

We hurtled down the hill, put in the wooden centreboard and were towed out of the harbour, through Carrick Roads and round the headland into Falmouth Bay eating our sandwich lunch as we went. By the time we reached the Committee boat a light breeze was blowing and it was evidently freshening all the time.

There was a big fleet—more than fifty boats—and the usual build-up of dry-mouthed tension. Just before the start it had become a planing breeze. We were carrying *Lightning*'s old mainsail, a famous sail which had been borrowed by Stewart Morris for one of his wins in *R.I.P.* and used by John for his win in 1934. A sail which had won two Prince of Wales's Cups already, and been second in two more, had a certain magical quality quite apart from its proven excellence as a power unit. It was getting old now, and perhaps more suitable for heavy weather; through stretching it was flatter than it had been, but it seemed just right for a good whole-sail planing breeze.

I was to sail the first half of the race and I did not make a very good start. Immediately to windward of us and slightly ahead was Robert Hichens in his latest home-made dinghy *Venture II*. We were both on the starboard tack and in a matter of moments

John had belayed the jib on a cleat and was out on the trapeze. Standing horizontally out from the boat with his feet on the gunwale, he was a startling sight even to me. To the other competitors the spectacle was irresistible. At an important time a great many of them gave their attention to our trapeze at the expense of sailing their own boats. Robert Hichens was now almost directly ahead; his crew looked at John with amazement, drew Robert's attention to him and for a critical ten seconds Robert sailed his boat 'off the wind', which allowed us to luff across his wake and get our wind clear. At one stroke we had escaped the consequences of my bad start and with John's weight keeping the boat much more vertical, with much less effort than any of the others, we forged ahead and rounded the weather mark first by thirty seconds. But what about the jinx? Still in all the history of the Prince of Wales's Cup no one had ever won the race who had been first at the first mark. I said something about this to John, whose sharp reply was, "There's got to be a first time." Stewart was lying second for a while, until he was overtaken by Colin Ratsey, sailing brilliantly in a very broad-beamed ugly-looking dinghy called *Hawk*.

We finally finished nearly four minutes ahead of him, with Stewart third. Although it was satisfactory to win and as a race it was exciting in the extreme, it could not quite compare with the thrill of my first success in *Thunder*, the year before. The holder of a Championship has more to lose than to gain. If he wins, so he should; if he does not, eyebrows are raised.

But as soon as the race was over the trouble began. Was the trapeze legal or was it not? When it was pointed out that the rest of the fleet had had an opportunity to say whether or not they thought it illegal before the race and had not done so, nobody was ready to enter a protest against it after we had won. All that was left was to say that in future it must be banned and, on the principle of setting a thief to catch a thief, I was asked by the Yacht Racing Association's Dinghy Committee (of which as a Cup-winner I had now become a member) to draft the wording of a rule which would ban our exciting new invention.

I am still sorry about this decision. It may be that it would have radically changed the fourteen-footers, yet here was a system of keeping a small dinghy upright in strong winds which was eminently enjoyable, required no very great skill, but looked spectacular, appeared to have no danger, and reduced the compression strain on the mast. Most important of all it made the body weight of the crew a little less critical, because it enabled a light crew, for example a girl, on a trapeze to compete on even terms with a heavy man in wind strengths up to fifteen knots, whereas previously the light ones had been at a disadvantage in any wind above ten knots. All these advantages were there for the taking, but because of a prejudice against what appeared to be too difficult and acrobatic and what was imagined to be dangerous, and perhaps most of all because we had won the Prince of Wales's Cup by its use, it was outlawed and did not in fact return until the design of the Flying Dutchman seventeen years later. Now it is also carried in the 505 class and one or two others as well, and greatly enhances the enjoyment of sailing on a hard day. It is tremendously exhilarating to stand out, comfortably supported by the trapeze, almost horizontal and skimming low over the waves.

It is sad that a handful of people who did not have the vision to see this should have outlawed the trapeze for so long.

CHAPTER 38   *Anabel*

THE collection of tame waterfowl living round the lighthouse had
been developing over the years, and now occupied about seven
acres of saltmarsh and the sea-wall, enclosed with a fox- and dog-
proof fence. What had begun as an assembly of British wild geese
and a few ducks was gradually developing into something a
great deal more comprehensive. But delightful though it was to
have the rare exotic species wandering in the enclosures and
coming up each morning and evening to be fed on the gravel
drive outside the front door, my greatest pleasure was in the wild
birds that came in of their own free will to join the party. There
were usually twenty or thirty Wigeon on the tidal pool, occasionally Shovelers and Tufted Duck, but the geese were the most
exciting. Often there were Pinkfeet in ones and twos, and family
parties, and for one winter a pair of Whitefronts. A Pinkfoot
called Anabel brought the greatest thrill of all.

She first came to the lighthouse on 25th September, 1936.
At that time the enclosure contained a flock of twenty-nine
Pinkfeet, and Anabel, who was a lost child, came sweeping down
to join them. Although she had already flown from Iceland at
least—perhaps from Greenland—she was at the most three and a
half months old, had somehow lost contact with her family and
was delighted to find some of her kind. She did not get a very
friendly reception from the other geese, but bad-tempered company was better than none. Although I was probably the first
human being she had ever seen, she showed no fear of me as I
stood watching her less than twenty yards away. Clearly she
supposed that if her elders and betters were not afraid there was
no reason why she should be either. Anabel was finally accepted
by the other geese and spent the winter at the lighthouse. By
March the thousands of Pinkfeet which had been wintering on

the Wash had started their northward migration, but Anabel stayed with the twenty-nine. I began to think that perhaps she would stay all summer through, but on the morning of 16th May when I went out to feed the birds there was no sign of Anabel. The migratory urge was not to be denied. During the moonlight night she had slipped away and set off to catch up with the great flocks already back in Iceland and Greenland.

At noon on 9th October, 1937, I was standing on the bank outside my front door when I heard Anabel shout, high up in a dappled autumn sky. She was a tiny speck when I first saw her, almost straight above me, and with bowed wings she hurtled downwards. She came in confidently, without circling at all, and settled at the foot of the bank a dozen yards from where I stood with my usual bucket of corn. I called to her and she walked straight up to me. Any doubt I might have had that this really was Anabel immediately vanished. There she stood, a plump little round person, with her queer angular forehead, her unusually pink bill pattern, and the few white feathers at its base. To me she was as recognisable as a stray sheep to a shepherd or a stray hound to a huntsman.

Again she stayed all winter and again she delayed her departure in the spring, this time till 10th May. But sadly she never returned. In October 1938 I waited in vain. Perhaps she went elsewhere— I hoped so, but there are many hazards in the life of a wild goose. By far the greatest is the wildfowler's gun. It is now thought that eighty per cent of those Pink-footed Geese which reach the flying stage are killed by shooting. Probably Anabel shared the fate of the majority of her kind.

The lighthouse birds first warranted the title of 'Collection' after I had visited what was at that time the largest collection of 'ornamental waterfowl' species in Britain at Walcot Hall in Shropshire, where two brothers, Ronald and Noel Stevens had enclosed the very large lake in front of the house. The birds were in the care of Denis Wintle, an enthusiastic young man who soon found himself the greatest expert of his day on the breeding habits of the many rare species brought to Walcot. My visit there at the end of a breeding season was the start of something much bigger than I recognised. Having previously set my face against foreign species I now found them irresistible, and indulged my basic extravagance. My exhibition in the summer had done rather well and it had been established that the birds in my collection were an essential part of my painting. Without tame wildfowl living round me I could not so effectively have painted them. The lighthouse collection had come to be known as 'Bird Models' and was therefore regarded for the purposes of Income-tax Assessment as part of the expenses of being a bird painter. To be able to acquire these enchanting exotic species such as Emperor Geese (£50 a pair), Ross's Geese (£40 a pair), and the like, on that part of my income which was not to be taxed required only that these species should appear in my paintings, and they were so beautiful and charming that this was not in the least difficult. I remember driving back from Walcot Hall across England to the lighthouse with a hamper in the back containing a pair of Emperor's and a pair of Ross's, and I remember how the Emperor's chirruped at me all the way.

My expedition to the Caspian led to a series of lectures and to an invitation to stay with the Duke and Duchess of Bedford at Woburn Abbey. They had read of my unsuccessful attempts to catch Red-breasted Geese in Persia and I knew that they kept, and had bred them, at Woburn. Apparently nearly thirty years before, a single pair of Red-breasted Geese had been obtained, which had not bred until they had been in captivity for thirteen years; thereafter they had rapidly increased until now there was a flock of some forty or fifty birds.

I arrived at Woburn as instructed after tea and was duly impressed by the vastness of the Abbey. I was led first to my room by a liveried footman of such presence that I felt that he must be a Chamberlain at least. Then I was led to the Library, not as I expected in order to meet my host and hostess, but rather to select a book to read until it was time to dress for dinner. I selected an ornithological work and returned to my room along the endless red-carpeted corridor lined with marble busts. In due course I emerged for dinner where for the first time I met the eighty-year-old Duke, and Mary Duchess of Bedford, herself a distinguished ornithologist, who was at that time acting as trained anaesthetist in her own clinic in London, and had flown herself back to Woburn that evening in her own light aeroplane.

After dinner the Duke told me about his herd of Père David's Deer. The species had been discovered in 1865 by the French Missionary Père Armand David, when he looked over the wall of the Imperial Hunting Park south of Peking. Apparently it was already extinct in the wild state. Later the forty-five miles of brick wall round the park was breached by floods and all the deer were believed to have been eaten by the famine-stricken peasants. But some must have survived, for there was still a herd there to be destroyed in the revolution of 1900. The last female in Peking had died in about 1920, but meanwhile a few had been obtained by various zoos, and the Duke told me how he had set to work to collect as many of these as possible in order to breed them up again at Woburn. As I recall he had found eight animals and from these he had built up a herd of about 200. I remember being tremendously impressed by this. The vision of one man on the opposite side of the world had saved a Chinese species from extinction; and it was not some obscure animal barely distinguishable from its relations, but a magnificent great beast with antlers quite different in shape from those of any other stag in the world. This, I remember thinking at the time, was in itself an achievement to justify the work of a lifetime. Such was (and still is) my reverence for the evolution of species, and my horror of the extinction of any single one of them.

The Duke also told me about the waterfowl collection in the park which was still one of the finest in the country, with Trumpeter Swans and full-winged flocks of Upland and Ashy-headed Geese, and full-winged Cape Barren Geese.

That night I was asked what time I would like breakfast and said, "Oh, whatever is the usual time—eight o'clock or half past eight—whenever it is convenient." I was told that eight o'clock would be very suitable and that Her Grace would be with me, as she would like to talk about Red-breasted Geese and show me her own flock in the garden after breakfast. She would herself have had breakfast at half past six as she always did. So as I ate my breakfast we talked of Red-breasts. I was shown the little flock of twenty birds which lived in the garden (there were twenty more in a walled paddock on the other side of the park). It was my first really close look at a flock of these exquisite little geese. If my Caspian trip had been successful I too might have had such a show in my enclosure round the lighthouse. More than anything else, the sight of these little Harlequin birds cropping the grass at terrific speed with their tiny bills brought home to me the basic failure of my journey to Persia.

As I was getting into my car to leave the Duchess said, "May I send you a pair of Red-breasted Geese for your collection?" I was overjoyed and accepted delightedly. I said, "You must come over and see them; could you not fly over in your aeroplane and land at Sutton Bridge aerodrome which is only three miles away?" This she said she might very well do. But I never saw her again. A few weeks later she was lost in her plane somewhere in the North Sea. Whether or not it had been her intention to land near the lighthouse will never be known.

The two little Red-breasts which came to the lighthouse from Woburn turned out both to be females. It was not so disastrous as it might have seemed, for a year later, when this first became evident, I had the opportunity of acquiring fifty wild caught Red-breasts from a dealer in Belgium. The market price in Britain was £50 a pair and one or two pairs had recently changed hands at £100. My twenty-five pairs could be had for £350. It seemed a big outlay and clearly they could no longer be 'bird models', but the expense was justified when I found eager customers for seven pairs at the full price and had a fine flock of thirty-six of the glorious little birds for nothing. Wild caught geese of any species seldom breed until they have been a dozen years in captivity. That the Red-breasts obeyed this general rule had been demonstrated by the original pair at Woburn. Hand-reared females, however, are likely to breed as soon as they become adult at three (sometimes two) years old. So now I had two potential breeding birds to be mated from the new arrivals, which was even better than if I had originally been given a pair.

CHAPTER 39   *The Hectic Trip*

AT the time of the Munich crisis I was on the other side of the Atlantic. I had been appointed Captain of an International fourteen-foot dinghy team taking three boats to race again at Toronto, and I had planned to have an exhibition of pictures in New York in November. In between the two I planned to see some American wildfowl and to paint some pictures of them to augment the ones sent over from England. My book *Wild Chorus*—the successor to *Morning Flight*—was also due in the autumn and there was still some of the text to be finished and sent back to the publisher. Finally I had brought some slides made from photographs I had taken in Persia with which I proposed to lecture. Altogether it was going to be rather a hectic trip.

A week after winning the Prince of Wales's Cup at Falmouth with the trapeze, we set off for Canada, as before in the *Empress of Britain*. Michael Bratby came as team manager and the helmsmen of the other two boats were Charles Curry and Colin Chichester Smith. John Winter was unable to get away from his business making grinding wheels at Stafford.

It was a happy but unsuccessful team, for the Canadians had learned much about dinghy design since our first victorious sortie and the winds were light throughout. This time Charlie Bourke and his team were too good for us, though the racing was very close. But for the disqualification of one of our boats we should have taken the series to five races for a decision. As it was, Canada won by three races to one.

Living in Toronto at that time was Elizabeth—pretty, gentle little Elizabeth from my Cambridge days. She was as sweet as I remembered her and radiating happiness. Her husband was in broadcasting, and her son, Peter, was six weeks old.

As soon as the races were over I went for a cruise down the lake in a schooner with Hank Hill, the most successful of the Canadian helmsmen in the series, and his charming wife Libby, who knitted me a pair of spotted socks while I wrote the concluding chapters of *Wild Chorus*.

The political situation in Europe looked very black. From New York I cabled to my mother "HAVING LOVELY TIME. VERY HOPEFUL SUCCESS SHOW. CABLE IF YOU CONSIDER NECESSARY RETURN FOR WAR. LOVE. PETE."

The answer by cable forecast that there would be no war in 1938.

A two-day trip to Canada to see the Greater Snow Geese came in mid-October. Three months before we had passed their gathering place on the north shore of the St. Lawrence estuary, on our way up the river in the *Empress of Britain*. Standing with Lady Tweedsmuir, wife of the Governor-General of Canada (John Buchan, who had opened one of my early exhibitions), we had looked across at the bluff headland of Cap Tourmente which overlooks the Snow Goose marsh. Colonel Eric Mackenzie, who knew the place, had pointed it out to us, but in high summer the geese had been in north Greenland and the Arctic Islands.

Now, in company with Eric Mackenzie again, I was to see the place with its geese. The adventure is described in a letter to John Winter:

"In the early morning we motored from Quebec out to the village of St. Joachin (pronounced in the French way). The countryside was brilliant with the reds and yellows of autumn, and the hills sloped down to the edge of the river with just a narrow marsh along the shore. At the end of Orleans Island the flat ground is wider, and there are rolling fields, rather like the fields at East Park on the Solway. The woods and copses were aflame and the great hill of Cap Tourmente behind rose, scarlet, to its peak to the eastward, and then sloped steeply down to the river. As we motored along through the fields, I suddenly saw my first Greater Snow, and a moment later several more circling in ones and twos before settling with some on the ground but still out of sight.

"After driving through two farmyards we arrived at the club, which is a nice little green shack on the very edge of the salting. There is a verandah enclosed with glass, an inner room and two or three bedrooms opening off it. From the verandah we could see a great many white geese out on the marsh, but the main lot could be heard as the distant hum of a big city, a mile up the shore under the sun.

"Our host was a charming French-Canadian banker, Henri Des Rivières and with him was a nice old ornithologist from Vancouver, Ted White, who spends a week there every year."

The club was, of course, a shooting club, but its membership was limited and each hunter was allowed five geese per day and only fifty geese per season. In effect this meant that about 400 geese were shot out of about 16,000 geese which assembled there.

Eric Mackenzie was keen to co-operate with me in getting wingtipped birds for sending home to my lighthouse, and I was also trying to take photographs with my Leica. In both of these objectives we were successful. We collected two young birds which were only slightly wounded and which were subsequently shipped to England in the *Empress of Britain*, and I took some remarkable pictures, afterwards reproduced in *Life* magazine.

The Greater Snows were striking to photograph with their white plumage and black wing tips. Most of the adults were stained with iron deposits on head and neck, and sometimes on the breast too, which gave them a beautiful orange glow.

It was on the following day that the Snow Geese provided their greatest thrill. What I saw that afternoon had a special influence on the distant future. We had been out in the morning in pursuit of the American Woodcock in the Dogwood thickets:

"As we returned we could see that the geese were feeding near the club. We went round and in by the back door so as not to disturb them, and we had lunch. The geese were then feeding 120 yards away, about 900 strong. During lunch they got nearer and nearer, and more and more geese came in to join them.

"Further down the marsh was another big lot and these came pouring up to settle with those in front. Eventually there were fourteen Blue Geese in our immediate vicinity.

"We kept fairly still inside the verandah of the club, though we were more or less in full view. I managed to get a window open and took innumerable photos. It was amazing. The geese came closer and closer, and as they worked towards us the greatest concentration always seemed to be near us, urging them to come nearer still.

"There was a ditch at about seventy yards but that did not

hold them up. They flew across it, and to finish with we had them within, believe it or not, nine yards of the open window. The window was six or seven feet from the ground, so we looked down on to the geese. The only flaw was a fence across about three yards away with a bar which cut across the white mass of the geese.

"During all this time geese were circling about within twenty or thirty yards. I took ninety photos and once, in my excitement and haste, I opened the back of the camera before rewinding the film. Fortunately this was at an early stage, and later pictures when the geese came closer will cap the spoiled ones (I hope). But wasn't it stupid!

"By now there were between four and five grand within a quarter of a mile on three sides of us, and plumb in front was a thick mass of 600 or 700 birds, all between ten and fifty yards away and so thick that you could not see grass between them. They were fighting and squabbling and feeding and drinking in a little puddle, and preening and flapping and flying ten yards and settling again, and making such a babel that we could hardly hear ourselves speak.

"They had been like this for about an hour and a half, with two or three young blues in the forefront when the climax came. A good many geese were sitting down with their wings drooped in the warm afternoon sunshine. Suddenly all the heads were up. A dog from the farmyard had appeared. In a moment or two they were up.

"If you can imagine 600 geese, the nearest at ten yards, filling the entire view-finder, you will have an idea of the photograph I think I have got.

"So ended an hour and a half of thrills piled upon thrills and a never-to-be-forgotten day. The geese flushed out a few hundred yards and went to a field by the railway and later a little train came chuffing by lifting them again. They settled further out like snow-flakes, looking blue against the pink of the setting sun. Soon afterwards a car arrived to take us away, and we left with a last look at the carpet of white across the marsh. Within a hundred or two which perhaps had not yet arrived from the north, we had seen all the Greater Snow Geese in the world."

But if the Snow Geese were impressive, the window through which we had watched them impressed me even more. One day my home must have such a window looking out over birds: and one day, sure enough, it did.

On 1st November, 1938, my exhibition opened according to plan at Ackermann's Gallery on New York's 57th Street. That evening I cabled to my mother:

"GREAT CROWD ONE SOLD BADLY MISSED YOUR ORGANISATION."

After a fortnight, during which sales at the exhibition were sluggish, I escaped rather guiltily to travel across the continent.

"Last week-end," I wrote to John Winter, "I went out to Connecticut to stay with one Dillon Ripley, a most charming young man of about twenty-five who has lately been round the world as an ornithologist. As far as New Guinea he went in a sixty-foot schooner, stopping at all the most attractive islands in the Pacific—Galapagos, Tahiti, Solomons, Fiji, Bali, and lots of others; he has also been into Tibet. He keeps ducks, has the only Eiders in captivity in America—two females—and knows a great deal about birds.

"He invited me down to his family house at Litchfield, especially to try to catch some ducks on a neighbouring lake with a flare and a gong. They were living in a small cottage on the estate, as the big house was closed for the winter.

"On the lake on the first afternoon I saw my first Hooded Mergansers and my first Buffleheads. There were Scaup, Canvasbacks, Goldeneyes, Black Ducks, Mallard, Greenwinged Teal and Coots. But there were not more than 150 ducks on the three-mile-long lake which was quite open, with no reeds, so I was not very sanguine about *murdab* methods.

"However we had bought a cymbal and as a flare we had a round lamp which looks like a bomb and which is in standard use over here where road repairs are in progress. Hugh Birkhead, a shy and quiet friend of Dillon's, who is at present working at the Natural History Museum, had picked it up on the roadside, and it was planned to put it back next day. We had a beautiful net which had been made to my design, and we made a hood out of a petrol can (oddly enough indistinguishable from the oil company cans which had been used for hoods in Persia). In a large canoe we set off up a river towards a pool where many ducks were said to feed. Dillon was paddling, Hugh in the middle beating the cymbal which made a noise almost exactly like the Persian gong, and I balancing perilously in the bows with the net. Standing up with a ten-foot net in the bows of a Canadian canoe with two other people in it, on a dark night when you may hit sudden snags is not one of the pleasanter occupations, but when we got under way and slipped along under the overhanging trees, with the gong ringing away it was amazingly like the Caspian again; even the paraffin smoke of the flare was the same and agreeably evocative.

"Several things were slightly different: the flare, and therefore the hood were much higher above the water than they should have been, and it was impossible for me to get far enough into the bows, because the canoe was too narrow and tipply . . .

"We had not gone far up the river when we saw two drake mallards. The flare was not really quite bright enough, but the mallards behaved exactly according to plan and swam skulking into the reeds, where they immediately went ashore, and of course we could not follow. I clapped the net across the reeds and one of them splashed out towards us, hit the boat and, once behind us in the dark, got up and flew off. The other came out too, and I switched the big torch on to him. This was an immediate signal for him to rise. I was very much encouraged by this as undoubtedly the birds were behaving just the same here as they did in Persia. My *murdabchi* would have caught both these ducks . . ."

The letter describes that night and the next in the greatest detail, and it is a tale of ducks nearly caught, but not quite. We even got within forty yards of thirty Canada Geese. We loaded the canoe into a trailer and took it over to the large lake, where I record that we saw great numbers of Musk Rats—"huge things as big as rabbits, but otherwise like Water Rats". Bass and pickerel jumped near the boat, coots clattered into it, and the ducks just evaded us. The first night had been clear, but the second was rainy and inhospitable. We had rigged a pressure lamp with red cellophane round it, on the ground that ducks do not see the red end of the spectrum so clearly as we do, but the lamp was knocked over and the two mantles broken before the idea could be put to the test.

The water was rough on that second night. The wind kept catching the net and rolling the canoe. A capsize in that cold deep water would have been no joke.

We were spinning along quite fast with the wind on our port

quarter when suddenly we saw the Buffleheads—eight or ten of them—the principal objects of our search. Some took wing but some dived. They were only six or seven yards away. One female came within six feet of the boat, but dived again at once before I could plunge with the net. We saw it, or another, about fifteen yards away, and then nothing more.

It had been, we felt, a good try.

Van Campen Heilner, sportsman and writer on fishing and wildfowling, had already taken me to stay with Winston Guest at Gardiners Island, and to a famous Duck Club at Grand Island, Illinois, to see great concentrations of Mallards which were not there. On a wild week-end when it was blowing what Van called 'a living gale', he took me to see the Atlantic Brant and the Black Ducks on Barnegat Bay. Next I was to join him at Cape Hatteras which juts out from the coast of North Carolina. But before that I had made my own plans for seeing the great concentrations of wildfowl in California, though I doubted if I could properly afford the time or the money.

From the plane I wrote to my mother:

"I suppose I really should not be going to California, but the last six weeks has been hardish work, and social stuff—fun in a way but dull in other ways, and I need a breath of fresh air and to hear a wild goose call. The Californian ones are exciting— eight different kinds and six of them entirely new to me, so don't blame me too much. I plan to be back in England by 20th December. I have three lectures arranged for two days just before I sail.

"The show has not been going with a swing so far as sales are concerned, but enormous numbers of very smart people are there all the time. So far I have sold only four, the largest £160 . . .

"The gallery is small and principally occupied with selling antique clocks, and furniture; most of the time the pictures in one room have sporting prints leaning against them. No doubt if they had sold more I should think it a marvellous gallery.

"I have made a portrait drawing of Lillian Gish who is one of the most revered actresses on Broadway. Long ago she was a movie star; but last year she scored a great success as Ophelia in John Gielgud's *Hamlet*. She was staying with the Hammonds at Syosset for the week-end. I found her enchanting.

"I did a broadcast interview the other night with a young

man who runs a sporting programme. We had a quarter of an hour in which to slap each other on the back and call each other by our Christian names. When the broadcast came on we got to the end of our script with one and a half minutes to go, so we had to extemporise, which was great fun. So far I have not met anyone who heard it. They don't seem to listen to talks much over here.

"Immediately afterwards I had to dash off to a dinner at the Explorers' Club at which I was to speak. Three hundred people and my pictures hung round the walls. Stef [Stefansson, the polar explorer, who had opened my Exhibition] alas, was away, but several rather interesting people were there—Henson, the Negro who went to the pole with Peary, and Bartlett, also of that expedition, who did the first part of the journey, and a nice young fellow who had met David [Haig Thomas] last summer in Greenland and who had news of the *Terra Nova* [my father's ship on his last expedition]. He says she is to be broken up next year. He had seen her a few weeks ago and says she has been beautifully kept.

"I am starting to collect some material for a scientific work on the Wild Geese of the World. It is, I hope, going to be a king amongst Monographs. I hear you say 'One thing at a time.' I know, and I agree, really, but it is a good chance to make contact with the people who know about geese over here.

"Frank Chapman [head of the Bird Department at the American Museum of Natural History and an old friend of my mother's] has been the kindest and nicest person in the world. He and the Paul Hammonds, with whom I have been staying at Syosset on Long Island, have been my guardian angels . . .

"I have just had dinner, and we have come through a mountain pass, as bumpy as I have ever met in an airplane—oh, *very* bumpy! It is rather exciting to see a huge great plane like this being simply thrown about by the air. Next stop Douglas, Arizona, then Tucson, then Phoenix, and at last Los Angeles. There's something terribly thrilling about crossing a continent in a day at an average speed of 180 m.p.h. . . ."

CHAPTER 40 — *California, Here I Come*

THE birds in California exceeded all expectations. The Caspian had hardened me to the spectacle of large concentrations of ducks and geese, but I had new and incredible sights waiting for me in the marshes of the St. Joachim (pronounced this time in the Spanish way, San Wakeem) and Sacramento Valleys.

Los Banos State Refuge is a large one—about 3,000 acres, consisting of a vast reed bed with pools and open patches in it. The reed is green and luscious and the white geese eat it. Flying over it I saw my first Lesser Snow.

There were said to be no geese at all at Los Banos, but in fact there were something over 4,000. Quite a lot of them were Whitefronts, although the majority were Lesser Snows. The reeds or rather bullrushes which surrounded the pools were in places yellow with autumn tints. These are called tules—pronounced toolies. Among the tules there were one or two 'Mallard holes'. One in particular we photographed—a pool in the reeds about 150 yards long and sixty yards wide. There was quite literally (and when I say that I mean it) no water visible whatever. Short of firing a shot there was no way of getting them to fly at once, but they got up in wave after wave and they took several minutes to do it. There were without doubt 80,000 Mallards on that pond.

The largest lake of open water had a nice bunch of geese on it —about 2,500—which included a lot of Cackling Geese and some Lesser Canadas. There was also one very small bunch of Big Canadas which are rare in these parts and twenty-five Whistling Swans.

We left Los Banos Refuge and motored along twenty miles of perfectly straight track northward through the marsh, passing a line of duck clubs, their little shacks spaced out every mile or so.

Here there were still plenty of ducks but few geese. I saw my first Ruddy Ducks but they were mostly immatures or females.

A telephone wire had created havoc among the Coots; there were quantities of dead ones all along the road, but for every dead Coot a hundred squattered across the water. Towards the end of the twenty miles there was a lovely golden sunset reflected in the still marshes below it.

About ten in the evening we arrived at Grey Lodge Refuge, Gridley, which is another State Refuge. As we had motored 350 miles in the day we were quite ready to turn in in a little shack. I borrowed a sleeping-bag and had a very comfortable night.

This Grey Lodge Refuge is about 2,500 acres and most of it is thick tules with pools and a few open places. On the way in we had stopped the car and heard the Snow Geese calling and chattering in the tules, and all night I could hear them and the ducks calling.

In spite of the geese we had heard in the tules in the dark on the way to the Refuge—a goodly roar—I was told that the geese fed out in the fields at night and returned at dawn. There was no moon, but it appears that, surprisingly, this is just what they do. I was woken at six and it was just getting light. Almost immediately afterwards the geese began to come in, together with the ducks —mostly Pintails—from the rice fields. Not even in the Hortobagy nor at Kara Tappeh have I seen a more impressive flight. For the next half hour the geese—nearly all Snow Geese and Whitefronts (about seventy/thirty ratio) passed over at the rate of about 1,000 a minute. They were coming high downwind and completely filling the sky. Ducks and geese circled and weaved in clouds over the tules and eventually settled among them. The combined roar of the oncoming masses in the west and the hordes which had already settled, was deafening. I think I certainly saw 50,000 geese go down into an area of about the size of Brogden (500 acres) at one end of the Refuge.

The Pintails went on coming out of the sky, hurtling down from all directions, long after the geese were only straggling in.

It was Sunday morning and that is the day of hunters. At precisely seven o'clock the battle commenced and really it was astounding. I do not think for the first twenty minutes that there was a single second without a shot—near or distant. The result was that, as in Hungary only more so, the birds pay no attention to shooting. Geese will sit with shooting going on all round quite close, deeming (quite rightly) that the safest place they can possibly be is on the ground just where they are.

To give you some idea of the problem of hunters in this country and why refuges are so necessary, on the opening day of the pheasant shooting in the Sacramento Valley alone, 14,000 pheasants were shot and the bag limit per man is two cocks each. At least 7,000 gunners were out that day. From the exhibition I beheld yesterday morning they most of them had as little idea of range as the folk who line the bank on the Wash. They are allowed to shoot ten ducks a day and most of them do so on Saturday and Sunday. An awful lot are wounded and one finds dead ducks decomposing all over the place.

The California weather was wonderful: brilliant sun and blue sky, cool at night with very slight frost and warm but not too hot during the day. The light is perfect for photography and for looking at birds, the atmosphere so clear that looking at far-away birds through glasses is especially exciting because they seem so close.

The setting of the Gridley Refuge is magnificent. Not far to the south lie a strange clump of volcanic mountains sticking up in the middle of the Sacramento Valley; these are the Marysville Buttes (pronounced Butes). They make a marvellous background to the snowstorms of white geese. Thirty miles away to the east is the silhouette of the Sierra Nevada and to the north lies the snow-capped volcano of Mount Lassen.

In 1938 the Federal Wildlife Refuge at Willows, California, was still known as the Spalding Ranch. On a sunny November afternoon we drove along the public road which cuts through one end of the 12,000-acre sanctuary.

The Warden—Van Huizen—told me that the geese roost on the 400-acre lake, the largest body of water in this great refuge. Later there will be more water but at the moment they cannot get it. It is dispensed by the farmers and must be paid for. The rice farmers hate the ducks and are therefore loath to provide water for the refuge. Van Huizen said that this year he only had about 20,000 geese there so far, as Tule Lake, the Federal Refuge in the north of California, was not yet frozen and the geese were all up there still. The previous year they had made careful counts, as it was the first year of the refuge, and there were 300,000 geese all roosting on the 400-acre lake—nearly 1,000 geese to the acre.

There was a striking contrast between these Californian valleys and the Caspian Sea: the concentrations of birds were in many ways comparable, but this time it was a trip rather than an expedition. The trappings of civilisation—automobiles, gasoline, shower-baths, spring mattresses, hamburgers and cole slaw, canned beer, paved highways—these were with us all the time. Inescapably the scale of the adventure was reduced, even though the wildfowl were more numerous and less familiar. There were, however, compensations. The best places were known; experts were available for consultation; films were not liable to be confiscated; and although the language was still quite different from my own, I found I could understand it, and be understood, more easily. In any event I did not waste time on comparisons. For anyone with a special interest in wild geese I was in Wonderland, and I was content to be thrilled by what I saw.

To join me in the Sacramento Valley that evening came Jim Moffitt, who almost certainly knew more about wild geese in North America than any other single person. He was a keen hunter too and had made a collection of skins, especially of the Canada Goose and its various sub-species. Jim was a delightful companion for several wonderful days among the geese round Willows and Colusa. We talked eagerly about geese from morning till night, and I wanted nothing better.

On the second morning we watched the great skeins go out at flight in their thousands and then at about eleven in the morning we saw them returning and tumbling down to the water where they had roosted. This I remembered was the habit of geese in many dry countries where no water is available to them on their feeding grounds. Had not Zhitnikov described it in Transcaspia?

By now here in California I was definitely more interested in photography than in shooting and, I arranged to go again to the Grey Lodge Refuge where the photographic opportunities were so remarkable. A burst of 400 or 500 Snow Geese rising within ten yards makes a splendid picture if you shoot it fast enough to stop the movement of their wings. The light in California enabled the shutter to be set at a five-hundredth of a second.

On the following day I collected my photographs in San Francisco (some of which were gratifyingly successful) and took the plane to return eastwards. When we boarded it we found on each seat, as was the custom, a complimentary copy of the local newspaper. This had two-inch headlines: "United Airliner Crashes in Sea, five lost". We felt that this was one day when the courtesy might have been forgotten.

At ten o'clock next morning I was in Washington *en route* for

Cape Hatteras and took a small Boeing plane to Norfolk, Virginia. There to meet me was Dave Driscoll, a pilot who has flown a great deal for Van Campen Heilner, who was to be my host at Hatteras. In Dave's 'Stinson three place ship' we took off from Norfolk and flew out over Currituck Sound and along the Outer Banks which consist of a strip of sand dunes protecting a vast area of marshland and lagoon from the Atlantic rollers. Here and there are tiny villages on the banks. We flew southward eighty miles along the banks, passing over Kittyhawk where the Wright brothers first flew, and where there is a big memorial to them. Part of the marsh behind the banks was the Federal Reserve of Pea Island and there we saw not less than 2,000 Greater Snows and a lot of Honkers. Finally we landed on the beach at Hatteras at the tip of the Outer Banks, where Pamlico Sound is about forty miles wide. Van Heilner was there to meet us as we taxied up the hard sand beside the surf and he drove us and the baggage a few hundred yards to a most charming little club, small but luxuriously appointed. This is the Gooseville Gun Club.

Our main occupation was to be the pursuit of Black Ducks and Canada Geese. The Canadas were especially interesting to me because they belonged almost certainly to the Labrador form, *Branta canadensis canadensis*, in which the base of the neck below the black 'stocking' is almost white, front and back. On the second morning we shot some of these geese, and I knew that Jim Moffitt wanted the skin of an old gander, so I selected one fine bird which weighed eleven pounds five ounces and skinned it out. I had not skinned a bird since Oundle days and never a goose in my life, so it took quite a long time. However with the able assistance of Addie the cook, a rather beautiful girl, wife of a Hatteras fisherman, who wanted to learn how to skin and thought she was watching an expert, the job was done. Little did she know that I was only just remembering how to do it as I went along. I managed to complete the job in about two hours and made only one small hole by the tail.

From Hatteras Van and I were on our way to see the Blue Geese on the Gulf of Mexico, so two days after he had landed me on the beach Dave Driscoll arrived again with his Stinson ship and stayed the night in the village. At eight o'clock we took off heading for Charlotte, North Carolina, to catch the Eastern Airlines ship to New Orleans.

It was a fine morning with high grey clouds and a slight following wind. We flew west from Cape Hatteras and the ceiling got gradually lower and lower until it began to rain. Van was doing the navigation and, as he had got hopelessly lost getting into place on the marsh before the dawn the morning before, I was rather apprehensive. I had been writing a letter and had just finished it when the weather became really bad. We thought we were over a place called Warsaw. We circled round once or twice to check up on it and saw an aerial signpost on a roof top saying 'Goldsberg 30', which confirmed our whereabouts; so we set off towards Fayetteville which was west and the next airfield, about forty-five miles away. We had flown about ten of them, following the main road, when the ceiling became even lower. We were just clearing the tree tops and Van suggested to Dave that we ought to land. I was for going on to Fayetteville which would only have taken another fifteen minutes, and landing on an airfield; but they decided not and so we circled round in the rain looking for a suitable field. We went down close and looked at one but it was full of sticks (part of some crop) so we went and looked at two more and chose the first. Then we came in to land well bolstered with cushions and with our seat belts especially tight. Unfortunately Dave did not get the wheels on the ground right at the start of the field and it was not a very big one. At the end was the main road and a line of telephone wires, so there was no chance of opening up and going round again. We touched down perfectly, about half-way across the field but the road was too close. Dave jammed on the wheel brakes and she swung round just short of the wires. The wheels stuck, the ship pitched forward quite slowly on to her nose and petrol began pouring out of the wing tanks. We opened the door and leapt out, mighty pleased to be on terra firma and unhurt.

In three minutes 100 people had materialised from nowhere. We pushed the nose up and put her back on her three wheels— not before I had taken a couple of photographs. Then without delay Van chartered one of the dozen autos which had arrived on the scene and we were driving to Fayetteville, where with minutes to spare we caught a train to Charleston, South Carolina. From Charleston to Atlanta we caught the Airline Flight in a Lockheed Electra and from Atlanta we took the night train to New Orleans. Quite a day!

But the Blue Geese were worth it all. They rose like smoke from the marshes of Louisiana Furs Inc., our hosts. I crept to within 10 yards of one of the vast flocks and got the best flight photographs of geese I have ever taken.

6

On the *puszta* of the Hortobagy in Hungary in search of Red-breasted Geese.

8

Forced landing in "the Stinson three-place ship" in North Carolina, on the way
to the Blue Geese.

1938

The prototype of my window at Slimbridge. Greater Snow Geese from the window of the Gun Club at Cap Tourmente on the St. Lawrence River.

1938

From the same window as they rose. At that time the total population of Greater Snow Geese was estimated at 16,000 and they were all at Cap Tourmente when I was there. The population is now nearly ten times as many.

We went on to spend a couple of days with the fabulous Ned McIllhenny of Avery Island, New Iberia, a great traveller and story-teller.

"Avery Island is a little Empire. McIllhenny has a factory which makes Tobasco sauce, of which he has a monopoly. He has salt mines, a flourishing fur business, the largest duck banding station in the States, a show garden with the finest collection of camellias in the world and also of bamboos. He keeps alligators of which there are a great many in the marshes. He has one tame one thirteen feet long. He shot the record Kodiak Bear in 1896 and it has not been beaten."

Van and I were privileged to shoot with his famous single-barrelled twenty-bore gun with a forty-inch barrel, a fascinating piece with which we found, because of its perfect balance, that we could shoot extremely well.

From his small flock of tame Snow Geese and from his duck banding traps, he gave me a number of birds for the collection at the lighthouse and I left with ten geese, thirty-two ducks and four baby alligators. To meet me in New York came thirty geese which had been assembled in California, and with a baggage list which would have done credit to Noah, I boarded a liner for Europe at the end of my hectic trip.

K

CHAPTER 41   *"Peace in our Time"*

I ARRIVED just before Christmas 1938 in the German liner *Bremen*.

"Peace in our time" was the slogan to which I had returned, but it seemed wise to get my name on a Reserve list. I applied to be enrolled in the Royal Naval Volunteer Supplementary Reserve, and was accepted.

Wild Chorus had appeared—a picture-book full of colour and half-tone reproductions of my paintings, with line drawings as tail pieces to the chapters. It had been well received by the critics. My lighthouse home was becoming well known, and people were coming from far and wide to see the birds which lived round it. Prince Bernhard of the Netherlands took films and stayed to tea, and it was rumoured that the King and Queen would like to come over from Sandringham.

A regular visitor from his North Norfolk home was the Chairman of Vickers, Archie Jamieson, who had bought a number of my pictures—some of them to hang in the wardrooms of his new aircraft carriers.

Brian D'Arcy Irvine flew over to Sutton Bridge for the day as a Cambridge University Air Squadron pilot. The bombing range on the Wash mudflats was in use now on Saturdays and Sundays as well as week-days. "Peace in our time" was wearing thin.

The lighthouse was very comfortable and pleasant in those days. Bella, the buxom and good-natured wife of a neighbouring farm worker, came with the mail in the morning, cooked my breakfast, did the housework, put out a cold lunch and a tray of tea-things, and returned in the evening to cook the supper. Mr. Grimwood came as a secretary for a couple of hours in the morning. Kenzie Thorpe fed the birds, painted pictures in the basement and was ready to be taken for me by casual visitors when I was away. When I did not go to Westmorland for my winter week-ends, or to sail *Thunder & Lightning* for the summer ones, I had guests to stay at the lighthouse or visitors who came over for the day. I hoped I might one day soon marry Deirdre.

The prospect of war and change was exciting and unsettling. For the adventurous there was no particular merit in the comfortable security of my present existence, but I bitterly resented the prospect of its interruption.

For one week-end at the lighthouse I drove from London accompanied by Gillie Potter, the comedian. Some years earlier he had been engaged by my mother to entertain a party at Leinster Corner consisting chiefly of Civil Servants from the Ministry of Health, at a time when my stepfather was Minister. Later Beecher Moore and I had been to one of his shows, and went round to his dressing-room. When we arrived Gillie was on the telephone and he continued to talk for the next half-hour, which might appear ill-mannered, but it was not so. The audible half of his telephone conversation was just as funny as his stage performance; indeed it was so brilliantly done and so witty that we were, for a while, doubtful whether, in fact, there was anyone at the other end.

It was then that the week-end arrangements had been made, and on the long drive he entertained me with the more intimate details in the life of Lord Marshmallow of Hogs Norton and his family. We stopped at several churches on the way for Gillie to study the memorials and tombstones, for genealogy had been his life-long interest.

There had recently been some question of reviving the office of Court Jester and had anything come of the proposal Gillie's name might have been on the short list. The idea was apparently abandoned, which I have always thought rather sad, because it would seem to be an entertaining and suitable office for revival.

A Christmas card led to an affable correspondence with Lord Baldwin, now in retirement, and I had a most cordial letter asking me to come and see him in London and tell him what I had been doing in America. "Had I," he asked, "been watching the flight of capital? Surely Long Island was a better place for observing the habits of millionaires than of birds. . . ." After his contretemps with my stepfather, I was not sure how this fraternisation would be received at home, but there was no smallest sign of disapproval.

One spring night I went with my family to Covent Garden to hear Melchior singing *Siegfried*. The great Danish tenor was said to be past his prime, but the power was still there. He was certainly the finest Siegfried I have ever heard, though I remember

thinking of him more as an actor than as a musician. Afterwards
we went round to see him in his dressing-room. After his gruelling
performance he was remarkably fresh and hearty. We met his
charming and beautiful wife and at the same time the singer Lily
Pons who had been in the audience, and had also come to con-
gratulate Melchior. Thinking of the noble proportions normally
required to produce an adequate 'sounding-board' for opera
(Lauritz Melchior himself was no exception) it was to me astonishing to find so small a woman as Pons with so famous a voice.

Early in the summer of 1939 my mother and I were invited to
stay in Venice with the pianist Prince George Chavchavadze. He
had recently been married and was living in a palazzo overlooking
the Grand Canal, with a private gondola and his own gondolier.
This to me was the ultimate luxury and my mind went back to
1919 when I had learned to propel a gondola. Once more I tried
my hand at it mounted on the *poppa* and found that after rowing a
duck-punt the gentle art held no insuperable problems. Perhaps, if
all else failed, I could find work as a gondolier.

George Chavchavadze was a beautiful pianist, then not yet
perhaps at his highest peak but already wonderful to listen to, with
a large repertoire. I made two drawings of him, one of which was
rather successful in conveying the musician's far-distant look.

Besides being a very promising pianist George was charming and
amusing. One of his parlour tricks was to convey a thunderstorm
by facial expression, starting from the dim flickerings of distant
lightning and finishing with the cloudburst overhead. He had set
to music in operatic vein the legend on the current packet of
Bromo toilet paper.

Our days were spent in much the same pattern, bathing before
lunch at the Lido, going to see pictures or churches or the Doge's
Palace or Verrocchio's magnificent equestrian statue of Colleoni
in the afternoon and bathing again when we got too hot. And what
pictures and architecture there were to see! From twenty years
before I remembered the gondolas, and San Marco, and the glass
factories, but I hardly remembered the pictures at all. Now I
found myself bowled over by the vast frescoes of Tintoretto in the
Scuola di S. Rocco and the church next door, and the huge
'Paradise' (supposed to be the largest picture ever painted on
canvas) in the Doge's Palace. But oh, the Giorgione in the Giovan-
elli Palace, the Titians, the Veroneses and even the brilliant
baroqueries of Tiepolo!

In the evenings George played for hour after hour as we sat on

the balcony and watched the moonlight shimmer on the Grand
Canal. So much beauty. But the 'handful of wicked men' were at
work; European politics hung like a great cumulo-nimbus cloud
over our summer.

"Peace in our time" my foot!

In August 1939 I was invited to give the Caspian lecture with
slides at the Duke of York's Camp. This was a camp for boys from
all walks of life, and since the accession of King George VI it had
been held annually at Balmoral. I was invited to stay at Balmoral
for the night of the lecture. All the Royal Family were there, but
I met them only at tea and at breakfast next morning.

I had not seen the King since, as Duke of York, he had come to
Leinster Corner to sit for my mother's two busts of him. I had
made a quick pencil drawing of him then, but although a reasonable likeness, it had been an indifferent work of art. Now I was to
sit next to him at dinner in Camp with the boys after my lecture.

After dinner there was a splendid concert; a young member
of the camp with a delightfully fresh tenor voice sang Scottish
songs in which the audience, including the King, joined in. It was
exciting and very moving.

Now I began to make plans for the lighthouse and its birds
when war came. I arranged that the valuable flock of Red-breasted
Geese should go to Walcot Hall in Shropshire, that others should
be taken to my farmer friend Will Tinsley in Holbeach Marsh,
and that the rest should go down to Horsey Island on the Essex
coast which David Haig Thomas had lately bought.

I had no idea how long there would be for these dispositions
though I imagined that the services of all reservists would immediately be required. But until war broke out no action could be
taken about all this, so I went over to Fritton to sail *Thunder &
Lightning* in the local regattas.

PART 2

CHAPTER I   *Outbreak of War*

THE last races of Lowestoft 'Sea Week' in 1939 had an air of
unreality. It no longer seemed important to win a fourteen-foot
dinghy race. In the season before, and in the season before that,
the winning of a yacht race had seemed all-important during the
time that one was doing it. But now, as the war clouds gathered,
all the significance and excitement of it seemed to drain away as
we sailed round in a kind of trance. I remember leading the fleet
home in one race and looking back into the afternoon sun and the
silver brightness of the sea. A dozen dinghies were following us with
spinnakers set on the run up the coast from Pakefield past the
Claremont Pier. The nearest was more than fifty yards astern. As
we approached the finishing line it should have been a moment of
triumph, but instead I felt a sudden fierce sadness. Not only was this
the end of a sailing season, but the end of an era, for nothing could
now avert the war. Perhaps we should never sail dinghies again.

I was staying at Stafford with my old friend John Winter on that
morning in September when Neville Chamberlain came to the
microphone to give his famous and sombre message which meant
that we were once again at war with Germany. Ever since Munich
I had been thinking a good deal about what I should do when war
came. I was at first drawn towards the R.A.F. after flying in a
Tiger Moth with Alan Colman who had been my skipper in the
dinghy races in Long Island Sound. He had let me fly it for a bit
("You're losing rather a lot of height, you know."). But since my
father had linked me more strongly with the Navy and my yachting experience had qualified me for the Royal Naval Volunteer
Supplementary Reserve this was where I had finally been enrolled
at the beginning of 1939.

The Supplementary Reserve was a special band composed
largely of yachtsmen who believed themselves to have an assured

place in the war-time navy from the very beginning of hostilities. I was soon to discover that my impatience to start a new life in the Navy was most unpopular with the authorities. When I wrote to the Admiralty I had no reply for three weeks, and I spent the time designing a cryptic camouflage for the Universal Grinding Wheel factory at Stafford in which John worked. In accordance with my own notions of camouflage I carefully painted a little model of the works in a pattern which was subsequently transferred to the buildings themselves, and I can only record that no bomb was ever dropped on the Universal factory.

I made a broadcast about watching badgers and related it to the war. However irrelevant natural history might seem, I was more than ever convinced of its deep-rooted importance to mankind in general and to me in particular. It was in the nature of an escape, but with an urgency which I was to recognise increasingly as the war dragged on.

When an answer finally came from their Lordships of the Admiralty, it was to inform me that I should on no account communicate with them again on the subject of being called up, that I was not wanted now, and it was even quite possible that I should not be wanted at all. About a week later I was called up. I went first as a Temporary-Acting-Sub-Lieutenant to H.M.S. *King Alfred*, the famous 'stone frigate' at Hove. Here in a huge underground garage hundreds of oddly assorted professional men, a large proportion of whom had spent some part of their holidays messing about in boats, were assembled and converted in a masterly ten-days' course into fully fledged naval officers. Among us there was an extraordinary atmosphere of rejuvenation.

"This is all exactly like school again," I wrote, "and makes one feel delightfully young. It is fun too. The life is not too hard —breakfast any time after eight—Divisions nine—fifteen minutes P.T.—lectures till lunch—including heaps of parades (there are 400 of us). Lunch at twelve in mess—lectures from one-thirty to four and then off till nine next morning with dinner in mess. Plenty of home-work, of course, which it is well to do—Morse, navigation, etc. It keeps one busy."

Our neighbours at morning P.T. were as like as not a distinguished actor on one side and a K.C. on the other. It was the first term of a new adventure and inevitably the greatest for all of us. We were preoccupied with the dreadful possibility that the war might end before we got to sea.

My sojourn at the *King Alfred* lasted longer than the usual ten days, for in some way I had managed to persuade someone that of all the types of vessels at sea, the one which would clearly be best suited to my particular talents would be a destroyer. It would be another three weeks before a series of destroyer courses became available to the Temporary-Acting-Sub-Lieutenants of *King Alfred*; and so in the interim I became liaison officer between the regular staff of the training establishment and the officers under training. It was the first time such an appointment had existed, and it was up to me to make something of the job. In addition to the general training I had a number of official duties like showing newcomers how to find their way about *King Alfred* and discovering the hopes and fears and preferences of the officers awaiting appointment, but my most congenial job was the organisation of the Thursday evening concerts, which took place in the great underground garage which was used as a Mess. Among the professional actors and variety artists who took time off from their appearances in the theatres of Brighton to entertain the troops were Stanley Holloway, Elsie and Doris Waters and many others. But there was also a good deal of local talent among the sub-lieutenants of the Wavy Navy. Ludovic Kennedy, whose father as Captain of the *Rawalpindi* had just been awarded a posthumous V.C.—one of the earliest of the war—was there as a Midshipman, and did a superb burlesque of a political speech. Edwin Benbow, concert pianist, played and accompanied songs including some of my repertory of American Railroad Songs.

I remember that in return some of us were asked to appear in 'The Dome' in Brighton, with an audience of 2,000. I was to sing a Railroad Song, and 'Frankie and Johnny' as an encore, accompanied by Edwin Benbow.

Of a sudden, I remember, I got lost in the verses of 'Frankie and Johnny' and found myself back in a verse I had already sung. The only thing to do was to stop and explain to the audience what had happened. I hit upon the idea of explaining it in oversimplified language and almost at once I got a laugh. I went back over the whole thing and explained it in detail all over again, and this time got a better laugh. I believe it was widely thought to have been part of my act.

My special friends at this time were Charles Wood, who was to do the same set of Destroyer Courses with me, and Dick Addis, who wrote brilliant comic songs and sang them at the piano at the weekly concerts. Both these two were later killed.

Gillian Dearmer, whose family were old friends of my family, was Personal Assistant to the head of the A.T.S., Dame Helen Gwynne-Vaughan; also she was enchanting. I invited her to one of the weekly concerts at *King Alfred* where she met Dick Addis, and soon afterwards married him. Dick had unbounded charm and wit. He wrote and sang a song which described our life at *King Alfred*; and after he had left I sang it each week with newly added topical words. Here it is in its original form:

THE WAVY NAVY

A Song Written and Composed by Dick Addis
for H.M.S. *King Alfred*, Hove

The Lords of the Admiralty wrote to me
And gave me this information:
They'd come to a decision to grant me a commission
To last for the duration.

The Lords were as friendly as Lords can be,
But they thought it only fair to say
That if I couldn't tell green from red,
Or had a discharge from the ears or the head,
Or any such habits as wetting my bed,
They'd send me right away.

But now I can start
To learn what is a chart
And the meaning of every pennant,
For at length I was told
That my name was enrolled
As an Ordinary Voluntary
Acting Probationary
Temporary Sub-Lieutenant.
I said an Ordinary Voluntary
Acting Probationary
Temporary Sub-Lieutenant.

We're the Wavy Navy, that is what we are,
Tho' we can't tell a bottle-screw slip from a spar;
We feel pretty nervous
At joining the Service:
The Wavy Navy is all at sea.

We spend our time here getting our fun
Taking to pieces a six-inch gun,

Tho' we don't know what to do
With a 'Sear part two',
Still the Wavy Navy is all at sea.

The good ship *Alfred* is a noble craft
And we're proud of her as can be,
But however we hanker
To make her up anchor
She *won't* put out to sea.

When first we paraded the Officers laughed
And told us to cut our hair,
But though we're a pretty good failure at drill,
For our gunnery makes the instructors feel ill,
We know that the government's paying the bill,
So why should anyone care?

We're the Wavy Navy—amateur sailors
Running up bills with expensive tailors;
Our ranks however puny, form
A fine array of uniform.
The Wavy Navy is all at sea.

Just to show how the Admiralty hate us
They've sent us an officer wearing black gaiters;
His methods are similar
To those of Herr Himmler.
The Wavy Navy is all at sea.

As soon as the war is over
They tell us our services cease;
But as long as they are slaying us
They have to go on paying us
So it looks like an early peace.
Doing our bit, serving the state,
(Our stripes may be crooked
But our characters straight);
We have the effrontery
To think we serve our country.
The Wavy Navy is all at sea.

The ever so brave-y
Know-how-to-behave-y
Wavy Navy
And we're all at sea.

Whether it was the dampness of the underground garage or the unaccustomed morning P.T. or the generally germ-laden atmosphere of H.M.S. *King Alfred* I do not know, but I spent some time during those first weeks at Hove with a cold and bronchitis. But I was enjoying it; from *King Alfred* I wrote to Michael Bratby.

"I've just been earmarked for destroyers, which is an absolutely plum job. It's *the* thing which every Wavy Navy man dreams of getting into and I'm so terribly cock-a-hoop about it. There's no doubt that it's the most active and exciting branch of the Navy, and I shall probably be in the West Country and am to be under Admiral Nasmith, who is an old friend. In fact I'm in luck.

"Most of my friends have moved on to jobs of varying interest but none that I would exchange for mine in destroyers. I expect to be sent on on Monday—or perhaps before.

"One's mind is too fully occupied to think about (a) the war, (b) wildfowling, (c) one's past life, (d) anything at all outside work. But I'd be angry if the war stopped before I got to sea . . ."

At last the Destroyer Courses were ready for us and with about twenty colleagues I was sent to do an anti-submarine course at H.M.S. *Osprey*—another 'stone frigate' at Portland. Here I met Robin Jenks who was in command of the little H-class submarine which was the target for our anti-submarine exercises. Robin invited me to go out in the submarine and dive with them on the exercise, and the delicious possibility arose that she might be diverted to patrol during the exercise and that I might have to go with them. But although there were H-boats on patrol at the beginning of the war (including this one) they were generally considered only suitable for training. Nevertheless diving in a submarine was tremendously exciting to me, and especially so because I was at the time reading *We Dive At Dawn*, an account of the submarine exploits of the First World War.

H.M.S. *Defiance* consisted of a group of old wooden ships lying on moorings in the River Hamoaze at Plymouth. These constituted the Torpedo Control School, and there I went next, with all the other officers on the Destroyer Course. We were to be sent to destroyers as Asdic Control and Torpedo Control Officers, with watch-keeping duties. I rather enjoyed learning about torpedoes, perhaps especially because my father had been 'a torpedoman'. We were living on board *Defiance*. One morning our appointments came through and each of us learned with great excitement to which destroyer he would be sent. Mine was *Acasta*, an 'A'-class destroyer which was considered quite modern by comparison with the old 'V.' and 'W.' destroyers to which many of the course were to be sent. The luckiest of our band seemed to be those who were being appointed to 'H'-class destroyers, then among the more modern in the Navy. Soon after they had joined their ships the flotilla of the 'H'-class destroyers was involved in the Battle of Narvik, and we envied them the more.

I discovered that *Acasta* was working out of Plymouth and that she happened to be in harbour at the moment; furthermore I knew that her First Lieutenant was an old sailing friend, Charlie Robinson, from Norfolk. That very afternoon I decided to go down to the Dockyard at Devonport and pay a social call, in order to make my number with the officers of my new ship. I had tea in the wardroom and was taken to see the Captain, Commander Glasfurd. I was shown the cabin I would occupy and made friends with the other officers with whom I should serve. On the following morning I woke up with a slight sore throat and by the same evening I had a high temperature. The Torpedo Control Course lasted a week and I was laid low after only four days of it. The officer in charge of the course came to see me in bed on the following day and said: "You know I don't think you will have done enough of this course to be able to take up your appointment at the end of the week; I am afraid we shall have to put somebody else in *Acasta* and keep you for another week." This was a bitter disappointment, but there was nothing I could do about it. I had to spend another week learning about Torpedo Control. When the time came I was appointed to H.M.S. *Broke*. Not many weeks later, at the conclusion of the disastrous Norwegian campaign, the aircraft carrier H.M.S. *Glorious* was returning from Norway, escorted by the two destroyers *Ardent* and *Acasta*, when she was waylaid by two German heavy cruisers, the *Scharnhorst* and, I think, the *Hipper*. In an action of incredible gallantry *Ardent* and *Acasta* tried to protect the carrier with smoke-screens and to attack with torpedoes. They were both blown out of the water at close range by the German heavy ships which went on to sink *Glorious*. From the whole force there were only a handful of survivors. Commander Glasfurd and all his officers went down with their ship.

Chapter 2   *H.M.S.* Broke

H.M.S. 'BROKE' was built in 1926 as a Flotilla Leader of the 'V. and
W.' class. It was in her predecessor of the same name that Commander Evans—afterwards Lord Mountevans—who had been
second-in-command of my father's last expedition, had won fame
in the Dover patrol in the 1914 war.

This second *Broke* was already an old ship at the outbreak of the
Second World War. She was to be my home, my pride and my
joy for two long years. When I joined her she was commanded by a
fine and open-hearted man of immense courage and noble character. Bryan Scurfield was a Commander with the Albert Medal
which he had won by diving into the oil tank of a previous
destroyer to rescue some men after a collision during the Spanish
Civil War. He was universally loved by his ship's company. I
first met him in the Captain (D)s office in Devonport Dockyard a
few days before I was due to join the ship. He was a big man, tall
and well built, with very bright blue eyes. He was easy to talk to
and I knew at once that he would get the best service out of me.
And so a few days later I joined the *Broke* at Devonport and my
ambition was realised. I was in a Destroyer. I began to write a
diary in an exercise book. It did not last long chiefly because this
form of recording was frowned on for the information it might
give if captured. It was full of technical detail and the jargon of
the job; all times appeared in four figures using the twenty-four-
hour clock, and I delighted in using initial letters wherever
possible. There were two reasons for this: first I have always
liked the authenticity implied by technical jargon. Pay
your reader the compliment of supposing he will value the
additional atmosphere to be derived from it, and that he does
not want to be 'talked-down' to. The second reason was my
passionate determination as an amateur naval officer to be

more professional than the professional. My exercise book began:

"9th March, 1940. On this day I am at sea in H.M.S. *Broke* serving as a Lieutenant R.N.V.R. We have been at sea about three days fetching a convoy from St. Helens and escorting it down channel. It is the Outward Bound Convoy for Gibraltar and we take it to about 27° N. where a French escort meets it and relieves us. Then we find the Homeward Bound Convoy and chaperone that up to the Downs.

"Our convoy of eighteen ships was joined, whilst I was on watch (afternoon watch) by a section of seventeen ships from Milford Haven. They were brought by the destroyer *Winchelsea*. We had the destroyer *Wild Swan* with us so now the three of us are looking after this fine fleet of ships.

"Details of happenings, they say, are not so much worth recording as thoughts and ideas; and yet life in a destroyer at sea is made up mostly of happenings—exact happenings, positions for rendezvous, signals from the C.-in-C., submarine reports—so much so that it is impossible to write of abstractions until the course of events has been recorded. And so here is some of the record.

"When I reached the bridge for the first dog watch we were at full speed—thirty-one knots and leaving a trail of black smoke that must have looked like the fire of London. The *Wild Swan*, newly re-engined, was falling back, unable to raise the steam in time. There was great excitement on the bridge. A Dutch ship had been torpedoed during the night and we were to pick up the survivors. In an hour we should be there. I was left alone on the bridge. It was a marvellous feeling to be in charge of this racing beast dashing to the rescue.

"Out to port beyond the *Wild Swan* I saw a flying-boat approaching and reported it to the Captain down the voice pipe. He came up and we altered course towards it—and again more to port, and then suddenly there they were—three little white specks on the water—the sails of three ships' boats. The *Wild Swan* was level with them almost past them, and the Captain signalled: 'You pick up survivors whilst I circle round.' *Wild Swan* said there was another boat bearing up under the sun, but we couldn't see it—only a distant French fishing boat, which presumably *Wild Swan* had mistaken for another ship's boat. It was a disappointment to the Captain and all of us that we had not picked up the survivors and it meant a lot of extra signalling too.

"The ship had been torpedoed at 0145, they had returned to her at dawn but she was on fire so they abandoned her again, and had been sailing ever since—ten hours—all together which was good organisation. There was a freshening breeze and a moderate sea. No sea is small at this time of year that far out in the Atlantic so it seems.

"The whole crew had been saved without a casualty—forty-two of them all told. They thought the ship might still be afloat and a few minutes steaming brought us into sight of a short-looking ship on the horizon. The aircraft were circling over it. They did not seem to have sailed far in their ten hours if this was their ship—I almost doubted it at first, but at length we ascertained that it was indeed the luckless Dutchman—the for'ard half of him only. We made to *Wild Swan* 'Does Captain want to go aboard his ship again?' Answer came, 'Doubt if this half will be much good to him but will ask.' He didn't.

"The ship had split in half just abaft the bridge and main superstructure (she had been a motor ship). The bridge was still smouldering, but on the for'ard end and the starboard bow the paint still looked clean and new—EULOTA—HOLLAND—in enormous letters and a Dutch flag ran the visible length of the ship's side. A neutral ship of about 6,000 tons.

"We steamed round her and through the wreckage. Rafts, casks, buoys, upturned boats (two fine white ones, all wasted like the three from which the crew were rescued, which had just been cast adrift again—and such nice smart boats too), a notice which must have read 'keep clear of propellers', but was split in half.

"Stretching upwind into the distance was a lane of oil. 'When you have had a look I shall engage her' we made to *Wild Swan*, and we fired at the half ship at about 1,200 yards range with H.E. shells. The hits made a metallic clonk—the shorts made a better show and a better noise. The smoke was lemon yellow. We hit her about seven times, but all too high above the water line. We went to look, but she was still not sinking, so *Wild Swan* fired about ten rounds. She took longer to get the range but fired from the better side and soon the hulk turned over. She rolled right round and then her stem floated up like, as the Captain said, 'a tribesman's tent' and like that she remained. We decided to administer the last few shots. An H.E. shell hit the very stem head and in a couple of seconds she was gone. So sank the *Eulota*—100 miles from shore. The submarine had had a long time to get away and we swept northward with a needle-in-haystack sort of feeling. Next day *Wild Swan* was recalled. 'About time,' was her signal. 'I am being eaten out of house and home by half Holland!' The wind was rising and a gale was forecast so we were told to go and hunt for a submarine which might be sheltering in a cove at Round Island, Scillies. Later that night we got there and hunted fruitlessly till dawn, then we made off for home and came into Plymouth after lunch. I didn't feel very good during my watch although it was interesting enough, with the Lizard appearing and disappearing in the mist—and I saw a whale and a great skua. Next day I was in bed with a temperature and only got ashore the last evening before we left, still feeling very groggy. The next morning we moved down to the Sound and anchored in a gale of wind, ready to leave at 0400."

The exercise book contains no more than this. I was, as I had feared, so preoccupied by the precise detail of what happened that there is little record of what I thought or felt. Yet I can remember even at this distance of time some of my feelings—my first misgivings. I was now installed in my destroyer and I suppose it is not surprising that in some ways I was disappointed. I had created so firm and so false a picture of what it would be like that it could scarcely have lived up to my hopes. There was, for example, seasickness for which I had not bargained, and a curious loneliness. My mother had always been seasick and as a small child I had been seasick in sympathy. In small boats it did not affect me but in larger ships I had continued to feel poorly in even slight motion. How much of all this was psychological I shall never know, but in *Broke* when the weather was rough the Captain ordered a bucket to be brought up on to the bridge and lashed behind the Direction Tower. And somehow because the bucket was there I found it difficult not to use it. Eventually there came a rough trip when I felt so ill and was so sick that I could no longer carry out my duties. I was forced to stay in bed, and the R.N.V.R. Medical Officer—my good friend Gerald Gibbons—had me transferred to the sick bay, a small cabin below the bridge. Here I remained for the whole ten-day trip, drinking orange juice and vomiting. I remember the Captain coming to see me and saying as he left, "Well, Scott, I hope we shan't have to put you ashore for good with chronic seasickness." But there was nothing I could do about it by then. I was very weak and next day I was yellow with jaundice. I had a month's sick leave to get over the depressing disease. I had no idea, and neither had anyone else, which of the two—the sickness or the jaundice—was cause, and which effect.

I went to Fritton whither my mother had invited the two children of an old friend of hers, Kit Howard, who had been a ballet dancer and whose father was Arthur Somervell the composer. The children were to be Easter holiday company for my brother Wayland. Jane Howard was sixteen and Robin was two years younger. I was jaundiced and depressed, and I should not have believed anyone who had told me that in two years' time Jane would be my wife.

During this sick leave the *Broke* was sent with all despatch to Scapa Flow in order to take part in the Norwegian campaign. I joined her there, making the last part of the journey by air in an Anson, and had no sooner gone on board than she was as suddenly ordered to return to Plymouth. The passage back took place in flat calm weather in fog, and off East Anglia we ran aground due to the wrong position of a Channel buoy. The ship had to be docked for examination. So far there had been nothing to test my resistance to seasickness now that I no longer had jaundice. When next we sailed it was late at night and in the morning we were at anchor among the Scilly Isles. When I went up to the quarter deck there was a barely detectable swell underlying the glass-calm sea; but it was the first swell since my sick leave. Surely *this* was not going to make me seasick. Or was it? There were a number of ratings working on the quarter deck. I was sure they could see how green I looked, and the more I thought about it the greener I felt. At last I was overcome and had to rush to the quarter deck rail. The scene is still with me eighteen years later— St. Mary's in the morning sun, the calm shiny sea, the remains of my breakfast sinking in the clear water, the sharp thick taste at the back of my nose, the ratings trying not to look scornful. Without doubt this time my sickness must be of purely psychological origin, and as such it could surely be mastered.

I remained at sea for most of the next five years. I do not think I was actually ever sick again, at least without some adequate alternative cause; but I always felt poorly for the first thirty-six hours out of harbour. Antidotes to seasickness were not readily available in the early days of the war. Somehow or other I discovered how best to tide over those first thirty-six hours. I had, for example, either to be lying prone or to be out in the fresh air where I could see the horizon. Thus I managed to weather my watches on the bridge and retired to my bunk when I was not up there. Prolonged perusal of a chart made me feel sick. And so did meals in the wardroom attended by the smell of fuel oil which seeped up from the after fuel tanks in rough weather. But a *modus vivendi* had been found, and lasted me all through the war.

Once back in the ship in April 1940 I found it very difficult to think of anything but the job in hand. I had promised to illustrate Michael Bratby's new book *Grey Goose* with line drawings of birds. Michael had an interesting Army job in Intelligence at his Divisional H.Q. On 1st May I wrote to him chiefly about the difficulty of getting on with the drawings.

The letter went on:

". . . Life is excessively exciting, and we've been about a bit, but the insides of envelopes have ears—half a mo' . . . I've just had to go up and salute a destroyer coming up the harbour, being Officer of the Day, and at the moment, as it happens, the only officer in the ship. I pop up, the quarter-master blows his pipe, the bosun's mate of the destroyer coming up harbour blows his, the officers in charge of the fo'c'sle and quarter-deck parties call them to attention, and the Captain returns my salute if he isn't too busy navigating his ship. His bosun's mate blows twice, I say 'carry on', my quartermaster blows twice—the destroyer is past and I return to this letter and my dinner which will soon be ready. It is all fun except that I have so little in common with any of my shipmates. The only responsive people are the Captain—and one sees all too little of him—and the R.N.V.R. doctor, who is nice and human and has the same amateur approach to the Navy as I have. The Sub-Lieutenants, on whom I turn all my available charm with no visible result, have one big hold over me—their knowledge of the service—and they do their best to keep me in my place by withholding as much as they can from my prying curiosity. The Engineer Officer who fought in the Battle of Jutland has one adjective only (which rhymes with looking) and one noun (which rhymes with sugar) but is none the less a pet. He is simple and unspoiled, but our conversation does not reach any great intellectual heights. The First Lieutenant is small and palefaced; he is not unusually clever, but this he manages to hide under a sort of impassivity. When you address him he says nothing for several seconds whilst you shrivel a bit under his steadfast gaze wondering what particular sort of fool you have disclosed yourself to be. In this way he 'terrorises' the whole ship. Not one of us but wonders 'what the First Lieutenant is thinking', and in reality it is, most times, I believe, nothing. But he is quiet and kind, and ashore, when he discards his professional mask, he does not mind admitting that he gets hopelessly lost in the black-out. Even aboard when I beat him at chess he's quite human. He has a kind sweet wife too.

"But the Captain's the man. If only we saw more of him—but at sea we only see him on the bridge, and very little in harbour.

"It's a lonely life being captain of a ship. He's had very bad luck as we've been aground, not really through any fault of his, but it has been very nerve-racking for him. However I think all will be well. The trouble about a destroyer is that there are so few officers that the chances are small of finding a shipmate with common interests. I suppose you're isolated nearly if not quite as much . . ."

This *cri-de-cœur* came from the very earliest period of my life in the *Broke* and did not last very long, because soon we began to have adventures which, in themselves, constituted a common interest. The ship was the point. For all of us she seemed to have a living character. We were part of her, and her adventures were our adventures, which all of us shared.

When the British Expeditionary Force was retreating to Dunkirk, H.M.S. *Broke* was in Devonport Dockyard undergoing a refit. I remember the awful impatience of those hot days of early summer. I was given a special appointment for about a week, and on 2nd June, 1940, I wrote:

"I am First Lieutenant of a destroyer [*Venetia*] but it is only a temporary job. She is a ship which copped it in Boulogne, but got back. She looks like a colander—they had twenty-one killed—and I am now in sole charge of her—but only in harbour. Tomorrow I shall go back to my own ship which will be a good thing as I have a lot of work to get on with. We are having a race to get the ship ready before Dunkirk falls. We may get there in time to help. It is just like getting a dinghy ready for a race—and it is accompanied by just the same hollow feeling in the tummy. I have a lot of new jobs in my own ship—

amongst others training the look-outs. In these days of aircraft and M.T.B.s they are a pretty important item.

"It is interesting being on the edge of it all with the feeling that so soon one will be in the middle. The drama of *Venetia*'s action would make your hair curl. I have beside me at this moment a bloodstained log which is the most superb presentation of the story you can imagine. Destroyers versus tanks must have felt very queer. Destroyers had the better of it.

"There is at the moment a desperate air of hurry—not much time left now, and yet, short of train and train and train, there is not much one can do. You cannot go and get a reefing kicking-strap made at the last minute as you can in a dinghy. They have not got spare anti-tank guns for us. Fifteen or twenty Tommy guns would do us a lot of good from a morale point of view. The air raids, it seems, are especially hard on morale simply because the ship's company can do so little against the aircraft. The few who man the A.A. guns are all right but the rest have nothing to do but watch . . .

"I have just written an article for *Country Life* on Greater Snow Geese. You wouldn't know how hard it is to make oneself think of something else these days—so my job must be quite absorbing really. Destroyers are now, to me, a subject by themselves, just like dinghies or geese, and I'm 'keen on them', which it isn't difficult to be when they are doing such terrific work. I'm determined to be a pukka 'No. 1' instead of just a temporary one in a derelict ship in harbour. Maybe one day . . . But anyway this has been useful experience."

Broke remained in the dockyard till after the fall of Dunkirk, and I had to remain with her. I tried to get leave to go up to Dover and help with the boats, but I was firmly told to get on with my job in my own ship. Nevertheless it was not long before we moved from the edge of the war into the middle of it. Our first adventure ended in frustration and bitterness, but it did not lack excitement. Although Dunkirk was over, there were still British troops fighting in France, and falling back into Normandy. The enemy had crossed the Somme and was driving on to the west.

CHAPTER 3   *St. Valery*

ON the afternoon of Sunday, 9th June, 1940, H.M.S. *Broke* was engaged in anti-submarine exercises with the submarine *Otway* a few miles west of the Eddystone Lighthouse when she received a signal from the Commander-in-Chief Plymouth to proceed with all despatch towards Portsmouth. Before we got there we were re-routed to Le Havre in company with two Canadian Destroyers —*Restigouche* and *St. Laurant*. At seven o'clock that evening I came on deck to see a strange and beautiful sight. Ahead was what looked like a terrific storm. The sky was black as ink, and already the dark cloud covered the sky overhead. From behind us the low sun shone in under this cloud and lit up the two Canadian destroyers racing along on our starboard beam. We were in line abreast at twenty-nine knots, which with our new boiler tubes was our best speed until they were 'run in'. The sea was mirror calm. The scene had something sinister and unnatural about it, and indeed, as we gradually came to realise, it was unnatural, for this black pall above us was oil smoke from the burning fuel supplies on shore still eighty miles ahead of us.

The newspapers told us that the Germans had reached Le Treport, but that Dieppe was still in our hands. Surely Le Havre could not yet be in danger! But an hour later it became evident that it was, for we passed an unfinished submarine being towed away and at half past nine we sighted two large oil fires ahead, which were causing some of the smoke-cloud under which we had been steaming for two and a half hours.

When we arrived outside Le Havre we looked for the Senior Naval Officer Afloat who was supposed to be in the destroyer *Saladin*. But *Saladin* was nowhere to be found, so we anchored off, while two air raids took place on the town. I managed to get one and three-quarter hour's sleep until we were called to Action

Stations at half past three in order to enter the harbour. In the cold of the dawn we passed through the anti-submarine gate in the obstructions outside the harbour, and crept up the channel in the early-morning light. A French battleship, the *Provence*, was at anchor on one side and one or two destroyers on the other. There was no visible activity on these ships.

Very cautiously we entered Le Havre harbour still peacefully asleep, so it seemed, under its high protection of balloons, but with the great cloud of smoke, blue in the morning haze, rising like a steep cliff and sweeping away to block out the whole of the northern sky. High above the balloons came a reconnaissance plane— almost certainly German. There were no crowds of troops on the quays, indeed except for a few refugees with their luggage and a couple of British Balloon Barrage men, there was little sign of life. We steamed right up the harbour, turned and, as there seemed nothing to be done, came away again having gained useful knowl-edge of the harbour should we be required to go back again. It was five-thirty a.m. on the morning of 10th June when we left; ten minutes later we passed *Saladin* going in. Outside again we were instructed by radio to go off with the two Canadian destroyers and the *Harvester* to turn back any ships heading for Le Havre, because the evacuation had been postponed, and a concentration of ships near the French coast would be vulnerable to air attack. We spread out—four destroyers in an extended line and headed north. Almost at once we steamed under the smoke pall and it was dark and cold and inhospitable. We did not immediately appre-ciate how much safer it made us from attack by German bombers. The pall extended in every direction as far as the eye could see. Just before eight o'clock we met a string of motor-boats from Hamble—civilian motor-boats just like the ones which had been used at Dunkirk. We turned them back, knowing that these instructions were surely wrong, for their fuel must have been strictly limited and they must in fact be wanted quite soon at Le Havre. It was not until nine-thirty-five that the mistake was rectified and we turned the convoy south again.

Half an hour later we ran out of the gloom of smoke into a sunny blue sky with a rather thick haze and correspondingly poor visibility. We were zig-zagging along in front of the nine little motor boats when we heard a loud explosion in the haze ahead. The alarm bell was sounded at once for Action Stations. About thirty seconds later the starboard look-out said "Here they are, sir" and almost at the same moment I heard bullets whizzing by, all

round the bridge, so it seemed. We all ducked down and grabbed
our tin hats. As I was putting mine on I glanced up and saw a
twin-engined machine just flattening out—we afterwards identified it as a Ju. 88. There were at least two, possibly three of them—
no one was afterwards sure which; the mist and the suddenness
and the machine-gun fire were bewildering. As I looked up I saw
the bombs coming. They came absolutely straight for the ship, so
that it appeared that they could not possibly miss us. It looked as
if they would go down the after-funnel. They were not very big and
looked white or silver. There were four of them. An instant later
there was a series of heavy explosions and the whole ship shuddered. The stern seemed to lift out of the water, and we had to
hold on to keep our feet. I was looking along the starboard side aft
and saw one bomb fall about eight feet away from the ship's side
and burst on the surface with a puff of dark-brown smoke. Two
bombs fell even closer on the port side just abaft the torpedo
tubes. One exploded on impact and the other went off perhaps ten
feet down raising a great column of water. I glanced up and saw
little parallel streaks of tracer bullets, pale grey like cigarette
smoke, and at the top of the streaks a diving aircraft which was
machine-gunning our little convoy of boats. The fourth bomb must
have fallen just off the starboard bow as we steamed into the
column of water thrown up by it and were drenched through as
the water fell down on us. Somehow miraculously we had not
been hit though the ship was heavily shaken and the gyro alarm
bell (indicating that the gyro compass was out of action) was
ringing insistently to add to the confusion. Almost at once the ship
was leaping forward at twenty-five knots, but the bombers were
already far away. The whole attack was over in fifteen seconds and
we had not been able to fire a single shot at them. We had escaped
very much more lightly than we deserved. It was a grave and
salubrious warning. It had been intensely frightening but somehow
exhilarating so that I wrote a few days later "conjuring up that
fleeting glimpse of the diving aircraft is now more pleasing than
otherwise". (A revealing measure of our greenness.)

This was a dark period on the bridge. By signal we learned that
Italy had declared war; and that the *Glorious*, *Ardent* and *Acasta*
had been sunk with almost all hands during the evacuation from
Norway. The German advance through France was even more
rapid than anyone had expected. And, finally, that three destroyers had been hit during our own operation. Into this gloom
came a new signal which seemed at the time of very minor

importance. It was from the C.-in-C. Portsmouth. "Following received from Naval Liaison Officer 51st Division: Request a ship may close Fecamp at 2359 today Monday to embark forty stretcher and forty walking cases." At this time one of the new Flower Class Corvettes *Gardenia* was in company with us, so the Captain detailed *Gardenia* for this service, while we went on with our search for the Destroyer *Boadicea* reported disabled by bombs. But as dusk fell the fog became much thicker and it was useless to go on searching. We learned by radio that Fecamp was in enemy hands. We hoped that *Gardenia* had not run into a trap. The fog cleared as we approached the coast on our way back to Le Havre. There was a big fire at Fecamp and a considerable battle was being fought to the westward of the town. Star-shells were going up from time to time, and curved red streaks of tracer buzzed about. We intercepted a new signal from the Naval Liaison Officer to the 51st (Highland) Division: "Isolated enemy armoured force is now operating westward of St. Valery-en-Caux. Request ship may close St. Valery at midnight to embark wounded. Boats should only be sent if two green Verey's Lights are fired from pier." The time-of-origin of this was four in the afternoon.

As we were evidently the nearest ship to St. Valery, the Captain decided that we should undertake this job and accordingly turned eastward again, back past Fecamp which was now blazing more fiercely. We had nearly reached St. Valery, which being east of Fecamp was therefore many miles behind the German line of advance, when the Captain told me that I was to be the one to go ashore. I was to take the whaler, to make contact with the army, to embark the wounded and any others who needed evacuation and to come off again before daylight. I was to return on board to report with the first trip made from the shore.

I had about a quarter of an hour in which to get ready, while the ship eased in towards the coast. I had a look at the chart of the place, unfortunately only on a very small scale. I strapped on a pistol and ammunition for it, and with binoculars round my neck all was in readiness. Just then up went a green Verey's Light followed by a second—the signal that it was safe to close the shore. I took a bearing of it by the stars. Then the Captain arranged a signal for me to make when I had established contact with the army: 'Jake', and another if all was not well. He detailed a signalman called Moorman to go with me and I went off to see if the first whaler was ready. But it wasn't, so I went to my cabin, fetched a torch, loaded my revolver as I returned on deck and

climbed into the whaler which was immediately lowered into the
water. The sea was quite calm and there was a haze. There was no
moon, but bright starlight and a glow in the northern sky where
the sun was not very far below the horizon. I pointed out my star
to the coxswain of the boat and the four hands gave way together.
There should have been five to row, but one was unaccountably
absent. They were all armed with pistols; but whether they knew
how to use them I largely doubted.

We pulled away and the ship began to creep in after us. The
land was not in sight. The ship kept so close behind us that we had
the feeling we were making no headway at all. The Captain had
told me that the tide was going to the east, so I made what I judged
to be an appropriate allowance for it and we rowed on for over
half an hour. Then the ship loomed even closer behind and beside
us, and the Captain shouted down through a megaphone that he
was sending the motor-boat to tow us in. By now the land was just
visible in the haze (it was in fact still two miles away). As the
motor-boat was launched two more green Verey's Lights lobbed
up into the air away to the westward. We had drifted a very long
way to the east. When the motor-boat reached us the signalman
and I transferred to her, and we started to tow the whaler. At
first the motor-boat went well, but then it spluttered and we had
to stop to adjust the water jacket. Five minutes later we were off
again, but still the load of the whaler seemed to be too much, so,
as the ship was still with us, I slipped the whaler for her to collect
and proceeded with the motor-boat alone. At first the motor
spluttered a lot and as the motor-boat's crew were not all armed
(they had two rifles between three of them) I thought this might be
why the spluttering was not more quickly cured. It was only when
I had made it perfectly clear that, splutter or no splutter, I did
not intend to turn back to the ship that the splutter finally disappeared and we chugged in towards the shore. When later I
discovered the calibre of Leading Seaman Laughlan, the Cox'n,
and Able Seaman Cooke, the Bowman, I knew that the engine
improved only because it was now properly warmed up.

By this time it was well after two a.m. and we were already
more than two hours late at the rendezvous. I did not want to go
close under the cliffs before reaching the harbour as they might
well be in enemy hands and any approaching motor-boat might
have been machine-gunned. On the other hand it was fairly dark
and slightly hazy and I did not want to miss the entrance. At last I
made out the end of a pier and we approached it as slowly as the

engine would run. The entrance was about thirty yards wide between two piers surmounted by little beacons. We could see no sign of life whatever on either pier—no sentries, no one who might have fired the Verey's Lights (and it was from the end of the pier that they were supposed to have been fired). It was two-thirty a.m. by now—nearly an hour since the last set had been fired. Meanwhile there had been intermittent dull explosions which I took to be mortar fire. What if the Germans had entered the village during that hour . . . We steered as close under the eastern pier as we could and kept the engine clutched in. This meant that we made a good speed, but it made so much more noise in neutral that it was the lesser of two evils. Going in at that speed it was difficult to scan both piers with my glasses and I cursed that the signalman had not also brought a pair. I had a man in the bows sounding with an oar, as the harbour was said to be almost dry at low water. However he could not reach the bottom.

There was a bend in the harbour, to the right, so we crossed over to the west side so as to creep round the corner. We passed a boat moored near the quayside. There was still no sign of life at all. The houses along both sides of the harbour seemed to be deserted. There was silence. It was extremely eerie. Ahead was a drawbridge and I decided not to go under it, but to land in the outer harbour. There were apparently no sentries at the bridge, but I heard what seemed to be a whistle. I whistled back. Silence. Was it a trap? Over to the left of the bridge I suddenly heard the sound of a motor-cycle engine, and then more engine noises. Some mechanised unit was passing through the village, and I felt fairly sure it would be an enemy one. I decided to go ashore at once and find out. The motor-boat was turned and came alongside heading outwards at the east side quay, and I climbed ashore. I said, "Wait here, and I'll be back in five minutes," and the Cox'n said, "Hope so, sir—Good luck, sir." I drew my revolver and ran across to the houses opposite, then keeping close to the wall I went towards the corner. Just before I reached it I saw the legs of a sitting sentry showing round it. I stopped for a few seconds to listen, hoping I would hear a language spoken, but I heard no word. So brandishing my pistol without much conviction I popped round the corner and said "Hands up." He jumped up and said, "Yes, sir, certainly, sir," and I said "Thank God, I thought you were a Jerry. Where's the C.O.?" He took me across the village square. There was a light tank in the middle with a high rod aerial. He called for the officer by name, but he was not in the tank. I found a subaltern among a lot of men who were standing about, but he said he had just arrived and knew nothing about any wounded, nor did he know where I would find anyone who did. A Military Policeman was very efficient. I told him I was in a desperate hurry and he bustled up a line of transport which was in a traffic jam on the far side of the square. It was moving slowly on. I spoke to a motor-cyclist and to a lorry driver but they didn't know where I would find an officer. The Military Policeman said he thought the Brigadier would be passing soon and that he would stop him.

My five minutes being up, I ran back to tell my crew that the village was held by the British. I found that they had already made contact with the sentry I had challenged and his mate. One of these said he believed he knew where the wounded were hiding in a house. He said he believed that the Germans had been through the village in the afternoon, but I doubt if this was true. We hurried down the quay, having already wasted precious time trying to find an officer instead of asking the sentry at once what we wanted. The price of my pomposity was ten precious minutes of darkness. As we passed the motor-boat I gladly gave the crew permission to commandeer the moored boat we had seen on the way in. Turning along the sea front we passed an abandoned tank in one side street and a lorry in another—put there no doubt to block them against enemy tanks. After walking about half a mile, during which the sentry often expressed doubts about the way, we came to a small square on the sea front and a man walking up and down on the promenade, who turned out to be an officer in charge of the wounded. I could not resist the phrase made famous by the *Cossack* when rescuing the prisoners from the *Altmark*. "The Navy's here!" I said. We walked quickly over to the house where the wounded were hidden. It was satisfying to hear the tone in which the officer shouted through the door, "They've come, boys —they've come to rescue us." A doctor, named McConachie I believe, came out and quickly told me that he had forty-seven stretcher cases and about sixty walking cases. I told him the position. It was already well after three a.m. and dawn was break-ing. I said we had about three-quarters of an hour in which to embark them. We could not stay long after dawn, as the chances were we should be sunk by bombs and then the wounded would have been better off where they were until the next night. The only thing was to get them along to the quay at once and embark as many as possible. From the sea front I got the signalman to call up

Broke with our little shaded lamp. "Jake," I said, "and send as many boats in as possible."

There was talk of getting ambulances to transport the wounded the 500 or 600 yards to the quay, but this was impossible as the ambulances had gone. I found my Coxswain trying to start the lorry in the side street for this purpose, but it had been effectively immobilised. Back at the motor-boat I found that the motor of the commandeered boat was also a non-starter, but they had it alongside and I told them to tow it down to a camber which sloped down into a recess in the quayside. Already some of the walking wounded were arriving here. Then I saw two drifters heading for the beach. My signalman was on the front and shouted to them, directing them towards the entrance. Apparently they very narrowly avoided grounding but they got in and berthed alongside right out at the end of the east jetty. They could not come further up owing to the shallow water and the falling tide.

Now that they were alongside I decided to put as many stretcher cases as possible into them and that only walking cases should be taken on board *Broke*'s motor-boat and its tow. So we moved the stretcher cases out to the end of the pier as quickly as possible. I had never realised what hard work it was carrying one end of a loaded stretcher. My Coxswain and I carried the first one out; the drifters were berthed one outside the other and there was a fifteen-foot drop to their decks. I left instructions with an officer to proceed as best he could with the embarkation, lowering the stretchers with ropes; then I went back to hurry on the work of moving the stretchers. I filled up the two motor-boats with the walking wounded, including a Paymaster called Morris who had a suitcase with 600,000 francs in it, and sent them out to *Broke*. In spite of my orders I did not feel I could possibly go with this trip; there were far too many wounded to be embarked, far too many things to be organised, and seemingly no one else much to organise them. I went out to the drifters again—they were the *Golden Harvest* and the *Golden News*—and spoke to the Lt.-Commander in charge of them. He said he had only a foot of water under him and that he would not be able to stay more than another half-hour. A Motor-Landing-Craft, a square metal vessel, at that time very new in appearance, had just arrived towing a string of four cutters, and having almost beached had then withdrawn and entered the harbour. It was clear that I should be able to embark the remaining wounded in these boats, and transfer them to the drifters outside, so I made this plan with the Lt.-Commander.

By this time it was quite light and my chief anxiety was for the ships outside. All through the dawn there had been this terrible urgency to get the wounded men away without risking the ships in a stationary cluster outside the harbour. Two or three more destroyers and other ships had joined *Broke*, and at any moment I expected to see the dive bombers attacking them.

There did not seem to be anyone other than the wounded who wanted to be embarked, as the subaltern in the square had said that the British forces intended to hold the place strongly to cover an evacuation which was being planned. I knew that the remaining wounded could be satisfactorily accommodated by the drifters and therefore made the following signal to *Broke*. "Request permission to remain until all wounded have been embarked. Consider you should not remain here as drifters can fulfil all present requirements." The signalman and I returned towards the camber, meeting exhausted stretcher-bearers and carrying their stretcher to the drifters while sending them back for more. As I returned I passed one more stretcher going out along the pier, and directed that it should be the last, as the drifters must leave. Then I began to embark stretcher cases in the M.L.C. alongside the camber. The warships were still lying off and I was in an agony of apprehension, as their safety seemed to depend on the speed of my operation. A Major came along the jetty. He told me that his troops were going to hold the village, but that there would be about 8,000 to evacuate that night. I told him we had heard that 12,000 might have to be evacuated from some part of this coast and that a lot of ships were being prepared for it. I passed this information out to *Broke* and said I hoped to be off by four-forty-five a.m. The Major went away and returned ten minutes later with the Chief of Staff of the 51st (Highland) Division, who said, "What are your orders?" I said, "To evacuate wounded and after that anyone who is ready to be evacuated—but it is already daylight and it will be a dangerous procedure." I told him that three destroyers had been hit the day before, but that if he could not hold out until the evening I would signal to my Captain and we would begin the evacuation at once. In a very tired voice he said, "No, I think we can hold on till tonight—but no longer. Some of us will try to cut through to Havre." "How many will there be to come off here, sir—about 8,000?" I asked, using the Major's figures. He said, "It'll be a lot more than that." I said, "Well, sir, you really think you can hold out till we get back tonight?" and he replied, "Well, if we don't there won't be

Lesser Snow Geese against a Californian afternoon sun.

1938

Rescue of the crew of H.M.S. *Comorin*, Armed Merchant Cruiser (ex-P. & O. Liner) on fire in a North Atlantic gale, by H.M.S. *Broke*, 6th/7th April, 1941.

anyone to evacuate. We're the last remnant of the B.E.F." Then he asked me if I thought we could get them all away in one night. I said I thought that if all the ships arrived that we had had signals about, then 12,000 could be got away in the night provided that enough small boats were available so that the beach could be used, and provided that the troops were really well marshalled ashore.

I made a signal to *Broke*. "Suggest ships should disperse so as not to attract attention of aircraft. Will join drifters and make contact with you later." *Broke* replied by asking who made this suggestion and I said that I did. The Chief of Staff was standing beside me at the time, so I asked him whether he approved it, which he said he did, agreeing that as many ships as possible would be needed at nightfall and that therefore they should not be laid open to aircraft attack during the day.

This was my last (and unsuccessful) attempt to get rid of the warships outside the harbour. As well as *Broke* they now included the Destroyers *Restigouche*, *St. Laurant*, the Sloop *Wellington*, the Corvette *Gardenia*, and a large troop-carrier—the *Hampton Ferry*. All this time there had been intermittent fire from what sounded like mortars up the valley a mile or two away to the south-east. The embarkation of the wounded was almost complete. The Chief of Staff went away in his car. I wished him luck and promised we would be there at dusk. Another Major who seemed to be less affected by fatigue stayed and talked, though I do not recollect anything that he said. I was nevertheless impressed with his quiet confidence and we said a most friendly good-bye ten minutes later when I left.

During the last half-hour of embarkation my very misty French was frequently called into play. A young girl and a man came down to the quay and asked if I would take them. I said if they were quick they might be able to get into the drifters. They said they had two elderly sick ladies and would have to fetch them. I told them that under no circumstances could I wait for them, but that they would be embarked if they were ready. This question of refugees and of the French in general, both civilians and soldiers, was an unexpected complication for which I was not adequately prepared. There was, I supposed, always the remote danger of Fifth Columnists, but on the other hand the French, as allies, were entitled to all the help we could give them. No one felt very favourably disposed towards them, as they were reputed to have fled the town earlier but apparently had been driven back into it.

L

I thought it unlikely that the civilians would be seriously mal-treated by the Germans and that the able-bodied soldiers should be remaining to fight. However when three officers arrived in a car and asked to be embarked, giving me the car as a present . . . "plein d'essence. . . ." I decided, as there was plenty of space in the cutters, to embark them. One French *poilu* showed me a scratch on his knee and another on his hand where he had fallen on the road, and kept repeating "Blessé". None of these men had arms, and I considered that they could be of little use to the defenders of the village, so I agreed to take them all.

Some of the British wounded were in pitiful case. Quite a num-ber of the walking ones were shell-shocked—quite dazed and unable to understand what was going on. One wounded man could just walk. He came hobbling along, thinking he would miss the boat. I went back to help him along. With an effort and a wan smile he made some joke about his wounds. It was not a very good joke, but the spirit was there. Others smiled up from stretchers. One Frenchman called in English for water. We had none, but there was a piece of damp cloth near-by on the top of a box and I damped his forehead with it. I told him he would have water in a few minutes when he got out to the ship. There were many other terrible cases, including a man who had lost both legs. But there was no time to dwell on these horrors. At four-forty a.m. I pushed the last cutter off the camber and jumped in. The M.L.C. and one cutter fully laden had already been taken away without my orders by the Chief Petty Officer in charge in order to put their wounded on board the drifters which he believed still to be alongside the pier further down. So I directed that the oars should be got out and the remaining three cutters should be rowed down the har-bour on the ebb tide. I said that the French able-bodied soldiers should be made to work for their passage. But as soon as we could see down the harbour I observed that the M.L.C., finding the drifters gone, was coming back for us. The cutters were made fast astern amid a good deal of fumbling. Only one man, a Petty Officer named White, was really efficient and useful, working quickly and intelligently; as he and I moved the boats about and secured the tow ropes, I pondered on the diversity of man.

Just as we were getting under way two ratings appeared on the jetty. They were part of the cutter's crews, and said they had found one more stretcher left in the house. McConachie, the doctor, who had been wonderfully competent all through the embarkation, explained that the man was dead, so the two ratings clambered

down a ladder to jump into one of the cutters as we went by.
Already at the bottom of the ladder was a French soldier waiting
to jump. They tried to make him climb up again, but I foresaw
trouble and ordered them to come down after him. Then I told
him in French to jump. In this way all three were embarked and
we steamed out.

The crowd of ships was still there. I asked *Broke* for instructions
(our little box lamp was only just visible in broad daylight) and
was told to transfer my three stretcher cases to the Corvette
Gardenia. I replied that I had twenty-seven stretcher cases and
about forty others, and then I took them all to *Gardenia*. She had no
doctor on board, but McConachie was with them and I heard
afterwards that another doctor was in the party. I had also brought
off twenty-two stretcher-bearers. They were unarmed and it
seemed useless to leave them behind. They were quite exhausted
and the way they had carried their stretchers close on half a mile
from the house to the drifters and then gone back for the next one
was beyond praise.

I spoke to the Captain of *Gardenia* and then took a small white
motor-boat from there back to *Broke*. It was five a.m. and had been
full daylight for an hour and a half, yet no single aircraft had
appeared in the clear blue sky. The motor-boat was one of the
Hamble lot who had been with us when we were attacked by
bombers on the previous morning. She was handled by her owner
—a civilian. He had one naval rating with him who told me he had
been in the Navy for two weeks. What he chiefly wanted to know
was whether he would get free cigarettes. As we came alongside
Broke rather untidily, the First Lieutenant shouted down to me,
"We're only waiting for you, you know," as if I were not in as
much of a hurry as he was. But it brought home to me again the
awful responsibility of keeping all these ships in so vulnerable a
cluster. It appeared, however, that the Captain had already told
them to disperse—including the *Wellington*, who happened to be
senior—and that they had not done so, or were still only just
doing so.

It was ten past five when I returned on board and went straight
up to the bridge to report to the Captain that all wounded had
been evacuated. I had left the ship just four hours before, and it
was just over two and a half hours since I had landed. One
hundred and twenty people had been evacuated, ninety-five of
them wounded. As we steamed away from St. Valery we heard
gunfire to the westward. The two drifters *Golden Harvest* and

Golden News were being shelled by a gun on the cliff top about three miles away. They escaped unhit. We told *Gardenia* to follow us and set off for Portsmouth—and still we had seen no enemy aircraft. Well on the way we met a lost motor-boat to whom we gave the last of our petrol (kept only for our own motor-boat) and the course for Le Havre, which latter he declined to accept, preferring one for Portsmouth.

At nine a.m. we sighted the bomb-damaged destroyer *Bulldog* at anchor and took her in tow. There was a thick mist soon after, but it cleared before we reached the Nab and further to the westward, on a parallel course, we saw the *Boadicea* in tow of *Ambuscade*. *Boadicea* with her engine-room flooded, was very low in the water. She had had six killed and five wounded. *Bulldog* had had three hits but no casualties at all. Later we slipped *Bulldog*, who was taken over by a tug, and at ten minutes to two in the afternoon we secured alongside in Portsmouth harbour and disembarked the wounded soldiers we had on board.

Half an hour after we arrived, the Captain and I went up to the Commander-in-Chief's office. We had received a signal that we and *Restigouche* and *St. Laurant* were to return at once to Plymouth. We could not understand why and we did not at all like it. Our job, we believed, was at St. Valery making good our promises to be there for the evacuation. The Chief of Staff told us that destroyers were not to be risked any more on the French coast. The group of senior officers round the blue baize-covered table did not seem to me to grasp the situation at all. I told them all I knew, including, of course, the conversations I had had with the G.1 of the 51st Division, but I had only had three hours' sleep in the last forty-eight, and I was at a disadvantage too with my Captain there, as I could not say nearly so much as I should have liked. Alone, claiming amateur status for my un-Service behaviour, I believe I could have roused them. The tantalising part was that they seemed to be undecided. Had this been an Admiralty directive it would no doubt have been useless. But here they were visibly making up their minds, and, as we thought, wrongly. While we were in the room a signal came from the Naval Liaison Officer 51st Division to say that 60,000 troops would have to be evacuated. For a moment we assumed that this would tip the scales. Surely now every available ship would go. I thought of my promise to be there, I thought of the tired voice saying, "I think we can hold out till tonight." I tried a new tack. "I do know St. Valery harbour and the beach fairly well now, sir," I said, and my Captain followed up

with "And we have been into Le Havre harbour in daylight too."
But it was not to be. "I'm sorry, Scurfield," said the Chief of Staff,
"but I'm afraid your sailing signal will have to stand." And so that
evening we went to sea and turned angrily westward for Plymouth.
"I feel like a bloody blackleg," the Captain said as we came to the
parting of the ways. That night another signal was intercepted
saying that it would be the last chance of evacuating 54,000 troops,
about half of them French. If they can do it, we thought, well and
good. But if they can't. . . .

The next day (12th June) was spent in doing nothing at Plymouth and on the following morning *The Times* reported a German
claim that 20,000 prisoners were taken at St. Valery-en-Caux.
The B.B.C. news gave out on the following day that 6,000 British
troops had capitulated there. It was explained that fog had
delayed the evacuation and that there were no extensive beaches
as at Dunkirk. Though many had been embarked many more had
not.[1] We felt very bitter about it. Our little operation had succeeded in its small-scale object, but failed miserably on the major
issue.

---

[1] 1,350 British were evacuated and 8,000 were taken prisoner by the 7th Panzer
Division under the command of Rommel. (Churchill. *The Second World War*, II, 134.)

CHAPTER 4   *Brest*

ST. VALERY fell to General Rommel on the morning of Wednesday, 12th June. On that same day Lord Alanbrooke (then General Sir Alan Brooke) went to France "to form a new B.E.F." with the only two fully formed divisions that remained to us—the 52nd Lowland Division and the First Canadian Division. Two days later, on 14th June, the Germans entered Paris, and on the same evening Sir Winston Churchill accepted Lord Alanbrooke's assessment that the "new B.E.F." which had only been in France for a day or two should be re-embarked forthwith. These details were not known to us in the *Broke* when we sailed for Brest at nine-fifty p.m. on 17th June. We had previously embarked scaling ladders and no doubt evacuation would be part of our job, for troops were being evacuated from most of the French Atlantic ports. That very morning the liner *Lancastria*, about to leave the harbour at St. Nazaire, had been bombed and sunk with the loss of 3,000 men in a sea of flaming oil. Evacuation was also proceeding at Cherbourg, St. Malo and La Pallice. France had by now completely collapsed. Pétain had succeeded Reynaud as Prime Minister and had asked for an armistice. It was towards a situation of extreme confusion that we were sailing through the calm seas on this summer's night. This record of our adventures is taken from an account which I wrote a few days after it all happened.

I went on watch at two o'clock on the morning of 18th June and there was an orange light in the north-eastern sky when we passed Ushant an hour and a half later. At five o'clock we turned east past Pierre Noire Lighthouse towards Brest. Half an hour later we passed a barrage balloon floating on the water, and sighted a number of vessels at anchor in the bay at Bertheaume. The signal station on the cliff told us not to proceed further because magnetic mines had been laid by aircraft during the night, so we anchored. We had only just done so when there was a brisk barrage over Brest, and eventually three enemy aircraft appeared flying very high. They were Heinkel He-III and we opened fire with our three-inch gun. They came on over us at about 15,000 feet, and we decided that they were too late to drop bombs on us that time. Someone had just said this when we heard a screaming whistle and a salvo of bombs fell just off our starboard bow. They were not very near. In one place there were a number of small splashes, probably made by incendiaries. The last bomb to fall made a loud unnerving wail but did not appear to explode.

The British Naval Liaison Officer—Commander Mackay—was ashore at Bertheaume. From him we learned by signal that the Senior Naval Officer Brest had left the night before in the destroyer *Mackay*. From now on there was sporadic air activity all the time. I saw a German aircraft shot down over the shore and watched it dive down behind the hill. At half past eight I was sent ashore in the motor-boat to collect Commander Mackay. He left an hour later and immediately afterwards I was sent off again in the motor-boat to go to each of the sixteen merchant ships at anchor in the roads. If they could carry troops or refugees I was to retain them; the rest were to be sent to Falmouth. The French ships, of which there were five, were later visited by a French Pilot Cutter, so that I finally only boarded eleven. It was an extraordinary feeling going on board these ships, some of them quite large, and telling their masters what they must do. I wondered if they would do my bidding, and was surprised afterwards to find that they all did. Two were British, with scaling ladders ready for evacuation. One was a big Norwegian who went to Liverpool, the others, Dutch and Greek, went to Falmouth. I also visited a Dutch passenger ship, the *Princess Josephine Charlotte*, to which 200 R.A.F. men had just been sent. With them they had taken two dogs and the master tried to persuade me to take the dogs back to *Broke*. The *Cutty Sark*, the Duke of Westminster's yacht which had been built as an 'S'-class Destroyer and was now a Destroyer again, was lying alongside *Broke* when I got back. She had a demolition party on board which was being transferred to us. The party, under the command of Commander Congreve, consisted of six sub-lieutenants directly from *King Alfred*, sixty-eight petty officers and men, as well as a party of twenty-two sappers under a lieutenant. Three of the six sub-lieutenants were Canadian and one of them I had met when we were sailing in Toronto. So now we were to be involved in blowing up the harbour installations as well as bringing away troops.

At noon the *Cutty Sark* went off and soon afterwards we weighed anchor and started up the harbour towards Brest. The sky was absolutely clear and out of it dived two Heinkels to attack the *Princess Josephine Charlotte*. She was completely hidden by huge waterspouts, although most of the salvo seemed to fall just astern of her. A third Heinkel followed and again missed, though not by much, a fourth Heinkel unaccountably did not dive. They must have been large bombs, for the great columns of water towered far above the ship's masts. What was most remarkable was the surprise achieved by the aeroplanes. The bombs were the first warning and they cannot have been released much above 500 feet. We opened fire on the retreating enemy, and the direction was quite good, but the fusing was hopeless. We never began to reach them, but the noise was a great encouragement to our ship's company.

It was a beautiful day with a fresh wind, blue sky and green water. French soldiers waved to us from the batteries on the south side as we passed through the narrows and came in sight of the inner harbour. Lying there were the new 35,000-ton battleship *Richelieu* and about six destroyers as well as an old cruiser, and away to the south-east an aircraft carrier. These ships had not sailed partly owing to the magnetic mines, and partly owing to the lack of instructions from their government. Just as we arrived at the breakwater a tremendous explosion occurred a few hundred yards on our port bow. A mixture of black smoke and spray went up 200 feet into the air. When it cleared there was a circle of floating debris. Two or three motor-boats soon arrived on the scene but there was no sign of anyone to rescue. It appears that there had been a lighter there, and it had almost certainly been blown up by a magnetic mine. A few seconds later a barrage went up to the northward and we spotted three aircraft. *Richelieu* was firing and we joined in. Two of the planes remained very high, but one dived down suddenly, perhaps because the guns ashore had got his range.

Thus in the din of battle we entered the inner basin of the Port du Commerce and secured alongside the quay, which was to be the scene of great activity for me during the next few hours. It was long enough for two ships, and behind it, running the whole length, was a range of warehouses. It formed the western side of a small basin full of fishing craft. There were four large cranes along the quay, and a number of abandoned motor-cars which had evidently been left by the re-embarked B.E.F. As we lay alongside our bows pointed towards the town. A steep slope ahead of us was traversed by a slanting road with a corner at the top. It was on this corner that we kept our guns trained, in case German tanks should come round it. At the top of the slope was a belt of trees, evidently a part of some public park, and just to the left of them a castle or fort. The town stretched away on both sides. To our left and to west of us was the Naval Basin, to the right more quays of the Port du Commerce, and beyond them some oil tanks which we had pointed out to the demolition party as we arrived. Commander Congreve and I landed at once and went to see whether any of the abandoned motor-cars could be pressed into service. But all had been effectively immobilised. The electrical leads had been slashed and the tyres punctured. All that remained of use was the upholstery, and most of the seats found their way into the *Broke*. We had been alongside about ten minutes when the British Naval Liaison Officer arrived on board with two officers who were said to be Belgian but were, I think, actually Polish. They left soon after and the B.N.L.O. went off too. He embarked in the French Destroyer *Le Hardi* with Admiral Ouest, and left the port. Later a car turned up to fetch him, which proved to be very useful. One of the Canadian subs went foraging and returned with a lorry in good working condition which he had fortunately found by the roadside. Two more lorries were found later and these were invaluable for transporting the demolition charges.

An Englishwoman turned up, governess in the family of a very charming French lady who had brought her to us for embarkation. At this stage there was much debate on whether or not refugees should be embarked. I went to see the Captain who said we might take her, but did not want her on board at once. The French lady said she could take her now to the house of a Countess Toulouse-Lautrec, but that they had no telephone. Eventually I handed this tangle over to the First Lieutenant and began to organise a party to collect Bren guns. There was a great air of hurry and bustle on the quay with the demolition party fitting charges and loading them into the lorries. There was not much more I could do there and I turned all my attention to collecting automatic weapons. We were still pitifully ill-equipped for replying to air attack. If we could only get together a few machine-guns we should be able to do *something*. Furthermore the Captain had instructed me to get these guns if I possibly could, so I must not fail.

The car, driven by a French sailor, which had been sent down

L*

for Commander Mackay, was now commandeered and I loaded
in a party of petty officers. These included the Gunner's Mate,
the Ordnance Artificer, my Asdic Petty Officer Baxter, and a
private soldier who had been left behind during the evacuation
of his unit. He said he knew where there were Bren guns in lorries.
So we set off up the hill past rows of abandoned and wrecked
lorries. At the top was a vast car park with hundreds more in rows
filling the whole square. All these vehicles were British. They
belonged to the soldiers who had brought them a few days before
and had now been evacuated leaving all their gear behind them.
How this evacuation must have appeared to the French sentries
who were now guarding them we could easily imagine.

There were two ways of getting any guns from the lorries
should we find any (and my petty officers very soon did). One was
to ignore the sentries and risk trouble, the other was to get leave.
The second seemed the best thing to do first and I was finally
directed to the castle which was on the far side of the square.
Before I knew what was happening I was talking to a Colonel who
was leading me in to see his General. The General spoke no English
at all and my French was stretched to its limits. However 'six
mitrailleuses' were promised and I took my leave after making a
few appropriate remarks about the bravery of his garrison and the
admiration which all must feel for his noble stand against impossible odds. I told the Colonel some more as we left and he said
in a very tired voice: "They will not take us alive." I said it was
just that fine spirit which was so much admired by us in England.
"Is it really?" he said, like a child who has been told something it
does not quite know whether to believe. He said he would come
with me to help to find the mitrailleuses—that he would drive
there and meet me (the whole distance was not more than 200
yards). Unfortunately, he said, he could not give me a lift as his
car was so small. It was indeed. There was barely room for the
little man and his chauffeur. Just as I left I was buttonholed by
three Polish officers, one of whom talked French. He said he had
his wife with him and could they go to England? As an after-
thought he said he also had 200 Polish troops with him. I told him
where the ship was, that I was not sure about his wife but that the
troops were one of the things for which we had especially come.
They went off in the direction of the ship and I thought I had lost
my little Colonel, but I found him again in his little car at the
drive gate of the great castle, where the first of the lorries were
parked. He laughed and said he would have walked had he known

which lorries I meant. We walked across the square and a very pretty young girl ran up to me and asked in French if we could take her to England. I said "No" and she said, "You are in a hurry? All right, I'll wait until you are not," and came running along behind. She watched while I arranged for the machine-guns to be released.

The Colonel was most helpful. There were some already in a lorry, but more than the six and a great deal of ammunition. I must transfer the six to a second lorry and some of the ammo and then I could go. His "Good-bye" was friendly—very tired—resigned. He said "They will be here by nightfall." I believe he really did not intend to surrender. As soon as he had gone I instructed that a few extra guns should be loaded into the lorry. The young girl was still beside me and with her two men. They said they were all three Poles. "Well, that's different," I said. "I thought you were French when I said we couldn't take you. I still don't know for certain, but I think we shall probably be able to embark you." The girl, who looked about nineteen, said her husband, also a Pole, was in the R.A.F. They had a car with them so I directed them to the ship. Then, with a French driver who had been detailed by the Colonel for the lorry, we set off back to the ship. I was standing on the running board. We had a longish way to go owing to one-way streets, which seemed a little absurd when the Germans were expected at any moment. On the hill we passed a party of B.E.F. with a lorry and some anti-tank rifles, and we told them to follow us down to the quay. Back at the ship, I went at once to report to the Captain. He was shaving and changing his shirt. He looked wonderfully cool, and there was I, hot and dusty and panting, in the doorway. I made my report.

We loaded the machine-guns and ammunition aboard, and also some car seats and a motor-cycle. The Captain objected to the motor-cycle as loot, but it was allowed when it was discovered to belong to one of the B.E.F. fellows. Sub-Lieutenant Mason returned with a lorry load of three-pounder ammunition. It was useless to us but we embarked it. Then Mason and I took over one of the lorries and formed a party for another Bren gun search. It was a poorish lorry and was to be driven by Williams—one of my Asdic ratings. The party included Petty Officer Baxter, the Gunner's Mate, Ordnance Artificer Clements and two or three other hands. At the top of the hill we found a better lorry and changed into it. P.O. Baxter drove it—very fast. Again I found myself travelling on the running board, for no good reason except that it seemed vaguely more flexible, but probably because it was what people did in the movies. Over the hill we came down again into the square full of lorries. We overshot the place where we wanted to stop, so we dashed on through some more streets and back into the square. The same French officer was there who had queried and finally approved our departure last time after complaining bitterly that the Colonel had given us no chit. He had forgotten all about the six machine-guns. I said we had sent back the lorry we had originally taken and that we were now looking to see if there were any more spare guns. Instead of the expected outburst he said, "By all means! I will send my sentry round to help you look." But we only found two Lewis guns and some tracer ammunition.

The square was full of people, mostly French civilians. They would all be in German hands before morning. Most of them were calm—dazed it seemed. Once or twice I saw men taking leave of each other with handshakes and kisses. "Bonne chance, mon vieux," and the tears flowed. The agony of France; but there was little time to contemplate it. We had been away from the ship for some time and I suddenly had the feeling that we should get back. It's getting late, I thought. The town was more deserted than it had been. The long lines of sailors with their gear, who had been marching down through the square towards the docks, had disappeared. Mason and I held a quick conference. There seemed to be a sudden urgency. A siren had blown down in the docks, perhaps just another impending air-raid . . . We collected the men together, and quickly raided an abandoned Red Cross van, from which we took four stretchers to replace the ones we had lost after St. Valery, and some blankets. By now people were running down the road leading into the square. At any moment we expected to see enemy motor-cycles or tanks following them. We bundled the last of the gear into the lorry, had a quick muster of the men (which was miscounted) and set off. But the panic was only an air-raid after all. The ships were firing away in the harbour as we drove down the hill at breakneck speed. I had to keep reminding Baxter to keep to the right. We hurtled along the quay, only just stopping in time to avoid collision with another lorry. The First Lieutenant shouted to us to get aboard at once; the ship was leaving. We rushed the gear across from the lorry and leapt after it. I went up to the bridge to apologise to the Captain for being away so long. He dismissed it in a word and said he was only relieved we had made it. The Polish Colonel was on board, and so was his wife, as I found when I went below for a cup of tea.

We had moved out from the quay to allow a French troopship to berth alongside. At four-fifteen p.m. we secured to No. 3 Buoy in the Outer Basin, and ten minutes later I was sent ashore in the motor-boat with a signalman named Wilcox and the Polish Colonel. My instructions were to try to commandeer enough boats to ferry the 200 Polish troops across to the *Broke* at No. 3 Buoy. As well as these troops 200 Polish civilians were expected; it was hoped they would arrive before the Germans. I landed, established my signal base on the quay and went immediately to the Office of the Prefect of the Dockyard Police which was at the end of the quay. It took some time to penetrate to the Commander within, but when I did he was friendly enough and came out with me, asking where the Poles were. I said airily, "Along there." Actually the Colonel had disappeared as soon as we landed, after saying:

"Will you promise me something?"

"I'll try."

"Promise that you won't go without us."

"I cannot promise what circumstances may force the ship to do, but I shall not leave until I have seen you again."

"I am satisfied." And he trotted off.

So I could not put my finger on the 200 Polish troops, to show them to the French Commander. He was nice, but he could not help. He had no small craft and he could only suggest that the destroyer return and 'accoster' alongside the large passenger ship which had taken our place at the quay. I signalled *Broke*: "Absolutely no boats available at present. Poles not yet arrived. Only suggestion you should come alongside French ship, if still no boats when Poles come." On the quay I unexpectedly found my Asdic rating Williams, who, as a result of our miscounted muster up in the square, had been left behind. He was surprisingly cheerful about it all. Five minutes later I saw *Broke* entering the inner harbour again, and went up to see the Captain of the French ship. He agreed that the Poles should be embarked across his ship. *Broke* signalled that I should ask him to move a lighter which was alongside his stern. I went up again and arranged this, but before anything could be done *Broke* was coming alongside ahead of the lighter. I was on the deck of the French ship as she did so. It was a tricky manoeuvre as there was an overhanging flare on the troopship; this was the downfall of our No. 2 (Port side) Whaler, which got crushed. I was standing a few feet immediately above it as it was squashed in like a basket. However the *Broke* was made fast alongside and a door on B deck of the troopship opened on to the destroyer's deck amidships. I went ashore again to look for the Poles and found them straggling along the quay. I gathered them together and was told to proceed with the embarkation. So directing the leaders through the French ship, I hurried up the stragglers. Half an hour later the 200 Polish soldiers had been embarked.

CHAPTER 5

Free Frenchmen

DURING this time the same gangway—one of the French ship's 'ladders'—was being used simultaneously by hundreds of French sailors and soldiers as well as civilian men of military age who were being evacuated by the French authorities. Ahead of this ship was another evacuating almost entirely sailors. There were poignant scenes around the gangways of these two ships. Thousands of men were being shipped away and even the officers of the ships did not know where they were going. Many were leaving their wives, children, parents, sweethearts, knowing that a few hours later they would be in the hands of the conquerors; and before that they would be under fire and bombed from the air. The atmosphere of the quay was charged with human suffering.

One man was hysterical. At his side were his mother and sweetheart. He had dropped his rifle and stood there in tears. "Je ne quitterai pas la terre de la France," he kept shouting, while his womenfolk urged him to go. They picked up his rifle and led him towards the gangway. He struggled and refused and at last another soldier picked him up and carried him, kicking and screaming, up the gangway. I saw another soldier standing watching, and biting the back of his hand.

An old woman came to me. Had I seen a sailor called Pitot? I said I was afraid I had not. She asked me if I would go aboard and seek him out as he was her son, and she wept when I explained that I could not do that either, as I had work to do on the quay. I shouted to a sailor up on the deck of the ship, "Do you know a sailor called Pitot?" She heard and smiled through her tears. But the sailor didn't know, and neither did another further aft. I had to go then in search of the Polish civilians who were said to be scientists and should by now have arrived; but I could not find them. A man and a boy came to me. They were French. The boy said, "Will you take

313

me to England? I know England, I have often been there, I have
friends there. If you will take me I will sign a pledge to join your
fighting forces at once." The man said, "This is my son, and I
have another. Take them both to England—they will fight. They
have money with them." "I am afraid it is impossible," I answered.
"We are not embarking any French subjects." Then the mother
came to me and asked if there was no way in which they could go to
England. I said that they should embark in the French ship, but she
said, "Where it goes there will be no organisation. In England they
will use them better." The elder boy was tall and dark and asked
again in English, "Please take me." I explained that the decision
was not mine but that, although I did not think there was the least
chance, I would ask my Captain. I had to go off again then to look
for the Poles who ought to have arrived. Ten minutes later I saw the
French family again. They smiled. They realised that I had not had
time to ask about them. They said nothing but waited by their car—
a large car for they were rich folk. The next time I crossed the
French troopship to the *Broke* lying outside her, I dashed up to see
the Captain and asked him if I might embark any French people. In
reply he asked how many I had embarked already. I said none at all,
but that I would like to take two boys who said they were prepared
to join the Forces. "All right, bring them on board—and anyone else
you think we really ought to take. Use your discretion." I went back
to the quay. The father and mother were pathetically grateful that
I had arranged to take their sons away from them. The boys kept
repeating that they would fight as soon as they reached England.

I was still waiting on the quayside for the Poles to turn up. Also
missing was the young Polish girl with the aviator husband whom
I had met in the square. She had apparently gone ashore to
telephone just before the ship moved out to the buoy and had not
been seen since. I supposed she had given up hope, thinking she had
been left behind, but in fact she must have got back on board
without anyone noticing because I found her in the wardroom
next day.

A French sailor who had been attached to Commander Mackay
as interpreter presented a note from him, and was embarked; and
so too were a couple of ex-B.E.F. interpreters to the Advanced Air
Striking Force. Another Englishwoman arrived and later an Englishman. I had arranged that no one after this should be allowed on
board unless they had my signature in red pencil. This seemed the
only way to embark people through the crowded French ship and
still remain on the quay myself.

My signalman and some of the motor-boat's crew, who had been helping the demolition parties to load their charges into the lorries, went down the quay to try to sink a trawler in the dock, but the French said it was useless anyway and that they would sink it themselves. I was fairly sure they had no intention of doing so. I went up the quay to the Prefecture Office and asked for news of the enemy advance. Rennes at noon was all they knew. I said, "Good-bye and thank you" to the little Commander and went back to the gangway. My signalman and Sub-Lieutenant Williams R.N.R. were there, having collected two abandoned French rifles and ammunition for them. This seemed to me to be scraping the bottom of the barrel, but if every man had something to point at an attacking aircraft it would, I supposed, make some contribution to morale.

A message came that the Captain wanted to see me at once. When I went to his cabin he handed me a signal from the Commander-in-Chief Western Approaches which said that the Germans were expected in Brest at seven p.m. It was then seven-thirty. "You must try to get a message through to Commander Congreve. He was going to start demolition at midnight—he must begin at once." I went ashore again. Only one of the demolition parties—a rating—was there and he was guarding some charges for the cranes along our own quay. I had to wait for some of them to return, which the rating said they would do at any moment. Meanwhile we carried the charges down the quay and placed them under the cranes. There were four cranes. Suddenly I had a vision of those four cranes loading a transport for the invasion of England; what I was doing had suddenly a purpose that was personal to me.

At last the lorry came back, and I turned it about and sent it posthaste to start demolishing and to get through to Commander Congreve if possible. I went on taking charges along to the cranes on the quay beyond. The French ship packed with sailors which had been lying astern of *Broke* was now leaving the quay, like a holiday liner with everything but the streamers. The dividing line between human happiness and human sorrow seemed very slender indeed. They were singing and shouting and cheering; and on the shore the women were waving and weeping. I passed one with a pram and a two-month-old baby in it. Under each arm I carried twenty pounds of wet gun-cotton, with detonator fitted and fuse trailing. As I placed the charges beside the outer legs of the crane the scene around me seemed as artificial as the cinematic device of 'back-projection'.

There was a column of French soldiers arriving on the quay. I spoke to some of them. One was truculent. He had been driving an ambulance. He asked what happened next, and when someone said he would have to embark in the troopship he said he would not leave French soil. He was going to stay and fight where he was. It was all very well for us British. We could run off and we had somewhere to run to, but the French had not. That was the difference. "Moi, je suis Français," he said, beating his breast to emphasise the contrast. The only officer with this party was very young. I wanted him to move the column away from the cranes, but he wandered about as if in a dream. As an officer he was useless.

Near the gangway there was a workshop lorry full of tools and equipment. Our motor-boat's crew had already removed all they wanted. A French soldier asked me whether he and his mates could have what was left. He was very voluble. "It *was* your lorry," he said, "but now that France and England are one, it is our lorry." This was a reference to the proposed Franco-British Union which had been announced two days before on 16th June. I did not bother to tell him that his Government had turned down the proposal, but instead I said that of course he could take what he wanted. Three or four of them clustered into the lorry looking for loot.

Back on board the Captain told me that no demolitions must take place near the quays, as the French had 6,000 to evacuate that night. One of the Canadian R.N.V.R. Sub-Lieutenants (his name was Grand) returned and reported that he had not been able to get across the main bridge to his demolitions as the bridge had been swung open. For the same reason he had not been able to get the message through to Commander Congreve. He thought that his was the only party to the east of the gorge which cuts up through the town. The party was mustered, and after ditching their surplus explosive in the dock they came aboard. *Broke* was about to slip and move into the Naval Basin, when some members of another party appeared. The officer, Sub-Lieutenant Proctor, leapt across the French ship and clambered on to the flag deck rail to ask permission to start his demolitions. He was very quick about this and jumped back again when he was told to carry on. The lorry hurtled off and a few minutes later there were a number of loud explosions and a big oil fire began to the eastward. Soon after he was back and all but four of his party were embarked.

As we were casting off from the French troopship, which was full of mixed troops, a grey hand grenade was thrown down on to the iron deck of *Broke* which was crowded with people—mostly Poles. The Chief Bosun's Mate—Petty Officer W. F. Beer—did not hesitate. He bent down, picked it up and threw it into the sea. In

the words of the Captain's Report of Proceedings: ". . . Whether
the grenade was at safe or not is not known and does not affect the
meritorious nature of Petty Officer Beer's action."

It was half past nine in the evening as *Broke* opened away from
the troopship. One of the four demolishers who had been left
behind—a petty officer—appeared just too late. The Captain
shouted to him across the widening gap, saying that he would be
collected, and immediately sent me away in the motor-boat as the
ship was turning, with instructions to collect the rest of the party and
rejoin the ship on the far side of the Naval Basin, where he was
picking up some of the west side demolition parties. I landed at the
point of the quay again and collected the petty officer and three
ratings, and also a French interpreter who was wearing a British tin
hat. Once more there seemed to be a sudden urgency. The confusion
which had filled that hot afternoon and evening seemed suddenly
to be sorting itself out like a bird's nest of string which is finally
disentangled. We had a ship full of troops, the demolitions were
under way. All that remained for tidiness was to get the demolishers
back on board and our mission was successfully accomplished.

Before leaving the quay I was accosted by a senior French
Naval Officer who asked by whose order the demolitions had been
started. "The Admiral," I said airily. "Which admiral?" "Admiral
Ouest, of course," I said, this being the title I had heard earlier in
the day. Apparently this was the wrong answer. It should have
been the Admiral of the Port—or the General of the Port. He was
greatly infuriated, for he said the demolitions should not have begun
until the morrow. I did not think I could do much to soothe him,
beyond saying that I thought the Germans would be here long
before the morrow dawned, so I left him fuming and returned to the
ship. The whole basin was swathed in smoke from several oil fires
that were now burning fiercely. I had no idea whereabouts the ship
would be and we had almost gone past her in the dusk before we saw
her nestling in the smoke right against one of the biggest oil fires.
We returned on board having wasted very little time indeed. As I
was climbing up to the bridge some floating cranes in the basin just
astern of us were blown up. It was a stirring sight to see them fall.
This was like breaking crockery on a titanic scale with a bit of Guy
Fawkes thrown in—and correspondingly satisfying. Our destructive instincts were having full rein.

The oil fire was just astern of us as we lay alongside—port side
to facing east—and there were two large cranes, one opposite the
bow and the other opposite the quarter deck. We told the demolition

party near us to be sure that these were not blown up till we had moved. We hoped, in their enthusiasm, that they would not forget. It was now nearly dark; there was lurid flame coming from the fires, and thick smoke swirling round the whole harbour area. The explosions were now almost like a barrage. I had no idea that the parties had brought so much explosive with them.

At a quarter past ten a petty officer of the demolition parties made his way on to the bridge and came up to me. He said that he and two ratings would like to volunteer to go up the harbour in the motor-boat and light the demolition charges which they had laid but had not been able to reach because of the open swing bridge. These were under a 150-ton cantilever crane and two pontoon bridges. I asked the Captain who was at first doubtful. We should very soon have collected everyone and be ready to leave. He did not want any more dispersal at this stage. I said it seemed a pity to leave so important a target and finally he agreed to let them go and gave me permission to go with them.

I collected Sub-Lieutenant Grand, to whose party the volunteers belonged, and in a matter of minutes we were away again in the motor-boat. The First Lieutenant called after us that the Captain would allow us an hour, but no more. It was ten-twenty-five p.m. We chugged to the mouth of the river and turned up it, passing fifty yards from a power house which we knew was to be blown up at any moment. We nearly got rammed by a tug round the first bend, and we passed a good fire burning on the corner. We never knew what it was, but it was not oil. Underneath a very high main bridge we could see our crane. I was for going on up to the pontoon bridges and doing them first, but Grand said he thought it would take too long, and that if Jerry was about he might stop us from doing the crane, which was far the most important. Round the next corner we came upon a congestion of moored tugs and boats. There was one tug dangerously close to the crane. We came alongside and said we were going to "démolir ce machin-là," pointing up to the huge bulk of the cantilever arm which jutted out almost over our heads. The French tugmen were sceptical. I thought I had aroused them when I told them that they only had ten minutes to get clear. They began bustling about, but they evidently changed their minds, for they made no move. We came alongside some boats lying at the steps at the foot of the crane, and four of the party landed. They scrambled up the slope to the foot of the crane. They looked tiny beside the huge girders. They had some trouble with the French sentries guarding the crane, and had to draw their pistols. They lit one fuse, but a little later returned and lit it again. There was a subsidiary charge that would blow up a side bridge when the crane went up. Then the party came dashing down the steep slope to the boat. We had kept the engine running as our motor-boat was notoriously bad at starting, especially when hot—in fact under such conditions she was often impossible to start. As the party jumped aboard I gave the order to let go. The engine was clutched in and immediately stalled. There was no self-starter. The stoker worked hard at winding but she gave no kick. Above us the fuses were fizzing away. They had seven minutes to burn; and there we were cranking away at the engine. The petty officer said, "Well, boys, we're going to be blown up after all!" and at that precise moment she started. The engine could not have been stopped for much more than thirty seconds but it seemed like as many minutes. This time she was very carefully clutched in and we turned out into the stream. We shouted to the tug that she had six minutes to get clear, but there was no one on deck.

We managed to get right down the river and past the power house before the explosion occurred. In fact we were beginning to wonder if something could have gone wrong. The fuses burned for something like fourteen minutes. Then there was a small bang followed by another and then lastly a most terrific report, which was, until then, easily the loudest explosion of the evening. We just saw the top of the crane tip and begin to fall before it was swallowed up in the smoke of a near-by fire. We wondered how the tug had fared and hoped that there had been no casualties.

Ten minutes after the explosion I was back on the bridge reporting to the Captain. "Hundred-and-fifty-ton train destroyed, sir." He said "Don't you mean 'crane'?" and we both laughed. Then anti-aircraft fire broke out and a few seconds later there was a vast explosion much louder even than the bang we had made under our crane. We think it was a magnetic mine which fell on land—the thing which afterwards was called a land mine. It fell not far away ahead of us and further demolished the power house. It was satisfactory to find that Jerry was helping us in our work. The aircraft appeared quite low overhead, showing black against the flame-lit sky. Red tracers sped after it from the French destroyers still lying outside the harbour. It circled over a second time but we did not open fire. Five minutes later the air-raid alarm was sounded in the town, but the plane was far away by then.

Just before midnight we embarked most of the west side demolition party and moved out into the basin so that the near-by cranes could be destroyed. We left the whaler in charge of Sub-Lieutenant Williams to bring off the rest of the party. Only one of these cranes went up according to plan. Great pieces of metal fell into the water well beyond us. Then the whaler came alongside and was hoisted in and the *Broke* turned and moved out of the harbour.

I was almost overcome with fatigue, but I stayed on the bridge as we went down the narrow channel. I was afraid that if I did not, I would not be selected to go ashore—and I knew there would have to be another shore party in order to collect the last of the demolition parties, including Commander Congreve himself, from the hotel at Bertheaume, where I had met the British Naval Liaison Officer that morning (though it seemed like a week ago).

The smoke from our fires came down parallel with us, thick and black across the sky to the northward. There was a bright moon, but as the channel turned north into the smoke, all was blotted out. We crept forward as in a fog—but a black fog in which nothing was visible ahead. The Captain decided to anchor, but five minutes later we saw a dim white line ahead which seemed to indicate that the smoke belt was quite narrow. So at one-fifteen a.m. we weighed again and came into Bertheaume Bay. In the moonlight the hotel was plainly visible. I made ready to set off on my sixth expedition of the day in the ship's motor-boat.

I returned to the bridge for last-minute instructions and at that moment a light was seen flashing on shore. It was a mile and a half to the east of the hotel. We tried to read what it was saying, but it made no sense. For some time the Captain debated whether I should go to this light or to the rendezvous. I don't think we thought very seriously that it was likely to be a trap, but there was always a possibility that the Germans had come round Brest in order to encircle the town. Eventually the Captain decided that the best plan was to go to the rendezvous and investigate the light on foot afterwards. This would be preferable to approaching a potentially hostile shore in the motor-boat. So at one-thirty-five a.m. I set off with Signalman Wilcox and we towed the whaler with us so as to be able to land on the beach. As we came near to the shore a body of men detached themselves from the shadows and came along the beach from the cliff to the west. I whistled and then looked at them very intently through the glasses. The overwhelming probability that they were our demolition party was momentarily swamped by the remote possibility that they were Germans—or even French who might deal with us like parachute troops. A moment later we were shouting across the breakers to the Canadian

Officer and I waded ashore. Only one of the two missing demolition parties was there and Commander Congreve was not among them.

I made a signal at once to *Broke*, using the old code word from St. Valery—'Jake' (which was misread in the ship as 'Oke') and proceeded to report how many men I had found. I arranged to send half of them out to the ship and keep the other half to embark their surplus explosive while waiting for the Commander who was expected to arrive at any minute. The party had bogged their lorry in the soft sand at the top of the beach. We started to drag the charges down to the edge of the incoming tide. A signal came from *Broke* to say that the explosive was not to be re-embarked but to be ditched, and another to say that the Commander and one other officer had arrived on board. I sent the Canadian Sub-Lieutenant off with half his party in the motor-boat and set to work with the petty officer and half a dozen hands loading the explosive into the whaler to be rowed out to a distance that would not be uncovered by low tide. We made a sort of jetty out of gun-cotton boxes, but we soon found that we must get our feet wet if we were to do the job with reasonable dispatch. So we waded about lifting charges into the whaler. The motor-boat had now returned and towed her out so that the charges could be ditched in the deeper water.

There was still a party of twenty-two soldiers missing and I decided to walk up to the hotel to see if they could be there; but they weren't. A signal from *Broke* said "There is flashing on the cliff to the east of you," and I replied, "Will investigate. How far along?" The answer was "Half a mile." We walked up towards the road, and tried to start a car, but it would not go. We tried to back the lorry out of the soft sand, but that was no use either. So leaving the petty officer to organise the loading and ditching of the rest of the explosive and to blow up the lorry with a small charge, Wilcox and I set off to walk along the cliff. We turned up a little road with houses on either side, standing haphazard in their small gardens, and came upon another car, but it was locked; a third we could not start, though in the attempt we woke a dog in the house, which began to bark. The road was getting narrower and the houses fewer, so that we doubted if a car would help us much in any case. The last house was a sort of tower. We climbed the steep slope of its 'drive', went past it and to the end of its little garden. From there we must strike out across country. The undergrowth of gorse and broom was thick and it was quite hard to find a way through. We were walking up to our waists in luscious summer herbage drenched in dew. The hillside was steep and we had been actively on the go without a break for twenty-seven hours. Dawn was breaking and we were very tired. A small bird flitted from a gorse bush close above us. It was barely light but there was no doubt of its identity—a Dartford Warbler. We could hear a droning of aero-engines. High in the blue some German aircraft—probably Heinkels—were circling, though it was too dark to see them. They meant nothing to us as we walked through the broom along the cliff top. They went off and dropped their bombs in Brest. We were wet to our knees from wading in the sea, but the dew washed the salt from our trousers. There was a glorious summer smell about the hillside.

Rather suddenly and unexpectedly we reached the summit of the cliff, and looked beyond. Something caught my eye on the far side of a sandy cove three-quarters of a mile further on. There were people on the beach. More were coming down by a path from the hilltop. I followed the stream back up the hill to where it sprang from a group of a dozen lorries. There were several hundred people, and in the dim light I was sure that there were women among them. They were surely French refugees. Some small boats were entering the cove and two ships were at anchor just outside. We came down the cliff a little from the skyline so that our lamp could be seen and then signalled what we saw to the *Broke*, which looked like a toy ship away below in the bay. I was told to embark the rest of the demolition party and return to the ship, which would by then have moved out to take cover under the smoke cloud which floated out from the oil fires we had started in Brest.

Wilcox and I turned back down the slope. We took a wrong path once—a narrow path which plunged down deep into the bushes and steep over the cliffside, twisting and turning. This would only lead to the shore in the wrong place, so we climbed back up it and returned thereafter exactly as we had come. As we neared the beach our landing place was hidden by the seaside houses. We had still 200 yards to go when we heard a series of incomprehensible shouts, not apparently in French, and coming from what seemed to be offshore. My first thought was that something was amiss in the whaler and we ran the last 150 yards to the corner where the lorry was standing on the soft sand of the upper beach. The scene was observed and interpreted by us in a fraction of a second though it takes longer to describe.

The whaler was 100 yards offshore and the men in it were shouting like maniacs. Standing at the water's edge was a Frenchman with his hands in his pockets and beside us was the lorry. Wilcox said, "I smell burning," and I said, "So do I." A thin wisp of smoke was blowing away from the fuse which nestled underneath the engine, waiting to ignite its demolition charge. With the same glance I saw that the fuse was still a foot or so long. We were then ten yards from the lorry but ten seconds later we were 100 yards away. The Frenchman stood, perplexed at all the shouting, within fifty yards of the lorry. "Venez ici," I shouted, but he would not come. "He's all right there," shouted the petty officer from the whaler as I started back to fetch him away. But when I stopped he turned and strolled up towards the lorry. We yelled with renewed vigour and he stopped and turned again towards us—now forty yards from the lorry. A moment later up she went. Parts of the engine hurtled into the sky. Some fell quite near us; many lobbed up over the Frenchman's head and fell in the sea beyond him. He was quite unhurt. Two lads arrived and joined him. Together the three of them cautiously approached the lorry, but not closer than a dozen paces.

We embarked in the whaler and were towed back to the ship by the motor-boat. It was five-fifty a.m. and she lay at anchor covered by the smoke which still swept westward in a great pall from Brest. I went up to the bridge for a conference with the Captain and Commander Congreve, who had come out in a small boat from the cover where I had seen the refugees.

The military party were to have come off in a fishing boat. It was decided that the Commander should take the motor-boat back about six miles towards Brest where they were to have embarked, to see what was keeping them. I was not required for this journey so I made my way aft among the sleeping Polish soldiers who littered the iron deck and quarter deck. My cabin was occupied by an Englishman, his French wife and their four-year-old daughter. I had some breakfast in the wardroom and turned in on a camp bed in Sub-Lieutenant Mason's cabin in the after cabin flat.

While I was gloriously asleep (at about eight-thirty a.m.) Commander Congreve returned on board, having found the lorry his demolishers had used, but the fishing boat had gone. Either they had been picked up by some other ship, or had set off under their own steam to England, so *Broke* weighed anchor and proceeded down harbour on her way to Plymouth. Soon after she passed the destroyer *Sturdy*. *Broke* was studiously keeping underneath the black smoke cloud and made a signal to *Sturdy*, "What do you think of my umbrella?" The Captain of *Sturdy* professed himself duly impressed and went on to enquire of Bryan Scurfield's son David, who was his godson. At nine-thirty *Broke* spoke to two French submarines *Minerve* and *Junon*, both in tow of tugs. They were on their way into Brest so we turned them about and escorted them to Plymouth. This was a very slow business, as they only made five knots.

It was to this situation that I surfaced to keep the first dog watch (four to six p.m.). It was a calm and lovely evening. Of a sudden there seemed to be no more hurry. There was a wonderful air of relief, almost a holiday elation among the hundreds of people on board. At five p.m. there arose from Brest a most enormous smoke cloud. The smoke from the oil fires, still streaming out to sea on the easterly breeze, was plainly visible, but this cloud, white at the top, rose thousands of feet higher. We were about eighty miles away at the time. We heard later that this was believed to be the demolition of the arsenal at Brest. It took us until nine a.m. next morning to get to Plymouth—not a very comfortable journey with more than 500 people on board a ship which normally carried 200. I had to sleep on a motor seat on the deck in the after cabin flat when I came off watch at four a.m. The stewards did splendid work in the wardroom, serving meals for sixty officers and refugees in relays. The wardroom was full of Polish officers. The Canadian officers shared with us such cabins as were not given up to refugees and their families. The Captain's day cabin flat was devoted to the ladies. The Doctor as ever was continuously full of good cheer. In his own phrase, he was "extremely benign", and fortunately had little to do in his professional capacity. On arrival the French lady who had occupied my cabin gave me a tiny medallion of St. Teresa, in return for such comforts as I had been able to provide, and my autograph. Her gratitude was moving.

It was nine-twenty on the morning of 20th June, 1940, when we secured to a buoy in Plymouth Sound and a hospital boat came alongside to disembark the demolition parties and all the civilians. Later a drifter took off the Polish soldiers, who sounded a bugle call in a leave-taking ceremony. The Captain, rising to the unexpected occasion, took the salute. He had been given a Polish badge and a German parachutist's badge taken in Norway. In return he gave the Polish colonel a ship's cap band. With the help of our Polish engineer officer under training, he was able to shout "Good luck" in Polish after the departing drifter. From its decks came three resounding cheers as it chugged off up the harbour.

Finally the two French submarines were towed into the Hamoaze —perhaps the most important result of our operations at Brest. The same evening we sailed on anti-submarine patrol.

CHAPTER 6

Our First Convoys

AFTER Brest we were sent one night up the River Gironde, but our orders were suddenly modified by radio and the adventure fell short of our expectations. When France had finally been overrun we found ourselves on convoy escort duty. We went up Channel to meet the convoy at dawn off Start Point. As day broke we could see ships everywhere scattered around the horizon. Some were being gathered together by the corvette *Clarkia* and we asked her what was the matter. She replied that a dive-bombing attack during the previous afternoon had sunk seven of the thirty-six ships and damaged three others, which had put in to Portsmouth and that during the night four more had been sunk by E-boats. The *Clarkia* was gathering the sadly depleted convoy like a hen gathering her brood, and we helped her.

During the afternoon when we were south of the Lizard and two small additions to the convoy had joined—one from Plymouth and one from Falmouth—we were aroused in the wardroom by an under-water explosion followed by the alarm bell calling us to Action Stations. We went round and through the convoy and discovered that either two or three bombs had fallen in a bunch from the clouds, doing no damage, and that the aircraft had been sighted for a few seconds by the nearest ship. We had an air escort of three Spitfires and an Anson at the time, but they failed to find the enemy in the clouds.

An hour or so later I was walking on the quarter deck when another bomb fell in the middle of the convoy. This time I could see the aircraft as the clouds were much higher. I could quite easily have pointed the machine out to the three-inch gun's crew as I went forward to the bridge but I imagined that this would already have been done from the bridge. A timely shell burst from us might have directed the attention of our fighter escort. But it seems that I was the only person on board who saw the enemy and I had not told the gun's crew. "This," I wrote rather pompously at the time, "was a bad mistake on my part."

Some minutes later when the German plane had disappeared to the eastward the fighters went off that way to look for it, without, of course, any hope whatever of finding it.

On the following morning a Sunderland flying-boat came and said by light: "I can lead you to a submarine fifteen miles away." It was in the path of the convoy, so we went off at once and as Anti-submarine Control Officer I was sent for. I arrived on the bridge just as we were reaching the position. There was a streak of oil and the Sunderland fired a smoke flare. Almost at once we got Asdic contact on the starboard bow and did a pounce attack with depth charges. We thought we heard the submarine move after it and then we lost contact. "Actually I am convinced it did not move," I wrote at the time. But there seemed little excuse for losing our target. Maybe it was a shoal of fish anyway, or a wreck on the bottom.

For an hour we circled round whilst the convoy approached and when it was abreast of us we suddenly picked up the contact again within 1,000 yards of the convoy. The streak of oil was still there, about forty yards wide and stretching away in a curve, which was probably caused by the changing tide. We had wasted much time on another patch of less convincing oil. The Sunderland was said to have bombed the submarine before summoning us, so perhaps the oil was an indication of its success.

We attacked twice with a pattern of depth charges—the first time causing large air bubbles. Then we tried a new method of attack which was carried out successfully only at the third attempt, and finally we put down two more charges to go off on the bottom.

"It is very unlikely," I wrote, "that this was a submarine but it has been allowed that if it *was* a U-boat it was 'almost certainly destroyed'."

The *Winchelsea* and *Vanquisher* turned up whilst we were hunting. They signalled congratulations on "avenging the *Whirlwind*". *Whirlwind* had reported a U-boat in a position not far away the day before and had subsequently been torpedoed and sunk by the U-boat as she was hunting it (the first time this had occurred in this war). We were far from convinced that we had been dealing with the *Whirlwind*'s attacker. We went on at once to catch up the convoy, which we were due to leave at dusk in order to meet an important incoming convoy from Halifax. About ten destroyers had been detailed to join it, and we were to be one of them. The afternoon was uneventful. I kept a showery dog watch. Dolphins were squeaking and bubbling on the Asdics and jumping all around.

During the night I was awakened by what I took to be either a ship in the convoy being torpedoed or a depth charge going off. In either case I decided I should be on the bridge and so I got moving at once. On deck there was some activity on the port quarter and someone said we had been rammed. I paused a few seconds to examine the damage, which consisted of a hole about eighteen inches in diameter bitten, as it were, out of the angle of upper deck and ship's side. The guard rail was gone for about twenty feet, but the damage apart from the hole was slight. The weather was calm, the night very dark and the ship which had rammed us was nowhere to be seen. This was because she was painted pale grey. On the bridge I heard that we had received a signal addressed to the little gunboat *Yusbashi Hakki* which was being delivered to Turkey, via the Cape of Good Hope. But she had done the bashing. We had ranged alongside to pass the signal by loud hailer. The man at the wheel had come out on deck to hear the message, the gunboat had taken a sheer and come into us. She was not badly damaged and could still steam at five knots, but she had to turn back for England and we accompanied her as far as the Scillies.

On the way we sighted a ship's boat. It contained fifteen survivors of the Esthonian ship *Vapper* and in a few minutes we had them aboard and had removed everything of value from the boat, into which we then fired a few rounds from a Bren gun which had signally little effect. Finally we rammed it (at the second attempt) so that other ships would not be bothered investigating it. A Sunderland appeared and we signalled that the other boat from the ship should be somewhere to the westward. It was subsequently found by another destroyer, I forget which—*Vanquisher*, I think—and I went down to tell the old Skipper that the rest of his crew were safe. He told me that two torpedoes had been fired at his ship and said it must have been a 'macaroni submarine', else why would it have wasted two fish on a small ship which would certainly have sunk in due course from the first?

That afternoon we left the *Yusbashi Hakki* near the Bishop Rock and turned west again to meet the convoy. There had been a signal from a British ship to say that she had been attacked by two U-boats on the surface. The first had shelled her. The second was "disguised as a fishing smack." We met her but could get little more out of her than the signal originally told us. A few miles further on we came upon a derelict which at a distance looked not unlike a fishing smack and may perhaps have been the 'disguised U-boat'. We tried to sink this by gunfire but it was full of pit props and our five hits in ten rounds had little effect on it, though they were useful gunnery practice.

That evening I turned in early—about eight-thirty—and was awakened by someone calling me to say I was wanted at once on the bridge as a ship had just been torpedoed. When I got up there I saw a vessel sinking about three-quarters of a mile away. Why I had not heard the explosion was obscure, as by all accounts it was quite loud below decks. Bit by bit in the excitement I gathered that the Captain had been observing the vessel through his glasses—a Swede—and wondering whether she was bona fide or whether he should send a boarding party, when the torpedo had struck. She was then no more than a mile and a half ahead of us, and it was altogether extraordinary that the U-boat had not seen us approaching, or if she had, that she selected that precise moment to attack when we were heading directly towards her.

We circled the sinking ship, which was herself still steaming in a small circle, heavily down by the bow. We made two mistakes at this juncture. We went too fast (sixteen knots) and we went too close to the sinking ship (half a mile). A wider sweep would have been much better. For about one and a half hours until it was dark we hunted without success for the U-boat and then turned in and picked up the two boats. There were twenty-two survivors and no casualties whatever. The ship was the *Bissen* with a cargo of wood.

During the night we cast to the northward hoping to catch the U-boat charging its batteries but without success. I had the middle watch and we saw nothing whatever. The morning watch however was more interesting. We had ideas of saving the *Bissen* and at dawn we returned to her. She seemed to be about the same as the night before, but when we were about two miles away without warning she sank. The convoy was in sight to the south-west hull down. Suddenly the two officers of the watch—the First Lieutenant and the Gunner T. saw a column of white rise above one of the ships. They were sure it was a torpedo and told the Captain. He was very tired and sleepy, and did not really take it in and they were not nearly definite enough. He knew that the convoy was well escorted anyway, and so he decided to wait at the rendezvous for the convoy to come to us. Meanwhile, just over the horizon, the *Leith* and about four destroyers were conducting a series of spirited attacks as a result of which they believed that the U-boat was sunk. But we took no part and finally returned with our two lots of survivors without further adventures.

Shortly afterwards we camouflaged the *Broke* on my scheme. It was designed to make her as pale as possible at night because ships nearly always appear as dark blobs on the horizon against the sky. Only down moon on a very bright night would she look too pale. Otherwise she could hardly be white enough. Accordingly one side was a compromise dazzle scheme. The best dazzle schemes, for deception, deceiving the enemy about the class of ship, the speed and angle of approach or inclination, are those which have contrasting patches indicating edges and surfaces which do not exist. The best contrast is one of tone—that is to say, black and white. But black or very dark tones ruin the night invisibility idea. At night, of course, colour is not visible, therefore provided that the colours are pale and of the same tone, the ship will look pale grey all over no matter what colours are used. At the same time, within the scope of paleness, bright colours juxtaposed may, in bright sunlight, produce the desired dazzle effect suggesting non-existent edges and false planes. The other side of *Broke* was therefore painted in pale pastel shades of blue, green, buffish pink and white.

The early reports from our sub-divisional mate *Vansittart's* Captain, Lt.-Commander Evershed, who years before had once written me a fan letter about my book *Wild Chorus*, were most encouraging. At dawn and dusk too, he reported that the ship was remarkably invisible.

I found myself thinking more and more during that summer of Jane, the gay child who had been staying at Fritton when I was recovering from jaundice. She was lanky and young with steady grey eyes, a mouth which turned up at the corners and a dimple in her chin. She was inventive and adventurous, full of original ideas and unexpected turns of phrase. At Fritton we had sailed boats, played running games on the lawn and acting games in the house (at which she was especially good), talked about music and painting and acting and writing, laughed inordinately—and begun to fall in love.

Through those critical months Jane was at a dramatic school in Ebury Street, and when I was on leave I called there of an evening to pick her up. We used to drive to Kew or Richmond Park and not talk about the great air battles which were now beginning, nor about the imminent invasion. All the same the war pressed heavily round us with a nagging urgency. There seemed so little of life that was not bound up with the uncertainties of my ship.

The nightly patrols from Plymouth went on through the late summer, and I gained experience as a watch keeping officer in *Broke*. Among my papers I found recently a couple of manuscript sheets on which I had tried to capture the atmosphere of those nights full of suspense and the feeling of great impending events:

"'Which is the lee side?' I asked of the Torpedoman on watch aft as I pushed aside the canvas 'darken ship' screen and emerged on to the quarter deck. 'Starboard, sir,' said a voice from the blackness, and I turned left and groped my way for'ard past the ends of the torpedo tubes which were trained on either beam. The faintest glimmer of paleness showed in the eastern sky, but the waves from the destroyer's bow were lit more brilliantly by an internal glow of phosphorescence. She was steaming at speed, her bow raised so that the walk along the upper deck was slightly up hill. I climbed to the bridge and was greeted by the officer of the middle watch.

"'No excitements,' he said. 'The course is 320°—twenty-five knots—there's a position on the chart: the others are in open order astern and the fighter protection will be here at dawn.'

"'All right,' I said, and he went off to bed.

"Beyond the compass stood the Second Officer of the Watch, for there are always two during the dark hours.

"'Like some cocoa?'

"'Thanks.' He disappeared behind the curtain of the chart table. I swept the horizon for the sight of a white spot that would be the phosphorescent bow wave of a returning E-boat.

"Gradually dawn broke. At first there were thin grey clouds framing a greenish patch of clear sky, and then the green turned to yellow and to gold. The gold became red hot; the grey clouds caught fire and burned to a deep scarlet ember, while thin streaks of dazzling silver marked the place where the sun would rise.

"To the northward, clear and blue, lay the land, the Devon coast which our nightly patrols served to protect from the threatened invasion. That strip of deep blue was the England that had suddenly become so much more precious to us because of her danger.

"A month before France had fallen and our world swayed on the brink of the abyss. We were still in the grip of the

1942   The Senior Officer S.G.B's on the bridge of *Grey Goose.*

1945   My mother.

The hazards of the iron deck in H.M.S. *Broke* in a heavy sea.

The sinking of S.S. *Apapa*, hit by a bomb in North Atlantic convoy. Note the overturned lifeboat, the man in the water and the man clinging to the extreme starboard quarter of the ship.

nightmare. But the land to the northward was real and the sunrise was real and so were a hundred sunrises of memory in days of peace.

"I thought, then, of one of them when I had stood in the bottom of a narrow creek at the margin of the saltmarsh. That morning across the eastern sky, so like the one I was watching, the skeins of wild geese had swept inland from the mudflats of the Wash. Beside me with his seaboots as firmly bedded in the soft mud as my own, a boy was standing, watching the morning flight of the geese for the first time. He stood entranced, caught up in their magic as the glorious chorus of their calling rang out across the marsh.

"All the geese came in to the east of us that morning and Brian's dream of returning with his first goose slung over his shoulder remained a dream for many months to come. . . ."

The manuscript goes no further. The Battle of Britain had begun and Brian D'Arcy Irvine was missing in his Hurricane after an attack by Stukas on a South Coast convoy.

M

CHAPTER 7   *The* Empress of Britain

As the autumn days of 1940 slipped by the prospect of immediate invasion receded almost imperceptibly, until all at once it became obviously too late in the year, and with sudden relief we realised that we had a winter's respite. At the same time the focus of the naval war switched from the Channel to the North Western Approaches, and the Battle of the Atlantic was on.

Broke was sailed for Londonderry, which was to be her new base. She was, I think, only the second destroyer to steam up the narrow and winding River Foyle and secure alongside the quay in this pleasant market town, which was to be our home port for about a year.

Our First Lieutenant had moved on to command his own destroyer, and Bryan Scurfield, greatly daring, had put me up to replace him, which surprisingly the Admiralty had accepted. This was the first R.N.V.R. appointment to such a job in a destroyer. To begin with I was terrified by the complexity of the work, but my Captain nursed me along until I began to feel first adequate and later even efficient.

I had not long been Number One when, on 26th October, *Broke* and the destroyer *Sardonyx* were ordered to raise steam and sail from Londonderry to the assistance of the great Canadian Pacific liner *Empress of Britain*, which had been set on fire in a bombing attack and abandoned. She was being used as a troopship, and as she was capable of fairly high speeds, she was not normally sailed in convoy, but 'independently routed' like the *Queen Mary* and *Queen Elizabeth*. It was therefore as a single unescorted ship travelling at high speed that the *Empress* had been attacked by a four-engined Focke-Wulf Condor. She lay burning a couple of hundred miles west of Ireland and we reached her as the light was fading. There was nothing we could do that night but screen her from U-boat attack.

Next morning two tugs arrived to take her in tow and our boarding party climbed up an immensely long Jacob's ladder to her fo'c'sle to secure the warps for towing. I remember that they found there a small Gladstone bag full of money—£100 or more—which was finally turned over to the Receiver of Wrecks. By eleven o'clock the *Empress* was in tow and proceeding at five knots. The fire on board seemed to have subsided and hopes were high that we could get her back to port. It was at this stage that another Focke-Wulf Condor circled round the horizon observing and reporting what was afoot. Soon afterwards a Whitley aircraft of Coastal Command reported that she had sighted a U-boat about fifty miles south of us and steering north. At this time the 'wolf-pack' tactics of the U-boats were already well under way, but on the other hand according to the Admiralty's estimate of the situation this was the only German submarine within probable reach of our position during the night.

As dusk fell over a glass-calm sea the huge liner, painted grey and still smoking slightly from the invisible fires below, was towed eastwards at four knots by the two tugs—while *Sardonyx* zig-zagged about a mile away on her port beam and we did the same on her starboard beam. The whole convoy was under my Captain's command. By tradition the First Lieutenant normally keeps the morning watch from four to eight a.m., but I was awakened long before that by two loud underwater explosions. I looked at my watch; it was one-forty-five a.m. I went up on to the quarter deck at once, for if there was a U-boat to be hunted, as the ship's Asdic Control Officer, I should be needed on the bridge. From the quarter deck I rang up the bridge and spoke to the officer on watch—a stout and bonhomous R.N. Lieutenant called Alan Jeayes. "The *Sardonyx* has dropped some depth charges," he said. "The Captain says he doesn't need you at the moment." I went down to my cabin again, kicked off my boots and was about to climb into my bunk when I thought "If there *is* a U-boat about I ought to be on the bridge, and somebody must think there is or those charges wouldn't have been fired." So I pulled my boots on again and made my way up to the bridge as fast as I could.

It was black dark and pouring with rain. The signalman was trying to read some dim flashing on our port beam, apparently from one or other of the tugs, but he was unable to make any sense of it. Apparently *Sardonyx* had fired a red Verey's Light indicating that she had made an attack on a U-boat, and we could hear her calling by radio, but the signals were jammed by traffic from the Admiralty. When we finally got close enough to her to signal by shaded light she indicated that she had lost contact by Asdic and had no real reason to suppose that her contact had in fact been a submarine. In the black darkness of the heavy rain storms I had not seen the *Empress of Britain* since coming to the bridge, indeed it had been almost impossible to use binoculars, and even in the clear patches between the storms it had been very difficult to keep in touch with *Sardonyx*. We continued our Asdic sweep on the northward side of the convoy's track, but to us it seemed doubtful if there had been a U-boat there at all. It was all, we felt, a false alarm and we headed back to resume our station on the *Empress*. We could not find her, though the dark loom of the heavy rain showers often made us turn in their direction. This was before the days of shipborne radar. Just before dawn we turned away from *Sardonyx* to investigate a light which turned out to be a steam fishing trawler, and when dawn broke we were alone. A Sunderland flying-boat came lumbering past us and we signalled by light, "Where is *Empress of Britain*?" but he did not seem to read us. It was not until nine-forty a.m. that we sighted *Sardonyx* steaming towards us. Then and only then did we hear for the first time that the *Empress* had sunk nine minutes after the initial explosions. *Sardonyx* could not believe that we had not seen the sinking and throughout the rest of the night had assumed that we knew all about it. In fact a heavy rain squall at the time had obliterated everything. *Sardonyx*'s signal that she had no real reason to suppose her Asdic contact had been a U-boat, meant no more than it said, but without the knowledge that the *Empress* had sunk it meant something quite different to us.

Meanwhile the U-boat Captain—the celebrated Jenisch—had reported his success and the news was broadcast as a German claim before we, who had been less than a mile away at the time, even knew of the sinking. This chapter of accidents was of course very bad for my Captain, though there was only one thing for which he could rightly be blamed; he should not have released and sent home three anti-submarine trawlers which had been patrolling round the burnt-out *Empress* when we first arrived on the scene. He had done this because they reported having been at sea for a couple of weeks, which would have been a long time for us and left us short of fuel. This was not applicable to Asdic trawlers. But he very soon lived down this mistake. The loss of the *Empress* after she had been burnt out was a loss of so much scrap iron but the prestige aspects were a good deal more important.

The Battle of the Atlantic was tough and bloody. We fought the elements as much as the enemy. Some of us used to talk of it as 'the Battle *with* the Atlantic'. During that first winter the U-boat wolf-packs had it more or less their own way until new methods of defence began to even up the balance. It was a pattern of burning ships, floating bodies, crowded lifeboats and a dreadful feeling of help-lessness. The U-boats attacked almost entirely at night. In the daytime the Condors came in with their bombs. For example, it was ten o'clock in the morning of 15th November, 1940, when a Condor appeared from the westward, bombed and missed the leading ship of the port column of our convoy and then came round at about 200 feet to attack the Commodore's ship *Apapa*. One bomb dropped at the foot of the funnel and another opened a great gash in her port side aft. Immediately she was enveloped in flame and smoke, and listing heavily. Terrible as the burning ships were at night, there was something even more awe-inspiring about this ship in her death throes in the middle of the forenoon. In the broad daylight we were watching the drama as if it were under a magnifying glass. The boats got away but one overturned, and there were still men on the forecastle who had been unable to get to the boats at all. A merchantman, the *Mary Kingsley*, had been standing by, and her master now gave a demonstration of fine seamanship by bringing the counter of his ship close enough to the *Apapa*'s forecastle to take off the men, among them *Apapa*'s master. In the heavy swell it was most skilfully achieved.

As we circled sweeping with Asdics and watching, Gerald Gibbens, our Doctor, took a series of photographs which included what must be one of the most striking shipwreck pictures of the war. In the background rages the fire behind the gaping hole in the ship's side, in the foreground is the capsized lifeboat and another coming to the rescue of those clinging to it; nearer still is a swimmer.

One boat only came off to the *Broke*. It contained the Commo-dore, Admiral Knowles, and a number of wounded men. It also con-tained a man who was obviously dead and another who showed no signs of life, but on whom we immediately set to work with arti-ficial respiration, which was carried on for an hour and a half to no avail.

Three minutes after noon the *Apapa* broke in half, the two ends rose up in clouds of billowing steam and smoke and she sank. The casualties were light and yet of all the ships which sank before my eyes during the war, the *Apapa* is still the most vivid recollection of that terrible, irrevocable last moment.

CHAPTER 8   *Winter and Rough Weather*

THE winter of 1940–41 was not very enjoyable for those who sailed
the North Atlantic and the ship's company of the *Broke* were no
exceptions. At the beginning of December I wrote to Michael
Bratby:

> "We are in unexpectedly to mend a bent condenser before a
> week on the job. These weeks are not anything to look forward
> to. They are absolute hell. If one thinks in terms of doing this
> work all through the winter it is unbearable. If optimism
> prevails one can think that by April the weather won't be so bad
> and between then and now, what with our refit, we shan't have
> much more than five or six more trips, then it doesn't seem too
> bad. The saving thought about it all is that we really are doing
> something worth doing . . . not far off the most important job
> a ship can do nowadays . . ."

When the refit came there was some relaxation in wildfowling.
I joined Michael and John Winter at Sandside on Morecambe
Bay, and heard again the whistle of Wigeon and the call of Grey-
lags. The marshes were under deep snow.

Back in the dockyard at Belfast I wrote to Michael on 19th
January, 1941:

> ". . . Lots of good memories to be stored. I shall remember
> our walk over the moss; and eating snow; and how invisible you
> were in your white coat at the first drive; and watching your
> shot from the rocks at the corner of Birkwood; and their stalk
> looking out across the silver-streaked sand. I enjoyed Grange
> too, and pulling out the punt there at dusk—such a nice friendly
> adventure. Those are the right kind of adventures even if they
> are less terrific than the war ones . . .

"I got back here safely but have been having a hellish time since. They had pulled all our cabins to bits in the refit, and I now live in the after cabin flat. The Gunner and I are the only Officers on board and we both sleep down there. On Thursday after lunch we sat in front of the stove in our topsy-turvy wardroom when suddenly there was a loud report on the other side of the bulkhead. We ran up on deck and towards the cabin flat hatch. As we went Guns said, 'My God—that Polish hand grenade we got in Brest was in my drawer—I wonder if it was that.' It was. The flat was full of smoke and lying over the threshold of the Gunner's cabin was a young Able Seaman who was acting as his servant. When I got down there I could see his legs only. I looked into the cabin and saw that there was not much that could be done. He was still technically alive I suppose but his face and both hands had gone and he had terrible wounds in the stomach. He was far past first aid—or indeed any aid at all, poor chap. Of course we sent for doctor and ambulance, but the awful thing was not being able to do anything. There was nothing that doctors or anyone else could have done but wait for the ambulance to take him away, but it was a dreadful wait. In ten minutes he was dead without, of course, regaining consciousness, but it was a nightmarish ten minutes. I had to try to keep everyone else away from seeing him, because it was very unnerving. Twenty minutes later the ambulance came and took away the body. Then I had to examine the cabin. This was also not a pleasant job. The cleaning up, which involved bulkheads and even the deck head above, was done by my best petty officer who was very good about it.

"The extraordinary thing was that my servant—a nineteen-year-old Able Seaman—was working in my cabin. The other boy called to him to come and have a look at something, and he just came out of the door of the cabin as the thing exploded. He was ten feet away and the paintwork round my cabin door was spattered by the fragments, but he was not touched. He saw the chap fall backwards, ran to help him, saw through the smoke how bad it was and ran up for help, meeting us as we ran aft.

"The boy who was killed was just twenty-one—a nice, stupid, rather lazy lad who was not very much use as a seaman, but was very cheerful and therefore very popular. So the ship is plunged in gloom. Poor Guns is very upset. The grenade was his responsibility, but being Polish he was not allowed to 'return it to store' with the other ammunition, and as it was locked up in

his drawer (even though the key was on his desk) I do not think
he can get into serious trouble about it. He was very good and
refused to allow himself to get jittery. He slept like a child in the
cabin that night; I know because I heard him snoring.

"Since then there have been an endless string of official
reports, inquest, court of inquiry, funeral and so on and so forth.
I sent the Gunner off for the week-end and dealt with them all
myself. But it is also very annoying because I had hoped to finish
all the remaining drawings for your book over the week-end.
However they shall be done . . ."

In March 1941 came an interesting, and in a sense prophetic
proposition. I wrote about it in a letter to Michael Bratby which
began:

"I am delighted to hear you're now a major. It really is fine
news, and I shall have to remember to call you 'Sir'. I came to a
turning off my road the other day, but I didn't take it. A chap
called Captain Agar—V.C., D.S.O.—who was Captain of the
Emerald when I did that broadcast at the Reserve Fleet Review
in 1939, which was such a flop, and with whom I stayed then,
wrote and said he was Chief of Staff to the Rear Admiral Coastal
Forces and would I go and have an M.L. (Motor Launch) in his
command with a prospect of a flotilla of them. My first reaction
was 'No! No! A thousand times no!' because they are miserable
little things at which all of us destroyer boys look down our noses.
Then I thought that maybe I was thinking the old conservative
thoughts, and that, practising what I so often preach, a change
would be good for me—pull me out of the rut.

"On the credit side were: a command of one's own (the dream
of most naval officers, but oddly enough not a particular dream
of mine. I would rather have an exciting and interesting sub-
ordinate job than a dull command any day); a chance to work
with the dashing Agar; and not much else.

"On the debit side were: a miserable little slow speed vessel
rather like the *Bella May* [a yacht we had used as a tender for
dinghy races]—only a bit bigger; a wasting of my destroyer
experience and at least a postponement of my chances of a
destroyer command which are fairly rosy at the moment. It
would also—here's our old friend now—put a stop to this very
pleasant life (*sic*) serving a man worth serving and with a nice
team of chaps most of whose little ways one knows.

"Lastly there is no doubt where the key front of the war is

now, and if one trusts oneself at all, it is nice to feel that one is making a contribution in a place where it really counts. A first-hand knowledge over a good many months of North Atlantic convoy is not an experience to be lightly cast aside when so few people have it. So rather pompously I have felt it my duty to stay on in destroyers and this I have told Agar, though leaving the door ajar for changing outlooks.

"I think there *is* a chance of getting a destroyer within the next twelve months, with a lot of luck. It would be nice to be the first R.N.V.R. to drive one in this war—or don't you think so? I believe I am still the only V.R. Number One (except for the old American destroyers which don't really count). At last I am beginning to feel confident—to feel I could do it. I'd be bad at some of it, of course; the navigation is too mathematical for me, and so is the gunnery. But I could handle the ship now—just like a dinghy—and the men, I think.

"It is amusing how inordinately proud of my wavy stripes I have become. If they were straight I should not somehow be nearly so pleased with myself, which many think would be a very good thing!

"We're just off on another trip and we've anchored because we're early, so I'll send this away in the motor-boat. Life has been too hectic to get away much but I went down one afternoon to see old William McAvoy at Strangford Lough. There were a few Brents around his island. One lot of a dozen flew past as I crossed the causeway.

"The other day I went to the Bewick's Swan place up here [near Lough Swilly in Donegal]. I went over to see an old fowler called Riley who lives on the edge of the flood—or 'slob', as they call it hereabouts. He gets oysters from the bay over the bank and catches a few sea trout with a worm. I wanted to get some of both off him for the wardroom mess. We got there at dusk and the water was very low, but swans were calling from the middle of the slob. Then we saw a bunch of about twenty geese— Whitefronts—rather high up, but sailing down into a field at the far end. Some if not all of the swans were Whoopers, and there were only about a dozen instead of the 102 I saw there before Christmas, then all of them Bewick's.

"Apart from that the work has been deadly hard. The ship is *just* beginning to look like a ship again, but it has taken three weeks to get rid of the dockyard filth. They mended a lot but broke nearly as many new things and left a good few unmended too. I

M*

find myself wondering if we achieved anything by the refit. I suppose we did really, but six weeks' leave does no one any professional good, and it will take weeks more to get the efficiency of the ship's company back again. But it is all fun, and we live and learn. We go out for practices that are bad and find the holes in our training. We don't have nearly enough training because at this game one just can't have enough. If you want to keep a ship running and also have the crew properly trained you should have two crews, one to do each—one to fight the ship at sea and the other to look after it in harbour, like the flying boys do. It's a hard life! . . ."

CHAPTER 9   *Fire at Sea*

ALL through that winter one of the brightest aspects had been the
Goodliffes. Guy and Grace Goodliffe lived in a delightful house
only a few miles from Londonderry, though it was over the border
in Eire. It was therefore necessary for us to wear civilian clothes
if we went there. Guy was tremendously keen on snipe shooting
and knew all the best snipe bogs within twenty miles of his
home. On every possible spare afternoon when *Broke* was in
harbour I used to go out with him after snipe, or ducks, or even,
occasionally geese. But it is the snipe I remember most vividly.
Guy taught me how their whereabouts depended on the phases of
the moon, how when they were in the red bogs it was useless to look
for them in the rushy fields, but if the moon was full there would
be none in the red bogs. Then we would come back to a wonderful
tea at Birdstown in front of a great log fire, and Grace would pour
from a silver teapot. It was all in glorious unforgettable contrast
to the life at sea. I took my Captain and other friends over to
Birdstown. I doubt if those dear gentle people ever quite realised
what a tremendous contribution they made to our lives. Somehow
as we returned in the darkness it had made the whole thing just
bearable again, and we could face another gruelling ten days
at sea.

On Sunday, 6th April, 1941, I came on watch at four p.m. for
the first dog watch and found a wild grey day of heavy seas, driving
squalls, and a moderate south-easterly gale.

We were on our way to meet a homeward-bound Gibraltar
convoy, having parted company with the outward-bound convoy in
the early morning, and we were plugging into a head sea at seven
knots which was as much as we could do with comfort.

We were in company with *Douglas* (an old Destroyer Leader like ourselves, and Senior Officer on this occasion) and *Salisbury* (an ex-American destroyer) and our position was on the port wing of a sweeping formation.

When I came on to the bridge three other ships were in sight, which was unusual because chance meetings were not common in 21° West—600 miles out in the Atlantic—more especially on days of poor visibility like this one.

These three ships were already some way astern and steering west, and I learned that we had 'spoken' to them half an hour before when they had first come into sight. They were H.M.S. *Comorin*, ex-P. & O. liner of 15,000 tons, now an Armed Merchant Cruiser, the *Glenartney*, a smaller merchant ship, and *Lincoln*, another ex-American destroyer, who was their escort.

They soon disappeared into the smoky haze and my watch passed uneventfully as I kept station on *Douglas* and contemplated, from the cosy depths of my duffle coat, the white foam streaks which patterned the grey mountainsides of wave, and the green curling crests that were the only traces of colour in that inhospitable scene.

About twenty minutes after I had been relieved I was informed in the wardroom that the starboard fore-topmast-backstay had parted, and I went at once to the bridge to organise the repair. While I was there a signal was received from *Lincoln* at six-twenty p.m.:

"H.M.S. *Comorin* seriously on fire in position 54° 39′ N., 21° 13′ W. join us if possible. 1600/6."

We passed this to *Douglas* for permission to go and were detached at six-forty.

Having told *Lincoln* by radio that we were coming, we made a further signal: "Expect to sight you at 2015. Is a U-boat involved?" to which came: "Reply No."

During this time we were able to increase to eighteen knots and with the following sea the ship's motion was so much easier that the backstay was quickly repaired and secured. We then began making preparations for what might turn out to be our sixth load of survivors since war began.

Scrambling nets, lifebuoys, oil drums (to pour oil on to the troubled waters), heaving lines and heavier bow and stern lines for boats, line-throwing gun, grass line and manilla—all these were got ready and the mess decks were prepared for casualties.

At eight minutes past eight in the evening *Glenartney* was sighted fine on the port bow at extreme visibility range—about eight miles

—and four minutes later *Comorin* was seen right ahead, which was exactly three minutes earlier than expected. There was a lot of white smoke coming from her single funnel.

We asked *Lincoln*, who was lying just to windward of the burning ship, what the situation was and she told us that *Comorin* was being abandoned, that no boats were left, that the *Glenartney* was picking up some rafts and that she, *Lincoln*, was hauling over rafts on a grass line.

When we drew near the scene was awe-inspiring. The great liner lay beam on to the seas drifting very rapidly. A red glow showed in the smoke which belched from her funnel and below that amidships the fire had a strong hold. Clouds of smoke streamed away from her lee side. The crew were assembled aft and we were in communication by lamp and later by semaphore. From the weather quarter the *Lincoln*'s Carley rafts were being loaded up—a dozen men at a time and hauled across to the destroyer lying about two cables away. It was a desperately slow affair and we went in close to see if we could not go alongside.

Various objects were falling from time to time from the *Comorin* into the sea. Each time one looked carefully to see if it was a man but it was not. Some of the things may have been oil drums, in an attempt to make the sea's surface calmer. We looked at the weather side first and passed between *Lincoln* and *Comorin*, only discovering that they were connected by line after we were through. But the line did not part, it had sunk deep enough for us to cross. We turned and tried to lay some oil between the two ships. This meant that we nearly got sandwiched. There were two raft loads going across at the time and the sailors in them waved us to go back. They seemed incredibly tiny and ant-like in their rafts on those angry slopes of grey sea.

The *Lincoln* was rolling wildly and once when her propellers came clear of the water we could see that she had a rope round the starboard one. Her starboard side was black, which we thought at first was burnt paintwork, but discovered afterwards was oil which they had tried to pump out on the weather side and which had blown back all over their side and upper deck.

To go alongside *Comorin* seemed an impossibility. The waves were fifty to sixty feet from trough to crest and the liner's cruiser stern lifted high out of the water at one moment showing rudder and screws and crashed downward in a cloud of spray the next. I thought a destroyer could not possibly survive such an impact.

Round on the leeward side we got our grass line out on to the fo'c'sle and dropped a Carley raft into the water attached to it. The liner drifted to leeward and so did we, but the raft with less wind surface did not drift so fast. So it appeared to float away up wind towards the other ship, and in a very short time was against the liner's lee side. There was a Jacob's ladder over the side and one rating went down and eventually got into the raft. We started to haul in on the grass but we had allowed too much grass to go out, the bight of it had sunk, the great stern had lifted on a wave and come down on the near side of the rope; the bight was round the rudder. When we hauled on the grass it pulled the raft towards the liner and under her. Each time the ship lifted it pounded down on the man in the raft, who began to cry out. At this time we drifted round the stern and could not see him any more. I am not certain if he was drowned, but it can only have been a miracle that saved him.

We were close to the stern now and we fired our Coston line-throwing gun. We fired it well to windward, but a little too high and the wind blew it horizontally clear of the ship like straw. But we were close enough to get a heaving line across—after many had missed—and we connected the Coston line to the departing heaving line as we drew astern and finally pulled an end of the grass rope to it and passed it over to the other ship. Then we put another Carley raft in the water so that they could haul it in to windward but for some time they made no effort to do this and finally their Captain made a signal that he thought the only chance was for *Broke* to go alongside and let the men jump. This was at nine-fifty p.m.

I had various discussions with my Captain as to which side it should be. I must confess that I did not believe we could survive such a venture. By this time it was almost dark and the *Lincoln*'s raft ferry had failed owing to the parting of their grass line. I do not know how many people they had rescued by this ferry, but it cannot have been very many as it was desperately slow. Not that it wasn't enormously worth doing, for at the time it seemed to be the only way at all.

I saw one body floating away and wondered if it was the chap from our raft. Indeed I felt sure it was, though I heard a rumour afterwards that he had managed to climb back on board, and I know that several men were drowned embarking in the *Lincoln*'s ferry service. Obviously a raft secured to the upper deck of a heavily rolling ship cannot be secured close alongside. If it were it would be hauled out of the water by its end whenever the ship rolled away and all those already embarked would be pitched out. The rafts therefore had to remain ten or fifteen yards from the *Comorin*'s side and men had to go down the rope to them. It was here that several men were drowned.

As it gradually got dark the glow from the fire shone redly and eventually became the chief source of light. As soon as we knew we were going alongside I went down to the fo'c'sle, got all the fenders over to the port side, and had all the locker cushions brought up from the mess decks.

I suggested that hammocks should be brought up, but Angus Letty, our Navigating Officer, said that since it was still doubtful if we should get alongside he thought it would be a pity to get them all wet. I wish I had pressed the point but I didn't. Letty had been doing excellent work on the fo'c'sle all the time, but I think his judgment was at fault in this and so was mine in not seeing at once that he was wrong. What are a few wet hammocks by comparison with broken limbs?

So we closed the starboard (leeward) quarter of the *Comorin* and in a few minutes we had scraped alongside.

The absolutely bewildering thing was the relative speed that the ships passed each other in a vertical direction. The men waiting on the after promenade deck were forty feet above our fo'c'sle at one moment and at the next they were ten feet below. As they passed our fo'c'sle they had to jump as if jumping from an express lift.

The first chance was easy. About nine jumped and landed mostly on the fo'c'sle, some on B gun deck. They were all safe and uninjured. As they came doubling aft I asked them how they got on and they were cheerful enough.

One petty officer came with this lot—P.O. Fitzgerald—and I immediately detailed him to help with the organisation of survivors as they embarked.

There was little, if any, damage to the ship from this first encounter and we backed away to get into position for the next. As we closed in for the second attempt the terrific speed of the rise and fall of the other ship in relation to our own fo'c'sle was again the main difficulty for the jumpers, added to which the ships were rolling in opposite directions, so that at one minute they touched, at the next they were ten yards apart. This very heavy rolling made it almost impossible for us to keep our feet on the fo'c'sle. We had to hold on tightly nearly all the time. I remember I had started the operation wearing a cap as I thought I should be easier to recognise that way, but I so nearly lost it in the gale that I left it in the wireless office for safe keeping.

The second jump was much more difficult than the first. Only about six men came and three of them were injured. From then on I do not remember the chronology of events as one jump followed another with varying pauses for manoeuvring. Our policy was not to remain alongside for any length of time as this would have been very dangerous and might well have damaged us to the point of foundering in these monstrous seas. Instead we quickly withdrew after each brief contact in order to assess the damage and decide upon the seaworthiness of the ship before closing in again for another attempt.

The scene was lit chiefly by the fire, as it was now pitch dark. Occasionally the *Lincoln*'s searchlight swept across us as they searched the sea for the last Carley raft which had somehow broken adrift. At each successive jump a few more men were injured.

We decided to rig floodlights to light the fo'c'sle so that the men could judge the height of the jump. These were held by Leading Telegraphist Davies and Ordinary Seaman Timperon all the time. The pool of light which they formed gave the whole scene an extraordinary artificiality, as if this were some ghastly film scene and I can remember, as I stood impotently waiting for the next jump, feeling suddenly remote as if watching through the wrong end of a telescope.

As soon as the jumping men had begun to injure themselves I sent aft for the doctor who was in bed with a temperature. He came for'ard at once and started to work. At the third jump we drew ahead too far and the whaler at its davits was crushed but several men jumped into it and were saved that way. Another time the Captain changed his mind and decided to get clear by going ahead instead of astern. The ship was struck a heavy blow aft on the port for'ard depth charge thrower.

At this jump there had been a good many injured and as we went ahead into the sea again to circle *Comorin* for another approach the decks began to wash down with great seas. This was awkward for the disposal of the injured and I went up and asked the Captain if in future we could have a little longer to clear away and prepare for the next jump—to which he readily agreed.

My routine was to be down by 'A' gun for the jump. There was a strut to the gun-cover frame which was the best handhold. Here I saw that the padding was properly distributed, the light properly held, the stretcher parties in readiness and hands all ready to receive the survivors.

Then we would crash alongside for a few breathtaking seconds whilst the opportunity did or did not arise for a few to jump. Sometimes there would be two opportunities—first while we still went ahead, and then again as we came astern. The great thing was to get the injured away before the next people jumped on to them. As soon as this had been done I went with the Shipwright to survey the damage and then up to report to the Captain. This was a rather exhausting round trip and before the end I got cramp in my right arm through over-exercise of the muscles.

The damage to the ship was at first superficial, consisting of dents in the fo'c'sle flare and bent guard-rails and splinter shields. But at length one bad blow struck us near the now-crushed whaler on the upper deck level. I ran aft and found a large rent in the ship's side *out* of which water was pouring. I did not think the boiler room could have filled quickly enough for this to be sea water coming out again, and came to the conclusion that it was a fresh-water tank. This was later confirmed by the Shipwright. As I had thought, it was the port 'peace' tank. This was an incredible stroke of good fortune, as a hole of that size in the boiler room would have been very serious indeed in that sea.

Several of *Comorin*'s officers had now arrived and we began to get estimates of the numbers still to come. There seemed always to be an awful lot more. I detailed Lt. Loftus to go down to the mess decks as chief receptionist and went back to my usual round—fo'c'sle for a jump, clear the injured, view the damage, report to the Captain and back to the fo'c'sle.

By now some of the injuries appeared to be pretty bad. There were a good many broken legs and arms and one chap fell across the guard-rail from about twenty-five feet. Letty came aft to me and said "That fellow's finished—cut his guts to bits." It appears that A.B. George, a young Gibraltar seaman who was doing excellent work on the fo'c'sle, had put a hand on his back—felt what he took to be broken ribs and withdrawn his hand covered with blood. No such case ever reached the doctor and although there is a possibility that an injured man could have gone over the side owing to the heavy rolling, I am inclined to think that the account was an exaggerated one.

It filled me with gloom, and since at least one-third of the survivors landing on the fo'c'sle had to be carried off it, I became desperately worried by the high percentage of casualties. True, they had improved lately since we had ranged all available hammocks in rows, like sausages. They made very soft padding but a few ankles still slipped between them and got twisted.

On one of my round trips I met an R.N.V.R. Sub-Lieutenant survivor trying to get some photos of the burning ship (I never heard whether they came out). There were a good many officers on board by this time, mostly R.N.R. Of course they did not recognise me, hatless in duffle coat, grey flannel trousers and sea boots, and it took a few moments to persuade them to answer my searching questions.

Still the estimated number remaining did not seem to dwindle. Sometimes there were longish pauses while we manoeuvred into position. Twice we went alongside without getting any men at all. Once the ship came in head on and the stem was stove in, for about eight feet down from the bull ring, and we got no survivors that time either.

Somewhere around eleven-thirty p.m. the fire reached the rockets on the *Comorin*, which went off splendidly, together with various other fireworks such as red Verey's Lights and so on. Later the small arms ammunition began to explode, at first in ones and twos and then in sharp rattles and finally in a continuous crackling roar.

The sea was as bad as ever and at each withdrawal we had to go full astern into it. This meant that very heavy waves were sweeping the quarter-deck, often as high as the blast shield of X gun (about eight feet). When these waves broke over the ship she shuddered and set up a vibration which carried on often for twenty or thirty seconds. All this time the hull was clearly under great strain. As we got more used to going alongside some of my particular fears grew less, but the apparent inevitability of casualties was a constant source of worry and there was also the continual speculation upon how much the ship would stand up to.

Once on the first approach there seemed to be a chance for a jump. Two men jumped, but it was too far and they missed. I was at the break of the fo'c'sle at the time, and looked down into the steaming, boiling abyss. With the two ships grinding together as they were there did not seem the slightest chance of rescuing them. More men were jumping now and theirs was the prior claim. The ship came ahead, men jumped on to the flag deck and the pom-pom deck amidships was demolished: then as we went astern, I ran again to the side to see if there was any sign of the two in the water, but there was none that I could see.

Having got the injured off the fo'c'sle I went aft to examine the damage to the pom-pom deck and see if the upper deck had been pierced. I heard a very faint cry of "Help", and looking over the side saw that a man was holding on to the scrambling nets which I had ordered to be lowered as soon as we arrived on the scene. We were going astern but he was holding on. I called to some hands by the torpedo tubes and began to haul him up. Eventually he came over the guard-rail unconscious but still holding on by his hands; his feet had never found the net at all. He was very full of water but we got him for'ard at once and he seemed likely to recover.

About this time too they had an injured man on X gun deck who was got down by Neill Robertson stretcher (the kind in which a man can be strapped for lowering). These stretchers were being used all the time. I went for'ard once to find a petty officer. There was a big crowd outside the Sick Bay and I trod on something in the dark shadow there. It was an injured man and I had tripped over his broken leg. I hope and believe it was still numb enough for him not to be hurt, but it was very distressing to me to feel that I had been so careless. I ought to have known that the congestion of stretchers would be there.

When I was reporting damage to the Captain on one occasion we were just coming alongside so I stayed on the bridge to watch from there, as there was hardly time to get down to the fo'c'sle. The Captain was completely calm. He brought the ship alongside in the same masterly manner as he had already done so often. He was calling the telegraph orders to the Navigating Officer who was passing them to the Coxswain in the wheelhouse. As we ground alongside several jumped. One officer was too late, and grabbed the bottom guard-rail and hung outside the flare, his head and arms only visible to us. There was a great shout from the crowd on *Comorin*'s stern. But we had seen it and already two of our men (Cooke and George) had run forward and were trying to haul the officer on board. The ships rolled and swung together. They would hit exactly where the man dangled over the flare; still the two struggling at the guard-rail could not haul the hanging man to safety. Then as if by magic and with a foot to spare the ships began to roll apart again. But still the man could not be hauled on board; still he hung like a living fender. Again the ships rolled together and again stopped a few inches before he was crushed. As they rolled towards each other for the third time, Cooke and George managed to get a proper hold of the man and he was heaved to safety and this time the ships crashed together with a rending of metal. The two seamen had never withdrawn even when the impact seemed certain and they had thus saved the officer's life. It was a magnificently brave thing to see.

Another man was not so lucky. In some way at the time of jumping he was crushed between the two ships, and fell at once into the sea as they separated. On the other hand I saw a steward with a cigarette in his mouth and a raincoat over one arm step from one ship to the other, swinging his leg over the guard-rails in a most unhurried manner, just as if he had been stepping across in harbour. It was one of those rare occasions when the rise and fall of the two ships coincided. One man arrived on board riding astride the barrel of 'B' gun and another landed astride the guard-rail. Both were quite unhurt.

During all this long night Lewis (our Gunner 'T') was with me on the fo'c'sle. He was a great stand-by, always cheerful and helpful. As we saw the damage getting gradually worse we found a chance to speculate on the leave we should get and even to hope that the ship would not be 'paid off' because of the terrible paper work involved and the number of things that each of us had 'on charge' in our respective departments which we knew would never be found and for which we should have to account. Letty was full of activity too on the fo'c'sle head and was doing excellent work among the survivors as they arrived on board, tending the injured, heartening the frightened, organising the stretcher parties.

After the terrible vibrations set up by the huge waves which broke over the quarter-deck each time that we had to go 'Full astern both', I became anxious about the state of the after compartments and sent the Gunner and the Shipwright aft to find out if there was any extensive flooding. They had not long been gone when one of our officers came up and said that there was six feet of water in the wardroom. I was inclined to take this with a grain of salt and it was lucky that I did so, for when the Shipwright returned he reported that there were a few inches of water slopping about on the deck but nothing whatever to worry about in any of the after compartments. The officer's explanation was that someone had told him this, he didn't know who, and he told this 'someone' to go aft and verify it and then report to me. Nothing of course had been reported to me.

This same officer only impinged himself once more upon my consciousness during that night. That was when he came up and told me in a rather panicky tone that the damage was really getting very bad on the mess decks and that he did not think that the men would stand much more of it. His explanation of this remarkable contribution was that an Engineer Lt.-Commander survivor who was down there and evidently (and, I hasten to add, with every justification) slightly shaken, had told him that he had better report the extent of the damage to his First Lieutenant.

Actually, of course, all this damage was above the water line, although, owing to the rolling and pitching a good deal of water was coming inboard through the numerous rents along the port fo'c'sle flare.

Back on the upper deck we saw a man working at the edge of the fire on the weather side of the *Comorin*'s main deck. We couldn't make out what he was doing, but we discovered afterwards that he was burning the confidential books in the blazing signalmen's mess.

Still we were periodically closing the *Comorin*'s bulging stern, with the wicked-looking rudder and propellers bared from time to time as the massive black shape towered above us. Still the men were jumping as the opportunity arose. Each time there was a chorus from the fo'c'sle of "Jump!—Jump!"

Although we were keen to persuade as many to jump as possible, I thought that it was better to let them judge the time for themselves and told my men not to call out "jump".

From one of the survivor officers I discovered there had been two medical officers in *Comorin*—one the ship's doctor, Lt.-Commander, R.N.V.R., and another taking passage, a Surgeon Lieutenant, R.N.V.R., but the latter was believed to have gone in one of the boats.

So next time we went in to the *Comorin* I shouted that I wanted the doctor at the next jump if possible, as I knew that our own doctor would be hard pressed with so many casualties. No chance arose that time, but a little later as we closed again I could see the Surgeon Lt.-Commander poised on the teak rail waiting to jump. Here was the one man that I really wanted safe but he missed his best opportunity and took the last chance, a jump of twenty feet. He landed beyond the padding, at my feet as I stood on the layer's platform of 'A' gun. He fell flat on his back and lay there quite still. But in a few moments he had come round and ten minutes later, very bruised and stiff, he was at work amongst the injured. He too had barely recovered from 'flu and was quite unused to destroyers; I believe also that he felt very seasick. His work that night was beyond praise.

Casualties were not so heavy now, but there were still a good many owing to the fact that jumpers on the downward plunge of the *Comorin* often met the upward surge of *Broke*'s fo'c'sle. This meant that they were hurled against the deck like a cricket ball against a bat.

We were all soaked through with rain and spray and sweat. It was very hot work in a duffle coat. My arms were still inclined to get cramp if I went up ladders by pulling instead of climbing. However I don't think this interfered with my work at all. I still continued with the wearisome anxious round—fo'c'sle for the jump, assess damage, up to report it, and back to the fo'c'sle for the next jump.

These last jumps were very awkward because the remaining ratings were the less adventurous ones whom it was difficult to persuade to jump. Two of them, senior petty officers, were drunk. They had been pushed over and arrived on board in an incapable condition. I thought they were casualties but was relieved, and at the same time furious to discover that they were only incapably drunk. It seemed too much that my stretcher parties should work on two drunken and extremely heavy petty officers, especially as they were the very two on whom the officers in the other ship would be expecting to be able to rely to set a good example to the rest.

Once I sent up to the Captain and suggested that we might perhaps consider rescuing the last few by raft if the damage got any worse, as with well over 100 survivors on board it would be out of proportion to risk losing the ship and all of them to get the last few if there were a good chance of getting those last few in another way. We agreed that we would try this as soon as the damage gave real cause for alarm but not before.

Quite suddenly the number on *Comorin*'s stern seemed to have dwindled. At last we seemed to be in sight of the end. There were about ten, mostly officers. The Captain and Commander were directing from one deck above, with a torch.

At the next jump they all arrived, unhurt, except the Captain and the Commander, who remained to make sure that the ship was clear.

Five minutes later we came in again. The Commander jumped and landed safely. The Captain paused to make sure that he had gone, then jumped too. He caught in a rope which dangled from the deck above, and which turned him round so that he faced his own ship again. At the same moment the *Broke* dropped away and began to roll outwards. The Captain's feet fell outside the guard-rail and it seemed that he must be deflected overboard. But he sat across the wire guard-rail and balanced for a moment before rolling backwards and turning a back somersault on the padding of hammocks. He was quite unhurt, smoking his cigarette, and he had managed to return his monocle so quickly to his eye that I thought he had jumped wearing it.

He turned out to be Captain Hallett—a destroyer Captain of the First War who had served under my father some thirty-five years earlier.

I took him up to the bridge to see my Captain and at forty minutes past midnight we made the signal to *Lincoln*, "Ship is now clear of all officers and men."

Rescue operations were now successfully completed. During the past three hours no less than 685 telegraph orders had been passed from the bridge to the engine room and executed without a mistake. Captain Hallett told my Captain that there were still some confidential books in the strong room of the *Comorin* and that he would not feel safe in leaving her until she had sunk. He asked us to torpedo her. Having discussed the possibilities of salvage and decided that they were not practical, we prepared to fire a torpedo. It was fired at rather too great a range and did not hit. Nor did the second or the third. Some time elapsed between these attempts and I went below to examine the situation on the mess decks. "Anyone here down-hearted?" I asked and received a rousing cheer of "No." A lot of water was slopping in through the numerous holes and I started a baling party with buckets. The casualties were mostly in hammocks, some on the lockers and some in the starboard hammock netting. The port side of the mess deck was a shambles. However, since everything seemed to be under control, I went aft to the wardroom and found some thirty-five survivor officers ensconced there. The deck was pretty wet and the red shellac colouring had started to come off so that everything soon became stained with red. The flat outside was running with fuel oil and water and baling operations were put in hand.

Then I went back to the bridge and instituted a count of the numbers of survivors which turned out to be correct and never had to be altered. We had exactly 180 on board. Back in the wardroom I found the Engineer Officer baling away with buckets. He told me that the Gunner had been washed overboard, but had been washed back on board again by the next wave. He was very shaken and had turned in. I discovered also that earlier in the evening when struggling with the manilla, P.O. Storrs had been pushed over by the rope, but had managed to hold on and be hauled back to safety. At some time or other A.B. Bates had been washed off the iron deck just by the for'ard funnel and washed back on board again on the quarter deck, a remarkable escape.

As it was now after two a.m. and I had to go on watch at four I tried to get a little sleep in Jeayes's cabin. My own cabin was occupied by a Commissioned Gunner whose arm had been crushed. He had caught hold of the outside of the flag deck. His arm had got between the two ships and been pinched whereupon he had let go and would have fallen into the sea but for the fact that his raincoat was pinched in and held. He hung by it and was hauled in from the flag deck ladder. I afterwards discovered that he had served with my father as an A.B. in the *Majestic* in 1906 when my father had been Cable Officer in her. He occupied my cabin for the rest of the voyage.

I did not sleep much and I missed the torpedoing of the *Comorin*, which was achieved with either the fourth or fifth torpedo. The sixth had a seized-up stop valve and could not be fired. At 0400 I relieved Jeayes on the bridge. The *Comorin* had not sunk; she was appreciably lower in the water and had a marked list to port instead of the slight one to starboard which she had had during the rescue. The Captain had turned in in the charthouse, but came up for a few minutes. I was on watch by myself and we were patrolling up and down to weather of the blazing wreck until dawn.

By about five-thirty the whole of the after promenade deck of *Comorin* from which the survivors had jumped was ablaze. It was satisfactory to know that we had been justified in attempting the night rescue and that time had been an important factor. At dawn we left *Lincoln* to stand by *Comorin* till she sank and set off home with *Glenartney*.

The return journey entailed a lot of hard work. Baling was continuous for the whole two and a half days. *Glenartney* was ordered to proceed on her journey calling at Freetown to disembark survivors, and we were left alone. The weather worsened and on Monday night we had to reduce speed during the middle watch from eight to six knots owing to the heavy head sea set up by the easterly gale. The water on the mess decks was more than the balers could cope with and was running out over the watertight door sills in waterfalls. There were about sixty tons of water on the upper mess deck—about one foot six inches of water when the ship was on an even keel, and four feet or more when she rolled, with a corresponding cataract when she rolled the other way. Life on the mess decks became very uncomfortable. The forepeak and cable locker were flooded and the fore store was filling. It was an anxious night. But when I came on watch at four a.m. on Tuesday the gale began to moderate suddenly. One of the survivor officers—an R.N.R. lieutenant—was keeping watch with me. By five the wind had died away to nothing and an hour later it began to blow from the west. Almost at once the sea began to go down and we were able to increase speed. By noon we were steaming at twenty knots for the Clyde and we arrived there on the morning of Wednesday, 9th April. I spent those two and a half days mainly amongst the survivors for'ard. Lewis and the others were looking after the officers as well as possible in the wardroom. The for'ard mess deck seemed to need most of my efforts, and besides I enjoyed the company of the rating survivors, so I spent as much time as I could on the mess deck amongst them. The *Comorin*'s Commander co-operated most kindly by providing three watches of baling parties with two officers in charge of each watch and by helping with other work. Three survivor officers shared the night watches with us on the bridge.

In spite of the apparently heavy casualties during the rescue, so many of these recovered quickly that there were finally only about twenty-five hospital cases out of the whole 180. The worst cases were compound fractures. There were three legs and one arm. The worst of these cases was an old Chief Stoker who was sixty-nine years old. He was in bad pain all the time and to begin with he had been placed on the lockers in the doorway on the starboard side of the mess deck, from which he had had to be moved later on. He was remarkably brave. The doctors were afraid he would die of shock, but on the last morning I had a half-hour's talk with him in which he described in spirited terms how he had once been presented to Queen Victoria. I believe he survived.

I found the youth whom we had pulled up on the net; he was lying stark naked in a hammock. He was still a bit under the weather but I got his clothes brought up from the boiler room and made him sit outside in the afternoon. Next day he was quite well and very bright. He was only eighteen and had been one of Carroll Levis's discoveries. His name was Sturgess and when he left he said, "Thank you, sir, for saving my life—I'll put in a request as soon as I get to depot to join your ship."

We arrived at Greenock at about ten-thirty in the morning and were alongside for rather less than one hour before slipping and proceeding to Londonderry. During that hour the hospital cases were taken into the ambulances, the remainder were put into buses, the two P.O.s who had been drunk on the Sunday night and had been under open arrest ever since were taken away under escort from H.M.S. *Hecla*, and our bread and meat that we had ordered by signal were embarked. I went ashore to give parting encouragement to the injured in the ambulance, and met an old school friend, David Colville, Lt. R.N.V.R. That same evening we were back at our base in Londonderry.

To complete the story—we learned that the fire in *Comorin* was an accident. A broken oil pipe at the top of the boiler room had dripped hot oil on a Stoker and made him drop a torch which had ignited the oil on the deck. In a flash the boiler room was blazing and had to be closed down at once. This meant that there was no power on the fire main and therefore nothing with which to fight the fire.

Lincoln came into Londonderry two days later and told us of the sinking of *Comorin*. They had fired sixty-three rounds and two torpedoes at her. The torpedoes—not supposed to be fired at all being American pattern—had not hit. They did not reckon at first that their shells did much good. But as the fore hatch cover was near the water, owing to her pronounced list they pounded this and made a hole there large enough to flood the forehold. One of the motor-boats floated off undamaged. Then the ship heeled over and finally the stern came right out of the water and she plunged down. She had sunk by about noon Monday, 7th April. *Lincoln* had saved 121, *Glenartney* about 109. *Lincoln* had most of the army survivors one of whom had been crushed between boat and destroyer. There was a story that an army officer after embarking in the *Comorin*'s boat had shouted up, "Of course you'll be sending the boat back for our baggage!"

Just after leaving Greenock for the Foyle we received the following signal from the Flag Officer in Charge, Greenock:

"I have heard with great pleasure of your outstanding display of seamanship in rescuing survivors and send you and your ship's company warm congratulations. I am proud that my old ship should have done so well. 1245/9."

And on the following day we received this signal:

"To *Broke*, Repeated C.-in-C. Western Approaches, F.O.I.C. Greenock, From Admiralty and First Sea Lord personally: Congratulations on the fine seamanship you displayed in going repeatedly alongside *Comorin* in heavy weather. 0400/10."

After the *Comorin* adventure *Broke* was once more back in the dockyard at Belfast.

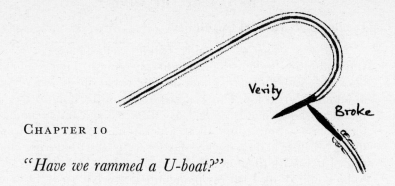

Verity
Broke

CHAPTER 10

"Have we rammed a U-boat?"

IN the summer of 1941 three things changed the immediate pattern of my life. Bryan Scurfield was given command of a Tribal-class Destroyer—*Bedouin*—much bigger and better than *Broke*; the Gladstone Dock at Liverpool became *Broke*'s operating base instead of Londonderry; and one morning when I was on watch *Broke* collided with another destroyer.

It was useless for me to ask to go with Bryan to his new ship. We both of us knew that this is virtually never done. I should certainly have to stay on to bridge the transfer. Before he left, we heard that Bryan had been awarded the O.B.E. for his magnificent seamanship during the *Comorin* rescue. I was Mentioned in Dispatches and three others of the ship's company were recognised, including the two who had pulled the survivor over the ship's side when he and they were in imminent danger of being crushed. Not many months later *Bedouin* was sunk in the Mediterranean and Bryan was taken prisoner. At the very end of the war in Italy a column evacuated from his prison camp was shot-up by our fighters. Bryan, regardless of his own safety, was tending a wounded fellow prisoner instead of taking cover when the next attack came in and he was killed. He was, I think, the bravest man I served under in the war, the most absolutely noble character, and the most likeable too.

Broke, with a new Captain, was soon to be transferred from Londonderry to Liverpool, and for most of us it was going to be an unwelcome change. The green hills round Loch Foyle and the beautiful salmon river up which we steamed to Londonderry after each wretched tour with the convoys was itself refreshing and reassuring, and we knew from an earlier visit to Liverpool that being based there would introduce a new drabness into our lives. There were blitzes there too, but curiously they seemed to be one of the lesser drawbacks of the change.

In a letter to Michael I wrote:

"The war seems to be going awfully well. There is a great wave of optimism here that it might stop soonish. That would be very nice, wouldn't it? There's no doubt that our bomber boys are doing a great job. I went down to one of the Bomber Command Stations when I was on leave six weeks ago and spent four days there waiting to go on an Operational sortie. They were flying Stirlings and on my last day we were all set to go on a big raid. I flew with them in the afternoon and we took the aircraft to be bombed up. I left my parachute in it while we went back for a meal and 'briefing'. Then at nine o'clock it was suddenly cancelled—very disappointing. I'm hoping to go during this next leave. I can hardly bear the prospect of more dockyard time. God, how I hate dockyards!

"If the war *is* on its final lap (personally I think it'll take another two years, but if . . .) it might be an advantage not to have the Americans with a finger in the peace pie. That is the only consolation I derive from their interminable shilly-shallying.

"But if we can win soon it will be the bomber boys who'll do it. I was greatly impressed with them, and they are the only folk who are doing anything offensive on a large scale. Really wonderful chaps! The pick of the best young men are in the responsible positions—Squadron Leaders and Wing Commanders, all about twenty-five and we should have to look out if they all started sailing dinghies after the war . . ."

My new Captain was Commander Walter Couchman. At first I found him a little frightening, but later when I had explored his sense of humour and found its subtlety, I grew to like him very much. There had never been any momentary doubt about his professional brilliance. In those days it was quite clear that he was bound for the top, and to the top he has gone.

I think it was his attitude to the collision which initially broke the ice, for at first we had remained rather aloof from each other. Obviously there was much room for improvement in the ship's efficiency, and I was wondering how many changes he would make. But the new Captain was trying hard not to be too new a broom. And then suddenly we were all in trouble with the collision. I had been on watch at the time, but of course the Captain, as always, was responsible, and if blame was attached to us he would inevitably share some of it.

The collision was quite a simple one as collisions go. It took place early one morning a couple of hundred miles west of Ireland. *Broke*, as Senior Officer of the Escort Group, was keeping station on the starboard quarter of a large convoy and the destroyer *Verity* was zig-zagging across the stern of the convoy. A U-boat attack from astern had been anticipated on the previous evening but had not materialised. In the half light of a pearly dawn I watched *Verity* on our port bow heading to pass about a mile ahead of us. In those relative positions it was *Verity*'s duty, by the rule of the road, to keep out of our way. Soon after she had crossed our bows I noticed from her silhouette that she was altering course, and at first I assumed she would be turning away from us and parallel with the convoy before 'zagging' back across its wake to the opposite corner. A few moments later, however, I realised that the turn had been towards us and she was on opposite course to us heading to pass down our starboard side. We should pass 'green light to green light' (although of course there were no lights in war time). I recalled the little rhyming mnemonic which says:

> Green to green or red to red—
> Perfect safety, go ahead.

So we held our course. If *Verity* held hers we should pass on opposite courses at a quarter of a mile. But there were two things that I did not know. The first was that no one on board *Verity* had seen *Broke*, perhaps because of our pale camouflage, perhaps because of the light of dawn which fell on us but showed *Verity* to us in silhouette. The second thing I did not know was that in order to use her fixed radar aerial, which required the whole ship to be pointed in the direction of radar search, *Verity*'s Officer of the Watch had ordered "Starboard ten" and was describing a loop at the end of his zig-zag so as to check that no U-boats were following the convoy.

Things moved fast now, for of a sudden I realised that *Verity* was still turning towards us and rapidly closing us. Furthermore she was now approaching on a collision course from our starboard side and it was therefore incumbent upon us to keep clear of her. My first impulse was to put on the brakes and then to alter course. "Stop both," I called down the voice pipe. "Full astern both—hard-a-port." Then I moved to the Captain's voice pipe. "Captain, sir, I think you should come up at once as I am afraid there is going to be a collision." There was nothing more to do. You cannot stop ships dead in their tracks. The two destroyers swept on inexorably and interminably towards each other. In a few seconds the Captain was beside me. "You know, Number One, I think you're right; are you going full astern?" "Yes, sir," and we stood and waited. From right to left, still going at her previous speed, the *Verity* streaked across our bows. For one brief moment I thought she might clear us, but then came the rending crunch of metal as we ploughed into her port side thirty feet from the stern.

I'm not sure if it was then or only later that I realised my most serious mistake. Had I said "Hard-a-starboard" instead of "Hard-a-port" she would probably just have cleared us. Here was the simple problem. If you are converging with someone and appear about to ram him, do you alter course away so as to minimise the blow as I had done, or do you alter course towards in the hope that you will pass behind him? If your judgment is wrong on the second course then you cut him in half. But in this case we might have cleared.

Immediately after the impact there were explosions caused by some of *Verity*'s depth charges which we had dislodged. But they were deep down and caused no damage. The Captain sent me at once to examine the damage, and I remember collecting the Ship-wright and making my way towards the forepeak through the hammocks on the mess decks to a chorus of questions: "What is it, sir? Have we rammed a U-boat?" Ah, if we only had! Decorations and congratulations all round, instead of a Court of Inquiry and perhaps a Court Martial. The damage was not dangerous in either ship and, thank goodness, there were no casualties, although we had ploughed into the bunk which the *Verity*'s Engineer Officer had left only ten minutes before. But at a time when Escort Vessels of all kinds were in desperately short supply the collision had taken us out of circulation for eight weeks and the *Verity* for fourteen. It was a horribly sobering thought.

I think my Captain knew the strain I was under before and during the Inquiry. No one could have been more considerate. At the end it was recommended to their Lordships of the Admiralty that the blame for the accident, although perhaps attaching rather more to *Verity* than to *Broke*, must nevertheless be shared, and, referring to *Verity*'s Officer of the Watch and to me, "that these officers should be cautioned to exercise more care in the future".

In peace time no second chance would have been given, but the wisdom of this more lenient course is perhaps demonstrated by the fact that for the rest of the war I never again let a ship approaching on my starboard side come within half a mile. In this respect I was much less likely to have a collision in the future than someone who had not had this vivid and unforgettable experience. But I had learnt my lesson the hard way.

CHAPTER 11   *The Stirlings*

ON Private View Day of the Royal Academy's summer exhibition
in 1941 I met Sir Courtauld Thompson in company with Air Commodore Sir Victor Goddard, who had been having a great success
with a series of brilliant broadcasts. While looking at a war picture
of mine which showed a German aircraft attacking H.M.S. *Broke*
on the calm morning off Le Havre a year before, I told the Air
Commodore how much I wanted to fly with the R.A.F. It was a
good thing, I argued, for all of us to discover at first hand how the
other half of the world lived. It could do nothing but good for me to
see the R.A.F.'s night bombing effort at first hand. No better way
could be found of fostering inter-services relations. "Well," said he,
"I dare say it can be arranged." And so in due course 15 Squadron,
who flew the great new Stirling bombers, became my friends. My
first visit to their base at Wyton in Huntingdonshire was abortive.
Their projected operation was cancelled. But not so long afterwards
Broke was boiler cleaning on the Tyne and I set the wheels in
motion for a second attempt.

The air-raid sirens sounded just as the train steamed into the
station at Newcastle at half past one in the morning on the 19th
August, 1941. The train was full, and because of the air-raid it was
in darkness. Not a seat was to be had, so I planted my suitcase in the
corridor and sat down upon it. During the night its thin cardboard
sagged and buckled under my weight as we trundled southward
at twenty miles an hour, with the glow of searchlights and the
flicker of anti-aircraft fire lighting the eastern sky. The coastal towns
were being attacked, and the white flashes of the guns were interspersed with the longer redder glow of heavy bombs exploding. It
was one of those raids referred to in the news bulletins as 'slight
enemy air activity over the North-east coast'.

By nine o'clock I had arrived at Huntingdon, where a telephone call brought an R.A.F. van to meet me from Wyton aerodrome. After a wash and breakfast in the Officers' Mess I walked over to the office of the C.O. 15 Squadron who was Wing Commander Pat Ogilvie, D.S.O. He had already told me by telephone that the Squadron was due for operations that night and after giving me the Squadron's news since I had last been there, during which time they had done several weeks of daylight operations, we went down to the Operations room to ascertain the 'Target for Tonight'.

The Operations room, behind steel doors, was already familiar from my previous visit. The controller sat at a table with a battery of telephones, the walls were hung with maps, aerial photographs and boards with the 'order of battle' chalked up on them. On a large central table were smaller target maps, more photographs and intelligence reports.

The target for the night was 'the Big City' and I was delighted that I had hit on a night when Berlin was to be attacked. The operation was to be a large one, and routes were requested from each Squadron so that they might be correlated. The C.O. stretched the tape across the sloping map and worked out a course which avoided the known opposition. Petrol and bomb loads were discussed.

Half an hour later, back in the C.O.'s office in one wall of a hangar which housed three Stirlings in various stages of repair, I was introduced to Pilot Officer Conran, the Captain of Aircraft A for Apples, in which I was to fly. We collected flying kit and walked over to the parachute department—a small building hung with scores of white parachutes in a dense curtain down the centre. Here I had a harness fitted and drew a 'chute of the Observer type, which one carries about like an attache case. Night flying tests were to be made at two-thirty in the afternoon so I went off to lunch with Pat at the Mess.

After lunch the adventure really began. We went up to the hangar and thence over in a lorry to A for Apples which stood on the far side of the grass aerodrome. I had flown once before in Stirlings, but again I was amazed by their vast size and tremendously powerful appearance.

The plan was to take off and do a landing again, so that Conran could get the hang of A for Apples, which he had not flown before. We should then take off again and fly to Alconbury (seven miles away) landing there on the concrete runway, where the aircraft would be bombed up and whence we should take off for the raid, for only from a runway could a Stirling prise itself off the ground with a full bomb load.

N

The four Hercules engines were started as soon as the crew had piled in and after five minutes slow running each was opened up in turn to full throttle, the airscrew pitch gear and each of the two magnetos tested on each motor. When one of the switches on the starboard inner was flicked off the revs came rushing down and the engine looked like stopping. This had to be repaired and the engines were stopped whilst it was done. The repair took over an hour during which time I sat in the second pilot's seat and talked to the second pilot who sat in the Captain's seat. He told me in detail what had happened to them on their last operational flight exactly a week ago. They had been to Berlin and had been hit by flak and had spun down 5,000 feet. On pulling out they had been hit again by what they believed to be a night fighter. The port outer engine had been set on fire and had burnt itself out, so that the airscrew had fallen off. They had limped home and when they got there the starboard inner had packed up too. They decided to land at Honington and were not familiar with the aerodrome. The controls were hit and were very sluggish. They made a crash landing and finished up in a sand pit. The aircraft was written off but the crew were all unhurt. They got three days' leave. "It must have been a bit shaking," I said. "Oh, well," he replied, "don't let's talk about it any more."

While we had been sitting there the mid-gunner had been ploughing up the aerodrome by firing unexpected bursts at a cigarette packet about thirty yards away. There were some men working roughly in line with it, and just right for ricochets, but that didn't seem to worry anyone.

At last the repairs were complete. The engines were started one by one. The starboard inner, the one which had needed repair, would not even turn over. It was left to the last and tried again. At first it did not move, but at the next attempt it turned, and started. The engines were tested at full throttle, 2,850–2,900 revs and plus five-and-a-half boost. Then we taxied across the aerodrome and turned with the wheel brakes. We pulled ahead a couple of times to straighten the tail wheel and then revved up with the brakes on. When the engines were roaring the brakes went off with a hiss of escaping air and the four knobs of the throttle controls—two red and two green—were pushed forward to their full limit. We began to accelerate with that tremendous force which is to me one of the greatest thrills of flying. There seems such terrific power in that thrust which sweeps the stationary aircraft into a speed of 150 miles per hour in a matter of seconds. The great aircraft rushes forward in a wild bouncing bumping career across the grass. Suddenly the bumping grows less and a moment later stops. A for Apples is airborne. So it was at a quarter past four on that Monday afternoon. Up went the wheels and up went the flaps. The airscrews changed into top gear and we made a circuit of the airfield. Passing over Huntingdon I looked down on the old war memorial of my mother's which stands in the market place, and the old bridge, and the church, and a Wellington in a corner of a field where no doubt it had force-landed.

Ten minutes later we were coming in to land. I stood with slightly bent knees behind the two pilots. Stirlings do not, of course, glide in to land. They have to be flown in on the engines, which means a low approach. We made a perfect landing, and taxied back to take off again for Alconbury, requesting transport by R/T on the way.

The second take-off was as impressive as the first, though for some reason we were longer on the 'under-cart' than the time before. We climbed to about 3,000 feet and flew round for a while, testing our inter-communication R/T and W/T. O for Orange was also in the air and looked as though she would land at Alconbury first. "Where is this Alconbury anyway?" said the Captain. "Oh, somewhere about west," said the Second Pilot. We found it when nearly past it, as it was, in fact, north-west of Wyton.

We came fairly close to a Wimpey (Wellington) in the air, and I was amazed at how swiftly we swung towards each other although on apparently about the same course. It made one realise the quickness of thought and action required in a fighter doing twice the speed.

O for Orange began to lower her undercart and we decided to make another circuit. I noticed however that she had only got one wheel down and said so over the intercom. so we swung round to port again and came in to land. We made quite a good landing, though we ran off the runway at the end. Then we taxied round the three Stirlings which were already parked in the middle, and came to rest beside them.

We watched O for Orange, both of whose wheels were now down, make a perfect landing and waited for our transport which did not arrive. The 'tanker' lorries clustered round to fuel the plane and a little tractor came grunting along with a string of bombs—1,000 and 500 pounds—each on its own little wheeled carriage.

In spite of an impending rain storm we decided to walk over to the gate at the main road and get transport from there. We found a lorry and all piled in—two crews, A and O, for the seven-mile drive.

The chat was of chances:

"Anybody's thirteenth trip tonight?" asked someone. "Last time we came back with another crew the other crew 'went for a Burton' —that was C for Charlie. . . ."

"Old George told me that—of course he's the only one of our lot left now."

"Nice chap Bill—just the sort of cove to be a prisoner of war with."

I heard for the first time the following story.

"Navigator—where are we?"

Pause.

"Better take your helmet off, skipper. By my reckoning we should be inside the dome of St. Paul's Cathedral."

Back at Wyton we called at the hangar. Some fellows went to fetch their kit and returned with the news that the target had been changed. The weather was no good further east and so it was to be Kiel. This was variously received.

"Pretty hot place Kiel."

"Not so bad as Berlin."

"Well, we had a proper pasting there last time."

"They can throw everything from Kiel bar the kitchen stove."

"Well, it's an hour and a half shorter anyway." And so on.

Back at the mess we went off to get some dinner.

I must confess that I did not have much of an appetite. There was a 'before the big race' feeling, and though we talked gaily enough, I would have been extremely grateful for any reasonable excuse for not going.

After dinner we went up to the crew room in the hangar for the briefing. Some of the crews were late and it was after seven-fifteen when Ogilvie kicked off. The room was full and the crews crowded round and leaned on a great central table covered with a large map. A strand of wool was stretched between pins to indicate the route which had a kink in it to avoid enemy night fighter patrols.

The target maps, with which each crew was provided, were marked with yellow pencil. The target was a 'cocked hat' where three railways joined rather to the south of Kiel and right opposite the very end of the fjord. The course for the approach was left to individual pilots. It was suggested we should follow the fjord south. We were told to bomb from as high as possible—18,000 at least.

Then the Met. expert made his report—four to six-tenths cloud over the target—thunderstorms which should be avoided on the way. The intelligence report said that *Tirpitz*, *Lutzow* and *Hipper* were in Kiel.

Three Stirlings were going there, A, O and S. V for Victor was a freshman who was going to Havre for experience.

We were each given a bar of chocolate and an orange.

After briefing we returned to the mess and put on jerseys and flying boots. The crews had climbed into buses and gone straight off to Alconbury.

Colonel Smith (another passenger) and I were joined by Tyson, Shorts test pilot (the Stirlings were built by Shorts), and the three of us were driven over by Ogilvie at great speed to Alconbury.

Tyson and I sat in the back and I talked as intelligently as might be about aircraft production. He told me how the flow of Stirlings had been held up by two direct hits on the fuselage assembly shop at Belfast.

It was raining when we arrived on the airfield. The Stirlings were ranged as we had left them in the middle of the triangle of runways. The only difference was that each now contained 9,000 pounds of bombs, made up of five 1,000-pounders and eight 500s, and the corresponding load of petrol.

We pulled up beside A for Apples and I sorted my flying suit, Mae West, helmet, gloves, chocolate and orange from those of the Colonel and joined the rest of the crew who were standing round the door of the aircraft.

I got dressed up and climbed up the very slippery deck of the machine to the front compartment, where I parked my helmet and gloves, and then re-emerged and wandered round the aircraft with the crew. The flight sergeant was cracking jokes. The rear gunner was playing about with his guns from outside the turret with someone else inside. He had his hands over the barrels, and the belts were in the guns, but he didn't seem to care.

The rain had passed and the golden sunset streamed in under the heavy clouds. Above us towered the huge black machine. The crew—seven of them—stood round bathed in the mellow orange light, smoking and talking; a Canadian navigator, a New Zealand rear gunner, a second pilot from Barbados. I thought "This is the way to keep our Empire in one piece," and wished that we did it so in the Navy.

Was there an order of take-off? someone asked. The Captain didn't know. The flight sergeant said he thought it would be the same as the Order of Battle. At last the Captain said, "Better start 'em up now—we've only got a quarter of an hour." The crew piled into the aircraft. Take-off was to be at nine-fifteen p.m.

The engines were started and turned over for five minutes before the throttles were opened in turn.

"Starboard outer—twenty-nine hundred—five-and-a-half." The rev. and boost readings for each engine were passed by the Captain from the panel to the flight engineer who wrote them down. My position for the take-off with full bomb load was the 'bed'—a sort of bunk at the centre of gravity. The rear gunner and I were to sit on this until we were airborne. I put on my parachute harness and moved off to the bed where after a search I found the inter-com. plug and plugged in. After a while the rear gunner joined me.

There were eight of us in the plane. Front gunner (standing behind the pilots for the take-off, but later in the very nose of the plane), Captain and Second Pilot. Navigator at a table just behind them, flight engineer at a panel of instruments on the starboard side behind the armoured bulkhead and the wireless operator on the port side of the same compartment. Abaft that was the 'bed' with me and the rear gunner, who afterwards went right aft to the tail turret.

It was almost dark when we took off. I watched the twinkling red and white air beacons and sat by the navigator's table as he marked in the dead reckoning positions on the course line. There was constant talk over the intercom., testing, discussing the engines and passing readings. We reported the lights to the navigator who checked up on our course. We could dimly see the line of the coast, and crossed it near Cromer.

We flew on a course of 065°, always climbing. About three-quarters of an hour later we were at 10,000 and started using oxygen. I was still very hot, for the kit was tight and quite stifling at low altitudes. I plugged in my oxygen tube to the connection beside me. It was impossible to tell if I was getting any through except by the hardly detectable relief from a slight quickening of the rate of breathing. I assumed that it was coming through and indeed it was.

When we were at about 14,000 feet heavy flak was reported ahead, but all finally agreed that this was a 'thunderstorm'. Soon afterwards genuine flak was seen on the starboard bow. This was my first view of it from the air. There was thin haze or cloud and the gun flashes were below it. Just above the cloud but far far below us were the sparkling pin-points of the shell-bursts. It was rather beautiful. This flak was held to be from ships, but I believed it to be from Heligoland. A little later, as we crossed the coast of Schleswig Holstein the flak stretched right across in front of us. We altered course because of this, twenty degrees and then forty degrees to port.

Suddenly above the clouds to starboard a flare lit up. We flew on towards it. It seemed most likely that this was dropped by a Hun night fighter who hoped to see a bomber in silhouette. At the time we wondered if it was dropped by one of our aircraft to try to get a position.

The flare entered the cloud, leaving a trail of white smoke as it fell. In the cloud it was even more effective as a background illuminant. The Captain asked if we were lit and on being told that we definitely were affected by it, banked steeply to port to evade it. By this time it was nearly below us.

A cone of searchlights had been visible far to the south. I suddenly noticed what I took to be more searchlights above us and shining up from above a high cloud bank. This was most puzzling until I discovered that it was the same cone of searchlights, seen as we were banking steeply to starboard to resume our original course.

Some flak began below us and it was an interesting feeling that the guns were definitely trying for us. The sparkling bursts were in line with the gun flashes, but nothing reached us at our handsome height of 19,000 feet. From time to time the flight engineer would ask for the readings which now included the thermometer—ten degrees below zero, but it did not seem unduly cold.

By now we were getting pretty near to Kiel and there was very heavy flak and almost continuous flashes from the port bow which I believed to be Kiel.

The flak was still heaviest on the port side and I thought that we were to the south of our course. By D.R. (dead reckoning) we had overshot the mark and planned to fly on seeking a gap in the clouds. If none could be found we should turn back and bomb by D.R. on the reciprocal course. Below was a white blanket. Ten-tenths cloud obscured the land altogether.

When we did turn we turned to starboard. As we were, I was convinced, already south of the target, this simply put us further south. I therefore suggested that we should go back to a course beyond the reciprocal so as to work up north towards the heavy flak. This was done and a few minutes later, at midnight exactly, with an unbroken 'sea' of white cloud below us we unloaded our thirteen bombs. There was no noticeable effect on the aircraft.

The navigator who had gone down into the bomb-sight compartment as bomb aimer, let them go. There was some momentary confusion as to whether they had gone or not, mainly owing to the native taciturnity of the Canadian navigator. Then there was the business of letting go a flash eleven seconds later for photographic purposes. There was some discussion as to whether it was worth letting it go at all since the cloud was so thick. But it was done.

There was a brilliant flash from the flare. At the time I took this for the bomb flash which I must actually have missed. We were at 19,000 feet when we released the bombs, and immediately afterwards we climbed to 22,000.

The main flak was still to the northward, where, beneath the thin cloud, there was a great area of continuous flickering fire. The gun flashes were white and so were the sparkling bursts. Most of this fire was directed against other aircraft of which about 160 were attacking Kiel that night.

We were now steering a very snakey course owing to the flak—a good deal of which was directed at us, though it was all bursting well below. Some of the bursts were close enough to see the little fountain of orange fragments. Far away to port we saw close-range flak firing red tracer at some other aircraft. It seemed very small and distant. During all this time I had looked on very much as a spectator at the films, with a curious detachment. Everything seemed so remote. The flak was so far below, the whole episode was so very improbable. Since the take-off the nervousness had completely left me and a complete fatalism had taken its place. We should get home or we should not. No action or decision of mine could possibly affect the issue.

Suddenly a searchlight was exposed almost below us. I was looking down on the starboard side and saw a dark patch approaching the glare. This was clearly a gap in the clouds and in a moment the light was in it and we were illuminated. The whole aircraft was brilliantly lit and I expected a heavy fire to be opened on us, or a fighter to attack. But about ten seconds later the beam slipped away from us as we banked steeply to port. We dropped an incendiary bomb with one fin knocked off to make it scream. We had three or four for the purpose of frightening searchlights. I wonder how effective they were.

There were holes in the clouds now and the gun flashes illuminated the fields and roads and woods of Germany. At last there was sea below and occasional flares in the distance. One fell gently over Heligoland (or so I believe it was, as there was an area of barrage fire about where the island should have been). The flare illuminated nothing but sea and we were far enough to the north not to be affected. The Captain and Second Pilot changed places and there was a sudden relaxation of tension. When we were half-way across the North Sea a flare was dropped on the starboard quarter and everyone was suddenly alert again. The rear gunner reported what he thought was aircraft below on that side. Then a few minutes later he saw a curious light astern with a beam stretching to another light. He asked for someone to go to the astrodome and check up on it make sure he was not seeing things. The navigator went. I wished I had gone but we could not both go and the oxygen question was complicated. The mystery, like so many of the strange sights of that night, was never solved. Soon after this we came well down so that, at about 10,000 feet, we could eat chocolate and smoke.

An hour later we were approaching the coast. Suddenly it showed up ahead and a beacon flashing D's. The Captain asked what was the letter of the day, and then the engines slowed a little. I thought that having sighted the coast we were perhaps losing height so as to save time. The next twenty seconds were a jumble. The slowing down continued and then the weight departed from my feet and we were stalling, falling; "Push the nose down!" said the Captain— "Right down!—what's the matter with the engines? Flight engineer—why have the engines cut?"

All this time we were in a steep dive—about seventy degrees. The coast, which had been nearly directly below was now a dim line right ahead. The navigator was standing beside me, holding on. I grabbed my parachute just as the Captain said, "Stand by to abandon the aircraft." Then, before anyone could move, the engines began to pick up. He had switched the airscrews to fine pitch to rev. them, and the engines had responded. We were coming out of the dive. The crisis was over. We had lost 4,000 feet.

At the same time as this it seems that the airspeed indicator also failed but gradually came back again. This was more important than it might seem, as it is one of the vital instruments without which the aircraft would be extremely difficult to land safely.

Even after the engines had picked up and the indicator was working again the position was still very uneasy. "What are you going to do, Skipper, gain height and bale out?" asked the Second Pilot. "No," said the Captain. "We'll get her in somehow." In looking back at this incident it seems possible that the failure of the airspeed indicator—perhaps due to the melting of ice—had caused the air-

N*

bed at five o'clock after forty-six hours without sleep. We never discovered the cause of the bump just before landing. It was thought at the time that we might have been hit by a night fighter, but in the absence of damage it was decided that the slipstream of O for Orange terribly close must have been the cause.

Next day, in the afternoon Pat Ogilvie flew me in a Lysander over to Horsham St. Faith's at Norwich. We went by way of the Washes and Ely and south of Norwich to Fritton. He circled Redmond Buxton's house, next to ours, for some minutes before I could indicate to him that it was the wrong one. After that we circled Fritton at 200 feet several times while I took photographs. Then we went back to Norwich, over the goose marshes of Reedham, and the island where I had shot those six geese one morning during the previous winter. It was very obvious why they were so much frequented by the geese. From above it looked very remote and attractive. Coming in at Horsham I saw the family's yellow car just arriving to meet me. They picked me up at the control tower, and we returned to Fritton for the next week of my leave.

cushion there. It is an
was a most enjoyable h
and streams and hop

It was very hot and s
stood behind the pilo
parallel with some Hu
In an hour and a half

Pat Ogilvie introdu
taking me on the Op. i
its night flying tests, s
noon. When we arriv
the wireless and we ha
During this time Tarr
this and that. Knowin
only a very little pe
quiet, rather good-loo
no way profound, ye
crew instead of a deta

When all was read
ground staff on board
tests than usual so we
hunting ground. Ther
that there would prob
was a large 'slappy bi
Fish Inn at Sutton, a s
son's special flood jus
Cathedral came up t
interesting Gull hole v
the new bank had circ
pond. It was on the so
and Mepal. On the wa
vapour from our wing
During this we lost t
landed at Alconbury.

As we taxied in th
Singh, and who wore
excited about a hare w
front gunner to shoot
piece of excellent ad
taken outside its con
looking out of the wi
look out of a differen

CHAPTER 12   *Fritton and Jane*

IN a letter to Michael Bratby soon afterwards, I described this leave at some length. After telling him of the Kiel raid I went on to write of my family and my girl:

"Jane came up to Fritton. She has been a lot there and fits in perfectly—one of the nicest things about her. She and Wayland get on wonderfully well. Wayland at Trin. Coll. Cambs. is now in a ground floor room in Great Court. He plays the piano well and composes interestingly. He is concentrating on music now at Cambridge much to the disappointment of his father who wanted him to follow up his History exhibition with more History. He is really *very* good company, even witty. We went and sailed at Wroxham and I won two races and was last in two, in twelve-footers, about seven or eight of them. One day it rained and there was no wind at all, and I won. The next was lovely and sunny with a nice breeze, and I was last! Jane is quite a good crew though not strong enough for fourteen-footers, she's too willowy altogether.

"I went 'duck shooting' with Frank Somerleyton which involved standing in the decoy at Fritton whilst the reeds were beaten out and then after lunch standing in a field in a row whilst some ponds were beaten out. We got fourteen ducks and a woodcock of which I shot one duck and renewed my determination that I should never allow ducks to be shot that way myself.

"The garden at Fritton was glorious. There were six or seven Comma butterflies on the Buddleia bushes. They really were a remarkable sight. Fourteen species of butterflies:—Comma, Red Admiral, Painted Lady, Peacock, Small Tortoiseshell, Wall, Brimstone, Green veined white, Meadow brown, Gatekeeper, identification on and off and had thrown out two screamers—incendiaries with a fin taken off. Satisfactory results were reported after these actions I was of the opinion that such were to be observed with the eye of faith only!

By now we had lost 1,500 feet and suddenly a searchlight caught us full in its beam. Evidently we were visible from below, for at once half a dozen more swept on to us and held us firmly. The whole inside of the aircraft was brilliantly lit and we could see nothing whatever outside except the dazzling lights that shone up at us. It is difficult to describe the overwhelmingly naked feeling which assailed us. One felt like saying, "All right. It's a fair cop. I'll come quiet!" The game seemed to be up, and one could not immediately see how it could end unless in tragedy. I had seen an incredibly accurate cluster of bursts at the point of intersection of one of the other cones we had been watching—and yet the seconds dragged on and no flak came at us at all. But this was small consolation, for it only made us more than ever sure that fighters were in the vicinity, and were about to pounce. Meanwhile the pilot was making frantic efforts to escape. He put us into a tight turn, then dived out of it and jinked the other way. It was astonishing to me that the heavily laden Stirling could cope with such aerobatics. But still the fierce beams held us. At first I had been very frightened, but then I became quite fatalistic about it as I waited for the burst of fire which must inevitably come. In the brilliant glare I could see the pilot's violent twisting of the wheel on top of the control column as clearly as by day. The Stirling pulled into a steep turn to port and suddenly, miraculously, we were out in the blessed darkness again. Someone aft had just said, "Here come the fighters!" but they didn't. Someone else said, "Well done, Skipper!" Thirty seconds later four red lights in a row were reported passing overhead by no more than a few hundred feet, from starboard to port. We were all so unnerved at this stage that these lights were taken for enemy fighters, but it seems more likely that they were the glowing nacelles of another Stirling above us.

Some of the crew said afterwards that they thought we were held for five minutes, but I think two minutes would be nearer the mark.

All this evasion had cost us a good deal of height and we were now definitely within the scope of the flak. A river appeared below us and we got a reasonable fix of the position. But afterwards the cloud thickened up ahead and was again ten-tenths. This did not prevent the enemy from firing at us. Occasionally I heard a strange knocking sound, which I discovered was the explosion of the closest shells. The burst of sparks was followed by a black puff which flashed past my window. Once we felt a bump as we passed through one of the little black mushrooms. This, then, was flak.

"About ten fighters in formation" came a report from aft, but it turned out to be the smoke from flak bursts.

At just about E.T.A. (estimated time of arrival) a small hole in the cloud showed a big bend in the Rhine—apparently the one due south of Cologne. There was a great deal of accurate heavy flak coming up; flares were dropping all about, and bombs too, bursting with a deep red flash. This was much hotter than anything I had seen on the Kiel raid. I found myself speculating on the laws of chance. How long could the shells go on bursting so close without scoring a direct hit? Surely it was only a matter of time—and not a very long time at that. Under the clouds were various glows, some from flares that had gone through, some from incendiaries (very white), some redder ones maybe from fires or maybe from dummies. The Captain ordered, "Open bomb doors." We were down to 14,000 feet owing to the earlier searchlights but the cloud protected us from them. I doubt if there were many there anyway as the main lot were in the belt we had passed through. The flak however was still heavy and accurate and often bursting all round. We flew north still weaving slightly and saw a fire on our starboard bow. This was clearly a building on fire. It shone dimly through the thin clouds, but one could see the square perspective outline of a house on fire.

The navigator was down in the lower compartment and kept asking if we could not go in and bomb each fire we passed, but the Captain kept saying, "This is no bloody good. We'll have to look around for something better." When we saw the building on fire, however, he agreed that it was a reasonable target and since it was very near our dead reckoning position, being a little east of the centre of the city according to our calculations, he turned to run in. Only half our load was to go in the first stick. "Right right," said the navigator—then "Left left—left left—steady—left left—steady —right right." There was a sudden heavy bump—the bombs had gone. We were slightly turning when they went and this may have been the reason for the jolt, for at Kiel I had not been able to feel the bombs go. There followed a lot of counting on the intercom. to find the time to let the photographic flash go. Then a rich prolonged red glow was reflected on the clouds for about a second. The bombs had exploded. This was followed by a white flash as the photograph was taken. Below there was thin cloud and the dim searchlights would shine on the clouds or through a hole in them, or flak would appear twinkling somewhere ahead of us. Once there was a tremendous burst of light flak—red and yellow tracer. Some searchlights began to be troublesome then. Singh—the Second Pilot—was flying and weaving slightly, as we plugged on at 15,500 feet. Suddenly the searchlights picked up a Wellington far below, flying just above some smoky, thin cloud. They could evidently see him quite well through it, for they held him without difficulty. He was nearly underneath us and about 5,000 or 6,000 feet lower. He looked almost on the ground. He was twisting and turning and several times he nearly got out ahead of the beam, but it always caught him up again. If we had been a German fighter we should have had ample time to get down to him. Then he escaped for a few seconds but was caught again. At last he was out altogether and the searchlights groped blindly. By this time they were almost immediately below. Singh, who was sitting on the starboard side, had not been watching all this as Tarry and the gunners and I had. Twice Tarry said, "I wouldn't fly straight over this," but Singh did not seem to understand what was meant. It occurred to me however that we might be helping the Wimpey by confusing the sound detectors and suggested this to Tarry, who did not seem to be much comforted by it. Nothing came of it, however; the search-lights were dowsed and we flew on our way unmolested. Some very heavy tracer was coming up to over 5,000 feet on our port bow but it was not at us, and anyway it only came up to a third of our height. It came very slowly in amber streams. They say you can see that sort of tracer coming long enough to dodge it, but I think you'd have to be pretty nippy to do it in a Stirling. Pat Ogilvie met some in his low-level Stirling attack a few weeks before when he flew over the Ruhr, by mistake, on his way back, at 300 feet. For fifteen minutes they went through very tough close-range stuff and got hit twice. He said he was too close to it to do much avoiding then, but the 5,000-foot tracer gave you long enough to get out of its way.

By this time we were half an hour overdue at the coast which we were supposed to be crossing over the southern end of the Friesian Islands. I thought I saw an estuary but it turned out to be a patch of cloud.

At last I did see the coast below and told the navigator. He pointed hopefully to the Friesian Islands, held his thumb up, and pointed down below. I had looked at the long beach line. It was slightly concave for as far as I could see to the northward. Wherever else it was, it was not Holland.

The very lateness of reaching the coast indicated that we were far further south than we thought. The first concave stretch of coast was south of Dunkirk. I pointed to this on the map and told the navigator I thought that was where we were. He shook his head in shocked incredulity. A few minutes later the Captain said, "There's a curious red glow underneath the moon." I said, "It's the reflection of the moon in the sea." He said, "Why so red?" and I suggested it was the effect of the haze. Whatever the cause that was quite clearly what it was, because one could see the coastline just above it. "Anyway we aren't over the sea at all yet," said the Captain. "I can see searchlights and flak just ahead." I said, "That must be Kent then." "Crikey, it can't be!" was the comment, and then a bright two-coloured signal showed to port. "What the hell's that?" said the pilot. We soon discovered it was the British recognition signal of the day. A moment later we saw the same to starboard. A few minutes after this the coast showed up ahead and it was agreed that it must be Kent. Now to me this clearly showed the existence of a very strong north-west wind. The new course of 012° parallel to the coast did not allow for that wind. We turned up the coast and struck out across the Thames estuary. For a long time we saw no land and the moon began to set. At last we picked up the Honington radio beam and turned to fly in on that. For twenty minutes we flew west seeing nothing below. At last we reached the coast. We had been blown right out into the North Sea. Navigation as an art did not seem to have been brought to any great degree of finesse in the R.A.F.

As we crossed the coast two searchlights came on and followed close astern illuminating us though they could not see us. "Get ready to fire a recognition cartridge." The pistol was being screwed into the socket. "Are you sure the I.F.F.'s on?" "Yes it's been on for half an hour." There was a good deal of comment about those searchlights. Eventually they were dowsed but two more came on ahead of us. So we fired our coloured lights. They lobbed up from the fuselage and lit us momentarily in lurid light before falling far astern. The searchlights went out immediately.

There were flashing beacons now to check our position, but the radio beam was the main aid to navigation. I felt full of confidence that we should now get back safely. Tarry had that effect on one. He seemed so completely in control of the situation—smoothing over difficulties. Next to the searchlight belt and the heavy flak the home landing is the most dangerous part; due to fatigue, many crashes occur then. Also, over the flare path there is a greatly war, the precise odds which are to be accepted in amassing human experience? If A for Apples or U for Uncle had failed to return the risk might scarcely have appeared justifiable, but in the event it seemed then, and still seems now, to have been rather more than just 'worth while'.

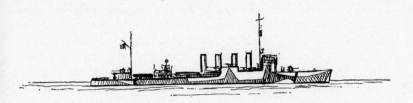

CHAPTER 14   *Camouflage and Explosions*

BY the middle of September 1941 *Broke* was ready for sea again and in front of us was another miserable North Atlantic winter. On the fourteenth, which was my thirty-second birthday, I wrote to Michael Bratby, who was now G2 Intelligence in Reykjavik, describing my latest aerial adventures, and went on to talk of the technicalities of my job.

"Back at the ship I had a week of bloody dockyard and then masses of work getting her to look like a ship again and getting the troops trained. It is fantastic how much they lose in a few weeks of idleness. They are twenty seconds slower loading ten rounds of 4·7 for example (it should take one minute or less). And correspondingly slower with all the rest. However we have certain compensations. One of them is that we can get and have got the very latest devices. Indeed so much of our time has been spent in dockyard now that we are probably (no, certainly) the best equipped destroyer at sea today; this last time you should just see the bathrooms we've had built! But all the same I'd prefer to have been at sea. Now we've got a b. winter to look forward to. I'm still hoping we may get up your way, but we seemed to be fated not to.

"Did I tell you my Captain was a great wildfowler? I'm hoping to get some days in Crawshaw's part of the world [the Ribble Estuary]. My Captain is an extraordinary and outstanding man. He's very brilliant and considered to be the most go ahead thing in the way of war winners. Actually he is all that, which is surprising considering that his voice is scarcely audible even when he is trying to shout. My main worry is that he is extravagantly critical of people, so that once someone has done something wrong, it seems he can thereafter never do anything right.

This becomes so extreme sometimes as to be exasperating. I used to think I didn't suffer fools very gladly myself, but I am a paragon of patience by comparison.

"I am still often resentful when he jumps down someone else's throat, so much so that I don't mind him jumping down mine now. He doesn't need so much looking after as Bryan did. My maternal instincts are not so often aroused as they used to be! But on the whole I like him very much and he has a wonderful way with Admirals and obstructionists. He sweeps both aside and the Admirals love it.

"Meanwhile Jane acts at Stratford-on-Avon in Shaw's *Doctor's Dilemma* (in a tiny part) and writes two letters a week of the most entertaining nonsense coupled with a modicum of extremely good sense and unusual understanding. She's so frightfully young and yet, like so many young people with fire (and make no mistake, she has more than a touch of it), there are sudden flashes of the wisdom of age. Heaven knows how they get there, but out they pop. . . ."

The whites and pale greys and blues in which I had first painted *Broke*, following my conviction that night invisibility was of value in the U-boat war, had now spread to many other ships. In the first instance *Broke* had been compared with destroyers painted a curious purplish mauve colour. These destroyers belonged to the Fifth Destroyer Flotilla commanded by Captain Lord Louis Mountbatten and the colour, having been his idea, was called 'Mountbatten pink'! It was based, I believe, on the invisibility of a Union Castle liner on a particular occasion. At night it was better than the standard grey because it was a little lighter, but the pink colour (as opposed to the tone) did not seem to be of any significance. I stuck to my original opinion that there was nothing magic about Mountbatten pink except the name.

Meanwhile the then C.-in-C. Western Approaches—Admiral Nasmith—had been sufficiently convinced by my arguments in favour of the pale blues, pale greys and whites, to commission me to design camouflage schemes for the fifty obsolete American destroyers, which we had acquired in exchange in the fall of 1940, long before the United States entered the war. Soon, however, all the destroyers in the Western Approaches Command had turned near-white. It must have been a little before this that a question had been asked in Parliament: Was the First Lord of the Admiralty aware that ships painted white had been allowed to sail in convoy thereby endangering all the other ships in the convoy? . . .

But the idea was now becoming generally accepted. At night no paint could ever make a ship *whiter* than the sky behind it. A white ship would match it most nearly, and be less easily seen than a dark one.

I wrote the following notes on the scheme at the request of C.-in-C. Western Approaches:

CAMOUFLAGE OF VESSELS OPERATING AGAINST U-BOATS

1. The first all-important principle is its operational object. In this case it is to avoid being seen by a U-boat on the surface at night. The scheme must be designed for this purpose, and this purpose alone; all questions of rendering a ship less liable to successful torpedo attack by confusing dazzle painting; and realistic false bow waves, etc., are considered, at the present stage of U-boat tactics, to be irrelevant.

2. Compromise is usually fatal in a camouflage scheme. Invisibility at night must be the *only* objective.

3. To make a ship less visible at night it must be painted a very pale tone, especially that part of it which is likely to be seen from conning-tower level against the sky.

4. Any one scheme cannot be completely successful under all weather conditions, therefore the best plan must be to seek invisibility in conditions which obtain on the majority of nights in the north-west approaches.

5. The very pale ship is not effective when lit directly by a bright moon, but it is effective on all dark nights and on all overcast moonlight nights; on bright moonlight nights the pale ship will still be better than the dark one against the up-moon half of the sky, only worse in the down-moon half, a fifty-fifty chance. Fifty per cent of the dark hours are moonlit, but a large number of the moonlit hours are overcast. Every overcast moonlit hour weights the scale in favour of the pale camouflage scheme, as the most suitable for the majority of the conditions.

6. A number of variations of the pale scheme have been tried, and have proved successful under the conditions described above. It has turned out by chance that they are also effective under certain day conditions and at dawn and dusk.

7. When, under bright direct moonlight the pale scheme

makes the ship show white, it still has a slight advantage over the ship that shows black, as nearly all ships do. This advantage is the psychological one that all look-outs are expecting to see a ship as a dark mass. Recently a look-out reported to me a 'Town'-class destroyer (painted with a form of the pale scheme) under a bright moon, about five cables away as "something making white smoke on the surface".

8. In conclusion the scheme should work to the best advantage on occasions when a U-boat might be surprised on the surface, and to make the *Vanoc*'s feat [the destroyer *Vanoc* had recently sunk a U-boat by ramming] more likely to be repeated, or on occasions when a U-boat might select what he thought was a gap in the screen, and find to his mortification that there was in fact an escort that he had not seen, right ahead of him.

9. It is emphasised that the variations within the range of the 'pale scheme' are still experimental and capable of improvement.

10. Notes on the general application of the scheme which have been issued for the guidance of First Lieutenants of ships I have camouflaged are appended.

P. SCOTT
Lieutenant, R.N.V.R.

By early 1941 C.-in-C. Western Approaches was making the following signal to Captains (D) Londonderry, Greenock and Liverpool, repeated Admiralty, Flag Officer Commanding North Atlantic, C.-in-C. South Atlantic:

"Four corvettes having been torpedoed up to date every endeavour is to be made to hasten camouflaging of corvettes in accordance with Peter Scott scheme."

But then a new factor arose. If the enemy could not see the escorts there was an improved chance of surprising U-boats, but if the escorts could not see each other there was also an increased chance that they would collide. *Broke* and *Verity* were not the only escort ships to be involved in collisions for which good camouflage was accepted as a primary cause. The Admiralty called a conference to consider whether these disadvantages outweighed the advantages, and finally came down on the side of the camouflage. I made designs for escort trawlers, and later for the Motor Gunboats and Motor Torpedo Boats of Coastal Forces. I wrote memoranda on the theory and practice of ship camouflage for Combined Operations. I wrote practical hints for First Lieutenants who had

2

Elizabeth Jane Howard.

1942

Motor Launch 291 and Steam Gunboat No. 8 (afterwards *Grey Wolf*) during the Dieppe Raid.

1942

Smoke Screens off Dieppe photographed from the bridge of my boat S.G.B.9.

to paint their ships. With these First Lieutenants I was far from popular, for my light colours showed dirt and rust immediately, whereas against Mountbatten pink they were hardly noticeable.

One morning in September 1941 we were lying alongside the destroyer *Whitehall* in the Gladstone Dock at Liverpool when from the other side of the dock came a series of loud explosions which lasted for about fifteen seconds. They had evidently occurred on board the loaded troopship *Franconia* and we immediately mustered a fire party on the jetty in accordance with the standing orders of the port. About a quarter of an hour after the explosions, one of the *Franconia*'s officers who was on the way to the telephone called down to us from the jetty that a number of anti-aircraft rockets had exploded and a lot more were scattered all over *Franconia*'s boat deck; he said that no one on board knew enough about them to deal with them, and could we help. So I sent for our Gunner (T) (Mr. Lewis) and asked the Captain of *Whitehall* whether I could borrow his Gunner too. He agreed and said that his Gunner's Mate, Petty Officer Robinson, had some experience of these particular rockets and would come with us too. So the four of us walked round the dock and went on board the troopship which was crowded with soldiers. The explosions had apparently taken place while experts were examining and checking the rockets and while soldiers were playing a game on the deck below. Rockets had shot all over the place and many of their explosive heads had gone off. Many more had not, and were lying about on the deck. Seven people had been killed and several more seriously wounded, and although the casualties had all been taken away by the time we arrived, the scene on the boat deck was not pretty. Bits and pieces of the rockets were all in among bits and pieces of the seven. The Gunner's Mate went forward at once, carefully picked up a slightly smoking rocket and threw it over the side. He came back and picked up a second, and then a third. After that I said, "Wait a minute, let's just take stock of the situation and see what has happened, before we go any further." There was still a strong smell of explosive and the rockets were warm to the touch—much warmer than they should have been. It seemed that at least five rocket heads had exploded. We could only see two more loose unexploded ones. On the first of the two, the little propeller blades, which 'armed' them and then became triggers, were bent and Robinson said, "I think we had better ditch this one too, sir, as quickly as possible." I agreed and he immediately did so. The second had its trigger blades, indeed,

o

its whole explosive head, deeply embedded in a wooden fairing piece attached to the deck. I gave orders that this one should not be handled for the present. At this moment a young Special Branch Lieutenant, R.N.V.R., came up and said he was a U.P. rocket specialist and had just arrived in order to deliver a handbook on the rocket mounting. Most of the remaining rockets were still in the 'ready-use' lockers, although these were open, and the Lieutenant said they felt to him well above the safe temperature. The first thing obviously was to flood them, so a hose was rigged and Robinson used it to fill the ready-use lockers. As the situation now seemed to be in hand, Lewis and I left. On the way down from the boat deck a policeman handed an unexploded rocket to Lewis saying, "I wonder what this is?" Lewis ran straight to the ship's side and dropped the thing overboard. Petty Officer Robinson was later awarded the George Medal.

Our Convoy Escort movements altered during the winter of 1941. We sometimes left the outward-bound convoy to refuel in Iceland before joining the next homeward-bound convoy and this gave me the hoped-for opportunity to see my old friend Michael Bratby. He had regaled me with the comic story of how the British Occupation Forces had arrived with a number of railway trucks although there is no railway line in Iceland, and we had laughed at the inefficiency and absurdity of it. Now as we drove to his headquarters just outside the Icelandic capital he told me the sequel. With much merriment he was recounting this delightful story to a guest in the mess, an officer newly arrived from England, whom he had been detailed to entertain, when he noticed a certain lack of response. Unsmilingly the visitor turned on him and said: "I sent those trucks, and you'd have been damned angry if there *had* been a railway and I *hadn't* sent any trucks." Thereafter Mike did not dare to broach the subject of the maps. It seems that for 1,000 maps of Iceland which had been ordered, the War Office had sent 750 maps of Ireland and, unaccountably 250 maps of Madagascar. History does not relate whether this or some other confusion caused the Prime Minister to lay down that Iceland should henceforth be designated Iceland (C).

The tanker from which we refuelled was anchored at the head of Hvalfjördur (pronounced Qualfiurther), the Whale Fiord, which runs in past Reykjavik for twenty miles into the bleak black volcanic hills. After refuelling one night in November we berthed alongside the destroyer depot ship *Hecla*, then so appropriately in the land of the volcano after which she was named. We had not long been secured to *Hecla* when the destroyer *Oribi* berthed alongside us on the outside. Both ships then reverted to 'four hour's notice for steam'. We were there for the night.

The *Oribi*'s ship's company were old friends and the party which followed in her wardroom was very cheerful. In the middle of it the signalman brought in the night signals, among which was a warning of severe gales in our area. We gave thanks for our luck that we were not on the high seas and thought no more about it. Soon after midnight we retired happily to bed. I was awoken about three hours later by the patter of running feet on the quarter deck above me, and a few moments later a breathless quartermaster stood in the doorway of my cabin to tell me that the gale had parted the wires—three of them—which attached our bows to the *Hecla*. I rushed up on deck to find that *Broke* and *Oribi* were drifting out, still secured together, and still very fortunately attached to *Hecla* by the stern 'ropes' (also wire hawsers). The two destroyers swung round so that instead of being head to wind on the inside, *Broke* was now stern to wind on the outside. *Oribi*'s smart little motor-boat which had been secured outside her was now acting as a fender between her and *Hecla* and was soon crushed to matchwood; and *Hecla*'s own boats were damaged before they could be pulled clear. But there were much more serious considerations than these.

Four hours' notice for steam means that even in emergency no power can be raised on the ship's own main engines for the best part of an hour. If the stern ropes were to part also we should be in real trouble, for the Hvalfjördur is very deep and getting an anchor to hold in that gale before we were drifted ashore on the rocks would have been more than problematical. The first thing, obviously, was to double up on the stern ropes as soon as the duty watch could be roused to pass across the necessary hawsers. The next thing was to raise steam. When done in a hurry this creates immense volumes of thick, dark brown smoke. Hanging as we were, stern to wind, this smoke blew from our funnel in clouds across the bridge where my justifiably disgusted Captain paced up and down impatiently in a duffle-coat over his pyjamas. Together we choked and coughed until suddenly I caught his eye and we roared with laughter. Dangerous though the situation was, it was also immensely comical. That he was able to laugh at this juncture, when once more I had patently let him down, was to me a sign of his stature as a Commanding Officer. The stern rope did not part, steam was eventually raised, and with it we were able to creep away and anchor safely on our own. There were a few sarcastic but on the whole understanding signals about the crushed motor-boats and there the matter ended.

In all this period the pattern of our escort work remained essentially the same, though the emphasis was gradually changing all the time. From a desperation in the winter of 1940–41 we had turned the scales in twelve short months. By January 1942 the Escort Groups were definitely on top of the U-boats, the convoys were getting through. But the weather gave no respite even if the enemy did. In December I wrote to Michael:

"We have had *the* bloodiest trip ever. One gale has followed another—twice we've had to go back because of damage. Our convoy has been held up so long that we shall be about three days late in. Altogether we are in low spirits. The after cabin flat got flooded and all the boys living there—young Jimmy Holmes, the Sub, and the Pilot, and the Gunner, and the old Belgian—have had their gear ruined; four feet of water slopping all over everything. We very nearly had four officers washed over the side—me one of them—trying to take primers out of depths-charges in the gale.

"Now the barometer has just gone down to 938—quite a phenomenon, and as we go forth again tonight we shall no doubt encounter the father and mother of all gales. I suppose we are getting fairly hardened, but, oh dear me, it is bloody while it lasts. I sit waiting for reports to come in of what has broken or carried away or been flooded and wonder what it will be next. . . .

"I've been amusing myself by writing a short story, but under difficulties. My cabin deck-head drips on the paper, and if I leave the manuscript for a moment it is swept on to the deck, which is running with water, by the first malicious roll. God, how these ships do tumble about. . . ."

One moonlight night in the gale I had to get up to the bridge from my cabin aft to see about some damage. There was no way of doing this under cover, and I had given instructions that no one was to go out on to the upper deck in the dark hours unless we were called to action stations, because of the risk of being washed overboard. The full moon shining in a very clear cold sky made it almost as bright as day when I emerged from the wardroom flat and clanged the door to behind me, locking on the clips. I was now out, entirely alone, with about 150 feet of wave-swept 'iron deck' to traverse before I reached shelter at the break of the fo'c'sle. For this fairly perilous passage I knew I should have to depend mainly on my arms and the arboreal ancestry of the human species. We had two overhead wires which ran the full length of the 'iron deck', one on either side, and running on rings on these were a number of short lengths of rope designed as handholds. I grabbed one of them and started up the lee side. Before I could reach safety at the far end the ship would roll that way at least twice and white water would cover the deck each time. It was just a question of whether these waves happened to be big enough to pull me away from my handhold—a sort of gamble. I got through the first wave without trouble. The second one soaked me through but I managed to hold on and struggled into the welcome lee and up to the bridge where the Officer of the Watch was pleased but slightly shocked to see me. "You shouldn't have done it all alone, Number One—disobeying your own orders!"

The perils of the upper deck in a heavy sea were more alarmingly and disastrously demonstrated a few weeks later, when we were running before a south-westerly gale from Londonderry to Loch Ewe on the mainland shore of the Minches. We were due to refuel at Loch Ewe and were in a hurry to catch up our outward-bound convoy. We ran before the gale at eighteen knots, and being exceptionally low in fuel the ship had less stability than usual, moreover, so much new electronic equipment had been added during recent refits that *Broke*'s top-weight was almost certainly above the safe limits. It was early afternoon as we ran up towards the rocky islet of Skerryvore, and I was lying reading in my bunk, when the ship rolled more than usually severely. A few minutes later a petty officer came to report that a wave had swept into the whaler at the davits, doing some damage, but that Leading Seaman Cooke, who was in charge of the whaler was at work in it, and clearing up as well as he could. I went up on deck and had a word with him as he worked above me. It was a murky spray-filled scene, and as there was still an hour to go till my watch and everything seemed to be under control, I went back to my bunk and my book. I was not very happy about the heavy rolling which I thought was probably caused by our fairly high speed in the very heavy Atlantic swell, but I had no idea that anything more serious could develop from it until it happened.

The ship rolled to port, further and further, but she did not roll back. I was pitched out of my bunk and found myself standing on the bulkhead—the wall of the cabin; and at the same moment the lights went out. I was in total darkness, for all the port holes in the living-quarters in a destroyer are battened down and blacked out when she is at sea, and below decks one is entirely dependent on artificial light. I had no time to pull on sea boots or duffle coat; I groped my way to the ladder and up it to the dim daylight coming through the door into the wardroom lobby. The door framed nothing but sky for the ship still lay over at a desperate angle. Very slowly, however, she seemed to be coming up a little, but she was still listing alarmingly to port. In my stockinged feet I remember making my way along the starboard side. The engines were stopped and the ship was losing way as she turned in a sharp arc to starboard. A few moments after I reached the bridge a message came in that two men had been washed over the side—one a look-out who had been on the port flag deck just outside the wheelhouse, and the other Leading Seaman Cooke from the whaler.

What appeared to have happened was that the ship had 'broached to'. From time to time in that big swell the rudder had been coming clear out of the water. When it did so the ship would begin to turn, only to be checked by the opposite rudder. Then on one great roll the rudder had not checked the swing; as she began to turn the centrifugal force on the upperworks of the ship heeled her over so that the rudder would bite less well, and as she came broadside on to the gale the wind itself added to the forces holding her over on her side. So far had she lain over that water had come in through the boiler room intakes and the dynamo had 'gone off the board' plunging the mess decks into darkness. In some of them especially the Stokers' and Petty Officers' messes two decks down —the hands found themselves standing on the ship's side, and many of them believed that the *Broke* had rolled right over and was upside down. But as we lost way, the centrifugal force was reduced and gradually the ship came back to a less alarming angle.

The next thing was to pick up the two lost men. We circled very slowly round searching the sea's surface. Both had been wearing lifebelts; surely they must be floating there somewhere on the great grey slopes of the swell. But we found no sign of them. A fishing trawler happened to be quite close and we made a signal by light asking her to help in the search, but she found nothing either. Cooke had been swept out of the whaler as he worked to square off the gear after the previous big roll. The young look-out's loss was even more extraordinary. He had been on the flag deck, only a few feet below the upper bridge and just outside the wheelhouse. When the 'broach to' came the Coxswain at the wheel had found himself looking at the door of the wheelhouse which was filled with the surface of the sea. Below the surface he could see the hands of the look-out, holding on to the topmast forestay—a heavy wire which came down diagonally across the flag deck. For ten, perhaps fifteen seconds the hands held on, and then the boy was gone. It was unbelievable that the sea could reach up almost thirty feet from the ship's normal waterline to drag one of our crew to his death.

The principal cause of this disaster was the fact that we were very low in fuel. This accentuated the effect of all the new and heavy equipment which had recently been fitted and found the ship in an unstable condition running rather too fast before a very heavy sea. Low fuel loads combined with speed were conditions which, once we knew the dangers, we could avoid in the future, but it was obviously going to be a long time before the ship's company regained their faith in the seaworthiness of the *Broke*, and many men spent their off-duty hours standing or sitting at the break of the fo'c'sle instead of sleeping comfortably in their hammocks on the lower mess decks.

Faith had not yet been fully restored when we were ordered to pay the ship off for a long refit at Portsmouth. Although we did not know it, she was being prepared and specially equipped for the North African landings. Very few of the old ship's company returned for the new commission which did not last very long. *Broke* was badly damaged in action against the French at Oran and sank while under tow towards Gibraltar.

Meanwhile, however, we were concerned with paying her off at Portsmouth and finding ourselves new jobs. When I finally left I had been in her for two years and a day. I was offered, and accepted, command of a Steam Gunboat building in the yard of Messrs. John Samuel White at Cowes. At the time of my appointment she was Job No. 6095. One chapter of my naval career was ending and a new one was about to begin. In between was a respite—a chance to get married.

CHAPTER 15   *Respite*

FOR a while now Jane Howard and I had been engaged. She was
sharing a basement flat in St. John's Wood with Dosia Cropper.
Early in my leave a dinner party was planned. Dosia had invited a
friend, Kit Dodds, who was working in the Admiralty, and his girl
friend Philippa Talbot-Ponsonby. In an elaborate hoax, I was
introduced to Kit and Phil as Jane's deaf uncle, and for the first
part of the evening the assembled company was forced to shout at
me, until the jest was abandoned. Afterwards a no less elaborate
game was played in which telephone numbers were selected with a
pin and the winner was the player who managed against a stop-
watch to conduct the longest conversation with the stranger at the
other end. In spite of these rather anti-social games, it was for me a
delightful evening. I remember Phil as a quiet rather shy girl, with
some sort of hidden character which I did not discover; but that
night I had eyes only for Jane.

With the new boat being built at Cowes, Isle of Wight, this
familiar place of so many happy sailing memories was obviously
going to be my headquarters for many weeks. The Admiralty had
explained that as no destroyer command was currently available,
the Steam Gunboat job would be a useful stop-gap which would in
no way jeopardise my chances of my own destroyer in due course.
Steam Gunboats (or S.G.B.s) were a brand-new type of vessel,
attached to the Coastal Forces although much larger than the
M.T.B.s and M.G.B.s and M.L.s with which that branch of the
Navy usually dealt. Unlike the smaller wooden boats they had
steel hulls. My S.G.B. was the last of a series of nine which
had been laid down in various yards, but two of them had
been blitzed and abandoned on their slips. The remaining
seven were to form a flotilla under the command of Lieutenant
George Pennell, R.N. The boats were 150 feet long and

finished up with a displacement of about 230 tons and a crew of forty.

As soon as I was appointed, it was suggested that I should visit some of the operating bases of Coastal Forces to gain experience. I lost little time in following up the suggestion, for the same evening I took a train to Dover and before dawn I found myself at sea fighting a fire in a sinking Motor Torpedo Boat.

But apart from this adventure, the paying-off of *Broke*—the pause in my war—was the opportunity I had been waiting for. At last Jane and I could get married. The wedding was at St. Mary's Church in Lancaster Gate only a few hundred yards from the family house at Leinster Corner. Jane was just nineteen. For our honeymoon we went to the Lacket—the family cottage at Lockeridge in Wiltshire. It was early spring, a spell of fine warm weather, primroses and catkins, and a chance to show my darling wife the countryside in which I had spent so much of my boyhood—our own beautiful dene, the West Woods, the downs, the 'Valley of dry bones', where the sarsen stones are in greatest profusion, the Kennet running clear after a spring drought, the great stone circles of Avebury. They were romantic places exactly fitting the pattern of our mood. It was, I believed, for these that we fought our war, for these we faced the winter gales in the North Atlantic, the U-boats, the bombing. For these we'd fight on till they were free and safe for our people. It was for this beauty that the ugliness must be borne, for this heritage that we wanted to bring children into the world. We rode over the downs to high Temple Wood, on horses hired in Marlborough. We followed the crest of Hackpen to the ancient British camp of Barbary Castle. We walked south to the Kennet and Avon Canal, and picnicked in Savernake Forest. The April landscape of Wiltshire held all our love and all our hope. Time stretched before us; and danger was still a long way ahead. After all the Steam Gunboat had still to be built, to undergo its trials, to be commissioned and 'worked up' before she could be ready for operations. All this would take most of the summer—all the time in the world.

After our honeymoon Jenny and I went to Cowes and stayed in the Gloucester Hotel, so as to be on the spot as the ship was completed. My mother had come down to launch her and now she was growing apace. The yard of Messrs. John Samuel White was curiously different from the dockyards which had refitted *Broke* and which I had come so wholeheartedly to detest. This was a smaller yard, closer to the front line than most, and perhaps the little Steam Gunboat was a challenge. The work progressed apace. I

O*

never found the dockyard maties playing cards on board as I had done in a famous yard on the Tyne.

When S.G.B.9 came to do her speed trials over the measured mile in Stokes Bay she returned a mean speed of thirty-six knots which compared quite favourably with the speeds of her smaller counterparts powered with the less reliable and more inflammable petrol engines. While these trials were in progress some operation was obviously being prepared in the Solent. Two other Steam Gunboats, completed earlier than No. 9, were to take part but it was not until much later that we learned it was the first projected raid on Dieppe. Because of a suspected leak to the enemy the whole scheme was abandoned for the time being.

At this time I was called upon to be best man at the wedding of my old friend Uffa Fox, and at the same time was involved in a rather delightful mistake on the part of the security authorities. During a week-end staying with Jane's parents in Sussex I had found a few Puss Moth caterpillars; back at Cowes I had amused myself by adding the larvae of Poplar and Eyed Hawk Moths to the collection of live caterpillars, and one or two of the rarer Poplar Kittens. In a letter to my mother-in-law I listed the different species and the precise numbers of each. The censorship suspected that this was some elaborate code by which details of the shipping in the Solent were being conveyed to an enemy agent, and in due course every caterpillar had to be shown to an investigating officer. As he was also an amateur entomologist it all ended happily with a discussion on where to look for Elephant Hawk Moths.

At this time I made a number of drawings of Jane, mostly in ink. The ink line was simple and uncompromising. It was also virtually inerasible. It had to be right first time. These were probably the best portrait drawings I have made in all my life. Drawing was an urgent and essential escape to a creative life; if my drawings could not be good under that kind of pressure, they surely could never be good at all.

By midsummer S.G.B.9 was ready to be commissioned and we took her down to the shore-based training establishment called H.M.S. *Beehive* at Weymouth. My new ship's company included three ratings from *Broke*—Frank Brown, a Leading Telegraphist of great efficiency, Jimmy Jones, my servant who had so nearly been blown to bits by the hand grenade in Belfast, and Tom George, the Maltese lad who had earned a Mention in Dispatches in the *Comorin* rescue. For five weeks we 'worked-up' until we were a fairly efficient team. Many of the exercises took place in Weymouth Bay at night.

A small pleasure steamer was used as target vessel and we conducted dummy torpedo and gun attacks on her. Also working up his M.T.B. at the same time was a very tall and entertaining officer named Alan Lennox-Boyd, and because I had joined the Navy a few days or weeks before him, he was always under my orders when we operated together. Alan's boat arrived at Weymouth when we were already half-way through the course, and at first he found the greatest difficulty in keeping his bearings during the night exercises. On one black dark night we had the Training Commander of the base on board when I saw that Alan was no longer astern of us as he should have been. He had somehow lost contact with us but the Commander did not seem to have noticed, so I wrote out a signal and sent it down to the wireless office. In due course came the inevitable query, "What's happened to Lennox-Boyd?" "I detached him some time ago, sir, to attack independently from the opposite side. I imagine he'll be crossing astern of the target at this moment." "Ah, yes—good."

By the beginning of August S.G.B.9 and her crew formed a reasonably well-knit fighting machine. We were sailed for Portsmouth quite evidently for something special, though of course we had no clue what it might be. Four Steam Gunboats were to be ready by 16th August and as we were already on the top line there was a week's leave for the ship's company.

I received the orders for the Dieppe raid five days before it took place—sixty or seventy pages of them with a portfolio of relevant photographs and charts, and I sat far into the night trying to form a picture of our particular jobs in the Combined Plan for this one-day frontal assault on a part of Hitler's Atlantic Wall. Two days later we were 'briefed' in the underground fastnesses of Fort Southwick on Portsdown Hill (which I was later to know so well) by Commander R. E. D. Ryder, V.C., who had led the fabulous raid on St. Nazaire. S.G.B.9 was to support the landings at two beaches on the extreme right flank—Orange I and II—and I met Lieut.-Commander Mulleneux who was in command of these landings. Our force was to be the Fourth Commando led by Major Lord Lovat.

The preparatory signal for 'Operation Jubilee', as it was called, was postponed one day, but on the 17th the code word 'Buttercup' came through, and on the following morning the executive signal— 'Tulip'—which meant that the expedition would sail that evening. This set us into a ferment of last-minute preparation. The ship's company knew that time was short but only the Officers, the

Coxswain and the 'Chief' (Chief Engine Room Artificer) actually knew that we were off that night, at least until about four o'clock in the afternoon when it became altogether obvious that the party was on. Soldiers were embarking in the Infantry Assault Ships ahead of us. Tank Landing Craft had already left to embark their tanks. Extra ammunition was taken on board and extra life-saving apparatus had to be stowed on the upper deck.

We slipped at half past eight in a clear golden evening and followed the great Infantry Assault Ships down Portsmouth harbour while the siren sounded 'All Clear'. The German evening reconnaissance had been a few minutes too early to see the movement of the assembling ships.

There was a great feeling of relief and elation to be started at last. In the last light of that calm summer evening the force looked very impressive forming up to pass through the East Solent Gate, a gate of netting in the barrage stretching, by way of the old forts, from the Isle of Wight to the mainland shore. There were Infantry Assault Ships (L.S.I., or Landing Ships Infantry), Destroyers, M.L.s, Gunboats and the French Chasseurs of the 'cutting-out party' (to bring back any ships found in Dieppe). They lay stopped all around Spithead awaiting their moment to dive through the gate in their correct order. At one moment we were the unnoticed jam in a sandwich of *Prince Albert* and *Glengyle*, from which we only extricated ourselves with considerable agility and anxiety.

After passing through the gate speed was increased to nineteen knots and S.G.B.9 took station on *Prince Albert* and M.G.B.312 (Lieutenant Nye, R.N.V.R.), and so to the channel through an enemy minefield which had been swept a few hours earlier by a special force of minesweepers.

The Senior Officer S.G.B.s—George Pennell—was on board as S.G.B.3, his own boat, was not ready in time. As he was sleeping in the charthouse, I curled myself into the bridge sponson and tried to get some sleep there. This was so uncomfortable that I had a deck chair brought up and sat at the after end of the bridge in that. It was a clear starry sky that moved gently around the foremast rigging. I lay wondering upon the outcome and thinking of many things past. This was the sort of operation I had always wanted to take part in—something so different from the routine work of the destroyers in the North Atlantic, different even from the routine torpedo attacks on channel shipping which we had been practising for at Weymouth. It was a special party with its own special dangers and I realised that I had suddenly got more to lose than I had had before. I wondered how brave I was going to manage to be now that I had personal responsibilities. Jenny had been wonderfully good and brave at our parting, but what sort of a strain was this to put upon a young girl? . . .

My courage, I realised, was not so robust that I could afford to undermine it. Such things were not to be thought of in too much detail. One would be as brave as the chemicals in one's body allowed. It was all a question of adrenalin anyway.

Once past the mid-channel minefield, through which the lane had been swept and buoyed, the various groups fanned out so as to arrive simultaneously off their respective beaches. We split up at 0144 and S.G.B.9 went up on to the port beam of *Prince Albert* in accordance with the screening diagram.

A warm wind was blowing from the south, laden with the smell of hayfields. At 0258 the *Prince Albert* finally stopped in an estimated position seven miles due north magnetic of Pte. d'Ailly lighthouse. Whilst we were stopped we suddenly saw a light ahead. It flashed three times and then twenty seconds later it flashed three times again. The Germans had left their lighthouse burning to guide us. Then we *were* achieving surprise. There it winked at us—group flashing three every twenty—just as shown on the chart. We wondered for a moment if it were a trap to mislead us. Perhaps it was not the Phare d'Ailly but a fake light five miles to one side of it to take us to the wrong beaches. Just as the Landing Craft were forming up the light stopped. Had the alarm been given? A quarter of an hour later the light popped up again and winked for three or four minutes.

The L.C.A.s formed into two columns of four and kept close to port of M.G.B.312 who was leading the Orange force towards its beaches. We followed astern.

Suddenly starshell went up away to port. It must be German starshell because no one on our side would risk giving away the quantities of small craft that were approaching the coast. It was 0350, exactly an hour before the touch down, so it could not be the first of the landing. By the light of the starshell I could see a large ship, perhaps a German merchant ship (we suspected a German convoy must be passing because of the Pte. d'Ailly light being on), perhaps the *Glengyle*—the largest of the L.S.I.s—late at the lowering position [which in fact it was]. Near it was a smaller ship, perhaps a destroyer. The starshell died and a tracer battle broke out, fierce white tinsel-like tracer being fired from the south and purposeful red tracer, much of it aimed far too high, from the north. This battle went on for twelve minutes and then subsided, and still the lighthouse winked periodically. Red and green lights on the port bow showed from the breakwater ends of Dieppe harbour. These and the lighthouse were in fact no attempt to mislead us and prove one of two things: either the enemy was completely surprised at least in the timing of the raid, or if he *had* been forewarned, the liaison between his intelligence and the authority which operates his lighthouses was not very good. Historically it now appears certain that the force of about ten large transports, eight destroyers and numerous coastal craft approached to within seven or eight miles of the enemy coast totally unperceived and that had it not been for the chance meeting of S.G.B.5 and the boats for Yellow beach with the enemy convoy described above, the tactical surprise would have been complete. As it was the battle was enough to send all the Germans ashore to Action Stations.

CHAPTER 16   *"Let Battle Commence"*

THE precise moment for landing was to be four-fifty a.m. when the first grey light would come into the clear eastern sky. Twenty minutes before this, we stopped a mile and a half offshore whilst Mulleneux transferred from 312 to the Support Landing Craft (L.C.S.) from which he was to direct the actual landing. Then our eight landing craft divided—three going off to the left to Vasterival with 312 in support and the other five going towards the Quiberville beach with us in support. This included Lord Lovat himself and the L.C.S. with Mulleneux. At four-forty-two the first aircraft appeared—Bostons and Hurricanes—and streams of the same white tinselly tracer went up from the battery round the lighthouse which seemed to consist of about five guns. To the eastward along the coast was more tracer, but all going upwards—still the landing craft were undetected.

About a minute before the touch-down a single white Verey's Light or fire ball lobbed up into the sky above the lighthouse, and the party was on. The pillbox at the eastern end of Orange II opened fire along the beach, and the fire was returned by the L.C.S. The Huns behind the beach fired a six-star green firework— no doubt an invasion signal, and another went up further to the eastward. All along the coastline battle was joined.

The Senior Officer directed us to turn stern on so as to present a small target and be able to fire our three-inch gun. I agreed in principle except that I did not consider we were close enough for accuracy and since no fire had been directed at us I would have liked to have been able to mop up the pillbox from closer quarters. However at a range of about 1,000 yards we opened fire on the pillbox. One or two of the bursts seemed fairly near although we had only open cartwheel sights. The pillbox ceased fire after we had fired about six rounds. Ten minutes later however it started up again so at five-fifteen we opened fire for a further three minutes bombardment. The L.C.S. was firing most accurately with Oerlikon and the pillbox was silenced for good. Unfortunately during this bombardment a non-flashless shell was loaded by mistake and the attention of a shore battery was drawn. It was not accurate fire, but since the pillbox was no longer giving trouble we made some white smoke and retired behind it to a range of one and a half miles while the shells continued to fall short. The L.C.A.s of the Orange landing party, having landed their troops, withdrew towards us while the shelling continued. We closed Bobby Nye in 312 who had also been shelled apparently equally inaccurately. By now it was broad daylight and at five-fifty a new battery to the east of the lighthouse opened up on us and as our first job was successfully completed we drew yet further offshore.

All this time there were explosions ashore from mortars, guns and bombs. At times there were great sheets of flame, at others very heavy detonations. All the while Bostons and Hurribombers kept coming in to attack the defences. One very loud bang was Lord Lovat's Fourth Commando blowing up the ammunition dump of the six-inch battery he had been detailed to destroy. At about six o'clock we sighted S.G.B.8 coming towards us through the smoke to the east. This smoke drifted seaward like white mist on the light offshore breeze. S.G.B.5 should have joined us, but as there was no sign of her by six-fifteen (she had been badly damaged in the encounter with the convoy but we had no knowledge of this until the evening), we told S.G.B.8 to take station two miles on our starboard beam and set off on a course of N. 60° W. at ten knots to carry out 'Task I', a prearranged sweep fifteen miles to the westward in order to give warning of the approach of surface craft. We had been given this job because five German T-class torpedo boats were known to be in Cherbourg harbour, and there was also a possibility of E-boats.

Low-flying aircraft which passed near us turned out to be first Blenheims and later Mustangs of Tac. R. (Tactical Reconnaissance). We steamed slowly along the enemy coast as bold as brass. At this moment in the bright morning sunshine we were lulled into a most curious and entirely false sense of security. There, four miles away on our port beam, shone the cliffs and the brilliant summer green of the fields and woods. St. Valery-en-Caux, scene of my adventures in 1940, nestled in its hollow with a haze of chimney smoke above it. We remembered that we had been told the Luftwaffe would be fully occupied elsewhere and indeed we had seen the milling clouds of Spitfires arriving as we left. They had come wave upon wave, in numbers the like of which I had never before seen. We forgot our own assessment that unprotected ships outside the fighter umbrella would be exactly what the Germans would be looking for. We did not imagine as we might have done the watchers on the cliff tops feverishly telephoning for the German Air Force to come quickly and bomb the two unprotected ships to the westward.

I turned to Nigel Buckmaster, my First Lieutenant: "Better send someone to get some breakfast for the ship's company, No. One" and I went back to examining the coastline with glasses. A light westerly breeze turned the sea deep purplish-blue. Twelve Bostons flying in perfect formation passed inland high above us shining in the early sunlight.

Two aircraft slipped between us and No. 8, unseen until they were past, low over the sea. "Friendly," I said at first, but I got the glasses on them and saw the black cross on the side of one—probably Focke-Wulf 190s.

We altered course fifteen degrees offshore. We were not in a healthy place and we suddenly realised it. Two more square wing-tipped planes came back from the westward—the Tac. R. Mustangs. But a few minutes later at seven-twenty there were "Aircraft right astern". Two fighters were weaving about and working their way round into the sun. In a few moments it was evident that they had designs upon us and as they turned their noses down I could see the bomb hanging under the first one. "Hard-a-starboard", and I rang up the revs. to twenty-eight knots. Off came the bomb just as the guns opened up. Not many fired, the pom-pom jammed, one of the point-fives had a misfire. The bomb fell in our wake close astern.

The second Hun was circling towards No. 8. Whether he misjudged the attack or saw that his mate had missed will never be known, but he transferred his attention to us, coming in on the port bow while we still turned to starboard. As he steadied up towards us in the shallow dive I saw splashes in the water short of us and then our own guns opened up. The F.-W. 190 was only firing machine-gun—not cannon—and he was himself enveloped in a haze of our tracer. I saw his bomb take the water twenty yards short on our port beam. There was a pause and then a heavy shock and a huge waterspout—but the ship was still afloat and still steaming. I remember thinking it must have been a very small bomb not to have damaged us more. Then I looked at the Focke-Wulf. A trail of wispy black smoke was coming out of it and it was losing height. But when it was nearly down to the water it picked up again and began to climb. I stopped watching it and became concerned with the fact that the ship would not steer, that the alarm bells were ringing continuously, that in fact we had been badly shaken. Those in No. 8, however, watched the damaged Focke-Wulf falter again and crash head-on into the bottom of the cliffs.

Meanwhile the 'Chief' had arrived on the bridge, "My vacuum's gone, I'd like to stop, but we *can* keep going slowly if we must." I rang down, "Stop both" and told No. 8 to take us in tow. Grif [Lt. I. R. Griffiths, R.N., her Captain] came alongside with a rush and a bit of a bump, but five minutes later (and only fourteen minutes after the bombing) we were under way in tow—very quick work.

Six minutes later Jimmy Grout (Flotilla Engineer Officer) appeared grinning and sweating on the bridge, "We've found it— you can go ahead in a minute or two," and he disappeared again like a rabbit. Never was such a report more welcome, for our position was very sticky. We were still in full view of the coast—one Focke-Wulf had returned to base to report that we were disabled. It obviously could not be long before further aircraft were sent to complete the job and dispatch us for good. At seven or eight knots we were still two hours from the fighter umbrella. But by seven-fifty-five the tow had been slipped and we set off at thirty knots to the eastward. A signal had just been received that E-boats had been sighted southward-bound from Boulogne. After a short stop a few minutes later for the engine room to make an adjustment, we proceeded at twenty-five knots and less than an hour later we were closing the assorted destroyers and small craft to the north-west of Dieppe while hordes of Spitfires milled comfortably over-head. But soon no doubt we should be sent out to the eastward to meet the E-boats.

Away in that direction were three sources of smoke over the horizon. We wondered what friendly craft would be making smoke right out there, and thought perhaps it was the E-boats. As we approached the destroyers we identified ourselves but got no answer. No doubt they were fully occupied one way and another, but we thought it was rather careless, and supposing we had been the E-boats . . .

Beyond the smoke which drifted idly north-east from Dieppe the battle spluttered and rumbled. Heavy fighting was going on by the sound of it. The westerly wind was now falling light as the sun blazed hotter—the sea was glass calm. Cloud upon cloud of Spitfires circled above us between 3,000 and 10,000 feet. There were no enemy aircraft in sight at all. The German flak was still lively when-

ever our fighters or fighter-bombers went low over Dieppe—
especially to the eastward. Every twenty minutes or so a fresh bunch
of Hurribombers came in low from the sea and shot up and bombed
the defences ashore. I saw one of these hit and watched him circle
very slowly before crashing into the trees.

Presently a Dornier came very low along the coast. It was spotted
by some Spitfires and soon one was on its tail. Smoke came first
from the Spitfire—probably smoke from his own cannon—and then
from the Dornier, which at once caught fire and went straight down
into the wood behind the Phare d'Ailly. A huge cloud of dark
brown smoke burst into the sky and curled up from the burning
wreck.

We closed *Calpe*, the Hunt-class destroyer which was H.Q. ship,
to ask for instructions but our loud hailing equipment remained
resolutely silent. She was lying stopped and surrounded by small
craft. Some were alongside, others lay round the other destroyers—
Brocklesby, *Bleasdale*, *Fernie* and *Albrighton*.

A smoke-screen began inshore of the assembled pool of craft
and drifted sluggishly north-east, but to the south and south-
west the coast, no more than a mile away, was clearly visible in
every detail. No sign of opposition came from it. Lord Lovat's
party had done their job well. The feeling of peaceful inactivity was
most strange and incongruous. The smoke itself was white and
friendly—the protecting aircraft circled unmolested and the boat
pool of perhaps fifty or sixty craft were equally unmolested. The sun
was so hot and the sea so smooth that "Hands to bathe" would have
seemed a perfectly appropriate signal. We leaned lazily on the
bridge screen waiting for orders from the *Calpe* whilst even the din
of the battle to the eastward seemed to be muffled by the smoke.
The boat pool had drifted to the westward so that it lay between
Pourville and the d'Ailly lighthouse. How inviting looked the
luxurious woods on top of the cliff and the brilliant fields, but the
powers-that-be wanted them blotted out. "Maintain a smoke-screen
half a mile inshore and to the westward" came over the loud
hailer from *Calpe*. We led off with Grif following on our starboard
quarter.

The smoke floats were ignited much more quickly than I expected
after all the trouble we used to have with them in *Broke*, and
before I could say knife, about five had been dropped in a bunch
and far too near the boat pool. We steamed on up the coast and
dropped more floats.

Half an hour later we were back beside *Calpe* with hardly any smoke left. She told us to take M.L.s 309 and 190 under our orders and continue to maintain the screen. Both these M.L.s had been damaged and were steering by hand with large tillers: 190 had a big hole in her starboard quarter. Our loud hailer had been brought to life by the magic attentions of S.G.B.3s Leading Telegraphist who was with us. Through it we directed the M.L.s when to drop their smoke floats. As we went off a formation of three Dornier 217s unloaded their bombs in the middle of the boat pool from about 4,000 feet without, as far as we could see, doing any damage. The Spitfires were on their tails before even the bombs were released, and almost at once one was set on fire. The crew baled out and the aircraft crashed in the sea a few hundred yards offshore and two miles to the westward. The first two to bale out fell in the sea, the others drifted in over the cliffs before coming down, for the sea breeze had set in; such very light wind as there was blew now from sea to shore.

Although the two parachutists who fell in the sea were about opposite Quiberville—a part of the coast which had not been attacked—we decided that the further offshore of the two was a reasonable risk as prisoners had been asked for, and we set course accordingly at twenty knots. Grif, however, came up on our starboard side and raced for the position, so we altered in, steering for the inshore airman's position—scarcely a mile from the cliffs. At last we sighted the bobbing head and slowed down. I overshot him a little, a heaving line was thrown and he grabbed it and was pulled along, his head submerged in his own bow wave. He let go and drifted a little astern and I began to go astern to get him when —whoosh crumph—and a shell landed on the port bow close aboard. "Full ahead both, hard-a-starboard." The pilot waved pathetically from the water, but his friends had sealed his doom. Another shell arrived within thirty or forty yards. We made C.S.A. smoke and zig-zagged sharply at twenty-eight knots. For eight minutes the shells continued to arrive with remarkable accuracy for range but out for line. They all fell to port. I did not know whether to expect them to correct for line but kept altering to starboard and it was as well that I did for the shells kept falling to port. The last salvo was a two-gun salvo just ahead after which we ran clear and reduced speed at 1035. We had got off a good deal more lightly than we deserved for it was, on the face of it, *not* a justifiable thing for which to risk a Steam Gunboat.

Twenty minutes later when we were back amongst the boats and the smoke a heavy air attack began. The log reads thus:

1102   Opened fire on Dornier
1103   ,,   ,, ,,   ,,
1104   ,,   ,, ,,   ,,
1107   ,,   ,, ,,   ,,
1110   ,,   ,, ,,   ,,
1115   Stopped to pick up pilot

All these engagements were separate and for a while the air was thick with enemy aircraft.

One bomber blew up in mid air and the bits fell slowly like autumn leaves. Later a fighter was disintegrated by a shell in the same sort of way. None of the bombs from these Dorniers seemed to have troubled the ships at all.

We had just received a signal that the withdrawal was commencing, and the battle on the beaches seemed to increase in intensity as the Landing Craft went in to take off the troops. At this time we were manoeuvring in thin smoke. It was possible to see the aircraft overhead but most of the ships were hidden. When they did appear they loomed enormous. 'B'-class M.L.s looked like vast transports. The effect was like a fog in a bad film. It was steamy and rather eerie. Parachutes were coming down all round. Two fell near the *Locust*, which was dimly visible in the smoke. I thought it would be rude to race her to them but a few moments later she moved off again and signalled, "Pick up two pilots astern of me." We went ahead and began to pick them up. Whilst we were doing it a fierce air battle was going on overhead and whenever possible we engaged enemy aircraft that were in range. Once we opened up on a Boston, which came low directly at us out of the smoke. We managed to stop the gunners before it was hit. This and a few rounds unordered from one of the point-five turrets at a Spitfire were the only times we fired at friendly aircraft. Other ships were much worse and sometimes the fire was general throughout the boat pool at an obviously friendly aircraft—a sickening thing to watch.

While we picked up the first parachutist—a German—the second one was shouting "Help—speed." We took rather a long time getting the first on board and he was finally hauled in over the transom. Picking up survivors with the air full of enemy aircraft and all our guns firing requires a high degree of concentration and I did not usually make a very good job of it. However we finally got the second Hun on board (also over the transom) and he was almost drowned. We decided to transfer him, on the advice of the Sick Berth Attendant, to a ship with a Medical Officer.

L.C.F.(L)5, a beach protection craft flying a medical guard flag, was near-by and we went alongside. After some argument and delay the man was transferred. By this time the air attack was less fierce but fairly regular. The Dornier 217s—Germany's latest bombers—were coming in in formations of three. One of the three was always shot down, often two and once or twice all three. Once I saw three come in from seaward. The leader went into a steep dive, the other two only shallow dives. I could not see the target for smoke but the Dornier who concentrated on the bombing run—a brave fellow—came out with six or eight Spitfires on his tail. He barely pulled out of his dive before he was heading down again on fire.

I watched another Dornier lining up for his attack. The Spitfires were elsewhere at the time except for one which was below and ahead of the bomber. This Spitfire turned up towards the Dornier and made a sort of lunge at it. The Dornier flinched and the Spitfire made a second lunge. The attack was spoiled and the Dornier jettisoned his bombs to escape a host of newly arrived Spitfires. We did not have time to follow his fortunes, but I doubt if he can have escaped. The Dorniers usually seemed to drop four bombs. Once or twice I saw more—six or possibly eight.

All this time it was very hard to know what was going on either ashore or afloat. From time to time signals came through calling for closer support. But how to do it, that was the question. How to know where our own troops were. The blanket of smoke between us and the shore was almost complete. Only occasionally glimpses of a silhouetted cliff showed in the gap between belching smoke floats. At eleven-forty-five we had made a signal to *Calpe* (H.Q. ship): "We have plenty of three-inch ammo. but no smoke, can we help?" to which we had received reply, "Closer support is required, offer of help appreciated." A few minutes later we signalled to *Calpe* again, "Can you give us a bearing on which to lob shells?" but got no answer to this.

There was a terrible feeling of helplessness at this time, and also a strange aloofness from the awful happenings so close to us but hidden by the thick white curtain. Every few minutes salvos of shells arrived on our side of the smoke, and occasionally there were plops from spent bullets and small shells.

It was an hour after it had been sent that I first saw a signal to *Locust* timed 1112 which said, "Give support at rising ground at end of Green beach." It was a bad signal; Green beach had of course rising ground at either end, and without more precise instructions anything other than moral support was impossible. We called up *Locust* by lamp and made, "Can we help you support Green beach?" to which came reply, "Yes—go in." A general signal had just come through: "All ships. Make smoke. Executive signal." And then a most marvellous spectacle developed before our eyes. The destroyers were making clouds of brilliant white C.S.A. smoke which shone in the sun, crowned with deep chocolate billows of fuel smoke from their funnels. I took some photographs of this as we steamed in to 'Give our support', making the last dregs of our own C.S.A. smoke as we went.

Then we plunged into the fog of it and at last emerged with alarming suddenness on the other side. There was Green beach and the village of Pourville about 600 or 700 yards away. We turned to port and opened fire at some tracer coming from the top of the cliff at the left-hand end of the beach with our three-inch gun. There was no sign of activity at all on the beach. A light on-shore wind had set in so that the smoke drifted slowly to the south-east over the front of Dieppe; heavy fighting was still going on at Red and White beaches. As we turned away from our bombardment bullets whistled around and Oerlikon shells plopped in the water beside us. But it was wild desultory fire and none hit us.

All this time shells were coming from the cliffs to the eastward of Dieppe—they were not accurate but they were fairly constant, so that hanging about even in the thick smoke was not very restful. We closed *Berkeley* and shouted, "What is happening?" But Yorke shrugged his shoulders. No one knew. That was the most difficult part. Help was undoubtedly needed, but no one could tell us where or how. We intercepted a signal from *Brocklesby* (Nigel Pumphrey) saying she was aground, but it was evidently ancient history; we saw her steaming out a couple of miles offshore. (Before commanding the Hunt-class destroyer *Brocklesby* Nigel had been an almost legendary leader of M.T.B.s at Dover.)

At 1243 we suddenly saw three aircraft heading straight for us about thirty feet above the sea. We quickly saw that they were Bostons but all the other ships opened fire. When they were quite close suddenly a dense cloud of white smoke came from them and left a wonderfully thick screen. It was magnificent the way it was done in face of so much fire from friendly craft. I heard that one was shot down but I didn't see it. *We* had seen that they were Bostons, why couldn't the others? It made one bitter and angry to see the ships shooting at our own brave chaps. Ten minutes later we headed in to carry out a further bombardment from closer—this time with pom-pom as well as three-inch. We were receiving such signals as "Situation critical behind Red and White beaches, can you hasten close support as requested—1144" and later "Enemy holds all beaches."

As we came through the smoke-screen for our second bombardment, the coastline loomed up far closer than we expected. The Hunt-class Destroyer *Albrighton* was there half shrouded in her own smoke and terrifyingly close to the shore. She was commanded by Hanson who had been driving *Lincoln* during the *Comorin* rescue. Her guns were firing and she seemed to be moving slowly ahead, and not, as we first feared, aground. We turned again to port, opening fire with three-inch and pom-pom at the eastern outskirts of Pourville which consituted the 'high ground at the end of Green beach'. We passed between *Albrighton*, who had ceased fire, and the shore at slow speed and turned back into the smoke. A good many shells and bullets were whistling both ways and plopping in the water all about us, but miraculously we were not hit.

Back on the off-shore side of the smoke we engaged a Dornier— then another, and at 1308 a formation of three dived down. One of them pressed home his attack on the group of ships all bunched together, which consisted of *Calpe*, *Fernie*, *Berkeley*, *Albrighton* and *Bleasdale*, to say nothing of S.G.B.s 8 and 9. The bombs came out and I saw one slanting down into the water close to the port side of *Berkeley*. Its slant took it right under the ship and when it exploded she reared like a bucking horse. The bridge went up and the fo'c'sle went down as if there were a hinge. Then for a few moments as the ship subsided again into the water the half-detached fo'c'sle waggled up and down.

We turned at once towards the damaged destroyer (not knowing at the time that it was *Berkeley*). She was steaming at high speed in a circle, heeling over steeply and with steam escaping with a roar. Grif was quite close—indeed, he had to go astern to avoid a collision, and as soon as she slowed up he laid his ship alongside the port side of the sinking destroyer and the crew trooped off on to his fo'c'sle. All the time that she had been steaming in a circle men had been falling off her steep decks and the wake was dotted with the heads of swimming survivors. As we closed in towards them we suddenly saw a bunch of three or four F.-W. 190s coming at us with their nasty little bombs hanging underneath them. We were close to *Calpe* at the time, stern to stern, and one of the bombs fell between us—thirty yards from us and fifteen from them, but it must have been a small bomb. *Calpe* lurched but was none the worse, and nor were we. Neither did any of the other ships appear to be damaged by this last attack in spite of the shocking way in which they were all clustered together. We followed the circular string of bobbing heads and threw over two lifebelts and a rubber dinghy (to hold five). Then we went on to a Carley raft and collected half a dozen men from that. By this time the other swimmers had collected at the rubber boat and we were able to go straight to that and pick them up. This seems a good idea when there are many people to rescue.

Berkeley was now stopped and down by the bow listing to star-board. Grif pulled away from her side with the last of her survivors and a signal came to us from her Captain (Lieutenant Yorke, R.N.) in No. 8: "Sink with torpedo" followed shortly after with a negative. Meanwhile *Albrighton* placed her stern opposite *Berkeley*'s stern and took off the Torpedo Gunners Mate who had been below and left behind.

Still the destroyers were clustered most dangerously together into a marvellous bomb target. But no attack came. Instead a Hurricane crashed in the sea close beside us, its pilot having no doubt baled out some time before. *Albrighton* lay off to the north of *Berkeley* and fired a torpedo. It hit under the bridge and blew off the bows which sank immediately. The rest of the ship, however, relieved of the weight floated more level. A second torpedo was fired and hit the after magazine which blew up. A huge reddish purple burst of smoke and flame belched out of the wreck and went up into the calm sky in a tall column with a mushroom of dense blackness at its top. This was an extraordinary and unforgettable sight, as indeed is the sinking of any ship—but the curious forma-tion of the smoke cloud was especially unusual. For a few seconds part of the ship floated so that we imagined she was resting on the bottom, then she disappeared altogether.

CHAPTER 17   *"Home, James . . ."*

BY half past one in the afternoon the ships were forming up into a
convoy for the return journey, and soon after the Naval Force
Commander made the signal "Negative Smoke." What remained of
it did not take long to clear, although there still seemed a lot of
work to be done. *Albrighton* was getting a Chasseur in tow. The
withdrawal from the shore was complete—no more boats were
coming off. All who were left behind must now be taken prisoner.
But the *Calpe* turned back towards the beaches as the *Albrighton*
came away. *Calpe* was firing her forward guns in a duel with a shore
battery whose shells landed on her starboard side close between her
and *Albrighton*. Under *Calpe*'s starboard bow came an L.C.A.
heading shorewards. This was evidently a last attempt to get a boat
ashore to take off further troops. It was a grand sight to see them
nosing towards the shore with hardly any smoke cover. But it was
quite obviously a forlorn hope. They could never make it. They
turned away and we turned away with them. Twenty-millimetre
shells plopped in the water round us.

All the destroyers were making black smoke, sometimes so
diligently that flames belched from their funnels. I thought one of
them must have a fire in the boiler room, but it was only over-
enthusiastic smoke-making. By 1341 the gallant attempt to get the
L.C.A. ashore had been abandoned and all ships were withdrawing.
The raid was over.

A second L.C.A. had appeared from somewhere and the two of
them brought up the rear. We went to look after them and rounded
up astern of them. A new battery was firing and the shells fell near
the last destroyers just ahead. Meanwhile occasional single Dorniers
managed to penetrate the fighter cover, and deliver fairly accurate
bombing attacks on the destroyers further out. Twice I saw them
completely enveloped in splashes. The Germans afterwards claimed

these as sunk but in fact they were not even damaged, though they lurched and shuddered at the explosions of the near misses.

Calpe and *Albrighton* increased speed to outrange the new battery. The two L.C.A.s chugged on slowly through the regular three shell splashes while we brought up the rear. *Calpe* signalled, "Take one L.C.A. in tow," and at the same time a 'C'-class M.G.B. dropped back to take the other. Actually she took both of them while we watched *Calpe* go off to the south-east in response to a Spitfire which was circling low and tipping its wings to indicate a pilot in the water. She made smoke as she went. A Dornier spotted her away from the Spitfires and did a shallow dive attack. We couldn't see *Calpe* at the time, only the pinnacles of the bomb splashes. A few minutes later another Dornier came out of the thin grey clouds which were now forming overhead. We fired a round from the three-inch to warn *Calpe*. But the Dornier dived down unopposed by our Spitfires which were all over the convoy of retiring craft three or four miles to the northward. Again the spouts of brown water appeared above the white smoke screen. Surely the *Calpe* must be hit—and if she was hit there was only us to go to the rescue. And we knew she had many hundreds of wounded soldiers on board as well as the Headquarters Staff.

We increased speed and headed towards the smoke. There was no sign of the destroyer, but a breaking bow wave came out of the smoke across the glassy sea. That bow wave might have been started before the last bombing attack, the *Calpe* might still be sinking in the middle of the 'fog bank' in front of us. Should we creep into it or skirt round it at high speed? I turned to port to keep north of it—the side on which the destroyer was most likely to emerge, and there at last she appeared steaming out at twenty-five knots. We all heaved a deep sigh of relief and made: "Interrogative O.K." to which came back, "Yes, thanks—please search two miles astern of me for six men in the water." Two miles! And we were no more than four miles offshore—with hardly any smoke left between us and Dieppe. We turned on to an opposite course and set off at twenty-five knots. Two miles back we still saw no sign of the missing men. The last of the smoke had gone and the sea was so completely smooth that I thought we could not possibly miss them. We turned to starboard in a wide sweep and suddenly something caught my eye—a flock of gulls on the water? No—five heads. As we approached, the swimmers waved and cheered from the water. We stopped amongst them and they were all on board in a sur-prisingly short time. It appears that the first attack on *Calpe* in the smoke had caused a cordite fire on No. 2 gun deck (the upper after mounting). Some of the men had been blown overboard, others had jumped to extinguish their burning clothing. The five were none of them more than slightly injured. It is not clear if there had ever been six as *Calpe* signalled.

Although we must have been perfectly plain to see, the shore guns did not open fire. By now, even the belated bombing attacks by our Bostons and Hurribombers which had gone on after the withdrawal, had ceased. The shore looked peaceful except for some columns of smoke rising lazily above the town.

Five miles to seaward the Spitfires milled above the convoy but only very occasionally did a small band of them circle out in our direction. Small parties of F.-W. 190s circled there too, so that every fighter had to be watched. There was a breathless urgency to get back to our protective umbrella and every moment of delay caused an ever-growing impatience. As we increased speed to rejoin, I swept the port side with the glasses and saw an L.C.A. away inshore of us. At first I took it for one of two derelicts, one of which had been blazing half an hour before: but this one was under way. I looked round the bridge to see if anyone else had seen it. No one had. Already we had been messing about unhealthily close to the shore for much too long. This would mean going at least a mile closer still. Was it a fair risk of the ship? Had I still the guts to give the order to turn south again? How much difference did it make that no one else had spotted the boat? Could I really leave the men in it, and have them on my conscience for ever after? . . .

I should like to say that I weighed all these things and decided to turn back, but that is not how it happened. As I wondered what I should do, I saw George Pennell put up his glasses and sweep towards the shore. In a moment he too would see the boat. "Port twenty" I called to the cox'n, and with sinking hearts we turned once more towards Dieppe at twenty-five knots.

As we closed the boat I aimed a little to one side so that I could sweep round and take it swiftly in tow till we were clear of the shore and the guns, which must, we all thought, open fire as soon as we stopped. The L.C.A. turned towards us. I aimed the other side and the wretched thing turned and came for us again. Eventually I had to go straight to it and turn beyond it. As we approached we saw that it contained three soldiers, two of whom were completely naked except for their Mae Wests. One of them was busy semaphoring "S O S". After turning we passed them a rope and they managed to secure the eye. Then, miraculously still unshot at, although we were no more than a mile off shore, we set off again to rejoin the now-distant convoy and its cloud of protecting fighters. On the way one of the periodical air fights developed overhead and a pilot was seen floating down to the north-east of us. I decided that trying to get the L.C.A. home was a secondary commitment compared with parachuters, so I took off the soldiers and abandoned it.

We found the airman sitting in his rubber boat; a large red flag with a white spot flying bravely over it. He was grinning and seemed perfectly well and happy. It was a striking contrast between our efficiency and that of the Germans. Their airmen had all been half drowned before we got them on board. This lad—a Norwegian officer—was on board in a few moments and we turned at once Dieppe-wards to collect another pilot whom we had seen descending. A near-by M.L. made over towards the same pilot so we signalled "Suggest you rejoin convoy at your best speed", which he proceeded to do.

We found the pilot without difficulty. He too was sitting quite comfortably in his rubber dinghy in spite of a badly broken leg and an injured arm. With his good arm he caught and secured a heaving line to the dinghy. Being in a dinghy instead of in the water halved the time that it took to get him on board and in a very few minutes we were off again on a course to rejoin the convoy. The second pilot was an American and was in some pain. An injection of one 'Omnipon' ampoule (half-grain morphia) seemed to do little to relieve him.

As we overtook the M.L. he signalled "This is my best speed." It was twelve knots, so we made "All right, we will stay with you." Just then a Dornier appeared out of the clouds. By now we were very familiar both with the appearance and tactics of these bombers. They were immediately recognised. This one came from right astern and dived down as we increased speed. We and the M.L. were the only unprotected targets—money for jam. All guns opened fire and I watched the bombs come out. At once I saw that they were travelling in the same direction as us and at about the same forward speed, perhaps a little more. They would fall just ahead so above the uproar of the guns I yelled to the coxswain, "Full astern both." He didn't hear me the first time, but when he did the result was most striking. Unlike the *Broke* after a similar order, the S.G.B. pulled up dead in her tracks and the bombs went on to fall about sixty yards ahead with four great spouting splashes. Meanwhile the guns had been doing well. The Dornier, which was about 2,000 feet up, was hit by a burst from the three-inch gun under its starboard engine. This caught fire and a thin stream of smoke came from it as the aircraft plunged almost vertically downward. There was great excitement on the bridge. "We've got him! We've got him!" But when he was a couple of hundred feet up he flattened out and, still burning, disappeared into the haze of smoke over Dieppe.

At four-forty-eight p.m., when we had almost caught up the destroyers, a parachute was reported two miles astern and away we went again. The sea was now so completely glassy that we expected to see him easily but after a search four miles in rear of the convoy we gave it up. Had he been English we should have seen his rubber boat. Unfortunately the parachute was not seen from the bridge and so no compass bearing could be taken.

By now the Benzedrine tablet I had taken was having a marked effect. I found myself singing away merrily and shouting exhortations to the Dorniers to do their worst. George Pennell, Jock Henderson, my navigator, and the coxswain, all of whom also had tablets, declared that they noticed no effect at all. (The after-effects on me were also noticeable. I felt very sleepy and listless for at least forty-eight hours.)

At five p.m. we came up with the convoy at last, just as it entered the southern end of the swept channel. Since the sinking of the *Berkeley*, enemy air attacks had been totally unsuccessful. An M.L. was stationed to mark the entrance to the lane of flagged dan buoys, the same M.L. that had so nearly rammed us in the darkness sixteen hours ago. When we came up to *Albrighton* I signalled by light to Hanson:

"I think I'd rather have the Atlantic even with the *Comorin* thrown in."

"I quite agree," was his answer.

"Did you have many casualties?" I asked.

"Only six killed but many wounded."

We decided that close between *Albrighton* and *Bleasdale* was a dangerous place to be should a determined Dornier turn up, so we crept past and up into the rearguard of the convoy itself. It was formed up in four columns with a speed of advance of eight knots. Ahead were *Calpe* and *Fernie*. One of the centre columns consisted of Chasseurs towing assault boats (L.C.A.s). The rest were M.L.s and M.G.B.s and one or two L.C.M.s (Landing Craft Motor), mostly towing L.C.A.s. Altogether there must have been between sixty and seventy craft and it was most surprisingly orderly. Many of the motor craft were flying flag Harry (one of my engines is out of action). Following the starboard column was the river gunboat *Locust* (with Ryder on board). Grif with the *Berkeley* survivors had long since gone on ahead to Newhaven.

As soon as we were through the minefield we gradually overtook the convoy so as to tell *Calpe* that we had his five chaps.

I went down to talk to the survivors and found one of the prisoners, a likeable youth who could speak no English, sitting with our black kitten on his lap, between his guard who was fast asleep with his head on the German's shoulder, and the Norwegian pilot. We had a short philosophical discussion on the senselessness of war to the limits of my German. He had apparently much impressed the ship's company by the way he had helped with the wounded. One of them told me that in spite of the blitzes when he had vowed no quarter for any German he would meet, he could not help liking this one; "'E's a gentleman, sir!" His reputation was the more remarkable as it was achieved without a word of the language. He was Feldwebel Richard Braun.

The other German—Oberleutnant Hans Wauka—asked a curious question in English: "Where shall we be landed—England or France?" Evidently he was convinced that the invasion had begun in earnest.

One of the Canadians from the L.C.A.—Private L. A. Nelson—told me that he had had conversations with French villagers indicating that the raid had been expected for some time.

The Norwegian told me he had shot down his first Jerry that day. It was the Dornier we had seen crash on the cliff top early in the day. After that he had got home with a damaged plane, got another and come out again only to be shot down himself by a F.-W. 190. His name was Olav Djonne.

We listened to the nine o'clock news and I had half an hour's nap in the charthouse from which I was roused by the alarm bell. When I emerged it was quite dark and raining hard, and the south-west wind was rising.

A Dornier had just passed over low, and had been fired at by the destroyer ahead. It did not come back. Perhaps it was one of the force sent over to attack us at dusk or after, which owing to the change in the weather had not been able to find us and had gone on to unload their bombs somewhere inland—afterwards claiming great successes against the returning armada.

We turned up the Portsmouth swept channel half an hour later, and as we passed the Nab Tower clouds of black smoke came from the funnel and we began to slow down.

For more than twelve hours the engine-room staff had been fully extended, nursing badly shaken machinery. Now a combination of 'stuck-up valves' and extreme fatigue was beating them. For the next hour and a half we proceeded in fits and starts in the inky darkness, having lost touch with the destroyers altogether.

Finally, however, we found the gate at about midnight in spite of a steering compass that showed fifteen degrees difference from the standard and a completely unknown speed which varied between nought and ten knots.

We crept up the Channel and groped our way into the harbour, turned with some difficulty and berthed alongside S.G.B.4 at forty-five minutes past midnight, just over twenty-eight hours after we had left.

In a short while the eleven casualties, five survivors and two prisoners had been disembarked, an operation which was not made more easy by a failure of the shore lighting, so that the wounded had to be moved by torchlight. The prisoners were taken on board S.G.B.3 and subsequently to the cruiser *Durban*, who lent us thirty blankets most promptly as all ours had been used by survivors and were wet or blood-soaked.

It was about three o'clock before we finally turned in to sleep late into the following morning.

S.G.B. 9, the Flotilla Leader (afterwards named S.G.B. *Grey Goose*) on her trials in the Solent.

1942

1957

1948

The rocket-nets in operation. In the top picture taken on the Yorkshire Wolds, the dark line is a solid mass of geese, which are mostly rather beyond the nets. The catch was 155. Below it is the first catch ever made with a rocket-net.

1948

Keith Shackleton and I are extricating the 30 Whitefronts and one Pinkfoot after the first rocket-net catch ever made—on the New Grounds at Slimbridge.

CHAPTER 18   *A Meeting with Charlie*

HISTORY has delivered a number of rather conflicting verdicts on the Dieppe Raid. Immediately after it, we knew only that on the debit side a great number of prisoners had been left behind, and on the credit side a great number of German aeroplanes had been shot down. We supposed also that some fairly useful experience of the techniques of frontal assault had been gained, and we knew that the naval losses had been much lighter than had been expected.

S.G.B.9 had come through her baptism of fire virtually unscathed and no single member of the ship's company had been scratched. They had all been splendid and I was delighted with them. This was just how I had hoped they would be. All doubts about the wisdom of leaving the destroyer world of the North Atlantic were now behind me. I was especially pleased with Jock Henderson, my navigator, and later to be my First Lieutenant, and with young Jimmy Jones, the able seaman who had come on with me from the *Broke*. He had been layer of the three-inch gun all day—it is the layer who fires it—and his marksmanship had been outstanding, but in addition all were agreed that his cheerful high spirits had been an inspiration to the gun's crew. This tall, quiet lad was one of those invaluable people who suddenly come out of their shells when in danger and show new and unsuspected qualities of courage and leadership. Jones was Mentioned in Dispatches as a result of his day's work.

While S.G.B.9 had been building at Cowes, the S.G.B.s already in commission had fought a battle with the escort of an enemy convoy off the coast of France. At that time the armament which they carried was extremely inadequate, and one boat, commanded by a Free Frenchman—René Barnet—was stopped, and had to be scuttled by her crew. This loss brought home to the powers-that-be how vulnerable were these new boats, for although they did not carry high-octane petrol, and the fire risk was thereby much reduced, they had only one boiler, only one feed pump, only one extractor pump. If any of these were put out of action by a machine-gun bullet the boat was bound to stop, and once stopped could only be brought home under tow. Towing was therefore going to be a very vital drill for all boats in the Steam Gunboat Flotilla. In due course the Admiralty felt that efficient towing drill was not enough; something more must be done; the machinery spaces must be pro-tected with armour plate; and until that had been done, said the Admiralty, the S.G.B.s must be employed only in defence. So in turn the steamers were taken in hand for this drastic modification. No. 9's turn did not come at once and she was used for South Coast Convoy Escort, based at one end on Portsmouth, at the other on Plymouth or Dartmouth.

Jane and I had lately taken a small furnished house in Seaford, so as to be handy for the main S.G.B. base at Newhaven, but with the new plan we only lived there for a few weeks.

If *Broke* had been unsuitable for convoy work in winter, S.G.B.9 was no better. At speed she behaved well, but at eight knots in a big sea it was a full-time job to keep her on a straight course. On one such desperate night with a south-easterly gale we were detached to take shelter in Dartmouth. It was pitch dark and raining hard, and the entrance to the harbour was hard enough to find in the first place, then came the added hazard of trying to keep the ship straight as we ran in with heavy following seas which tried to sweep her broadside on. I remember asking the Port War Signal Station by shaded light for permission to enter and thinking that all would be lost if I had to wait long for the answer. The only thing was to keep steerage way into the mouth. I had forgotten all about the boom, the curtain of steel netting which hung from buoys across the entrance. Suddenly the boom defence vessel loomed up ahead to remind me, though much too late to stop. At that precise moment the signal station on the cliff top began winking at us. Permission was granted, and as we came up to the boom ship we could see that the gate was opening, though the great buoys had so far been pulled less than half-way back. "Hard-a-starboard!" I shouted. The cox'n made three violent turns on the wheel and we dived through the gap. In a few moments we were in the calm water and inky black-ness of Dartmouth Harbour, and half an hour later we were safely secured alongside the Coastal Forces Depot ship. Now, all these years later, I can remember the feeling of relief, the sense of victory and sheer satisfaction as we sat in the wardroom and contem-

plated our achievement before we turned in. We had come successfully into a difficult harbour in a gale, but even that would scarcely
be appreciated by anyone who did not know of the S.G.B.s' steering
problems. We had had phenomenal luck, of course, that the gate
had been opened in time. But between us we had also exercised
some skill. No one but ourselves knew or cared how much, but the
knowledge amongst us bred a great comradeship and confidence.
We were a real team now. How maddening that we were given no
offensive work to do!

One of the brighter aspects of this new operating area was a
chance of some wildfowling. The Staff Officer Operations at
Dartmouth was George Newman, in peace time an estate agent, a
wildfowler and a keen amateur cricketer. He had taken a house
quite near to Dartmouth and immediately below it was a tiny marsh,
to which at night time came a surprisingly large number of mallards
and a few teal to feed. The evening flight on this little marsh was a
pleasant thing to look forward to at the end of a rough passage with
the convoy, and I was grateful to George for what was, in the true
sense of the word, a recreation.

Even the defensive role of the S.G.B.s involved us occasionally in
action. In the small hours of 19th November, 1942, we fought a
short battle which was to have interesting repercussions two years
later. It was on that morning that I first encountered Kapitänleutnant 'Charlie' Müller, an already famous E-boat Commander.
We were in station astern of a west-bound convoy near Start Point
and I was asleep in the charthouse when the alarm bells rang. In
a second I was on the bridge, and could see a starshell floating down
to seaward of us. "What's up?" I asked. "Just a starshell, I think
the trawler on the port bow of the convoy must have fired it," said
Jock Henderson. Then suddenly 'Clang!' as a torpedo hit the
merchant ship just ahead of us. As I hauled out to port and increased speed there were three more explosions and then we saw
the tracks of two more torpedoes approaching. One passed ahead,
the other right under the ship, or so it seemed, though most probably
the torpedo itself was just ahead of us, for the wake of bubbles is
some way behind the 'fish' itself. We and the other escort ships all
fired starshell now, and by its light we could see five E-boats about
a mile and a half away. As we made after them they disappeared
into a cloud of their own smoke. A few moments later we saw
tracer bullets buzzing across in front of us. One E-boat was firing at
another. It was cheering to find, after an unfortunate incident a
few weeks before, that we were not the only ones to make this kind

of mistake. Meanwhile we ourselves were sighted by the destroyer *Brocklesby* who was Senior Officer of the Escort, and a moment later her starshell burst over us. By its light, however, we spotted another E-boat and briefly engaged it as it sped away to the south. We followed for a bit but suddenly we heard another underwater explosion. So there were still E-boats harassing the convoy—we must go back at once.

We had not long turned back to the northward when we saw an E-boat silhouetted against the light of starshell. It was heading exactly towards us. I felt like a fielder in the deep field—could I prevent a boundary? Clearly the E-boat was unaware of us. We reduced speed so that he would not see our bow wave and turned on to a parallel course, not 200 yards away from him. Our own very meagre supply of starshell was exhausted, but so long as the illumination was provided by *Brocklesby* and the trawlers of the screen, we could hardly miss when the moment came to open fire. Still the E-boat had not seen us and gradually he drew level with us. Now was our chance. "All right, Number One, open fire," I said, and exactly at the moment that he gave the order the last starshell petered out and there was utter darkness. With the light behind it for another fifteen seconds we could have blown that E-boat out of the water. As it was we fired towards it and the tracer sprayed around it, but there was no sharp black bull's-eye for the gunners to aim at. The critical half minute which it took the enemy to make his white smoke, and turn away into it, passed without the decisive blow being struck. After all, one direct hit on the waterline with the three-inch gun would probably have done it—would have slowed him down enough for us to try conclusions. But it was not to be.

For a long time after that, I used to lie in bed at nights and imagine that I had given the order fifteen seconds earlier (which I could quite well have done, for we had waited only for the absolute optimum), or that *Brocklesby* had fired one more starshell and thus given us those precious seconds, or that we ourselves had had another round of starshell for the three-inch gun. Paragraph thirteen of my Action Report to the Commander-in-Chief Plymouth reads: "It is submitted that the allowance of fifteen rounds of starshell should be greatly increased and that additional ready-use lockers should be fitted to contain it."

CHAPTER 19   *The Flotilla*

WE needed a home, Jane and I, and the only sensible thing seemed
to be to make it in London. It so chanced that 101 Clifton Hill,
St. John's Wood, was to let. This had been the home of Jane's
distinguished grandfather, Sir Arthur Somervell, the musician, and
to it Jane had frequently come for tea parties as a little girl. The
house was the right size and had a nice garden at the back; towards
the end of 1942 we moved in. It was a good time for this because at
last S.G.B.9 was in Southampton Dockyard having the armour
plate fitted round her boiler room and engine room that would
once more make her eligible for offensive fighting. At this time too
there was to be a change in the command of the Steam Gunboat
Flotilla. George Pennell was to hand over to a school friend of
mine, Tom Dorrien-Smith, another professional N.O., but Tom
was anxious to stay with the Fleet Destroyers in which he had been
serving, and in due course I was promoted Lieutenant Commander
and became Senior Officer of the First S.G.B. Flotilla.

For some time I had been campaigning for a much heavier
armament for the Steamers. The three-inch gun had been fitted in
S.G.B.9 for trial. It would now be fitted in the rest, but I was
determined that many more guns of other kinds should be fitted at
the same time. My boat was to be in dockyard hands from mid-
January until the end of April 1943. During this time I made many
visits to the Admiralty both in London and also in Bath, where the
Naval Constructors and Ordnance Departments had their headquarters. And then on 2nd February our daughter Nicola was
born in a nursing home in Kensington, ten days earlier than she
was expected. At eleven days old, the day on which she and her
mother returned to Clifton Hill, I made my first drawing of her—
the first of many. I was a proud and wondering father, proudest
perhaps of my young wife. It was so hard to think of her as a mother.

I had still to travel about from London to Southampton, to Portsmouth, to Newhaven, to Bath. The frequent partings, although they had not yet the overlay of danger—the sense of potential finality, were nevertheless partings and were sadly frequent.

The Captain of S.G.B.6, Howard Bradford—a peace-time architect—had broken his arm at the conclusion of his 'work-up' period at Weymouth, and I was temporarily appointed to command his boat early in April. It was the first of the Steamers to complete the new modifications. The others would be ready later in the month and my own in early May.

There were still two professional Naval Officers commanding boats in the flotilla. Lt. Griffiths—Grif, who had shared the Dieppe adventures with us—came to the Navy from the merchant service, and Jock Ritchie, also a R.N. Lieutenant, had been in M.G.B.s before, and had been Second-in-Command to Pennell. Jock was himself an outstanding leader, and might well have been disappointed that he did not become S.O. of the flotilla, but if he was, I was not allowed to see it. We had become close friends as C.O.s of our own boats and he was my closest colleague now in the affairs of the S.G.B.s. Indeed for me, as an amateur, the loyalty and support of these two professional Officers was one of the most heartening things in my naval career.

Now that S.G.B.6 was ready for sea, there began a grim summer of fighting in the Channel, perhaps the most hazardous and certainly the most nerve-shredding part of my life. I now found myself often making mental reservations about the future—for the first time seriously allowing the possibility that I might not survive the war. I believed only thus far in life after death: that if I were killed some of my works—my own creations, pictures, books—might live on a few years after me, that the love of living people would do the same, and that my child and her descendants would move and talk and feel a little like me long after I was dead. But this feeling of continuation of my line was small compensation for the awful partings with my wife. By what right had I blighted her life with this perpetual anxiety? How could I justify myself in acquiring these new family responsibilities when I knew that I must go on fighting my war all out? It was the only way I knew how to do it; perhaps the only way I knew how to do anything.

On the evening of 9th April I found myself once more on the bridge of a Steam Gunboat, leading three small M.T.B.s out of Newhaven harbour on an offensive sweep along the enemy coast. That night, I remember, there was exceptionally brilliant phosphorescence in the sea, so that the boats made beautiful luminous green bow waves as they sped across towards France. This would have seriously affected our chances of a surprise attack had enemy shipping put in an appearance, but they didn't. As we lay stopped and waiting we were apparently picked up by the German radar, which was very much less effective than our own. Nevertheless the shore batteries opened a fairly accurate fire on us, which made us move on. Later, at a range of at least seven and a half miles, they started up again and put a salvo of four shells very close to us indeed.

Four days later we were half-way across the Channel listening to the nine o'clock news from the B.B.C. on our way to the German convoy lane when a shattering announcement came over the air. 'Hitch' had been killed in action off the Dutch coast. Robert Hichens, my old friend of fourteen-foot dinghy days, the Falmouth solicitor who had won more decorations than anyone else in Coastal Forces, had been struck and killed instantly by a stray shell right at the end of a successful battle. I remember that we stopped, as was our wont, to compare positions at the entrance to the swept channel through the minefield, and at the same time passed the news to the other boats. There was a shocked incredulity in their tone as they answered. Surely there must be some mistake, they seemed to say. Others could be killed in action, but not Hitch.

It was another blank night with no sign of enemy shipping. I spent most of it thinking of Robert, and the day he had first appeared with the home-made fourteen-footer which we had all been snooty about until it came third in a twenty-knot breeze. I remembered how he had started just in front of us in the Prince of Wales's Cup at Falmouth when John and I had first tried out the trapeze and how in his surprise he sailed off the wind just long enough to give us our wind free and let us through. I remembered how he had taken me to sea on my first visit to H.M.S. *Beehive*, the Coastal Forces base at Felixstowe a year before; how we had met only a week or two before in London to plan a new assault on the Admiralty in order to get our policies on heavier armament through; how I had heard that he would very shortly be asked to take on a training job at H.M.S. *Bee* at Weymouth as a rest from operations, and how I had greatly doubted if he would accept it.

For me it was a cheerless, empty night.

Soon after I was scheduled to make a broadcast about the Coastal Forces. For some time I had been wondering on what central theme to hang it and it seemed to me now that to tell Hitch's story would infuse the whole programme with his inspiration; and it would be a story I could tell with all sincerity. The broadcast, when it came, seemed to catch the imagination of many who listened. It even made headlines in the daily press. It was 'produced' by George Barnes (long later head of B.B.C. Television) and was the first of several which I made after the nine o'clock news on Sundays. To the present time I have kept in touch with Robert's wife and two sons, and after the war I was commissioned to paint a portrait of him to hang in the R.N.V.R. Club. It was a difficult portrait to paint, as there were few war-time photographs to work from and I had to rely largely on my memory.

Three nights after Robert was killed I took S.G.B.6 and two D-class M.G.B.s to patrol in the Baie de la Seine. One of these M.G.B.s was commanded by John Hodder, in whose previous boat at Dover I had had my first introduction to the Coastal Forces. The other was commanded by Dickie Ball.

In bright moonlight we fought a lively battle against a defensive patrol of armed trawlers. The bare bones of the story are told in the covering letter from C.-in-C. Portsmouth when forwarding my report to the Admiralty. More interesting perhaps are the details which I sent in a letter to Jock Ritchie, the Captain of S.G.B.4, soon afterwards, and which follow the official account.

SECRET

Coastal Force Action of Night 15th/16th April, 1943

From......COMMANDER IN CHIEF, PORTSMOUTH.
Date.......25th April, 1943.   No. 2102/0/9683/29.
To..........SECRETARY OF THE ADMIRALTY.
Copies to:

Commander in Chief, Plymouth (2 copies)
Commander in Chief, The Nore (4 copies)
Vice Admiral, Dover (2 copies)
Naval Officer in Charge, Newhaven.
Commanding Officer, H.M.S. *Bee*.
Commanding Officer, H.M.S. *Attack*.
Commanding Officer, H.M.S. *Aggressive*.
Commanding Officer, H.M.S. *Hornet*.
Captain (D), First Destroyer Flotilla.

1. Be pleased to lay before Their Lordships the following report of an action between S.G.B.6 (Lt.-Cdr. P. M. Scott, M.B.E.,

R.N.V.R., Senior Officer of Force), M.G.B.608 (Lt. J. Hodder, R.N.V.R.), and M.G.B.615 (Lt. R. Ball, R.N.V.R.) and three large armed enemy trawlers.

2. The force had been ordered to proceed through passage II in QZX 771 [a minefield] and carry out a search in the Baie de la Seine with the object of destroying enemy shipping.

3. At 0014, 16th April, an enemy plot was detected by the H.P.T. R.D.F. Station [radar], Ventnor, at a range of seventy miles, and the position was passed to the force, which proceeded to close. The relative positions of the two forces were passed until S.G.B.6's sighting report was intercepted.

4. During the first stage of the action, which lasted eight minutes, S.G.B.6's steering gear was shot away and M.G.B.615 expended all her six-pounder ammunition and her pom-pom became irremediably jammed by a round stuck in the barrel.

5. The Senior Officer ordered M.G.B.615 to stand clear, and forty-five minutes later, having rigged hand steering, proceeded with M.G.B.608 in pursuit of the enemy, whom he correctly assumed to be retiring towards Le Havre.

6. During the second stage of the action, which was mostly fought at ranges of under 500 yards, the leading trawler was silenced, stopped and set on fire, while her consorts kept a distance of 1,500 yards, firing inaccurately.

7. S.G.B.6 endeavoured to sink the trawler with a torpedo which missed, and then owing to the lack of ready-use ammunition and the late hour, and being only ten miles from the enemy coast, the Senior Officer correctly decided to return to harbour.

8. Lt.-Commander Scott reports that the first stage of the action was opened at too great a range, owing to his turning to an opposite course too soon, and the ammunition was wasted at long range.

9. It is disappointing that the expenditure of some sixty rounds of three-inch ammunition failed to sink the enemy, but this would not be probable without a lucky shot in a magazine or certain hits on the water line at very close range. In pressing home such an attack considerable damage and casualties would have been expected as the estimated armament of each trawler was one four-inch (estimated from splashes), one forty-millimetre, four twenty-millimetre, and several light machine-guns.

10. A technical enquiry on the gunnery of the action was carried out by a representative from H.M.S. *Excellent*, and a copy of the report is attached. This discloses an unsatisfactory state of

affairs in the gunnery training, and action is being taken on this.

11. The remarks of the Commanding Officer, S.G.B.6, on the necessity for fitting extra ready-use lockers are concurred in: and the remarks on material forwarded by the Commanding Officer, M.G.B.608, are also commended to Their Lordships' consideration.

12. I consider that Lt.-Commander Scott showed skill in the handling of his force, and great determination in his engagement, pursuit, and re-engagement of the enemy.

13. Recommendations for awards will be forwarded in a separate submission.

(Signed) Charles Little
Admiral.

Paragraphs 12 and 13 were sweet music, of course, but it all seemed rather bogus. Our object had been to destroy enemy shipping and we had signally failed to do so. Really we had not been all that clever or brave. John Hodder seemed genuinely to think that I had not led the force too badly, and I took some comfort from that; but it now seemed important to give the unvarnished story to the flotilla. I wrote a long reply to a letter from Jock Ritchie asking for details:

"You were quite right about the brightness of the night. It was virtually a daylight action. Fortunately, the Hun shooting was very wild, partly because they thought we were a destroyer and were correspondingly scared, and partly because—well, after all, they were only old trawlers stooging along. We sighted them at three and a half miles. Unfortunately they turned 180° just then, otherwise we might have been able to sneak up from astern. I made a balls because Sandy [Sandy Bown, First Lieutenant and Gunnery Officer of S.G.B.6] kept repeating (quite rightly) 'three-inch gun won't bear', so I turned to open 'A arcs' much too soon. The trawlers turned away and the result was 600 yards. I tried to get back to starboard but the steering had gone. The reason for this has not yet been traced as we can find no hits affecting it.

"The action lasted eight minutes—the last four of which only the two D's were firing as I reckoned the range was too great. When we stopped firing (we had been using tracer owing to the brightness of the night) the enemy concentrated on the two D's and left us alone. They had hit us a few times and killed the loading number of the three-inch gun. We hit them fairly hard—the second ship principally and also the third. Two or three times there were sudden 'flare-ups' on the gun platform of the second ship, as of small cordite fires. Tracer was very blinding and so bright that the moonlight seemed to make no difference to it. The targets were almost directly up moon for all the first part of the action.

"We tried steering by engines but the rudders were at Port 20 so it was hopeless. We could see the Germans about 2,000 yards away flashing to each other. I passed a signal to John Hodder and Dickie Ball 'Attack again' and they went off. Meanwhile, I managed to get the ship pointing well to starboard of the course and then rang down half ahead port and in this way progressed slowly in the right direction, stopping when the course did not help and turning to port with main engines, thus describing a series of loops.

"Meanwhile, Ball in 615 saw me coming and thinking very reasonably that it would be nicer to attack with an S.G.B. than without, he turned and closed me, leaving John proceeding at slow speed towards the enemy and already quite close (1,200 yards) but not being fired at. Well, I did not think much of him going in alone so I called him up and made 'Rejoin.' The signalling was very good all the time and it was a most curious feeling all signalling to each other and the Huns doing the same only a mile or so away. By this time I was stopped again and it was clear that until my steering was right, there was nothing much to be done. Dickie Ball came alongside me, went astern and nearly rammed me stern first but just went ahead in time (two feet, but a miss is as good as a mile). He told me by hailer (which I was afraid the Germans would hear) that he only had four rounds of six-pounder left and a shell jammed in the barrel of his pom-pom. I reckoned he was a liability and told him to withdraw to our rendezvous five miles north-east of the action, wait there half an hour, and then return to harbour independently. This was undoubtedly an error. He still had a single Oerlikon and his point-fives and I reckon he would have been most useful if only to draw the enemy's fire. After all, many an M.G.B. has had to fight with less than an Oerlikon and two twin half-inch machine-guns.

"We didn't get our steering right for half an hour, indeed it was quite a relief when we did. We set off, in hand steering, to get down moon again before attempting to intercept. The chap who came over from *Excellent* to investigate our gunnery short-comings, put in his report that too much importance was attached to the moon aspect. That is actually a rather inept criticism, I think. My own view, and that of everyone who was there, is that had we approached from the up moon side, we should have been at a grave disadvantage. The trawlers could *see* us down moon, but they couldn't see us well enough to aim straight. I am con-vinced that they fired substantially more bullets at us than we did at them and the reason they were hit and we were not was very largely, if not entirely, because we kept them against the moon.

"Well, we beetled off eastward at twenty knots with John Hodder astern and then after half an hour (rather less) we turned south, thinking we were ahead of them by then, and started to sweep back at slow speed. I had a fear, however, that they might have gone more to the southward, so we turned back to south-south-west and suddenly sighted them right ahead about three and a half miles with terrific bow waves, obviously legging it at speed.

"I must own to a sinking feeling on sighting. The moon was so bloody bright. Whilst there was a doubt about finding them, the cowardly subconscious was saying hopefully, 'Perhaps you won't', although the conscious went on working out every possibility to make sure we did find them.

"The leading trawler opened fire on us when we were turning towards and were still about 1,200–1,400 yards away. I do not think it is possible to stop guns crews from ducking (at any rate, not until they are veterans, and this was their first action) if they have to be shot at without replying, so rather earlier than perhaps was advisable, I gave the order to open fire. The range was closed to about 600 yards and then it was quite obvious that we could not turn far enough to starboard to cross the leader's bow. I was not at all anxious at that stage to swop punches on parallel courses at close range as the enemy was firing four-inch, at least one if not two two-pounder, and at least four Oerlikons. So I turned away to port, and checked fire so as not to waste ammo. This, more by chance than design, worked a treat, as the Germans went on firing away with very little success as we turned to port and set off to the eastward to regain our lost bearing. (I reckon they were doing something like twelve knots.) We got a bit of a pasting as we got in line with 608 on the turn, as the overs (and everything was high) were hitting us.

"But the point was that the Hun pans were good and empty when we were ready to turn hard-a-port and go straight for him with the *full advantage of the moon*. Up to this point I think (mainly by chance as I say) that we had adopted the best tactics for getting to close range under what were virtually daylight conditions.

"We opened fire at about 500 yards at Red 30 degrees and by the time the leading trawler was abeam it had been silenced. The moment of realisation of this was extremely exciting. I turned to starboard to come in again, and 608 hauled a little out of line to starboard because she thought the trawler was trying to ram her as it was turning to port. I think this was a bit far-fetched as I am convinced the trawler was unable to steer by then and was rapidly losing way, with a loud noise of escaping steam. The result of 608 hauling out of line provided an interesting exercise in gunnery control. For a short while 608 fouled the range. Fire was checked easily for a few seconds and reopened again as soon as the target was clear of 608—a matter of no more than ten seconds. This was possible largely because of the brightness of the night and Sandy's very good handling of the guns.

"Now I checked the fire and tried to get the three-inch gun to carry on firing, but communications to it had failed. After this it only fired two more rounds before it broke down for good. The semi-automatic gear was not properly disengaged and the gun ran out and would not come forward again, as it had bent the rod. We did one more run by which time practically all ready-use ammo. was expended.

"It was now getting very late and it seemed to me to be too late for a boarding operation, particularly as the trawler had manned a ·303 machine gun and was evidently not quite ripe for boarding. She was spraying us with inaccurate bursts. I therefore decided to fire a torpedo and drew off to about 500 yards on the down moon side. The trawler had now swung back to starboard and I reckoned it had stopped. The first torpedo to report 'ready' was the starboard one and so that was the one I fired—at a range of about 400 yards or possibly a little less.

"It is a remarkable feeling as soon as you have fired, isn't it? The awful irrevocability of it and the rather abandoned feeling —'Well, for better or worse, that's done.'

"The torpedo ran all right as far as I could see but the track passed about two or three yards astern of the target. Then I realised that I had been a complete ninny to assume that she was stopped, as being a very big trawler she would be bound to be carrying a little way still. Actually the torpedo may have passed under as the range was probably less than I thought.

"Anyhow, I was so horrified by missing that I decided (quite incorrectly) not to fire the other one. Instead we ranged up alongside the trawler at about 100–150 yards and fired at her with all that would still fire—which turned out to be the starboard point-five and nothing else. Pom-pom supply had broken down owing to one yellow supply number; Oerlikon pans were empty and so were ·303 pans, and the three-inch, which owing to the breakdown in communications we were expecting to open fire at any moment, was irreparably bent.

"The point-five was using no tracer and was raking the target from end to end. You could hear the clatter of it against the trawler. But suddenly, the after Oerlikon on the target came to life and its first burst went into our bridge and into the caboose below. One incendiary shell came into the bridge and exploded knocking us all down (five of us) but only wounding Harris (the navigator) and him only slightly. The bridge was full of smoke and luminous incendiary composition and splinters of the binnacle and there was a goodly fire going in the caboose amongst the point-five ammunition boxes. I had been going slow both, but decided that I had better disengage until the fire had been dealt with so I drew off to about 1,500 yards.

"Meanwhile, John Hodder had silenced the German fire with a beautifully placed burst of Oerlikon at 200 yards range. He followed me and came up alongside, reporting that his pom-pom was out of action, he had used his entire outfit of six-pounder and that one of his twin Oerlikons was also out. This left him with one Oerlikon and his point-fives.

"Our own position, when the fire had been put out, was that we had no ready-use ammo. left for anything. Sandy said it would take about half an hour to be ready again. By this time it was pretty late and I didn't think we could afford to wait half an hour. Actually, of course, it should have been possible to be ready in less than that.

"This is a part of the proceedings about which I am *not* very proud. We ought to have had another go. If there had been any guns to fire we would have gone in again at once, but with what I took to be an inevitable delay of half an hour, and with John Hodder's guns more or less finished, I decided to go home—

without even trying a depth charge. Rather a poor show. We had a long way to go and as it was, we were pretty late.

"During the last part of the action we were struggling on the bridge with coils of wire, as the aerial had been shot down. However we rigged a jury aerial and made a signal to Ball (615) to return to harbour, in case he should be hanging about waiting for us. The Germans switched on Cap d'Antifer light so as to give us a nice departure and we sped homeward. Our side were less thoughtful about navigation and gave us no R.D.F. [radar] position. Nor did they give us any information about 615, although they must have heard that we got no answer to our call —and should have realised that we should be anxious. She must have been on the Portsmouth Plot. But then Duty Commanders never did have much imagination.

"Since that party we had a rather bad do last week (night of 29th/30th April). We went to cover a minesweeping operation which was cancelled owing to the darkness of the night. We went on and did a sweep between Fecamp and St. Valery—four boats—S.G.B.6, M.G.B.s 608 (John Hodder), 614 (Peter Mason) and 615 (Dickie Ball).

"It began to blow up so I decided to start back in good time but we had not gone far when I lost sight of 608 astern. It was shocking weather—wind force six and rain—so I switched on my overtaking light. John was so taken aback by the bright light that he stopped, thinking that we had either stopped too, or dropped a flare over the side. I went on, reducing to twelve knots for a mile or so and then, supposing them to have had a breakdown I turned back (a mistake), reduced to ten and flashed all round ahead. Presently, I picked up 608 on the starboard bow and signalled to her. She passed on opposite course about 150 yards away and 614 (Peter Mason) astern of her and out on her starboard quarter passed very close. 615 (Dickie Ball) passed closer still—fifteen to twenty feet. All very hair raising. While this was happening there was a splintering crash astern and 614 took 608 amidships on the starboard side. 608 had been turning to starboard to follow me. 614 had been on her quarter because of the A.I.X. gear on her pom-pom which obscures the view ahead.

"This was 0438 and the position was twelve miles from St. Valery, i.e., in full view when dawn should break. 608 had a huge hole in her engine room and seemed to be sinking. 614 was hardly damaged. In the dark it was extremely hard to make contact with all the boats and it took ages to find 608, but eventually I got alongside and had her in tow by 0515 at seven knots but it was too ambitious in that swell, and after fifteen minutes it parted.

"I was in a desperate quandary about W/T silence. A signal pin-pointed by the enemy at that time would be bound to stir up trouble. The weather was bad for aircraft—low cloud and rain. On the other hand, if I made nothing and the weather cleared it would take ages longer to get air cover. This was the sort of decision which might well have been made by the spin of a coin, but when seventy men's lives may depend on it, there is real agony of mind.

"When we got 608 in tow again I finally decided on a signal and made it. Ten minutes later the tow parted again. By this time our towing pendant was in poor condition and I told Dickie Ball (615) to take over. It was now daylight and thank God the coast was hidden by rain. Dickie did a very good job. He got 608 in tow in a very short time and we had to accept a speed of four knots. However, the weather seemed so impossible for aircraft that we breathed more freely. Meanwhile, 608 got lower and lower in the water. 615 passed pumps and hose astern on heaving lines and generally displayed considerable initiative.

"We fell out one watch and I went down to the bunk in the charthouse for a few minutes but at 0730 I shot on to the bridge when R.D.F. reported aircraft bearing Red 120 and soon after I got up there a Ju. 88 came out of the cloud and circled to the west of us where the horizon had suddenly cleared. The clouds were still low and the Hun turned up into them. He came out of the cloud heading straight for us and the three-inch was told to open fire. The Ju. 88 crossed from port to starboard quarter and the three-inch gun was spoiled by the after depression rail. When they got back on to him he had turned steeply up towards the clouds and a moment later had disappeared. No shot was fired.

"The next two hours with visibility ten miles and cloud base about 1,000 feet were fairly nerve-racking—but nothing came of it. By 0930 the rain had come down again, and we could breathe freely once more. At 1100 two M.L.s joined us and at 1200 we got a signal to say fighter escort could now be expected, but this was cancelled at 1230.

"The sea got calmer in the afternoon and we got into thick fog off our own coast. They gave us a few plots and we found that our dead reckoning was only one and three-quarter miles

wrong since 2300 the night before, which considering the towing
and messing about we had done, was pretty good.

"Three miles off Newhaven 615's tow parted. We had
decided to let him finish the job, so he went alongside and took
608 in, berthing her, without assistance, at 1605. John Hodder's
ship's company had been at the pumps continuously for eleven
and a half hours. Really Ball's seamanship was excellent, but
apart from that it was all rather a black show.

"Principal causes of the collision were:
1. Darkness of night—very exceptionally dark.
2. 614 being on quarter instead of astern of 608, because of
   the special fitting on the gun which obscured the view
   dead ahead.
3. 614 altering to starboard, when she lost 608's stern light,
   instead of to port.
4. S.G.B.6 switching on the overtaking light in the first
   place.
5. 608 misunderstanding it.
6. S.B.G.6 going back to look for M.G.B.s.

Board of Enquiry is on Friday!"

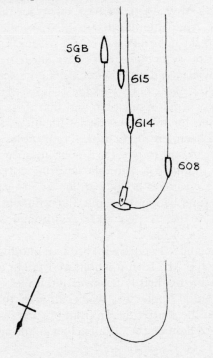

CHAPTER 20   *More Fumble*

FORTUNATELY the Board of Enquiry was kind about the collision. But even now, all these years later, I remember that morning because it brought me, I think, more acute anxiety than any other of the war. The Seine Bay battle brought, in due course, a D.S.C.

S.G.B.6 led Motor Torpedo Boats and Motor Gunboats to sea two or three nights a week usually without incident. When incidents arose they seemed to be equally divided between those caused by enemy intervention and those caused by some error on the part of our own side.

On the night of 5th May, 1943, we were escort for the six Fleet Minesweepers of the Ninth Flotilla during a large-scale sweep on a very dark night off the coast of Normandy—one S.G.B. and six 'B'-class M.L.s. At the conference before we started much had been said about six German destroyers at Le Havre. One Elbing-class, one Kondor-class and four 'T'-class. It appeared that the enemy might have got wind of our plan and that these destroyers might well be waiting for us. So, to deal with them, four Hunt Class destroyers had been lent by C.-in-C. Nore (*Fernie, Cattistock, Cottesmore* and *Quorn*) to add to two Portsmouth destroyers (*Bleasdale* and *Glaisdale*) to make a suitable covering force for our operation. In short, we were to be the bait for a destroyer engagement, at the same time as carrying out the valuable sweeping operation that was to cut a new passage through an enemy minefield.

The night was calm and very dark with brilliant phosphorescence so that the sweepers and M.L.s with whom we were in close company were chiefly visible by their bow waves and wakes.

From position Apples Apples we swept through the field to position Beer Beer on the south side. In front of each sweeper but the first bobbed the red light on the Oropesa float of the next ahead, kiting its cable and cutter out to one side. Each sweeper but the first steamed therefore in swept water and the escort followed in the swept water too.

A green lighted dan buoy was dropped to mark position Beer Beer and the whole force followed the leader round to starboard to sweep back to the northward again. One of the M.L.s had been detailed to retrieve the light from this dan buoy after the leader had passed and to sink the buoy itself. The first sweeper was to pass it fine to port so that its mooring rope would be cut by the sweep, but by mistake she left it to starboard. The buoy was still moored, and as there was a strong tide running it was obviously very much more difficult to get alongside than if it had been cut adrift and floating free.

S.G.B.6 brought up the rear and as we came to position B.B. we passed the M.L. struggling with the light. He had evidently failed to get alongside, as the light was still on the buoy and still 20 yards from the M.L.

The M.L. immediately ahead of us turned out of line and went over to help his friend, and about three minutes later at three-forty-eight a.m. a cluster of starshells burst overhead brightly illuminating the S.G.B., four of the M.L.s and the last two Mine-sweepers.

Up till that time I had not really believed much in the likelihood of a sortie by the German destroyers at Le Havre, but here they were. I had a vague feeling of annoyance that my appreciation had been wrong.

The two M.L.s collecting the buoy were a quarter of a mile astern and it was from astern that the starshells were being fired. The next two M.L.s hung back to wait for them, but our job was to protect the Minesweepers, not the M.L.s, who could quite well make their own smoke.

We did not start making smoke until the high explosive shells began to arrive, and at once they were unhealthily accurate. "Make smoke" was the order and clouds of white C.S.A. smoke belched from the stern whilst clouds of black fuel smoke belched from the funnel. And all the time the starshells hung overhead so that it was almost as bright as day.

We tried to fire starshell back but there was a slip-up in the drill. A new crew was the cause and although the fuses of the starshells in the ready-use lockers were already set, the crew were trying to fuse them and solemnly setting them to 'safe' by mistake. So the first four starshells failed to burst.

Meanwhile the enemy shells were falling all round. Spouting splashes rose up close astern, close to port, and very close to the last two of the line of Minesweepers. Nasty black bursts of shrapnel exploded close overhead with a spluttering crump.

One of these burst directly above and fragments clattered down on the upper deck. The wireless aerial fell in coils on to the bridge.

We turned to port to hide for a moment in our own smoke with the intention of bursting through it to deliver a torpedo attack. But the Minesweepers soon ran clear of our screen and the enemy were evidently gaining bearing on the starboard quarter. They were still a long way away but we could occasionally see them illuminated by their own gun flashes. We steered back to starboard to run up the starboard side of the sweepers with our smoke screen. The sweepers had cut their sweeps. We passed some of their floats, with the red lights glowing on them and we sped up their line leaving our white blanket astern to hide them. Far astern we saw tracers flying and occasionally some was directed at us.

For some strange reason the enemy seemed unwilling to close the range and presently his fire died away. The radar indicated that he was still on our starboard beam and we fired more starshell which lit this time but we saw nothing. It was dark again over us so we stopped the smoke waiting for the next attack.

Then came an ominous signal from the Senior Officer of the Destroyer Force. "Am engaging E-boats in position so-and-so" and the position he gave was within a mile of B.B.

E-boats! There was something wrong here—and in a flash I realised what must have happened. The Destroyers had taken the two M.L.s picking up the light from the dan buoy and the S.G.B. for E-boats. And we, not suspecting the possibility of the error, had made no attempt to identify ourselves.

So the action had lasted twenty-five minutes before any of us discovered that we were all on the same side.

We closed up on the Minesweepers and when dawn began to break we discovered that only two of the six M.L.s were in company. We called up M.S.9 and asked him if we should go and search for them or stay as anti-aircraft escort. He told us to stay. When it became broad daylight we saw the four missing M.L.s away to the eastward and presently they came trundling in to join up again.

So ended a sad fiasco. The passage had not been swept and had to be done again. Not only must the Germans have watched the battle with glee, but the jettisoned sweeps with their Oropesa floats and the dan buoy remained to mark the spot where we had been.

Fortunately no serious damage had been done to any of the ships though a shell had hit one of the Minesweepers and failed to explode. More fortunately still there had been no casualties at all. Paragraph 12 of my report read:

"It is submitted that the onus of identification did not rest with the escort force which was in company with the sweeping force within half a mile of position B.B. and within fifteen minutes of the time ordered, and that there was no reason to suppose the attacking force was anything other than the enemy destroyers about which information had been received."

Later on the day of the operation I met the Senior Officer of the Destroyer Force ashore, and he was full of the most abject apologies, which, of course, had to be accepted as gracefully as might be. But I was still of the opinion that we were playing at war in the Channel. Altogether too much fumble.

Ever since my appointment as Senior Officer S.G.B.s I had been trying to get names for the boats instead of numbers. I thought it would increase everyone's pride in his ship; so I made an approach to the Admiralty. I was advised to call upon a certain Lt.-Cdr. Walker, oddly enough in the Press Division, but apparently he was also secretary of the Naming Committee. At our first meeting he started off:

"Sorry, old boy, there's not a hope. You see we've got a length limit of 130 feet. We're simply not allowed to name any boats below that overall length." I let him go on.

"You see if we made any exceptions we'd be inundated and the postal problems would be impossible, so we've got to stick to our rule. I'm terribly sorry but I'm afraid that's it."

"Oh yes, of course," I said. "Obviously you must stick to your rules. Under 130 feet have to have numbers, above that can have names. That's it, isn't it?"

"Yes, that's it."

"Well, in that case," I said, "we ought to be all right. You see, the Steam Gunboats are 150 feet long."

It was, of course, not for many weeks that the final authority came through, but we were told that the Naming Committee would view sympathetically any names which we might propose. You could, after all, scarcely put it fairer than that. My working notebooks of that period are full of lists of possible names. A series of six was needed which were somehow linked together. I was keen to use bird names and immediately thought of geese. I particularly wanted my own boat to be called *Grey Goose*, after the first boat I had ever owned, the duck punt built to my own design in Cambridge. The others I thought could be *Snow Goose*, *Brent Goose*, *Blue Goose*, *Bean Goose* and *Kelp Goose*, with *Black Goose* as a spare. But on the whole the flotilla did not want to be geese. We tried other birds—waders like Sanderling, Dotterel, Whimbrel, Turnstone, or finches like Chaffinch, Bullfinch, Goldfinch, or ducks like Goldeneye, Garganey, Merganser, Harlequin. We tried butterflies like Swallowtail, Fritillary, Grayling, Tortoiseshell, Brimstone, and moths like Hawk Moth, Tiger Moth, Ghost Moth, Dagger Moth, Fox Moth and a series consisting of Goblin, Bogy, Demon, Spectre, Wraith, Ghost. We put all these to the vote in the flotilla, but only at the last moment did we hit on the suggestion which was finally selected. If I wanted my boat to be *Grey Goose*, why did we not use the word 'Grey' as the link? And so it was. The Admiralty insisted that the letters S.G.B. should officially be retained in the ships' titles. But this was a very minor limitation to what was, after all, a delightful gesture on the part of Their Lordships in allowing us to choose our own names. So my boat was S.G.B. *Grey Goose* while the others took the names that each had chosen. No. 3 was to be *Grey Seal*, No. 4 *Grey Fox*, No. 5 *Grey Owl*, No. 6 *Grey Shark* and No. 8 *Grey Wolf*.

My own *Grey Goose* had been delayed in the completion of her refit at Southampton by the other campaign I had been fighting for the Steamers—the increased armament. My notebooks are full of little plan diagrams of S.G.B.s in red ink showing every possible permutation and combination of guns which might turn the boats into really formidable warships. With the addition of the armour plate round the machinery spaces, it was clear that *Grey Goose*'s thirty-six knots on trials was a thing of the past. All that weight would pull down her speed drastically. While it was useful to have a high cruising speed in order to be able to make interceptions, the art of attack depended largely on the stealthy approach, and the speed at which it was possible to disengage after a battle was not so very important. What matter if you could only 'get the hell out of it' at twenty-six knots instead of thirty-six? It just meant that the enemy had a little longer to shoot at you. By comparison, it was surely vastly more important to give the boats some teeth so that while they *were* in contact with the enemy they could really make their presence felt. And so more and yet more guns were piled into the S.G.B.s, until they were more than a foot below their designed waterline.

At this stage of the war a very interesting psychological influence was making itself felt in the naval war of the North Sea and the English Channel. Air power was still the major limiting factor and almost all operations of surface forces were confined to the dark hours because of the vulnerability of ships to air attack. The German E-boats came across to our convoy routes under strict and very Teutonic orders. Their business was to fire torpedoes or to lay mines. If they were disturbed in their business they were to make a smoke-screen and run for it. Materially this was eminently sensible, for even superficial damage meant boats out of operations. Far best to keep clear of trouble and be ready to come again the next night.

The British Navy on the other hand cherished the spirit of its greatest sailor of the past. Was it not before the Battle of the Nile that Nelson had issued his famous directive, "No Captain can do very wrong if he lay his ship alongside that of an enemy"? One of the signals in our Coastal Forces signal book which had also been in Nelson's was "Engage the enemy more closely", and it had several times been used by our Gunboat leaders. As a result, in almost every encounter between our Coastal Forces and their German opposite numbers, we turned towards and the Germans turned away; we were the hounds and they were the hare. I do not for one instant believe that the young Germans who manned the E-boats and R-boats and Channel escort vessels were any less brave or determined than the boys in the British boats, but this curious directive which had been given to them gave to us, at the same time, an incontestable moral ascendancy in all our battles and must, I believe, have played a significant part in the eventual outcome

CHAPTER 21   *Dawn off Cherbourg*

THE refurbished *Grey Goose* was not finally ready for sea till mid-June 1943, and then we were sent off to H.M.S. *Bee* at Weymouth to get 'worked up' once more into a fighting team. On the staff there now was my friend Jock Ritchie, who had had to leave S.G.B.4 because of an old wound in his knee. His influence on the training programme was already apparent. A month later we were back at Newhaven to join up with four other Steam Gunboats. For the first time since I had taken over the flotilla a unit could be mustered for offensive operations which consisted exclusively of S.G.B.s. The patrols began again two or three nights a week, but there were only minor adventures, until on the early morning of 27th July we were involved in a fairly desperate battle. At this time we were trying to co-ordinate the night bombing efforts of the old Albacore biplanes with our own attacks, and the shore-based radar on the cliff tops of the Isle of Wight were able, on nights when conditions were good, to give us some details of the movements of enemy shipping though they were not always accurate and often incomplete. The Cherbourg Peninsula was just within their range but the Seine Bay was outside it. When they detected shipping the details were passed to us by C.-in-C. Portsmouth and were called 'Enemy plots'.

On this particular night we had left Newhaven five strong, and in order to understand the story a brief *dramatis personae* is necessary. As we steamed south across the Channel, I was leading in *Grey Goose*. I used always to try to sleep on the way over, so that until the next alteration of course my First Lieutenant, Jock Henderson—an indomitable Scot—was, no doubt, keeping watch. Immediately astern was *Grey Shark* with Howard Bradford now back again in command. His First Lieutenant was Sandy Bown who had served me so well during the brief weeks when I had been commanding

her, and had done such an outstanding job controlling the guns in
our Seine Bay battle. Astern of *Shark* came Grif in S.G.B.8, now
Grey Wolf, with an admirable First Lieutenant in Tim Langridge.
Then came *Grey Owl* with Richard Hall, and finally young Jimmy
Southcott, who had taken over S.G.B.3 from George Pennell; she
was now *Grey Seal* with Mike Barrett as First Lieutenant. This was
the proud force that set out to intercept an important merchant ship
which was expected to cross from Cherbourg to Le Havre during
the night. It was soon to be reduced by one when *Grey Owl*
developed a defective feed pump and I had to send her home. We
drew blank in the Seine Bay, but went after a patrol—which
turned out to be rather a strong one—just outside Cherbourg as
dawn was breaking. Here is the letter I wrote to Jock Ritchie a
fortnight afterwards:

"My dear Jock,
"I dare say you'd be interested to have the inside story of our
do. I already seem to have written about fifty pages on the subject,
but an action report—even with all its enclosures—is never more
than about half the story. The only good thing about the affair
was that we learnt an awful lot. If our experience can be used
then we shall have gained something, I suppose.
"To begin with, our patrol was designed to meet a merchant
ship and not to concern itself with the R-boat patrol off Cherbourg. However, since our co-operating Albacores had swept the
Baie de la Seine (we supposed) and found nothing, we decided
that we should make all speed for the enemy plot off Barfleur.
"Our Albacore boys had spent the whole of the afternoon
before with us—and that was their second visit to Newhaven.
We had made what we thought were fairly watertight plans for
identification; furthermore if they met the enemy they were to
illuminate after bombing. Somewhere about 0200 they did bomb
the R-boats off Cherbourg and illuminated them, but they were
round the corner from us and still about thirty miles off so that
we didn't see the flares. If we had it would have saved the twenty
minutes delay in getting the first enemy report out to us.
"Portsmouth gave us two enemy plots which were quite good
but the third and last one was phoney I think. Anyway it looked
like a right-angle alteration of enemy course from west to north.
We didn't get to the position until nearly an hour later but
received no more plots although I believe the enemy were being
plotted all the time. This resulted in our slowing down much

earlier than necessary and finally, after passing through the positions, stopping to discuss the situation. Grif came up to starboard. We were north of Cap Levi and if we were to go back the way we had been told to go (010° from Barfleur) we could not afford to go further west. On the other hand, the enemy was clearly still at sea, and probably heading for home. If we went westward after him, we could always go home to the north-west if we missed him, and we could go on hunting for another fifteen minutes. Grif said, 'I think it's hopeless now without another plot. I think we ought to call it a day.' I said, 'We'll go on towards Cherbourg for ten minutes anyway before we give up.' It was one hour and twenty minutes since the last plot had been received.

"By this time the moon—which was after the last quarter, not much more than a crescent—was well up and giving a little dim light, but not much. It was almost directly behind us. We cracked on again at twenty knots, course about 240° and a few minutes later, I suddenly heard four explosions astern. I had seen no flashes but nevertheless assumed it must be shore batteries as we were about four miles off Cap Levi where we knew there was a radar battery. So I immediately altered course to about 330° to open the range. Actually it was an Albacore which had straddled Jimmy, who was tail-arse Charlie, but I did not dis-cover this until we got home. The Albacore was from Exeter, and not one of our friends from Tangmere. It had been allowed by its controller to come as far east as Cherbourg and thought it was off Alderney. Actually, it was due north of Cap Levi, four and a half miles. Two bombs fell neatly to port and two to star-board of poor Jimmy and a burst of tracer passed across his bridge.

"As I steadied on the new course I got a radar contact at Red 80 [this means 80° on the port bow—that is to say, almost on the beam] 3,500 yards two or three small echoes. So we immediately came back to port to bring them ahead. I asked Ian what the time was and he told me 0355 to which I am alleged to have replied 'We've just got time for a quarter of an hour's fun and games.' It was within five minutes of the last possible time I reckoned we could stay with safety from air attack on the way home.

"*Note:* the *correct* thing to have done from the point of view of the war effort and material would have been to have turned north at once and returned to Newhaven. From a morale point of view it would no doubt have done harm and I expect I should have been court-martialled, but I am sure it would have been a most sound and sensible thing to do—as we knew we had only fifteen minutes and we knew that a good attack takes an hour at least. We also knew that the patrol was a strong one and that it would be there another night. So it would have been right to wait until conditions suited *us*. However we didn't.

"We didn't know exactly how close to the shore we were. I thought the shore batteries were already firing and I did not fancy being hemmed in by a strong force and so when I saw the Huns ahead I turned slightly to starboard so as to engage them on the port side firing to southward. A turn to port to go inside them would almost certainly have been better as it turned out.

"There seemed to be no end to the Germans. They looked like a flock of wigeon with two or three geese amongst them. The sea was so glassy that you could see the reflections of stars. The moon was nearly behind us—slightly on the port quarter. Also behind us was a faint north-east glow of the dawn. The geese were on the left—two or three trawlers—and the wigeon were sitting still apparently, and all clustered together. Being a punt gunner I aimed for the thickest part of them—not, of course, a very good idea unless I was going to use my 'punt gun' (torpedoes) which I wasn't. Actually, of course, I should have, as it was a good chance of a flock shot—if they had been set to three feet. About three or four of them in the middle were quite solid. In fact at first I thought there was a longer target there—but there wasn't. There were far too many Huns to count—at least eleven.

"At about 500 yards the radar reported: 'Echoes lost in the ground wave, sir.' One of the R-boats challenged with quite a dim blue light—I'm afraid I couldn't read the letter—?R, ?F. We came to the trawlers first and I let them go past so that the other boats would have something to shoot at when we opened up. I think the line was a bit longer than it should have been just then. (The order was Howard, Grif, Jimmy.) *Closer station keeping*.

"When it is very calm it is hard to judge range but we were certainly not more than 300 yards and possibly a good bit less when I said 'Open fire.' Then a tragedy took place. The port point-five gunner lost his head and fired his guns without aiming, about twenty degrees into the air. This was blinding to the other guns and from that moment all hell was let loose."

Here I must break into the narrative to give some idea of what the scene looked like. I hardly needed to describe it to Jock, for he had seen this kind of thing more often than I had. But assuredly of all the actions I fought in the Coastal Forces, this one produced the greatest volume of tracer shells and bullets. At least fifteen ships had opened fire simultaneously and the air was thick with the red and green and white streaks. They ripped away from our guns towards the enemy line, they fanned out of the enemy ships and came lobbing towards us almost as though you could reach out and catch them, until they whipped past just over our heads singing as they went; they criss-crossed ahead and astern, they ricocheted off the water and popped as they exploded in the air, and they thumped into us from time to time with a shower of sparks. It would all have been very beautiful as a spectacle if it had not been so dreadfully frightening. But for me, thank goodness, there was no time at this stage to be frightened. The letter goes on:

"I'm afraid the Albacores' bombs—only 4,000 yards away—had fully aroused the Germans and every gun must have been trained on us. I suppose they were blinded by tracer too, because considering how close we all were to each other it is odd that more damage was not done on both sides.

"The Germans must have got under way fairly quickly because by the light of sudden flashes which I took to be hits—but which may have been gun flashes (I think they were hits though)—I could see the R-boats creaming along on a parallel course about 300 yards away. At this stage it would have been nice to have had some starshell. Our three-inch had been doing very well and I saw three hits with it, which caused big showers of sparks. It would have been quite impossible to convey any speech to the guns—the only way would have been to check fire altogether and I was not keen on doing that. So we had no starshell. As a matter of fact, I don't think I thought of it myself till afterwards. In any case far too many R-boats seemed to be shooting at us and my gunners were not firing at more than two of them at most. I looked back and could not see any S.G.B.s following. In truth I could see very little at all as the tracer was completely blinding.

"I remember seeing the leading R-boat on our beam and shooting at us and thinking, 'Thank God there aren't any more to pass.' We had passed at least six overtaking at about five knots, and they had done us a bit of no good. We were burning a bit aft—with a lot of smoke; and a scare report came to the bridge. 'All the three-inch guns crew killed, and we are heavily on fire.' We kept on a steady course still because three guns were still firing quite well, it seemed. The fire aft died down, but then suddenly flared up very bright again and all the Huns started shooting at us so I decided to disengage. A long way astern and on the starboard quarter I could see two S.G.B.s flashing on their recognition display signals (two green). As I turned away more and more ships seemed to be shooting at us, some from the starboard quarter and fancying that this must be the S.G.B.s I switched on my display, too. It lasted about ten seconds and then—pink—and out it went, shot out by Grif or Jimmy or both. However, they only got two pom-pom hits on us. We found the fuses afterwards and neither of those did any damage to speak of —one went into the mess deck and one through a splinter mat and into X gun ready-use locker where it spoilt some pom-pom ammo. but didn't explode it. I found afterwards that my starboard sided guns had fired about 200 rounds back. Shame on us!

"Jock Henderson who was wounded and Able Seaman Wendon and Stoker Clelland put the fire out very quickly with a hail of bullets whistling round their ears. It was a three-inch ready-use locker full of starshell which had gone up.

"Also an entire ready-use locker full of Z guns and pom-pom ammo. had vanished in one 'pooff' and left the locker looking like a tulip.

"I reduced to ten knots as soon as the worst of it was over in order to let the others catch up. From time to time some hopeful German would direct a burst at us and they would come lobbing towards us. I planned to go to the standard rendezvous two miles north of the action so that we could reform and see if we could go in again.

"As I looked back I saw a line of all three S.G.B.s in the light of some starshell which the Hun had just put up.

"I watched them go in to attack and suddenly saw one ship get the most terrible pounding. I hoped it was one of them but I feared it was one of the Steamers because it was very near where I had seen them in the starshell. For about twenty seconds shells were bursting and sparkling all over it. The battle roared on very fiercely and then rather suddenly ceased. There was a pause of a couple of minutes and then the distress signal—a short burst of tracer going vertically upwards directly astern of us. I said to the Coxswain, 'Starboard thirty—steady on south', and my heart sank into my boots!"

CHAPTER 22   *Meanwhile*

"NOW to go back to the others . . . The action had begun at
0357 and early on *Grey Shark*'s steering had gone. If you remember
it went in a previous action in a rather unexplained manner as
the pipes were found to be slightly dished by a shell which was
believed to have hit in the second phase of the action, *after* the
steering failure. Again, although the pipes were well and truly
shot away this time, there is some reason to believe that they
were not shot away until after the failure. The mystery is still
unsolved, but still being investigated. Anyway the effect was that,
before it was definitely established that the steering had gone and
the wheel could be changed from power to hand steering the
ship had turned nearly ninety degrees to starboard and contact
with the leader had been lost. Grif did not know whether to
follow Howard or not, as he couldn't see me—indeed he couldn't
see anything much and nor could anyone else, so completely
blinding was the tracer. So the line was broken and for a bit
Grif and Jimmy took on principally the trawlers whilst I was
taking on the best part of the line of R-boats up front.

"But as soon as Howard's steering was fixed up he saw me
burning brightly and decided that I must be in a very poor way
and must be protected from the rough Germans. So without a
thought he plunged into the mêlée between me and the R-boats
announcing to Sandy his intention to ram. He missed, unfortunately (?), and passed about twenty-five yards from four of
them, getting a horrible pasting as I had seen. He managed,
however, to give a pretty fair return, I gather, and saw a lot of
hits on the enemy. They also (Sandy and some of the guns'
crews) saw two men in the water clinging to some wreckage. They
wondered if they could be chaps blown overboard or washed off
us (as they quite thought that we had sunk by now—and so did

the Germans according to their communiqués). They also say they saw a ship very low in the water which looked as though it was sinking.

"At that very close range some of the enemy's armour-piercing shells were bound to go through; in fact seven entered the boiler and with a hiss poor *Grey Shark* came to a standstill. The boiler room crew escaped unhurt either by the shells or the escaping steam, which is quite remarkable.

"Grif was too blinded by the tracer and starshell even to observe that Howard had been stopped. All he knew was that he couldn't see the next ahead and that he was being shot at by ships at Red 30 and Red 130 and at every ten degrees in between. He could still see me burning on his starboard side and decided to follow round to starboard. His bridge had been hit, his First Lieutenant and navigator and coxswain all slightly wounded and he was at the wheel and coming round to north. The coxswain had been cracked on the head by a large piece of perspex windscreen dislodged by a two-pounder shell on the bridge armour. He picked himself up from the deck and took the wheel again and went a little past the course, altering back to port.

"Meanwhile Jimmy had seen Howard buy it. He stood on for a few seconds and then said to himself 'Oi, you can't leave old Howard there' and turned back hard-a-starboard.

"Half-way round his turn he suddenly saw Grif on his starboard bow and as Grif altered back to port he suddenly saw Jimmy. There was nothing to be done. They both went full astern but they hit pretty hard. Grif's forward mess deck was holed very badly—a hole about fifteen feet wide at the upper deck and going down to a point about three feet below the waterline. Fortunately the bulkhead between that and the old officers' space was undamaged, and so although he thought at first he was going to sink, he was in fact quite well able to keep the damage under control.

"All those things had happened pretty quickly while we had been putting out our four fires (two forward and two aft)—and before Sandy had pointed his bridge Vickers guns into the air and fired a burst to summon assistance. We turned at once and steered south towards the distress signal and then in the binoculars I saw *four* ships lying more or less stopped, and a dozen possibilities went through my mind. Were they all Huns? Were three of them Huns mustered round the damaged S.G.B.? The fire parties went back to their guns—but I must confess I wondered how many of them would still fire all right. Only two of the three-inch guns crews had been laid out. I was a bit worried too because our recognition display had been shot away (as well as our W/T and radar aerials). Identity was the key to this situation and the best and quickest method was not available to us.

"Certainly one of the four was an R-boat—he came more or less straight towards us. The others were directly behind him— and which were they? The next one looked all wrong. Surely another German. Actually it was Grif down by the head after the collision, about which of course I knew nothing.

"Now came a regrettable moment. The first boat had been identified as an R-boat. It looked exactly like the photograph we have in our intelligence room. It altered course to starboard and passed close down our port side. It should have been blown out of the water. But it wasn't. Ever since I have been wondering just *why* it wasn't. The answer is a combination of reasons I suppose. I was still not sure that two more R-boats were not trying to board the damaged S.G.B.; I did not know exactly where the remainder of the enemy were, but I did know from the distress signal that one S.G.B. was fairly certainly going to have to be towed. It was getting light pretty fast and any inter- ruption of the towing would probably spell disaster. A fresh battle would produce shore starshell and the towing operation would be detected. If the enemy knew what was afoot we should never be allowed to pull away our lame duckling. The other S.G.B.s (with commendable loyalty!) stoutly maintain that the issue was a straight swop and that my decision was right. No doubt the R-boat in question is also quite happy about my decision. I am pretty well satisfied it was wrong, but I didn't have awfully long to make it in, and you know I'm mostly pretty slow about things.

"By the time I had identified the other three boats as S.G.B.s the R-boat was too far past us to make it worth starting anything. One of the S.G.B.s got under way. I made 'Follow' to him by light, but although he gave an R for it, Grif didn't receive the signal and in any case he was best out of it. I, of course, did not know how badly damaged he was, until a little later when he made a W/T signal saying he was disengaging.

"It appears that the R-boat had closed Jimmy whilst he was trying to get Howard in tow and started flashing, and Jimmy replied with E.B. ('Wait' in German signal procedure) and the

Starshell and tracer. Steam gun-boats in action, 1943.

R-boat had waited. Actually of course the R-boat must have had a nasty shock finding himself so close to the enemy and must have been very glad of the opportunity to creep away. During this time *Shark* saw and heard a German shouting in the water about fifty yards away.

"As soon as Grif had gone off I circled round the other two. I watched the R-boat circling to the north of us, and following round to the west with binoculars came suddenly upon a whole bunch of them, seven at least. The wretched things were clustered in the darkest part of the horizon whilst we were completely silhouetted against quite a bright dawn, and what was more, it rapidly became apparent that they were closing in at slow speed. And still the two S.G.B.s lay stopped. I could distinguish, now, which was 'tower' and which was 'towee' and suddenly I saw the 'towee' start to pivot round: the strain was on the tow, they were under way.

"By this time the enemy were less than 1,000 yards away and the obvious course was to lay smoke to cover the tow. I increased speed and started to make smoke and immediately the Hun saw what was happening and opened fire. However, I had already passed between them and the tow and the smoke had hidden it perfectly. The R-boats' fire was very poor and our B gun, which had had a stoppage in the first action was in particularly good form. This was Hitch's pom-pom gunner and he was firing in short but admirable bursts. We saw quite a number of hits on the second R-boat. *Seal* and *Shark* saw the glow of it through the smoke. The first R-boat turned towards and I expected him to come through the smoke after us but the second one turned away and the others seemed to follow. Some starshells were fired and several big splashes appeared about fifty yards away, either from the trawlers or from the shore batteries, probably the trawlers.

"Meanwhile the tow had whacked it up to about ten knots and Jimmy, with most excellent judgment, refused to attempt anything faster, realising that if the tow parted all would be up. We dropped astern of them again so as to be able to repeat the smoke run, and we did in fact make another puff of it for good measure. A few minutes later we ran into what we took to be a fog. Actually it was some smoke which Grif had made ten minutes earlier with the object of providing cover for us. 'Do you think it might come in useful to them?' he had said to the wounded Tim, who had just completed a big shoring-up job. And so the smoke had been made. I had been looking astern for

Q

signs of a pursuing enemy and when I looked round both *Seal* and *Shark* had disappeared. The sea was so calm that the smoke was completely invisible, and as we were still in the clear I could not for a moment imagine what had happened to the two ships which had been about half a cable away only a few seconds before. I asked the starboard gunners if they had sunk, but they seemed to think they hadn't and suggested fog, and then we ran into it too. In the middle of it we passed only five yards under *Grey Shark*'s stern. Very hair raising. After that we ran through several patches of real mist—so much so that I began to feel more sanguine about the risk of air attack.

"By now it was broad daylight—I did not think the enemy ships would dare to follow long because of our air support which they would expect. We had a message by light from Sandy saying he was the only unwounded officer in *Shark*. Portsmouth made us signals about some destroyers which were coming to meet us and eventually we met the *Stevenstone* and soon after the *Bleasdale* with Grif in company.

"We all stopped and, while *Seal* remained attached to *Shark*, I went alongside *Shark* and shunted her backwards alongside *Stevenstone* so that their casualties could be transferred—and ours also. This took about half an hour or more, in a position about half-way between St. Catherine's Head and Barfleur.

"Howard, though quite seriously wounded in the leg, was still hopping about on his bridge. Johnny Harris, his navigator, was pretty bad, with a compound fracture of the thigh, and is only just off the danger list now. His Midshipman (Tomkinson) died on the way back in *Stevenstone* and so did another of his chaps. Our Bill Williams-Ellis was badly wounded in both legs, but he's getting on all right now.

"Howard's coxswain—himself badly wounded, amputated another man's leg (with a razor blade) in an attempt to save his life, but it was no good. The coxswain went on working till they got back when he collapsed.

"Grif had already transferred his wounded to *Bleasdale*. One—the Captain of the three-inch gun—had had his leg severed by a shell bursting on it. Supporting himself on the gun he had taken over breech worker and gone on firing the gun for six minutes until the action finished when he collapsed and died soon after—three others of Grif's crew were killed.

"While *Shark*'s wounded were being transferred we went off about half a mile and tested our guns—all firing at once. This was a very good idea as we felt ready to tackle any F.-W. 190s that might turn up and the noise put heart into everyone.

"There were seven killed and over thirty wounded and many of those thirty kept going, some of them for nine hours or so—till their ships were back in harbour—Howard did—and Tim Langridge—and my leading seaman and Howard's coxswain. Jock Henderson with a bullet in the back of his neck and blood pouring all over him, dashed about the place unceasingly. Once on the way home I looked up and saw him at the top of the mast in a bosun's chair trying to repair the radar aerial! At last his enthusiasm came to grief when we were detached to return at twenty-five knots and he set out to rig a bottom line. The chain carried away and wrapped itself round the screw and, presto! we were a docking job.

"The whole do lasted only thirty-six minutes, but I reckon quite a variety of things took place in that time. There were a lot of opportunities for exceptional resource and initiative and courage and there were a lot of chaps who were not slow in taking them.

"Jimmy's towing was the star turn—and Howard's headlong plunge.

"The results? A lot learnt—some good experience, a few Germans killed, a few holes in some R-boats—and four S.G.B.s out of action for periods varying between seven days and six weeks, with seven of their gallant men gone for good.

"It appears that two R-boats had to go into dry dock and two more were not used after they had returned under their own power to Ouistreham. There is no indication about the trawlers. So far as is known nothing was sunk. One interesting thing is that according to the radar plot after disengaging at about 0436 the R-boats went back to Cherbourg, but just before entering one apparently turned back to the scene of the battle—possibly to look for the men seen by *Shark* in the water.

"And the merchant ship we had been after moved from Cherbourg to Havre about five nights later!

"The Germans say that two 'M.T.B.s' were sunk. They say there were five of us and that one was set on fire and was seen to sink. Later during what they call a second patrol only three British boats were seen indicating that another had sunk. Very little return fire was encountered and they were able to close in without much danger to themselves. 'Piles of dead and wounded were observed on the decks of the British boats.'

"Well, there's the tale. Another battle spoilt by bull-in-a-china-shop methods, but they were rather forced upon us by the time of day.

"I would very much like to hear any comments you may think of. We have worked out a long list of lessons learnt. Some are fairly controversial, but we put them in so as to make people think. You will be getting a copy at *Bee* in due course, I expect.

"Love to Phyllis and Jean.

"Yours ever,

Peter."

After that action I had two special worries. The first, which I could never quite escape in any battles where there were casualties, was the degree of my own responsibility for the deaths and injuries of my chaps. Perhaps if I had been more skilful, if I had turned to port instead of to starboard at the beginning and had thereby got the advantage of the breaking dawn, perhaps if I had thought of using torpedoes at the outset and approached more slowly, perhaps if I had *recognised* that this was a sort of ambush we had fallen into and needed special cunning to turn to our advantage—so many perhapses. It was easy enough to talk about not making omelettes without breaking eggs, but what sort of an omelette had we made anyway?

And then, at the other end of the scale, was that wretched R-boat that got away. Down the years I have lain awake at nights and thought about it. Was it really just plain cowardice that prevented me from saying those two words "Open fire"? Like a film editor I find myself winding back the film and starting it again at that moment when the R-boat detached itself from the other three. Clearly it had not seen us at all. It was heading almost directly towards us, so as to pass down our port side at no more than fifty yards range. All guns were given the bearing to train round on to. If they had all been on the top line and ready to fire, I should think it must all have been over in ten to fifteen seconds with the R-boat a shambles in front of us and no one left alive on the upper deck. But *were* all the guns on the top line? How many would have fired when I gave the order? Perhaps less than half of them. And then what about the three ships ahead, at least one of which looked like another R-boat? Perhaps two of them were at this moment trying to board and capture the disabled S.G.B. These were my friends who had made the distress signal and who counted on me to come to their rescue. There were still long seconds before the R-boat would be past, still long seconds in which to make my decision—my decision to say just two words. I was looking most of the time through binoculars at the dark shapes ahead, trying to identify them, and glancing occasionally at the R-boat. I was waiting for a report from the three-inch gun that it was 'on target' and ready to fire—a report which never came. Of course at that range neither ship could easily miss and certainly the R-boat's guns were trained on us. He may not at first have identified us, but as we drew level he must have known for certain that we were his enemy. Yet he did not open fire. Obviously he would not, for on the face of it we were the more powerful ship—larger and with heavier armament. If we didn't start anything, certainly he would not. But of course if we did, so would he. No doubt we should get a pasting if as I feared we could not muster the fire-power to smother him in the first few seconds. Try as I will I cannot remember consciously thinking of this argument at all, but how large did it loom in my subconscious and influence the other thoughts that raced through my mind? Now the R-boat was exactly abeam passing on an opposite course, the ideal moment to open fire—one tremendous shattering burst from all our guns and the job would be done. But what about the ships ahead? What about my friends in distress? I put up the glasses once more to look at them; two of the ships were certainly S.G.B.s, even the third, odd though she looked, must be an S.G.B. too. Now I must open fire of course. I turned back to the R-boat, which was on the quarter now—the best opportunity was past. A pity to start anything now that the best chance had gone. Better get on with the rescue of the damaged S.G.B. which must be got in tow unmolested.

Paragraph 10 of the C.-in-C. Portmouth's covering letter says:

"The Senior Officer, when he turned back to the distress signals of *Grey Shark* was faced with a difficult decision when he found himself passing close to an enemy vessel. He could have done no wrong in engaging, and such would have traditionally been the correct course of action, but he was summoned by a consort in distress, and this might have made the difference between her loss or safety. As the battle eventuated, had *Grey Goose* been delayed, diverted or damaged by this potential encounter, she would not have been able to screen the damaged vessels at the critical moment.

"11. The taking in tow of *Grey Shark* by *Grey Seal* in four minutes under fire shows a high degree of seamanship and training.

"12. The action of the Senior Officer in laying a smoke-screen between the concentrating enemy and the tow, and drawing the fire on himself, was a well judged and gallant action which met with the success that it deserved."

Soon after this battle I was awarded a bar to my D.S.C. But I still lie awake at night sometimes and wonder.

CHAPTER 23   *The Seven Minesweepers*

IT was not long before enough S.G.B.s were available again to form
a striking force. *Grey Fox* had been the last to complete her face-
lifting refit, and now that Jock Ritchie had gone to H.M.S. *Bee*,
her new Commanding Officer was Peter Mason (whose M.G.B.
had collided with John Hodder on that wild morning off St. Valery).
I was particularly glad to have him in the flotilla, for he had shown
a complete understanding of the kind of fighting tactics in which I
believed. Although most of our operations were in the broader
parts of the Channel opposite Newhaven and Portsmouth, occasionally we were lent to the Vice-Admiral Dover for operations in
the Straits. One great advantage here was that enemy shipping
passing through at night was much more certainly and accurately
plotted by the shore-based radar than it was further down. Furthermore we were only moved up to Dover if some kind of a 'party' was
expected, and so the summons was always rather welcome. Those
were the days when from time to time the great guns would
exchange shots across the Straits, and one could imagine oneself
steaming up like a wedding procession through the archway of
their whistling shells.

My recollection is that we had been at Dover for several days
waiting for some important torpedo target which was expected
nightly, but that nothing happened till the night of 4th September,
1943. Four of us were out that night, *Goose*, *Fox*, *Seal* and *Owl*, and
I remember that a strange and rather puzzling explosion took place
just after dark. An unidentified aircraft had been heard passing
low across our bows and then two minutes later came this very
heavy explosion. We saw the flash and the waterspout and, as we
steamed past the place, we smelt strong explosion fumes. But we
never knew whether it had been meant for us.

Soon after nine p.m. an enemy force left Boulogne and began

to steam southward rather fast along the coast. The radar plotted their movements and Dover reported them to us. With my ear to the voice pipe on the bridge I could hear the high-pitched Morse messages being received down in the wireless office. The signals were passed up to the chart table on the bridge where the Navigating Officer—a new and very young navigator who had only just joined the ship—was working away feverishly with roller-ruler and dividers, plotting the enemy's course and speed and laying off a course to intercept. Unfortunately he made a small but vital mistake, so that we did not aim far enough ahead of the German ships. The sea was exceptionally phosphorescent that night and the speed necessary to make a successful approach, now that the error had been corrected, was obviously going to produce a brightly luminous bow wave and wake. Time and the phosphorescence were against us; and so it was that while trying to move up into an attacking position, but still a mile and a half from the enemy I heard the sound of distant gunfire.

"Damn and blast," I said, "that'll be starshell"; and a moment later, hopelessly, "It is!"

Suddenly a brilliant light burst overhead, and then another and another. We were bathed in a dazzling white glare while the starshells floated lazily down on their parachutes. Tracers and the heavy shells followed, streams of green and white shimmering out across the calm sea and great shell splashes spouting up all round. The tracer seemed to be a barrage, for it criss-crossed about in a tangled network of flying sparks. Very little of it came directly towards us. Nevertheless the tactics had to be changed, and as the German force hurried down the coast we yapped round its heels like terriers waiting for a chance to bite. Once we passed through the enemy's wake in order to try to gain bearing for an attack on the landward side in the mouth of the River Somme. There was a strong smell of smoke as we passed astern, and we pitched and rolled for a moment as we met the waves thrown up by the enemy formation. Three times we closed in to attack, but each time the starshells went up, followed by cascades of tracer and the leaping waterspouts of heavy shells. Once a single white flare went up far away over the coast, and by its light the enemy force was perfectly silhouetted— seven 'M'-class Minesweepers in line ahead.

"Two of the middle ones," I wrote a few days after the action, "were old-type sweepers with tall, thin Woodbine funnels, the others seemed to be of the squat-funnelled kind. They were all smoking like hell and obviously legging it as fast as ever they could go.

"Seven 'M'-class Minesweepers—solid great ships of 600 or 700 tons with four-point-one-inch guns and a large number of automatic weapons—were fairly formidable opposition for four S.G.B.s, but the night was still young and we decided to keep on trying.

"Next time their starshell went up when we were still 3,500 yards away, and the high explosive arrived shortly after, but we soldiered on in at twenty knots. I remember looking astern and seeing the rest of the force snaking after us among the tall pillars of the shell splashes. All round it was as bright as day, or brighter, and it was an extraordinarily beautiful spectacle. The sea was a brilliant unreal green under the starshells; some of them burned through their parachute strings and fell into the water, where they went on burning as they sank, with a wonderful luminous greenish glow. Above, the sky was full of curling question-marks of smoke left by the flares as they floated down. I thought one flare was going to land on the fo'c'sle, but it fell just clear ahead. There were still torrents of tracer trickling and streaming away from the enemy ships, and our boats were occasionally hit. The Huns were using a multiple twenty-millimetre gun, which put down a strip of bursts in the water that would have been most unhealthy to be in. There were also some bursts of self-destroying stuff which exploded in a neat little row in the sky.

"We fired back very little at this stage, for it would have been wasted in the dazzle, and we were concentrating on the torpedo attack, but it soon became apparent that that was not going to be possible. Four-inch shells were arriving thick and fast and getting rather accurate. I saw the next astern spattered by a near miss. Another fell directly ahead of us and many whistled narrowly over. I had another look with the glasses. Was there a hope of seeing the target and firing torpedoes? My impression was no, so we turned away in order to try another plan. The four-inch followed us out to about 5,000 yards, and I don't quite know why none of us got a direct hit, considering the average accuracy. At last the starshell stopped and there was a sudden darkness— the after-dazzle darkness which seems darker than the night.

"New tactics were necessary; we planned this time to get well ahead and then lie in wait, so we set off to get into position. On the way we ran full-tilt into a new German patrol which was lying to seaward of the convoy route. We tried to slip past

Q*

unobserved so as to continue our efforts to torpedo the Mine-sweepers, but at less than a mile it was impossible, and the new enemy, who must have been watching the fireworks for some time, now joined in the battle. At once starshell came up again and immediately after it the streams of tracer.

"Here was a sudden opportunity, and I decided to take it. We were already close to some enemy ships, and it seemed we had a better chance of doing them down than we had of getting at the Minesweepers. I came hard round to port and opened fire, and again the tracers began to buzz about like purposeful red bumble-bees, the smaller machine guns burst forth in tinselly white and yellow showers like Golden Rain, and all the while the scene was lit by the bright white starshells hanging overhead.

"As we closed in to 500 yards and came round in an arc, we seemed all to be firing at the centre. I have never seen nicer shooting—there was nothing wild about it, just deliberate bursts ploughing straight into the targets. We took the right-hand one, and in a matter of seconds the stream of tracer from him had dwindled to nothing.

"Peter Mason, who was next astern in *Grey Fox*, was putting up some prettily placed starshell, and by its light Jimmy Southcott, who was following in *Grey Seal*, picked out a Hun going from left to right. With amazing quickness he turned out of line, reduced speed and fired torpedoes, one of which apparently hit. I didn't see the explosion myself, but all the other boats did. Meanwhile the enemy we were engaging was firing only spasmodically but still steaming fast, and we were converging on him and fairly raking him with everything we had. Clouds of smoke were coming out of him, and a fine red glow showed under the bridge aft, apparently through a hole in the ship's side. He was about 150 yards away. If only we could illuminate him our fire would be twice as effective, but we had run out of starshell. I shouted for the searchlight, and Dearing, my leading signalman, jumped up to man it. But, before he could switch on, a twenty-millimetre shell had mown him down. He was badly wounded in both legs. As usual, the wireless aerial fell in coils all round us on the bridge, the result of a hit on the mast.

"We were overtaking the enemy, and I got a good view of him by the light of someone else's starshell. He was one of the con-verted landing-craft type known to the enemy as an A.F. boat and to us as a T.L.C., type III. The sloping bow and stern and the little high bridge after were very distinct. When he had fallen just abaft the beam he suddenly got one of his eighty-eight millimetre guns going and clocked us a couple of times in quick succession. They made a terrific 'bonk'. I felt sure the first one had got the engines and was not surprised to feel the ship lose speed. It was a very curious feeling. I knew for certain that these two hits were eighty-eight millimetre shells, for they pushed the ship over quite a lot when they hit. I remember thinking that if he hit us a couple more times he would finish us; and then miraculously we were still going—and not only that but increasing speed again and turning away to starboard. It seemed almost too good to be true.

"'Midships, and steady as you go,' I cried hopefully. But no, we turned to starboard and to starboard, and I realised that the steering had been shot away. In a few moments we should be heading straight back towards the Hun.

"'Stop both.'

"'Telegraph's shot way, sir.'

"I pressed the engine-room bell, but all the lighting and electrical circuits had gone. The seaman torpedoman popped up beside me, 'Port tube badly holed, sir.' We did not realise in the din of the battle that a direct hit on the firing mechanism had actually fired the torpedo without our knowing it. By the time a messenger could get to the engine room it would be far too late to stop the ship before she had completed her circle and was back in action again.

"Many of the guns' crews had been hit (for we had been under fire on and off for two hours) and one gun was jammed, but we would have to tackle the Hun with what we had—including the starboard torpedo; not a very good chance perhaps for a torpedo attack with the rudder jammed hard-a-starboard, but it seemed likely to be the only chance.

"During our turn away both Peter and Jimmy had gone past making a smoke-screen and, so far, the enemy was invisible, but a few moments later we were through the smoke and there was a Hun. I set seven knots for his speed on the sight, and as we swung on I pulled the starboard firing lever and yelled 'Fire Sugar.' The lever came back freely in my hand. The connections had been shot away, but a couple of seconds later the torpedo went off, fired from the tube. I could see by then that the slight delay would be enough to make it miss ahead as the ship was still swinging to starboard. The fish jumped once and then went away straight, and it passed well across the bows of the enemy, making a bright phosphorescent wake as it went. The range on firing was about 400 yards and we closed to about 250 in turning, engaging with all guns that were still working. If it was the same Hun as before, he had put out the fire in between whiles, but I think it may have been a different one. He scarcely fired back at all, and continuing our willy-nilly turn to starboard, we plunged back into the smoke again.

"At last we had established a sort of 'bush telegraph' between bridge and engine room and had stopped engines. This seemed the only way to end our mad gyrations. The Chief (Chief Engine Room Artificer W. Bird) got the rudders amidships and reported to the bridge that although there were two gaping holes in the engine room he thought he could keep the ship going, but we should have to steer by main engines.

"It was evident that we were in no case to undertake any more fighting, so we came round to northish and rigged a jury wireless aerial to find out how the others had got on. At first we could not get through to them and we were rather anxious, but later we found that Jimmy in *Grey Seal* and Richard in *Grey Owl* were all right, although, in disengaging, they had been illuminated by what appeared to be a third enemy force to the westward. As we went we had the greatest difficulty in keeping the rudders amidships. From time to time they worked over until the ship was circling again, and for a while we progressed in a series of loops.

"Sometime later we had a quick brush with some E/R boats which appeared on our starboard beam. We couldn't do much about it, as we couldn't steer to pursue them, and the problem of identity was rather acute, as Jimmy and Richard had just joined up with us. The E-boats crossed astern of us and were lost almost at once. They were the fourth enemy force we had encountered that night.

"On joining up Jimmy had signalled with a blue light 'My fish hit', which was the first we knew of his torpedo attack, and splendid news it was. But we had also received a signal from Peter Mason which was too weak to read. We could only make out a part of it, but that said, '. . . require assistance', and we were immediately in a ferment of anxiety. I planned to send Jimmy or Richard back to look for him, but before doing so we asked for a repetition of the signal from Dover. When they answered I went down to the wireless office and we decoded it feverishly, 'My position . . .' and we knew that it ended '. . . require assistance'. The position followed, and there was one more group before

'require assistance'; it was sure to be 'disabled' or 'broken down'
—it was neither—it was simply 'interrogative require assistance'.
I have seldom felt a more delightful glow of relief.

"Towards dawn the wind began to rise, but in spite of the two
big holes and the many small ones in our ship's side, the engine-
room crew managed to keep the ship going under her own steam.
The work of improvisation that they did down there in the
darkness and the heat (for the fan circuits had been shot away)
was beyond all praise.

"At daybreak we found that Peter Mason was about four
miles ahead of us, and he got into harbour first, followed a few
minutes later by the other three. Amongst all four boats one man
was killed, one died of wounds and eleven others were wounded.
My ship was the only one that was damaged, except for the
superficial bullet and splinter marks with which each was
liberally spattered."

The German claim, which they put out on the radio, was quite a
different story:

D.N.B. IN GERMAN FOR EUROPE. 10.47 a.m. 5th September, 1943.
"BERLIN: The International Information Bureau reports
that during last night German coastal covering forces engaged
two British motor torpedo boat formations off the west coast of
France. During the first action about midnight, two of the enemy
boats were sunk by direct shell hits. One hour later a second
engagement took place in the waters off Le Treport, in which
another two motor torpedo boats were sunk and a third one was
set on fire. Thus the British light surface fleet lost four of its boats
and probably a fifth within a few hours, in an attack against the
German convoy routes off the coast of Western Europe."

Our return to harbour was marked by a sad little comedy.
Grey Goose had been steering by main engines from the end of the
action—that is to say, by differences in the revs. on the two pro-
pellors instead of by using the rudders, and furthermore all these
alterations were being passed by word of mouth from the bridge
to the engine room by a chain of ratings one of whom had to shout
down through the engine-room ventilator. The system had worked
so well that when a tug approached us just outside Dover breakwater with orders to take us in tow, I declined the offer and we
steamed into the harbour and round into the Submarine Basin.
Here a formidable array of Senior Officers was waiting to greet the

returning warriors, but before we could go alongside we had to turn round, for we were to berth on *Grey Fox* which Peter Mason had already turned round and you could not berth S.G.B.s head to tail. The standard method of turning is to go ahead on one engine, astern on the other and the ship then slowly revolves; if she gains head way or stern way you either stop one of the engines until she is once more revolving on one spot or increase the speed of the other engine to achieve the same result. In this case I had the port engine going slow ahead and the starboard going slow astern, and when *Grey Goose* was about half-way round she began to gather stern way, towards the jetty alongside which a number of vessels were berthed. To check this stern way I ordered "Half ahead port" and then the only mistake in the chain of communication to the engine room took place. The order reached the Chief E.R.A. as "Half astern port." That's funny, he thought, the old man is usually so meticulous about stopping engines between going ahead and going astern. But still, if that's what he said, that's what we must do. And so *Grey Goose* began to gather more stern way. "Stop starboard" that was the one that was going astern. Surely the port engine if it was going ahead would now check the stern way, but it didn't (because of course it wasn't going ahead). Suddenly I realised that something was wrong. "Stop both—Full ahead together"; but it was too late. Inexorably our stern bore down on a Norwegian minelaying M.L. There was a splintering of wood as her frames and bulkheads were crushed before the errant Steam Gunboat could be stopped. And all this was directly under the eyes of the Brass Hats on the jetty above. When my Action Report was forwarded to Admiralty the covering letter ended with a paragraph which said:

> "While it is realised that the Senior Officer was anxious to berth his ship under her own power, it is considered that he would have been better advised to accept the tow which was offered."

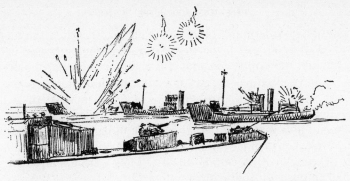

CHAPTER 24   *Both Sides of the Story*

THE reports called for after these actions had now grown so formidable, and took so long to compile that there was a danger they
would interfere with the operations themselves. Of course it was
important to wring every last drop of information and experience
from each battle for use in future operations, but it was obviously
getting out of hand when the Senior Officer was too deeply involved
in writing up the last action to go out and fight the next one. On
the other hand I had no illusions about the importance of the paper
work. The might of the pen was not to be underestimated. If we
were not meticulous and, at necessary moments, eloquent it would
be even more difficult to get the equipment we wanted. On the
whole, however, we had wonderful backing from our Senior Officers
all the way up the line to the C.-in-C., and I shall always be
especially grateful to Admiral Sir Charles Little, under whom I
was to serve again later in the war. The Naval Officer-in-Charge
Newhaven was old Captain Hardman Jones, a First World War
shipmate of my stepfather's. It was he who had taken me to sea
for an exercise in the Light Cruiser *Champion* at the age of fourteen.
But at Newhaven we were directly under the Coastal Force Base—
H.M.S. *Aggressive*—commanded by Captain G. W. Heaton. By
reason of their size and the fact that they were fairly frequently in
action at that time, the Steam Gunboats were probably the most
important ships working from *Aggressive*, and as such we were
Captain Heaton's blue-eyed boys and could do no wrong—a very
agreeable state of affairs.

Aggressive was housed in the London and Paris Hotel which was
on the platform of the Southern Railways Terminal. We lived on
board our boats, but I had an office in the building, overlooking
the harbour, and had set up an intelligence room which was used
for briefing meetings before going to sea. After a night patrol we

473

normally had a bath and breakfast in *Aggressive*. Often the night's activities were discussed over the partitions in the bathroom which accentuated the impression that it was all an outsized schoolboy's game. I have often wondered since how much better we played it because of its game-like qualities. They are more than faintly ridiculous to look back on, but they probably helped at the time.

We had now discovered, so at least we thought, that against the wide awake German patrols and escorts it was impossible to make a surprise attack with Steam Gunboats. They were too large for the kind of ambush which the seventy-foot Motor Torpedo Boats could so often bring off. Our torpedoes were our best weapons but how could we get in to a decisive range—say 600 yards—without being seen? Yet we must still think first of our torpedoes. Peter Dickens, the greatest M.T.B. exponent of them all at that time, used to say, "You can knock things about with guns, but if you give it half a chance a torpedo will do the job for you, suddenly and completely." How to get close enough to give the torpedo its chance, that was our problem. It was illustrated in a running fight on the night of 21st September, 1943. The three Steamers were *Seal*, *Owl* and *Fox*, and I was embarked with Jimmy Southcott in *Seal*. We found a strong enemy patrol just up the coast from Le Havre at half past midnight, but they saw us at the same time as we saw them and began to illuminate with starshell. For about an hour we let them shoot at us at long range, and then suddenly they seemed to have run out of starshell. By this time however we were almost at the entrance to the channel leading into Le Havre. At a range of 1,000 yards Jimmy fired his two torpedoes, but they did not hit the target, though one of them exploded, probably on the bottom. Like rabbits, the enemy ships bolted into their harbour and no torpedo target was available for the other two Steamers. We had reason to think that a part of the enemy force had turned back to the north, so off we went after them, but we never found them. It was an abortive night which confirmed our belief that some drastically new tactics were needed. Only five nights later, however, we achieved complete and devastating surprise in the same area in a most satisfactory little battle which did a great deal to restore our self confidence. For that night's patrol I had decided to embark in *Grey Fox* with Peter Mason. The other boats were *Grey Seal* (Jimmy Southcott), *Grey Shark* (Roger King, a Free Frenchman under an assumed name, who had taken over when Howard Bradford was wounded in July) and *Grey Owl* (Richard Hall). A few days after the action I wrote the following account:

"The four of us had been down to Le Havre and drawn blank, and we swept northward again towards Cap d'Antifer. Just before two a.m. we found the enemy by radar and stalked him for about an hour. It was a curious night with bright phosphorescence and heavy storms with lightning but no thunder. I wondered if he would sight us in the lightning flashes, but I finally came to the conclusion that, unless someone happened to be looking directly at us at the moment of the flash, he probably wouldn't. A very black storm was approaching from the nor'-nor'-east and we decided that there was a good chance of an unobserved attack if we could time it to coincide with the arrival of the storm. Our radar plotting and amplifying reports were exactly like an exercise at *Bee*.

"Finally, about an hour after our first contact, when we were just north of Etretat, I made the signal 'Form port quarter line' and turned in to close on a steady bearing. The hail pattered down on our tin helmets and the night was inky black. It was useless to try to use glasses because of the rain. When the range was 1,000 yards the enemy was still invisible in the blackness but we were just abaft his beam according to the plotted enemy course. I was standing just behind Peter and kept saying impatiently 'For heaven's sake—can't you see them *yet*?' for I knew we must be getting close. Suddenly he said very calmly, 'Yes I can see them now. Port ten', this in order to bring the torpedo sight on. The range was below 600 yards when he fired both torpedoes. I had still not seen the enemy, and what was much more important, he had still not seen us. A look-out into that driving hail must have been quite impossible to keep.

"Having put the force in port quarter line, we turned to starboard and immediately fired a spread of four starshells. By their light we saw two trawlers quite close together. The First Lieutenant, John Erskine Hill, put the guns on to the second one, and opened fire at once. From that time on the illumination was continuous, partly supplied by *Grey Seal* and partly by the Germans. Although the rain restricted the area of starshell illumination, the scene directly below the bright white light seemed to be quite as bright as day. The two trawlers, however, did not reply at all. All guns ripped into the second trawler which was at about 300 yards, and a small fire was started at once just forward of the bridge.

"Suddenly I saw a third trawler right ahead, and as we turned to starboard it came down the port side at very close range.

Just as John, without a moment's delay, made all his guns change target to this trawler, there was an explosion on the after end of the leading trawler. A vivid flame of bright cherry red with streaks of blue and green in it shot out of the trawler—not vertically, but sloping to the right, and after it had gone there was a white column of either smoke or spray which must have been at least 100 feet high. At the same time all guns engaged the third trawler, now no more than sixty yards away. I think that one small machine gun was firing back at us but that was all, and everything we had was going into it. The three-inch hit four times in quick succession. The two forward pom-poms put five belts each into it. They couldn't miss. There was a roar of escaping steam and suddenly a white cloud came out of the ship's stern. Whether this was steam or white smoke I don't know. At the same time she altered course to port round our stern. Bits were flying off the upperworks as every gun hit. At that range and with bright starshell illumination it was quite impossible to miss.

"When the leading trawler blew up I felt vaguely that it was rather later than I would have expected our torpedoes to hit. I thought it very likely that it was a torpedo from one of the other boats, but since none of the others fired torpedoes at that time it must have been ours. There is one other rather remote possibility—that it was a three-inch hit (or even smaller calibre) which blew up the magazine. In any event it seems certain that it sank, as Jimmy Southcott says that nothing of it remained after the explosion worth shooting at, and it is confirmed that one trawler was sunk that night.

"As soon as we had passed the third trawler two ships began firing at us out of the rain. The fire was not very accurate although we sustained a few hits, and we increased speed. We were 3,000 yards from the shore, the Hun was now fully roused, we had expended our torpedoes, and the ready-use lockers needed topping up. Of the rest of the force only one S.G.B. was in sight, and he was a good way astern (it was *Seal*). So I made a signal 'Rendezvous on completion of attack', and we proceeded north-west to the rendezvous position five miles away. As we went we were shelled by the shore batteries which were apparently firing tracer shells. They were not very accurate. It seemed to me that we could do nothing more until we had reformed.

"At the rendezvous I found that *Shark* and *Seal* had already joined up. Neither of these had, I discovered, fired torpedoes. I decided, wrongly I think, to wait for *Owl*. *Owl* signalled that she had not fired, then signalled that she had completed an attack. The latter signal should have been 'Am about to attack.' If this signal had been correctly made we could have gone in to create a diversion. Pity! As it was this attack of *Owl*'s was carried out single-handed. There was continuous starshell, and by its light *Owl* had sighted two largish ships, two or three trawlers and at least eight R-boats. That *Owl* was able to approach to within 900 yards under the continuous glare of starshell and herself firing starshells over the target can only be attributed to mis-identification. In some way the Germans must have thought that she was one of them returning perhaps from the pursuit of the rest of us. The shore batteries only were firing at her and they were fairly accurate. One of *Owl*'s torpedoes had a leaking stop-valve and could not be fired, but the other was fired using the flashing lamp of one of the German ships as a point of aim. It seems likely that the Hun was either stopped or nearly stopped at the time, and the torpedo probably missed ahead. At any rate no result was observed. *Owl* then disengaged, still unshot at except by the shore batteries, which got fairly close. She could still see a ship burning to the westward, which was presumably the trawler we had shot up fifty-five minutes before. She arrived at the rendezvous at four a.m. By this time the wind was north, force five, and the sea was rising. You can't aim torpedoes very well in that stuff, nor can you shoot very straight.

"I signalled to both *Seal* and *Shark* saying that I thought the weather was unsuitable for another attack, what did they think. They both agreed. So as soon as *Owl* arrived we set off for home. We all four entered Newhaven in company at 0720. The only damage whatever suffered by the whole force was two twenty-millimetre holes in *Fox*'s port torpedo tube, and the only casualty was Peter Platt, the Midshipman, with a scratch on his ear. He was most annoyed when I insisted he should go to the sick bay and have the blood washed off it before he came in to breakfast."

Not long after this battle I was shown translations of various broadcast reports in German purporting to describe the same encounter. At the bottom of the page I wrote a short paragraph and then attached the German transcripts.

"The above account was written before reading the German broadcast accounts. Both cannot be correct. I think mine is not exaggerated, and it forms a picture, as well as I am able to describe it, of exactly what I saw. The accounts that follow are picturesque, but not very closely related to the facts."

GERMAN TELEGRAPH SERVICE (D.N.B. EUROPEAN) 0854 27.9.43.

BERLIN (International Information Bureau). (MORNING): In the early morning hours of today, a naval engagement took place in the waters of Fecamp between the escorting vessels of a German convoy and British light naval forces. According to reports so far available, several British light naval craft suffered heavy damage.

GERMAN TELEGRAPH SERVICE (D.N.B. EUROPEAN) 1215 27.9.43.

BERLIN (International Information Bureau). (MIDDAY): As already reported, German naval covering forces engaged and severely mauled a formation of British E-boats in the early morning hours of today.

The International Information Bureau learns that two large British E-boats were set on fire and sank. Three other British vessels received hits and had to break off the engagement [this makes five out of four].

GERMAN EUROPEAN SERVICE IN ENGLISH.

'Matters of Moment.' 1730 1.10.43.

'News from the Front'—"Here is a recording we have just received from one of our reporters on the Channel coast."

Reporter: "On September 28th the German Supreme Command announced the destruction of two English motor gunboats. The patrol boat flotilla has just arrived at their base on the French coast, and we have received first-hand information. The flotilla is one of the most successful ones in the Channel area. So far, one man has received the Knight's Cross of the Iron Cross, and ten others the German Cross in gold. These high decorations are only awarded to men who have accomplished something extraordinary.

"Well, this night was again a night full of action. The crews had to stay on board for orders had arrived to leave port and take up positions. While the formation was on the way, the starlit sky changed into a pitch-dark night. The flotilla leader, a Commander, was embarked in one of the boats, and this was the one which received the wireless message that in square XY enemy ships had been made out. Immediately orders were given to the crews to keep careful look-out in square Y.

"For about half an hour nothing happened, but all of a sudden several look-outs reported wakes of torpedoes. What that means only a man who has been on board a torpedoed boat knows. With great skill the torpedoes were out-manoeuvred, and a few moments later the shadowy shapes of several English motor gunboats appeared out of the rain squall. The concentrated fire of the German patrol boats covered the enemy boats, but they had made up their minds to fight this time, and for a few minutes it was just a free-for-all affair. One of the motor gunboats stopped, developed smoke and fire, and sank very close to the German boats. Another enemy boat wanted to make an especially dashing attack. It tried to break through the German line. A leading seaman, the gun captain of the fo'c'sle gun, on one of the German boats had noticed this. With his automatic gun he commenced to rip the enemy boat apart, even though a shell splinter had caused a wound on his forehead. Blood was trickling into his eyes, but all he did was to wipe his eyes a few times with his fore-arm, and fire till the enemy boats disappeared, leaving nothing but a cloud of smoke behind. This was too much of a dose for the remaining English seamen. They turned their boats and disappeared into the dark of the night.

"The patrol boat had also suffered casualties. A four-centi-metre shell had entered the chartroom. A leading seaman in the room, as well as the helmsman, was badly wounded. The mate, who saw the helmsman sink down on the wheel, jumped across and kept the boat on the right course. Again, German seamen and German weapons proved to be unequalled in skill and quality."

GERMAN HOME SERVICE 1430 2.10.43.

The German Navy does not limit itself to defending the immediate vicinity of the coast; on the contrary, light German naval forces carry out daily thrusts into the Channel, to attack the enemy wherever possible. The little ships of the German Navy remain victorious in numerous encounters with enemy naval forces and bombers. Only a few nights ago a naval action took place at night in the Channel, and was mentioned by the High Command. The fighting is usually severe and demands real men and cold blood. This being in constant contact with the enemy, the necessity of bitter fighting which often leaves no alternative than either to destroy the enemy or perish oneself, has marked them. They are not easy to bring to the microphone, because they claim that they were doing nothing special, and in their modesty they believe that the other fellow has done more. This is the case with the Commander of one of the patrol boats which played a major part in the sinking of the two M.T.B.s reported in the High Command Communiqué of 28th September.

I am now in the Commander's cabin, and he sits opposite me with members of his crew. The Lieutenant now tells his story:

Lieutenant: "It was one of those encounters we have fought out so often, except that it was the most recent one, and, therefore, we all remember it well. It was typical Channel weather, a light sea and squalls of rain. Suddenly we saw torpedoes racing towards us out of the darkness of a thunder cloud, but we were able to turn away. In the glare of our starshells I saw an English 'Gun Speed Boat' [in English] quite close, about fifty metres to port. I immediately gave orders to open fire, but the British opened up at the same moment. I received a direct hit in the wheelhouse, and was thrown down. As both my legs were stiff I thought at first that my spine had been injured. I dragged myself up by the compass, and was surprised to find that my boat was still manoeuvrable. The man at the wheel had been mortally wounded and was groaning heavily. His place was taken by the Quartermaster. I was especially pleased with the performance of the gun served by Ordinary Seaman First Class Boerzer, who calmly poured one round after the other into the English boat [this may be literally true as two rounds hit *Grey Fox*]. He had better continue the story."

Boerzer: "There is really not very much to tell. I saw an M.T.B. quite close to us to port, trying to turn, and opened fire. There was a short but severe exchange of fire, in the course of which we received several hits as well, and several guns became total losses. After that the M.T.B. directed the fire of its front gun at me and I aimed at it in return, silencing it. After that the M.T.B. just lay there, its engines stopped, and it became an easier target. I then directed my fire at the bridge and at the stern-gun and suddenly after several hits I had been able to score, there was much smoke and then an explosion, and the boat was no longer to be seen."

Lieutenant: "We too, however, had received several more hits on the water line and the Mechanician Second Class had better continue the story to tell us what happened below."

Mechanician: "When the noise started I was just working on the engine. We received several hits in the boiler-room (Heizraum) as well as on the hull. These leaks were immediately stopped. The artificial-fog containers (Nebelkannen) had been hit and when we started manoeuvring the fog got into the engine room through the ventilators. It was very difficult to continue working in the biting smoke, but when the Commander asked whether we were all right, we had put everything in order and were able to continue on our way."

There was something rather depressing about reading these German reports, because we had considerable respect for the enemy we were fighting. We hoped he did not really believe all these claims he made on the radio. Of course excessively optimistic claims are part of human nature. We knew that our own claims were often far too hopeful. We knew that British claims for aircraft destroyed erred in this direction—even the famous days of the Battle of Britain had been marred by shameful exaggeration. But when the Germans talked about ripping us apart in the action off Etretat we hoped and believed they had been got at by Dr. Goebbels's Propaganda Ministry. It is interesting that during the six months ending on 30th September, 1943, the Germans claimed to have destroyed twenty-seven M.T.B.s and six M.G.B.s for certain and to have "so badly damaged that their loss can be assumed" a further fourteen M.T.B.s and two M.G.B.s in the waters of the Channel and North Sea. In fact during that period and in those waters one M.G.B. was sunk by enemy action and one rather old one was lost through stress of weather—two instead of forty-nine.

As the autumn of 1943 advanced I heard rumours that the role of the S.G.B.s was to be changed again. They were to be attached to Combined Operations. Although I would not have admitted it at the time, it was becoming inescapably evident that as an experiment they had not been altogether a success. Originally I had been Senior Officer, First S.G.B. Flotilla, with the implied suggestion that there would one day be a second. Now I had become S.O. S.G.B.s and it was abundantly clear that no others would ever be built.

I think at this time I had begun to recognise in myself the symptoms of operational fatigue. When the battles began and the tracer began to stream out towards us I found myself saying, "Oh dear! Not again!" I had amassed, of course (as I had done in North Atlantic Convoy Escort) a useful amount of experience, but I needed a rest from beating myself against the patrols and escorts off the French coast. I should soon have been two years in Coastal

Forces and the idea of a rest from operations was now generally accepted.

It should not have been difficult to broach the subject but I was prevented from making my thoughts known by a curious and tiresome circumstance which developed. During the summer the Naval Intelligence Division had suggested a series of lectures on escaping from prison camps to be delivered to the crews of the S.G.B.s. On the face of it this seemed a sensible idea, but when the officer came to give the lecture I suggested that if it could be given as a general lecture to all the operational boats at Newhaven, that might be better than singling out the S.G.B.s as the only ones, on the grounds that they were the most likely ones to be captured. With their particular vulnerability and the aggressive nature of our work this was in fact so, but I did not particularly want my chaps to think of themselves as more greatly handicapped in this way than the crews of the M.G.B.s and M.T.B.s. The foolish young man who came to give the lecture went back to the Admiralty and put in a report to the effect that all was not well with the morale in the S.G.B. Flotilla. I learned then that the whole subject of morale is dynamite in time of war. It is the unmentionable of unmentionables, and once it *has* been mentioned it must run its long course. The whole affair did not come back to me till several months and many dozens of operations later. When it did the S.G.B.s had already been transferred to Combined Operations and I was summoned by Admiral Hughes Hallet, then living in the Royal Yacht Squadron Castle at Cowes, to tell him what it was all about. Being a newly elected member of the R.Y.S. myself it was arranged that I should stay the night there. Hughes Hallett, who had been the Naval Force Commander in the Dieppe raid, listened to my story and then said, "Well, let that be a lesson to you to keep off the subject of morale from now on. Now tell me about the S.G.B.s at Dieppe." Thereafter we had a most delightful evening.

The change in the S.G.B.s' function would have provided the rest I needed, but more drastic changes were in store for me. I had hoped that the promised destroyer command might now come up, and that perhaps I would get one in the Portsmouth Command, which seemed to me to be a sensible combination of the two kinds of experience which I possessed. But when I made this happy inspiration known in the Second Sea Lord's Office in Queen Anne's Mansions they said, "Oh dear me no! You must go and do your training stint at *Bee*. The destroyer? Well, maybe after that— shall we say six months?"

This no doubt was good sense, for the teaching had to be done by people with action experience, and far the most useful thing I could do with my experience was to impart it to others. But at the time it was a bitter pill.

It had, however, one great advantage. H.M.S. *Bee* had been removed from Weymouth to Holyhead—far enough away from the war—and I could be reunited for a reasonable period with Jane.

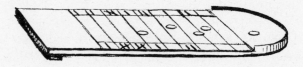

CHAPTER 25   *The Tunnel*

HOLYHEAD was a backwater of the war. Here I was at school again, but this time as a master. There were lectures to give and long days, and sometimes nights, to be spent at sea in other people's boats on various exercises. It was a wonderful opportunity to use my accumulated experience and the ideas which stemmed from it to teach the tactics I should otherwise have been trying to put into practice. But I could not really see it as more than marking time. The work was hard, but there was also some leisure. In the winter evenings I went Wigeon flighting with Nigel Conant, agent of the Stanley estate, and sometimes we were out too for morning flight.

Our baby was staying with her grandparents, and Jane, freed from maternal chores, undertook the production of *The Importance of Being Earnest*, in which she also played Gwendolen. Jack Lambert, the literary critic, then commanding an M.T.B. under training at Holyhead, played Jack Worthing. I was Stage Manager, and understudied the part of Dr. Chasuble. It was probably as well that I was never called upon to play it, for I scarcely had time to learn even those few lines. The part was ebulliently and most successfully played by Basil Ward. The production, though hard hit by last-minute changes occasioned by the movement of H.M. ships, was a considerable success, and I have found that familiarity with so many of the lines of this enchanting play is a constant source of pleasure.

When the spring came, however, I was all ready for the fray again. I looked forward excitedly to my Destroyer. The war was moving to its decisive stage. The summer must see an Allied invasion of Hitler's Europe, and however small it might be, I wanted desperately to have my part in it—at sea in my own Destroyer. But the Admiralty had another disappointment in store for me. "Look," they said, "we know we promised you a Destroyer, and we'd like to keep our promise. But you've been specially asked for by the Captain Coastal Forces Channel, who is setting up a staff at Portsmouth, and we can't really refuse him. You'll be working with Christopher Dreyer, planning for the big show—we think it's really more important than an independent command . . ." All of which I took to be sales talk at the time, though I had occasion to recall the conversation later. But mention of Christopher Dreyer was a powerful influence. I had known him at Newhaven and we had many ideas in common. As Senior Officer of a flotilla of M.T.B.s he had operated in company with me several times, and we got on well. I knew that working together we could get things done.

After Newhaven, he had taken his flotilla to the Mediterranean. Many stories of his exploits were current in Coastal Forces circles, the best perhaps being his encounter one night in the Straits of Messina with a U-boat on the surface which bore down upon him as he lay stopped. It passed twenty yards ahead of him which was much too close to fire torpedoes. He went full speed astern to get far enough away so that the torpedoes would not run under in their initial dive, but the U-boat had gone. He was about to give chase when he saw a second U-boat following the first. Still going astern, he fired one torpedo at a range of scarcely 100 yards and the submarine blew up. A further torpedo attack on the leading one failed, though it may have been damaged by depth charges. It was then that Christopher made his classic signal to C.-in-C. Mediterranean (Admiral Cunningham): "Two U-boats in position so-and-so. Regret only one sunk."

As a regular Naval Officer, Christopher remained only a Lieutenant R.N. (albeit with a D.S.O. and two D.S.C.s) for the whole six months of his appointment as Staff Officer Operations to the Captain Coastal Forces, but his influence on the plans and operations and his worth to the Portsmouth Command during that fateful period rated the rank of Commander at least. Had he been a temporary Naval Officer like me, no doubt that is what he would have become, but such were the inflexibilities of promotion in the Regular Navy, that a Lieutenant he had to remain. I was to be S.O.O.(2)—Christopher's right-hand man. For me it was to be a very happy partnership.

At first we worked in an office in Fort Southwick which stands on Portsdown Hill. Our Mess was in the red brick fort too, and we slept in a dormitory hut behind it. Later we moved our office down into 'The Tunnel' (more properly Portsmouth Combined Headquarters) which was a series of mine-like galleries cut down into the chalk beneath the fort and deep in the interior of the hill. Our offices had vaulted roofs and were in a gallery leading off the main tunnel which had a larger diameter, and in which an Operations room and Radar Plot had been set up. Other galleries were full of the offices of other departments, of radio equipment, of telephone exchanges, of air conditioning plant and emergency generators. It was an underground village with a population of a hundred or more.

In this setting we had a twofold job to do. We were responsible for the day-to-day operations of the Coastal Forces in the Portsmouth Command and we were charged with the planning for all Coastal Forces to be used in the impending invasion. For this we were given full details of the plan as early as March—at least, as full as they then were. At no time did I ever enjoy knowing important secrets and I can remember the conflict in my mind between curiosity to learn where the invading forces would land and my general distaste for the responsibility of possessing the knowledge. There was also a time when the advantages of the Seine Bay as a landing place seemed so overwhelming that it was impossible to imagine any doubt in the enemy's mind where the blow would fall.

After the initial landings on D-day, the build up was to be poured across the Channel down a wide sea lane which became known as 'The Spout'. The flanks of this spout were to be largely protected by the Coastal Forces. Against what? This was the question we asked ourselves over and over again. On paper the Germans still had a fleet in being, though it hardly seemed likely that they would bring it into the confined waters of the Channel in spite of the successful passage of the *Scharnhorst* and *Gneisenau* two years before; the balance in the air had swung too much against them since then. And if they did, of course, more powerful forces than M.T.B.s would at once be involved. But there were German destroyers and torpedo boats and 'M'-class Minesweepers in some numbers, both on the Atlantic coast of France and in the Low Countries. There were E-boats, too, based at Cherbourg to the west and further up the Channel to the east, and there were also large numbers of U-boats which might come into the Channel from their bases at Brest and Lorient and St. Nazaire, or all the way from Germany. Besides all these there was the possibility of secret weapons. Flying bombs and V2 rockets were unlikely to have a direct effect on the war at sea, but there were always midget submarines, human torpedoes (which had already been used at

Anzio) and explosive motor-boats. Against all these possibilities the Spout had to be protected and the main weight of this defence was going to fall on the shoulders of the Coastal Forces.

At the same time as we were making the plans for it all, we were also responsible for the nightly operations in the Channel—the defence of the convoy routes, the offensive patrols off the French coast, the minelaying operations. E-boats were more than usually active during this period. Evidently uncertain of the time when the invasion would be launched, and insufficiently supplied with intelligence and aerial reconnaissance, the German High Command was using E-boats regularly during April and May to reconnoitre the approaches to the Solent area, as well as for their more normal functions of laying mines, and attacking our assembling ships with torpedoes.

Only once in that period did the E-boats achieve anything of any consequence. That was during an invasion exercise when they got in amongst a convoy of landing ships in Lyme Bay and wrought serious devastation and heavy loss of life; it was their sole success although they were at sea night after night. Mostly we seemed to have the measure of them, because, near to our coasts, they were detected by radar and their movements were recorded on 'the Plot'.

In the Naval Plotting Room was a great map of the Channel like a huge low billiard table with a white perspex top. On it the positions of all ships, friendly or enemy, were shown with numbered models. Their movements were shown by the constant attentions of Wrens with special wands, like billiard rests. When the E-boats came over to operate on the South Coast Convoy route they were immediately detected and the whole course of the subsequent action could be controlled by the Commander-in-Chief, or his Chief of Staff, or most often by one of a team of Duty Commanders. Further up Channel in the Dover Command, where the enemy convoy route was only twenty or thirty miles from the radar sets, such radar control was the standard practice for offensive as well as defensive operations. In 'the Plot' where the movements of all the ships were plainly visible on the map, it was possible for the Controlling Officer to make the interception calculations, and put his ships in touch with the enemy simply by giving them courses to steer at a given speed. This of course was the R.A.F. technique which had won them the Battle of Britain. How could we harness this technique to the defence of the Spout when it stretched seventy miles and more from the radar sets on the cliff tops of the Isle of

Wight? True, on certain nights with special weather conditions the range of detection was enormously extended—'anomalous propagation' it was called—and shipping could be plotted off Cherbourg and well down into the Baie de la Seine. Two of our actions in the S.G.B.s had been brought about by this 'anomalous propagation', but clearly we could not depend on it for the defence of the Spout. If we were to have radar cover over the defence areas on the flanks we must take it with us in ships, and to be really effective the radar aerials must be on taller masts than were carried in Coastal Force craft.

It was from this conclusion that a new technique in naval warfare emerged. It provided that a whole battle should be controlled by an officer watching the movements of the ships on the cathode ray tube of the radar set—the Plan Position Indicator, or P.P.I. as it was then called. This was usually a horizontal dial (sometimes vertical) about ten inches in diameter. Revolving round it was a line of light representing the beam of the radio impulses and any objects which gave an echo from the beam showed as luminous greenish-white dots on the 'tube'. These gradually faded but were rejuvenated each time the beam passed over them. The result was a map. The face of the tube was calibrated with circles at various distances from the set, and by the turn of a switch different scales could be used. At that time most sets could use either a seventy-five-mile, twenty-five-mile or five-mile scale. The last was of course the most accurate and it would therefore be desirable for the control ship to remain well within five miles of the scene of battle. The Control Officer was simply to sit there in the darkened Plot poring over his P.P.I. as a player might pore over a chessboard, and talk in plain language or in a simple time-saving code over the radio telephone to the forces he was controlling.

This was the revolutionary idea which Christopher Dreyer and I had to get across to the powers-that-be. The first step was not difficult. Our immediate boss, the Captain Coastal Forces, Channel, was Pat McLaughlin, a small but energetic man who at once saw the significance of the whole conception. Further up the line there were difficulties, because of course every available ship was going to be needed, and to earmark any for this new and untried system was taking a considerable chance. Eventually we were told we could have four Frigates—destroyer-sized vessels though with less speed—and that they would be fitted with the very latest American radar sets which were better than anything available from Britain at that time. We were also told that use could be made of the radar Plot in the cruiser H.M.S. *Scylla*, which was to be Admiral Sir Philip Vian's Flagship and would be at anchor in the British Assault Area.

This was better news than we had dared to hope. With such a demonstration of faith in our plan, it seemed more important than ever that it should succeed. Now we must select our Control Officers, train them and train the men in the boats they would control. For all this there was not a moment to lose. Lieut. Philip Lee, D.S.C., R.N.V.R. (who had played Algernon in Jane's production of *The Importance of Being Earnest*) was still at Holyhead. No one was in a better position to work out the details of our plan, to incorporate them in the training at H.M.S. *Bee*, and to hold himself in readiness to be a Control Officer when the time came. Appointed at the same time was Lieut. Guy Hudson, R.N.V.R., who had been teaching navigation at Holyhead.

These two were later joined by Tony Hollings (Lieut., R.N., and the only regular officer doing this job), George Bailey, who was lost when the Frigate *Trollope* was torpedoed, Guy Fison and Pat Edge, who was to operate from the cruiser *Scylla*.

Opportunities for realistic exercises in the new technique were rare before D-day. On 18th May, however, a large-scale exercise was held in which Admiral Vian tried out off the English coast the defence measures he was going to use in the Assault Area, in his capacity as Naval Commander, Eastern Task Force. It was a complex exercise in which certain M.T.B.s were to represent E-boats and attempt to penetrate a defence line and reach an 'anchorage' off Worthing. Outside the whole exercise area was another defence line to prevent the real E-boats from getting mixed up in the exercise. Christopher and I watched the Plot in the Tunnel under Fort Southwick until dawn. We were responsible for the outer defence line, and what happened in the exercise inside was of intense significance to us. The real E-boats came out, but were intercepted by the very outermost fringe of the patrols. Two S.G.B.s —*Grey Owl* and *Grey Wolf*—engaged them and they turned tail at once and fled. Meanwhile the sham E-boats went on with their exercise attack, and penetrated much more deeply into Admiral Vian's defences than, when the time came, any genuine E-boat ever managed to do. Nevertheless, it seemed that once the snags had been ironed out, our system of control was going to work.

All through that spring Christopher and I worked away in the Tunnel. The normal access to our office and the Plot was down interminable flights of stairs with a central banister, like the stairs to an Underground Railway Station. But we had found a pleasanter way of returning to the fort above for lunch. If one walked for a long distance along the tortuous galleries one came eventually, past various steel doors and gates, out on to the chalk hillside, and could then climb up a pleasant, if steep, white path among wild flowers sometimes crowded with migrant Painted Lady and Red Admiral butterflies, to the fort above. From the slope of Portsdown Hill we overlooked the harbour below. As the invasion fleet assembled so obviously in this and all the other South Coast ports, it seemed absurd that we should regard surprise in any form at all as a factor in the coming operation.

In our daily round those walks up the steep hillside in the sun were a happy contrast to the life in the artificial light and doubtful air conditioning of the Tunnel. In the wardroom above ground in the fort was a shove ha'penny board and Christopher and I formed the habit of a quick game before lunch and another after it before plunging down again into our burrow. "I'll run you up the board" was the phrase, and with it in my mind goes another. Christopher and I were both cigarette smokers but someone had told one or other of us that cigarettes were nothing but another nail in our coffins. "Have a nail," we always said thereafter, "And there's just time to run you up the board before we go down again."

But although so much of our time was spent underground, sometimes we went down to H.M.S. *Hornet*, the Coastal Forces base in Haslar Creek on the west side of Portsmouth Harbour, to discuss the new technique with the Commanding Officers of the boats congregating there for the great day. I remember one afternoon standing overlooking the busy scene with a positive pain of disappointment in my stomach at the thought that I should not be going with them on this, 'the greatest military undertaking in history'. To be sure, we had perhaps played quite a useful part in its preparation (during which we had been expressly forbidden to go on any operations for fear of capture), but it was going to be hard watching it all in model form on the Portsmouth Plot. Long later I have learned that a similar problem of personal participation was exercising the minds of the King and the Prime Minister at this very time.

On the night of D-minus-one, 5th June, 1944, our Coastal Forces boats were out in full strength in spite of the strong wind and heavy sea. The assault had already been postponed for twenty-four hours because of the weather. General Eisenhower had taken a bold decision to accept no further postponement, a decision which alone may have preserved the vital surprise element. On such a night the

German defenders had been assured by their meteorologists no invasion could take place. But it did! The spearhead of the assault convoys and the Minesweepers which preceded them were escorted by M.T.B.s, M.L.s and Harbour Defence M.L.s, some of them acting as navigational leaders, others as smoke layers. There were two strong patrols in position on either flank as well as the special force of H.D.M.L.s which were providing a diversion. Many miles up the French coast from the real landing beaches this ingenious force equipped with fireworks, smoke, gramophone records, and balloons to make ship-sized radar echoes, went about the hazardous task of drawing attention to themselves, and pretending they were an invasion.

In the current phrase Operation Overlord was 'a big party'. At dinner that night in the Mess at Fort Southwick there were about twenty officers and it was as if we were going to quite a different kind of party—perhaps a first night. There was an air of unreality—a pinch-me-and-I'll-wake-up feeling. We talked of trivial things which bore no relation to what was uppermost in all our minds. After dinner we were going down to watch the curtain go up on one of the decisive dramas in human history. We should see it in a detached impersonal way, as numbered models on a table, the more detached because Command had passed a few days before from C.-in-C. Portsmouth to the Allied Naval Commander Expeditional Force (A.N.C.X.F.) Admiral Sir Bertram Ramsey, and ours was only a repeat of the Plot at his Headquarters. Nevertheless like everyone in the land we had an immeasurable stake in the operation's success; we should be watching the table like gamblers with their last penny on their chosen number.

After dinner we walked out into the ante-room. "Have a nail." Christopher took a cigarette from my case. "I'll run you up the board before we go down," he said. It was no doubt a fanciful notion that our game of shove ha'penny had anything in common with Drake's game of bowls.

Portsmouth Plot had never had so many models on it as there were that night and not one of them was enemy. I had drawn the proposed routes to the Seine Bay so often in the preparation of the plans that its spout-like shape was utterly familiar; but there was a new thrill in watching its outline gradually fill out with models, and realising that that very shape was at this moment being marked out in full scale by the wakes of the great armada as it plugged into the choppy seas of the Channel.

My most vivid memory of that night was the sense of amazement

R

that we were after all achieving tactical surprise. If the date and place were known to the enemy, he must surely move in ships to spread confusion in the advancing convoys. The chance encounter with a patrol of the eastern spearhead at Dieppe two years before had shown how disruptive such an engagement could be. And yet as the night wore on it became evident that the German High Command possessed no such foreknowledge. This realisation brought the first great sensation of relief. The first bridge had been crossed, the most important perhaps from the naval point of view. In the dark hours there was no contact whatever with enemy ships. When the battle had been joined ashore the *Möwe*-class torpedo boats near-by in Le Havre put to sea. Visibility was not very good that morning, but as they closed towards the invading armada they suddenly saw warships so much larger than themselves that after one torpedo attack they retired again into harbour. One of their torpedoes hit the Norwegian destroyer *Svenner*, which subsequently sank; but their brief sortie did not affect the progress of the landings in the very smallest degree. The E-boats in Cherbourg also came out, but they achieved even less; indeed they were not in action against our ships at all.

So the Spout was a reality. Could it now be protected by the units of Coastal Forces deployed and controlled by the young officers sitting at their P.P.I.s in the Radar Frigates and in *Scylla*?

Although Captain Coastal Forces, Channel, was responsible for all the Coastal Forces in the Channel, the Vice-Admiral, Dover had been entrusted with the east side of the Spout, while C.-in-C. Portsmouth looked after only the west side. Thus operationally Christopher and I only dealt directly with the patrols off Pointe de Barfleur and not with those off Cap d'Antifer. We were none the less interested in the progress of our new technique wherever it was being used. From the beginning it was more wholly successful than we had ever dared to dream. The finer points were quickly evolved as the teams got used to working with one another, and they provided as good a protection of the Spout and the anchorages at night as the Allied Air Forces did during the day. After each night's operations they returned to Portsmouth and the Control Officer, and very often the Senior Officers of the units would ring up our office in the Tunnel and speak either to Christopher or me, telling us of any lessons they had learned which might have a bearing on the next night's plans. Then in the light of these, and the reports of the boats available, we would lay out the patrols for the next night on a special portable perspex map of the Channel which I had prepared for the purpose.

This proposed plan would be taken first to the Captain Coastal Forces—Pat McLaughlin—for approval, and then to the C.-in-C.'s Chief of Staff, Commodore Bellars. It was usually approved without modification and the patrol lines and details, laid out in coloured wax pencil, had then to be translated into signals addressed to all the ships and authorities concerned which would set the operations in motion. In the afternoon Christopher or I would take the same little perspex-covered chart down to H.M.S. *Dolphin*, the Submarine base which had temporarily become an additional Coastal Forces base, where the Commanding Officers of the M.T.B.s and the Frigates, their Navigating Officers and the all-important Control Officers were assembled for briefing. The room was not very large and it was always crowded. Our job was to explain to them every detail of the plan which we had ourselves prepared that morning, to give them all available intelligence and to clear up any ambiguities which might have arisen from the signals which of course they had all received. Having gone down a long list of technical points from tactics to communications, we wished them good luck and returned to Fort Southwick, there usually to spend the best part of the night on the Plot. Even when the radar could not 'see' them in their positions off the coast of France we could often follow their adventures from the signals.

Once the bridgehead was firmly established in Normandy it seemed that radar mounted on high ground in France might give us valuable additional cover first on the vulnerable eastern flank facing Le Havre and later perhaps on the west flank too. I was instructed to go forthwith to France to explore not only these possibilities, but also the prospects of basing some of the Coastal Forces in the British Assault Area so as to obviate the long plug back to Portsmouth each morning and the long plug out again each night. I was attached to the Flag Officer British Assault Area (F.O.B.A.A.) with instructions to establish a small Plot over there with radar sets which I must myself set up and with communications which I must myself organise. I was also to hold myself in readiness as a relief Control Officer in the Frigates and at the same time to make full use of my close liaison with Christopher Dreyer in Portsmouth. It was technically quite a formidable task, but the prospects of returning to France, and of being in action again were irresistible.

I crossed the Channel on the afternoon of D-plus-9—15th June, 1944—in an M.T.B. and for me a new adventure began.

CHAPTER 26   *Normandy 1944*

I SPENT a large proportion of the next two months in France and wrote of these events soon after my return, while the impressions were still fresh in my memory. The manuscript was written in a number of notebooks and the flyleaf of the first carried the following note:

"This notebook was found in the office of the Chantiers Navals Shipyard near Caen, on 21st July, 1944, while it was still under fire from the German mortar batteries across the Orne.

"At the time of writing there are probably a million British fighting men in Normandy. From among them hundreds will no doubt write their impressions of this summer of 1944. An extra one will hardly be noticed.

"Like so many records this was started almost as a diary, and because events moved swiftly, I soon found myself far behind-hand with my writing; I made one or two attempts to keep up by jumping on to record a recent adventure and going back to fill in the gaps afterwards; and I made one or two alterations and additions at a much later date, among them the paragraph I am now writing. For those who would wish to, there is no way of distinguishing wisdom after the event from brilliant prophecy of events to come. Perhaps the story contains both, but it is mainly a straightforward narrative.

"In July 1944 the Allied bridgehead is, as it were, an island surrounded by war—an incredible Alice-in-Wonderland island. Along the landward perimeter is the front line with the din of artillery bombardment and the frightful destruction of towns and villages. Along the seaward side is the war of E-boats and mine-laying aircraft, and the destruction from the D-day landings.

"Only in the middle of the island—five miles inland—is the

country undamaged except by the presence of the vast armies and their motor transport and armour. Here in the peaceful centre the houses still stand and there are rest camps for the troops in the chateaux and the farmsteads. The war engulfed them quickly, passed them by in a day, as it did the town of Bayeux. And by contrast with the war so near, the peace in the centre of the island is all the more strange and impressive.

"I spent my first night in the Assault Area (15th June) on the seaward side of the island, in one of Don Bradford's flotilla of M.T.B.s (682—Bill Beynon). He brought me over in the afternoon of D-plus-nine. At the time the most remarkable feature to me of all the remarkable things was that this mass of shipping lying at anchor off the beaches—warships, merchant ships and landing craft by the hundred—was entirely without apparent air cover. Two distant Lightnings were the only aircraft we saw all day. The shipping lay there peacefully within a few hundred yards of the coast which so short a time before we had dared to approach only at dead of night. Yet here was this great armada tightly packed together in the anchorage, and there just behind them was the shore, with trees and fields and villages and the afternoon sun shining on it all. It was a scene which took a little while to get used to.

"I went on board *Scylla*, the flagship of Admiral Vian, the Naval Commander Eastern Task Force, or N.C.E.T.F. for short, where Pat Edge, the Coastal Forces Control Officer, was welcoming the M.T.B. boys as they arrived, and afterwards I went on patrol with Don Bradford's unit on the eastern flank opposite Le Havre. The night was comparatively quiet. It was only twenty-four hours before that Le Havre had been heavily blitzed and nothing came out to us from the stricken port. In the early morning we steamed into 'Sword Gooseberry', the easternmost of the Gooseberries or short-term artificial ports. This consisted of a harbour formed of sunken merchant vessels and warships lying stem to stern, touching to form a continuous breakwater for the protection of the landing craft which were ferrying supplies to the beaches.

"I went on board the River Gunboat *Locust*, who lay in the harbour, and from there took a Duck (or D.U.K.W.—amphibious vehicle) and having gone back to collect Don, set off for the shore. It was my first trip in these strange amphibious creatures. It was raining hard as we grounded and rolled up the sandy beach. All around were piles of the dreaded beach obstructions which had exercised us so much when we looked at photographs of them before D-day.

"The beach itself had not come to life as it was still no more than seven o'clock in the morning. All along the dunes were canvas signs stretched between poles which served as landmarks for the various craft coming in to the beach. There was (how should there not be) an inevitable thrill as we jumped down from the high side of the Duck on to the sand of France. I remembered the beach at Berhaume which I had left on that summer morning in 1940. Don Bradford and I walked up the wire laid road along the high watermark. This was the coast that we had so often sighted at night, which had for four years, up till nine days ago, been a hostile coast full of the menace of shore guns. The dark line of it had been a symbol of the enemy during our night patrols. But now we were walking along its beach in the early morning rain."

Next day I went back to England and did not return to the Alice-in-Wonderland island for about a week, when I arrived at Courseulles with a definite job as Staff Officer (Coastal Forces) to the Flag Officer British Assault Area (F.O.B.A.A.).

My job at Courseulles was to see that the operations of our M.T.B.s were sensibly conceived, that the orders were properly made out for them and that sufficient information on how they were carrying them out came back to the Admiral's plot during the night. E-boats were very active again by now, for they had been extensively reinforced since the heavy raid on Le Havre. As well as the E-boats there were regular patrols of 'M'-class Mineseepers and R-boats, which steamed up the coast towards Cap d'Antifer and back again. The patrol was so regular that it was known as 'the night train'. We had a number of battles between our M.T.B.s and the night train, and we got the E-boats' morale down so much that they used to come out about eight miles from their harbour, and then as soon as our forces began their interception they would turn and bolt for home at forty knots.

Our Plot in the dugout consisted of a chart under perspex on a trestle table. At the back of the table sat plotters connected by head and breast telephone sets to the Mobile Naval Radar sets which were set up along the coast. Across the tiny room sat four telegraphists opposite four wireless sets. An additional pair of earphones for me was connected to the R/T set, so that sitting at the left of the table I could keep control of the whole situation. At the right of the table was the Plotting Officer who put the enemy reports on to the perspex with a wax pencil and small cardboard ships to represent the last known positions. The whole of the front of the table was left clear for the Admiral or Chief of Staff or Staff Officer, Operations, to come and watch at any time. Admiral Rivett-Carnac used to come and sit by the Plot most evenings taking great interest in the battles, but making no attempt to interfere with the way I was handling them. The Chief of Staff was Grant and the S.O.O. was Tom Masterman (Commander, R.N.). It used to be dreadfully hot in the dugout so that we all worked in shirt sleeves, which gave us a very businesslike appearance. From time to time we went out into the fresh air to cool down and smoke a cigarette. Each night there were enemy aircraft about and the guns banged noisily outside whilst the news of the sea battle came to us on the radio telephone. Slips of paper and more slips of paper were the keynote of those nights. Signals pushed in front of me as I sat at the side of the table were slipped into bulldog clips and hung on a board with six-inch nails in it—one each for W/T in and out and R/T in and out. 'R/T in' was always the bulkiest clip.

I was on duty most nights until between three and five a.m., after which I could usually get some sleep. Normally I slept until ten a.m. and cleared the plans for the next night at a ten-thirty staff meeting to which Captain (P) and the Control Officers, who had been at sea, always came. I used to take a little chart in a perspex case with the proposals drawn in on it. These could be altered quickly and simply if the staff discussion demanded it. Then Tom Masterman took the details off the chart to make his night disposition signal, which ordered it all to take place. After that I used to telephone by landline to Portsmouth and tell them our proposals and hear theirs. This we did by using a transparent grid of our own which I had made before leaving. Only two of them existed. I had one and Christopher Dreyer in Portsmouth had the other. By using this method we could pass our secret dispositions over the ordinary telephone lines. After lunch I could sometimes make up sleep, but more often than not there were journeys to be made ashore visiting mobile radar equipment and harbour installations as well as various liaison missions with the Army.

The military situation in those days was that Caen—one of the D-day objectives—had not been captured. The Germans had counter-attacked and made themselves a salient north of Caen. They held Lebissey, Epron, St. Contest, Buron, Authie and then down to the Carpiquet area. And our troops sat opposite them at

Beuville, Cazelle, and Vieux Cairon, waiting for the materials of war to accumulate behind them. And accumulate they did. I first saw this accumulation when I went over in a jeep to see our mobile radar stations (Monrads). About a mile inland it started. On either side of the road for mile after mile the fields were full of dumps— ammunition, stores, motor vehicles—disposed and scattered against the possibility of air attack, though such was rare enough by day and surprisingly ineffective at night. Indeed at this time the enemy's air activity was limited almost entirely to night minelaying with an occasional sweep with Me 109s on cloudy days.

One evening we heard that there was to be a great heavy bomber raid on the enemy positions round Caen. The vanguard of Lancasters was due to arrive at ten past eight, and at eight o'clock we climbed to the top of the 150-foot water tower which stood in the precincts of our camp. Tom Masterman came up as well. The view from the top was superb. If you faced south the cornfields stretched five miles up the gentle slope to the crest of the hill. Little woods, occasional wooded hedges, but mostly the green gold of the corn in the late evening light. As far down the other side of the crest, but hidden by the high ground, were the enemy's positions before Caen, the objective of the raid. To the east were the villages of Tailleville and Douvres and the twin spires of La Delivrande. To the west were the marshes stretching along to the cliffs of Arromanches, under the sunset. In the sky along the shore-line, both east and west and directly behind us to the north, were clusters of little low balloons with the sharp fins of the naval type. Behind, too, was the anchorage and the Gooseberry with its sunken merchant ships protecting the fleet of small landing craft; and ships and more ships stretching for miles out to sea.

This was the scene that surrounded us when the first Lancaster bomber appeared from the north. Closely following it was a cluster of the great black things emerging from amongst wisps of dappled cloud. And then as we looked into the distance we could see even more and still more bombers coming. As the leaders reached the target the flak began to burst in the sky until the air was peppered with little puffs of smoke. But still they flew in. They were not very high, perhaps 6,000 or 7,000 feet, no more (so it seemed); they came in crowds, not flying in any formation, but just filling the sky so that a great stream stretched across the zenith. Big clouds of grey smoke came up above the woods on the horizon from the target area. Rivers of tracer poured upwards, and the bombers flew on into it. One circled back left-handed and made a forced landing in a field or perhaps on an airstrip. Another lost height over the enemy lines in the far distance. A third, burning fiercely, crashed also far away, too far to see if the crew had been able to bale out. But most of the Lancasters turned right and flew on to the west-wards before turning north. One was losing height and suddenly it turned downwards and went into a vertical dive. A few moments later it plunged into the sea with a burst of flame which flickered and burned on the surface after the wreckage had disappeared. We watched in awe, for we had seen no parachutes emerge, but then we thought maybe they had jumped earlier and we looked back along the course it had taken. And there were the parachutes—two, three —we looked further back, yes, there were more—five, six, seven— against the dark clouds of the dusk there might have been others. The light southerly wind was blowing them over the sea. As the parachutes came floating down, we glanced round to the Goose-berry. Three Air Sea Rescue Launches were already on the way, creaming out of the little artificial harbour. They would be there waiting before the parachutists reached the sea.

A second wave of bombers followed less than half an hour after the first and we watched that too. This great raid must, we realised, be heralding the push that we were all waiting for.

That night the guns thundered and the light of the barrage flickered in the sky as I walked back to my tent in the early hours after the night's patrol activity off Le Havre. By three o'clock it was usually possible to know what was likely to happen. So far the human torpedoes and the explosive motor boats, which appeared a week or two later, had not been used. If there was no activity by three it was usually safe to get some sleep.

R*

CHAPTER 27   *The War on Land*

ON the day after the big air-raid and the night barrage, the first
great attack was launched on the Caen salient. On the following
afternoon I was offered a place in a staff car which was going up to
the front. The Military Liaison Officer on F.O.B.A.A.'s staff—
Captain Pat Meredith Hardy—was to make contact with various
units. Tom Masterman and another came too.

We started at the eastern end calling on an Artillery H.Q. at
Coleville to hear the latest news of the battle. Then we moved on
to Bieville and Beuville, two tiny adjacent villages which had been
our front line. As we came up to the battlefield there were burnt-out
tanks in the cornfields. We came to a haystack which had been
used as an observation post. We climbed to the top of it in a drizzle
of rain and looked across a shallow dip of green fields with a wood
on the right in which, we were told, the enemy was still holding
out. There were great concentrations of tanks behind the wood and
moving across the hollow under the cover of a big hedge. This
looked very exciting although no enemy could be seen. Through
the hollow ran a road on which vehicles dashed at high speed. We
did not imagine that half an hour later we should be cruising along
this same road, stopping to look at the dead enemy tanks.

Beyond the hollow was the skeleton of a wood with a water tower at
one end. This was Lebissey Wood, which had been captured
during the earlier part of the day. As we came down from the
haystack, on which we were photographed by a Press man who
was passing and thought our naval uniforms looked odd, we saw
twenty or thirty prisoners being herded along the road in their
spotted camouflage suits. They looked neither more nor less
miserable or bedraggled than one would expect prisoners to look
after a major battle.

We moved westward along roads which ran parallel to the front.

The first was one we had looked down on. Now we were close to the tanks hiding behind the hedges. One field was entirely full of 'Priests', the mobile twenty-five-pounders which were firing away at objectives out of sight beyond Lebissey Wood and over the crest. In spite of the din of the guns a herd of cows was lying down in the field a few yards from them. One of their number had strayed into a minefield and been blown up. It lay dead, belly downwards in a ghastly spreadeagle with the gases within it swelling it to a horrible bloatedness. The minefields were wired off here, as elsewhere, and hanging on the wires were the familiar German stencilled skull and crossbones notices with the word 'Minen'.

We came to a village where there was said to be an observation post in a chateau and we found the chateau, although it appeared deserted. There was a sentry in one of the downstairs rooms, who showed us the way up to the attic which had been the O.P. There were a few tiles of the roof missing but no worse destruction. Through the holes left by the missing tiles one could look out on the troops advancing across the open cornfields. In this area a concentration of Germans was holding out in the woods near St. Contest and the white smoke-screen which began whilst we were in the attic was evidently to cover an attack on these positions. But there was little to be seen. The artillery barrage continued unabated but otherwise there was no activity. The inside of the chateau was a sad shambles, though no doubt much could be salvaged. The owners had some taste in furniture and pictures. There were fine old family portraits, a few modern landscapes and some Chinese prints. The adjoining farmyard was full of dead animals. We drove to the edge of a wood which had been our front line at the start of the push. There was a shattered shrine but the figure of the Virgin was intact. A dead and bloated cow lay on the opposite side, its legs sticking out stiffly from the inflated body. The wood was thick and leafy. A soldier standing at the corner said that it was inadvisable to go further and a notice on the verge said 'Road not checked beyond here', meaning that it had not been cleared of mines. Half a mile ahead up the straight road we could see another wood, or what had been a wood, with a village nestling in it. It was now a row of tattered bare tree trunks with a few shapeless walls sticking up above the rubble. Over to the left, a thick green wood, which had not been touched by our devastating bombardment, still held an outpost of Germans. There was the crackle of machine-gun fire as our troops went through it, mopping up resistance.

We drove on through Cairon and Vieux Cairon. Our guns were

hidden, barking from woods and orchards and hedgerows—but not to be seen. Occasional German shells came amongst them—a crump as opposed to the clean bang of the discharge of our own guns. The whistle of the shells overhead seemed to make an arch and the din was appalling. In the midst of it a very old lady was sitting in a field milking a cow.

We stopped the car in a dip in the road beyond Vieux Cairon. The next village was Buron, reported to have fallen. On the right Authie was being assaulted and on the left St. Contest was still holding out as a pocket on the left flank of the sector. From the dip, where a dead pig lay by the roadside, we walked forward along the road. On either side was open country with arable fields and grassland. The country rolled gently away into the haze of battle. On our right was a hollow up which tanks were advancing—mostly Shermans. Behind them were strings of infantry, waist deep in the corn, spread across the opposite slope. Ahead were the smoke-screens which hid them from the enemy beyond Authie. Occasional enemy shells burst in their midst; occasional big explosions seemed to indicate mines. Further up the hollow, between Buron and Authie, there were tanks advancing at the furthest limit of visibility. One was on fire with a column of black smoke curling into the sky. On the ridge the infantry were strung out between the tanks. As they reached the crest they began to crouch and finally nothing but an occasional tin hat showed above the corn.

The road we walked along was typical of a battlefield. Such roads, I learnt afterwards, all have the same desolate look. The surface is pock marked with bullet and small shell holes. The dust and dirt thrown up have not been disturbed by the passage of cars, so that the surface has the appearance of disuse. There are odd bits of debris about the road and the verges—splinters of wood from shattered telegraph poles, disordered coils of wire, spent cartridge cases, empty ammunition boxes, the wooden handles of German hand grenades. Here and there a tin hat, a haversack, a battledress tunic or a ground sheet, an empty and punctured petrol tin. There are mounds of earth by the roadside made perhaps by a bulldozer, or perhaps by spades which cover the remains of a cow or a pig, or maybe a man. Such a road was the one we now walked up. Overhead the larks were singing, loud above the noise of battle.

Stopped by the roadside, drawn on to the grass, were a dozen Churchill tanks, fitted with mortars. They were waiting to go forward, standing in the open with engines running. We met two Guards officers and stood talking to them in the middle of the road.

As we stood, two German prisoners came along the road in the charge of a Canadian walking behind them with a tommy gun. When they came to us in our naval uniforms, they thought that we must at least be the Army Commander and his Intelligence Officer. So they stopped and came to attention with a click of heels. This was not at all what their guard had in mind. He told them to go on in forceful language and fired his tommy gun into the verge to lend encouragement to his words. The Germans' arms flew up again and with an apprehensive glance over their shoulders, they set off once more at a brisk pace. We climbed into the Churchill tanks and talked to the crews about the progress of the battle so far and what they would be doing in half an hour's time. They seemed to like to talk in order to reduce the tension of their wait. I was struck again by the way danger makes the world a smaller place for me and all the people in it are my friends. I believe those tank crews felt the same at that moment.

Buron, a crumbling ruin of a village a few hundred yards ahead, was under heavy mortar fire from the enemy and we decided not to go into it. Instead we returned down the road to our staff car.

Caen fell on the following day and we were sent up, the next afternoon, to look at the results of the shelling of Lebissey Wood and the 'ring contour'—the highest point north of Caen—by the battleship *Rodney* and the monitor *Roberts*, during the great bombardment before the push. Lebissey Wood was still under mortar fire when we stopped in it. It is on the crest of a ridge, which falls away steeply to the east, down to the Canal and the Orne and, across it, the factory of Colombelles. Some of the Colombelles chimneys had been knocked down but the majority still stood, fully a dozen towering high above the steelworks, to make observation posts for the German gunners. On this afternoon we had two jeeps. In one I rode with Hugh Mulleneux, the Gunnery Officer on F.O.B.A.A.'s staff whose boats we had covered in the landing at Dieppe. In the other was Pat Hardy and a little Frenchman called Meurville.

The road into Caen from Lebissey was under observation from the factory chimneys and was said to be under fire. We saw many cars and lorries coming through, but after consultation, it was decided to cut back through Bieville and across to the main road down over the ring contour. We went back and along the road where the mobile guns had been firing the last time, past the dead cow that had been blown up on a mine. There were troops on the ring contour. We took the jeeps past the road fork and a little way down the hill and then walked back to look at the huge craters which covered the highest ground. Who could tell which were from bombs and which from the *Rodney*'s bombardment? Whilst we were there a queer rumbling, moaning noise came up from Colombelles. Several of the troops dropped into their foxholes. We lay down behind a wall. Nothing came. It was apparently the discharge of 'Moaning Minny', the multi-barrelled mortar, but it had not been coming our way.

We decided to go down into Caen to check on the situation at the main bridge over the canal. Sniping was still going on, particularly in the east side of the town; and Vaucelles, the half of the town across the River Orne, was still apparently entirely in enemy hands. Just as we left the top of the hill I saw signs of a battle away to the south-west, beyond Caen. A slope up to a distant ridge had burning tanks on it—flames and columns of smoke. From where I stood it was impossible to see more than a tiny patch of the battle through a gap in the trees. Further down the road it seemed that the view would be clear. We drove down and the road went into a cutting. Here we stopped and I scrambled up the slope on the west side to gaze across at what I afterwards discovered were the first battles for the famous Hill 112. It was very distant, perhaps four miles away, and at that range until one has watched a battle for some time it is almost impossible to follow the course of events or even to tell friend from foe. I had not been there long when I heard some desultory popping behind me on my left, and turned round for the first time. In climbing to the top of the cutting on one side I was in full view of the whole of the town behind and below me. Most of the foreground was shambles but beyond were buildings in which apparently the snipers were housed. One of them had just begun to shoot at me. The bullets sang overhead and then closer, and in a second I had slid down into the road. Even here we did not feel secure. The higher houses were still in sight. We went back to the jeep, engaged its four-wheel drive and started into the town. The route had been used by tracked vehicles and perhaps jeeps but nothing else. It went straight over the desolation of the north part of Caen. It went down into the bomb craters and up the other side and over the rim into the next. "In peace time," we said, "you would pay a shilling for such a ride on the scenic railway."

Suddenly we came to the end of the desolation and to houses. The other jeep was there and another, belonging by chance to a Marine Officer who had been Forward Observation Officer for the *Rodney*'s shoots. He and Hugh Mulleneux had a long talk about the problems of bombardment. There were a French couple with whom Meurville talked and another Frenchman wearing a French tin hat painted white who leant over the map as we outlined our route and the front line. I wondered if he was a spy. It was impossible to get through into the centre of the town by car so we went back over the scenic railway and up the hill to the ring contour and then worked round using the map. The main tank routes down into Caen had been marked by white tape stretched on either side of the tracks to indicate the parts cleared of mines. We drove down a grassy track so marked which led into a little hollow. The hollow was full of carefully camouflaged foxholes dug by the Germans before the push. Branches of trees still unwithered lay over some of them.

So we came into the centre of Caen, where miraculously the cathedral had escaped almost untouched. Here in the main street it was possible to look up and down and see no sign of damage beyond a few broken windows. Here too was an amazing scene, for the streets were full of people—men, women and children, laughing and smiling, shopping and gossipping. It was not the hysterical welcome which I later saw so frequently, but at the time it was remarkable enough when the sniping was going on only a few streets away and less than half a mile separated us all from the enemy at Vaucelles. As we examined the map in the middle of this scene a cluster of little boys crowded round us demanding "cigarettes pour papa".

West of Caen is the suburb of St. Germain la Blanche Herbe. We drove along until the road begins to climb on to the hill. From here at the edge of the town one could look out across the Orne to the south where the Germans were still holding out and to the south-west in the fork between the Odon and the Orne where the battle for Maltot and Hill 112 raged beyond the aerodrome of Carpiquet. For a while we watched the tanks, tiny ants crawling up the slopes or sitting dotted about the distant fields. Near the crest several had 'brewed up'. It was impossible to know which they were, ours or theirs, as they blazed away with tall pillars of black smoke curling above them. One Sherman was hit with a flash and began to burn at once. I had a feeling that most of the burning tanks were ours, but it was probably quite unjustified.

On the way home to Courseulles we agreed that we had a new understanding and a new admiration for the boys who had to fight in tanks. Like the aircraft in which I had flown over Germany, I saw the tanks as the counterpart of our own boats, and had watched their ordeal with my own eyes.

CHAPTER 28   *The Chantiers Navals*

HALF a mile downstream from the Colombelles factory, on a strip
of land between the canal and the River Orne, is the great shipyard of the Chantiers Navals de France. The Flag Officer British
Assault Area (F.O.B.A.A.—my boss) proposed an expedition to
this shipyard to discover its state of repair, and I was instructed
to go and examine the possibility of establishing a Coastal Force
Base there. The position of the front at that time was that Ouistreham—the town at the mouth of the Caen canal—was still under
shell fire and the line ran up the valley to the outskirts of Caen.
Even in Caen itself, the far side of the river—the suburb of Vaucelles
—was still enemy held.

Roughly the enemy held the line of the Orne and we held the
line of the canal. The narrow strip of marsh between the two
waterways was 'patrol ground', and on this strip was the shipyard,
opposite to Blainville. Immediately below Blainville, the Sixth
Airborne Division had been holding a bridgehead across the Orne
since D-day. The right flank of this bridgehead came to the river a
little below the shipyard. Recently the Highland Division put in
an attack southward along the far bank in order to take the steelworks at Colombelles. They had reached the factory but a counter-
attack with Tiger tanks had dislodged them and they had fallen
back. We did not know exactly how far back, but we heard that two
or three officers of the Thirtieth Assault Unit (whose job it is to get
into such places as the shipyard and save all equipment and papers
of interest) had been mortared a certain amount the day before in
the Chantiers Navals.

We set off in a jeep, four strong—two Engineer Officers, a
Polish Commander and myself. As we left an attack by Me 109s
had just been beaten off. Four columns of black smoke indicated
where four of them had been shot down. We took the main road

through Tailleville to the eastwards past the twin spires of La Delivrande (one plain, one pearl)—the church undamaged in the D-day fight. One spire is plain and the other, exactly like it in shape, is decorated with elaborate ornamentation. Neither would be so satisfying without the other as foil. Through Cresserons, Hermanville, and Coleville to Blainville. We stopped to get news from Div. H.Q. and again in Blainville at the H.Q. of the Reconnaissance Regiment, whose patrols were said to be occupying the shipyard. The Colonel of the regiment was a cousin of one of the party; he was out but we arranged to return later.

From Blainville we turned down the hill and over the Bailey bridge crossing the canal. A little narrow road went off along the bank of the canal and the arm leading to the shipyard basin. We followed it. This was entirely different country from the open corn-fields and rolling land on the other side of Caen and it was somehow much less appropriate for war. The summer trees were rich and green; the willows were silver green, and the reed beds were blue-green. The country was thick and small and one could see no great distance in any direction. Only up the valley and just in front of us the tall factory chimneys of Colombelles, the eyes of the German gunners, towered above the treetops, looking down even into the secluded strip of marsh along which we drove. "Go slow, so as not to raise the dust," they had said at H.Q., "and they probably won't bother to shoot at you."

At this point the whole valley was no more than half a mile wide. On our right as we drove up it was the canal, on our left was the river and beyond it a wooded slope covered with scrub with a hedge at the top, about 500 yards away. This wood, we said knowingly, must be held by the 51st Highland Division and we spun happily down the road, nor did we discover until we got to the far end that it was in fact held by the Germans. Our three-quarters of a mile drive along the road had been parallel to the enemy's front line, most of the way in full view of it, at 500 yards range.

Half-way along we passed the burnt-out remains of an R-boat lying half submerged at the side of the channel. The shipyard, much overgrown with summer vegetation and thick reeds, consisted of a large basin with about half a dozen small ships scuttled in it, and another half-dozen ships on the slipways in various stages of completion and damage. The cranes and gantries had almost all been demolished. In the middle of the basin was a scuttled armed trawler lying in about ten feet of water and beyond were the buildings, most of them not seriously damaged.

We found the patrol in a large air-raid shelter. The C.O. was asleep, but the N.C.O. insisted on waking him and we went into the buildings. The C.O. who was a Captain in the Reconnaissance Regiment, explained that the whole area between the canal and the river was regarded as patrol ground or No-man's-land and that his platoon was an outpost. Across the river, 100 yards away, were the German outposts, one could hear them shouting orders, he said, particularly at reveille. The scrub-covered slope across the river had only snipers in it, as it was too exposed to our view. We moved into the shipyard and for some time browsed in the main offices to the shattering accompaniment of an artillery duel which rattled the few remaining windows. There were some interesting drawings in the drawing office of the ships building and refitting in the yard. The half-built tankers of about 400–500 tons were evidently a 'spécialité de la maison'. The managing director's office was full of Nazi propaganda books and pamphlets. The stationery store was well stocked. Foolishly I did not collect one of the very excellent notebooks we came upon and the next time I was there they had all gone; only a few rather inferior ones were available— like the one I am now writing in.

We wandered round the workshops, visiting the power plant and sounding the depth of water alongside the quay with a piece of wire attached to a bomb splinter to act as a lead-line. There were black redstarts nesting in the buildings, I saw a fine cock and what appeared to be two hens, but one may have been a fledged young one. A kingfisher flew across the basin. I decided to go on board the trawler out in midstream and the patrol C.O. gave me a little Cockney soldier as escort. This little man, with tin hat and camouflage net worn round the neck like a scarf, armed with a tommy gun, filled me with admiration for the British soldier's mastery of the art of war. He had been in the fighting since D-day but had had no battle experience before that. He was a Cockney from South London, yet in the six weeks he had assimilated all the habits and attributes of a seasoned hunter. He walked as a Scottish deer-stalker walks. He was perpetually alert and receptive.

Our way to the far side of the basin led us through the underbrush and the reeds, past the slipways and gantries and through various fences and barbed wire. In this patrol area there was always the chance that one might come suddenly on a Hun patrol lying up for the day in the thick cover. Against this possibility the tommy gun was held at the ready. As he walked and I followed him, he

trod softly picking his way, watching for trip wires or newly disturbed earth that might indicate a mine. At the same time he kept
looking up towards the enemy slope and selecting our course to
give us maximum cover from the buildings and the trees. All this
he did apparently by instinct—or was it perhaps sound training?
Two things, he said, must be avoided; first, never run because it
catches the sniper's eye, and secondly, never come back by the same
route that you went out.

We reached the bank of the basin. The level was six feet lower
than normal, the shores were covered with dead fresh-water fish
and many live ones were rising out in the basin—perch, bream,
dace, chubb and a fish which looked like a grayling. From the far
side I had seen a little raft on the bank. This I found and launched
and climbed precariously on board. It was a very small Carley-type
raft and I found that the only way to keep dry was to kneel astride
it. The only available paddle was a plank picked up on the beach
and what little wind there was blew dead against me. However, I
struggled out across the fifty yards to the scuttled trawler. On the
way I had some qualms. Tied up astern of the trawler was another
raft with a paddle lying on it. What better place for an enemy patrol
to hide in during the day than the cabins of the trawler which were
still above water. Here was I, unarmed, about to walk straight into
the ambush.

I climbed aboard the trawler which was lying over at a steep
angle. There was a frightful stench of dead fish which were floating
in the engine room and in the after accommodation. The bridge
structure with the Captain's and First Lieutenant's cabins, was
undamaged, although fairly thoroughly gutted, partly by the
Germans when they abandoned her and partly, no doubt, by the
Thirtieth Assault Unit people who had been on board the day
before. Needless to say, no German patrol was there to ambush me.
I spent about an hour on board and found a number of interesting
documents, including a diary of the Captain's with a full account
of a recent visit to Berlin. The First Lieutenant had a notebook in
which he and his French girl friend (or friends) had attempted to
settle the language question—"Je vous aime" and "Geben sie mir
einen Küss" had pride of place. On the bridge were two signal
lamps which I knew would be invaluable in any M.T.B. I picked
one up and pressed the switch. Being a battery lamp it lit and a
brilliant searchlight beam shone out across the German front line.
I hoped no one had noticed or would think it worth shooting at me.
I took notes of the exact armament and whatever other details

seemed to be of interest, then I paddled myself back, to the accompaniment of the squattering of moorhens. My little escort had been sitting all this time motionless at the edge of the rushes with his camouflage net pulled over his head, invisible if you did not know exactly where to look for him. We struggled up the bank and set off back towards the main buildings. Through a gap in the barbed wire it was necessary to break one of his golden rules; we had to come back the way we had come. I did not think much about it until a queer popping broke out from the top of the scrub-covered slope on our left. It was accompanied by a 'piew-piew' as bullets came about our ears. The snipers were shooting at us; and forthwith we broke the other golden rule—we ran like stoats. Fifty yards and we were in cover, proceeding again at the appropriate catlike pace.

The rest of the party had collected some oddments of souvenirs, including a huge photograph of the *Burza*, the Polish destroyer, which had been built there and in which the Polish Commander had once served. Whilst I had been away on board the trawler a few mortar shells had landed on the buildings which I had heard, for the crump of arriving shells is quite different from the bark of departing ones. All the while our shells had been singing over into the Colombelles factory and bursting with a crump and a cloud of brown smoke. At times they went so fast and the German shells came back so regularly that one could imagine oneself standing under a vault of whining shells, just as we had imagined the much greater arch over the Dover Straits two years before.

With our new-found discovery that the enemy overlooked our return route, the rest of the party was ready to agree that my plan of putting the hood up over the jeep to hide the unusual appearance and number of its occupants, was not so cranky as they had claimed when I insisted on stopping to do it at Blainville on the way down. We returned thither without mishap, however, and went to call on the Colonel, who received us sitting naked in a small green canvas bath, whilst our fighters shot down a Messerschmitt overhead and our anti-aircraft shot at our fighters. Afterwards he gave us some gin in the parlour of the farmhouse. Our driver, who was the Colonel's cousin, was invited to stay for dinner, and so we took the jeep on back to Courseulles. Stupidly we allowed the Polish Commander to drive, and for three-quarters of an hour we were in far greater danger than at any other time during the day.

CHAPTER 29   *A Rash Adventure*

AFTER a brief visit to England where I bought myself a khaki battledress, I was off again to Courseulles for a further term of office as Coastal Forces Staff Officer. As before, I was to do an occasional night at sea as Controller in one of the frigates in order to give Tony Hollings and Guy Fison a chance of a night off to sleep ashore in France or to get back to England for some clean laundry. With two frigates in the area these two were required every single night (after George Bailey was killed when the *Trollope* was torpedoed) unless I stood in for them occasionally. This was useful experience for me and became exceptionally valuable later on in the Channel Islands.

My normal routine was still to sit on the Plot in the orchard at Courseulles listening to the R/T with a pair of headphones and talking to the Controller from time to time on the V.H.F. telephone. There was, in fact, very little that we could do except keep track of events and leave it to the Controller, who had Captain (P) on board (Captain Pugsley for most of the time, though for a short spell, a remarkable man called Captain Gotto). After about three o'clock I could usually turn in, in the spare bunk in Tom Masterman's caravan near the Plot.

As before, in the mornings I organised the operations for the next night and in the afternoons I either slept or pursued the various missions with which from time to time I was charged. It was decreed at one time that the Commanding Officers of various ships operating in the area would benefit by a brief visit to the front, and as I now knew the roads fairly well I was detailed to act as their guide. Thus it was that on 26th July I wrote of an adventure which had taken place the day before.

"Yesterday I took Peter Dickens, Tony Hollings and Guy Fison to see the slow-going advance south of Caen. We had

decided to go via Colombelles which had lately fallen, out
towards Troarn, but time was short as all three of my companions
had to be back in time to go to sea at dusk. We cut out Colombelles and struck east into the dust and milling tanks moving up
into the line. A jeep coming in the opposite direction was driven
by Charles Tryon—a Major in the Guards. We had not met for
ten years but he recognised me and shouted. We stopped and he
told us how the battle went, drawing in chinagraph on his
perspex map case. The Canadians were pushing south from
Caen on the Falaise road and the going was very slow. The tanks
were to have attacked that evening but it did not look as if they
would be called on yet. The breach had still to be cut for them. To
the south was, he said, the place to see the battle, so we went
back through Vaucelles and turned south, not on the Falaise
road but on the next one, leading to André and Mai-sur-Orne,
which passes over another ring contour on the crest of a down.

"We found ourselves bowling down a road that was comparatively deserted and I explained my theory that if you saw
soldiers shaving beside their transport the odds were that they
were not actually under fire, a theory which I later disproved.
According to our information André-sur-Orne had been captured
that morning and Maltot which was on our right, had fallen the
night before but remained the front line. We passed the self-
propelled artillery scattered about the fields. On approaching
the front in this area it was always noticeable that the din of
battle was loudest some two miles or more behind the line, where
the artillery was concentrated. In the dead ground behind the
ridge the fields were full of 'Priests' (mobile guns) firing away at
the German positions beyond the crest, away down the far slope
to Mai-sur-Orne. Soon we came into the area where the troops
all wore tin hats. With some difficulty I persuaded Peter Dickens
that it was tin hat time. His tin hat was too small for him and he
looked uncommonly droll. At a cross roads sat a Canadian
Military Policeman. We asked him the situation and he said that
from there on the road was being shelled, and that it would be
unwise to hang around in the area, although the traffic was going
through to André and seemed to be all right provided it kept
moving. André itself, however, was being mortared.

"The crest of the hill was about half a mile ahead. Having
come this far it seemed a pity not to see what could be seen of the
battle on the far side. At the cross-roads there was a wall. We
decided to leave the jeep by the wall and walk the half-mile

along the road. There were a couple of dead horses in the field, and as usual the road was pock marked with small shell holes; the telegraph poles were splintered and the wires were lying about the roads and ditches. It was a straight road with open rolling fields on either side—no hedges and very few trees. On the right the fields fell away to the wooded valley of the Orne and just beyond it Maltot. The trees on the far bank about a mile and a half away were German-held and in full view. Beyond them the fields rose again to the famous Hill 112—the scene of the great tank battles of three weeks before and still the front line. By the side of the road there were many shell craters and many fox-holes hurriedly dug, some by the enemy and some by our own troops on the previous day.

"In a cluster we walked along the road, the other three dressed in blue naval uniforms. I was in my khaki battledress. After we had walked 300 yards it seemed to me that we were bound for a nasty place and that it was going to be a slow business coming away from it on foot should the shelling start again. As there were several jeeps and motor-cycles and occasionally even larger transport spinning along the road from time to time, I thought we should be much less noticeable in the jeep. One felt so very naked walking along that open road, ant-like, in full view of the enemy. It was therefore agreed that I should go back and fetch the jeep whilst they walked on and I would pick them up. This I did and shortly caught up with them and took them on board. We went on as far as a bend in the road, beyond which the hill sloped gently away to André-sur-Orne. Here we stopped and from this point, with one exception, our doings were distressingly ill-advised. The one exception was that I turned the jeep round. It did seem that it might be wise to have it pointing in the right direction.

"Still the jeeps and motor-cyclists flashed past as we stood by the side of the road with field glasses, looking across to the German woods. One of the motor-cyclists pulled up and even turned back to come to us. 'I wouldn't stop here long,' he advised, 'and if you do I should get near a foxhole.' We thanked him and he went on his way. A hundred yards back down the road we had seen one of his colleagues sprawled, dead, by the side of his shattered motor-cycle where a shell had hit the road. We took the advice. There did not seem to be much mining on this sector of the front. The verges were apparently clear and across the road were some convenient foxholes. We walked across to them and sat down on the mounds of earth. 'If we look carefully with glasses we'll probably be able to see tanks and things and follow the course of the battle,' I said, and we sat and looked. Across the valley there were hidden camouflaged tanks and troops, probably front-line troops, in foxholes sheltering behind banks and along hedgerows. Maltot was hidden in the trees on our right. Ahead and to the right were the burnt-out hulks of the tanks I had seen in the battles for Hill 112 which I had watched from Carpiquet. On the left the road disappeared down the slope to André and beyond André smoke rose in the air from Mai, still in enemy hands. Suddenly the air was full of diving Typhoons. They plunged towards Mai and, with a twin trail of smoke, their rockets went down on to the objective. As each pulled out of the dive the tearing roar of the rockets' discharge and the whine of the power dive reached us. In quick succession they dived down and great black mushrooms of smoke came up from the target area. The fourth Typhoon, more determined than the rest, pressed home his attack to a few hundred feet. It was much braver than the rest and at last he pulled out and his rockets went down. Up he went in a zoom and we thought that all was well, but then he did a slow roll over on to his back and went into a vertical dive, hitting the ground with a burst of black smoke in the middle of a wood below us.

"Peter said 'Oh! The suddenness and completeness of it!' I thought how short a time before the bravest of all the party had been having tea in the mess at the airstrip. And from the time that he screwed himself up to make that brave attack it was no more than five seconds to the final end.

"As we talked I stood up to see if I could see anything over to the left with the glasses. Exactly as I got to my feet there was a deafening crack and a shell burst about 100 yards behind us. Rather quickly we jumped down into the foxhole, except for Tony Hollings who lay flat outside in the grass. When I looked behind I saw that our jeep 100 yards away stood fairly and squarely on the skyline. In addition another jeep containing two soldiers who were concerned with joining a broken telephone wire had pulled up near-by. They had taken the precaution of driving off the road into a slight hollow so that at least their jeep didn't look like the side of a house. They had to be there and we did not. They cannot have regarded our presence or that of our jeep with any favour.

"We did not have very long to take in this situation. The next shell landed exactly opposite our foxhole and about twenty yards to our right. I bobbed down to the bottom of the foxhole, which was a slit in the ground some six feet long, two feet wide and four feet deep. At the far end of it I saw Guy Fison who had also bobbed down. Peter Dickens didn't move. He stood upright with his head and shoulders above ground and his beard jutting out towards the offending shell burst. With admirable reasoning, he realised that it was too late to duck for that one and there was plenty of time before the next. Tony Hollings scrambled into the hole and we lit cigarettes. The situation was unhealthy. More shells were arriving, many of them close to the jeep. Indeed one had landed on the road within about four or five yards of it, and from where we were we could not see whether or not the little car had been damaged.

"Evidently the German observers had seen us and deemed us a worthy target. The tricky part was that time was now short and within the next half-hour we should have to start back if the patrols off Le Havre were to sail on time. After about ten minutes the shelling ceased and we held a council of war. There were two schools of thought—one that we should crawl all the way back to the jeep and hope to avoid observation, the other that we should run like hell and hope to get going before they started up again. We started off crawling and finished by running. We ran across the road and along the far ditch. At one point it was full of corpses which had been hidden by a few hastily dug turfs, probably done during the previous night. Tony did not notice them and ran over the top of the turfs. I saw and smelt them and ran round the boots which protruded at the end. I remember shouting some fatuous remark to the two soldiers about our jeep being nearly hit. Considering what they must have thought of us and our jeep, they were surprisingly forbearing.

"We jumped across the road, leapt into the jeep, which showed no sign of damage, and trod on the starter. Much depended on the first turn of the engine for if it did not start first go, it was wont to choke and fail to start at all. We had had some embarrassing moments in traffic with it, but this time the engine came to life at once. I crashed into gear and we sped away down the road. We had gone less than 400 yards when a shell burst in the field opposite where we had been. Such was evidently the communication delay between the German observer and his guns. We bowled back at a good pace much relieved that we had escaped so lightly from our folly.

"We came away with increased respect for the soldiers who were fighting there. We realised how short a time we had been under fire and how little we had liked it. How many times during these trips to the front have we said, 'They seem to be mortaring down there—not a very healthy spot. I don't think we'll go down there.' We have seen the soldiers who have no choice in the matter. If the plan calls for them to go down there, they go, mortaring or no mortaring. And when they get there, they have to stay there. No rushing to a jeep and making off out of the area. They remain to be mortared, hour after hour, day after day, week after week. I had certainly done my job in giving these Naval Officers first-hand experience of the war on land, but it could not be said that our afternoon's work had achieved very much. Yet perhaps it was not entirely in vain if it helped us to realise what the infantry have been standing up to on the battle-fields of Normandy.

"And so back to Courseulles and the boys away to their ships in plenty of time for the night patrol."

The Hedge at Hill 112

CHAPTER 30   *A Most Satisfying Brief*

AT the beginning of August it was arranged that I should go to
Cherbourg to help to operate the U.S. P.T. boats—the American
M.T.B.s—and set up a Plot at the U.S. Headquarters of C.T.F.
125; in fact, I was to repeat my work with F.O.B.A.A.

Before moving to Cherbourg more permanently, I had to turn
over my job at Courseulles to Don Bradford, who was temporarily ashore whilst his flotilla reformed, and had been sent to
relieve me.

In Cherbourg, the Chief of Staff, Captain Clarke, gave me a most
satisfying brief. "We want," he said, "to lay on some operations
against the shipping in the Channel Islands; I want you to get
together with the P.T. boys, get the operation orders all set and then
go out and do it." Did ever a staff officer have a more admirable
prospect! Battles to be thought out and planned and then carried
out—and I was to do it all myself. No Admiral could have wished
for better.

There were a number of technical problems to overcome and
there was no time to be lost. The first was to find some form of
control communications, for the P.T. boats had no W/T, only R/T
with a very limited range. We decided that this communication link
would have to be through the radar station at Joburg, a little
village on the high moor at Cap de la Hague. The next was to
arrange with Plymouth for the P.T. boats to work in an area which
was laid down as Commander-in-Chief Plymouth's sphere of
operations. This was arranged by C.C.F. in Portsmouth. Another
problem was to obtain the necessary enemy intelligence and this
could only be passed to us on a land line from England using a
code.

Many of these problems had confronted us earlier in the summer,
first at Portsmouth, where we had set up a fairly efficient operating

mechanism in the months before the invasion, and then at Courseulles with F.O.B.A.A. Here there was an added problem; that
the Americans were deeply suspicious of British methods and that
international politics loomed large in all these matters. I was never
able, for instance, to persuade the Chief of Staff or the Admiral at
Cherbourg to speak direct, on the excellent land line, to their
opposite numbers in Plymouth. Communication was by signal,
in which a game was played to see who could make the rudest
answer. In all that appertained to the fighting in the Channel
Islands, it was left to the Staff Officer, Coastal Forces, at Plymouth
(Lieutenant Coleville) and myself to pour oil upon the troubled
waters.

At the same time as organising operations in the Channel Islands,
we were also trying to set up a Plot in the Headquarters in
Cherbourg. In charge of this was a most charming young American
Lieutenant called Maynard Fisher, who was also the Commanding
Officer of the radar station at Joburg (Monrad IV). He invited me
to make my home at the radar station and he took me out there that
very night.

It was about fifteen miles from Cherbourg, along a road which
gradually climbed through beautiful tree-filled country to moor-
land with heather and bracken. The site of the set was the old
German radar station with a central concrete emplacement above
which the tangled remains of the Giant Wurzburg set lay as it had
fallen when the Germans destroyed it. The aerial array was perhaps
sixty or seventy feet long and had been quite thirty feet high, although it now lay on its side like the skeleton of a vast bed. It was
an interesting commentary on our superiority in radar, to compare
the little mobile set, with its aerial array of no more than six or
seven feet, mounted on a trailer, and giving far better results than
the German monster had ever done.

Maynard Fisher had set up his plotting room in the concrete
dug-outs which had housed the German set, and his men lived
in the well-built huts which the enemy left quite undamaged.
They were sunk some seven or eight feet into the ground so that
they were like basements, but they were quite well appointed and
made a pleasant place to live in. Maynard rigged a camp bed in
his room for me and it became my home whenever I spent a night
ashore for the next three weeks, which was not very often.

There is a statutory time—I think it is about three weeks—after
which one is entitled to say "we used to do so-and-so" instead of
"we did". My time at Cherbourg consisted mainly of a routine

which seems to fall within this category. We used to take the P.T. boats to sea nearly every night. The Chief of Staff had conceived the idea that a Destroyer Escort—the American equivalent of a frigate—should be made available to mother them, and I was greatly in favour of this, for here was a frigate from which I could practise the control tactics which had been so successful in the earlier days of the invasion. The only trouble was that the P.T. boats and the D.E. (U.S.S. *Maloy*) were completely untrained, and the only training we could give them was harbour discussion and practice in action.

During my early days in Cherbourg I wrote an appreciation of the situation in the Channel Islands. I collected what intelligence was available and drew up a table of enemy forces and our forces. I worked out a plan to take advantage of any move which they might make among the islands, and put up a number of ambitious schemes involving the use of four British Fleet destroyers then in Cherbourg. Greatly to my surprise this appreciation was extremely well received by Admiral Wilkes and Captain Clarke, and was used as a basis for all our operations. In accordance with it, our nightly patrols continued. I arranged them usually to cover any shipping which might pass between Guernsey and Jersey, so that we used to spend the night a few miles west of La Corbière—the south-westernmost headland of Jersey.

On the first night that we did it, two units of P.T. boats were with us, from Squadron 34, whose Squadron Commander—Jack Scherertz—was with me on board *Maloy*. We had been on patrol since dusk, but it was not until about four-thirty in the morning that our radar first detected enemy ships coming from St. Peter Port in Guernsey and evidently bound for St. Helier in Jersey. There appeared to be at least five ships in the convoy and intelligence led us to believe that two would probably be 'M'-class Minesweepers, more dangerous customers than the trawlers which probably made up the rest of the escort. Somewhere in the middle would be the escorted ship, a smallish coaster, or perhaps two. Coasters were all that was left to the enemy in the Channel Islands, in the way of merchant ships, in those days.

I vectored one unit of three P.T.s on to the target, but they missed the interception astern. Then I moved in the second unit of two P.T.s. The sea was flat calm at the time and there was a fog. They all got in amongst the enemy and the two boats became separated. The second lost his head and fired his torpedoes blind into the fog because the leader had told him on R/T that the enemy was right ahead. Needless to say the torpedoes missed; so did the leader's.

At about this time I made a bad slip; I told the unit which had missed the interception that the enemy bore so-and-so three miles from him, which was true, but I used the wrong call sign, so that it went out as if addressed to the unit which was in action. This called forth a plaintive cry on R/T: "Hell, I'm in the middle of them." It was the last we ever heard from that boat. Some of the enemy appeared from the Plot to be slowing up, whilst the rest went on into St. Helier. It was now full daylight, but it was still foggy. We ourselves were about four miles from the shore, and we vectored the rest of the P.T. boats to join us. There was still no word from the 509 boat. When the others were alongside, we had a quick conference down on the iron deck of the *Maloy*. They were all anxious to go and look for the 509 boat, but I knew that two echoes remained on our scan, in the roadstead outside St. Helier. There was still fog although it was now nearly eight o'clock, and three boats still had torpedoes. By the first principle of war the object must be relentlessly pursued—and the object was the destruction of enemy ships, not the rescue of the 509 boat. I put this point of view to Jack Daniel, who was O.T.C. (Officer Tactical Command) of the unit, and he saw it at once. I was much tempted to go with him, but Jack Scherertz pointed out that the vectoring would be complicated in the fog and that I ought to stay in the *Maloy* to do it. Scherertz himself decided to lead the party and it was agreed that after the attack they should search to the westward for 'the 9 boat'. Only two of the three boats were to take part, as the remaining one had developed a defect of some kind.

It was an extraordinary scene as the P.T. boats pushed off from the D.E. in the bright light of day to attack a target only four miles away in the fog. I rushed up to the Plot and watched them closing in on the radar scan. At times I was in doubt about the enemy echo, which I began to think might possibly be a point of land, as it was so close to the shore and remained so stationary. But it wasn't a point of land.

Scherertz came to the edge of the fog, and 300 yards beyond it was a trawler lying bows on. He fired his torpedoes—though with a head-on target they had little chance of hitting, and disengaged at once, coming under heavy fire as he did so—fire which both his boats returned. On the radar scan we could see him coming away at speed with the shells splashing around him, and the overs and ricochets falling half-way out to where we were—sudden little white blobs on the disc of the P.P.I. He told us on R/T that he had casualties and he came straight alongside us to transfer them. Again, not more than twenty minutes since they had left, we had the P.T. boats alongside, as we lay stopped four miles south of St. Helier; and then the fog began to lift. We got the wounded safely across to the *Maloy* and then moved off as fast as possible to the westward. Soon, however, we ran into another patch of fog and this gave us our chance to turn north again in search of the 509 boat. We had no idea at all where she might be. If she was sunk we had little or no chance of finding the survivors in the fog; if she was only disabled we expected to find her by radar. Perhaps the enemy had stopped to pick up the crew—we had seen them split up and two echoes (the two which Scherertz attacked) had been well astern of the others. Perhaps she had gone ashore in the fog on disengaging, for the battle had been less than a mile from the Jersey coast. With the fog so patchy it would have been wrong to take the *Maloy* any closer to the shore and there was no sign of an echo on the radar scan. The P.T.s were about to make a cast across the scene of the battle, when the fog began to clear altogether and we had to withdraw at best speed, out of range of the shore batteries. We could only hope that the crew of the 509 boat had been, or would be, picked up and taken prisoner. There was nothing more that we could do to rescue them; and as the mist cleared and the islands came into sight, we set course sadly for Cherbourg, west about round Guernsey and the Casquets.

Jack Scherertz had been slightly wounded in the battle and his face was covered with blood. The C.O. of the boat had a lucky escape, for the back of his tin hat had a large dent in it from a splinter, but he was unscathed. Several of the crew had been wounded and I went down to the sick bay aft to see how they were getting on. Scherertz was helping the Sick Berth Attendant to give a blood transfusion to a man on a stretcher who was practically dead. Lying face downwards on a bunk was a man who had been hit in the back. He had a nasty wound, but there seemed no doubt of his recovery. Sitting on another bunk, sobbing into his hands, was a young lad who had been hit in the shoulder and was suffering from shock. He got up when he saw me and came over to talk hysterically. "It was murder," he said. "If that's what you call a bloody 'M'-class Minesweeper—it looked like a bloody Battleship." (Actually although we had thought that 'M'-class Minesweepers were with the convoy, there had been nothing larger than a trawler as escort.) "Bloody murder," he repeated again and again, "Bloody murder to send us in on to a bloody Battleship like that." Scherertz and I told him what a fine fellow he was, and that he'd be all right, and he quietened down. The blood transfusion had finished: it had failed to revive the pulse and it was clear that the man on the stretcher was dead.

That was the P.T. boats' first blooding in the Channel Islands. We sent aircraft to search for the 509 boat and we swept the area with P.T. boats the next night, but without success. Meanwhile the German broadcasts claimed to have sunk two, one after being rammed by one of the escorts.

Two days later Wattie (the Coastal Command Liaison Officer) and Sherwood, ex-C.O. of one of the P.T. boats and now Flotilla Operations Officer, went up in a Walrus to look for survivors. They saw a body in the sea off La Corbiere and landed to identify it. It was one of the 509 boat's crew, though they could find no identity disc. Sherwood recognised it and later identified it from photographs of the crew. The Walrus was unable to take off in the loppy sea and taxied up into the calmer water in the lee of Sark, without interference from the shore guns. It was still no good, they couldn't take off and they finally taxied across to the mainland shore, which took them several hours, and landed in the little harbour of Dielette, just south of Cap de la Hague. Here they beached themselves on a well-mined beach without mishap, had an excellent lunch at a little restaurant and came back to Cherbourg. The Walrus stayed there till next day, when it was successfully flown off. A week, or more, later, part of the 509 boat, badly burned, was salvaged by another P.T. boat. Those were the only clues that we ever had to the nature of her fate.

CHAPTER 31

We Drummed them up the Channel

Christopher Dreyer

IT was bad luck that we should lose a boat in the very first action, and, with her, one of the best officers in the flotilla, but the operations went on, with occasional breaks for a night of bad weather. Jack Scheretz rigged a camp bed for me in his room on the ground floor of a house which the P.T. boat squadron had taken over in the Rue Victor Hugo, but if possible I always tried to get out of Cherbourg to the radar station at Joburg for the night. Maynard Fisher was a good host. His S.B.A. (Sick Berth Attendant), an Englishman, looked after the creature comforts and was evidently well entrenched in the village, for there were always two eggs for breakfast, and many local additions to the compo rations—or rather their American equivalent, 'ten in one'.

At Joburg the Monrad crew were very comfortably installed. They had a couple of German lorries which they had put into commission. They had at first two, and later eight, excellent horses for riding; and the loud speakers round the camp played 'music while you work' from morning till night. The view from the camp was superb. The heather-covered moor sloped away on three sides for a mile or more to the cliffs and the sea. Alderney, barely ten miles away, looked very close on a clear day, because the camp was so high: to the left one could see Guernsey; further left was Jersey, and further still the coast stretching southward past Dielette, round the corner to Carteret. Only once when I was there was the weather clear enough to pick out Sark from the bulk of Guernsey behind it. All these islands were held by the Germans, and indeed we often expected the radar station to be shelled by the Alderney batteries within whose range it lay. But evidently they had not sufficient ammunition to regard us as a worthwhile target.

Maynard Fisher had about fifty men under his command. Some dozen of the technicians were American, and all the rest were British. He looked after them well; I found that he knew intimate details of British Naval Administration and had studied rates of pay and advancement. In return I found that the men were devoted to him.

The operations were now running on a firm basis, with a striking degree of international co-operation. One night we fought a running battle in which I had under my radar control two British Destroyers (one of them Captain (D)), a Free French unit of M.T.B.s, and a unit of Canadian M.T.B.s, as well as the U.S. P.T. boats. But as Simpson, the S.O.O., had forecast, it was a case of 'lean pickings' in the Channel Islands in those days.

C.C.F. brought my time at Cherbourg to a rather sudden close by summoning me to return at once to Portsmouth to complete the report on our part of the invasion. So I packed my bag and Wattie drove me out to the airfield at the west side of Cherbourg harbour. As we arrived a Dakota was about to leave and I managed to scramble on board. Our destination was Heston and I had then the problem of getting to Portsmouth. An R.A.F. squadron which lived on the far side of Heston aerodrome agreed to take me, a Czech pilot flew me down in a Proctor in time for lunch, and I reported to C.C.F. in the afternoon.

At this time I was full of schemes for intensifying the war against the Germans in the Channel Islands, but I found that there were more urgent commitments. There was a great deal of talk about 'ripe plums' when the Channel Islands were mentioned, but the Falaise Pocket and the German retreat to the Seine had turned the limelight on to the eastern end of the Channel.

A few days later C.C.F. decided to pay a lightning visit to the Continent to clear up a number of minor problems, both at Cherbourg and at Courseulles. Hugh Eaton, who was A.N.C.X.F.'s Staff Officer, Coastal Forces, and I accompanied him. Our flagship for the journey was S.G.B. *Grey Shark*, commanded by Roger King, the Frenchman wearing R.N. stripes. This was the first time I had been to sea in an S.G.B. since relinquishing command of the flotilla, and this ship, with many of the same crew, had at one time been under my temporary command (whilst Howard Bradford was away with a broken arm) during which we had fought that moonlight action against trawlers in the Baie de la Seine. In many ways I wished that I were still leading the S.G.B. flotilla. But then I wondered whether in fact it would have been a quarter as interesting as what I had been doing.

After our routine business I accompanied my boss on a visit to Monty's headquarters where we stayed the night but I never saw the great man himself.

Two days later I summoned S.G.B. *Grey Shark* to Arromanches from Cherbourg, to take us back to England. My message was that *Grey Shark* was to be at Arromanches, with fifty Camembert cheeses on board, by two o'clock on the following afternoon . . . and she was.

We crossed on a flat calm evening of exceptional visibility so that we had scarcely lost sight of the French coast, it seemed, before St. Catherine's Point on the Isle of Wight came up ahead. A U-boat had torpedoed a merchant ship a few hours before and we passed close to the destroyers which were hunting it, though not so close as to upset their Asdics. It was still strange to think of U-boats in the Channel, for there had been none there since the early days of the war. The invasion and the invention of the Snorkel had combined to bring them back into the Narrow Seas.

For the next week or two I remained working in my old job with Christopher Dreyer on C.C.F.'s staff in the Tunnel in Portsdown Hill. The Coastal Forces which we were operating were embarking upon their most productive period of the war, the evacuation from Le Havre. Each morning we laid on the operations at Fort South-wick and each afternoon we went down to H.M.S. *Dolphin* to do the briefing. Here, just as they had done before I went to France, the Destroyer and Frigate C.O.s met the Senior Officers of the M.T.B. units and the Coastal Forces Control Officers. Together they worked out the tactics which proved to be the most highly specialised co-operative technique yet seen in this type of night warfare.

Philip Lee was still the leading Control Officer and the greatest exponent of the art, and his colleagues were still Guy Hudson and Guy Fison. Philip and Guy Hudson had been doing it for ten weeks practically without a break, and Guy Fison only a very little less. The evacuation of Le Havre and its attempted reinforcement lasted from 23rd until 30th August. During that time the enemy is believed to have suffered the following losses and damage:

Sunk: Nine T.L.C.s, two trawlers, four coasters, one E-boat, two R-boats.

Driven ashore: One T.L.C., one coaster, one R-boat.

Damaged: One trawler, one T.L.C., two coasters, five E-boats, four R-boats.

This was achieved without loss to ourselves and with only very light casualties.

Mark Arnold Foster is the name most clearly associated with that period. Mark's Flotilla was constantly in action and with tremendous success during the whole period. Dudley Dixon, Stewart Marshall, Dave Shaw: these also led their flotillas in the battles off Cap d'Antifer. And there were P.T. boats from Squadrons Thirty and Thirty-five, under Sam Saltsman and 'Rosie'. I never discovered what 'Rosie's' real name was, but I suppose he must have had one. Perhaps it was Rose. Of the Frigate C.O.s there was Brown (C. G. H. Brown) of the *Thornborough*, Brownrigg of the *Retalick*, and Party of the *Seymour*, and of the Destroyers (mostly of the 'Hunt' class), which were the newest addition to our team, there were usually Geoff Kirkby of the *Melbreak*, and the Free Frenchman Patou of *La Combattante*. *Myddleton* (Cox) and *Talybont* were also there on some of the nights. Poor Keddie of the *Cattistock*, who joined towards the end, was killed on the very last night of the fighting in the Channel.

The room at *Dolphin* was daily crowded with officers for the briefing and in the background, but probably the most important cog to make these operations run like clockwork, was Christopher—Lieutenant C. W. S. Dreyer, D.S.O., D.S.C. and bar, R.N.—who, as Staff Officer Operations to C.C.F., planned them all in his own head. His strategic sense, his tactical skill and administrative ability, combined with his delightful manner, carried all before it, and I believe none realised how important he was in the scheme of things at Portsmouth so well as the officers he briefed daily in the crowded room at *Dolphin*, and who went out nightly to put his plans into execution. I never ceased to wonder at the flexibility of a Navy which in one of its most crusted bulwarks—the Portsmouth Command—gave such freedom and such responsibility to a young officer, and left him serving as a Lieutenant. "My dear chap," said a very senior officer to me once, "there's simply no mechanism for promoting him."

By 1st September the enemy ships had been drummed up the Channel. With the exception of the few that remained in the Channel Isles, still harassed by the destroyers and P.T. boats

I had trained, and what shipping attempted to move along the French coast south of Brest, no targets remained for Coastal Forces west of the Straits of Dover. Suddenly, overnight, we, at Portsmouth, found ourselves with nothing to do but write the reports and wind up our affairs.

It was then that I started my flying lessons in a Tiger Moth from Gosport. My instructor was Tim King, a Squadron Leader in Coastal Command, who had been a colleague of ours on C.-in-C. Portsmouth's staff all the summer, and was, in peace time, a flying instructor. Both Christopher and I had lessons and advanced quite rapidly. I was luckier with the weather and managed to get in about seven or eight hours, so that I would have been able to go solo had it not been that we were flying a borrowed aircraft and dreadful retribution would have descended on Tim if I had broken it.

We used to fly from Gosport aerodrome to Appledram—a disused airfield on which we could practise our 'circuits and bumps' without getting in anyone's way. Tim bought me a book which I dutifully swotted up before each lesson. At one point I read further ahead in the book than I should have done and on the following day as we ambled over to our practice field I put the nose down to gain speed and then pulled the stick back into a quick loop. It was almost a flick manoeuvre and Tim was rightly very cross with me. That was not what he had given me the book for. But secretly I think he was quite pleased at my progress.

One day in the first week of September we were flying at 2,000 feet along Portsdown Hill when I suddenly saw a single goose flying parallel to us at the same height. As he came closer I saw to my amazement that it was a Brent Goose of the Light-bellied form. It was incredibly early in the year for such a record. This same day was extremely bumpy and turbulent, and I remember hoping that these conditions were not too common, else maybe I should not take kindly to flying in light aircraft.

[Little did I know that thirteen years later I should be impatiently awaiting the bumpy days in order to get good lift for soaring in my glider.]

Karl Müller
Kapitänleutnant
P. O. W. Camp 7.

CHAPTER 32   *Charlie*

I WAS soon moved to Great Yarmouth, to join the staff of Captain Coastal Forces, The Nore. Off the Dutch coast the M.T.B.s continued to operate against evacuation convoys, but as usual the winter campaign was fought more against the weather than the enemy.

On the night of 18th September, 1944, two M.T.B.s led by Lieutenant J. F. Humphreys, D.S.C., R.N.V.R., and controlled from the Frigate *Stayner* engaged three E-boats off the coast of Belgium and all three were sunk. Our casualties were three killed and one wounded. A collision between two of the E-boats largely contributed to this startling result. The M.T.B.s picked up a number of survivors—among them Kapitän leutnant Karl Müller, Senior Officer of the Tenth Schnellboot Flotilla, known to his friends as 'Charlie'. The name of 'Charlie' Müller, one of the handful of E-boat Commanders to hold the Ritterkreuz, was well known among the officers of the Coastal Forces. I knew for example that I myself had met and engaged him at least once in my Steam Gunboat, in the action off Start Point.

Early in October I was instructed to go to a prisoner of war camp in the Home Counties in order to interview Charlie on technical matters relating to E-boats and Coastal Forces. I found a pleasant-faced young man of about my own height, with broad shoulders and straight dark hair. He was perhaps twenty-eight years old, and his English was better than my German. Our conversation was carried on in both languages, however, each speaking the other's until defeated by a word, when the language changed. On this first visit we talked for three hours.

I found that his attitude was quite definite, and perfectly realistic. The war was lost to Germany and the quicker it was brought to a conclusion the better for all concerned, particularly the Germans.

To this end he was prepared to help so long as he did not disclose details which might threaten the lives of his colleagues in the Schnellboot Service. All of them, he said, recognised that the war was lost when the first break-out from the Normandy bridgehead took place. They had come to accept that they were weaker at sea and in the air, but until then they had imagined that they were still stronger on land. Charlie kept repeating that the war must be made to end quickly. To me the most fascinating part of the discussion concerned the actions in which he and I had fought against each other. We spent some time discussing the tactical details of the battle in the early morning of 19th November, 1942. His had been the E-boat we had waited for as it headed directly towards us in the glare of the starshells—the E-boat which had been saved by the sudden darkness when the last starshell had burned out. His boat had been hit by us twice, but insignificantly. Nevertheless we conducted a long and fascinating post-mortem on the action. In equal detail we examined the battle which had ended in Charlie's capture. The loss of a whole unit of three E-boats was a serious reverse and Charlie had been searching his heart to see whether his professional skill could logically be called in question. I had to admit that extraordinary bad luck had attended the unit that night. Charlie had been in action, so he told me, 165 times. In this he was only exceeded by Götz von Mirbach with 170 actions. These actions only included contact with enemy ships and not minelaying sorties. This was far in excess of the most experienced officers in our own Coastal Forces.

Charlie was sympathetic when I told him of our disastrous S.G.B. action off Cherbourg on 27th July, 1943. He had seen the action taking place in the distance when he had been on passage from Le Havre to Cherbourg after a refit. He told me that the Senior Officer of the R-boats we had engaged was a certain K. K. Anhalt, who was regarded as a very brave fellow. He had at one time lost a hand, and in a later action had lost the same arm, but was nothing daunted and was still at sea.

About a week after this first talk Christopher Dreyer joined me for a second visit to the P.O.W. camp, and we spent four and a half hours in conversation with Charlie. He talked in general about the superiority of the E-boats as warships over our Coastal Forces. All E-boat personnel were quite satisfied that they had greatly superior craft. This was said very politely and without arrogance. Speed, reliability, non-inflammability, low silhouette, better sea-keeping qualities, all these he quoted as reasons for this conviction. For the last two years, he told me, he had never had to turn back because of an engine breakdown. The Mercedes-Benz diesels were wonderfully reliable engines. Coming back to Harwich, the D-class M.T.B. which had picked him up had been heading into a wind of force two to three and bumping considerably. This, he said, the E-boats never did even in the worst sea. Nor were E-boats very wet, except sometimes in quarter line when the bow wave of the next ahead threw up a lot of spray.

Charlie told us in detail about a colleague's visit to Berchtes-gaden in March 1944. His friend had been summoned to give details and advice on E-boat development. He was amazed to find that Hitler knew intimate details of the boats, asking whether the new four-centimetre guns had been a success and discussing technical features of the new engines. He had also heard Hitler confirming alterations to the *Gneisenau* and quoting the length of barrel of her guns and other exact figures. Hitler's day, he said, began at nine-thirty a.m. when he took his sheepdog for a walk, and ended at four a.m. (his staff having waited all through the night for a possible immediate summons). Lunch was at three p.m. and dinner at ten p.m. Charlie's friend said it was possible to have an ordinary conversation with Hitler without feeling that one was talking to the Führer of the Reich, but that there was something queer about his eyes, which seemed to look through you. He believed him to be remarkable, but definitely more than a little mad.

Charlie gave us an account of the personalities of the E-boat world—Berndt Klug, Götz von Mirbach, Klaus Feldt (whom he said looked rather like me), Baron Nikko von Stempel, Hugo Wentler, 'Bobby' Fimmen, Klaus Schmidt, Johannsen (who was killed in the air-raid on Le Havre at a party celebrating his award of the Oak Leaves to his Ritterkreuz), Zymalkowski, Matzen and the rest. The human details of these men brought home the futility of it all. It may well have been essential for the prosecution of the war to foster the idea that 'the only good German was a dead German', but among these, there were obviously good Germans and among them, but for the 'accident of birth', I might quite well have been serving. But then this war—which allowed only of the bright-est white and the darkest black—was absurd anyway. It was one of the rules that you were not allowed to think any good of your opponent. If you did you might not in this day and age go on try-ing so hard to kill him. In the past it had still been possible to honour your enemy. Or had it? Fraternisation in the trenches was something else, and there was war weariness and all that. What remained this time to keep up one's resolve? Belsen and the gas chambers? We did not know much of them at that time. Charlie had heard of them but believed they were much the same as P.O.W. camps. Technical efficiency, habit, service discipline—these were the things which kept us fighting far more surely than hatred. It was primarily a game.

At that time I had almost completed the manuscript of an official book on the Coastal Forces in the Channel and North Sea. At first it was envisaged as a companion publication to the series of which the first was the very successful pamphlet by Hilary St. George Saunders on the Battle of Britain. By the time I had compiled my history it was a much longer book and the war was nearing its end. The Admiralty had agreed that a longer, more historical book would be more useful at this stage, and had themselves recommended publication through the normal channels. The typescript of the book had not yet been through Admiralty censorship, but as I was anxious to achieve the greatest possible accuracy I asked to be allowed to show it to Charlie Müller and permission was given. Charlie evidently enjoyed the book and soon afterwards I received the following eulogistic letter from him, written in English. The opening phrase refers to a description and specimen copy, on page twenty-two of the typescript, of the Action Report rendered after any naval engagement:

"*From* Karl Müller,   3.11.1944.
      Kapitän leutnant,
           P.O.W. Camp.
"Sir,
    "I have the honour to submit my report (page twenty-two of your book) on my comments and opinions of your book about the Coastal Forces. In my opinion this book is a very good achievement; particularly attractive because of its close resemblance to life. There are many scenes so well described, that I—because I had quite the same often only on the other side—thought I was once more in those situations. The description of feelings during eventless patrols, sighting the enemy, the moment when the torpedo slips away, the endlessness of time until the fish hits his target or not, the sighting of phantoms after a hard look-out for hours, the eternal talking about the proceedings in the action after having got into harbour, the daily life of the Senior Officer, etc., are particularly genuine.

S*

"Summarising all this from my E-boat point of view I can say, that your book has genuine climaxes of life and seamanship. You are to be congratulated on this work. I am very glad of having had the opportunity of reading the book, and I shall not fail to buy one after the war—if possible.

"The German E-boat men have always acknowledged the deeds of the enemy of the Coastal Forces. Indeed you ever demonstrated a lot of bravery, initiative and above all 'Drauf-gängertum' in all situations. We appreciate this without any envy. You often made life a hell for us.

"I think this book will show the deeds of the Coastal Forces to the public in a right light besides adding another leaf of glory to the history of the Royal Navy.

"I didn't find any inaccuracy. In many cases I saw an absolute and surprising likeness between your life and ours. It seems to be nearly the same amongst all small forces.

"Thank you so much for your kind letter. I hope all C.F. men and E-boat men can see each other after the war; it would be very interesting.[1] I wish you the best of luck for the future. I have forgotten to say that I have taken some notes about the rise of the C.F. during this war. If you are not in agreement with this please ring up here, and I shall destroy them.

"And here are some notes of my remarks:

"P.12. It is quite right, that we have been trained to attack convoys and bigger ships in the beginning of E-boat activity. Those were our tactics. We avoided battles with M.G.B.s and M.T.B.s. That has not been out of fear of the enemy, but because it was not sufficiently remunerative for general purpose of our E-boat warfare. 'Es brachte nichts ein.' For the rest I must say in this connection, that we have always fought at a disadvantage in numbers during all the war. Breakdowns by actions with M.G.B.s, etc.—maybe only for eight or fourteen days—were very disagreeable, for we missed these boats attacking a convoy, because only some boats succeeded in coming through the screen of escorts, the bigger part being chased by destroyers. For this reason too we seldom had patrols. R-boats were better qualified for these tasks.

"P.13–21. The description of the base and the S.O.'s day (brief, orders, weather, etc.) seem to be especially true. I could write it with nearly the same words.

"P.43. When *Scharnhorst/Gneisenau* made their way through the

[1] Charlie will be visiting me with his family in 1961.

Straits, there were ten E-boats in action. I was on the last boat
of the first group. Both flotillas—yours and ours—roared very
nice alongside each other for a time. We all shot our tracers but
it has been useless in the rough sea. Our range from the big ships
was 6,000 metres, no less. They steamed ahead in line; *Scharnhorst, Gneisenau, Prinz Eugen* (not *Prinz Eugen* at the head). The
force did twenty-nine sm. (knots) during this time. The M.T.B.s
never closed nearer to us than 800 metres. They let their torpedoes
go when they were about 6,500 metres away. The fishes could not
hit because the range was too great. One fish broke the surface
not more than fifteen metres ahead of my boat. The appearance of
your flotilla was surprising for us, because the sea was rough. The
destroyer (*Friedrich Ihn*, not a Narvik-class one) and we too, did
not engage your boats for a long time, because this operation was
ordered to go on with as great a security as possible (R.A.F.).
"Extravagant Claims: For your own particular amusement may
I tell you that at the beginning of 1942 the English broadcast
reported sixty-seven German E-boats destroyed to date. It is
founded on fact that we lost two E-boats by enemy action.
'Hart im Raume stossen sich die Dinge' (Goethe). The escorts
destroy a great many, we know that well. Indeed not every small
burst of fire means that a boat has gone to Davy Jones's locker.
I myself was reported sunk five times by broadcast and I am
living now. The defensive forces are for ever straining every
nerve to cover themselves with glory in action so that they very
often see double or threefold. I am certain that it is the same on
both sides. But beyond that propaganda often finds on the 'green
table' its own conclusions from the military reports. One cannot
prevent that. We have always hated these people.
  "You can't too highly estimate the advantage which our
limited radar range gave you. Waiting for hours off the enemy's
shore was a thing unknown to *us* after the beginning of 1942.
Henceforth we used the tactics of 'jab and run'. During the last
year your shore radars found us up to about 25 sm. Under these
conditions attacking seems to me to be mere running the gauntlet.
  "I hope these points will be interesting for you.

Yours,
Karl Müller
Kapitän leutnant."

Here the story might have ended but for a proposal to send
Charlie to a P.O.W. camp in the southern United States. While he

was awaiting passage at a U.S. transit camp, volunteers were hastily sought for an exchange repatriation by way of the besieged port of St. Nazaire which was still in German hands. A well-known politician was to be returned in exchange for a German officer of distinction. At short notice and without consultation with the British authorities Charlie was selected and a few hours later he was back in Germany. When I heard of it I thought ruefully of the instructions I had received before the interviews: "Be as frank with him as you like," they had said, "he's in for the duration." And when, a few weeks afterwards, my new book went up to the Admiralty for censorship I told them of the notes which Charlie had taken from it, and reminded them of the proverb about stable doors.

Later the East Coast Convoy route was simultaneously attacked by a large number of E-boat units—so many that the radar plot was greatly confused. Next morning I rang up Christopher Dreyer, now at H.M.S. *Vernon*, the Torpedo School.

"Did you see the details of last night's E-boat activities?"

"Yes."

"Did anything strike you about it?"

"If you mean did it remind me of how we asked Charlie why the E-boats never tried a mass attack to swamp our radar plots, the answer is it did."

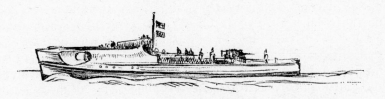

CHAPTER 33   *The 'Surrender' of the E-Boats*

AT long last the Admiralty had come up with the promised Command and a choice one it turned out to be—the *Cardigan Bay*, a brand new anti-aircraft Frigate building at Leith. It was not a destroyer (as originally promised) but it was in many respects better: a really last-word ship. In the early spring of 1945 as the German war was drawing rapidly to its climax, my time was divided between various courses and visits to the shipyard to see how the building of my Frigate progressed. I went through the famous tactical anti-submarine course run by Captain Gilbert Roberts, C.B.E., R.N., at Liverpool; through the damage-control course at Baron's Court which taught me how to keep a badly damaged ship afloat; and through an advanced Tactical Course at Greenwich. I went also to see the other ships of the 'Bay' class which were being built, in order to see the snags which arose and how they were dealt with.

At the time of my appointment 'to *Cardigan Bay* in Command', it had been evident that the war in Europe would be over before she was commissioned. There would remain, of course, the war against Japan. At that time a Japanese capitulation seemed very remote. How, one wondered, could unconditional surrender be obtained from a people who by tradition believed in death before dishonour—who were already fighting their naval war with suicide bombers? Could the Allied war aims be achieved short of killing the last Japanese? I had never been to Japan; I simply did not know the answers to these questions, but I foresaw a long continuation of the Pacific War. And it would all be happening a long way away from my wife and child.

Then with mounting acceleration Germany was overrun and the European war was suddenly at an end. The principal aim of five long years had been won, and yet it was not quite all over.

I could not pack up and go back to my family brushing my hands together and saying "*That's* done." It had long been evident of course that we could not be beaten. But now more than ever the urgency seemed to have seeped out of it; even the booster "Let's get it finished with" had largely been expended on Germany. I remember being fortified at that time by Drake's famous (and often misquoted) phrase written in a letter to Sir Francis Walsingham in 1587 after he had destroyed the assembling ships of the Spanish Armada in the harbour of Cadiz:

"There must be a beginning of any great matter, but the continuing unto the end, until it be thoroughly finished, yields the true glory."

At lunch time on 12th May, 1945, I was standing on the half-built bridge of another Bay-class Frigate in Belfast Dockyard listening to the one o'clock news on a portable radio. It was announced that some E-boats were to surrender at noon on the following day at Felixstowe. This was an event at which it would have been nice to be present, I thought, and there was in fact nothing further to detain me at Belfast. The only problem was how to get from Belfast to Felixstowe in time. By boat and cross-country train the prospect was hopeless. The only possible chance was by air. There were a number of Very Senior Officers, not one of them known to me personally, who had to be persuaded that it would be good and useful for one particular rather junior Naval Officer to be at Felixstowe when the E-boats arrived. Once the point had been accepted, developments were rapid and by half past three an official car had deposited me at Aldergrove aerodrome where a twin-engined Oxford Trainer was ready for take-off. That evening I had supper in the Mess at Felixstowe, where H.M.S. *Beehive* was fairly buzzing with activity and already most of the Senior Officers of the flotillas on the east coast were assembled. Here my luck was in. I found that the Senior Officer of the unit which had been detailed to go out to meet the E-boats was my old friend John Hodder with whom I had first gone to sea in Coastal Forces and who had fought with me in my first action as Senior Officer S.G.B.s against the trawlers in the moonlight. I was therefore assured of a place in his boat on the morrow.

Ten M.T.B.s left Felixstowe to meet the E-boats. On board one or other of them were a great many of the leading personalities in the Coastal Forces. In line ahead we steamed out to the South Falls buoy, off the Thames estuary, the prearranged meeting-place, and there cut engines to wait. It had been announced that the E-boats were coming to surrender, and to us the gesture had a dramatic finality about it. It was the right conclusion to the Coastal Forces war; it rounded the story off for us. At about two in the afternoon two specks came up over the horizon and in a few minutes the E-boats had reached us. Hodder ordered them to stop, and the two boats quickly lost way and lay there gently rolling. Here they were—long and low and menacing—our opposite numbers, our special opponents in all these years. One had a black panther painted on its side, and both flew the white flags which had been stipulated before they left Rotterdam. This was for most of us the first view of an E-boat in daylight, a dream view, for taking an E-boat in prize had been a universal dream in Coastal Forces, yet it had never been done. No E-boat had yet been brought into a British harbour. That would be done by us today, but the occasion was more interesting than triumphant. Hodder manoeuvred his M.T.B. alongside the black panther. It had been agreed that, because of my few words of German, I should be put on board together with 'Jake' Wright, Maurice Pryor and two signalmen. A few moments later we jumped across. Then the M.T.B.s formed up on either side and the formation set off for Felixstowe. On the E-boat's bridge was a German Admiral. I saluted formally and he saluted back. It seemed to me that we should be scrupulously correct. The Admiral was a small man, dressed in a leather coat. He told me that he was on a mission to the Commander-in-Chief Nore, and was carrying charts of the German minefields. I said I understood that they had come to surrender. "We have already surrendered," he said. "Germany has surrendered. I am merely to bring the charts to the Commander-in-Chief and then to return." I made no comment on this, but somehow I did not see the two E-boats going back, at any rate for some time, and I was a little doubtful about the Admiral. His name, I discovered, was Bräuning and he was not pleased when we insisted on having White Ensigns flown above the German ensigns in the two boats, but it was finally agreed amicably. Also on board were Korvettenkapitän 'Bobby' Fimmen, Senior Officer of the Fourth E-boat flotilla, and Korvettenkapitän Rebensburg. As Staff Officer Operations to the E-boat chief (Kapitän zur See Petersen) Rebensburg had been my opposite number during the previous summer. It was against him that Dreyer and I had planned and counter-planned. But Korvettenkapitän Rebensburg was not very forthcoming and what had been a potentially interesting meeting came in fact to nothing at all.

On the passage from South Falls to Felixstowe the formation

made twenty knots—the best cruising speed for D-class M.T.B.s—
although the German boats had been making thirty-two knots
from Rotterdam to South Falls. The wind was freshening as we
turned in towards the Orwell estuary and we watched John Hodder
in the boat ahead putting on his oilskins as the spray burst over his
bridge, while we in the E-boat sat up on the canopy at the back of
the dustbin and remained perfectly dry. There was no doubt about
which was the drier type at twenty knots. But it was noticeable that
the E-boat rolled much more than the M.T.B. and was therefore a
much less steady platform for gunnery.

With some difficulty we persuaded the Germans to fall their
crews in on deck as they entered harbour, where a great crowd of
spectators was assembled on all the piers and jetties. The E-boats
berthed alongside Hodder's boat, a manoeuvre which, because of
their large screws and considerable astern power, they performed
with spectacular speed in the small basin. At once the armed
guards filed on board and the Germans were hustled off their boats.

No doubt the scuttling of the surrendered German Fleet at Scapa
Flow in 1918 called for special precautions this time. No doubt we
were dealing with a ruthless enemy whose defeat called also for
humiliation. But as I saw it these things did not relieve us of the
responsibility for being 'correct'. The more strongly we might feel
the more correct we must be. This view was not shared by everyone
at Felixstowe and before the end of the day I was angry and
ashamed. It was of course essential to see that no opportunity was
offered for the scuttling charges known to be fitted in all E-boats
to be ignited, and for this reason once the crews had been hustled
off the boats they could not go back. I went down into the engine
room of one of the boats during the hustling to make sure that the
engineer in charge was not busy lighting the fuses, and found that
he wasn't. When I came up again I found I was in demand as interpreter. It was a difficult assignment. It seemed important to me
that these men should have respect for the British Navy, and that
we should therefore behave with proper dignity, and correct service
procedure. In this way the ignominy of defeat would be most
effectively brought home to them. To be beaten by someone you can
respect, it seemed to me then, is more shaming (and more permanent) than to be beaten by a barbarian you despise. The Admiral
might be treated with lofty disdain, but he must be treated as an
Admiral. We might regard the Germans as uncivilised, but that
made it all the more important to be civilised ourselves.

As their interpreter I found myself in the position of prisoner's friend and advocate. In a very short while my efforts on their behalf had been interpreted as fraternisation. The crews of the two boats had been hustled away without opportunity to collect their personal effects and I made a plea for some special arrangement to be made to remedy this. I was told that one officer would be allowed on board to assemble all the personal effects which would then be transferred to the temporary prison where they were held. Woe betide me, they said, if this led to any damage to the boats. That was fair enough, and when they had selected the young officer who was to go, I thought it worth getting a promise out of him. "Look," I said, "I have had some difficulty getting this concession for you. I want you to promise me on your word of honour as an officer that you won't try to sink, or otherwise damage the boats." "I promise," he said, and we went back to the basin. We were on board the two boats for more than an hour, collecting the clothes and belongings of the crews. In the course of it the young man kept asking me if I would like this or that as a souvenir. He finally thrust a large calendar of pin-up girls into my hands. "You must have something."

I believe Admiral Bräuning was finally allowed to deliver his charts at Chatham before being sent to a prisoner-of-war camp. Many years later he wrote to me, still from prison, to say that he had enjoyed reading my book on the Coastal Forces, and especially the brief account of our meeting. In this I had described him as 'a dry little man, full of salutes', but he had taken no umbrage.

CHAPTER 34   *The Hustings*

WE had fallen out of love with our St. John's Wood house and
after some hunting around London during periods of leave Jane
and I had found and bought a small terrace house in Edwardes
Square—No. 8. Not long after we had moved in, I was sitting at
my desk in the ground floor room when a burly and bonhomous
figure came through the little front garden gate and knocked on
the door. He told me that his name was Holbrook, that his brother
had been the famous V.C. Submariner of the First World War,
and that he was Chairman of the Conservative Association at
Rugby. Would I, he asked, join the short list of their prospective
candidates. Polling Day in the General Election of 1945 was then
only three weeks away and a quick decision was called for.

Here it was, then—the decision which had been at the back of
my mind for so long. Not the Navy versus Politics, but the War
versus my family. And for some time I had been worried about
the family. All was not well with my marriage. I had subjected it
to greater strains than it could withstand. My dangerous and
distant life in the Coastal Forces had taken me away from Jane.
Perhaps this was the point at which I could come back to her.
When the decision had to be made she was away in the country;
but we talked on the telephone, and I found that on the whole she
favoured accepting the Rugby offer. There was still my ship, my
beautiful new Frigate, the Command for which I had waited so
long. Was this to be denied me at the last moment? I had one night
in which to decide, and on the following day I was on my way to
Rugby.

My views about politics were of a very general character and my
knowledge of economics non-existent, but I knew exactly what kind
of an England I had been fighting for, and it was not in order to be
able to turn the whole thing upside down and start again. About

this I could make a fairly impassioned speech—but about precious little else. The short list at Rugby included a soldier and another sailor. The soldier was Lt.-Colonel John Lakin who had been at preparatory school with me and who lived in the constituency. The nomination finally went to him and I found myself in the crowded train on the way back with the sailor, Commander Alan Noble. What, I asked, would he do now? Go on being a Naval Officer? He thought probably he would. What would I do? Once more I saw my Frigate looming up. But then I thought: if the decision was right the first time, it is still right. "I think I'll go back to Central Office and see if they've got anything else."

Thus about three days later I found myself adopted as Conservative candidate for the newly delineated constituency of Wembley North, which, it was thought, should produce a Tory majority of between 1,000 and 2,000 votes. I had just a fortnight in which to make myself known to the electorate of Wembley, and there was no concealing from them that, in this new field, I was as green as a mallard's head. It was useless to pretend I knew; it was, I felt, much safer to admit that I did not, but to make it plain that I intended to learn. My Labour opponent, Charles Hobson, also new to the constituency, described me as "a self-confessed political ignoramus". It was a three-cornered fight and the Liberal was Ian Baillieu. One evening he had no way of getting home to London so I gave him a lift in my rather elderly and decrepit Vauxhall. After that I found it much harder to be rude about the way the Liberals were 'splitting the vote'.

I soon found that the speech making was not too difficult, nor did I have much difficulty in dealing rather light-heartedly with the occasional hecklers. The really terrifying part was answering a cleverly phrased question by an opponent in the audience. Question time became the bane of my life. Often to begin with I did not know whether the questioner was for me or against, and I had to arrange a sign language with my efficient and long-suffering agent when the questioner stood up. "He's a staunch supporter"; or "he's a dangerous opponent, be careful"; or "I don't know him".

"What," asked one unidentified questioner, "does the candidate think about Community Centres?" I had only the haziest idea of what a community centre might be. I was fairly sure that it did not have anything to do with Communism, but I had no idea whether this was an election issue and whether I should be letting the side down if I said they were splendid things and I only wished we had more of them. The word 'togetherness' had not, so far as I know, been coined at that time, but I proceeded to give an account of the philosophy which it describes and drew a round of enthusiastic applause; after that we went on to the next question and my personal views about togetherness were never disclosed, which was perhaps as well.

A number of distinguished men agreed to come and speak at my meetings, Harold Macmillan, Peter Thorneycroft, Sir Donald Somervell, Lord Hailsham (then still in the House of Commons), Lord Simon, Sir Alan Herbert. I remember at the A.P.H. meeting there was a disturbance among the hecklers and from the uproar the only audible words were "Stinking fish". Alan shouted back, "What was that? A declaration of policy, or merely a statement of identity?" and brought the house down.

By the eve of the poll I was getting into my stride, and almost beginning to enjoy the campaign. There followed the three-week delay while the votes came in from the Services, and then on 26th July in the Town Hall at Wembley we watched the packages of votes building up in two long lines down the table and for a while I was several hundred ahead. At one point near the end of the count Charles Hobson came over and said, "Well, it looks as though you'll be in," but almost at the same moment came a stack of Hobson packets which put him in the lead. I was beaten by 435 votes in the Labour landslide which had so unexpectedly swept the country.

It was of course a great disappointment at the time. Jane had worked as hard as I during the campaign, and had had a great personal success, but I think both of us were too basically unconventional to be wholeheartedly accepted by the inhabitants of Wembley. We should have done better perhaps in a rural community. I felt that we did not have very much in common with the people who so nearly became my constituents, friendly and hospitable though they were. Thereafter I nursed Wembley North as Conservative candidate for a couple of years, but it was only a few weeks after the election that the narrowness of my escape first began to dawn upon me. In 1939 the course of my life had been broken abruptly when I joined the Navy. Now it had been broken again as abruptly when I left, and to start on a political career at this stage had seemed reasonable. It might have been a good thing to have a painter and naturalist in the House, but before the *next* election I should probably be on my way again, on some active peace-time ploy. I was in no mood to mark time for the duration of this Parliament, nursing my constituency and waiting. I wanted to get on with my peace, so I plunged back into ornithology and conservation and began painting hard. I returned to my birds with a new and passionate delight.

During the war Paul Gallico had written a story called *The Snow Goose*, in which a hunchbacked painter of birds, who lived in an East Coast lighthouse, had one day been brought a wounded Snow Goose by a village maid and tamed it so that it followed him about —followed him to Dunkirk and returned alone when he was killed to give the news to the heroine Fritha. I first learned of the story when a copy published in America was sent to me by my old friend James Robertson Justice with a covering note saying, "I think, if properly handled, this should be actionable." Certainly at the beginning of the story I was only lightly disguised and I remembered how I had told Gallico about my lighthouse and my painting —and indeed had invited him to come and see the place, though he never came. I had been introduced to him at a World Skating Championship by Maribel Vinson, long the American Champion. Somehow I did not see a court upholding a claim that the hero of *The Snow Goose* had injured me in any way. An alternative and more agreeable proposition now appeared. There was to be an English edition of the little book, and Michael Joseph (whose son Stephen had been with me in the *Broke*) asked me if I would undertake the illustrations for it.

I had not long been out of the Navy when I decided to take an exhibition of pictures to New York and at the same time to consult Gallico on the proposed illustrations. There was some urgency about one of the colour plates which was to be a portrait of Fritha bringing the wounded goose to the lighthouse door. Jane and I had taken passage in the *Aquitania* bound for Halifax with a load of young Canadian brides—mostly English girls married to Canadian soldiers. Among them we looked for a blonde girl who might make a suitable model for Fritha, and eventually found one who seemed just right. I drew her during a concert played by a fellow passenger, violinist Ida Haendl, and later made a small complete painting.

Paul Gallico saw it in the exhibition at the Harlow Galleries, but showed no great enthusiasm. He moved on round the gallery and stopped opposite a pen and ink drawing, "Ah, now that," he cried, "*that's* the face I imagine for Fritha. Who is this . . ." glancing down at the sheet in his hand " . . . this Jane?" "It's easy," I said, "she's my wife and she'll be here in five minutes. Mind you, she's nothing like the description in your book—she's a dark girl for a start. . . ." "Never mind," said Paul, "that's the face I want—you can easily make her blonde, can't you?" And so that is what I did.

The frontispiece of the illustrated editions of *The Snow Goose*, which have been selling well down the years, show a blonde version of my beautiful and much-loved Jane.

Jane was now writing seriously and with great promise. She had half a novel called *The Beautiful Visit* written in her own hand in a notebook from which she had been reading extracts to a publisher, and the notebook was left in a New York taxi, nor were all our efforts to recover it of the slightest avail. It was gone for ever. No doubt the rewritten chapters were, as she has always maintained, much better than the original version. There were, after all, distinguished precedents for this particular disaster. In any event the book had a startling success when it finally appeared.

We returned from New York in the *Queen Mary* with a large consignment of terrapins and tortoises and a few snakes, some destined for the London Zoo and some to be kept in vivaria at Edwardes Square. A number of harmless Garter Snakes, a couple of King Snakes and a Blanding's Turtle were being exercised in the bath when one of the little Garters slithered up the chain to the overflow hole and disappeared inside. This was clearly a crisis, for I did not know much of the plumbing connections in this liner, but in the next-door cabin on one side were Lord and Lady Halifax, while on the other side was Mr. MacKenzie King. The errant snake, even if meaning to return meekly to its home bath, might easily, it seemed, mistake the turning and appear in the wrong one. After an anxious twenty-four hours however it homed unerringly into the right bath and was duly returned to its proper container.

CHAPTER 35   *Slimbridge Discovered*

IN the autumn of 1945 I received two letters from ornithologist friends which, taken in conjunction, were to have a very profound effect on my life. Both these letters were from farmers and both concerned wild geese. The first was from Howard Davis, an experienced observer of birds living near Bristol, who sent me a copy of a paper he had written on the great flock of White-fronted Geese which has wintered on the Severn Estuary from immemorial times. If I could spare the time to come down, he wrote, he would like to show them to me. I remembered my brief visit there before the war, at a time when the main flock had just left on the spring migration. I had seen, as I recalled, a bunch of twenty or thirty and that was all, and I had examined with interest the old duck decoy in the little wood. It would be nice to go there again, but I wondered when, if ever, there would be time.

The second letter was from my old and valued farmer friend Will Tinsley. At the beginning of the war some of the best birds from my lighthouse collection had been taken over to his farm to live happily in the orchard and about the farmyard. Among these had been a pair of Lesser White-fronted Geese, perhaps the most beautiful of all the world's grey geese which I had first met in Hungary and later in their thousands on the Caspian shore.

At that time the Lesser Whitefront was the rarest British bird; it had only been recorded once, and on any list you cannot have a rarer bird than that. It shared that distinction with some twenty other species which had only been recorded once in Britain. This single record was in 1886 when an immature Lesser Whitefront was shot in Northumberland by Alfred Crawhal Chapman, brother of Abel Chapman, the famous wildfowler and author. The Lesser White-fronted Goose breeds as far west as Scandinavia and from there eastwards across sub-arctic Europe and Asia almost to the

Pacific. Those Lesser Whitefronts which breed in Lapland fly south-eastwards on their winter migrations, through Hungary to Macedonia and the Mediterranean.

I had brought some slightly wounded Kis Lilliks (the first word, pronounced Kish, meaning small) back with me from the plains of the Hortobágy to my lighthouse home. When the war came and my collection of live waterfowl was disbanded, a pair of Kis Lilliks was taken over to join Will Tinsley's collection of geese which lived in the orchard beside his house. Now in his letter Will reported an extraordinary occurrence; he said that in 1943 a wild Lesser White-fronted Goose had come down one day out of the sky and landed beside his tame pair and had stayed there for several days. There was little chance that the bird could have escaped from any other collection, but as a truly wild bird it was only the second which had been so far recorded in Britain. I had no doubt whatever about the identification. I remember saying to myself, "If Will says it was a Lesser, then a Lesser it most certainly was." From this I fell to wondering how many people there were in this country who would know the difference between a Lesser Whitefront and an ordinary Whitefront.

It is, to be sure, a little smaller but not much; its bill is a good deal smaller and rather pinker, but the only definite distinguishing character is the golden yellow eyelid which encircles the eye of the Lesser Whitefront. How often, in the field, can a wild goose's eyelids be critically examined? Supposing, I thought, these Lesser White-fronts came regularly to the British Isles, who would recognise them? Of course, Will Tinsley would, but I could not think of very many others. And if they came, where should one look for them? It seemed to me that they would be most likely to mix accidentally with those species of geese which migrated to Britain from breeding grounds further to the east. Two species of grey geese do this—the Bean Goose and the Common or Russian Whitefront, and the largest flock of Russian Whitefronts in Britain in winter was to be found on the Severn Estuary. Here, then, was the chance of putting my theory to the test. If it was correct I might expect to find a stray Lesser Whitefront among the larger geese if I could only get close enough to see their eyelids.

A few weeks later I was staying in Stafford and suggested to my friends John Winter and Clive Wilson that we might take up Howard Davis's invitation; on the following day, after a telephone arrangement, we met him at Slimbridge. We walked from the bridge over the canal and down to the end of the lane, after which he led us out towards a war-time pillbox commanding a view of the saltings upon which the geese were feeding. Bent double, we crept across the field, behind the low sea-wall and into the dank concrete box. From the embrasures we had a most wonderful view of a great flock of 2,000 wild geese. Among them we saw, quite near-by, a young Bean Goose, then a Barnacle, and a Brent and later a Greylag. There were also a few Pinkfeet but the majority were, as they should have been, Russian-bred Whitefronts. That evening we went back to stay with Howard Davis at his farm near Bristol. As he drove me back in his car I outlined my wild idea about the Lesser Whitefronts and was rash enough to suggest that it was for this very purpose that we had come down to the Severn. On the following day we were back in the pillbox again overlooking the green Dumbles and the grey carpet of wild geese. Again the young Bean Goose was close in front of us.

We had been in the pillbox, I suppose, for a little over half an hour when Howard Davis said quietly, "There's a bird here which interests me. Would you have a look at it?" In a few moments he had directed me to the goose in question among the tight mass of geese in front of us, and the instant my binoculars lit upon it I realised that it was a Lesser Whitefront. My spine tingled delightfully as it does in the slow movement of Sibelius's Violin Concerto. Here almost too easily was a vindication of my far-fetched theory. It was, no doubt, a small recondite discovery, a minor ornithological technicality, yet for me it was a moment of unforgettable exultation —a major triumph, an epoch-making occurrence, a turning point; or is it only in looking back on it that I have invested it with so much significance because, in the event, it changed the course of my life?

From the pillbox we watched the little Lesser Whitefront for half an hour or more, satisfying ourselves that the eyelids were in fact golden yellow, that the bill was small and extra-pink, and that the white forehead patch rose high on to the crown of the head. The bird had that smooth, dark, perfect look, almost as if there was a bloom on the feathers, which is so characteristic of the Lesser Whitefront.

Later in the afternoon we moved further down the sea-wall to get a better view of a part of the flock which was beyond the fence that crosses the Dumbles at the half-way mark. Here among 200 or 300 more Whitefronts was a second Lesser Whitefront. To make certain, we went back and found our original bird still almost in the position in which we had left it. Here then undoubtedly were two Lesser Whitefronts; if Will Tinsley's war-time bird was to be accepted, as I felt sure it should be, these were the third and fourth specimens of their kind ever to be authentically recorded in Britain. It is not often that one sees so rare a British bird and it may be imagined with what excitement we telephoned that evening to a number of ornithological pundits. The meticulous and ever-sceptical Bernard Tucker after much cross-questioning professed himself convinced, but I was privately glad that he saw them for himself a week later. In the following year we saw three Lesser Whitefronts and in most of the succeeding years in this Severn flock there have been at least one, sometimes as many as six of them, appearing as strays among the Russian White-fronted Geese.

On that sunny day in December 1945 the third and fourth Lesser Whitefronts had brought the total number of kinds of wild geese we had seen together on that marsh to seven, and as we walked back from the pillbox I came to the inescapable conclusion that this was the place in which anyone who loved wild geese must live. Here were two empty cottages which might become the head-quarters of the research organisation which had been taking shape in my mind over the war years, the headquarters of a new collection of waterfowl, of the scientific and educational effort which I believed was so badly needed for the conservation of wildfowl. As we squelched up the track, past the 100-year-old duck decoy, into the deep-rutted yard and back along the muddy lane towards the canal, I looked at my surroundings with a new eye, an eye to the future, for this was the beginning of the Wildfowl Trust.

PART 3

CHAPTER I   *Gloucestershire and Ethics*

IN 1945 there were four other potential areas in which my new collection and research station might have been started. One of them was an old familiar place—Brogden—on the north side of the Kent Estuary in Westmorland. But during the war its grass fields had come under cultivation and the geese had largely given up going there. Another possible place was an old Keep overlooking a marshy valley in Wigtownshire. Two others had the advantage of being nearer to London: Amberley Wildbrooks in Sussex and the High Halstow marshes in Kent, where there was a fine old red-brick farmhouse called Swig's Hole, an ancient and derelict decoy and a flock of several hundred White-fronted Geese. At Slimbridge the geese were in thousands, rather than hundreds, and the decoy was less derelict, though the house was no more than a cottage: and besides, Slimbridge had its Lesser Whitefronts.

The day I had seen them had not been my first on the Severn Estuary. More than twenty years before, having read of the wild geese there in the books of Sir Ralph Payne Gallwey, I determined to visit the place. The opportunity came during a university vacation at the family cottage near Marlborough, whence I motored over with a friend in the family Austin Seven. This was the entry I made in my wildfowling diary next day:

"Tuesday, 18th September, 1928. Went by car from the Lacket to the rather depressing town of Berkeley on the Severn. Here after sundry enquiries we found that the best shooting was to be had on the 'New Grounds' but these are apparently too close to certain decoy pools and shooting is illegal. We therefore went down to the edge of the water some miles below the New Grounds and walked along a flood bank towards Bristol. There were a lot of very shy Curlew.

"A man at the farm where we left the car had told us we were too early for the Wigeon and geese. These all went to the New Grounds to feed.

"We tried unsuccessfully to stalk some of the Curlew, saw a fox and found an ox skeleton. Further on we talked to another farm hand who also said we were too early, but that later on the geese came past there. They flighted from the New Grounds out to sea. Most of them went along the channel, but in misty or foggy weather particularly they came low along the shore. Mist was better than storm for the geese. He said that last year the geese had been mostly the little goose instead of the ordinary big one, but a diversion came, and I forgot to ask him what he meant.

"We saw a small party of duck out in the channel. They were Mallard, but he was surprised they were not Burro' Ducks [Shelducks] though the telescope helped to convince him. We walked on along the bank but saw nothing. The tide was low and the mud stretched three-quarters of a mile to the river channel. As it got dark we still saw no duck, although we heard two shots further along. We walked back four miles to the car, and so home without mishap.

"The country around the estuary is very treey. The fields are mostly grazing and I saw no stubble at all, so that there is nowhere for geese or duck to feed inland [sic]. Presumably they feed on or around the decoy ponds or somewhere up above where we were, and flight on to the mud where the estuary broadens out. The next thing to do is to discover how the land lies on the New Grounds and failing this above them."

But I never did, and did not go to the area again until, with the permission of Captain R. G. W. Berkeley, I was taken there on the 27th February, 1937, after a lecture I had given in Bristol. I went this time to one of the two decoy pools, where there were a few Teal, and curiously enough a single Egyptian Goose. There can have been very few Whitefronts about at the time for we only found one small flock of about fifty in a field near the canal.

Neither of these pre-war experiences gave any clue to the perfect suitability of the place for my post-war purposes.

The last bridge over the Severn is the railway viaduct at Sharpness where the river narrows. Immediately above this the estuary is much wider, with an expanse of water at high tide which is three miles long and a mile wide. Further upstream the river gets gradually narrower round a series of great bends. At low water many hundreds of acres of sand are exposed—an ideal roosting place for wild geese and ducks. Over this part of the river the tidal range is more than thirty feet and the spring tides produce a wave over the sand which builds up as the river narrows, into the famous Severn Bore—a breaking wave five or six feet high which sweeps up the river at about twelve miles an hour.

Between Gloucester and Sharpness the tides make the river virtually unnavigable, and for more than 100 years sea-going ships have reached the deep water above Gloucester by way of the Gloucester and Berkeley Canal. Near Slimbridge the canal runs through flat meadows which have been progressively reclaimed from the Severn tide over four centuries. The pushing out of successive sea-walls to consolidate and perpetuate the natural silting of the river mouth has created an area of 1,000 acres known since the early reclamations as the New Grounds.

The main feeding grounds of the geese lie between the canal and the tidal shore. Early in the winter the birds feed largely on the 200 acres of grassy saltmarsh known as the Dumbles, which lie outside the sea-wall; and it was here from one of the four pillboxes built during the Second World War that we saw the first Lesser White-front. Later in the season the Dumbles become almost denuded of grass, and the geese move into the fields inside the bank.

The first, and perhaps most important advantage of this area over almost all other wild goose resorts in Britain was the Manorial Right of the Berkeley family over the foreshore to the centre of the river channel at low water. Held from immemorial times, it had been reaffirmed in a famous case finally decided in the House of Lords as recently as just before the First World War.

On this right the continued existence of this large flock of White-fronts mainly depended (and still depends). To be sure the geese were preserved for shooting, but the numbers of geese shot and the amount of disturbance caused by the shooting were negligible. The Berkeley Goose Shoot had been conducted in a reasonable and moderate manner ever since guns were invented; the geese owed their long and continuing sanctuary to this sporting interest.

The second advantage of this area for the purposes of studying wild geese was the sea-wall itself—the high bank which keeps the spring tides out of the low-lying fields and runs along the back of the Dumbles. Watchers can move freely behind it without disturbing the geese, and by happy chance it lies to the south of the birds so that the sunlight illuminates them throughout the day, without ever shining in the eyes of the watcher.

In most places the second-hand value of a war-time pillbox is strictly limited, but the four on the sea-wall, built when Hitler's invasion seemed imminent (we used to say he must have heard about them, as he never came), could, with minor modification, be well enough adapted to their new purpose. It was possible to enter them from behind, unseen by the birds on the Dumbles, and the view could be improved quite simply by opening out the embrasures. We also needed a number of new observation posts to be spaced between the pillboxes so that wherever the geese might be feeding on the marsh we could safely peep over the bank opposite them without being detected. In this way it seemed that the wonder of watching the wildest of wild birds at really close range could be enjoyed by many people who might never otherwise have had the chance.

The first of the new huts were built by German prisoners during the summer of 1946. They were of timber, thatched with straw, and were fitted with hinged shutters, so that if the geese were close they could be watched through a narrow slit, which could be opened wider if they were further away. They were also fitted with benches to sit on, with an arm rest for steadying binoculars and even a foot rest. It was my theory that intensive observation and study would be much better carried out if the observer was reasonably comfortable. One of the most important features of these hides was the covered approach to them from behind the sea-wall, but although they were frequently copied elsewhere during the next few years, they were always so sited that they could only be entered by first driving the birds from the area after which the observer hoped they would return. The whole secret of the observation huts at Slimbridge is that they can be entered by a party of twenty or thirty people when the geese are within ten yards on the other side, and provided that no one sneezes or coughs loudly the party can watch them and leave the hide again without the birds knowing anything about it.

On Sunday, 10th November, 1946, a meeting was held at the Patch Bridge Guest House, Slimbridge, where the road crosses the canal on the way to the New Grounds. It was attended by Captain R. G. W. Berkeley, the landlord, H. H. Davis, who had watched the Severn geese for many years and drawn my attention to the first Lesser Whitefront, James Robertson Justice who had come down with me that week-end to see the place for the first time, Keith Miller Jones, our family solicitor who had lately drawn up the rules for the Hansard Society, and my old friend Michael Bratby.

White-fronted geese in the green fields of Gloucestershire.

The following resolution was carried unanimously:

"That a Society be formed with the name of 'The Severn Wildfowl Trust' and that the draft rules produced to the meeting be adopted as the Rules of the Trust."

So the new organisation which I had been planning for so long was officially formed, for the scientific study and conservation of wildfowl.

I had more or less given up shooting. My personal doubts had increased and been finally crystallised by a particular incident.

During a goose-shoot the six or seven 'guns' were standing in a cluster when a single goose flew over. Each man (and I was one) raised his gun and fired two barrels. Twelve shots went off at the goose, which staggered in the air, flew on and then began to lose height. It came down far out on the mud flats in a place quite inaccessible because of the soft mud which in parts of that estuary amounts almost to quicksand. As it landed, I watched with my glasses, and saw that both its legs were broken. It crash landed, came to rest quivering on its belly, and put its head up. There was nothing that any of us could do. It was 500 yards away and inaccessible. We repaired later to the hotel for lunch, and a very good lunch it was; I remember that the cherry brandy was excellent. In the afternoon I recall that our marksmanship was a little below the standard of the morning. As we passed along the sea-wall I saw with binoculars that the bird still sat out on the mud, its neck still raised. At dusk we went back to tea, a bath before an excellent dinner, and after it a comfortable bed.

On the following day I came out again to watch the geese. The shooting of course was over, and many of the geese were feeding in the fields as if nothing had happened. But out on the mud, in precisely the same place (for there were small neap tides at the time which did not cover the high sand), still sat the goose with the broken legs. "What right," I said to myself, "have we men to do this to a bird for our fun—to impose that kind of suffering? I should not want this for a sworn enemy, and that goose was not my enemy when I shot at him—although I was his."

"That kind of suffering," I had said—but what kind of suffering was it, for without being a bird how could one know what pain they felt? Perhaps this is a question which will never be adequately answered, but there are, of course, observations which bear upon it. We know that wounds which would incapacitate a man do not do so to a bird. We know that cockerels will feed unconcernedly

T

immediately after a major abdominal operation. We know that although forty-one per cent of a sample of 825 adult Pink-footed Geese were shown by X-rays to be carrying shot somewhere in their bodies, the average weight of the forty-one per cent was no lower than the weight of the other fifty-nine per cent, and weight is one of the most sensitive barometers of a bird's wellbeing. It has been held, and I believe rightly, that pain in birds is something quite different from, and much less than, pain as we know it in man. I mean this in the physiological sense. But psychologically too, it is clear that animals suffer less, in that they are unable to reason about it and to anticipate pain or death. They do not think, "Perhaps this wound is mortal, perhaps I shall die." But in spite of all this the goose with the broken legs was upsetting.

I took the argument a stage further. I had in the past derived enormous enjoyment, good health, interest, and aesthetic pleasure from being out on the marshes at dawn and dusk and under the moon, in rain and gale and frost. The birds with their beauty and wildness had been an endless source of delight. The difficulty of outwitting them, the discomforts, the occasional dangers—these, and not the killing made the sport of wildfowling one of the most exciting in the world. I was not interested in 'the ultimate sanction'. I would have given anything (and I wonder how many others feel the same) for a handy portable device which for the same output of knowledge, skill and manual dexterity would bring a bird to hand alive and unharmed. It was inescapable to me that, had I never been interested in wildfowling, my enjoyment, and also my knowledge of the birds, would have been much less. Was there not a balance here? Perhaps so long as a man is deriving so much good as to offset the bad, the balance might still fall in favour of the wildfowler. If I were advising a young boy would I not say to him: "Of course you will enjoy wildfowling; it will bring you unparalleled thrills; and if you never experience those thrills you will probably never enjoy the birds themselves to quite the same extent, for you will not learn the subtle goose/rook, wigeon/starling distinction, the subtle difference between man's attitude to his traditional quarry and his attitude to all other birds"?

I am doubtful whether this argument that I might offer is sound, but I am quite sure that as soon as the doubts and the disquiet prevent you from enjoying shooting there can no longer be any good reason for going on doing it. So I have sold my guns, and I no longer shoot. It is easy for the young and keen to say, "Well, that's all right for him, he's shot all the geese he wants and now he says he doesn't think it's a good thing." But that merely confuses the issue; a dog-in-the-manger is something different again, something which I hope never to be. It can be argued that the final decisions should be made in the conscience of the individual. "Do I think this right, do I think this wrong? How much does my decision affect other people? Do I enjoy it so much that the overall good offsets the bad? Or would it be better to give it up?" Having decided to give it up the situation is not quite simple. If cruelty exists on a level comparable, say, with cruelty to children, then more is demanded than personal abstention. But if we must campaign perhaps we should be better occupied campaigning against the extermination of all life on earth, or for the alleviation of all suffering starting with human suffering. Should we not oppose worst things first?

CHAPTER 2   *The Blowlamp and the Snow-plough*

IN its earliest days the Severn Wildfowl Trust had one major
stroke of good fortune. We were able to enlist the support of Field-
Marshal Lord Alanbrooke, who had been Chief of the Imperial
General Staff and Chairman of the Chiefs of Staff Committee from
soon after Dunkirk until the end of the war. This great man, a
prime architect of Allied victory, had found recreation in its most
literal sense, in Natural History—and especially in birds—during
the heaviest pressures of the war. Now he planned in his retirement
to study and film birds. In his letter accepting my invitation to
become the first President of the Trust he wrote, "I may not be
able to devote much time to it", and it was never our intention
that he should do so. But from then on for the next fourteen years,
except on the few occasions when he was ill, he never missed a single
Council meeting. He has come regularly to film birds at Slimbridge;
he has presided over General Meetings and Annual Dinners; he has
brought his films to be shown on my television programme and he
has always been available for consultation. In retirement his life
seemed to be only a little less busy and active than it had been
during the war, and it was to us astonishing that he could spare so
much time for our new organisation. His acceptance of the
Presidency turned out to be one of the most important factors
in its success, and it demonstrated once more how really great
men can and do find time to go into the detail of quite small things
when they are interested. In a long correspondence with Lord
Alanbrooke over those years, each one of nearly 200 letters from
him is written in his own hand.

In the very first he wrote, "It will be a great move if you can get
Archie Jamieson to be Treasurer"; and we did. Sir Archibald
Jamieson had been Chairman of Vickers since the days before the
war when he came over to my lighthouse from his country home in

North Norfolk. He agreed at once to look after the finances of our new Society. In the years that followed many of his difficulties arose from my principle of spending the money first and finding it afterwards—a system which can be carried just so far but no further.

At that time I was living and working in London at 8 Edwardes Square, and driving rather fast to the New Grounds at week-ends in a green three-litre Jaguar which was my pride and joy.

Besides the wild geese there was, of course, the decoy, which lay in the little wood close beside the headquarters cottages. Berkeley New Decoy was its full title, as listed in Sir Ralph Payne Gallwey's *Book of Duck Decoys*. It had not been effectively worked for about thirty years, although it had been repaired with the intention of working it in 1937. There was stout string netting still on the pipes which needed only a small amount of patching. Only two of the four pipes were usable, the other two having at some time or other been filled with mud from the pond and blanked off. The first season's catch was only six ducks, but although they were only Mallards, they were, to us, six very important birds—our first. They were duly ringed and released.

We fed the decoy to attract the ducks and I remember watching an evening flight in that first season and counting twenty-nine Mallards as they splashed down with a ring of bright water on the twilit pool. Since then we have counted well over 1,000 birds coming in to the half acre of open water, but in those days twenty-nine seemed a lot.

It gave me great pleasure to have a duck decoy to develop which could be compared with Borough Fen Decoy where I had learned the decoyman's art. How we built up the lead and the catches from year to year is shown by this table:

	Total Ducks Caught
1946–7	6
1947–8	133
1948–9	269
1949–50	609
1950–1	1,203

Since then a record catch of 2,237 was made in the winter of 1957–8.

Around the new headquarters—the three cottages at the end of the lane—were some marshy fields, where we began to dig out ponds and to build fences to enclose a new collection of live waterfowl.

The first pond was scooped out by a dragline in a small orchard and the next among rushes at the near end of a field which was to become known as the Rushy Pen. For fencing we used Summerfeld tracking—a type of stout wire netting threaded with rods, which had been used on the ground for temporary airfields during the war and was therefore to be had at a very low price. The collection was to be started from a nucleus of birds brought together by Gavin Maxwell, a friend from lighthouse days, at his home in Wigtownshire. At this time he was developing his Basking shark-fishing industry on the west coast of Scotland operating from the island of Soay and he was anxious to find a home for about forty birds which he had assembled at Monreith—the family home in Wigtownshire during the war. To look after these birds I had engaged John Yealland, now Curator of Birds at the London Zoo, who before the war had for some time looked after the late Duke of Bedford's birds. I had met John near Brussels in 1938 when he was curator of an excellent waterfowl collection belonging to Dr. Derscheid, afterwards an important leader of the Resistance until he was executed by the Gestapo.

John Yealland and I went up to collect and bring back about fifty geese from Monreith. It would be touch and go whether the new pen would be completed in time for the arrival of these birds. We brought them down hopefully, only to find at the last minute that it was not.

The birds were in crates and could not remain in them overnight. The only place in which they could be released was in the rooms of the empty bungalow beside the Decoy. The quarrelsome Upland Geese had the larder to themselves, the Snow Geese were in one bedroom, the little Ross's Geese in another; the Emperors had the kitchen. They emerged from their boxes in the dim light of torches and we watered and fed them. By noon on the following day the pen was completed and the birds were herded out of the house, through the yard, and down the lane to the gate of their new home. To this nucleus of a collection were added a few pairs of birds which had been at the lighthouse before the war: the Lesser Whitefronts which had spent the war at Will Tinsley's farm, a pair of Red-breasted Geese which had been kept for me by Rick Pilcher, the surgeon in Boston; and there was a Spur-winged Goose which was said to be thirty years old. These were all under the care of John Yealland and later his two assistants, Eunice Overend and Tommy Johnstone. So once more I found myself occupied with the delights and disappointments of a collection of waterfowl. Some of the magic of my old lighthouse had been recaptured. I was keeping birds again.

But at that time the wild geese were to me the most marvellous aspect of the Wildfowl Trust and the observation huts worked better than I had ever dreamed they could. There was, during that winter, a period when the snow was on the ground and the geese were seeking out any snow-free patches. If we wanted to get close-up views of the geese all that seemed necessary was to clear the snow from the grass in front of some of the observation huts. I wondered how this could most easily be achieved. Perhaps, I thought, by sweeping the snow with a flame as one might mow grass with a scythe. We decided to try it out. A blowlamp was borrowed, and in due course was roaring out its blue tongue of flame. John Yealland and I advanced on to an area of undisturbed snow and began to sweep. The flame made no impression whatever. With two inches of snow on the ground we found that if the blowlamp were shone on one spot for a matter of half a minute a small dent the size of a mouse hole appeared in the snow; and a moment later at the bottom of it were a few shreds of red-hot burned-up grass. Blowlamps, we concluded, were not the right tool for the job.

Our next idea was to make a snow-plough. In those days timber was difficult to get but we finally acquired two large ancient beams and connected them with a railway sleeper to make the plough. This was put together by the local carpenter and took a fortnight to make. By the time it was completed and delivered at the New Grounds the snow had melted and by the following winter the snow plough had long since been cannibalised to make bridges and other more immediately important structures. The blowlamp and the snow-plough have now become symbolic each of a particular but different kind of folly, both of them peculiarly my own.

Late in the winter of 1946 my mother came down to Slimbridge to see the wild geese. It was a good week-end and the geese behaved well. From the slits of the new observation huts we watched them for long periods at less than twenty yards range. She wrote in her diary:

"The geese were terrific, so was the cold; but I wouldn't have minded if it had been ten times colder. We sat in hides behind the sea-wall for hours, but the movement of the geese was enthralling. And then the evenings back at the inn, very snug with a big wood fire; and then up early in the frost and back to the marsh!"

Early in 1947 she fell ill. She seemed to be aware that her illness was incurable before it had been diagnosed, but the awareness was itself a huge joke to her. On 24th July, at the age of 69, she died of leukemia in St. Mary's Hospital, Paddington. Through those last weeks she was full of courage and patience about it, but at the same time absolutely realistic. When a blood transfusion from me had patently failed to give more than temporary relief, she knew that her first assessment had been right. She was gay and carefree and magnificent until the very end. My brother Wayland and I motored with my stepfather to Sandwich to spread her ashes along the beach she had known and loved. It was done without ceremony and we were as gay as she would have wanted and expected us to be.

Memory is usually (but not always) kind, discarding the bad and retaining only the good. I had an easy and happy relationship with my mother, and rarely (even in the most oppositious school days) was it clouded with anger. I do not want to remember her ill or dead, and yet I cannot forget those last days in July 1947. They have led me to decree that my own children shall not be allowed to visit me on my death-bed, nor on any account whatever to see my body after I am dead, if there is any way of avoiding it.

My mother did not believe in 'life after death', and, in its conventional context, neither do I, but she qualified magnificently for the three kinds of immortality which I recognise—the three ways in which individual continuance can be assured and people may live on after they have died: in the creations of their art, in the memories of the living and in the persons of their descendants. Sculpture has a notable permanence, and my mother made more than twenty public monuments; in addition, there are remarkable diaries published as *Self Portrait of an Artist*. As a friend she was greatly loved and made life a better thing for so many besides her own family; and her two sons have so far produced eight grandchildren to perpetuate her gay laughter.

A week or so after her death I had a postcard from Bernard Shaw, then ninety-one:

"How jolly to find that the Severn Wildfowl Trust is your shop!

"The news from Leinster Corner reached me on my birthday and for a moment struck it all of a heap. But I cannot feel otherwise than gladly about her, nor imagine her old. She was a very special friend.

"I have sent in the documents and am now, I presume, a Wildfowl.

G.B.S."

CHAPTER 3

An Important Decision

MY marriage had gone wrong and Jane had left the house in Edwardes Square, happily without lasting bitterness. I had turned all my thoughts and energies to the development of the Severn Wildfowl Trust. Already my post-war activities were becoming complex enough to require the services of a small secretariat; it seemed essential to engage the services of an organiser as principal private secretary, and manager of my affairs. To this end I advertised and a number of evidently efficient young ex-service men replied. We decided to invite the most promising candidate to a dinner party after a film. Jane, who knew the requirements so well, was there too, and we invited my brother Wayland, and asked him to bring a girl so that Jane should not be the only one.

Quite early in the evening it became evident that the candidate was unsuitable, and once that had been established I turned to the charming and beautiful girl who was sitting next to me at dinner. Her name was Elizabeth Adams. From my stepfather I had often heard of her father, for both had been in the Zeebrugge raid. I discovered that she too was looking for a secretarial job and she thought that she could handle the one I was offering. In this she was quite right, for she ran my secretariat and the Severn Wildfowl Trust with great success for eight months until she left to get married to my brother Wayland. Her last assignment before leaving was to make arrangements for a successor. Thus it was that I sat one afternoon in the ground floor room of the little house in Edwardes Square interviewing a shy, quiet girl, who sat before me looking small and neat and serious. She had been working as archivist in the Embassy in Belgrade, and before that, most secretly, at Bletchley, and before that again in the Land Army, milking cows. Her father had been a naval officer. The interview was short. The appointment was urgent and she got the job. I should probably have laughed out loud had anyone suggested that I had made, that day, the most important personal decision of my life. If it is reasonable to regard as the most important those decisions which have brought the most evident happiness, then the train of circumstances I have just described is without question the most important in my story—the circumstances that led to my second marriage, which has so far brought me nine years of happiness in the highest degree I have ever known.

Driving between London and Gloucestershire in the early years of the Trust, I often broke the journey at Kidlington aerodrome just north of Oxford. It was time, I thought, to complete my training as a pilot and to get an 'A' licence. This involved starting again from scratch. My friend Keith Shackleton, the painter, who came often to the Severn estuary, had also decided to learn to fly at Kidlington, and so too had my new secretary Philippa Talbot-Ponsonby. Together the three of us took lessons with minor degrees of competition. Our teacher was the imperturbable and delightful Chief Flying Instructor of the Oxford Aeroplane Club, C. F. Cockburn, known always to us as 'Coe'. I found flying a Tiger Moth again immensely stimulating and at the same time 're-creating'. With goggles and helmet in the windswept open cockpit my noisy and rather smelly flying machine took me into a new and still unfamiliar world of three-dimensional freedom. There was a developing manual dexterity, the control of 'scenic railway' sensations in the aerobatics, and below the living map of familiar England. It was a first step towards the much greater enjoyment of flying gliders later to come.

In 1947 I was engaged by the B.B.C. to be one of the commentators for the wedding of Princess Elizabeth to the Duke of Edinburgh. My station was on the roof of St. Margaret's, Westminster, overlooking the entrance to Westminster Abbey. The assistant who was delegated to look after me and see that the equipment was in working order was a then unknown member of the B.B.C. staff, Rex Alston. I was, as usual, extremely nervous. I remember the voice of 'Lobby' Lotbiniere, the Director of Outside Broadcasts, coming over the line from Broadcasting House to all the commentators just before the programme started: "Good luck, boys. Don't forget this is the largest listening audience there has ever been for any broadcast, 250 million people will be listening to you." Surprisingly this did not add anything to my peace of mind. A few moments later Rex trod on the junction box of the headphones, cutting off our direct communication. Quickly we switched on the portable radio and were just in time to take our cue from that.

The Royal Wedding was my second post-war attempt at commentary. The first had been the Victory Procession, in which I had travelled in naval uniform in a D.U.K.W. amphibious vehicle. I was required to do three short periods of commentary, one somewhere in south London, another as we came through Parliament Square and the third as we passed the saluting base. Here, with my cap sitting slightly crooked on my head because of the headphones that I wore beneath it, I had saluted my King. The worst which befell me that day was in Parliament Square where I could not find an adequate word to describe the decorative pagoda-like structure which had been set up in the middle of it. As we came past I fought for words to describe it, trying without success to avoid using the one which first came to mind. On the following day *The Times* reported that "Words failed Mr. Scott when he came to describe the ceremonial erection in Parliament Square".

Running commentary was not and is not for me, except perhaps on a subject of which I have specialised knowledge and familiarity. I can get by on a sailing race, or a crowd of ducks being fed, or an aerobatic display in gliders, but for most other subjects it is not my line. A year or two later I was called on to do a running commentary job in the Albert Hall for a large rally of Young Conservatives. It was to be attended by Sir Winston Churchill and Sir Anthony Eden. All went reasonably well this time. I had heard that it was Eden's birthday, though it was not generally known. As I announced this to the packed hall, Churchill jumped up from his chair and went across to shake Eden's hand. Later I very much enjoyed introducing the Leader of the Opposition, as he then was, with surely one of the most exciting of all anticipatory phrases "Ladies and Gentlemen—Mr. Winston Churchill." In the Green Room after the meeting Churchill greeted me warmly not for the part which I had played in the rally or for my Conservative candidacy in the '45 Election, but because I had made arrangements for him to put down some Swallow-tail butterflies and Elephant Hawk moths in his garden at Chartwell. It was the only thing which interested him that evening and we talked about it for ten minutes, to the evident annoyance of the politicians who were waiting to speak to him.

The butterflies and moths were to come from the Butterfly Farm of my friend Hugh Newman, which I had first visited in my early childhood in the days of his father, L. W. Newman, who founded the business. I had been to Bexley again after the war, as part of the

process of recapturing the delights of youth and peace time. Hugh
was very keen to start a B.B.C. Children's Hour programme on
Natural History. Questions were to be sent in by the children on
postcards and he and I and Brian Vesey-Fitzgerald were to answer
them. To this end we met Derek McCulloch, the Head of Children's
Hour, at a lunch party and discussed the proposed programme. Its
title was to be 'Nature Parliament'. I did not care for it very much,
perhaps chiefly because it looked like being more of a quiz than a
'parliament', though the object was not to test our knowledge but
to answer authoritatively the queries sent in by the children. Surprisingly the programme was a great success and it has been heard
in Children's Hour once a month ever since. James Fisher is one
of the Team and we are now in our fourteenth year.

In 1947 I was granted permission to make portrait drawings of
Princess Elizabeth and Princess Margaret. For the sittings I went
to Buckingham Palace about half a dozen times with a drawing
board and a box of pencils. I made two drawings of Princess Margaret and three of Princess Elizabeth, all on plastic as lithographs
which were printed by Cowells of Ipswich through the good
offices of my friend Geoffrey Smith. The sittings at the Palace were
alarming only because I was afraid the drawings would not justify
the time given by the sitters. This became almost an obsession.
But the Queen seemed pleased with the results and the Princesses
were patient and charming.

I can still visualise a scene described to me by Princess Elizabeth.
The car given to her as a wedding present went so smoothly and
slowly in bottom gear that one day in Windsor Great Park she and
Prince Philip had got out and walked along beside it while it
purred along empty.

These were my first meetings with Queen Elizabeth II, who was
afterwards to become Patron of the Trust and a regular visitor to
Slimbridge.

I was painting hard at this time in the ground floor room at
Edwardes Square which was part dining-room, part office, part
studio. Keith Shackleton came there often. He elected himself
to the unofficial office of Scapegoat to the Severn Wildfowl Trust,
because he said he was always blamed when the wild geese were
disturbed. Besides learning to fly simultaneously at Kidlington I
often roped him in to help me with a picture. "Will you whizz in
some blue sky on that side while I get on with the water down
here?" and Keith would start 'whizzing'. I had first met him in war
time when he was a schoolboy at my old school, Oundle. During a

school holiday he was watching geese at Martin Mere near South-port, and together we had stalked up a ditch bottom to photograph them at close range. Together, when they finally flew away, we had agreed that there was no more romantic bird in the world than a wild goose.

My portraits in pencil were more successful than those in oils, and I was also using lithography. *Country Life* published a book under the title *Portrait Drawings*; it contained the thirty-six best drawings that I had then made, and I was very proud of the collection. Somehow the reproduction seemed to improve them. For a moment I thought they were a significant achievement, but soon after I realised that like so much of my work, they were just not quite good enough. Perhaps if there had been no war . . .

Before the war I had been on the brink of branching out into new fields in painting. I had been planning vast ambitious canvases, allegorical works, abstractions, goodness knows what. After the war, so far from a new branching out, I wanted only to return to the old things, to 'get back to normal', to recapture the happy pre-war life. I was keen to paint birds again in no particularly new way, but rather to revert to the precise point at which I had broken off and from there set out again; it was the manifestation of my safe return.

A part of this return was to sailing. Neither John Winter nor I had sailed dinghies at all during the war, and we felt convinced that we should now be outclassed by the younger generation. Nevertheless we entered *Thunder & Lightning* for the first post-war Prince of Wales's Cup race at Brixham in the summer of 1946. To our astonishment we found that she was still as fast as any of the boats and we won the race comfortably by about three minutes.

At that time I had recently joined the Council of the Yacht Racing Association and at one of its meetings, presided over as usual by Sir Ralph Gore, Commodore of the Royal Yacht Squadron, a letter was read asking for a representative of the International Yacht Racing Union to attend a meeting at Lausanne in Switzerland to discuss the forthcoming Olympic Games. Before the war the International Yacht Racing Union had been adminis-tered from London and its archives, together with those of the Y.R.A., had been largely destroyed during a London air-raid. Sir Ralph looked round the table to see whether anyone was ready to go to Lausanne. Having been in the home theatre all through the war I thought it might be rather fun to go to Switzerland, so I offered to attend. Sir Ralph said, "That's settled, Scott will go to Lausanne." I thought that when I got there I should find a number of other yachtsmen and between us we should thrash out the classes to be used in the yachting events of the Games which were to be held at Torquay in 1948. When I arrived however I found that I *was* yachting and the others present represented athletics, basketball, wrestling, cycling and so on. It was therefore up to me to decide on the classes which would be used and to tell the International Olympic Committee what the yachting fraternity wanted. It was a sudden and rather awe-inspiring responsibility.

Having become thus associated with the Olympic Games, I was appointed Chairman of the Y.R.A.'s Olympic Committee and told to organise the yachting in Tor Bay. For this I had magnificent support from Francis Usborne, the Secretary of the Y.R.A., in whose Cambridge sailing team I had been a junior member, and from Quintin Riley, the Polar explorer. The issue was confused by the fact that I had also put my name down as a competitor in the Selection Trials for the single-handed sailing event which was to be raced in the new twelve-foot Fireflies. Thus I found myself organising the trials as a dress rehearsal for the Games and, at the same time, competing in them. Perhaps luckily my performance did not impress the selectors and I was therefore free to devote my attention to the organising of the event itself.

Our headquarters at Torquay were the Public Baths in the Marine Spa overlooking the bay, where one crisis followed another in monotonous sequence through the fortnight of the Games. At times the organisation was sorely pressed. One morning Crown Prince Olav of Norway, whom I had previously met during the Jubilee Regatta at Torquay in 1937, came into the converted bathroom which was our main office saying, "Can I help you?" —and forthwith sat down at a table to add up the sheets of points scored on the previous day's racing, corrected by the results of numerous protest cases.

The President of the International Olympic Committee at that time was Siegfried Edström, who came to perform the ceremonial opening of the Games at Torquay. It was my job to look after him like visiting royalty from the moment that he arrived until his train left again for London. The ceremony was almost unbelievedly disastrous and soon acquired in my mind an irresistible resemblance to the School Sports in Evelyn Waugh's *Decline and Fall*. Yet about most of the things that went wrong there was still that lingering hope that not everybody had noticed.

After the Games I gave a private dinner in the Imperial Hotel at Torquay. It was attended by the Crown Prince, Sir Ralph

Gore, and a small number of others who had been helping with the organisation. I remember that at the end of the dinner I rose to propose the Loyal Toast and said, "The King." A few moments later Sir Ralph Gore asked me whether he could propose the toast to the King of Norway, to which of course I readily agreed and he then rose and said: "His Majesty The King of Norway." I have always concerned myself with perfection of detail and was immediately horrified at the thought that I ought to have said "His Majesty the King" in proposing *my* loyal toast. It was not until some long time afterwards that I discovered that we were both right. The Loyal Toast should correctly be "The King" or "The Queen" but His Majesty should be used for a foreign King.

It is ridiculous that so tiny and insignificant a point should have hung in my memory for so many years. I recount it only as an example of obsession with detail carried to a laughable extreme.

CHAPTER 4   *A New Race*

THOSE scientists who are interested in the evolution of species can usually be divided into 'splitters' and 'lumpers'. Collectively they are known as taxonomists. The splitters had their heyday in the years that followed the acceptance of the sub-species or race as a distinguishable unit of population into which a species might be divided. Races were separated and described often on measurements of a few millimetres until the reaction set in. The lumpers said that the splitters were confusing and complicating the issue, were unable to see the wood for the trees, were hiding basic truths about evolutionary relationship in their enthusiasm for subdivision.

Somewhere between the two, no doubt, lies the sensible course. If I must be one or other, I am a splitter. If one population differs recognisably from another, I am for taking note of the fact and giving it a name for convenience. But I never expected to go in for any active splitting myself until on a January morning in 1939, I saw that yellow bill which began something only concluded in the spring of 1948.

In the long ago before the Second World War, my friend David Haig Thomas came back from an expedition to West Greenland, bringing with him a pair of White-fronted Geese. They were kept on the lake at Millichope Park in Shropshire where he was then staying, and it was not for several months that I was able to go over and see them. The chance finally came when I went there to be 'best man' at his wedding. When I saw these birds, I was immediately struck by the fact that their plumage seemed very dark and that their bills seemed to be yellow instead of the Whitefronts' usual milky pink. Of course, I thought, this may be caused by the fact that David brought them back as young goslings so that they were reared on board ship with rather unnatural food. But it crossed

Marking Whooper cygnets in Central Iceland. With me are Dr. Finnur Gudmundsson (*left*), Director of the Natural History Museum, in Reykjavik, and Valentinus Jonsson, the farmer who was our guide.

Riding into the Central Desert of Iceland towards the Pinkfoot breeding grounds near the Hofsjökull Icecap. On the right is Finnur, in the middle James Fisher.

1953

The Trust's second expedition to Iceland reached the Pinkfoot breeding grounds by bus and lorry although there was no road. Here it is at the foot of the Kerlingerfjell.

1951

The edge of the Hofsjökull Icecap with Hjartafell in the background.

951

James Fisher photographing moulting (and therefore flightless) adult Pinkfeet and Goslings rounded up on the first Iceland Expedition, when just over 1,000 geese were ringed.

953

More than 3,000 flightless adults and goslings rounded up on Arnafellsalda during the second Iceland expedition when just over 9,000 were ringed.

1951

Philippa Talbot-Ponsonby and I were married on 7th August 1951, at Reykjavik.

my mind that possibly the Whitefronts of Greenland were always
dark and always had yellow bills.

Two years later, in 1937, David went again to West Greenland
and I arranged with him to send back some birds as soon as he
arrived and before he spent the winter there. In due course back
came eight more White-fronted Geese, four for Millichope and
four for my lighthouse. As soon as my birds arrived I realised that
they were identical to the two I had seen before. Surely therefore
there was a distinguishable race of White-fronted Geese breeding
in Greenland. The next problem was to find out where they spent
the winter. The first obvious answer, as the birds bred on the *west*
side of the Greenland Ice Cap, was that those few White-fronted
Geese which had been recorded on the eastern shores of North
America must come from the Greenland breeding grounds. But
these were only a few dozen stragglers. Surely this could not be the
whole population of the race.

Then I remembered something else. Years earlier I had read a
famous book, *Letters to Young Shooters* by Sir Ralph Payne Gallwey,
published in 1896. It includes a series of brief descriptions of the
various species of wildfowl, and under White-fronted Goose it
states: "The bill *all one shade, orange yellow* except the tip, which is
white" (his italics). As, at the time I first read this, the bills of all
the Whitefronts I had ever seen had been predominantly pale
pink I supposed this to be a mistake, which was surprising from the
pen of so careful an observer. But now I remembered that Sir Ralph
had done much of his wildfowling in Ireland. Perhaps the White-
fronted Geese in Ireland had got orange-yellow bills and perhaps
they came from breeding-grounds in Greenland. Furthermore I
found from the literature that the famous ornithologist, Gould, had
described as orange-yellow the bills of two White-fronted Geese
sent to him by Lord Enniskillen from the county of Fermanagh.
All this called for an early visit to Ireland to put my theory to the
test. So in January 1939 John Winter and I set off for Londonderry with a duck punt on a trailer. Our main objective was to
observe and if possible to secure some White-fronted Geese,
though our secondary objectives were the more conventional and
general ones of the wildfowler.

We tried to approach the Whitefronts as they fed on the near-by
slob-land at Eglington, but the weather was dull, the light poor,
and we were never able to get close enough as they fed to determine
the bill colour, still less to obtain specimens. We went afloat with
our punt on Lough Foyle just outside the sea-wall which protected

the Slobs, and we had good stalks at the Wigeon and the Brent Geese. Towards the end of a strenuous week it looked as though the Whitefronts had beaten us. On our last night in brilliant moonlight and on a falling tide we took our punt down a shallow creek which followed the curve of an old breakwater of weed-covered rocks jutting out from the corner of the sea-wall. It was a full night's operation for there was no chance of returning to the shore line until the tide began to make at dawn. The sky was clear, the moon full, and it was freezing hard. There were Curlews, and Redshanks, and Dunlins, half seen all round us except where they showed in sharp silhouette in the silver track of the moon. As we came to the calm open water we hauled the anchor ashore and climbed out of the punt to warm ourselves with exercise on the hard sand. We ran hither and thither, we danced about, and I remember we practised the Palais Glide (or was it the Pally Glide). We were perhaps 100 yards from the punt when we heard the geese—the wild liquid call of Whitefronts. They had been feeding on the Slobs under the moonlight, and for some reason they had decided to come back to their roosting grounds on the sand flats at the edge of the tide, perhaps for a drink or to wash. We ran to the punt and seized our guns, and then crouched low a few yards from the punt in a patch of black seaweed at the edge of the broken line of the breakwater. There was a thin cloud drifting across the moon making the sky a pearly white, and we could see the geese easily as they came clanging down over our heads.

We fired four shots and from the skein three birds fell out. Two dropped vertically, quite dead, on the sand beside us. The third fell slanting and landed 100 yards or more away. Immediately I began to run after it. It was only wing tipped and made off at a good speed ahead of me, but eventually I caught up with it and brought it back. In the punt we got out a nearly spent torch and looked at our three White-fronted Geese. By the dim yellow light it was impossible to determine whether the bills were yellow or pink. I had however ascertained that the wounded bird was not seriously damaged. Here was a goose which would eventually recover and become one of my collection of live birds at the lighthouse. I wrapped it up in a mackintosh, threaded its head out through a sleeve so that it could breathe, and laid it up under the combing alongside the great gun in the punt. We did not increase the bag at all that night but I remember the excitement with which, as the dawn began to break, we glanced from time to time at the bills of our three birds; and the triumphant thrill when it finally became evident beyond any doubt that the bills were yellow.

The dead birds were subsequently skinned and the wounded bird was brought home to the lighthouse where almost immediately it took up with the four birds from Greenland and became perfectly tame.

At that time, H. F. Witherby, the distinguished ornithologist, was completing the great reference work which was to be called *The Handbook of British Birds*. I wrote to him about my new Greenland-Irish, yellow-billed Whitefronts and told him that I was convinced they constituted a hitherto undescribed but well-marked race. At first he remained sceptical, so I invited him to stay at my lighthouse. There, on the gravel in front of the door he fed a typical pink-billed Whitefront from one hand, while from the other he fed a yellow-billed bird from Greenland. It was a convincing demonstration and before he left he said: "We have no name for your Greenland bird, but I'm prepared to put a footnote in the Handbook, and when you do the plate of the White-fronted Goose, I should like you to illustrate the yellow-billed Irish-Greenland bird as well as the typical form." And this soon afterwards I did.

All this had happened before the war, and now once more there was a chance to return to the subject. I discussed with my old friend Christopher Dalgety how it should be regularised. He had himself shot White-fronted Geese in the west of Scotland and also in Ireland bearing rings which had been put on in Greenland, where an extensive goose-ringing programme had been organised by Dr. Finn Salomonsen from Copenhagen. Salomonsen was already reaching the same sort of conclusion as we had reached about the Greenland Whitefronts, and although we did not know it, he had been planning to describe the new race. Meanwhile, however, I had mentioned it in a species list in a prospectus published by *Country Life*, and this mention qualified the name I had chosen as a *nomen nudum* (for no description went with it). Now we decided to describe the race officially, and we had to decide which bird to select as type specimen. It seemed important to select a bird which was known to have had a yellow bill, and this was not possible in the case of museum skins in which the bill colour is usually completely faded. In this respect perhaps live birds would be the best. A pair had recently been sent from Greenland via the Copenhagen Zoo to Whipsnade and a second pair had followed, joining the collection of The Severn Wildfowl Trust at Slimbridge. But measuring live birds is awkward, and a type specimen should be easy of access for study. So finally we chose an adult bird shot by

Christopher in Ireland in 1947. From the same group an immature bird was shot carrying a Greenland ring. Here was a type specimen whose skin was satisfactorily preserved, whose bill colour was recorded within a few minutes of death and whose breeding and wintering grounds were known and linked by the aluminium ring. To this we gave the name I had used in the prospectus, *Anser albifrons flavirostris*—the goose white-fronted and yellow-billed. There remained only the formality of presenting the story to the scientific world. The official channel we chose for this was a meeting of the British Ornithologists Club, the dining club of the British Ornithologists Union, which meets monthly in the Rembrandt Hotel, South Kensington. On Wednesday, 17th March, 1948, Christopher and I exhibited our specimens and read a joint paper after the dinner. Our description was subsequently published in the Bulletin of the Club, which for a long time has been regarded an an appropriate vehicle for such communications. The full designation of our bird is therefore the Greenland White-fronted Goose, *Anser albifrons flavirostris*, Dalgety and Scott.

In this way, ponderously, minute and perhaps unimportant fragments are added to the sum of human knowledge.

CHAPTER 5   *Delta and Bear River*

IN October 1948 I paid my first visit to the Delta Waterfowl
Research Station near Winnipeg in Canada. If the Wildfowl Trust
has an opposite number anywhere it is at Delta, at the southern
end of Lake Manitoba.

The lake shore is a narrow tree-grown sand-bar which divides
the open water from a vast wilderness of marsh three or four miles
wide and forty miles long. This is the summer home and breeding
ground of great numbers of ducks—a sea of reeds and bullrushes
with pools and bays and channels, bounded by the wheat fields to
the south. Al Hochbaum, the Director of the Station, is a big,
gentle, friendly man with a perpetual smile and a crew cut. I have
only a very few times been so certain I should like a man at the
moment I first saw him. We had many things in common, for we
had both reached our scientific interest in wildfowl from the sport
of wildfowling and Al enjoyed drawing and painting them as much
as I did. Already when I first met him his famous book, *The Canvas-
back on a Prairie Marsh*, with his own illustrations, had been published.

The research station was the last group of houses at the eastern
end of the village of Delta, a village standing on the sand-bar
between the lake and the marsh. In front of it was an artificial
two-acre pond excavated by bulldozer and beyond it the reed
beds stretching away into the distance.

"Living on the pond," I wrote in a news letter home, "were
about sixty Canada Geese, a Whistling Swan and a Richardson's
Goose, and beside the pond was a large aviary made of telegraph
poles with wire stretched between and wire-netting over the top.
In this was another little pool and about thirty more Canadas,
which were being kept full-winged and will be released for
nesting in the spring. Also on the pond were some Canvasbacks

and a few Pintails, Shovelers, and Gadwall, which had been reared by hand for subsequent release. All these birds attracted a good many wild ones and there were about seventy or eighty on the main pond on the morning I arrived, most of them Greenwinged Teal. Al told me that a few weeks earlier 700 or 800 wild birds were to be seen daily in these pools and he had caught and ringed ('banded' is the American word) about 700 in lobster-pot type traps each about the size of a motor-car."

Al was very keen to build a decoy pipe on to this pond so that he could catch at his convenience; he recognised that the great advantage of a pipe over a trap is that if untended for a few days its efficiency improves, whereas it is essential to visit traps daily without fail. I was equally anxious that he should build the first American duck decoy and drew out for him the design of a pipe. Later I pegged out the exact positions on the ground where it was to be built. In the following year I watched ducks being caught in it, and it has been operated successfully ever since.

I found that the research station consisted of a range of indoor pens, large rooms where the ducklings were reared, an incubator house where 900 eggs could be hatched and a large laboratory where the birds were examined, weighed, measured, studied, skinned, and so on. In summer there were between twenty and thirty students always working there from universities, game departments and other organisations. The main researches were in game management using ducks as game birds, and the finances were derived from the Wildlife Management Institute, a body financed by the firearms and ammunition industry.

If this kind of fascinating work could be done in North America, why could not the same sort of research be started in Europe, and who better to do it, I thought, than the Severn Wildfowl Trust? It was at Delta that I first heard about the X-ray examination of ducks and geese to discover how many of them carried lead pellets in their bodies, either from eating them or from being wounded. The proportion of wounded birds seemed surprisingly high. I decided that similar samples of European ducks and geese should be examined.

I saw the tail and wing feathers of individual ducks being painted for field identification and heard how dyes were injected into the eggs just before hatching so that the ducklings came out a bright colour and were thereafter identifiable.

A few days later I was at the Bear River marshes in Utah. In

early November 1948 they were stupendous. This was how I wrote
of them:

"The Bear River, which is about as wide as the Thames at
Maidenhead, runs into the Great Salt Lake through a delta. The
lake has receded and the fall is only one foot per mile across the
whole of the wide floor of the valley. The result is an area of
very shallow water, some of it grown up with reeds and rushes,
some covered with samphire (*Salicornia*) and some just bare
mudflats. This stretches for twenty-five miles across the valley
between the steep snow mountains to east and west.

"The Bear River Refuge covers altogether 64,000 acres. In
the middle of it is the headquarters which has a well-laid-out
Research Station, a highly Americanised version of what it would
be nice to have at the New Grounds one day. The headquarters
were dominated by a tower 100 feet high like an electricity pylon
with a hut on top, and the rest of the settlement consisted of
seven or eight little white red-roofed houses. The first unexpected
thing when we arrived was a car park with well over 100 cars
in it. These were the 'duck-hunters' cars. I learned that when
the area was first taken over as a Refuge it was agreed that
controlled shooting should be allowed on forty per cent of it
during the hunting season. Sixty per cent was to be rest area with
no shooting at all. At the entrance to the Refuge was the office
with a big notice: 'Stop. Check here'. All hunters registered there
on the way out to the marshes. The boy behind the counter was
young and dark and rather handsome. He knew nothing about
me, although I had written to the Superintendent, but he was
kind and friendly. Anyone who had come from so far away must
be taken care of. He would arrange it. I afterwards discovered his
name was Ray Glahn. He explained that Mr. Kubichek, to
whom he introduced me, was a department photographer and
would be driving round the Refuge in his pick-up and would
take me along. 'Won't you, Kubi?' Kubi said he would. Kubi
was aged about fifty with white hair and a friendly manner—
not so much a scientist as a meticulous photographer. We got
into his 'pick-up' and set off along the thirty-nine miles of dykes
to see the birds in the Refuge. Round the headquarters in the
pools and in the reeds were a few ducks. It is a sanctuary there,
for no shooting was allowed in a square of about half a mile round
buildings. There were Godwits and there were American
Avocets—black and white like ours but with no black on the

head or neck, which are a pale sandy colour instead. We were steering south along the dyke and had to pass through the shooting area. About 300 shooters were out on the forty per cent of the 64,000 acres and in fact they were much more concentrated as they had to keep to the reedy areas. As a result there were few birds to be seen until we got out to the deep water or southern end of the dyke. Then as we drove for ten or twelve miles along the dyke with two feet of water on the left and very shallow films of water on the right and a deep ditch beside the road, we saw an incredible sight. It was not that there were so very many birds in any one concentration but that they were scattered continuously along beside the road and only rose when the car was within twenty yards. In certain areas certain species predominated. There were places where there were mainly Gadwall and large numbers of Goosanders. There were bunches of Canvasbacks, and hordes of Greenwinged Teal. We saw everything in the course of the drive—1,000 Whistling Swans, numbers of small parties of Canada Geese, one small lot of Snow Geese. Many of the geese were sitting on the road in front of us. Pintails were easily the most numerous ducks and most of them were drakes. Greenwinged Teal came next but mostly in big flocks and only in certain areas. There were Shovelers known locally as Spoonies and Wigeon known locally as Baldpates. Cinnamon Teal which are common as a breeding species were now rare as most of them had already left for the south. Goldeneyes were common and so were Buffleheads. There were Redbreasted Mergansers and delightful little Ruddy Ducks. Golden Eagles, Roughlegged Buzzards, Harriers and Peregrines, Shorteared Owls, Great Blue Herons, Egrets, Kildeer Plover, Redwinged Black Birds—all these and many more. And if you say that is just a list of birds I have to admit that it is and hope you will add from your imagination the clear bright sunlight in which we saw them, and the staggering impact of the sheer numbers.

"When we got back to the office the hunters were coming in fast to check their bag. The ducks were being sexed and aged and recorded. By law shooting ceases one hour before sunset having started half an hour before sunrise. The bag limit was two Canada Geese, three Snow Geese and five ducks except that you could shoot up to twenty-five Mergansers if you wanted to, but nobody did. Swans were totally protected. The 300 hunters had an average bag of nearly three ducks apiece; a day's take was about 800-odd ducks. Only very few geese were shot."

I caught a bus from Ogden near Bear River to Salt Lake City. It was a lovely drive; as we left Ogden the snow-covered hills on the left were lit by the setting sun and later the sunset became very beautiful over the Salt Lake and the low hills to the south-west of the city. It was a desert sky coppery-bronze with blue-black clear-cut mountains and every now and again small parties of ducks circling over the fields as we went by.

That night my plane landed at Sacramento, and next morning it was California weather—a heavenly morning, temperature perfect, bright sunshine, air like wine. I took a taxi out to the airport where I was met by Ross Hanson, a big friendly young man with whom I got on very well from the outset. His opening gambit was that they were at my service to show me just what I wanted to see. I had only to say the word.

I found that he was a flying instructor. We had lunch together at a sit-up counter on the airfield, talked, planned ahead and made tentative plans for my return to New York. Then off we went, with me flying as soon as we were clear of the city.

CHAPTER 6   *Ross's Snow Goose*

I WAS back in California—in the Sacramento Valley—that wonderful area of wild goose concentration which I had visited with Jim Moffitt in 1938. But Jim, North America's greatest expert on wild geese and my potential collaborator on the proposed Goose Monograph, had been killed on active service in Alaska in a flying accident half-way through the war.

Here I was again flying up Butte Creek where Jim had shown me the Tule Geese, past the Marysville Buttes (pronounced to rhyme with newts) and on to the Federal Refuge at Willows, where ten years before, with Peter Van Huizen, the then Superintendent, and suffering from a blinding headache and an incipient cold, I had run after wounded Cackling Geese, Lesser Canadas and Snow Geese for my collection at the lighthouse.

"As we came over the refuge," I wrote of this return visit, "we saw some very thick concentrations of Pintails, and in the rice fields on the refuge itself, just in front of the Headquarters were a large number of Snow Geese—about 25,000. We landed on a strip next to the Headquarters, and the geese—the nearest no more than 300 yards away—paid no great heed. We taxied up to the buildings and went into the office to meet the boss, Vernon Ekedahl. He was a charming, unassuming, middle-aged man—more of an engineer and farmer than a biologist, though he knew his birds well. It was only his second winter on the refuge and Van Huizen had stayed to show him the ropes last winter. Almost at once he took me out by car into the refuge, with a good pair of binoculars.

"The refuge is a rectangle of farmland five and a half miles long and three miles wide, which has been flooded in parts; in some of it rice has been planted, but there are a few natural ponds and a great deal of what they call 'cat-tail' and we call bullrushes. The estimate of birds in the refuge that week were 60,000 geese and 250,000 ducks. The goose estimate may have been a little high but the ducks were about right. As one motored along the dusty roads the ducks within twenty yards rose continuously on either side—all the species of dabblers and a few divers. We came suddenly on open patches in the reeds which were entirely full of geese. In one of them was a crowd of Snows with a few Whitefronts, standing in shallow water; and suddenly I saw a bunch of nine all a size smaller—the first Ross's Geese. The whole lot moved, and we went round to look at another lot. Here were more Ross's or perhaps the same— two or three mixed in with the rest. I walked along ahead of the car and below the dyke. Then Ekedahl put them up and they came straight over me—about 2,000 geese—first Cackling Geese, then Lesser Snows. At last I picked out the three Ross's flying with much faster wingbeats; the short neck and short bill make them look quite different. The three picked their way through the flock in company with half a dozen Cacks, and presently as I watched them ten more Ross's joined in—thirteen little white Ross's, their black-tipped wings beating at precisely the same speed as the Cacks."

I had seen the neat little Ross's Geese in their winter quarters, and later we found 400 of them in a vast stubble field. Their entire world population was held to be about 5,000 at that time, though the estimate was probably not very accurate. Goose populations fluctuate sharply and since then there has been one season with at least 12,000 Ross's Geese in California. But the species is still insecure. Although protected many are shot each year by careless duck-hunters in mistake for Lesser Snows.

The next thing was to follow them to their almost unexplored Arctic breeding grounds in the middle of the north shore of the Canadian mainland.

Thus one day at the end of May 1949 I found myself sitting with two American companions, Paul Queneau and Harold Hanson (unrelated to my pilot friend in California) in a 'Diner', a small restaurant on the muddy track which was then the main street of Yellowknife, a mining town beside the Great Slave Lake. We were on our way to spend the summer in the Perry River region of the North West Territories. In the corner of the Diner stood a large and ornate juke box containing records from *South Pacific*, the

latest Broadway musical. There was also a record of a catchy little
waltz tune called 'For Ever and Ever' sung by a Mr. Russ Morgan.
During our two days in Yellowknife before heading north again
our nickels tinkled into the juke box and the waltz 'For Ever and
Ever' tinkled out of it, only occasionally varied by 'Some Enchanted
Evening' and 'Bali Hai'.

I have often associated popular tunes with specific events and
adventures, but I doubt whether any other tune has ever held such
powerful associations for me as 'For Ever and Ever'. In the days
that followed we flew north in our ski-fitted Anson aircraft meeting
all kinds of difficulties, through which I hummed the little waltz
incessantly. In due course came a rather hazardous flight in an
ever-thickening snowstorm through a narrow gorge with the cloud
down on the hills on either hand. "For ever and ever . . ." I sang
lustily to myself and from then onwards it became the signature
tune of the whole expedition. I have only to hum it now to see
again the golden brown expanse of the Barrens dappled with
snowdrifts, the pools of meltwater teeming with birds, the cheerful
consumptive faces of the Eskimos; to hear the Long-tailed Ducks
singing 'ow-owdely, laydely-ow' on the lake beside our camp and
to smell wet caribou hide.

This was my first experience of exploration. Hitherto my father's
Polar travels had inhibited me, but this seemed absurd when my
knowledge of a rare goose could only be completed by spending a
summer in the Arctic. It was a summer of unusually bad weather
and we were often confined to camp, where I was glad of a complete
Shakespeare which had been offered to me at the last moment before
leaving. But in spite of the late snowstorms the expedition was
entirely successful. We found and studied the colonies of Ross's
Geese, we explored and named new lakes and rivers, and we made
friends with the Kogmuit Eskimos—a cheerful friendly and altogether captivating tribe. We mapped, listened to the ticking of our
Geiger counter (which was never quite fast enough), collected specimens of mammals and birds and rocks, took films, and stills, re-
checked the position of the Perry River from sun sights and found
it was in the District of Keewatin and not in the District of
Mackenzie as shown on the map, counted the brood sizes of six
kinds of geese and finally in August brought back ten live Ross's
and two Whitefronts in the Fairchild Husky float plane which had
flown in to collect us.

CHAPTER 7   *The Britannia Cup*

THE story of our Perry River summer is told in a book *Wild Geese and Eskimos*, published soon afterwards by *Country Life*, and in the following winter I was commanded to show the film we had made to the Royal Family at Sandringham. It was a week-end invitation and on the Saturday I was to shoot pheasants. I remember that I took with me my Eskimo Parka with its hood lined with wolverine fur. We were told to take coats with us in the morning in case of rain between drives; I had none other than the Parka. In the shooting brake the King noticed it and said he hoped I should not have to put it on as I would look like a bear and this would not only frighten the birds but would frighten him.

Michael Adeane, an old Cambridge friend, who was Assistant Private Secretary to the King, lent me his guns and fortunately, though I did not shoot especially well, I did not disgrace myself. In the afternoon we were joined by the ladies, who stood beside a different gun at each drive. The Queen stood by me at one and Princess Margaret at another. Once the Princess urged me to shoot at a Woodcock which was heading for my neighbour, but as my neighbour was King George VI I refrained from poaching his bird. Surprisingly the Woodcock sailed over unhit by the King's four barrels.

During this visit to Sandringham I outlined to the King a proposal which had been in the back of my mind for some time for the establishment of a new Yacht Racing Trophy. For a good many years there had been no challenge for the America's Cup, and it seemed then that with the disappearance of the big J-class yachts the famous jug would pass into history and never be raced for again. A new Transatlantic competition for an equally important trophy might with advantage be established. My idea was that the old J-class yacht *Britannia*, which had been sunk at sea at the end of her long racing career, should be commemorated by a Britannia's Cup. The name of the trophy would have the apostrophe s in exactly the same way as the America's Cup named after the famous American schooner. The words in each case represented the countries. The parallel seemed neat and complete. For some reason the King did not like the idea of linking the cup to the old and famous sloop. He was, however, prepared to present a Britannia Cup and soon after he wrote in his own hand as follows:

> Buckingham Palace,
> 26th March, 1950.

"Dear Scott,

"Many thanks for your letter giving me the particulars of the 1851 Cup presented by Queen Victoria[1]. I will now discuss the matter with Sir Ralph Gore who happens to be both the President of the Yacht Racing Association and the Commodore of the Royal Yacht Squadron. I am very glad you mentioned this matter to me privately as it makes all further conversation so much easier. I was so sorry that my daughter's visit to you was spoiled by a too ardent well-wisher!!

> I am,
> Yours very sincerely,
> George R."

The last sentence referred to the first time that Princess Elizabeth came to the Wildfowl Trust, when the papers had run the headline 'Mystery Woman in Blue Spoils Royal Visit'. It was early in March and the wild geese, 2,000-strong, were feeding that morning in the Tack Piece immediately opposite to the Rushy Pen. They could not have been better placed in front of the observation huts, but by ill-luck a young girl who wanted to catch a closer glimpse of the Princess decided to come in by way of the sea-wall and the fields. In doing so, of course, she put the geese out of the Tack Piece and far out on to the mud banks about ten minutes before the arrival of the Royal party. The poor girl wrote afterwards saying, "Please I am not a Mystery Woman in Blue; I am a sixteen-year-old girl and I am very sorry to have upset the geese and the Princess." Her letter was sent on to the Palace.

In the summer of 1950 the International Ornithological Congress

---

[1] The America's Cup was the £100 cup of the Royal Yacht Squadron. Although often called the Queen's Cup, it was not presented by Queen Victoria as I had mistakenly told the King in my letter.

was held at Upsala in Sweden and after the Congress there were
excursions. I went first to Jamtland and then to Lapland, to the
great lake of Torne Träske; and from there further up the railway
line to Vassijaure and into the hills to look for Lesser White-
fronted Geese. I had been to the area on a flying visit (literally)
three years before, unsuccessfully attempting to catch Lesser Whitefronts alive for the collection at Slimbridge. This time we succeeded.
Knut Larssen, the local station-master led us into the wild country
round the lake of Pajep Njuorojaure, where we found Lesser Whitefronts which had moulted their flight feathers and were flightless.
We caught two males and a female, but kept and took back with
us only the males which we needed so badly for breeding at the
Trust.

My companion on the trip was the Trust's Assistant Secretary,
Philippa Talbot-Ponsonby. We visited a Lapp camp, caught a
lemming which ate its way through my coat pocket, found the
nests of Velvet Scoters and Buffon's Skuas, rode in leaky boats and
were devoured by mosquitoes; but above all we walked and walked
over the fells and through the birch woods. I was happier than I
had been for years.

In 1950 I was put up for election to the Council of the London
Zoo of which I had been a Life Fellow since the day of my christening. A week or two before the election I was to attend a meeting
of the Council of the Avicultural Society which usually met in the
Council room of the Zoo. I arrived a few minutes late, slipped into
the room quietly and sat down at the table. There were a number of
familiar faces around it and all seemed in order until I asked my
neighbour (who was Terence Morrison-Scott) whether I might
glance at his copy of the agenda. As I leaned over to look I saw the
heading, 'Meeting of the Council of the Zoological Society of
London'. I had come on the wrong day and had sat myself down
in the Council to which I had not yet been elected. With mumbled
apologies to the Chairman I crept out in a sweat of confusion and
embarrassment.

In spite of this gaffe I was elected and have served on the Zoo
Council (with the statutory breaks) ever since. It has been a
stimulating time. From the end of the war it was clear that the Zoo
needed replanning and rebuilding, and I felt that this should be
done by a top architect like Hugh Casson. When Solly Zucker-
man became Secretary things began to move and before long a
new Zoo had been designed. Already it is well on the way to

being built, in spite of the tedious red-herrings which brought so much unwelcome publicity to the Zoo's affairs a few years ago.

Soon after the formation of the Severn Wildfowl Trust I had begun lecturing on its behalf. I developed a patter which seemed to make the audience laugh—although I have never been able to remember set jokes of any kind. But I had discovered that an audience is most attentive when it is afraid of missing a laugh. The problem was to avoid facetiousness. All the fees went to the Trust. In order to keep the numbers of lectures within bounds I was forced to double my fee and then double it again. Finally I was left with the dozen lectures a year which I could conveniently manage though I felt uncomfortable about the 100 guineas fee. But I was never really happy lecturing and was always (and still am) dreadfully nervous before going on. If the first laugh does not materialise I get slower and slower and duller and duller.

One awe-inspiring setting for a lecture was the Royal Institution in Albemarle Street, with Lord Brabazon in the chair. Traditionally the lecturer must walk into the room and immediately begin speaking, without any preliminary address to the audience. No "My Lords, Ladies and Gentlemen" to break the ice.

In complete silence I went to the drawing board and began to draw a Dodo, the story of whose extinction I was wont to use in those days to lead me into the subject of conservation. Finally the Dodo was drawn; last of all came the expression in its eye. Sometimes the drawing came off and the expression was funny, sometimes it failed. It was largely chance. As I put in the final dot and turned to the audience there was no vestige of a laugh. I panicked and still without speaking went back to the drawing and fiddled with the eye, trying to make it funnier. Still no laugh. I went back a second time and there was a titter, a third time and they roared. To this day I do not know why, but from then on the lecture went well.

Lectures led to lecture tours and to a waterborne tour of the Midlands in *Beatrice*, the converted Narrow Boat belonging to the Trust which normally lay near the Patch Bridge at Slimbridge and was used to accommodate visiting ornithologists. Robert Aickman, the principal pioneer in the campaign to save our canals from decay and abandonment, had earlier invited me to join his newly formed Inland Waterways Association as a Vice-President, but this was my first adventure on the canals. There were others to follow. The principal difficulty of this tour was that *Beatrice* had been converted from an old Butty especially for the Trust and her engine was unreliable. At an early stage we found ourselves running behind-hand on our schedule and before long, after constant break-downs, we were something like forty miles astern of our lecture engagements. Thus on each successive night I had to drive further and further to the lecture venue in a hired taxi, or the Mayoral car. Fortunately we had arranged a break in the middle of the lecture schedule to cover just such eventualities. By the time we reached Southport we had caught up again. In spite of these vicissitudes— perhaps to some extent because of them—the tour was enormously enjoyable. The crew varied from six to nine and included Robert Aickman, Chairman of the I.W.A., one of the most erudite of men and most excellent company. We sailed out into the open estuary of the Mersey in order to get from Liverpool to Weston Mersey lock, a fifteen-mile journey on salt water in a fresh breeze; we crossed the Barton Aqueduct and descended in the famous Anderton Lift which carried the floating *Beatrice* in a tank eighty feet down from the Trent and Mersey Canal into the River Weaver Navigation. We got firmly stuck in Harecastle Tunnel which is one and three-quarter miles long and has subsided owing to adjacent coal workings. *Beatrice* was wedged against the roof 1,000 yards in, a situation about as conducive to claustrophobia as any I have ever experienced, but after a great deal of hard work pulling her back, loading her with bricks and trying again a number of times we eventually got her through six and a half hours later, and emerged black from head to foot into an April snowstorm.

In the month of the tour we covered 450 miles, and passed through 273 locks. There is a strange beauty and peace about these little-used thoroughfares running deep into England. We became proficient at working the locks and sliding our tight-fitting boat into them. We learned with nice judgment to slip the stern rope over the bollard on the lock gate in passing, so that the way on the boat pulled the lock gate shut behind her and the pulling brought her to a standstill before her bows hit the lock gate at the other end. The locks fitted *Beatrice* like a glove and there was a whole field of satisfaction in passing her through them smoothly and without mistakes. Above all we enjoyed the leisureliness (once we had caught up with our schedule). This voyage brought home to me the essential good sense in trying to save our canals and navigable rivers from abandonment and destruction. For two generations the railway companies had been trying to rid themselves of canal competition, buying many canals and letting them rot. Now many people thought that because they did not pay for commercial

v

traffic they should be abandoned and filled in. They had not the vision to see that here was a great new recreation ground for our overcrowded people. Perhaps the canals could not pay that way either, but with a combination of uses these multi-purpose waterways could (and can) be turned into one of the country's most valuable amenities. I remain convinced that the costly alternative of filling them in is stupid and wasteful.

In the following year after our Midland lecture tour, we took *Beatrice* to the Inland Waterways Association's Festival at Market Harborough. In a rash moment, I had agreed to take a part in Benn Levy's play *Springtime for Henry* to be presented at the festival. This was virtually the only stage venture of my life. In the four-part play the other three parts were taken by professionals—Nicolette Bernard, Carla Lehmann and Barrie Morse. It was exciting to work with them and they in turn were endlessly patient with me. For a week they carried me through the play, including one ghastly performance when I missed my entrance through sheer carelessness, and Barrie gagged away manfully until I got there. The audience never knew.

CHAPTER 8   *Rocket Netting*

EACH year in October a team heads northward from the Wildfowl
Trust to catch wild geese with rocket nets. The invention and
development of these nets followed logically from my efforts with
springs many years earlier. But whereas the original object had
been to catch a few geese for the collection at the lighthouse, the
new object was to catch them in bulk for ringing. If we could catch
enough, not only should we find out more about their movements and migrations and about their expectation of life, but we
might even be able to use a sampling method to measure their
populations.

James Robertson Justice claims that it was he who first suggested
to me, "Couldn't we throw a net with the Schermuly Pistol Rocket
Apparatus, as used for saving life at sea?" I claim that I put the
same question to him. He is probably right. Whichever way it was,
I found myself, one summer's day in 1947, in a grassy meadow in
Sussex which was the proofing ground of Messrs. Schermuly
Brothers of the S.P.R.A. works, Newdigate.

It was not until the following February that we had the first
chance to try out the complete equipment on the White-fronted
Geese at the New Grounds. Mr. A. J. Schermuly came down
especially for the attempt, and so did Keith Shackleton, and a
photographer from *Country Life*. There were only about 1,300 geese
on the estuary at the time and on the afternoon before the attempt,
we made a reconnaissance of the feeding grounds.

The geese were no longer to be found in the three small fields
into which they had flown at dawn, but we came upon them at last
much farther away round the edges of a 100-acre field at the
Frampton end of the New Grounds. Here, however, the wheat in
the centre of the field had been grazed almost bare, and the geese
had congregated in a thick swathe along two edges of the field. One

of these edges was formed by a barbed-wire fence, and the other by a shallow creek or 'flash', no more than a few yards wide. Along the top of the slope leading up from the flash the geese were sitting most thickly; indeed, we could not remember to have seen Whitefronts more tightly packed.

We flushed them gently from the field, and walked over to examine the area and select the most suitable spot on which to set the net in the darkness before tomorrow's dawn. In view of the north wind, we thought that it should lie along the drills of the wheat at the edge of the field where the shoots were longer because the geese had not grazed there so much. We then explored the nearest available cover, which was an old disused sea-wall some 100 yards away across the flash and beside the continuation of the fence. All this decided, we returned in the dusk, feeling that our chances were reasonably good if only the geese would come again to the area in which we had last seen them.

That night great preparations were made. Mr. Schermuly overhauled his wiring; Mr. Harris, the photographer from *Country Life*, checked a telephoto lens; and the rest of us made lists of the objects which must on no account be forgotten on the morrow— the net, the rockets, the cartridges, the battery, a pressure hurricane lamp and torches for setting the net in the dark, the rings for ringing, pliers for crimping on the rings, a pencil and notebook for writing down their numbers, sacks for setting up on sticks in the small fields in which we did not want the geese to alight, the portable hide, spare string for an emergency, sandwiches and a spade. Someone said it would be useful to have a 'nice little ferreting spade', but in the absence of such a specialised tool we substituted a spade (although it appeared on the list as 'spade, N.L.F.').

We rose at four next morning and set off in two parties, one by car with the heavy gear to go round to the Frampton Bridge, which was less than half a mile from the selected spot, the other to walk the mile and a half, planting the 'scare geese' in the small fields on the way. After arriving by car at the bridge, I was not very familiar with the exact route to our part of the 100-acre, so with our various hurricane lamps and torches we started on the right bearing by the stars. This led us across a number of awkward ditches, but they were successfully negotiated, and soon after five-fifteen a.m. we joined the other party on the old sea-wall, and went out together, all seven of us, like a party of smugglers or body-snatchers, across the flash at its lowest crossable point, and down the edge of the wheat to the corner of the fence. There we laid out all the equipment we had brought in a small heap so that nothing should be overlooked and be left to frighten the geese when daylight came.

The patch we had chosen for the net was about ten yards from the fence, and, like the rest of the field, it was covered with small lumps of clay which were frozen solid. We found, as we laid out the net, that the meshes caught frequently on these little lumps and were held firm and immovable. The chances that it would fly out freely, however neatly we folded it, seemed very small. But, having risen at four, and being on the spot, we felt that we could not do more than lay it carefully and hope for the best. So we laid it out very carefully, seven of us in a row, with the Tilley lamp hanging on the handle of the 'nice little ferreting spade'.

As soon as the net had been furled the party divided and some went off to fetch the portable hide which had been left beside the car. Three of us stayed behind to set out the rockets and lay the firing wires. It was getting late. Already the eastern sky was bright and we knew that we had a bare twenty minutes before the arrival of the geese. We stretched out the wire and then our rocket expert decided that he must fire a couple of cartridges in order to make sure that the wiring circuit was correct. The powder was removed from the cartridges and they were set up in the pistols; then we set off to run round the head of the flash to the end of the remote-control, near the place selected for the hide. We were in a hurry and we turned to cross the flash too soon. I had high waders and could cross it anywhere but my companion stumbled and filled one boot. We hustled to the end of the flex, found that it would not go into the terminal on the battery without paring away the insulation, and in trying to do this in the dark Mr. Schermuly cut the ball of his thumb badly. But eventually the job was done, the contact was made, and two little sparks of light flashed at each end of the net. The circuit was correct, all that remained was to set up the rockets in place of the trial cartridges. Back we rushed round the head of the flash again, crossing this time a little further up. The rockets were slid into their pistols, the head string of the net was attached. Grass was strewn over the heads of the rockets and plucked wheat shoots were strewn over the grass. Twenty yards ahead of the net, five yards less than the net should, in theory, be able to throw, I made two tiny cairns of lumps of frozen clay, one opposite each end of the net. These were to be the markers, to show when the geese were within the 'catching area'. With a last glance at the net, which looked painfully visible even in that early morning light, we collected together the spare equipment and started back once again round the head of the flash. As we walked along it we could hear the first geese coming and I extinguished the two hurricane lamps. The geese were heading for the small fields and it was still almost too dark for them to see the sacks on their sticks.

When we got back to the old sea-wall we found that the rest of the party had just finished erecting the portable hide. The flex, however, had not been laid the full distance and the roll of it still lay twenty yards away along the barbed-wire fence. At this critical stage a large skein of geese came up to the field and looked as if it would settle. But by great good luck, the geese swept back to circle yet again over the small fields, and while they did it I rushed down and collected the coil of flex, spreading it as I returned. It reached the portable hide with exactly two feet to spare and was laid under one corner to the battery (an ordinary high-tension dry battery taken from a wireless set). We went to collect grass with which to decorate the hide, and the party was split up when the geese returned. Five of us flopped down into the three-sided square of wire netting and barrage balloon fabric while the other two hid themselves in the ditch about fifty yards away.

About 300 geese came straight for the 100-acre and settled in the middle of the bare part of the wheat field. This was excellent, we thought, for they were directly down wind of our net and seemed likely in a few hours to feed up to it. Meanwhile more geese came slipping in over the belt of trees in the background—skein after skein in an almost unbroken stream. They came with great confidence, flying low and setting their wings as soon as they reached the edge of the field. By the time that the sun rose, oval and orange-red behind us, there were over 1,000 geese feeding in a tight pack in front. Then came a startling development. A family party of geese rose from the great crowd and flew low towards the corner of the field—our corner. They settled about forty yards in front of the net. They were followed by others, until a regular flight began. Bunch after bunch swept in and pitched in the ever-thickening crowd in front of our net. So far everything had gone unbelievably right. For the next hour we lay breathlessly in the hide as the phalanx of geese advanced into the 'catching area'. They were ten yards from the little clay cairns—five yards—two yards—passing between them, and then the cairns were swallowed up in the milling crowd of geese which advanced still closer to the net. Was all in readiness? The wireless battery, the leads—the leads, where were they? They were nowhere to be seen. Two feet of the end of the flex had been pulled under the edge of the hide in that hurried last minute but it was not there now. We peered out through the observation slit in the front of the hide. The black shiny insulated wire led towards us, but just outside the hide it turned off at right angles. While we had been camouflaging the hide someone must have kicked away the end of the lead; it was outside the hide, on the same side of it as the geese. What were we to do? Slowly and dexterously we lifted a corner of the hide and reached out towards the lead. My fingers closed over grass stems, over a bramble, but not over the missing flex. One of my companions squinted down through the observation slit. "Another four inches and you'll reach it." At last I felt the flex and pulled it into the hide. The crisis was over, and the geese were another five yards closer to the net.

The slit in the hide was at a very awkward height, so that one could only use glasses through it by supporting oneself on the other arm, and then only for short periods. During one of these quick looks, however, I noticed a Pinkfoot, no doubt one of the three young birds which we had observed scattered among the White-fronts all through the winter. As usual he was at the edge of the flock and in the forefront of those which crowded on towards the net.

Now was the critical time. At what distance would the geese first see and keep away from the net? Would they turn about and walk quickly away from it once they had detected its presence? We watched anxiously. A feature of the advance of a flock of wild geese when feeding is that from time to time the more powerful and influential geese drive others away from them; and so the leading edge of the flock keeps bulging where a bird or a family has run a few paces forward at the close approach of a quarrelsome gander. At length there came a time when the fugitive birds would no longer run forward. If pursued they turned and threaded their way back through the flock. They would not come nearer to the net than about four yards from it. The crowd in the 'catching area' could not get any thicker. It had reached saturation point. It was now or never. Mr. Harris got ready with his camera and Mr. Schermuly with the ends of his flex.

"All right, let her go!" The circuit was made and the rockets fired; simultaneously the whole flock of 1,300 geese rose into the air with the combined roar of wings and of voices. We all jumped up to watch. As the cloud rose we could see that a small patch of flapping geese remained on the wheat field. We had made a catch.

I set off to run towards the net, straight down by the fence to ford the flash with my high boots on, whilst the rest came round by the shallower crossing further up. I think the geese were more alarmed by the sudden appearance of seven people careering across the field in scattered formation than they were by the discharge of the rockets themselves, and on any future occasion we have planned to remain hidden until the uncaught birds are well clear.

As I came to the net I made a quick count, thirty-two geese. We had succeeded. We had made the first great catch of geese alive for ringing. It was a satisfying moment. Then began the laborious task of extricating the birds from the net. Almost before we had started one bird, however, extricated itself and flew off. But we lost no more. Among those remaining was the Pinkfoot which we had seen advancing into the 'catching area'. He was ringed and released. Some of the birds were released one by one, but sometimes they were released in couples, which we thought to be the better way, as the two then flew off together. Fairly soon it became apparent that many of them could not be extricated from the net without cutting some of the meshes. It was astonishing to what extent the birds had become ravelled up in so short a time. It was astonishing, too, how docile and resigned the geese seemed to be, and how little they struggled while being extricated. One old gander was full of spirit and continuously pecked my knee while I was disentangling his neighbour and finally himself. We ringed several young birds including a family of five with their parents.

We had pulled the net at eight-forty a.m. and it was half past nine by the time we had finished. Of our thirty-one geese, fifteen Whitefronts and one Pinkfoot had been ringed and released at once, and fifteen other Whitefronts had been put into the sacks for transporting to the pens.

As we walked back to the hide some of the geese were returning to the fields, and a large skein circled low over the 100-acre. They did not settle, but on the other hand it was evident that they had not been disastrously frightened by the discharge of the rockets.

We returned home greatly elated with our success which, in spite of the net's bad throw, was much greater than any of us in our heart of hearts had been expecting.

The next catch at the New Grounds in February 1950, using two nets, yielded seventy-one Whitefronts. Big numbers seemed to be on, so in March we took the nets to Scotland and tried them on Pinkfeet and Greylags. But although our hopes were often high twenty-five Greylags was our best catch. Yet on one of those spring days on the Solway Firth I can vividly remember a single moment of supreme anticipation. The geese had beaten us for most of the day, but in the afternoon they began to feed towards the net. Something flushed them suddenly, hopes fell and then rose as quickly when they began to settle much closer to it. I remember as I lowered my glasses catching Philippa's eye and saying "Exciting . . . ?" and her murmured reply, "Almost too exciting . . ."

We caught no geese that day but I realised more than ever that rocket netting was as thrilling a pastime as I knew. We might have invented a useful technique for the scientific study of birds, but we had also invented a first-class sport. If the equipment was cumbersome and the operations were exhausting, the results were especially satisfying, because the ultimate sanction was achieved but not exercised. We did not have to kill the geese to show we had outwitted them; we had to do something much more difficult—to catch them unharmed.

Since those days the equipment and the techniques have greatly changed. The record catch is 490 Pinkfeet, and a month of netting may yield a catch of over 3,000. We are more sure of our success than we were in those early days; and yet it is still possible to sit fruitlessly over a net from dawn till dusk for three days running and have to retire empty handed at the end of it.

For the Pinkfeet, whose population we have been measuring by this means, we set out two nets facing each other in the middle of the chosen field. The nets are sixty yards long and furled on a great drum from which they are unwound into position. When spread the nets stretch twenty yards, and as they are to be thrown towards each other they are laid forty yards apart. Spaced along each net, and half buried in the ground at an angle of about forty-five degrees are six rockets loaded with cordite, and wires which will fire all twelve rockets simultaneously are led away to the camouflaged trailer 'hide', parked inconspicuously beside the hedge—perhaps under a tree. The nets and rockets are hidden by straw in the stubble fields in which we usually set for Pinkfeet. The space sixty by forty yards between the nets is the catching area and in this not only must the geese be persuaded to land, but to concentrate. Much of course depends on the original selection of the site. If there is a mound in the field it should if possible be included in the catching area. The nets if they are to be properly hidden must lie along the line of the drills or along the tracks of the harvester. (Sometimes these are at right angles to each other.) If they are to fly out properly and make a good catch they must lie parallel to the wind direction,

V*

and as we usually set our nets the night before for a catch at dawn, the morrow's wind must be accurately forecast.

Supposing that the right field has been selected (and it is alarmingly easy to select the wrong one), the net has been properly set and adequately hidden, and that the morning's wind is in the right direction, there is still the problem of getting the geese down in precisely the right place. For this we use stuffed decoys of two kinds. Some are standing up with their heads stretched downwards as if feeding, and others are sitting flat on the ground with their heads turned back under their wings. In the twilight of the early dawn these must be set out with special knowledge of the reactions of the first wild geese which will respond to them. Those reactions will vary with the wind strength and this dictates the precise position of the two groups of decoys—the standers at the downwind edge of the catching area, the sleepers further up towards the middle but taking into account the slope of the land.

When all is ready the team withdraws, some to what may be a long and isolated vigil in the trailer 'hide', the rest to a convenient vantage point on the road which cannot disturb the incoming geese, and which becomes 'the grand stand'. Often the first geese come to the field before it is light enough for them to see the stuffed decoys. Geese have surprisingly poor eyesight in twilight. They probably settle elsewhere in the field and must then be driven away, otherwise the later arrivals will go to them in preference to the stuffed ones. But in due course, if all has been done well, the first party of live geese settles with the sleeping decoys. We call them 'live decoys' and if they are well placed we have then only to wait while the skeins come streaming from the roosting place and pour down into the catching area. Many things can yet go wrong. New splinter groups of arriving geese may draw the concentration away from the catching area; the geese may detect danger and after a pause with every head up they may suddenly flush and fly off to some other field: a shepherd may appear to tend his sheep in the next field: a car may stop in the wrong place on the road: a near-by shooter may fire a shot: a low-flying aircraft may put the whole flock into the air so that when they settle back they are scattered all over the field. In goose netting there are many potential slips 'twixt cup and lip.

But if none of these things happen, and the concentration builds up, the tension builds with it. Will enough geese come to give us a great catch, or ought we to dash round with the car and move over those extra 500 which have gone down three fields away? Are they thick enough already? Are there any more on their way from the roost?

The button-presser in the hide is probably in touch with the grand stand by field telephone or walkie-talkie. There is a hurried exchange of views.

"Fifteen hundred in the field, 700 in the catching area—it ought to make a catch of over 300."

"They look quite good from here but they're over the left-hand net. I don't think it's getting any better now."

"All right, we'll go as soon as this next lot's down."

The suspense is almost unbearable as the last birds flap down and fold their wings. A pause till all are feeding, a ten-second count down and . . . "Sheeee . . .", the nets are out and over the geese. There is a moment of surprised silence as the great birds leap into the air, followed by the clamour of the uncaught part of the flock. More than 1,000 geese circle round. Many begin to land again, some of them on top of the net. After the second circle the bulk of the flock heads off to settle with the 500 three fields away. A few small parties are still circling low and trying to settle again.

The Land Rover with the ringing and weighing equipment and the 'keeping cages' drives down on to the field and the long scientific job begins.

First the keeping cages have to be set up at one end of the nets— small rolls of hessian which when stretched on stakes form a row of small compartments each to contain a single goose sitting on the ground and covered by four walls and a roof of stretched hessian. Each cage has 25 such compartments and for this catch of 300, thirteen cages will be needed so that the whole flock can be held and released simultaneously, thereby making sure that the family bonds which evidently have survival value in geese are not unnecessarily broken. When half the cages have been set up the extricating will begin.

Philippa is the most expert extricator. We have found that girls are especially good at it. She and one other will take the birds one at a time from under the one-inch mesh net, in which they are much less tangled than they used to be in the days when the meshes were larger. The transporters take a goose under each arm from the extricators and bring them to the central position, where, sheltering in the lee of the vehicle the ringers, sexers, weighers and recorder go about their work.

It takes nearly three hours to clear 300 geese from the two nets. When all the work has been done and all the geese are ringed, the keeping cages are lifted off in quick succession so that the whole great flock flies off together. Then the nets must be cleaned of every stick of straw and refurled on their drums, the rockets must be recharged, the electric leads reeled in, and all must be repacked in the van and the trailer in readiness perhaps for a set the same evening, if a new field of adequate promise has been located. An essential feature of the population measurement study is that the samples must be taken from as many of the Pinkfoot's winter haunts as possible. This means that we seldom fire the nets more than two, or at the most three times in the same locality each year.

Perhaps the most extraordinary feature of all is the reaction of the geese themselves. They seem to regard the rocket explosions as something to be compared with thunder and lightning. Many times we have confirmed that they are less disturbed by it than by having a twelve-bore fired at them from the ditch.

Sometimes we have reset the net in the same field, and once we caught a bird in the second catch which had been ringed in exactly the same spot on the day before.

Recapturing birds which have been ringed by the same team in earlier years—meeting old friends again—is one of the nicest features, as well as the most useful scientifically. In a catch of 300 there are likely to be at least twenty such.

The rocket nets have been operated by our team in the same areas in Scotland and northern England for ten years, so that we know the places, and many of the farmers, well. We have developed an *expertise*, a whole range of specialised skills, a vocabulary of our own. It has almost become a cult. Perhaps fifty people have joined the team from time to time and have enjoyed the peculiar delights and frustrations, excitements and exhaustions which make up rocket netting.

Sometimes I feel rather defensive about my invention. 'Love me love my dog.' Those who enjoy it are *ipso facto* my friends. "Do you remember that field?" I say as we go past in the car, and the right reply is "1953, wasn't it? One of the rockets broke loose, but we got 262 all the same. That was where they came down with the tractor and trailer to feed the bullocks in the next field and the geese sat through it all."

For me rocket netting remains something very personal—the realisation of an early dream. "Just imagine," I say to myself when I see 300 geese under the nets, "Just imagine what I should have thought of this in 1932."

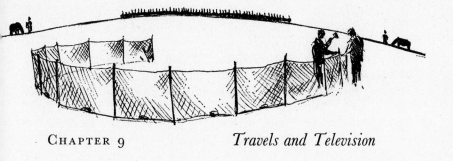

CHAPTER 9   *Travels and Television*

BY the spring of 1951 we had marked no more than 600 Pink-
footed Geese, using our nets mostly in Scotland, and although they
were scarce on the Severn estuary, they were evidently going to be
easier to study than our Whitefronts. They decoyed better and
were therefore easier to catch with rocket nets; the bulk of the
world population was in Scotland and England during the winter;
and their breeding grounds in Iceland and Greenland were a
great deal more accessible than those of the Whitefronts in Arctic
Russia.

Our next expedition, it seemed, should be to Central Iceland
to study the Pinkfeet in the summer and perhaps to find some
of the 600 we had ringed.

James Fisher, my old friend whose father had been headmaster
of Oundle and had so greatly encouraged my naturalist leanings,
Finnur Gudmundsson, head of the Museum in Reykjavik who
had been with us in Lapland, Philippa Talbot-Ponsonby and I,
with an Icelandic farmer, Valentinus Jónson, as guide, rode up
the River Thjorsá to the Hofsjökul icecap and camped for the
summer at the edge of the great breeding colony of geese. Our
adventures are described in *A Thousand Geese*, a book of which
James and I were joint authors.

During our time in Iceland Phil and I were married in Reykjavik by the British Minister, Jack Greenway, who in days of
yore had once been to visit me at the lighthouse.

It was only in the last few days of the 1951 expedition to the
Interior that we learned the proper technique for herding the
flightless geese into nets at the tops of the hills to which they
habitually run. For most of the month of July when the goslings
are still too young to fly the adult geese are also flightless, having
moulted their wing feathers. Thus the whole population is

grounded and can be herded together into great pedestrian flocks. We decided that our new-found technique should be given a better trial and that we should make a second expedition so that it could be exploited for the whole of the flightless period. In the summer of 1953 an expedition of five Englishmen and three Icelanders (one of them Valli, our faithful guide of two years before) returned to the meadows of the Thjorsá below the Hofsjökul icecap. Whereas in 1951 we had caught and marked 1,100 Pink-footed Geese, now in this 1953 expedition we marked over 9,000. Two of the round-ups enclosed more than 3,000 geese each.

It was a brilliantly simple technique which we now perfected. Several square miles of the marsh were surrounded by horsemen moving the geese very slowly and gently towards a prearranged hillock. Once the mass had assembled on the summit they were held there while a horseshoe of small-mesh nylon netting was set up on stakes near-by, forming a corral into which they could quickly be driven.

With the drives in Iceland and the rocket-nets in Scotland and England, we have marked more than 25,000 Pinkfeet in ten years, during which it seems that the population breeding in Iceland and Greenland and wintering in Britain has fluctuated between about 40,000 and 70,000. One individual bird was caught four times—first in Iceland in 1951, then the following year in Scotland, then in Iceland again in 1953 and finally a second time in Scotland. Many more have been handled three times by our team.

The film of the first Icelandic Expedition, made entirely with the tiny fifty-foot Magazine Kodak (with a three-inch and a six-inch lens), which had been given to me by Kodaks in Rochester after the Perry River expedition, was surprisingly successful. I developed a lecture around it, which included some drawings— one of them a caricature of Finnur Gudmundsson, who is a very large man riding on an Icelandic pony which was very small— and we decided to take the Festival Hall for a lecture in aid of the Wildfowl Trust. It was the first time that the hall had been used for a straight lecture. Since then it has been used by many others, including the Everest Expedition, and James Fisher on behalf of the Royal Society for the Protection of Birds. But ours was the pioneer effort and we were very doubtful of its success. To our own and everyone else's intense surprise, we filled the hall to capacity and had to turn 300 people away.

One day not long afterwards I was lunching with Desmond Hawkins, who produced on sound radio several of the natural history programmes in which from time to time I broadcast. "I'm going on a television producer's course," he told me.

"You know," I said, "I've often wondered whether those lecture things I do, with film, might not make television material."

"When are you doing the next one?"

"Not for ages."

"Well, when I get back from my course, would you do a special one for my son's school, so that I can watch and think of it in terms of TV?"

Fortunately for me the schoolboys were delightfully receptive and chortled away at the drawing of Finnur on his pony, and other sallies.

The pattern of the lecture was a short preliminary talk with drawings and a map followed by the first reel of the film. There was then a short pause while the film reels were changed, during which I progressed the story with more drawings; finally at the end of the second reel of the film there was a brief conclusion. This technique was obviously capable of extension, so that instead of two reels one might have three or four sections of film with spaces for discussion in between them. This would then become more like a lantern slide lecture but with film inserts instead of slides. Thus was the framework of the television lecture with film established.

I had appeared two or three times before on television, the first time at Alexandra Palace before the war after my return from Persia. Dressed in a Pustin or sheepskin cloak I had been interviewed by Leslie Mitchell in Joan Gilbert's Picture Page. Curiously enough my next appearance, together with Michael Bratby to talk about the Wildfowl Trust, was also at 'Ally Pally' in the revived post-war Picture Page with Joan Gilbert in the chair; once more the interviewer was Leslie Mitchell.

For my first few television lectures I used my own film, but it soon ran out. Either I had to give up TV or to find new film. Desmond suggested that I might be chairman of a series, and introduce other people who had taken natural history film. The recipe was moderately successful and the new pattern appeared once a month from the Lime Grove Studios, though it was still difficult to find enough good film.

In the summer of 1955 I attended the International Ornithological Congress at Basle in Switzerland and there saw a startling

film of woodpeckers taken by a brilliant young German cine-
matographer, Heinz Sielmann. He and I were invited to give
repeat showings of our films at a special evening entertainment
at the Basle Zoo. My film was in colour and described our recent
expedition to Tierra del Fuego; Heinz's film of the woodpeckers
was in black and white and stole the evening. It had been taken
inside the woodpeckers' nests by cutting into the back of the tree,
setting up the hide behind it, and finally accustoming the woodpeckers to sufficient illumination for photography. By any
standards it was one of the most remarkable achievements of wild
life photography ever screened. That very evening Heinz agreed
to bring his film to England and show it in my TV programme.
His woodpeckers got a listener research appreciation figure that
was second only to the Coronation.

It is often claimed that listener research figures are as likely
to be wrong as newspaper polls, and when one of my programmes
gets a low figure this is what I claim too. But when the woodpeckers got eighty-eight, and when quite recently Heinz outshone
them with an eighty-nine for his *Summer with the Storks* on which
I gave the commentary, I feel quite confident of the absolute
scientific objectivity and basic soundness of the results.

"Our series," said Desmond Hawkins one day soon after the
woodpecker success, "should have a title and a signature tune.
Do you like *Look*?"

"Not very much; it's the title of an American magazine which
is about quite different things."

"But it's a good title."

"Well, if you say so . . ."

And so *Look* it became; and a signature tune was commissioned
from Bruce Montgomery. At first it had been monthly but now
it became fortnightly, and later weekly for a series of six or seven.
This regular appearance on television has curious concomitants.
To be recognised wherever you go may be advantageous or
disadvantageous, but it cannot be ignored or forgotten about.
In deafening asides people 'whisper' your name, they turn to
look more carefully, they smile winningly as if you should have
recognised them, they rush up with scraps of paper to be auto-
graphed, and they make appreciative but embarrassing little
speeches about the programmes. But there are the advantages
too, which in my view far outweigh the drawbacks. Extra good-
will is invariably generated by recognition. People are at once
trying to be helpful, obstacles magically disappear, food comes

Ready to take off in my Olympia 419X at the Bristol Gliding Club at Nympsfield.

1956

The view from our bedroom window on a February mornir

1958

The Wildfowl Trust with the Severn Estuary and Sharpness Railway Bridge in the background, photographed from my glider.

re than half the birds are wild visitors.

Our house in summer. The window from which the upper picture was taken is
at top right.

1961

Philippa.

more quickly in a restaurant, service more quickly in a shop, and when I go to obtain permission to set our goose nets in a farmer's field I know beforehand what the answer will be if there is a television aerial on the chimney.

About this time I realised that my weight had begun to go up steadily. I was five feet nine inches tall and I weighed fifteen and a half stones (217 pounds). I was becoming a stout man. By 1955 I had decided that something must be done about it. I consulted my doctor, who said there was only one answer—to eat less. He would give me a simple diet and if I stuck to it my weight would drop. On 16th June I started the diet, which excluded butter, fats, bread, sugar and alcohol but allowed potatoes; I weighed in on the bathroom scales at fifteen stones six pounds and began to keep a daily chart on a piece of graph paper. I lost sixteen pounds in the first month and the process continued until by the end of October it levelled out at twelve stones three pounds. I felt very much more active and no longer had difficulty getting down to tie my shoe, but my clothes hung about me in folds and had all to be altered to my new shape.

Television viewers were startled by my change in appearance in so short a time and thought I must have been seriously ill. Certainly for a while I looked a little haggard and what had been my double chins became scrawny flaps like a chicken's wattles. It may be that I took too much off in too short a time, but the curious thing was that when I eased up on the diet my weight did not shoot up again. I have kept the daily weight chart going to this day. One stone crept back again, but after that it remained steady. At thirteen stones three pounds (which I recorded on the chart this morning, 29th June, 1960) I am not unduly concerned about overweight. Five or six pounds lighter I should like to be and perhaps will be for I have pious intentions of tightening up a little on the diet. But by and large I eat very much what I like again now—though rather less at home than when I go away. The secret of it all is the chart. If the zig-zag 'curve' trends upwards it bolsters my resolve. No second helpings for a couple of days until the position has been retrieved.

For some years after the end of the war my main home and headquarters had been the little house in Edwardes Square, and I had travelled each week-end by car to the New Grounds to watch the growth of the Severn Wildfowl Trust. But it soon became apparent that this constant shuttle service between London and Gloucestershire should be reduced to a minimum, and that maintaining two homes was not only uneconomic, but downright inconvenient. Gradually my main centre of activity changed from London to the New Grounds, to the little eighteenth century farm cottage which was to be my principal home for six years. It was in the old coach house of this cottage that I installed a picture window and the room became part sitting-room and part studio. Here I began the illustration of a four-volume book, *The Waterfowl of the World* by Jean Delacour.

The illustrations for the first volume were completed just before our departure on the trip to South America, which took Phil and me to Tierra del Fuego, and later to the High Andes of Bolivia. The original plates were painted in oils on thirty by twenty-five inch canvases. I remember working against time late into the night on these in the studio of the old cottage, encouraged and entertained by Konrad Lorenz who had been staying with us for several weeks studying and filming the behaviour of ducks. This great pioneer of ethology, whose original mind has given new impetus to the science of animal behaviour, had become a close friend, and has remained one ever since. A few years ago he moved his research station to a beautiful lake in Bavaria, where he installed the ducks and geese he was studying, and set up aquaria for his work on fishes. I went over to see it and to record it for a broadcast programme. Konrad met me excitedly in Munich. "I feel," he said, "exactly like a small boy who is going to show his new toy railway to his best friend."

In 1952 our daughter Dafila was born and two years later our son, Richard Falcon. 'Richard' after Richard Taillebot who came over with William the Conqueror and was an ancestor of the Talbot family, and 'Falcon' which was my father's second name. The two children were christened on board my father's old ship *Discovery* just as Nicola had been ten years before. In accordance with nautical tradition the ship's bell was the font.

For many years *Discovery* had belonged to the Boy Scouts Association, on the Council of which I now sat. She lay alongside the embankment in the heart of London and thousands of people came each year to see her. Sea Scouts used her as a centre for seamanship training and visiting Scouts from overseas could stay on board. The Wardroom and Officers' cabins were beautifully maintained and there was a collection of Antarctic relics connected with my father. But the maintenance was costly and in due course it became necessary to find some other plan. There were rumours that the Admiralty were prepared to take her on but proposed to use her 'for the storage of files'. This seemed a sad waste of a ship whose history and tradition could surely still be used to fire the imagination especially of young people. I decided to ask a number of eminent men among them Admiral of the Fleet Lord Cunningham, Lord Alanbrooke, the Bishop of Portsmouth, Sir Edmund Hillary, Sir Raymond Priestley and Sir Michael Balcon to join a Committee to examine the proposals. A Discovery Trust was considered but was never formed because the First Lord of the Admiralty came back with an entirely new plan for using the ship for training pre-National Service men and for allowing Scout and other youth training to continue at week-ends. My big guns had been trained but it was never necessary to fire them.

Quite recently the question of re-rigging the old ship has been raised in Parliament by my friend and war-time colleague in the Coastal Forces, David James. David, who finally got back to England after two astonishingly ingenious escapes from German prison camps, has many connections both with square-rigged ships in which he sailed and with the Antarctic where he has been. He proposes that the yards should be restored to *Discovery* so that she becomes again a square-rigged ship instead of what he described as 'a bastard schooner'. It remains to be seen whether it will be possible to raise the money for this either from the Admiralty or from some voluntary source. If it is considered worth keeping the old ship in the centre of London, there is certainly much to be said for keeping her rigged as she was in her sea-going days.

With an increasing family our cottage at the New Grounds, which had been our only home since the sale of the London house, was now bursting at the seams. We had decided to build a new house next door to it, and overlooking the birds in the Rushy Pen.

The building of the new house was to be accompanied by the conversion of an L-shaped cow-byre behind the old cottage into a staff hostel and laboratory wing. Beyond it, and connected by a passage, was to be our private house, and beyond that again my studio.

To create this building we invited Peter Bicknell, who was practising as an architect in Cambridge and had been a friend for many years, ever since he and his brothers had been at school and at Cambridge with me. For our purpose he was the best possible kind of architect. Very roughly I drew out various ideas and he took them away and turned them into a practical pro-position. It was a collaboration of the most stimulating and agreeable kind. Over my bed in our tiny attic room in the old cottage I had rigged a sheet of plate glass. Behind this I slid any kind of drawings about which I wanted to think deeply while lying in bed on the following morning: the design for a new painting; the layout of some new ponds or pens on the New Grounds; Peter Bicknell's latest drawings of our new house and the cowshed conversion—all were set up above my head as I lay in bed, including the detail drawing for an exactly similar sheet of glass above my bed in the new house.

There are few things more enjoyable than planning a new house and its surroundings. In this case the surroundings were of especial importance because the great picture window of the studio was dependent on the landscape design of the new duck ponds to be excavated in front of it. I was often late for breakfast as I lay in bed building in my mind's eye the picture of our home as it would be in that seemingly far-off day when it would be finished.

My year-old daughter Dafila tapped down the foundation stone with the handle of the trowel, and at long last the house was finished. My son was born three months after we moved in. Were I to have the opportunity of building the same house again there is hardly anything that I would change. As a home for our family, after six years it still seems to me almost perfect.

CHAPTER 10

*The Rarest Goose
and Some Swans*

MY interest in the processes of evolution has produced in me a kind of reverence for every living species. Many people, I know, share this feeling. The prospect of the extinction of any existing species then appears as a potential disaster which man's conscience should urge him to avert.

It was in the 1930s that I first became aware of the danger which threatened the Ne-ne or Hawaiian Goose, and in those days I wrote to Mr. Herbert Shipman of Hilo in the big island of Hawaii, who, I had read, kept in his garden a small flock of live Ne-ne. In the wild state the bird seemed to be becoming rapidly rarer. Mr. Shipman undertook to give me a pair of these geese on condition that I would go out to Hawaii to fetch them, and this I might well have done had it not been for the intervention of the Second World War.

After the war I learned from various sources that no more than thirty-two Ne-ne were known to exist and that the world population of the species was almost certainly less than fifty.

In the early days of the Severn Wildfowl Trust, a letter was sent to the Government of the Territory of Hawaii asking what steps they were proposing to take to save this last remnant from extinction, but the interventions of a well-meaning society on the opposite side of the globe are unlikely to be well received by Government officials in any part of the world. Our letter remained unanswered. A little later I was in correspondence on some other subject with an American scientist, Dr. Charles Schwartz, who mentioned that he had recently been invited to visit Hawaii in order to advise the Board of Agriculture on the management of its game birds. He added that he was very uncertain whether he would be taking the job. I wrote immediately imploring him to accept on the grounds that this was perhaps the only opportunity

607

of saving the Hawaiian Goose. Whether my importunity had any effect I do not know, but Dr. Schwartz took the job and focused the attention of the Department on this tiny remnant population so successfully that a new project was planned for the breeding of Hawaiian Geese in captivity. In charge of this project was an ornithologist, Don Smith, who had studied for some time at the Delta Waterfowl Research Station. When he sought advice from Delta, Al Hochbaum in turn suggested that he might consult the Wildfowl Trust, and in this way we found ourselves invited to help with the Pohakuloa Propagation Project.

It was not until the following year that this help took the form of sending to Hawaii our then curator, John Yealland, now Curator of Birds at the London Zoo. John inaugurated out there our standard rearing programme by which more than one clutch of eggs is laid each year by each female, thus greatly increasing the potential annual production. Before he returned after his breeding season in Hawaii John Yealland went to see Mr. Shipman, who had provided the original four birds for the breeding project at Pohakuloa. Was the offer he had made to me before the war still open? Mr. Shipman said that it was, and John returned to England with two beautiful Ne-nes.

This was in 1950 and in the following spring the two birds made nests and each began to lay eggs in them. Clearly there was something wrong somewhere. We sent an urgent cable to Hawaii for a gander, and meanwhile took away the infertile eggs, blew them, ate the contents in an omelette and preserved the shells. A week after the despatch of the cable a fine male Hawaiian Goose arrived at Slimbridge. He was called Kameha-meha after the greatest King of Hawaii, and his two wives were christened Kaiulani and Emma after a famous Princess and a famous Queen of the islands. In the following year both these two females nested and nine young were successfully reared. From that time onwards the stock in Europe has steadily increased until in 1960 there were 126 birds descended from those original three. They live mostly at Slimbridge, but there are pairs in various European zoos and collections. By a strange coincidence in 1960 there were believed to be exactly 126 birds in Hawaii, of which fifty was believed to be the total number of wild ones. The world population was therefore 252, or five times as great as at its lowest ebb.

On our way back from Australia, New Guinea, New Zealand and Fiji in 1957, Philippa and I visited Hawaii and were taken by our old friend Bill Elder, Professor of Zoology from the University of Missouri, who had spent a year studying at Slimbridge and was now spending a year studying the Hawaiian Goose, on a great tramp across the wild expanses of lava known as *a-a*, which is the natural habitat of the Ne-ne. Alas, on this gruelling day of walking across the jagged lava fields high on the slopes of Maunaloa we did not see a single wild Ne-ne. But Bill showed us the hatched nest of a pair he had been watching. It was hidden under a fallen tree in a *Kipuka* or island of vegetation in the sea of lava.

Although it has scarcely increased in the wild state and is still one of the world's rarest birds, it seems probable that, barring nuclear explosions, the extinction of the Ne-ne or Hawaiian Goose has for the time being been averted.

But many other species are in desperate straits. The Ivory-billed Woodpecker has probably gone, and so too, I fear, has the Pink-headed Duck of India and perhaps the Golden-backed Hanging Parakeet of the Philippines, but the Japanese Crested Ibis with nine individuals and the great Whooping Crane of North America with thirty-nine, the California Condor with sixty-five, the large flightless ground parrot of New Zealand called the Ka-ka-po and the Eskimo Curlew with unknown but tiny populations, these and many other species are hanging on by the narrowest margins. Controversy rages on whether the last remaining individuals should or should not be taken into captivity and reared artificially. This was successfully done with Père David's Deer and the European Bison, and when the prospect seems otherwise hopeless I have no hesitation in saying that it should be tried. Extinction is irrevocable. No technique to avert it should be overlooked.

Among the bird species less heavily threatened but still very rare is the Trumpeter Swan of North America. It is the largest of the world's swans and the 1,500 individuals which remain live in the Rocky Mountains and Alaska, except for a very few in captivity.

One day when the Queen, then Princess Elizabeth, was walking round the Wildfowl Trust's enclosures she told us that she was shortly to set out on a Royal Tour of Canada. Were there, she asked, any birds she might bring back for us? I murmured that we had for some time been trying without success to acquire some Trumpeter Swans. A couple of months later came a cable from Canada which said that three pairs of Trumpeter Swans had been presented to Her Royal Highness and asked whether the Trust would be willing to look after them for her. In due course five of the six swans were caught. The sixth pushed open the door of the trap and escaped. The five were sent to England and Her Majesty came down to see them only a few weeks after her accession.

Wild caught swans do not normally breed until they have been some years in captivity. We settled down for a long wait. After two years one of the swans, a pen (female) died. This left us with three cobs and a pen. We wrote to British Columbia reminding them that the sixth swan was still to come, and asking whether they could send two pens while they were about it. Not long after, two beautiful young females arrived and in 1959 one of them nested, but she only laid two eggs and neither hatched. In 1960 she laid five eggs, of which two were fertile, but again neither hatched. We have often noticed that the first attempts of young and inexperienced birds to breed are unsuccessful but that the chances of success improve with experience. We have high hopes for 1961.

All the species of swans in the world are represented in the enclosures at Slimbridge and many of them breed. One pair of Australian Black Swans regularly rears two broods per year. The cob of this pair was lent to us by Sir Winston Churchill. At a time when we had an odd pen we heard that there was some over-crowding at Chartwell and that an extra cob was making trouble on the swan pool. We wrote and asked if we might borrow him, and Sir Winston replied that we could have him "until such time as I may need him again". He is a splendid bird and must have sired more than thirty cygnets since he has been at Slimbridge.

In 1952 I was commissioned to paint a series of large pictures of swans for the Entrance Hall of the Worshipful Company of Dyers in the City of London. The Dyers Company is one of the two City Livery Companies (the other is the Vintners) which still retain a Royalty of swans on the River Thames. These oil-paintings were to be of Mute Swans.

Having painted the set, I was invited to join a Swan-Upping party on board a pleasure steamer to watch the traditional ceremony in which the Thames swans are rounded up and apportioned between the two livery companies and the Crown. Also attending this colourful function was Sir John Barbirolli, conductor of the Hallé Orchestra, who told me that in the winter a new symphony by Vaughan Williams, based upon the music he had written for the Ealing Studios film *Scott of the Antarctic*, would have its first performance in Manchester. He invited me to attend.

On the day of the concert, 14th January, 1953, there was a thick fog. Nevertheless Phil and I set off to motor from London to Manchester with all too little time to spare. After a nightmare drive we drew up outside the door of the concert hall with seconds to spare. We rushed up the empty stairs towards the dress circle, took a wrong turning and found ourselves heading for the gentlemen's lavatory, turned back in time and finally careered breathlessly down the central aisle to be met by Lady Barbirolli just as her husband came on to the rostrum. The *Sinfonia Antartica* occupied the second half of the concert.

Hitherto the symphonies of Vaughan Williams had been almost unknown to me, except in fragments over the radio. What I had heard had not so far excited me. Whether it was that I remembered the themes used in the film, or the first-night atmosphere, or family associations, I do not know, but I found that I was irresistibly and very deeply moved by the music. Since then I have become familiar with the work through a long-playing record, but I still remember that first wonderful performance and the impact of its rich orchestration, its great bold central melody, the tinkling ice, the exquisite sadness of the wordless voice, the withering chill of its wind machine. Without doubt it is noble music.

At the end we went to the Green Room for a small gathering and then on to a dinner of eight with the composer, conductor, leader of the orchestra, their wives and ourselves. There were short impulsive speeches. Barbirolli's and Vaughan Williams's were both moving and delightful. Mine was hopelessly inadequate.

It was my first meeting with Vaughan Williams, who was then eighty-one and rather deaf. I met him several times thereafter, and he came to see the birds at the Wildfowl Trust during the Three Choirs Festival at Gloucester. He told me once that he had never cared very much for the *Dream of Gerontius* and that on this day of the Festival, depending on the weather, he either went to the cinema or came to see the ducks.

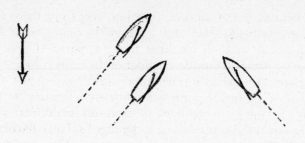

CHAPTER II   *Yacht Racing and its Rules*

IN pre-war years, when the Championship Race for the International Fourteen-foot Dinghies had seemed all-important, my summer holidays had been ordered by training and preparing for the Prince of Wales's Cup, to the exclusion of all else. After the war I had awoken to the thought that if I was to study wild geese on their Arctic breeding grounds, no such one-track objective could be allowed to buy up my summer leisure. Four northern summers followed this conclusion—the Perry River expedition, Lapland and the two trips to Iceland.

But these did not mean that sailing was altogether abandoned. After the summer with the Ross's Geese I returned to Montreal for an international dinghy series, with Keith Shackleton as my crew; and in 1956 John Winter and I brought out our trusty old *Thunder & Lightning* again for the Prince of Wales's Cup at Torquay. We bought new Terylene sails for her and in light airs she was still very fast. On the Monday of the week's racing we won, and all seemed set for a spectacular come-back, but when the big race came on the Thursday, in the lightest wind of all, we bungled it and finished half-way down the fleet.

Dinghy sailing needs practice and Slimbridge is many miles from any suitable dinghy sailing waters. But for Cowes Week one year John and I were lent a Swallow—one of a particularly 'hot' class of keel boats—and Phil sailed with us as foredeck hand. Although our performance over the whole week was unimpressive, on one day of light winds we won comfortably. Now to me there is a certain special *cachet* in winning a race in Cowes Week, and, although our success was almost entirely fortuitous, it was for some reason peculiarly satisfying. It was the sort of day when specialised local knowledge of the tides was all-important, and of this, of course, we had none. For a while we followed the pundits round the shores of the Solent, tucked as close in to the beaches as we could safely sail. Finally, as the leaders headed yet further up towards Southampton Water and away from the next mark we revolted. "Common sense dictates that this is nonsense," we said, "we must now strike out into the tide." In nine such days out of ten we should no doubt in our ignorance have been swept away towards the Needles, but on this particular day we were right. We ghosted out towards the buoy and rounded it without difficulty, romping down the tide to the finishing line almost before the others had noticed what we were at.

One summer I was invited to sail the Royal Dragon *Bluebottle* at Fowey Regatta, and to stay the while with General Browning and his wife Daphne du Maurier at nearby Menabilly where I had spent three summer holidays in my boyhood. The racing was not very fierce, for in the absence of other Dragons, *Bluebottle* sailed in the handicap class. They were pleasant days sailing but they lacked the tension to be found in class-racing. To me the most exciting part was revisiting the haunts of thirty years ago. As I sailed out of Fowey Harbour at *Bluebottle*'s helm I remembered the very first sailing race in which I had ever competed. It too had been in a handicap class, twice round this same unaltered harbour, last at the start and last all the way, but the beginning of a life-long delight.

And the great tumbledown house of Menabilly had not altered at all. It was still full of children and bathing dresses and slack tennis rackets, and best of all, there were still Greater Horseshoe bats in the roof hanging like pears from the same rafters as they had occupied all those years before.

Ever since before the war I had wondered why sailing should be almost the only form of locomotion for which no official speed records had ever been set up. The development of locomotory vehicles usually depends on racing and on ultimate speed. In yacht racing class rules had been designed to create fair competition for the helmsmen, but these rules had the effect of restricting speed. Why had no open competition ever been staged in which all such restrictions were swept aside? Why not a speed record for sailing boats over a measured mile, and why not races in which experimental boats of different classes raced against each other to find which was fastest? Speed still has an appeal for its own sake. Fair competition there should, of course, be; but fair competition in a fast boat will always be more fun than in a slow one. From the Dinghy Committee of the Yacht Racing

Association, to which, as a winner of the Prince of Wales's Cup, I was automatically elected, I put forward these proposals away back in 1938 but although both have now come to pass, the ideas seemed to fall on deaf ears at the time.

I was therefore surprised and delighted to read that in 1955 F. G. Mitchell, who has done so much for yachting in this country, had put up a prize of £50 for the fastest boat over a measured half mile in the Solent during Cowes Week. Charles Curry suggested I should have a shot at it in the Fairey Jolly Boat—an elongated decked version of the latest fourteen-footer design. My crew was Vernon Stratton [who represented Great Britain in the single-handed class in the summer of 1960 in the Olympic Regatta at Naples]. As we sailed out of Cowes a strong gust of wind came sweeping between the buildings. It caught us when we were still sorting things out and the boat capsized. Uffa Fox, who was watching, said it was touch and go, and if he had kept his window shut it might have been all right. We got the boat in to the steps below the Island Sailing Club, bailed her out and set off again for the transit posts in Osborne Bay. Two quick runs of almost continuous planing in a cloud of spray, one way faster than the other, and the average was eleven knots. We did two more for luck but they were not quite so fast. The competition was open for the whole week and there were other attempts, one by a large cruising Catamaran, but no one exceeded our speed in the Jolly Boat and we were declared the winners.

In the following year Tiny Mitchell offered the prize again and it was won by a Catamaran. These twin-hulled boats clearly held the secret of higher and ever-higher speeds in sailing and I became very much interested in their development. I arranged that Catamaran races should be given during Cowes Week by several clubs including the Royal Yacht Squadron so that their performance could be seen at first hand by the more conservative yachtsmen. The effect was interesting and although in some respects it pointed out the wide differences between Catamarans and conventional boats, it also showed the extraordinary speeds they could sail at and the exhilaration of sailing them. On one particular day in Cowes Week 1957 the Catamarans were the only boats racing, all others having been cancelled because of gale-force winds. I sailed a Shearwater and finished second. It was very wet but very exciting.

That same year I persuaded the Duke of Edinburgh to go for his first sail in a Catamaran. Unfortunately he travelled three-up in Ken Pearce's Catamaran *Endeavour* which, as a result of the extra weight, burrowed into the seas several times, though the Duke was nothing daunted. As we sailed past him in another Catamaran he shouted across: "They're wonderful so long as they stay on top!" After that we sped up into the calmer water of the Medina River and dashed wildly along in great juddering sheets of spray. There is no doubt that Catamarans in a fresh breeze offer a quite new sensation in sailing.

I have never thought much of my capacities as an organiser or administrator. From long ago I always promised myself that when I became too old for sailing small boats I would *not* get involved in their administration. But somehow this very thing had been creeping up on me. I had allowed myself to be elected to the Council of the Y.R.A. and from there I had become involved in the administration of Olympic Yachting in 1948. Soon afterwards I was rash enough to suggest that the international organisation—the I.Y.R.U.—ought to have a proper constitution. In the way that so frequently overtakes people who offer an idea, I soon found myself Chairman of the Constitution Committee. With the aid of David Pollock's able legal mind a Constitution was finally drawn up and adopted.

By now I was rather enjoying the challenge of delicate international relations and conflicting interests in yachting. The meetings of the Union were held for one week each year in November. They were attended by the world's technical experts on yachts and by a number of distinguished racing men, among them my old acquaintance, the Crown Prince of Norway.

One of the problems which occupied a great deal of attention was the question of the International Right of Way Rules for Racing. Soon after the war it was evident that the rules had accumulated so many additions, special provisions, and footnotes, that they were ripe for a complete redraft. Harold Vanderbilt, who had successfully defended the America's Cup and had also re-written the rules of Bridge, set about preparing a new code, which not only tied up all the loose ends but also, in the name of simplification substantially modified the principles. This new code was first presented to the Union in 'take-it-or-leave-it' terms, with the added comment that whatever the International Union did the United States, which was not a member, proposed to bring them in at once. This impatience back in 1947 meant that for ten years there were two conflicting sets of right of way rules to confuse the world's yachtsmen, and the sad part was that the

American set was the better, and would almost certainly have been adopted by the rest of the world had it not been rammed down their throats.

This was a situation which, in my earliest days in the Union, I set out to put right. Once more I was put in charge of a committee. But for a while we had to progress slowly. The first step seemed to be to get the U.S. into the Union. In 1950 I went over to New York and addressed an impassioned plea to a great meeting at the New York Yacht Club. That autumn they joined, and Henry Morgan, who as Commodore of the New York Yacht Club, persuaded them to do so, is now one of the Union's two Vice-Presidents.

The first stage of my campaign was satisfactorily concluded. But Sir Ralph Gore, President of the Union and of the Y.R.A., and Commodore of the Royal Yacht Squadron, was absolutely opposed to any change of rules, chiefly because the new American set was in contradiction to the sailing section of the long-established International Regulations for Preventing Collisions at Sea (often known as the Board of Trade Rules). What were the chances of getting the Board of Trade Rules changed to remove Sir Ralph's principal objection? It seemed they were negligible.

But gradually the climate of opinion in Europe began to change. Sooner or later, everyone felt, the *best* rules must surely prevail.

Meanwhile late in October 1955, at short notice, Sir Ralph Gore resigned his Presidency of the Union, and soon afterwards that of the Royal Yachting Association (as it had by then become). The I.Y.R.U. Conference was no more than a week away and the Permanent Committee was rocked by the news when it assembled at the Royal Thames Yacht Club in London. Someone had to take the chair to get the meeting going and as an English-speaking delegate I was invited to do so. In the course of the next few days the assembled yachtsmen had to elect a new President, and many were the earnest conversations which took place at corner tables in the various dark corners of the Club. For me too there was some heart-searching. Should I be a candidate or not? There were those among the members who urged that I should be. On the one hand it seemed that with a great interest in the subject, with an almost militant internationalism, with a moderate command of two other languages beside my own, and an open mind on technical matters, I might perhaps be able to bring something useful to the Union. On the other hand there was my technical ignorance, especially of larger yachts and ocean racing; my views on the right of way rules were not shared by everyone, my life was full of other activities and there were many people of greater distinction and seniority who ought surely to be considered before me. For a couple of days I was on the verge of withdrawing, but in due course I agreed to be a candidate for election. By the day of the dinner, which is held annually towards the close of the Conference Week, the special sub-committee set up to examine the Presidential candidacy had informed me that they proposed to approach the Crown Prince of Norway who had not been able to leave Oslo because of the illness of King Haakon, and to ask him to accept the Presidency; but if for any reason he found himself unable to do so, they told me that they intended to put forward my name unopposed at the final meeting. Between the afternoon session and the cocktails before the dinner, the sub-committee had been on the telephone to Oslo and when we met again for drinks they bowed slightly and said: "Good evening, Mr. President." They were premature, for I had still to be elected, but the meeting accepted their recommendation. The Crown Prince had agreed to be a Vice-President until such time as he came to the Throne. Since his accession he has become President of Honour.

Being President of the International Yacht Racing Union has not been quite as difficult and terrifying as I had anticipated. The idea of following so wise and distinguished a yachtsman as Sir Ralph Gore had filled me with apprehension. But my friends in the Permanent Committee have been kind to me. Although the organisation has grown rapidly, and now embraces Russia and the countries of Eastern Europe, it has retained an extraordinary atmosphere of friendliness which surely must arise from a common delight in the wind and the water, the sails and the boats. Our conferences are a gathering of fair-minded men and even a problem which arose between East and West Germany was satisfactorily resolved.

The controversies and delays in forging a universal set of racing rules are at last at an end. Gerald Sambrooke Sturgess, a dentist in Norwich against whom I often sailed in the old days on the Norfolk Broads, has made himself, over the years, the greatest expert on the wording and case law of both sets of rules. Already he has drawn them together in a series of steps. His meticulous care and skill has been matched by Gregg Bemis on the American side. Each heads a committee, and in astonishingly close collaboration a final draft of what is believed to be the best possible

set of racing rules that can be devised was submitted to the
Union's Racing Rules Committee under Commodore Niels
Benzon of Denmark. The preliminary meetings were at Naples
during the Olympic Regatta.

Now, as the second stage of my campaign reaches its climax,
comes the most striking news of all—that the International Con-
vention for the Safety of Life at Sea will alter its Regulations (the
Board of Trade Rules) so that they agree with the main principles
of the new yacht-racing code. The tangle is unravelling fast, but
there is still one serious problem ahead. Already European yachtsmen have accepted two sweeping alterations to their rules in the
last four years. Will they accept a third, and we believe final,
version? It should be a good one, and we intend to let it stand for
several years without alteration.[1]

[1] In November 1960 the new Code of Racing Rules was unanimously adopted by
the 37 Member Nations of I.Y.R.U.

Some of the 126 Ne-ne or Hawaiian Geese (exactly half the world population) which have been reared at Slimbridge from the original three sent from Hawaii in 1950.

The first year's production of nine Ne-ne at Slimbridge when the world population was under fifty.

1957

The family in the studio window.

1957

The ducks outside.

CHAPTER 12   *Rockets, Bees and Fishes*

ONE day in 1954 I was opening a new school, and talking as I
often did about Adventure with a capital A. When given this
sort of job to do I usually talk about Adventure and Enthusiasm,
and oh how ponderous I can get! On this particular day I began
to talk about people landing on the moon, and how I thought
this would happen within the lifetime of the children who were
listening to me. This was before the days of Sputniks, before the
Astronomer Royal's famous dictum that space travel was 'utter
bilge', back at a time when nothing much was written about it
except space fiction. But I noticed that there was absolute silence
in the hall—not a cough, not a shuffle. The children sat on the
edges of their chairs peering up at me expectantly. I told them
all I knew about the prospects, which was not very much, and
I decided there and then that it ought to be more. I applied for
membership of the British Interplanetary Society and was
accepted. I had quite expected this might be a body of cranks
and crackpots, but to my surprise I found a very well organised
serious scientific society.

I had been acting as Chairman of a sound radio series called
The Travellers, produced by Eileen Molony (later to become the
television producer of *Look*) and I suggested that interplanetary
travellers of the future ought to have a logical place in the series.
It was finally decided, I thought rather unimaginatively, by the
programme planners that any such programme should not be
broadcast under *The Travellers'* banner, but that a programme
should nevertheless be done, and this led to a series of fifteen-
minute pieces in the Light Programme in which I put simple
questions to such experts as L. R. Shepherd, Val Cleaver and
Patrick Moore.

There are many people who think space exploration is pointless

W

—a waste of money which might be spent on medical research, famine relief, refugees, education, and all the other problems which beset our time. There are good arguments on both sides. Perhaps it is my reverence for exploration and my belief in Truth as a principal objective of man which makes me side with the rocketeers and the radio astronomers. I can conceive of no greater adventure than to make the first journey to the moon or to another planet. All other exploration is insignificant by comparison. It is the most practical of all exercises in practical cosmology. You may look through your visual telescopes and listen to your radio telescopes, and send out your satellites and your probes, with their cameras and their television, but when the first *men* are on the way, that will be the real thing.

Man must survive on the earth. Scientists must help him to do so—help him not to exterminate himself, help him to get his food, help to alleviate his sufferings, help to increase his happiness. But to what end? Just so that his species can survive, not blow itself up, not starve, feel less pain, live more happily? Surely this is not enough. Surely he must evolve, aspire, explore, in order to justify his survival. He must sea ch perpetually for Truth in order to satisfy his soul.

But there are less high-falutin arguments in favour of astronautics and the part our country should play in them. The political influence of the Sputniks has been easy to see. The ascent of Everest announced on Coronation Day was not a bad thing for British prestige. If we believed that our particular brand of freedom and justice was worth fighting for in two wars, and if we still believe in it and in Britain's influence on world affairs, then we should try to catch up in the space race, perhaps leapfrog in it, as we have done in the aircraft industry. If you say we cannot afford to do it, I say we cannot afford not to.

One evening at a dinner in the Royal Yacht I put some of these arguments to the Duke of Edinburgh. Rather rashly he told me to put them on paper for him. The memorandum was headed: "Why Britain should put the first man on the moon." It was dated 8th August, 1955. But the document was so full of platitudes that I did not dare to send it in. Instead I asked if I might put forward four bees which had recently been buzzing in my bonnet. One was about direct power from the sun and the importance of backing British research in this field which will ultimately replace all other sources, including atomic energy; another was about giving more honours to the teaching profession; the third about speed records in sailing and the fourth about the importance of developing small boat sailing, especially if possible on some of the great new reservoirs.

My argument for the last one (and I felt it very strongly) went like this: The Human Race will either blow itself up or not blow itself up. If it does not, then the scientists will produce power and mechanisation on such a scale that more and more leisure will be available to all the people. We have at present a forty-four-hour week, sometimes a forty-hour week. If we are thinking ahead we must get used to the idea of a thirty-four-hour week and then a twenty-four-hour week. This new leisure will be no good to people unless they can be shown how to use it. This is why I think it is vitally important to foster outdoor sports and interests—such things as climbing, gliding, sailing, riding, bird-watching, wild-fowling, fishing, and skiing. In this field, sailing is a wonderful possibility; it builds character, encourages resource and initiative, re-establishes contact (and conflict) with the elements, fosters the team spirit. From being a rich man's sport, it has, in the last few years, suddenly become available in the form of dinghy sailing to very large numbers of people, especially young people. But this is only the very beginning of a movement which is, I believe, going to mushroom out still further in the next twenty-five years.

There is plenty of water round our islands but the requirements for small boats ashore cannot always be met. We have got to build 'Marinas' and provide ramps and 'dinghy parks' as soon as possible, so that these facilities are not left so far behind the increase in boats as the roads have been left behind the increase in cars.

We have already provided the boats with adequate buoyancy so that they are reasonably safe. They will never be *quite* safe and that is as it should be or the spice of danger would be lost. Sailing is all set to blossom out.

But we badly need more sailing facilities inland, and for these large reservoirs are ideal. The most important are those around London. Hitherto the Metropolitan Water Board has been adamant that sailing cannot be permitted on drinking water reservoirs. But the Bristol Waterworks Company has allowed sailing on Cheddar reservoir for a number of years and no one in Bristol has been poisoned by it.

One day I hope there may be facilities for sailing on at least two (one east, one west) of the London reservoirs, under the same sort of conditions as those which have been so satisfactory at Cheddar. Other reservoirs such as the new ones in Staffordshire and Essex might follow later.

The films of the journey Phil and I had made to Tierra del Fuego, the Land of Fire, and up into the Altiplano of Bolivia had had sufficient success on TV to suggest to the B.B.C. that other expeditions might follow. One to Uganda, at the invitation of the Chairman of the National Parks, to perform the opening ceremony of the new Safari Lodge in the Murchison Falls Park, was too short for serious filming, but it was our first chance to see the African fauna, and however many elephants you may have seen in films or on the TV screen, the first view of a wild herd is a stirring sight. It was satisfactory to find that the real thing was still so incomparably more exciting than the canned version.

As President of the International Yacht Racing Union I had been invited to preside over the International Jury at the Olympic Games in Melbourne in 1956. This seemed to be the opportunity for filming a series of programmes on Australian wild life, and we planned a round-the-world tour, to include New Guinea, New Zealand, Fiji, and Hawaii on the way home. With Phil and me came Charles Lagus as cameraman. Most of our adventures must wait to be described in another book, but in the course of the journey, something significant happened which must be recounted here.

We were at Cairns on the Queensland Coast on our way from New Guinea to New Zealand. It was Christmas time and unbearably hot and sticky; the children were 6,000 miles away, and Phil had a poisoned leg. It was all rather depressing, but although we did not know it, we were on the threshold of a revelation. To convey the nature of this revelation I must, for a moment, digress.

I have always been deeply moved by the great diversity in animal life and the amazing ingenuity of the selective processes in evolution. How and why have all these animals become different one from another? How has the Red-breasted Goose acquired its startling and complicated pattern of black and white and chestnut-red? Why is the caterpillar of the Elephant Hawk Moth to be found in two colour schemes, one brown and one green? By what incredible sequence of minute changes has the peacock evolved its tail? This sense of wonder and mystery has never left me—indeed it has grown stronger as I have grown older. In the study of evolution as in all other branches of biology, perhaps all other branches of science, the answer to one question prompts at least three more. It is a road which has no end, only a right direction, which leads to the Ultimate Truth, a road along which we can travel hopefully, without ever expecting to arrive.

The evolution of behaviour patterns (as much as colour patterns and shape) has given me especial cause to marvel. On the same visit to Australia we had seen the fabulous Mallee Fowl, one of the turkey-like Megapodes, which hatches its eggs in the centre of a huge mound heated at first by rotting vegetation and later by the sun. Consider the instinctive skill required by the male bird, who alone looks after the nest mound and measures its temperature with his tongue, to regulate this natural incubator by scratching off the sand or piling more on top. Most remarkable of all is that in the first weeks of incubation by the heat of the compost he piles on more to make it hotter, whereas later, when the sun must do the work, he has to scrape off sand to achieve the same result. Consider too the recent discovery that certain small night migrating birds like the Blackcap and Garden Warbler can orientate themselves in relation to the star pattern in the night sky; and this they can do without any kind of training or learning. Young birds, reared in captivity without their parents, took up a direction under the dome of a planetarium which could be altered by swinging round the pattern of the stars.

Until recently my thoughts on evolution had been confined mainly to birds and particularly to the birds of the family *Anatidae* —the ducks, geese and swans; and then came Christmas 1956, and the three days we spent at Cairns going out each day to swim with face mask and snorkel over the coral gardens of the Great Barrier Reef. The entry in my diary which covers this period begins:

"For part of these three days I have been in a new world. Nothing I have done in Natural History in all my life has stirred me quite so sharply as my first experience of skin-diving on a coral reef. Konrad Lorenz said when I saw him in Bavaria in September that this was one thing I must do before I died— and now I have done it, or rather started to do it. The dramatic threshold which is crossed as soon as one puts one's mask below the surface is, to a naturalist, nothing less than staggering in its impact. Much has been written already about the scarcely explored new 'continent' of the ocean; I have read these des- criptions in the books of Cousteau and Diolé, and yet I was unprepared for the visionary revelation when I first saw the real thing.

"I must try to describe it chronologically and in detail, but the effect on my mind is still rather kaleidoscopic and bewildering. First it should be explained that the adventure falls into four chapters and an appendix—and, by the way, I have no hesitation in using the word adventure, for this type of swimming cannot fail to be high adventure, nothing less, for any naturalist; indeed for any imaginative person who has never done it before. The four chapters were four separate dives, two on the first day and one on each of the next two. The appendix is two visits to the Underwater Observatory on Green Island. As befits such a sequence, each chapter was more exciting and more moving than the one before. The final effect was overwhelming, so that in spite of trials and tribulations with ill-designed equipment, and intense discomfort arising therefrom, I cannot see how I can ever escape from its lure. I am already an addict and I have not yet used an aqualung."

From then on my diary is full of drawings of fish—the common fishes of the coral reef. I drew the marvellous yellow and black striped and barred Butterfly Fish of the genus *Chaetodon*. I drew the black and white Damsel Fish *Dascyllus*, the superb Anemone Fish *Amphiprion* which are golden-red with pale blue bands, and the ridiculous Razor Fish which swim perpetually standing on their heads. But to begin with I did not know their names.

The first two dives were made in rather murky water at a place called Double Island near the mainland shore. There was a great profusion and variety of fishes, but it was on the second dive in the afternoon that I came upon a shoal of about twenty round fish like vertical dinner plates, about eight or ten inches across, which stayed in a decorative and sociable cluster just above the rocks. They were brown and marbled and their sociability was vastly impressive. I think it was this shoal that suddenly showed me the immense possibilities of all these fish in terms of comparative ethology—the comparative study of animal behaviour.

I wrote that night: "A very curious feature of swimming with a snorkel is that although one's eyes are only an inch or two below the surface, there is no feeling of being on the edge of the world one sees. On the contrary, one feels very much part of the scene, and of course one *is* in among the fish, for one's hand reaches out towards them and some are hardly scared by it,

moving quietly only a foot or so in front of it. It is as new a
sensation as gliding or skating; and with it all is the almost
agonising thought to a naturalist, of how much there is to learn
before one can use even a fraction of what one sees. Above all,
there is the unbelievable beauty of it."

Next day we were taken to Michaelmas Cay, a small islet
thirty miles from the mainland right out on the Barrier proper.

"The water here had a totally new clarity so that chapters
one and two were blurred and muddy preludes to a crystalline
brilliance which I had never believed possible in water. It was
as if the water was air. I noticed at once that most of the fish
were different from the ones at Double Island. There were two
kinds of bright blue Damsel Fishes, one about four inches long
in which the male has an orange and yellow tail and the female
is all blue. They lived in pairs and their blue was of such
brilliance that it appeared irridescent like a butterfly's wing.
The other kind was smaller with no orange tail and of a slightly
different shape. The blue was paler though no less brilliant.
These lived in shoals and when I first saw the first one hovering
around a coral head—about a dozen or twenty of them—I
found myself exclaiming with astonishment out loud: it was a
sort of shout of joy at seeing something so incredibly beautiful."

Next day was Christmas Day and found us at Green Island,
also out on the Barrier, about thirty miles from Cairns. Green
Island has tourist attractions, but this seems to have had no harmful effect upon the life of the coral reefs. Indeed one of these
attractions is an underwater observatory—a large tank sunk in
twenty feet of water, accessible by stairway from a pier above
and fitted with portholes through which the fishes could be seen
and photographed. This observatory—from which I distinguished
no less than fifty-two different fish species swimming freely in the
sea outside—provided the appendix to our new discovery, but the
climax was swimming once more in these incomparable coral
gardens. It was on Christmas afternoon that Charles Lagus filmed
Phil and me going into the water with our masks and flippers.
We had no underwater cameras, so once that had been done the
decks were clear for the fourth and last chapter of our underwater
adventure.

"It consisted," I wrote in my diary, "of about two and a half
hours in wonderland. Phil was having some trouble with an

ill-fitting mask and snorkel, and her flippers gave her cramp. About ten yards out in about three or four feet of water there was a kind of sea grass growing which contained a few fish, but the coral did not begin for another ten or fifteen yards in a depth of about five feet and this was just too deep for Phil to stand and adjust and empty her mask. At first I stayed with her, but later I realised that she would prefer to work it out for herself, so I set off to join Charles on a protracted cruise of the near-by coral. Just as each of the preceding chapters had outshone the last, so now this cruise was far and away the best of all. Once again most of the fishes were new—different from those on Michaelmas Cay. One of the most colourful and amusing looked rather like a pig with prominent blue stripes between its eyes and across the tip of its snout, and with a sharp radial pattern of black and white and yellow on its sides, (identified long later as *Rhinacanthus aculeatus*, the Pig-snout Trigger Fish). They ran up to ten inches long and were quite charming in their manner. Once again the loveliest sight was the shoals of blue fish—not the very bright ones of Michaelmas Cay—but a soft blue species in big shoals always near coral the tips of which were just the same colour. This was so delicate and in such perfect taste that I lay for a long time looking at the gentle combination. Presently Charles came and said he had seen what he thought was a young Hammerheaded Shark about five feet long which had 'scared the daylights out of him', but if we both went back . . . but alas, the beast had gone.

"I swam back to see how Phil was getting on. She had discarded her flippers but the mask and snorkel had been mastered and she had reached a patch of coral where she could see plenty of fish. Near by I found a pair of Razor Fish floating with head vertically downward. I chased them to see if I could scare them into any other swimming posture, but they kept easily ahead of me, still vertical. Crawling slowly up and down over the ripples on a patch of white sandy bottom was a hermit crab in a tall shell about five inches long. At the edge of the coral were shoals of large Parrot Fish—one or two rainbow-coloured males among a dozen or so drabber females. Everywhere we met saucer-shaped *Chaetodonts* or Butterfly Fish, always in pairs which were identical, but each pair seemed different from the last. Could all these be different species? Evidently they were."

Butterfly and Damsel Fish on the coral reef at Fiji.

Then and since I have pondered on how all these different species of Butterfly Fish can live on the same reefs, at the same depths, apparently with much the same feeding habits, and yet each with a different bold pattern of spots or stripes to assert its specific identity—each, so to speak, with its national flag. Can we suppose that an ancestral and perhaps ubiquitous Butterfly Fish was hit many thousands of years ago by a large climatic change and was only able to survive in a number of isolated patches perhaps on certain coral reefs? Each isolated population, subjected to slightly different conditions, might then have evolved upon slightly different lines so that, when a climatic amelioration came along and all the Butterfly Fish were able to emerge from their geographical isolation, each population was unwilling to cross with its neighbour—had achieved reproductive isolation and therefore by definition, specific status—and proceeded to develop conspicuous 'flag' patterns in order to avoid confusion.

This mechanism was unlikely to be confined to Butterfly Fish. I could draw parallels in the world of birds. And here the full significance of my new-found delight in fish-watching was revealed to me. Infinite possibilities stretched ahead.

Not long afterwards we were in Fiji and spent a week resting at the beautiful hotel at Korolevu, after a strenuous fortnight in New Zealand. We swam for long hours each day over the Fijian coral gardens. Phil was now completely at home under water and we swam hand in hand which was a good arrangement as we could signal easily to call attention to a new discovery. Again the fishes were different from the ones we had seen on the Barrier. I drew them as soon as I came ashore. There were thirteen kinds of Butterfly Fish.

We lived in a comfortable thatched cottage among the coconut palms within twenty yards of the sea. The Fijians danced and sang and drank kava. A great giant of a man called Walai came swimming with us on the reef, and took us to meet the chief in his village. One night I took a waterproof torch and went swimming over the reef. The night fishes were quite different from the daytime ones. Most of them were goldfish colour. I am told it was dangerous, that there might well have been sharks, and that they were more likely to be 'on the feed' when it is dark. This is probably true, but at the time I knew no better and saw no sharks. The memory of our week in Fiji glows romantically. As a South Sea island it was lovely enough but with the fishes as well it remains irresistible. We shall have to go back.

W*

Since then I have watched fishes through a face mask in Hawaii, the West Indies, the Panama Canal, the Galapagos Islands and East Africa. My knowledge of birds has helped me to understand them, and they in turn have clarified for me many problems in ornithology. But for me as a painter and a naturalist those first dives on the Barrier Reef were the revelation. The wonder of it seemed appropriate to that hot Australian Christmas Day.

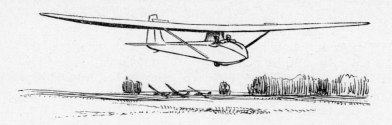

CHAPTER 13   *An Introduction to Gliding*

GLIDING had always sounded an adventurous business. It evidently
had much in common with sailing. It was one of those things I
had been meaning to try one day, but so far the chance had never
come my way. And then one day—it was All Fools' Day, 1956—
my neighbour rang me up:

"Have you been up to see the gliders yet?"

"What gliders; where?"

"Look out of your window and you'll probably see one flying
along the Cotswold edge. They belong to the Bristol Gliding Club
which has just moved to Nympsfield."

Half an hour later I was on the new gliding field being offered
a first flight by the Chief Flying Instructor, John Parry Jones, in a
side-by-side two-seater. John was a big enthusiastic man with a
quiet urgency in his voice. As we waited for the cable to be towed
out from the winch at the far end of the field, he told me what to
expect. There was a quick cockpit check, a shout of "Take up
slack" followed by a shout "All out" and our glider was pulled
violently forward. Almost at once it was airborne and heading
steeply into the sky like a kite—much too steeply for one only
familiar with the take-off attitudes of powered aircraft. Up, up,
while John prattled amiably away, and I gripped the bottom of
the instrument panel and wondered how he would know when he
had got to the top. I wondered too what it would be like then. It
was rather like the long preliminary wind up to the top of a
scenic railway. What would the downward swoop be like?
Unexpectedly it was far nicer than the climb. John released the
cable with a click and we floated out over the valley below. It was
no more than agreeably draughty in the open cockpit. There we
sat side by side 1,000 feet above the airfield, peacefully admiring
the view. At first the air was quite smooth, but then as we flew

along the Cotswold escarpment it became bubbly and buoyant. John tipped our wings sharply into a bank and we went round and round in tight circles.

"Look at the variometer!" he said. "Watch the green ball."

On the instrument panel among the standard instruments which I recognised—airspeed indicator, altimeter, turn-and-slip for blind flying—was one with two vertical glass tubes calibrated in feet per second. In one was a green pellet, in the other a red one. As I watched the green one moved up until it was nearly half-way to the top of the tube and reading five feet per second, pushed up, as I discovered later, by expanding air escaping from a flask. Briefly this meant we were going up. John patiently explained that a glider is always coming down through the air, and the only way it can go up is by finding air which is rising faster than the glider sinks. This we had found—a column of warmer air called a thermal, in which he was now keeping us by steering in tight circles. We rose a few hundred feet and then the thermal died, the green ball sank to the bottom of its tube and the red ball began to flicker up in the second tube. We straightened and flew on along the face of the hill. Presently we felt the burble of rising air again, and again we circled in another thermal. These were 'blue' or 'dry' thermals, John told me, for the sky was cloudless. Usually the tops of thermals formed clouds, and indeed summer cumulus clouds were nothing more than thermals which had reached condensation level. But today the thermals were weak and formed no clouds.

From 1,000 feet, but for the thermals, our flight in the T21 trainer would have lasted four minutes; in fact it lasted nineteen, and as we swept in to land at an increased speed and trundled to a standstill on the single wheel I realised that it was not the last flight I would make in a glider.

"How long will it take you to teach me to glide?" I asked.

"If you've had power flying experience, about thirty flights before you can go solo—three or four hours of flying all told, but it may take you a good many week-ends to get them in."

"Never mind," I said, "I'll have a bash!"

A whole new field of experience was about to open up, a new and, as it turned out, absolutely satisfying outlet for my occasional restlessness. To go sailing meant a long car journey from my home, but directly above it was an ocean of sky waiting to be explored.

On 9th June, 1956, I flew solo for the first time in a Slingsby

Tutor. To begin with I thought this might be the limit of my ambition. I knew how to do it. I could graduate slowly to the higher performance club sailplanes. Beginning at the age of forty-six it was absurd to think of doing much more. Perhaps I should have known myself better or perhaps I had reckoned without the cunningly devised 'Certificates' of the International Aeronautical Federation, designed expressly to lead on the aspiring glider pilot. There are, to begin with, A, B and C certificates which in these days of dual training in two-seaters are likely to be achieved in fairly quick succession, but after that come the Silver C, the Gold C, and, most difficult of all, the three diamonds. When I first learned of these things only one British pilot had all three diamonds and even today there are only four. Maybe, I said to myself, it would be fun to have a Silver C, and from then onwards I was committed.

For the Silver C I would be required to stay airborne for five hours, to fly across country for fifty kilometres, and to climb 1,000 metres (3,281 feet) above the height of launch or any subsequent lower point before the climb. It would no doubt be some long time before these three could be achieved.

My principal instructor was a cynical young man with blue eyes who always wore a blue jersey and wrote novels which did not get finished. He was a skilful flyer and knew no fear. He had a devastating turn of phrase, took life as he found it and may yet be a great writer; his name—Peter Collier. At the time of which I write he was instructing the club's weekly summer courses.

"Now that you've got your C," Peter said, "if you come up during the week there's no reason why we shouldn't fling you off from time to time in the Tutor, without interrupting the course."

So I went up to Nympsfield on the Thursday. The T21 was doing circuits and was back on the ground each time before the cable had been retrieved; but as the day developed, the two-seater began to stay up longer. After the first two soaring flights had been occupied with taping up some bad places in the cable and running out of petrol in the retrieving car, there was at last a cable waiting when the T21 was still airborne. Here was my opportunity—I must grasp it with both hands, or something . . .

Three minutes later I too was airborne. There was no wind at all and I barely squeezed 700 feet from the launch, but I found lift at once and began to circle. It felt nice and buoyant, but the green ball fell back and the red one bobbed up. I straightened and headed for where I thought the lift should have been, but the red ball only went higher. In two minutes more I was back on the ground—total, five minutes. This was repeated twice and then I found something better. The green ball stayed up at three, occasionally five feet per second. Even the altimeter needle moved up—very slightly. When the green ball dropped back I went on circling for a long time in 'no sink'. Rather weak, these thermals, but really there's nothing in this circling business! We could stay up for quite a while—in fact we've already *been* up quite a while. (We? All this 'me and the Tutor' stuff which always creeps into all solo pilots' accounts of their flights.) Hullo, that red ball's going rather high—worse than ten red. Oh dear, it's no good, we'll have to go in. But it was more like a flight, we must have been up at least half an hour. What did you say? Nine minutes? Oh well . . .

The next launch provided fifteen minutes of fumbling at 600 feet, and when I got back there was a cable waiting for an immediate relaunch. Now this was absurd—five launches and I still had not hooked myself on to the sky. Something positively must be done this time. If the T21 can stay airborne for half an hour, and the Olympia is up there circling at 3,000 feet or more, surely, having kept the standard work, *Soaring Pilot* by my bedside for the last month, I can centre on a thermal and *gain* a little height above the launch? I watched the Olympia circling effortlessly, and wondered how much mental effort the pilot was putting into it. The silent lazy circles gave no clue, and already the sailplane looked small away up there, a thin little cross, not much more than a speck in the sky. I wondered when I would be good enough, or lucky enough, to become a 'speck in the sky'. But the first thing to do was to make a positive advance on the launch height; that was the immediate objective. Well, let's have another shot.

"Can-I-Take-Her-Off-Safely"—the initial letters each stand for an item in the cockpit check—"All clear above and behind— Take up slack—All out!" Here we go again. Hold on to your hats! Screaming launch, let's try tail wagging (the signal to the winch driver that he is hauling in too fast). He can't have seen it. Oh yes, he did—I think we're going to stall. Ah, that's better. Considering there's no wind it's going to be quite a nice launch, 800 feet. Now, what did they say, "Turn right off the launch and try the little bowl on the slope?" Well, let's try it—but it's no good. Not a peep, and we're back to 600. We must turn back into the circuit. Hold everything—here it is, a strong turbulent surge, the starboard wing blown into the air—tuck it down again like it says in the book and start circling to the right. You're skidding, too much rudder again! That's better, and the green ball's still shivering at three feet per second. There's the winch immediately below and they're working on the cable again. Quite nice turns now, and still two or three green. Oh look, we're at 1,000 feet! A surge of lift, straighten for three seconds and then into the turn again. Oh yes, five green but not all the time. Now we're going to work at this, let's try the book methods. Worst heading, where's that? O.K., straight up the ridge it's only two green, now sixty degrees, straighten up and into the turn again. Golly, it worked! It's five green all the way round. This is fun! No wind at all; the winch is still directly below. Wonder if we're interfering with anyone's launch. No aircraft on the ground, and anyway they're still mending the cable. Hey, watch it, the lift's falling off. Green ball's dropping right back on one side of the circle. Let's try the *best* heading method. Five green there—what's just behind the left wing-tip now? Easy—my home beside the bend in the estuary. Round to it, straighten . . . and two and three and in again. There it is, a real surge of it. It's worked again. It's really quite simple; needs a bit of concentration though. I wonder why I'm so dry in the mouth—wish I'd remembered to bring those peppermints to suck. The winch is still more or less straight down there. It looks pretty small, we must be quite high. Cor! 2,500 feet and still going up; not only that but the green ball's going higher now—up to ten. Ten feet per second—that's pretty fast climbing. Time to look round and enjoy the scenery, but it's a bit hazy now and rather cold. It's also suddenly rather lonely and frightening with no windscreen, and nothing but a little plywood bucket to sit in. What the hell am I doing up here anyway, and at my age too? Hullo, not going up any more. Perhaps the thermal has 'thrown us out'—let's try over to the north. Yes, there it is again; really strong now, bursts of twenty green—3,500 feet and no barograph in the locker. Perhaps I could get Silver C height but it would not count if I did not have a barograph trace to prove it. "*Never* go without a barograph," one of the pundits had told me, but I had thought it could not apply at my level of proficiency. All the same we must get to Silver C height just for the fun of it. What's 1,000 metres? Three thousand, two hundred and eighty-odd feet. Well, we're higher than that already, but then there's the launch, another 800, call it 1,000 for safety and then add some to make a round figure. We must get 4,500 on the clock. We're really in the core of the thermal, fifteen green all the time, sometimes twenty, and lovely big lazy circles with the lift steady all round and the ground getting hazier and the curious flat cloud on top like a grey pancake. And there's Silver C height. But we might as well go on to cloud base now, though we must be careful not to get sucked into it. There are no blind-flying instruments in this glider, and even if there were I shouldn't be able to use them. It doesn't look a *very* big cloud, but with all this twenty green about . . .

And now suddenly there are dark wisps of cloud trailing below us and the horizon has disappeared. The altimeter says 5,500 feet. It's time to stop going up. Nose down, speed up to fifty-five, and a whole lot colder, in fact perishing cold in the open cockpit with no windscreen and clothing for a summer's day. And, look, the green ball is still up at five and the ground is hardly visible at all. Nose down some more and out spoilers. The little slats on the tops of the wings ought to counteract all this lift. That's better but the green ball won't go right down. It hovers between one and two. Oh golly, this is serious, we *are* being sucked right into the cloud. Maybe this is a Cunim—a thunder cloud in the making, maybe it's already too late to escape and the Tutor will break up in the cloud, and me with no parachute. And then suddenly we're out into sunshine, and blessedly the red ball has popped up. Panic over, but it's still horribly cold. I'm shivering uncontrollably from a combination of fear and cold. But the horizon is there again and the sun is comforting and the cloud is quite definitely *not* a Cunim. Let's fly out over the Severn estuary, over my house and enjoy the view in spite of the cold. I'm still shivering. I've throttled back now to thirty-five m.p.h. but I wish there was a windscreen on this fuselage. There's still this feeling of loneliness too. It's really very silly. After all, I'm much safer up here at 5,000 feet than I would be at 500, and yet I should feel quite at home dicing about over the ridge, and up here I feel definitely unsafe. I suppose it's all a question of what one is used to.

Now, how far can I go and make certain of getting back; there's not enough wind to worry about (or to warrant trying to get Silver C distance—thirty-two miles). What did it say in the book—"four miles for every 1,000 feet?" Well, it's about five miles to home and five miles back—ten miles, 2,500 feet—well, that ought to be O.K. and anyway there are patches of 'no sink', which, combined with the cold wind, indicate that we should fly as slowly as possible. And so out over the ponds of the Wildfowl Trust, a tight circle there and on out over the river, another circle, and now let's head back towards Nympsfield. Still nearly 4,000 feet on the clock. Another circle over my house; I bet nobody down below has seen me. Pity really, but it's too far to shout. Might as well go back by way of my cloud which is still sitting more or less where I left it. There's only weak lift under it now— that I can find anyway. But it's too cold to stick around, and so I go gently back, my world becoming gradually more and more familiar the nearer I get to launch height. Finally, the approach. This they had said was the time when one's judgment failed, after one had been high up for a while. I must exercise more care than ever. No wind. Much floating even with the spoilers out. Patience, there's no hurry. Hold off six inches above the ground, and then hold off more and . . . down. Quite nice really, and just as well with everyone looking. And down on the ground it's hot again, no need to shiver any more.

It was one minute under an hour since I had taken off, they told me. "You know," they said, "the Tutor looked absolutely tiny up there, straight above us—just a tiny speck in the sky."

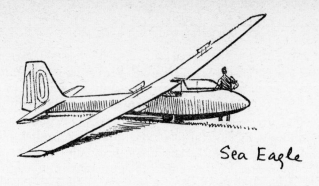

Sea Eagle

CHAPTER 14   *Soaring Progress*

PERHAPS the greatest appeal of gliding is the simplicity of its basic concepts. In a glider you are competing against gravity. When you are going up you are winning, when you are coming down you are losing. There is something satisfyingly direct about it. As the glider is always sinking, the pilot's skill is in finding air which is rising faster. In the early days the easiest up-going air to find was the wind hitting a hill face and being deflected upwards. The glider's scope is limited by the length of the hill and the height of 1,000 or 2,000 feet to which the updraught extends. But the time a glider can fly in hill lift is limited only by the pilot's endurance. It becomes comparable with pole-squatting. With the exception of the five-hour requirement for the Silver C badge, duration is no longer a measure of gliding prowess. The discovery that thermal up-currents could be used opened up a whole new field of long-distance flying. By finding thermals—the bubbles of hot air which rise from some part of the ground that has become hotter in the sun than its surroundings—and circling tightly in the up-going column, the glider gains enough height to set off in search of the next thermal, and so on across country until the sun gets too low to set off any more of them. The little white bun-shaped *cumulus* clouds of a summer's day are the tops of these thermals, and the pilot goes from cloud to cloud knowing, if the day is good, that there will be lift under each. In this country the record distance is 360 miles, and the world record— flown in the United States—is 550.

Cumulus clouds are not always small and bun-shaped. Sometimes they become vast thunderheads or *cumulo-nimbus* clouds (cunims for short) and these have very powerful up-currents. In this country such clouds have taken gliders to more than 30,000 feet—for which of course oxygen is necessary.

Still only half-explored is a third kind of lift called 'wave'. When water pours over a weir or a hidden stone in a stream there often arises downstream a series of standing waves which remain more or less stationary. The same thing happens when an air mass flows over a mountain range. In the upward part of such a wave a glider has been carried up to 46,000 feet.

All these things I read about and heard about in the talk that went on at the Gliding Club as I learned my new technique. I learned too about launching methods. At Nympsfield we used a winch with about 1,000 yards of cable which pulled the gliders up like a kite to about 1,000 feet—or a third of the cable length; but there were other methods. Auto-towing involved a fixed length of wire and a motor-car on a runway. This is even more like running with the string of a kite. Aero-towing—being tugged into the sky by a light aeroplane— is the most efficient way of all because the glider can release at an adequate height to be fairly sure of finding a first thermal. From 600 feet up the pilot should be planning his approach to land. A launch to 1,000 feet gives him only a very short time to look for thermals, whereas with a launch to 2,000 feet (the standard height for aero-tows) he has more than three times as long. For this reason in competition flying aero-tows are almost invariably used.

At the opposite end of the scale there is bunjy launching. In this the glider is catapulted off the top of a ridge into hill lift. The power is supplied by half a dozen people running downhill to stretch the bunjy. But the Bristol Gliding Club's new field was not a bunjy-site.

The Club had previously operated at Lulsgate, an aerodrome, a few miles west of Bristol, but when that was turned into Bristol's airport, it had to move. Two large and rather undulating fields on the brink of the Cotswold escarpment were bought and turned into one, and Nympsfield became a new name in the Gliding Movement.

For me this new training had an immense appeal. I needed an adventurous recreation. Not only was small boat sailing too far away, but I had reached the stage in dinghy racing when if I won people said, "Well, so he should," and if I did not, they said, "The fellow's slipping, you know." In the new game I started at the bottom. I was not expected to be anything but a rather elderly clot, and many were the clottish mistakes I made.

But one of the difficulties was time, and I soon realised that unless I was prepared to spend a tremendous amount of it waiting around for my turn to fly, I ought to become a 'private owner'. As I still knew so little I joined with a fellow member, Harry Daniels, to form a syndicate and we bought and flew a new flaming yellow Olympia

2, which we called the *Firebird*. In her I flew one day for five hours to qualify for the Silver C duration leg.

By the following year I felt I had learned enough to have a glider of my very own, and I ordered a new fairly high-performance two-seater from Fred Slingsby of Kirbymoorside in Yorkshire. It was a T42B Eagle in which Phil could fly with me, but which also had an excellent solo performance. We called it the *Sea Eagle*, and in it, one blustery day at Nympsfield the Duke of Edinburgh made his first flight in a glider, with Peter Collier in the back seat.

It was not very long before I had climbed my 1,000 metres and flown my fifty kilometres to complete the Silver C badge. Yet somehow it could not be left there. The Gold C badge loomed up ahead. For this I must fly 300 kilometres (187 miles) and climb 3,000 metres or 9,843 feet from the lowest point of free flight.

On 1st July, 1957, the clouds were gangling and loose-limbed like rather bedraggled chickens. Their feathery flanks trailed away to a damp and ragged fringe at the bottom. Twice I tried to get up to them, flying alone in the *Sea Eagle*, but each time I scraped in weak thermals for little more than twenty minutes. My third launch was at four p.m. and for half an hour I struggled to keep up. A thermal off the spur on the ridge took me very slowly to 1,500 feet but an excursion under the most promising cloud out in the vale drew a complete blank. Back at the ridge another weak thermal suggested that it was better to look down to the most likely thermal sources for lift than to look up to the clouds. I drifted back over Stroud, scarcely climbing above my glide-path home, until at 2,000 feet I suddenly noticed a slight improvement and at 2,800 feet I was among the trailing wisps of a small cloud. So far I had flown about four times in cloud and on one proud occasion had climbed over 1,000 feet on turn-and-slip indicator—no Artificial Horizon was fitted at that time—before using the air brakes to check excessive speed. Here, I thought, was an opportunity for some much-needed practice. So, with the green ball standing at a fairly steady five, I wandered into the murk. After a while my circles emerged on one side, so I moved further into the cloud and the lift fell away to nothing. I turned north flying through patchy cloud with glimpses of the ground. The cloud looked darker ahead—much darker. Almost at once I was in much stronger lift, with the variometer standing at ten green all the way round. I settled down to the routine I had read about not long before in an article in the magazine *Sailplane and Gliding*. Let the eyes rotate round the three main instrument readings and say them out loud. "Turn and slip and speed and turn and slip and speed . . ."

I said to myself out loud and unceasingly, breaking the monotony occasionally when the speed approached sixty m.p.h. to say (also out loud) "get that bank off—too much turn", for a colleague had recently suggested that too much bank was probably the cause of my earlier zoomings.

After a while the green ball went even higher up the tube and the altimeter ploughed round in the most purposeful manner. "Turn and slip and speed . . ." I kept saying, while I wondered how long it could last—6,700 feet was my previous highest: the Club record was eight-and-a-half: it would be nice to get to nine . . . The green ball stayed mostly at twenty. A little tuft of water appeared at the front of the canopy by the ventilator, then the canopy began to mist over, and there was an icicle on the pilot-head mounted on the nose; then it began to get lighter and much rougher. I pulled down my loosened straps and gripped the stick more firmly. With my other hand I held on tight to the connecting bar of the air-brakes (a safe hand-hold which cannot jerk them open in a bump). "Turn and slip and speed . . ." came from a very dry mouth. "Turn and slip and speed and turn and . . . get that bank off . . . and slip and speed and . . ." The hand of the altimeter wound on past 9,000 feet. I'm not quite certain at what stage the idea of a 'nice little exercise in cloud-flying' changed into an attempt at Gold C height.

A lot of things were happening now. It became very turbulent indeed; the *Eagle* had no oxygen; and then I could not remember how many feet there were in 3,000 metres, but I was too fully occupied to work it out. The speed became erratic, the sailplane was tossed about like an autumn leaf and then suddenly there was silence and the air speed indicator swung down to nought; we were in a spin. Now, I felt, was quite a good time to pull out the air-brakes and when a suitable airspeed had been restored I glanced across to the altimeter—10,800 feet. With the air-brakes out I was trying rather unsuccessfully to fly straight and level in a south-westerly direction and a few seconds later, just twenty minutes after I had gone into it, I burst out of the side of the cloud. It was dazzlingly bright and supremely beautiful: immediately below me was the cauliflower top of one of the foothills of my cloud; and far, far below that again were the straggly wispy *strato-cu* fragments which had been covering four-eighths of the sky all day. I made a 360° turn to look at the cloud behind me, and only then realised that it was a solitary giant—the only big cloud within twenty miles. From below I had had no idea it would be so big.

There did not seem to be very much more above, but I was so

close to it that perhaps, as with a mountain peak, the summit was hidden by the closest bastion. Most striking of all was the colour— a brilliant golden-yellow in the evening light. The grandeur of the scene was breathtaking, and I was still under the influence of the glorious relief that the sailplane was under control again. At the same time I was desperately trying to do mental arithmetic and to establish my whereabouts. "A thousand metres is 3,281 feet, so what is 3,000 metres? Three ones are three, three eights are twenty-four, four and carry two . . . ah! that must be Aston Down, and there's the green reservoir on Minchinhampton Common . . . and carry two, three twos are six and two is eight, three threes are nine— 9,843 plus 1,000 for the launch . . . Golly, aren't those clouds beautiful over there under the sun. Well, 10,843, but . . . but . . . I only went to 10,800. I've missed my Gold C height by forty-three feet! Except of course that I must have lost at least that after the launch and before my first thermal. But supposing the barograph did not agree with the altimeter. Obviously I had cut it dangerously fine. Incidentally from that height if I had set off straight away I could have made one glide to Lasham (sixty-five miles from Nymps-field) and we wanted the *Sea Eagle* at Lasham for a TV programme three days later, so that's another opportunity missed. Bother!

By now I was half-way home and down to 7,500 feet, with plenty of sink about. What should I do? If I went back to Nympsfield maybe Peter Collier could leap in and get *his* Gold C height, but that was rather unlikely as the cloud was now far downwind and no other clouds looked at all promising.

Very gradually it became more and more clear that there was only one sensible thing to do—to turn back, re-enter the cloud, make certain of Gold C height and then head for Lasham. Even after this conclusion became inescapable I found I was still pointing towards Nympsfield. I took a final screw on my courage and swung into a steep 180° turn. The die was cast. I was committed to a further 'short exercise in cloud-flying'.

Five miles to the eastward my cloud still brooded over its own dark shadow lying across the valley at Chalford. It was a bigger cloud now, and it seemed to be higher—a towering giant more frightening than ever now that it had come to manhood. Its top was apricot coloured and crisp, with purple shadows; its foot was murky blue almost merging with the darkness of the Cotswolds below. My first climb had been made in ignorance of the size and quality of the cloud I had been sucked up into, but this time I could see only too well my opponent. I would dearly have liked a really good reason for staying out in the friendly sunshine.

I must have been flying in some fairly strong down-draughts, because I only got back to the cloud at about 4,000 feet—a few hundred feet above its base. I switched on the turn-and-slip and plunged into the side having made a mental note that south would be the quickest way out. At once I found lift and began to circle, but it was not very good, and in searching around to improve it I burst out into the clear air to the north-west. Back inside again I ran straight into steady ten green, which soon improved to about twenty. "Turn and slip and speed and turn and slip and speed . . ." From the beginning the climb was more turbulent than the first. I kept trying to get into the darkest part, in the hope that it would be smoother away from the edge, but it was a vain hope. There was a patter of rain, and later a patter of hail; and there was icing at the front of the canopy as before. Did the hail make it a *cunim*, I wondered? It was not very loud hail, and there was no lightning. But, *cu* or *cunim*, I was steaming up at twenty feet per second and bouncing about like a pea in a pod the while: ". . . and turn and slip and speed . . . hold off that bank . . . and slip and speed . . ." The altimeter crept past my previous best and up to 11,000, and now the turbulence increased sharply. With no oxygen I had no particular wish to go much higher, but the attempt to straighten up on a southerly course proved disastrous; a few moments later rapid fluctuations of the airspeed persuaded me to pull out the air-brakes. Until then I was still going up and the altimeter needle now stood at 11,500. I was holding on tight to the air-brake control with one hand, gripping the stick grimly with the other, and occasionally pulling down my shoulder straps which kept working loose. Still attempting to fly straight and level I found that the airspeed continued to fluctuate disconcertingly; and then suddenly it increased very sharply so that the indicator read eighty m.p.h. The brakes were out, and at this speed we should have been losing height fast, but instead the green ball was at twenty and the altimeter needle was surging round clockwise. Fascinated and seriously worried, I watched it go up 700 feet in about thirty seconds before, with a frightful bump, we flew into a violent down. A few moments later the airspeed shot up again, and once more with full brakes out and eighty m.p.h. on the clock we climbed 700 feet; again there was a violent jerk and we were going down; and then suddenly we were out in the blessed evening sunshine. The panic was over. I tried to shut the brakes but they were frozen open. Ahead two great walls of cloud were closing together and I aimed at the gap. The

Sea Eagle just squeezed through and I could almost hear the clang as they met behind me. I tried the brakes again and they closed half-way but no more. And so my hard-won height fell away in a miserable glide with the red ball steadily at ten feet per second down or worse.

Nevertheless I headed for Lasham. The total distance from Nympsfield was sixty-five miles, but already my cloud had taken me fifteen miles to the eastward, so that I had barely fifty-five miles to glide. From 11,000 feet in still air, with the air brakes in, Lasham should have been in the bag with a little to spare. But with the air-brakes out and the sky full of sink it was quite another kettle of fish.

I flew out over the Cerney gravel pits half hidden by wispy cloud and headed for Swindon. Every minute or so I tried the air-brakes again and managed to get them a little more shut, but I was down to 7,000 before they finally clicked home. To get to Lasham now I must obviously find some more lift. Over Marlborough was another big cloud and beyond this and to the east were a couple more. I headed out west of my course to the Marlborough cloud. I was a few hundred feet below cloud base when I got to it . . . and found nothing. A bonfire was burning at the edge of Savernake forest and the smoke came up towards my cloud. There was even a tuft of slightly lighter cloud at the point where the bonfire's hot air appeared to enter the darkness of the decaying giant. Round and round I went muttering the familiar sailplane pilot's *cri de cœur*— "There must be something here somewhere." But the best I could find brought the red ball down to one for part of the circle. At a quarter past six in the evening it was perhaps only to be expected.

I headed on, working desperately at my gliding-angle graph, and soon saw that Lasham was just beyond my grasp. Clearly there would be no more lift so I had the choice of landing in a field a few miles short or turning off to the nearest aerodrome. Andover seemed to be within reach and from there I could be aero-towed to Lasham; so to Andover I went—forty-eight miles from Nympsfield. The long glide was not without its anxieties for the sunlit town far out on the horizon seemed an impossible distance, but when I remembered that I had 500 feet more than I had thought because of the differences in airfield height, I was able to sit back and enjoy the beauty of the countryside in the orange evening light.

I landed safely at a quarter to seven among gliding friends at Andover and the barograph had duly recorded a climb to Gold C height.

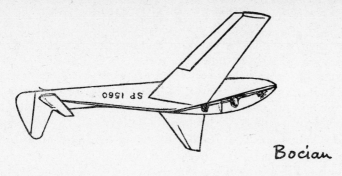

Bocian

CHAPTER 15   *Straight and Level*

MOST of us who glide say that we do so because it stimulates us. What we mean is that it frightens us. The question is: "How much?" If it frightens us too much we no longer enjoy it; if it does not frighten us enough we become bored. Somewhere between the two, we think, lies the special appeal of our sport, and it leaves a fairly wide scope for individual variation.

Ever since I took up gliding I have always been a member of the Straight and Level Club. Aerobatics are only enjoyable to me in their mildest forms. Chandelles are all right, loops are my limit, and anything which disturbs the dust from the cockpit floor is well beyond it. Thus when I arrived to watch the World Gliding Championships at Leszno in Poland in the summer of 1958 I was astonished, as I got down from the taxi which had brought me from the station, to see a two-seater Bocian glider circling at 500 feet over the middle of the aerodrome *upside-down*. It was not until the following day that two of my friends from the Midland Gliding Club told me that they had both been indulging in this doubtful entertainment and one of them—a Pole named Teddy Proll—said that if I wanted to fly during my short four days at Leszno he could arrange it. At this point I thought I made myself clear that although there was nothing I should like to do more than to sample the Polish thermals, there was nothing I wished to do *less* than to fly upside-down. An hour or so later Teddy Proll approached me excitedly and said he had arranged it all and that in a few moments I could have a flight in the two-seater Bocian.

Now this machine was not entirely new to me because a week before I had flown in one at Helsinki and had found it, although not to my way of thinking quite so attractive as an Eagle, nevertheless a perfectly gentlemanly aircraft of high performance and considerable comfort. I therefore looked forward to my flight with lively anticipation and soon afterwards, at the launch point, I was introduced to the charming young man who was to fly with me. He spoke a very few words of English and a very few words of German, and to make quite sure I explained to him at some length in both languages that the limit of my ambition was perhaps an hour of comfortable thermal soaring after which I hoped to return equally comfortably to earth. He seemed an intelligent young man and appeared to understand me perfectly. There was some delay because on the previous landing the air-brakes had become inexplicably jammed. When the seats were removed a screwdriver was found wedged behind the air-brake control. Apparently during inverted flight it had slipped out of a pocket. At least this particular hazard would not come my way. No inverted flight for me!

We were launched by aero-tow with a sixty-foot tow rope—half the length of the tow ropes I was used to. It was of a suitable thickness for towing a motor-car and wholly innocent of any 'weak link' arrangement which would be obligatory in England. I found that the climb to 500 metres required all my attention, for the tug—a low-wing monoplane—was terribly close in front of us. To begin with when I flew in the standard position, with the tug's wings just below the horizon I was looking down into the cockpit and could almost read his instruments. I was shortly corrected by my young colleague and told that I must keep all of the tug above the horizon. This I did and was surprised not to fall into his slip-stream, but it turned out to be quite a comfortable position. Nevertheless the short tow rope still required a high degree of concentration. At 500 metres we released in an indifferent thermal and I started to turn. My companion shouted "No, no! Not yet!" and seized the controls. We flew further into the thermal, which then admittedly improved, and was of such enormous dimensions that the straight period did not carry us through to the other side as it would have done in an English thermal. As we began to gain height I found that my companion was a confirmed 'pudding-stirrer'; the control column was in constant motion and as a result (so it seemed) we had quite a rough ride. After a while the thermal grew weaker and I asked if I could fly again. Here I was lucky, for I decided to move over to another thermal underneath a cloud which was just forming and this was so much stronger that we roared up at about 500 feet a minute. And so we wound our way to cloud base (but not into cloud because the turn-and-slip indicator batteries were flat). From 5,000 feet we headed back towards the aerodrome. "Now . . . aerobatic!" said my friend. Could it be that he had misunderstood me? Well, there was no harm in the simple ones. I performed a couple of fairly mild chandelles followed by a loop. "Is very nice," said my friend, "now I show you." He took over the controls and in a second we had half-rolled and were flying upside-down. A number of unfortunate circumstances dominated the next few moments. First I had not taken the elementary precaution of tightening the lower pair of straps. Tightly though my shoulders were held, my midriff was only loosely supported. In order to offset this disadvantage I had found a convenient hand grip for my left hand under the seat. Everything seemed under control although I was hanging rather far away from the seat itself. A few moments later my companion began an inverted turn. At this point the seat, unaccustomed to an 'upward' pull of one and a half times my weight, gave way with a splintering crash. This was greeted by a loud guffaw from behind me. I wonder whether you can remember as a child lying belly downwards in your bath? I was in just such a position, only the bath was the perspex canopy. It was at this stage, to my undying shame, that I could no longer withhold a stifled cry for mercy. With a flip back of the stick positive G was restored as we half-looped out. Hastily I tightened the straps, for clearly we had not seen the end of this business. In a few seconds we were involved in two consecutive slow rolls. But with the straps tighter I felt slightly more secure, although my toes were curled around something—perhaps the variometer bottle—which was quite certainly not designed to take the strain now bearing upon it.

The next thing was a half-loop to inverted-flight and at that precise moment we hit the edges of a thermal. "Ah-ha," said my companion and we began to circle upside down. It was only when he started to tighten the turns and we had already gone up fifty metres that I allowed a further expression of dismay to escape my lips. This time, in what I hoped was a firm voice, I followed it with "right way up now, please". A few seconds later a more normal world was restored to me. We were still regrettably high. "Now Immelmann," said my companion, and in quick succession we performed two half-loops, rolling off the top. After what I had already suffered these were, it must be admitted, comparatively mild and I even made so bold as to try one myself, but it was executed at too slow a speed, and my companion demonstrated with two more. As we now approached the lower limit of what in this country would be regarded as aerobatic height I began to breathe again, but my relief was premature. First came two rather charming little flick stall turns, a manoeuvre which only leaves you on the straps for a second or so. It is not unpleasant as a sensation and is quite spectacular in appearance, for the glider seems to cartwheel in the sky. We were now down to 500 feet. Down went the nose yet again. "What now?" I thought. At the edge of the aerodrome our Bocian half-rolled on to its back and we made a run across the whole width of the field upside-down. Oh dear, oh dear! But surely there could not be much more. We half-rolled out, went up into a chandelle, round, out brakes and a spot landing which trickled us up to the hangar door. An enthusiastic Teddy Proll rushed up to take a snapshot and to ask the inevitable question: "Did you enjoy it?"

Back in England I was glad enough to return to my beautiful *Sea Eagle* whose Certificate of Airworthiness specifically excluded inverted flight. That spring she had done me proud by taking me from Nympsfield to Penzance—a flight of 305 kilometres which completed my Gold C. It was the thirty-fourth Gold C to be issued to a British pilot.

Twice I used the *Sea Eagle* to combine business with pleasure. The first time was a short flight from Nympsfield to the Military College of Science at Shrivenham where I was to dine in the Mess and give a lecture afterwards. Strapped in the back seat of the glider was my evening dress and decorations. The second was a longer flight from Nympsfield to the Trust's branch establishment at Peakirk near Peterborough. I was anxious to establish that in the right weather a glider was a moderately reliable form of conveyance.

But just as racing had been for me the most fascinating part of sailing, now competition flying seemed the best part of gliding. The British Gliding Championships are held every other year, alternating with the World Championships. They are divided into a League 1 and a League 2. For my first attempt I competed without signal success in League 2, for my second even less successfully in League 1.

The basis of the competition is that, depending on the weather conditions a particular task is set. It may be a race to a goal, or round a triangle, or to a turning point and return. It may be free distance in which each pilot tries to get as far away from the starting point as possible. It may be distance along a set line, in which any distance you may land off the line will be subtracted from the distance you have gone along it. It may be a pilot-selected goal, in which you must declare a landing place which will stretch your prowess and the weather conditions to the limit. If you achieve the goal you may add thirty per cent to the points, and by the same token if you have underestimated your capabilities or those of the weather you may overfly your goal, but will have to fly thirty per cent of the distance before you begin to score more.

Whichever of these tasks is set by the organisers of the competition, the winner's points for each mile he flew are reduced to 100 marks, and the other competitors are scaled accordingly.

On the opening day of the 1959 competitions (held at Whitsun so as to make use of the spring soaring weather) we were set 'Free distance' as a task and I flew the Eagle solo from Lasham in Hampshire to Leeds—more than 180 miles. I was well pleased with the flight, but eight of the seventy entries had flown further, and one, Commander Nicholas Goodhart, had beaten all-British distance and goal flight records by flying 360 miles to the Scottish Gliding Union's headquarters at Portmoak, some fifteen miles north of Edinburgh. As each glider must fly twenty miles before it begins to score, my 160 was less than half Nick's 340 and against his 100 points I only scored forty-eight. But Lasham to Leeds was still a worthy flight by my standards.

As the competition advanced, however, I could not maintain even this level. My scores sagged down and down. Yet the flying was enjoyable enough, and the last day of the Championships produced one of the most enjoyable flights I had ever made. Peter Collier, who had taught me to fly gliders, came with me as navigator in the back seat.

The task was an out and return race from Lasham to Oldbury Castle near Calne. It was, let us face it, a difficult task: a slow race flying across the wind but slightly with it on the way out and across the wind but slightly against it on the way back. One of the things that made it so enjoyable to me was that we flew over friendly familiar country where I had spent so much of my boyhood. Another was that we were almost perpetually in company with other gliders in the race. In this context it is not quite like an ordinary race, for each glider is racing against the clock having crossed the starting line at a different time. Unless you know that someone else started after you did, the fact that he is ahead of you does not necessarily mean that he is beating you.

This day was beautiful, the atmosphere clear, the clouds very small. Under each the lift was for the most part spent by the time the cloud had made its appearance and the best thermals were the 'blue' ones that we found by chance out in the open. In the early stages we found ourselves circling in company with Lorne Welch in the blue Eagle. Lorne, who built a glider to escape from Colditz prison camp, and never used it because the war ended before it was finished, had test flown my Eagle when she was new. He and his wife Ann (Vice-Chairman of the British Gliding Association and manager of the British teams to the last seven World Championships, organiser of the British competitions and author of six books on gliding), were part owners of the blue Eagle, the machine which Nick Goodhart and Frank Foster had flown to win the World Two-Seater Championship in France in 1956. Today Lorne was flying his Eagle solo and we were two-up, but in spite of that the performance of the two aircraft, whenever we met, was astonishingly similar. The wind pushed us south of our course at one stage and we found ourselves over the great military camp at Tidworth. Here the sky was clear of cloud but in spite of that we managed to find a blue thermal without getting dangerously low. Things began to look up as we crept along the road leading north past the Collingbournes and over the Kennet and Avon Canal to Savernake Station. It was here that we came into a thermal some way below Nick Goodhart. A few minutes later Huish Hill was below, one of the earliest gliding centres in England and scene of some of the pioneer hill-soaring flights. Then on over the West Woods and the Lacket, our family home at Lockeridge—ground which I had known from the age of thirteen. As we circled in a thermal which took us slowly but steadily up at 300 feet per minute, I looked down on the middle of the West Woods and saw the still-familiar clearing we had known as Archer's Dene, where in the long ago I had taken Lord Grey of Fallodon, then almost entirely blind, to hear his first Wood Lark singing. We had sat on that bank there, and the nest had been across on the other face of the little valley. Further on we found a thermal over Boreham Wood—Sleepy Wood we had preferred to call it— where the Butterfly Orchids grew in profusion. And looking down Lockeridge Dene I could see our little cottage, the Lacket among its tall elms and poplars—the poplars which I had planted as a boy to feed my Poplar Hawks and Puss Moths. Here again we found ourselves thermalling with Nick Goodhart above us; his brother Tony joined us in the little French Fauvette and so did Wally Kahn flying his Eagle solo.

We were not far now from the turning-point, Oldbury Castle, where a monument stands on the top of the down beside the ancient British camp. The B.B.C. had announced this turning-point and holidaymakers had been advised on this Whit-Saturday afternoon to go there and watch the gliders turning. The scene as we approached was, of all the flight, most memorable. The downs below were gaily crowded with people and the sky seemed to be crowded with gliders. Wally Kahn had found a thermal just short of the turning-point and made a few turns in it. We marked where it was, joined it, and made a few more turns in it. From all directions gliders headed in towards us. The correct move seemed to be to nip out before we had drifted down wind, go round the turning point and head smartly back to the same thermal again before it died and while it was still marked for us by the column of circling gliders. So we flew out over the edge of the downs, gay with their picnic parties. Forming a centre-piece were the brilliant markers of our turning-point laid out by the organisers—orange and bright 'Dayglow' pink in the shape of a Cross of Lorraine. Over this colourful scene we made our turn and headed back towards the thermal. Most of the dozen or so gliders in it had not yet been round the turning-point. As we circled we looked back to the other side of the turning-point, near Yatesbury Camp where there was another thermal with perhaps eight or ten gliders in it. There, near the bottom of it, was the red-white-and-red wing-line of Nick Goodhart's Skylark III. We had last seen him 600 feet above us and now not only was he behind us but also nearly 1,000 feet below. This splendid indication of our progress gave us tremendous encouragement. We headed out from the top of our thermal back over the Valley of the Grey Weathers, the wide landscape dominated by sarsen stones, past the Lacket and over the West Woods again, back to the south-eastward with Savernake forest on our left. Here in a thermal we watched the little plastic Fauvette of Tony Goodhart circling in another thermal about a mile away. His was not such a good one as ours; we could see that he was not going up so fast as we were, which gave us further cause for encouragement. Circling with us was Dave Martlew in a Skylark III and eventually Tony Goodhart saw that our thermal was better and came over to join us. In due course his much smaller turning-circle enabled him to climb up to our level and the three of us set off in line abreast, looking for the next thermal. We flew along together at the same altitude until one came up between Dave Martlew and us. We turned to starboard and Dave turned to port and the two of us almost met head-on as we came towards each other in the best lift of the thermal. Dave, in the most courteous and airmanlike fashion, gave way and altered his circles to follow ours because he judged we were there first. Tony Goodhart came over and joined us; we thermalled and thermalled and thermalled all three, and then headed on to the next.

A few thermals later Tony Dean-Drummond joined us in an Olympia 419. He came in a couple of hundred feet above us, but two or three minutes later he was 1,000 feet above and speeding away on course, leaving us struggling to gain a little more height. At the time I wondered how this was done, but since becoming the owner of my own Olympia 419 I am less surprised. In weak thermals the Eagle is simply no match at all for the 419, and with two-up the scales were further loaded against us. Gradually we began to realise that we were dropping behind; everybody else seemed to be getting better thermals and going away ahead of us. Nick Goodhart was far above us again, and in time far far ahead. Suddenly we were getting low and the evening was getting late; our hearts were in our boots. It was a quarter to five, and the thermals were almost dry now, with very little cloud forming. Over Whitchurch we staggered to one of the last clouds of the day but it gave us practically nothing. Desperately we sought lift from a sunny slope of bushes, where we hoped the wind might be sufficiently broken to give shelter for a 'wind shadow' thermal, and sure enough we got one.

As we worked up from about 1,500 feet—uncomfortably low so late in the afternoon—five gliders, having seen us scraping and struggling, came in far above us, where the thermal was still much more powerful than it was at our level. One of them was Derek Piggott, the Lasham Chief Flying Instructor, another Dave Carrow who insures my glider, a third was John Williamson, R.A.F., son of the author of *Tarka the Otter*. Each circled half a dozen times and headed on towards home; below we struggled on up; and then who should come sweeping suddenly into the thermal at about our level, even a little below us, but Lorne Welch with whom we had shared thermals at the beginning of the flight. We had seen him briefly at the turning-point and now he was with us again. And so in close company we worked the lift laboriously almost to cloud base. But now it was late and, as we had been 'scraping', the wind had drifted us a long way south towards Andover. Our hopes of completing the course were low, but not extinct. Ron Rutherford in his Skylark II had been with us too and set off from the top of the thermal before us. He made for the last available cloud which was back at Whitchurch from which we had already drifted away once. Should we go straight for home or divert to the cloud? If we went up wind to it again it seemed we should have gained very little, on the other hand it was still a long way to Lasham. Ron went for the cloud at Whitchurch, Lorne, behind us, headed straight for

Looking across the excavated pond to our new house with its 10′ × 8′ studio window.

With our children Nicola, Dafila and Falcon, and the Decoy dog, Piper, (a Shetland collie) in the studio.

Lasham. We debated and finally decided on the cloud at Whit-church. By the time we reached it it was as dead as mutton.

There was no question of making a final glide from the height we were at, with the wind still fresh and so nearly ahead of us. A faint hope of getting back was raised by a dry thermal near Micheldever Station in which we climbed a few hundred feet. But our hopes were raised only to be dashed. The thermal petered out and we were left gliding on towards Lasham and getting lower and lower as we went. Far ahead of us was another glider well below us creeping snail-like across fields and woods all golden in the evening light. He was not going to make Lasham either. We were less than 1,000 feet up when ahead of us we saw a glider in a field and we realised that nothing would get us appreciably beyond this field. As we drew nearer we recognised it as Lorne Welch, who must have landed there a few minutes before. He had recently written an article on the selection of landing fields at the end of a cross-country flight. This then must surely be the best field for miles around, so we bowled in beside him. It was a difficult field with a rather steep slope to land on, but we got safely down and drew up at exactly half past six not fifty yards from Lorne's aircraft—two Eagles side by side, and only three miles from the finishing line.

Out and return tasks and triangle races in which the glider returns to its point of launch can only be achieved on days when the wind is not too strong. There are other days when travelling against the wind, or even across it, is difficult if not impossible. The thermal strength may be such that in circling round and round for a climb of 1,000 feet you may be drifted three miles down wind. If you then head back against so strong a wind you may have lost your 1,000 feet in the same three miles and be back where you started. Had you turned down wind from the top of your climb the 1,000 feet might have given you a glide of as much as nine miles, which with the three miles you drifted while climbing would mean twelve miles across country down wind, as opposed to no progress at all up wind. On such days glider pilots (who usually want to make as long a cross-country flight as possible) head off down wind. They probably declare some aerodrome as a goal but they may not always reach it by the time the day's thermals die out, or they may pass through difficult conditions where the thermals are widely spaced, where the cloud they head for is no longer giving lift, where in mounting despondency they can find no more up-going air and are forced to land prematurely.

x

There is plenty of time to choose a good field to land in. A high-performance glider in still air can fly more than six miles for every 1,000 feet. The six-mile radius imaginary circle is moving with the wind, so that in the down wind direction it will be more, and up wind less. This distance means that from 2,000 feet a vast tract of land is available from which to choose the best landing place. If all the country within his gliding circle is unsuitable for landing the pilot should not have set out to fly across it.

But landings can be made in 150 yards, and much less if there is a breeze of wind.

"How," you may well ask, "does a glider get home again after a cross-country flight and an 'away landing'?" The answer is simple to describe but more complicated to undertake. It must be 're-trieved', and retrieving is in itself an art and something of an adventure.

Gliders are so made that they can be taken to pieces. The wings, which may span more than sixty feet, divide up into two or three pieces (depending on the type of glider); the tailplane is either removable or folding; and the whole glider can be stowed in a long tunnel-shaped trailer.

For a long-distance flight the retrieving crew (which may be one, two or more in number) sets out by car with trailer attached, in the direction of the pilot's declared goal. Every hour the crew stops and telephones back to base for news of the pilot. No news is good news in this, for it means he is still flying. As soon as he lands the pilot himself telephones his precise position back to base and this is passed to the crew the next time they ring up.

In practice it works very well and the crew seldom overshoots the glider, but in a competition of seventy gliders it requires a major organisation at base.

After a very long flight the retrieving crew may not arrive till long after dark, and you may not get home again till next morning. Retrieving can be an eventful business.

Olympia 419

CHAPTER 16   *Diamonds*

BY the summer of 1959 I had been launched 550 times and had
flown in gliders for 300 hours with only one mishap. One day in
the previous summer the winch had failed during a launch; I
had wallowed on the wire and allowed the speed to fall off too
much; so that the *Sea Eagle* landed heavily and the little wheel
was pushed up through the bottom of the fuselage.

Then came the disastrous 31st May, 1959. I had been soaring
with a passenger on the west ridge at Nympsfield and was returning to land, a little lower than usual. It might have been prudent
to turn in early and land at the upwind end of the field, but the
hay had not yet been cut at that end, so it would be slightly
better to go on to the down wind end. Then I saw that the T21—
the side-by-side trainer—was also coming in to land. I felt that I
could not cross ahead of him. So I swept out to turn behind him.
I should have known—indeed I did know—that there would be
a down-draught curling over the hangar and down the ridge
behind it, but the T21 was in front of me. I was committed to
going astern of him. Then the 'curl-over' took charge. In gliding
circles it is sometimes known as 'the clutching hand'. As I turned
in, the trees in front rose up to meet us. We were evidently not
going to make it. The only thing to do was to increase the speed
by lowering the nose and trying to dive through the topmost
branches. We were still turning slightly and the low wing broke the
telephone wires; the Eagle slewed round a little and the bushy
top of the tree pulled down the speed, so that she stalled. There
was a nasty splintering crash and we were on the ground, still
sitting in the glider, neither of us hurt, but under my feet I could
see the grass covered with little broken bits of plywood.

Half an hour after the prang I was sent round on a circuit in
another Eagle, though I have since been told that the wisdom of

this time-honoured practice, which is supposed to restore the nerve, is now regarded as very doubtful.

The Eagle was going to take not less than two months to repair. I considered carefully what I should do. The accident had been caused by an accumulation of misjudgments. I had left the ridge too low, I had been unduly influenced by the insignificant factor of the uncut hay, I had failed to realise that I could safely have turned in ahead of the T21, I had underestimated the curl-over. Did all these mistakes amount to a conclusion that I was accident-prone? Or did they alternatively reduce the chance that I would ever make those particular errors again?

For a day or two my morale was at a low ebb. But then determination returned. I was not going to give up gliding. After all there were still the three diamonds to be added to my Gold C badge.

At the very end of the competitions I had had a trial flight in a single-seater Olympia 419x—a *ne plus ultra* in British glider design, built by Messrs. Elliotts of Newbury whose principal business is furniture. I decided to replace the Eagle with an Olympia 419, and placed the order immediately to restore my spirits. The new machine was ready on the afternoon of 18th July; I went to fetch it from Newbury, trailed it to Nympsfield and flew it for two hours in the evening in ridge lift. The weather forecast for the morrow was good and if the day fulfilled its promise I was going to try for the first of the diamonds. Of the three requirements perhaps the easiest is Diamond Goal: this involves a flight of not less than 300 kilometres (the Gold C distance) but to a declared landing place. The other two are Diamond Distance—a flight of 500 kilometres, and Diamond Height—a climb of 5,000 metres or about 16,400 feet.

Nympsfield is an awkward place for starting on a Diamond Goal flight. In a north-east wind you have to go to the very tip of Cornwall, and in the prevailing south-westerly wind you find that Great Yarmouth is not quite far enough; the 300 kilometre-arc falls four miles out to sea. There are two ways of getting over this difficulty. One is to carry a sealed camera and make a dog-leg, photographing the turning point on the way; and the other is to get the tug-plane to tow you four miles to the west of Nympsfield before you start. On this Sunday morning I was dropped off by the Club Tiger Moth, at the railway junction just beyond Berkeley Road Station at eleven-thirty-eight. It was certainly a good day; the thermals were abundant if not especially strong. My barograph chart shows only one achieved rate of climb of 500 feet per minute and I was led to that by three gulls. The rest are mostly 200 and 300 foot jobs.

I was not alone in my selection of task for the day. Four other pilots—Tony Gaze in his Eagle, Keith Aldridge and Tony Morgan in Skylark IIs and Doug Jones in an Olympia II were all Yarmouth-bound, and so, although we did not know it, was Mike Gee, dog-legging from Lasham. I was third away, with Keith Aldridge and Tony Morgan ahead of me. I came up with Tony soon after Cheltenham but I did not see Keith until he joined the same thermal near Newmarket. On the other hand the sky seemed to be full of gliders soaring locally. An unidentified red Skylark with white wings was circling between Finmere and Buckingham, and over Bedford I met *Ranunculus*, the syndicate Olympia from Cranfield though I could not see which of my friends was flying it.

A cloud base of almost 5,000 feet a.s.l. made the crossing of the airway (in which cloud flying is forbidden) quite painless. Near St. Neots I spent some time in a thermal studying the lay-out of the duck ponds on a friend's estate, where he keeps a fine collection of waterfowl. I was making fairly slow progress—a bare thirty m.p.h.—and quite evidently the twelve to fifteen knots of westerly wind which had been forecast had not material-ised. This immediately gave cause for alarm about the distance the sea breeze, with its stable unsoarable air, might have penetrated into East Anglia. But this bridge would have to be crossed when I got to it. I was surprised to find no gliders in the sky above the Cambridge Club, for the lift was magnificent at this time of the day, and a few minutes later I looked down at Waterbeach upon a crowd of stationary dinghies, utterly becalmed in the narrow river. No doubt a breathlessly exciting race was in progress, for, as I well knew, very light airs can sometimes be just as dramatic as a breeze; but somehow I was glad to be up here looking down, rather than down there probably not looking up.

By Thetford cloud base had gone up to 5,500 feet. At Snetherton Heath, south-west of Norwich, the silence in the 419 cockpit was broken by a sudden and unexplained roar which I finally located as a motor-cycle rally on the aerodrome 4,500 feet below. By Old Buckenham cloud base had gone up further to 6,000 feet, but ahead the flat base line was broken by trailing cascades of cloud which drooped 1,000 feet to a second tier—a new cloud base—caused, presumably, by the damp air of the sea breeze.

Here it was then, as far in as Norwich and giving, no doubt, a head wind from there sixteen miles to the coast. How strong would it be?

From 6,000 feet with Wymondham abeam to port, the Scroby Sand off Yarmouth was visible as a sharp yellow bar against the blue of the sea. In still air it would have been a final glide of twenty-five miles from here to North Denes aerodrome, and safer still with the promised twelve to fifteen knots of westerly wind. But with a sea-breeze of unknown strength against me I was taking no chances. It was just five o'clock and Norwich—several miles north of my track—might still be feeding thermals to some active-looking cloud above it. I turned forty-five degrees left towards it. Here was the crux of the flight. Beyond Norwich the sky was perfectly clear, over the town the cloud trailed its sad-looking streamers and wisps. To my inexperienced eye they indicated decaying cloud and sinking air. If I could not get 2,000 feet of height at this stage I was just not going to get there—yet another Yarmouth failure and I had already made four abortive attempts in the Eagle. But surely there would still be *some* lift under these clouds and over this large city; and so indeed there was. As I reached the outskirts I hit a nice thermal and began to work it; and then as I sat there with that glorious feeling that my goal was now within my grasp (provided that I made no major fumble), cloud suddenly started to form 1,000 feet below me in my thermal. Soon it was forming all round me, but only in wisps. The strongest lift was on the west side of the streamer, which provided a perfect marker. In due course the cloud thickened and I wandered about in it trying to drain the last dregs of its lift. It got me to 5,600 feet and a few minutes later I broke out into the open on the eastern outskirts of the city, with only fifteen miles to go. It would need to be a pretty strong sea breeze to bring a 419 down *that* fast.

As I flew out into the clear blue sky the glider was rock steady in the utterly calm air. I took my hands and feet off, stretched, and breathed a great big comfortable sigh. The next half-hour was the most enjoyable of the flight—a smooth straight glide over country I had known and loved well from early youth. The sailing boats on Wroxham Broad, away on my left, were moving faster than they had been at Waterbeach. I cast my eye over all the Broads where I had first become fascinated with birds, and where I had first learned to sail—the Hovetons, Woodbastwick and Ranworth, the River Ant leading up to Barton, and beyond, the

Thurne and Potterheigham Bridge, Hickling Broad and familiar Horsey Mere, where I had spent four summer holidays.

Immediately ahead was Acle with the parallel lines of road and railway following the River Bure to Yarmouth across the marshes where the wild geese feed in winter. The nearest Broads now were Filby, Rollesby and Ormesby, more lake-like than the marshy Broads to the north. On my right was Breydon—with its tidal mudflats uncovered (so *that* was why the Scroby Sand had shown up so prominently. Maybe at high water it would not be such a good landmark) and beyond Breydon I scanned the higher ground near Belton. Fritton Lake where my family home had been for fifteen years from the 1930s was hidden in the trees; and right ahead lay the railway swing bridge at Yarmouth so familiar from Ted Seago's lovely painting; I was going to get there with height in hand. Even though I knew where to look for North Denes aerodrome I found myself concentrating on the field next door to the south of it, which from a distance looked much more like a landing field. But then I saw one of the joy-ride Austers going down and saw that what I had taken for odd sheep in the field were in fact white runway markers.

I arrived over the coast at 2,000 feet, taking a number of photographs with my fixed camera, and then landed. The first diamond was in the bag.

No chances arose in the summer of 1959 to try for the other two diamonds. I improved my cross-country performance by flying triangles—100 and 200 kilometre triangles—starting from and ending at Nympsfield.

Soaring is for the most part a seasonal activity and midwinter is no time for distance flying. When the spring came I was waiting for chances of diamonds or of British records. Easter 1960 produced a day for an attempt on the British out and return record but I fumbled it and had to land nine miles short on the way home. Suitable days to fly 500 km. for Diamond Distance are very rare in this country. Philip Wills, the great pioneer of soaring, ex-world champion and chairman of the British Gliding Association, made nine flights of over 450 km. in various countries of the world, but the 500 eluded him until last summer in Texas.

In Britain it has only been achieved four times—once from Gloucestershire across the Channel and on to the eastern borders of Holland, once from Lasham to Scotland and twice from Norfolk to Cornwall. Of the four flights two were made by Britain's number one seed, Nick Goodhart. I had no illusions about it. I knew that Diamond Distance was very difficult indeed, but on 14th May, 1960, with a rather rare south-south-westerly unstable airstream the thing seemed worth trying.

The wind was strong though the lift was patchy. But it meant that while I struggled to gain height in rather weak and broken thermals, I was being blown up England at an encouraging speed. Twice in the Midlands I was convinced that the flight would end, but each time I managed to creep laboriously back up again. By Durham big storms had spread cloud over most of the sky. When the sun disappears thermals are few and far between. I was only 2,000 feet up as I passed over the great Norman cathedral. An opencast coalmine gave me a burble, but the day was evidently spent. I selected a field to the west of Sunderland in which to land, but approached it over a small junk yard full of old motor-cars. Perhaps it was the chimney of the adjoining workshop, or perhaps the old cars had retained some heat, but at 800 feet I picked up a very weak thermal. Scarcely rising at all I circled and circled and circled, drifting with the wind towards Newcastle. My rate of climb was less than fifty feet per minute, until I saw two immature Lesser Black-backed gulls circling below me. They made much tighter turns than I could make, but they were always in the best lift. All I had to do was to keep them in the middle of my circle and I knew I was in the most powerful part of the thermal. It pleased me a great deal to be using these birds as guides. From the start one of the appeals of soaring had been getting the bird's-eye view; I had often flown with gulls and buzzards before, watching their reactions to the invisible energy we were both using, but they had never been so useful to me as now.

But it was a long slow business to get up to cloud base from 800 feet at 100 feet per minute. The cloud which was forming at the top of my thermal was small and looked grey in the shade of the overcast from a black thunder cloud away to the west which was trailing rain curtains down to the ground. At 4,000 feet I circled into the bottom of my little grey cumulus, and then a re-markable thing happened. The lift suddenly and startlingly in-creased. Perhaps the curious physical phenomenon known as the Latent Heat of Condensation was the main cause, or perhaps a layer of hotter air from the roofs of Newcastle had been catching me up from below, and was now surging into the growing cloud. Whatever the causes the effect was astonishing. From 100 feet per minute my rate of climb had increased to more than 1,500 feet per minute. I popped a peppermint into my mouth. This was going to be interesting.

At about 9,000 feet I put on my oxygen mask balancing my half glasses (without which I find it a strain to read the instrument panel) on top of the nosepiece, and as the altimeter passed 10,000 I turned the oxygen switch to low. Still the needle went round half as fast again as the second hand of a watch. But at 13,500 it became lighter and turbulent and the lift fell off. I have learned that it does not usually pay me to wander about looking for lift in cloud, so when it becomes turbulent and difficult and the lift falls off, I lose no time in straightening up on the desired course. I turned to north-west and flew straight and level by my gyro instruments.

From a bright white mist I flew with absolute suddenness into almost twilight darkness, the glider dropped like a down-going lift, my glasses fell off in the turbulence and a hideous roar broke out as hail bombarded my perspex canopy. A moment later lightning began to flash, but so deafening was the roar of the hail that I heard no thunder. I was now back in lift again, and going up fast though not quite so fast as before.

Diamond Height had suddenly become a possibility. My low point of 800 feet immediately before this climb meant that the 5,000 metres need only have 800 feet added to achieve the necessary height—16,405 plus 800 equals 17,205—call it 17,500 for luck. Ice crystals were penetrating into my cockpit from the cracks round the canopy. Already there was a thin coating over my knees. The inside of the perspex was entirely frosted over and so were the faces of the instruments. When I put my glasses back over my oxygen mask for the fourth time, I noticed that the hairs on the backs of my hands were picked out in rime.

At 17,600 the lift began to fall off again and as my second diamond should be safely on the barograph trace, I turned on to a north-westerly course to concentrate on the third. Although I did not know it till later my altimeter had lagged behind the barograph, which, after recalibration, dutifully recorded that I had reached a height of 18,300 feet.

By now I had a serious problem on my hands. The great anvil of ice crystals had spread out from the top of the thunderstorm, and joined the overcast from earlier ones. I was flying in cloud which was probably unbroken ahead of me. Theoretically from this altitude at Newcastle I should have been able to reach my

X*

declared goal at Portmoak, fifteen miles north of Edinburgh, but the 419's wings were covered with ice, and her rate of sink was greatly increased. I could not expect the ice to melt until I was down to 5,000 or 6,000 feet. But there was worse than this. I had little idea of the direction and strength of the wind, and I was probably not going to see the ground till I was down to cloud base. This had been 4,000 feet before the storm, but behind the rain there had been cloud almost down to the ground. On my course of north-west, if I had allowed too much for the wind I might fly into the Cheviot Hills, 2,600 feet high, before coming out of cloud; if I had allowed too little I might emerge below the cloud and see nothing but the North Sea all round me. Perhaps the wisest thing would be to pull out the air-brakes and descend in circles while I was still near Newcastle, especially as the gauge showed not very much oxygen left. Yet somehow I could not bear to throw away all that height. I turned a little bit more to the westward and soldiered on through the grey blanket of cloud, while the hum of the Artificial Horizon began to fall in pitch as the battery ran down.

After about half an hour there was an irregularity in the grey and then a sudden break. In the open patch still 10,000 feet below, I could see the coastline and the unmistakable outline of Budle Bay. A moment later it was swallowed up in the cloud again. I adjusted the course accordingly and flew on through the clouds. When I next emerged Berwick and the Tweed were just ahead and still at 4,000 feet I crossed the border into Scotland. But unless I found more lift I had no hope of getting to Portmoak, and it was now late in the evening. I was flying almost at right angles to the wind by this time as I crept along the coastal plain near St. Abbs Head. Far to the west the evening sun was setting off thermals south of Edinburgh, but they were several miles out of my reach. At last I picked a field near the village of Cockburnspath and landed. I was 298 miles from my starting point and 500 kilometres is 312 miles. I landed at six-forty-five p.m., and by eleven p.m. my secretary, Mike Garside, driving single-handed, had arrived with the trailer. By driving alternately for two hours while the other slept on an air-mattress in the back of the car we were back in Gloucestershire by ten o'clock next morning. For both of us the excursion to Scotland and back had taken twenty-three hours. It chanced that no one in Britain flew further than 298 miles during 1960, so the flight qualified me for the Wakefield Trophy, but Diamond Distance remains to be achieved.

CHAPTER 17   *The Window*

THE wheel has come full circle. It is June 1960 and I finish writing
my story where I began it—in the window of my studio overlooking the Rushy Pen at Slimbridge. But this time there is a
summer scene on the pond in front of me. A Wigeon swims by
with four russet-headed downy ducklings, an American Ruddy
Duck fusses about her brood, scolding the gay chestnut-coloured
drake who patters his blue bill on his breast in vain courtship of
her. Over on the grass four broods of Barnacle Geese—tiny bubbles
of pale grey down—are feeding with their parents. A pair of
Fulvous Whistling Ducks crosses the pond with eight young ones
in a dark grey cluster between them; a Steller's Eider drake dives
in front of the window and in the background a party of nine wild
Shovelers rounds up into the eye of the wind and settles among
the rushes. The evening clouds suggest another lovely summer's day
tomorrow—just right for an attempt on the 'out and return' record
in the 419. But tomorrow must be spent rehearsing a television
show at Bristol for transmission in the evening.

No doubt more than half my active life has been lived, but
bringing my story up to date does not, in my mind, make a conclusion, or even a punctuation. Part of today has been occupied
with looking at the exciting new data which Geoffrey Matthews,
our Assistant Director (Research) has been collecting on the
orientation capacities of Mallards. When released one by one
they mostly fly out of sight on a north-westerly bearing provided
that the sky is not completely overcast. When it *is* overcast they
scatter at random. The direction is the same all the year round
for Mallards captured at Slimbridge and Peakirk. We have been
discussing how and why they do it, and we have been discussing
the architect's new plans for the new Research Centre to be built
here at the New Grounds. We've been talking about the African

Special Project of the International Union for the Conservation of Nature and our forthcoming trip to Kenya to open a new National Park for Flamingos, with its prospect of swimming again on the coral reefs off the coast. We've been looking at the plans for the new biological research station to be set up by the Charles Darwin Foundation in the Galapagos, a project which has excited Phil and me ever since we went there to make films for television in 1959. This morning, too, there were letters about the Loch Ness monster . . . As usual there seem to be rather too many things to do.

The evening sun streams in at the huge plate-glass window. Phil has just put the children's grey Shetland pony out at her tether post, and she is helping Dafila, now eight, to put the Poplar Hawk Moth caterpillars on to fresh branches of poplar and back into their polythene bags. Falcon, aged six, is drawing a tree, behind which is hiding what he calls 'a Danger'. Nicola, aged eighteen, has just come in from riding, and Piper, our Sheltie decoy dog, who was brought up with Dafila, is lying in an exquisitely elegant pose on the hearth rug.

After dinner I shall have to get down to the line drawings for this book. For that I shall need the Brahms Violin Concerto and a Sibelius symphony; either II or VII will do.

As I contemplate all these things I am more than ever convinced that I am the luckiest man I know. I say this not with smugness or self-satisfaction but because I can think of nothing sadder than to live a happy life without recognising it. Maybe I am an ostrich with my head in the sand. Maybe Fate or my own or other men's folly has all kinds of disasters in store for me, but they cannot take away these exciting and happy years. Not to acknowledge such good fortune would be inexcusable.

INDEX

INDEX